RELIGIOUS LIFE IN A NEW MILLENNIUM

VOLUME THREE

Buying the Field

Religious Life in a New Millennium
Volume Three

Buying the Field
Catholic Religious Life in Mission to the World

Sandra M. Schneiders, IHM

Paulist Press
New York/Mahwah, NJ

Cover image: Procession of the Virgins, detail of gold leaf on glass and colored glass mosaic in Sant'Apollinare Nuovo, Ravenna, Italy, c. 568.

Unless noted otherwise, the Scripture quotations contained herein are from the New Revised Standard Version: Catholic Edition, Copyright © 1989 and 1993, by the Division of Christian Education of the National Council of the Churches of Christ in the United States of America. Used by permission. All rights reserved.

Cover design by Cynthia Dunne, www.bluefarmdesign.com
Book design by Lynn Else

Library of Congress Cataloging-in-Publication Data

Schneiders, Sandra Marie.
    Buying the field : Catholic religious life in mission to the world / Sandra M. Schneiders, IHM.
        pages cm. — (Religious life in a new millennium; Volume 3)
    Includes bibliographical references and index.
    ISBN 978-0-8091-4788-5 (alk. paper) — ISBN 978-1-58768-257-5
    1. Monastic and religious life of women. 2. Catholic Church—Missions. I. Title.
    BX4210.S2545 2013
    255`.9—dc23
                                                            2012046106

ISBN: 978-0-8091-4788-5 (paperback)
ISBN: 978-1-58768-257-5 (e-book)

Published by Paulist Press
997 Macarthur Boulevard
Mahwah, New Jersey 07430

www.paulistpress.com

Printed and bound in the
United States of America

The Reign of God is like a TREASURE
hidden in a field
which a person FOUND…
and out of joy
SOLD ALL *she had*
to BUY THAT FIELD.
(cf. Matt 13:44)

This volume is dedicated
with love and gratitude

to
John S. Cummins
Bishop of the Catholic Diocese of Oakland,
California, from 1977 to 2003

who faithfully tends
the flame of the Second Vatican Council
in season and out of season
at home and abroad
whose zeal, hospitality, and joy in ministry
continue to make Christ and the Church real to so many
and whose friendship has been a great gift in my life.

Contents

Preface
to
Religious Life in a New Millennium
(Three Volumes)

In the twelve years since the publication of *New Wineskins*[1] the experience of Roman Catholic women Religious, who were the primary intended audience of that book, has broadened and deepened to an extraordinary degree. If in 1986 it was appropriate and necessary to talk of new wineskins (that is, of new structures and procedures), and even of new theological categories and constructs, to hold and give shape to the new experience of the life that was emerging in the wake of Vatican II, today it is time to speak of the wine itself, the substance of the life, which has matured during the past decade yielding both excellent vintage and some disappointing results. The new wine that demanded new wineskins a decade ago now needs decanting. It is time to pour, to taste, to analyze, to judge, to choose and reject, to blend and bottle, to store for the future. This task is already underway in a plethora of books and articles that have appeared during the 1980s and 1990s. This three-volume work, *Religious Life in a New Millennium*, is intended as a contribution to that lively discussion.

It is the underlying presupposition of this work that for Religious Life and those who live it in faith there is indeed a future full of hope (cf. Jer 29:11). But if that hope is to be realized Religious must do the difficult work of rethinking their life in the radically new context of a new millennium, which many cultural critics are characterizing as postmodern. I say that this is a difficult work precisely because the context is complex. If the experience is to be accessible to those contemplating it for themselves, and if it is to be presented coherently to those who appreciate it as well as those who do not, it must be examined and articulated anew and in depth.

In recent years I have been struck by the qualitative difference between the types of questions Religious were asking two decades ago and those that are at the center of discussions today. It seems to me that virtually every question raised today leads directly to the issue of what Religious Life is and means. In other words, whatever the presenting problems or issues— celibacy, permanent commitment, formation, new types of association, community, vows, ministry, feminism, Church, or prayer—the real question is "What is this life really all about?" Whatever one has to say about the particular issues must originate in and be expressive of how one understands the life itself. I think the explicit emergence of this question is a very positive development even though it greatly heightens the stakes in every discussion. It manifests the realization that, finally, Religious Life is a life; not a collection of disparate and separable elements, but a coherent whole. The question about the life itself is one about its wholeness, its integrity, and its authenticity as a way of being in this world. Consequently, this work, and especially the first volume, is not an easy read. Anyone looking for a possible answer to specific problems will probably be disappointed.

What I am offering is an understanding of the life itself in its contemporary cultural context (volume 1) as the framework for a reconsideration of its various constitutive dimensions and dynamics (volume 2), and an exploration of the way in which the authentic and integrated living of this life can help to transform not only the Religious her or himself but also the Church, society and culture of which Religious Life is a part (volume 3). This is a dangerous project for a writer because articulating a comprehensive view of any reality invites not only agreement and disagreement with particular points (always a welcome source of both affirmation and improvement) but complete rejection of the project as a whole if the underlying presuppositions are found unacceptable. This a danger I am willing to run because I am convinced of the value of Religious Life not only to the individuals called to it but also to the Church which is called to be a light to the nations and therefore to the world itself.

Recently someone asked me, "Does Religious Life need the Church?" and I replied that I thought the prior question is "Does the Church (and therefore the world) need Religious Life?" I am convinced that the answer to the latter question is yes (and for other reasons so is the answer to the first). The realization of the potential of Religious Life for our endangered cosmos, species, and culture, however, requires a theoretical basis that is clear and compelling. I am not arrogant enough to claim that this work supplies such a basis, much less the only one, but I hope it will generate focused discussion at the level on which I think this discussion must proceed at this point in history.

The primary intended audience of *Religious Life in a New Millennium* is the same as that of *New Wineskins*, that is, North American Roman Catholic women Religious in non-cloistered Congregations. This is not, however, the exclusive audience, for obviously much of the material in this work, as in its predecessor, is applicable to Religious in other cultures; to Protestant and Anglican Religious and members of ecumenical communities; to male Religious, especially those of non-clerical Institutes; to members of enclosed monastic communities; to members of Secular Institutes and of secular or third orders connected with Religious Orders; to members of Societies of Apostolic Life; and to various kinds of associates of canonical Institutes. I have learned from conversations with lay people, both Catholic and non-Catholic, that much of the material in *New Wineskins* was directly relevant to committed lay life and I hope that that will be the case with this work as well.[2] Indeed, it should be the case that Religious Life, rooted in and expressive of baptismal consecration and mission, would have much in common with, rather than be different from, Christian life in general.

The choice of the specific audience is dictated by very practical considerations. First, the forms of life in some way analogous or related to Religious Life are so numerous, and each is sufficiently specific, that "ringing the changes" on everything that is said to account adequately for the variations would make the text excessively lengthy and cumbersome, even if I were capable of doing it. Those living these other forms of life are much more competent than I to make the appropriate distinctions and qualifications in terms of their own life.

Second, this work is a reflection on experience, and even within canonical Religious Life itself (to say nothing of related forms of life) the experiences of female and male Religious, of North American Religious and those of other cultures, and of non-clerical and clerical Religious are irreducibly diverse. I am simply not competent to analyze experience I do not share.

Finally, while I attempted to include, as fully as possible, both apostolic and monastic Religious Life in my specifically-intended readership of volumes 1 and 2, this is somewhat less possible in volume 3, which is extensively concerned with ministry outside the monastic enclosure. Although the two forms of life have much in common, especially in terms of spirituality, and their mutual influence today is extensive, I will be concerned in volume 3 with the issue of why and how ministry beyond monastic or even ecclesiastical boundaries is intrinsic to non-enclosed Religious Life.

The choice to write a new work rather than to revise *New Wineskins* was dictated originally by two realizations. First, the essays in the earlier volume retain their validity as reflections on the experience of the two decades that followed Vatican II and therefore, at least in my judgment, can usefully stand as they are since many of the issues that arose in that period are still with us.

Second, the experience that now requires reflection is not generated by the same dynamics as was the experience of the 1960s and 1970s. Although this distinction is simplistic, I think it is indicative of something important to say that in the immediate aftermath of the Council Religious were dealing predominantly with changes *within* Religious Life itself as Religious encountered the "world" from which they had been rather hermetically sealed for centuries, whereas in the last fifteen years the concern has been much more explicitly with the interaction *between* Religious Life and the ambient culture, both secular and ecclesial. Furthermore, the life-giving spiritual energy generated by the Council dominated the first two decades after its close. Unfortunately, but importantly, the next three decades saw increasing polarization in the Church between those who continued to embrace the Conciliar renewal, including the vast majority of women Religious, and a powerful restorationist movement bent on neutralizing if not reversing the Council. This polarization, which seems nowhere near resolution, has deeply affected Religious Life and touches in one way or another most of the areas and issues to be discussed in volume 3.

There is a cause and effect relationship between the two phases. As Religious Congregations responded to the Council's reaffirmation of the world as the locus of salvation and reconceptualized themselves as existing not out of or separate from the world but in, with, and for the world, they began an extensive dismantling of the structural barriers between themselves and other people and between the privatized culture of preconciliar Religious Life and the surrounding culture. At first, the primary impact of this dismantling was experienced within Religious Life itself. Dress, horaria, dwellings, community life, and ministries changed. This called for revisions of Constitutions and from that followed changes in internal structures, institutional involvements, and relationships within and outside the Congregation. Foundational to these observable changes, of course, was a new theology and rapidly evolving spirituality, but it was the breakdown of the "total institution" of convent life that precipitated what was to follow.

The opening up of the institution, or what I call in this trilogy the deconstruction of Religious Life as "total institution," interrelated Religious with American secular culture in a new and much more intimate and pervasive way. To invoke only a few pertinent examples, permanent commitment through vows could not be proposed or explained without some reference to the cultural experience of ubiquitous career mobility, familial reconfigurations, indefinitely delayed marriage, and rampant divorce. Poverty had to be seen through the prism of attitudes toward money, lifestyle, and social class in a capitalist culture and in relation to a global economy that involved developing cultures that were not only income-poor but also newly aware of what was going on in so-called "developed," that is, income-rich cultures. Ministry had to take account of the categories of career and promotion, employment and compensation, insurance and retirement. In short, it was not just that ceasing to be a closed system had repercussions for the internal life of the social system we call Religious Life but that the system itself was now in pervasive interaction with its cultural environment in ways that have deeply influenced it. It is primarily this interaction between Religious Life and culture, both ecclesial and secular, that is the focus of this trilogy.

It has seemed to me that this task of analyzing and rethinking Religious Life could best proceed in three phases: the first a consideration of the global or general context (both cultural and ecclesial) influencing Religious Life; the second focusing specifically on the life itself through an exploration of its distinctive and constitutive relationships; and the third focusing on the influence of Religious Life on the context (again both ecclesial and cultural). In the global phase (volume 1), I address the larger question of "locating" or situating Religious Life in the multiple contexts that now qualify it in significant ways. It is a question of "finding" the treasure that is Religious Life. This task of "locating Religious Life" is a distinctly postmodern undertaking in the sense that there is no grand scheme or metanarrative within which all the influencing environments can be coherently related to each other and cumulatively create the single "space" or "place" of Religious Life. There was a time when we could describe the relationship between the Church and the world and within the Church the place of each form of life. This enabled us to properly place Religious Life in relation to all its significant publics: Vatican, hierarchy, local clergy, other forms of Religious Life, other Congregations within one's own form, Catholic laity, other "seculars." And none of the relationships overlapped in intrinsically contradictory ways. Religious Life was subject to some, superior to others, in opposition to still others.

Today, religious life is situated vis-à-vis a plurality of incommensurable, overlapping, or totally unrelated realities, movements, and structures, and each of these situations may affirm, challenge, or radically call into question the self-understanding and claims concerning the meaning and significance of Religious Life. How, for example, are Religious related to their obvious analogs in other world religions such as Buddhist or Hindu monastics or Islamic Sufis? How are Religious related to clergy or to laity within the Catholic Christian community? How are women's Religious Congregations related to feminism as a cultural movement? What kind of sociological reality is a Religious Congregation? What does the new cosmology and its effect on theological categories have to say to the fundamental christocentrism of Religious Life?

This list does not exhaust the questions but it does suggest how different they are from those we were asking in the 1960s and 1970s and how each question pertains to a sphere of reality, which may have little or nothing to do with the spheres from which the other questions arise. Answering one such question sometimes does not seem to help much in answering another. This fragmentation and pluralism are characteristic of postmodernism, and the pertinence of these questions to Religious Life suggests how involved in the cultural context of postmodernity Religious Life now is. It is not possible to put these complexes together into a single, unitary worldview. Rather, they have to be held individually and together in a pluralistic way. This engagement with the diverse universes to which Religious Life is related is the global task of this trilogy.

Second, there are the questions that are specific to Religious Life itself but which must be asked and answered differently because of the different contexts in which Religious Life is situated today. In volume 2, therefore, I am concerned with the relationships that constitute Religious Life as a "state of life," or, as I prefer to put it, a lifeform: the multiple relationships established by the commitment to Religious Life through Profession; the central distinctive relationship to God in Jesus Christ that is consecrated celibacy; and the relational context in which Religious Life is lived, namely celibate community. Struggling with questions about commitment, about the meaning of consecrated celibacy as the defining and distinguishing feature of the life, and about the varied ways in which the reality of community is embodied to form the life context of this commitment has generated an experience that was ripe for examination at the time volume 2 was published. This experience has been, in my opinion, predominantly life- giving and liberating, but it has also been, from some perspectives, frustrating and even traumatic. Wise people can learn from both positive and negative experience. My intention in volume 2 is to examine that experience in light of history, tradition, Scripture, theology, and the social sciences, but especially in terms of the spirituality involved in responding to the vocation to "sell all," that is, to give the all of one's life to the All who is God within this particular form of life.

Third, as Religious have engaged the new experiences arising from their much broader and deeper interaction with the world from which they were once virtually completely separated, they have encountered a whole new set of questions and challenges about how to live as disciples of Christ and Religious in this new context and what it means to participate in the salvation of the world which God so loved as to give the only Son. The attempt to describe and interpret this broadened experience is the subject matter of volume 3. It begins with an in-depth inquiry into the meaning of "world" and what it means to be missioned, as Religious, to that world. The second and third parts of the volume are concerned with how by Profession of evangelical poverty and prophetic obedience Religious construct an "alternate world," namely, a concrete realization of the Reign of God in opposition to the Kingdom of Satan, which is structured by possessive exploitation and oppressive power. The struggle between these two world constructions goes on in history, in the "field" of God's good creation (including humanity) on its journey to fulfillment. The struggle between these two world constructions, between the "wheat" of God's sowing and the "weeds" of Satan's project, takes place in the living by Religious of the economics and the politics of the Reign of God in community and ministry. From within the "alternate world" they create Religious are missioned to the world that is torn between God and Satan. This is a very different experience and self-understanding than that which characterized the preconciliar "flight from the world" theology of Religious Life.

Needless to say, this work is not, indeed could not have been, the product of one person's reflection. Numerous individuals and groups have offered invaluable assistance with different aspects of each of the volumes and are acknowledged in the appropriate places. However, some people and institutions have played a role in the entire project and I wish to thank them in this general Preface.

First, my gratitude goes to the numerous Religious Congregations that have invited me to reflect with them on their experience and have thus helped me to discern the real questions and to appreciate the diversity of approaches to them. I am deeply grateful to the writers and lecturers, women and men, who have been discussing Religious Life throughout the five decades that have elapsed since the Council. I am also much indebted to newer Religious, especially the members of Giving Voice, who have been seriously engaged in discussing this life from the standpoint of those who never experienced preconciliar Religious Life. It has been a special privilege to participate in various ways with national and international organizations such as the Leadership Conference of Women Religious, the Religious Formation Conference, and the International Union of Superiors General (women) and Union of General Superiors (men) and the leaders of Religious Congregations from all over the world who have participated in the symposia sponsored by UISG and USG, from whom I have learned so much.

I owe particular thanks to my own Religious Congregation, the Sisters, Servants of the Immaculate Heart of Mary, whose never-failing support and appreciation of my work has made me both proud and humbly grateful to be a Religious in these challenging times. I want also to thank the Carmelite community of Baltimore for their wonderful hospitality to me on numerous occasions as I have prayed and reflected on the issues discussed in this work.

The actual task of writing would not have been possible without the combination of financial resources generously provided by the Lilly Foundation and the Louisville Institute, and the precious resource of time provided by leaves of absence for research from my home institution, the Jesuit School of Theology at Berkeley. My editors at Paulist Press, Lawrence Boadt (of happy memory), Paul McMahon, and Donna Crilly, have been perfect collaborators. And a wonderful succession of research assistants—Jan Richardson; Joanne Doi; MM, Rev. Beth Ford Friend; Margaret Gorman, SND; Ray McNamara, RSM; Shari Roeseler; Jessica Taylor; and currently Amanda Kaminsky—they alone know how invaluable their tireless chasing down of facts and figures, meticulous attention to the details of production, careful proofreading, creative suggestions, and impressive skills with the computer have been.

I have been assisted in ways far too numerous and frequent to list by my colleagues at the Jesuit School and the Graduate Theological Union. It is a rare boon to work in a context that includes world-class experts in almost any field of knowledge in which one might need assistance and to experience their readiness at any time to help with matters as small as a reference or fact and as extensive as a lengthy consultation. My thanks to all of them.

My debt extends to the staffs of several libraries but especially those of the Flora Lamson Hewlett Library of the Graduate Theological Union and the Alcuin Library of St. John's University in Collegeville, MN, which serves the Institute of Cultural and Ecumenical Research at which I was privileged to spend a wonderfully fruitful Fellowship semester in the spring of 2005.

Finally, my heartfelt thanks to Bishop John Cummins, Ordinary emeritus of the diocese of Oakland, California, to whom volume 3 is dedicated. I have enjoyed his friendship since before his arrival in Oakland and continue to appreciate it since his retirement. His deep understanding of and fidelity to the content and spirit of Vatican II, his love of learning, devotion to scholarship, appreciation of the contribution of theologians and Religious to the local and universal Church, and his personal warmth and vibrant humanity has created an atmosphere most conducive to serious intellectual work in service of the Church throughout almost all of my theological career.

While I have learned much from those who have helped me with all three volumes of this work I have, inevitably, made the final decisions about the content of these volumes and bear sole responsibility for what has resulted. I can only say that whatever limitations they suffer (and they are surely many) they would have been much more numerous and serious without such help. I hope my readers will profit from what they find here, challenge what is questionable, and go on to enrich the conversation about the treasure of Religious Life, hidden in the field of Church and world, for which some, in their joy at finding it, have unhesitatingly sold all they possessed.

Epiphany 2012
Berkeley, California

Acknowledgments

Even more than was the case with the first two volumes of *Religious Life in a New Millennium* this volume has benefited from the extensive and substantive help of a number of people without which it would not only be far less adequate than it is but would probably never have seen the light of day. It has been my privilege to be associated with these people and my joy to acknowledge their contributions.

First, Margaret Brennan, IHM, Barbara Green, OP, and Rev. Elizabeth Ford Friend prepared the Study Guide for all three volumes, which will appear with this volume as a separate fascicule. Creating the Study Guide required not only reading the lengthy volumes and writing the texts of the summaries but developing the pedagogical tools to help people engage the material. My gratitude for their intelligent, creative, and generous contribution to this project will be multiplied many-fold, I am sure, by those who will study these books personally and in groups with the help of the Guide. This pedagogical tool will be of special benefit to Religious for whom English is not their mother tongue.

The meticulous work of Margaret Gorman, SND, on the format of the text and of Jessica Taylor who prepared the bibliography, two research assistants *extraordinaire*, has been a godsend.

A number of scholars have aided me, with expertise from their disciplines, on aspects of the subject matter of volume 3 about which they know far more than I. People who have read the whole, or a substantial portion, of the manuscript are the following: Mary Coloe, PBVM, who commented on the entire manuscript; Barbara Green, OP, who not only read and made suggestions on the entire manuscript but helped especially with chapter 4 on the Old Testament material on poverty.

xxi

Amata Miller, IHM, gave me significant help on chapter 5 in regard to economics and Catholic Social Teaching. Rev. Richard McBrien was very generous in written and oral consultations on Church history, especially by reading and critiquing chapter 7 in regard to the papacy and Vatican II; Kilian McDonnell, OSB, and Constance FitzGerald, OCD, read various chapters and were most generous with their consultations, especially in regard to the material on obedience and community. Ray Maria McNamara, RSM, helped me to understand pertinent material on the new cosmology and ecological issues. Whether or not I have followed their suggestions on any given point (and usually I have), I have learned much from each of these colleagues that has enabled me to ask better questions, see the topics more comprehensively, and arrive at more considered positions.

I owe special thanks to the following canonists and Canon Lawyers who have supplied endless references, judicious interpretations, helpful opinions including options of interpretation I would not have seen, and, at times, virtually tutored me on significant points: Francis Morrisey, OMI, and Lynn Jarrell, OSU, who each read significant portions of first-draft material and gave me a good deal of time in consultation. I also thank John Beal; Thomas Green; Sharon Holland, IHM; Rose McDermott, SSJ; Nancy Reynolds, and SP; and Rosemary Smith, SCNJ. I not only learned a great deal from these experts but grew greatly in my appreciation of the ministry Canon Lawyers exercise in the Church. There may well still be errors or poor judgments concerning Church law in these pages, but they are certainly not the fault of these scholars to whom I am so grateful.

For help in understanding the concerns and interests of younger Religious I am grateful to Paul Bednarczk, CSC, of the National Religious Vocation Conference; to Maria Cimpermann, OSU; to Julie Vieira, IHM, and Maxine Kollasch, IHM, of "A Nun's Life Ministries"; and to the women of "Giving Voice."

I am especially grateful to my colleagues at the Jesuit School of Theology who discussed the New Testament material on poverty in chapter 4 at a Faculty Colloquium, thereby giving me the advantage of interdisciplinary criticism of that crucial material.

Finally, I want to thank the Louisville Institute for financial support for the early stages of research for this book; the Board and administration of the Jesuit School of Theology, especially Dean Kevin Burke, SJ, for research and writing time; the administrative and support staff of the Jesuit School of Theology and the Information Technology personnel of the Graduate Theological Union for timely help on numerous occasions; and the Library Staff of the Graduate Theological Union for research assistance.

As anyone who navigates the exhilarating but arduous and often lonely journey of research and writing knows well, it is not only professional colleagues, technical assistants, and those who supply material resources who help bring the results of scholarship to publication. In a very special way, it is friends who offer companionship, understanding, the respite of shared recreation, interest that never shows boredom and ever-ready encouragement (and the timely cup of coffee or spontaneous phone call) who keep one not only sane but motivated as weeks become months and the end continues to recede. I cannot thank enough my dear friends Kathleen, Rich, John, Rita and Tom, Clare, Cornie, Barbara, Connie, Mary, and Dot. You know what you have contributed to my work, but even more to me.

In a very special way I thank God for the presence in my life and accompaniment in this work on Religious Life of someone who will never read it, my dear friend Mary Milligan, RSHM, who died a few months before it was completed. We met in Rome, two young Religious with our eyes on the Star that had risen at Vatican II, on the Feast of the Epiphany in 1972. Mary went on to became a major figure in American and international Religious Life as well as a revered leader in her own Congregation. Her wide and deep experience, both public and personal, were a resource ever at my disposal. I have no doubt she has had something to do with this book finally going to the publisher—on the Feast of the Epiphany 2012.

Although the positive contribution of others to this work has been enormous, the final responsibility for its shortcomings, of which I suspect there are many, rests solely with me. Because of the importance for the Church and the world of the gift that is Religious Life, this is an intimidating responsibility. (One always hopes that one's blunders will concern insignificant subjects!) But I am encouraged to risk offering these fallible and finite efforts by my trust that this text's intended readers, Religious and their friends, lay and ordained, will recognize any errors, poor judgments, or false starts and will be able to find better responses, perhaps because I have been able to identify some of the more significant questions.

Feast of the Epiphany 2012
Berkeley, California

Abbreviations

A.A.   *Apostolicam Actuositatem* (Decree on the Aposto-
              late of Lay People), in Flannery. vol. 1.

A.G.   *Ad Gentes* (Decree on the Church's Missionary
              Activity), in Flannery, vol. 1.

CARA   Center for Applied Research in the Apostolate.

BTB   *Biblical Theology Bulletin.*

CBQ   *Catholic Biblical Quarterly.*

CCC   *Catechism of the Catholic Church* (Collegeville, MN:
              Liturgical Press, 1994).

CCL (1917)   John A. Abbo and Jerome D. Hannon, *The Sacred
              Canons: A Concise Presentation of the Current Disci-
              plinary Norms of the Church (in Paraphrase)*, 2 vols.
              (St. Louis: Herder, 1951).

CCL (1983)   *Code of Canon Law: Latin-English Edition*, transla-
              tion prepared under the auspices of the Canon
              Law Society of America (Washington, DC: Canon
              Law Society of America, 1983).

C.D.   *Christus Dominus* (Decree on the Pastoral Office
              of Bishops in the Church), in Flannery, vol. 1.

CICLSAL   Congregation for Institutes of Consecrated Life
              and Societies of Apostolic Life (Vatican).

CMSWR   Council of Major Superiors of Women Religious.

CTSA   Catholic Theological Society of America.

CWS Classics of Western Spirituality Series (Mahwah, NJ: Paulist Press, various dates).

D.H. *Dignitatis Humanae* (Declaration on Religious Liberty), in Flannery, vol. 1.

D.V. *Dei Verbum* (Dogmatic Constitution on Divine Revelation), in Flannery, vol. 1.

E.E. *Essential Elements in Church Teaching on Religious Life,* issued by the Sacred Congregation for Religious and Secular Institute (SCRSI). English translation in *Origins* 13 (1983): 133–42.

Flannery *Vatican Council II: The Conciliar and Postconciliar Documents,* edited by Austin P. Flannery, 2 vols. (Grand Rapids: Eerdmans. 1975 and 1984).

F.T.T. Sandra M. Schneiders, *Finding the Treasure: Locating Catholic Religious Life in a New Ecclesial and Cultural Context* [Religious Life in a New Millennium, vol. 1] (New York/Mahwah, NJ, 2000).

G.S. *Gaudium et Spes* (Pastoral Constitution on the Church in the Modern World), in Flannery, vol. 1.

LCWR Leadership Conference of Women Religious.

L.G. *Lumen Gentium* (Dogmatic Constitution on the Church), in Flannery, vol. 1.

N.A. *Nostra Aetate* (Declaration on the Church's Relations with Non-Christian Religions), in Flannery, vol. 1.

NAB New American Bible.

NCCCL *New Commentary on the Code of Canon Law Commissioned by the Canon Law Society of America,* edited by John P. Beal, James A. Coriden, Thomas J. Green (New York/Mahwah, NJ: Paulist Press 2000).

NCR   *National Catholic Reporter.*

NIV   New International Version of the Bible.

NJBC   *New Jerome Biblical Commentary,* edited by R. E. Brown, J. A. Fitzmyer, R. E. Murphy (Englewood Cliffs, NJ: Prentice Hall, 1990).

NRSV   New Revised Standard Version of the Bible.

NT   New Testament.

O.T.   *Optatam Totius* (Decree on the Training of Priests), in Flannery, vol. 1.

O.E.   *Orientalium Ecclesiarum* (Decree on the Catholic Oriental Churches), in Flannery, vol. 1.

OT   Old Testament.

P.C.   *Perfectae Caritatis* (Decree on the Up-to-Date Renewal of Religious Life), in Flannery, vol. 1.

P.G.   *Patrologia curus completus: Series Graeca* (Paris: J. P. Migne, 1857–66).

P.L.   *Patrologia cursus completus: Series Latina* (Paris: J. P. Migne, 1844–55).

P.O.   *Presbyterorurn Ordinis* (Decree on the Ministry and Life of Priests), in Flannery, vol. 1.

S.A.   Sandra M. Schneiders, *Selling All: Commitment, Consecrated Celibacy, and Community in Catholic Religious Life* [Religious Life in a New Millennium, vol. 2] (New York/Mahwah, NJ, 2001).

S.C.   *Sacrosanctum Concilium* (Constitution on the Sacred Liturgy), in Flannery. vol. 1.

SCB   Sacred Congregation for Bishops.

SCRSI   Sacred Congregation for Religious and Secular
            Institutes (Vatican). Precursor of CICLSAL.

U.R.   *Unitatis Redintegratio* (Decree on Ecumenism), in
            Flannery, vol. 1.

Introduction

This final volume of *Religious Life in a New Millennium* bears as title the third action in the thematic scriptural citation that supplied the titles of the first two volumes, Matthew 13:44, which I accommodate as follows: Religious Life is like a TREASURE which a person FOUND hidden in a field and out of joy SOLD ALL she had to BUY THAT FIELD.

Volume 1, *Finding the Treasure*, is devoted to trying to "find," that is, *locate*, Religious Life in the overlapping fields of postmodern culture and the postconciliar Church. The thesis is that the once easily recognized and defined reality of Religious Life has become difficult to discern in itself or to distinguish from other forms of life in the Church, that is, it has been "lost" to view, not only to the view of those outside the Church or outside Religious Life itself but also, in many ways, to the view of Religious themselves. This predicament is not due to lack of commitment on the part of Religious or animosity on the part of others but to the radically changed situation in which it finds itself at this juncture in history. The undermining of the classical worldview with its ontologically based cosmology and post-Enlightenment self-understanding and the radical conciliar reorientation of the Church from rejection of the world to solidarity with the world subverted the theological self-understanding of the life and its sociological embodiment as the total institution we called "convent life." Consequently, if Religious are to create the renewed form of the life required by the new situation they need to understand the *context that is affecting* Religious Life. Volume 1 was an attempt to find new ways to position Religious Life as a prophetic lifeform in relation to that complex context.

The second volume, *Selling All*, engages the issue of *commitment* in Religious Life, the total self-gift that is not only the "cost" of the treasure but that internally constitutes the life itself. Thus, vocation to, preparation for, and perpetual commitment by Religious Profession provided the prelude to extended treatments of the constitutive relationships of Religious Life: to Christ in lifelong consecrated celibacy and to the community in the Religious Congregation. Volume 2 suggests that these relationships constitute the *internal reality* of the life.

In this third volume, *Buying the Field*, I am challenging the usual imaginative interpretation of the third action in the biblical text. I never recall anyone asking what the person in the text did with the field she or he had bought once she or he had dug up the treasure. But the fact that nothing more is said of it suggests that it was abandoned as its new owner was absorbed in appropriating the treasure. Indeed, that would be an apt description of the sequel to entrance into Religious Life in times past. The "world" in which the candidate had found the treasure of Religious Life was abandoned, indeed rejected. Its fate was left to "seculars" as it no longer concerned the one who had definitively renounced it. Did it become a vacant lot, an overgrown eyesore that hosted nefarious activities best carried on in the underbrush? Did someone else appropriate it? And, if so, did that person care for it and cultivate it or exploit it for personal gain until it was depleted? If these questions evoke those we are beginning to ask today about the natural universe whose treasured resources humanity has extracted and exploited, the evocation is intentional. The world, and the complex relation of Religious to it, is the complex and controversial topic of this volume.

In this extended biblical metaphor that has supplied the titles for the three volumes, I have suggested that the field in which Religious Life had been hidden from view has become, in fact, its new context. The postmodern world and the postconciliar Church constitute the reality to which Religious Life must develop new relationships if its distinctive identity is to be fruitful for a new situation. In other words, while *possessing the treasure*, at the price of *selling all*, is of consummate importance, so is the *field* in which this treasure is found. Religious Life, especially in its ministerial form, does not exist simply to be treasured by those called to it and used by them for their own purposes (however worthy), but also and equally importantly, this treasure exists for the sake of the Reign of God in this world. Religious Life is not only profoundly *affected by* its context as we saw in volume 1, but also must *affect* its context which is the burden of this volume. Its prophetic character situates it in the Church and turns it, through the Church, toward the world.

In part 1, I will propose a biblical and theological framework for a spirituality of world-engagement[1] that will be developed in parts 2 and 3. That framework will be constructed in two stages. In chapter 1 we will explore the variety of understandings of "world" that have emerged in the history of the Christian movement and bring them into relationship with the meanings of κόσμος (world) in the New Testament in order to discern more clearly the meaning of the tradition of Religious renunciation of the world and how that tradition needs to be criticized today as well as reappropriated for our times. In chapter 2, I will focus on the specifically Christian, that is, Resurrection-based, prophetic identity of Religious which empowers them for witness and ministry in and to the world. And in chapter 3, I will raise the question of how we can understand the mission of Religious to the world today. We need, in short, to discern the field, describe the harvesters, and delineate their task.

In part 2, we will be concerned with the economic dimension of the world. The lens for the theological analysis of and development of a spirituality for the participation by Religious in the coming of the Reign of God in relation to the handling of material goods is the vow of evangelical poverty and its role in the construction of the alternate economic system that characterizes the mystical-prophetic lifeform of Religious. After mining the Old and New Testaments in chapter 4 for resources for understanding the meaning of poverty, chapter 5 is devoted to the communitarian and ministerial dimensions of the alternate economic world that Religious create. And in chapter 6 we examine the unitive dimension of the vow, the spirituality of poverty of spirit and how it functions in the quest for God. The context for these considerations is the economic reality of the first world within a world economy that is marked by globalization (i.e., first world hegemony), increasing economic violence, and the ever-widening gap between the very rich and the very poor.

Part 3 will be concerned with the vow of prophetic obedience and its role in the construction of the alternate political system that characterizes the alternate world Religious create and live in and from which they minister. After developing a framework for a renewed understanding of Religious obedience that takes account of the horror that the Holocaust's sacralization of blind obedience wreaked upon the human race, what we can learn from the social sciences, the human sciences, and historical experience about power, authority, and obedience, and what Jesus as model of obedience teaches (chapter 7), we will turn to the community and ministerial dimensions of prophetic obedience as the politics of the Reign of God (chapter 8). In chapter 9 we will attempt to clear a space in the Church for a new understanding of prophetic obedience in the ministry and spirituality of Religious. Finally, in chapter 10, we will explore the unitive function of obedience at different stages in the spiritual life of Religious.

The conclusion of this volume will also be the conclusion and the synthesis of the project as a whole. After recalling the Conciliar context from which the renewal of Religious Life arose and the radical reorientation of the life, for so long self-defined in terms of world-rejection, to the world which God so loves, I devote a lengthy section to unpacking a descriptive definition of Religious Life as it has been interpreted and articulated in these three volumes. The description presents it as an organic lifeform that is intrinsically Catholic Christian (though not denominationally exclusive), mystical-prophetic (rather than hierarchical and institutional), and ecclesial (rather than ecclesiastical), and is constituted by perpetual profession of the vows lived in community and ministry. I discuss some of the implications of these constitutive features of the Life in relation to some of the disorientation and trauma Religious have experienced, particularly in relation to ecclesiastical power and authority, in the years since the Council. Without in any way minimizing the suffering these have caused I deny them the final word, preferring to read the future in terms of the paschal mystery, the triumph of life over death, which is at the heart of Religious Life.

As I said at the outset, I first considered as possible titles for this third volume "ransoming the field" or "tending the field." But both suggested to my imagination a kind of extrinsicism that seemed less radical than what I am proposing in this volume about the relation of Religious to the world. When we buy something, at least in first world culture, we become responsible for it. We can choose to relate to it from a position of dominative power. We can abuse it, exploit it, throw it away, destroy it, or neglect it. Or we can choose to relate to it interdependently, recognizing its God-given value and our own responsibility. We can treasure it, care for it, cultivate it, repair its defects, protect it from exploitation, maximize its creative potential by proper and reverent use, share it with others, and even give it as gift to the generations who will succeed us, and consecrate it to God. Ownership, in other words, can mean domination and exploitation, or it can mean participation, mutuality, and stewardship.

First world culture has, historically, tended to put the emphasis on the first, both in regard to material goods and in regard to our non-human cosmic environment. And the often imperialistic approach to mission on the part of the Church has tended to incarnate this proprietary attitude both toward other religious traditions and toward the "secular order." To acknowledge to ourselves that we have created the human culture and the Church as institution in which we find ourselves is to acknowledge our responsibility for them. We are not tenants who can move out when the place becomes uninhabitable, or benefactors who can make donations or send aid from a distance without dirtying our hands. We are the "owners" in the sense in which we own our bodies, our talents, our feelings, our relationships. And we must choose what we are going to do with what, in fact, is deeply, humanly "ours," namely, the cosmic home in which we live, the culture which shapes us and is shaped by us, and the Church which we are. Although "buying the field" is a metaphor for an "ownership" which is metaphorical rather than literal I hope it captures something of the seriousness of our challenge and our responsibility as Christians and as Religious for the world and the Church of our time and the future.

Once again, as in the first two volumes, I invite the reader to participate in the rethinking of the life we share as Religious. I make no claim to have definitive "answers" on any of the issues I engage. But I can offer some resources from the areas of Scripture, theology, spirituality, sociology, and cultural studies pertinent to them and which I have had the privilege not only of studying but of discussing with many Religious in North America and in other countries. If what I offer in these pages helps to stimulate reflection, personal and corporate, and generate further discussion and shared commitment among us it will have accomplished its purpose.

Part One

Theological Context

Chapter One
Naming the Field: Meaning of "World"

I. Introduction

As the title of this volume suggests, all the topics with which it will be concerned have something to do with the relation of Religious Life as a lifeform, and Religious individually and corporately to "the world." Consequently, our first project (part 1) is to construct a biblical and theological framework for talking about the world to which Religious are missioned (chapter 1), the identity of Religious as those who are missioned to that world (chapter 2), and the nature of the mission entrusted to them (chapter 3). Within this framework we can then attend, in the remainder of the book, to the particulars of world-construction and world engagement that are characteristic of Religious Life as a distinct lifeform in the Church.

A source of the confusion and misunderstanding which often arise in ordinary discourse is the assumption that the meaning of the term under discussion (e.g., "the world") is self-evident. Each person in the discussion assumes that everyone else understands it the same way she or he does. The resulting discourse, which seems unproblematic, generates certain rhetoric around the reality in question which becomes the accepted wisdom on the subject. It is only when serious confusion and clearly incompatible positions emerge that the discussants are forced to raise the questions, "What are we talking about?" and "Are we talking about the same thing?" This is the

3

situation regarding the term "the world" as it has functioned in the self-understanding of Religious and their understanding of their lifeform in the Church. However, the problem of the meaning of the term for Religious is a subset of the same problem at the level of the Church itself. The purpose of this chapter is to arrive at some clarity about the meaning(s) of "the world" which can then be invoked as we consider, in subsequent chapters, how Religious relate to the world in terms of material resources (poverty), power (obedience), transformative action (ministry), and daily life (spirituality and lifestyle).

II. Historical-Cultural Models of the World

It might seem logical to begin our reflections with the biblical and theological data on the subject of the world. But, in fact, the biblical material itself emerged from the Church's earliest experience of itself in relationship to its sociocultural context, that is, the world of late antiquity. Although, as we will see in the next section, Scripture contains nuanced theological reflection on the meaning of "world," the Church's discourse about its relation to the world was not theoretical reflection on an abstraction but a response to a concrete situation, namely, the real world in which the first Christians found themselves. As the Church moved through the first centuries of its experience it generated two models of Church-world relationship. These would be complemented in the Middle Ages by a third. The medieval model, which underwent modification in the early modern period, reigned until two radically new models were evoked by developments in Europe and the New World in the eighteenth century. With major variations in diverse times and places, until the complete turnabout in the twentieth century at Vatican II, these models have controlled, to a large extent, Christian reflection on the Church-world relation. Our primary interest is in the versions of the Religious lifeform that were called forth by and shaped by these models.

It is manifestly impossible even to sketch the twenty centuries of Church history in relation to a broad topic like "the world" or Church-world relationships, much less to attend to the nuances in understanding and the enormous variations within the diverse models that characterized each period. Furthermore, it is crucial to keep in mind that we are looking at only one aspect of the Church, namely, its understanding of its relationship to the world as that understanding emerged from its actual lived experience. Consequently, many—indeed most—aspects of the Church's identity and its ministry cannot be mentioned in what follows, not because they did not exist or are not important, but in order keep our focus on the question, "How did the Church understand the world and what did that understanding imply for Church-world relations?" in a given period. We are in search not of historical description but of a broad typology of Church-world relations that will position us to appreciate the remarkable reorientation of the Church toward the world that occurred at Vatican II and why incorporating that new orientation into the subsequent experience of mission and ministry has proved so confusing and problematic, especially for Religious.

The incoherence of much very well-motivated and generous involvement with the world on the part of Religious in the postconciliar period is not due to lack of sincerity or strenuous, even heroic, effort. It has been primarily due to lack of a coherent theological framework within which to discern, choose, and coordinate efforts, and to evaluate results. However, more than forty years of postconciliar experience of Religious in ministry provides us with considerable data in the attempt to analyze the problems and search for some answers. In what follows I will first propose a typology of Church-world relations as these types developed in successive periods of history. These models are not theoretical, that is, possible or ideal ways of understanding this relationship, but rather experiential, that is, real ways in which the Church-world relationship was imagined, understood, and lived. Then I will turn to Scripture, especially the New Testament, for resources for the project of rethinking that relationship today. The purpose of this enterprise is to suggest a framework within which to situate the distinctive ministerial identity and activity of Religious, particularly first world women Religious, within the mission of the Church as a whole.

A. The Church as Persecuted Minority: Self-defense

The Church emerged in first-century Palestine as a sect of Judaism, itself a colonized, religiously defined entity within the powerful Roman Empire which was virtually coterminous with the known world. Within a relatively short time (sometime between the 70s and 90s CE), the Church's relationship to its religious matrix, Judaism, became increasingly strained,[1] until it eventually became clear that the followers of Jesus of Nazareth, who believed him to be Messiah and Lord, were no longer simply Jews but "Christians" (cf. Acts 11:26).[2] Furthermore, their belief that Jesus alone was Lord brought them into sharp conflict with the Roman Empire, whose deified emperor the Christians refused to worship. In short, before it was a century old, Christianity was doubly marginalized: in relation to its native religious context (Judaism); and in relation to the reigning sociopolitical context (imperial Rome). Christianity was not only a minority, religiously and politically, but it was a *persecuted minority*. The earliest Christian reflection about "the world," therefore, was done in terms of the struggle of the community for survival in a hostile environment, defending itself against attack from without and the temptation of its members to self-protective apostasy from within. The world, quite simply, was everything that was not the Church.

The New Testament testifies to at least two responses of the first Christians to the Church's status as a persecuted minority. One, of course, was the courageous acceptance of martyrdom when the only alternative was apostasy.[3] The other, to which the Pastoral Epistles bear witness (e.g., 1 Tim 2 and 6:1–2;), was the attempt to "fit in," to neutralize persecution by demonstrating that Christians were responsible citizens from which the empire had nothing to fear. While the first gave unmistakable witness to the religious conviction and heroic fidelity of the Christians, the second involved them in practical compromises that have affected the Church ever since.[4] For example, Paul's unwillingness to confront the sociopolitical implications of his belief that slavery among Christians was contrary to the Gospel (cf. Phlm and Gal 3:28 in relation to 1 Cor 7:21–24; Eph 6:5–9; 1 Cor 7; 1 Tim 6:1–2) undoubtedly underwrote centuries of Christian acceptance of slavery as a legitimate, or at least inevitable, social institution. And the willingness of the Church to sanction the household codes (e.g., Col 3:18–25) of secular society in a Church that was called to a discipleship of equals unleashed in the early Church an increasingly repressive patriarchalism that began with the suppression of the roles of women in the early ecclesiastical community and continues to impede the recognition of their full equality as Christians and as ministers today.[5]

In short, "the world" for the early Christians was an essentially negative and threatening reality. The term designated, in effect, everything other than the Church, which was a relatively restricted network of small communities trying to survive in a basically hostile environment. From the beginning the Church had an active agenda of conversion (preaching the Gospel to every creature [Cf. Mark 16:15]), but it saw itself as an enclave of those saved from the world, not primarily as a force for the transformation of the world itself—something which was manifestly not even a remote possibility for a numerically small, persecuted minority group in the all-powerful Roman Empire. This situation gave rise to a *self-defensive* model of Church-world relations which, in one form or another, has been part of the tradition ever since.

The earliest form of Religious Life, *consecrated virginity*, arose in the first-century Church in the dangerous context just described. The virgins, both women and men, were quintessential Christians, motivated by their faith in the Resurrection, not only to ascribe divine glory to Jesus (the threat of Christianity to Judaism's monotheism and Rome's imperial cult), but to profess lifelong virginity (which deprived the empire of their reproductive capacity).[6] The consecrated virgins were esteemed and protected in the Church both as an elite group in the local community and as the doubly jeopardized members of a vulnerable minority. The choice of virginity was a particular form of "dying to the world," one that distinguished Religious not only from the world (as was true of all Christians), but also from their fellow Christians.

The choice of virginity was not motivated by defense against a hostile secular power as was the sect-like sociological organization of the Church itself in relation to Judaism. Nor was it, as some have suggested, a form of "unbloody martyrdom" embraced by Christians who lived after the time of the great persecutions. Rather, it arose during the first century and was a cause of martyrdom. Virginity was motivated by a particular appropriation of the Resurrection, a topic to be discussed at length in the next chapter. The majority of Christians continued to marry and reproduce, that is, to build themselves through their progeny into the ongoing process of history in this world. The consecrated virgins made a radical choice against not only reproduction for the empire but also reproduction for the family. In the virgin the family died out historically, something that the virgin considered not a tragedy (like barrenness in the Jewish community) or a curse (like being born or made a eunuch), but a triumphant espousal of the Resurrection as a present, intrahistorical but history-transcending reality.

B. The Church as Official Religion of the Empire: Partnership and Cooptation

The early period of official persecution drew to a close in the fourth century with Constantine's Edict of Toleration (313 CE), which established Christianity as a legitimate religion in the Roman Empire. Shortly after, Theodosius I (379–395), in collaboration with Gratian who was emperor in the West, made Christianity the state religion of the Roman Empire.[7] The Church was not simply free to be itself; it was now an honored partner of a larger and more powerful, indeed world-dominant, religiously sanctioned political system.

Obviously, such a privileged situation was, in some respects, beneficial to the Church and, from the standpoint of the Church's mission to spread the Gospel to all nations, beneficial to the culture that the Church could now evangelize without hindrance. But it also created interdependence between the ecclesiastical and political realms which could, and often did, undermine the Church's meaning and message. Maintaining a privileged position in society is a strong incentive to avoid confrontation with the regime that is the source and guarantor of that privilege. If imitation is the highest form of flattery, it must be admitted that the Church engaged in unfeigned flattery of the empire. The Church, rapidly becoming a worldwide institution, organized itself on the pattern of the Roman Empire into dioceses and provinces responsible and subject to strong centralized government. This organizational structure, reflective of a divine right imperial conception of government, persists to this day in the Church. With a certain feudalization during the Middle Ages, it has withstood the challenge of democratization for the nearly four centuries of the modern period. The cracks in this structure are becoming ever more evident in the contemporary Church's organizational preference for self-promotion and self-defense, even at times over the good of the People of God.[8]

In short, the second model of Church-world relationship is one in which the Church, to a greater or lesser degree, is *coopted* by the world. It was during the first period of such cooptation that the second major form of Religious Life emerged, namely, *eremitical monasticism,* the life of the desert hermits. Many Christians in the late third through the fifth centuries, convinced that the Church had become so worldly that authentic living of the Gospel within the day-to-day life of the institution was seriously compromised, literally "fled from the world" to the deserts of Egypt and Palestine. There they constructed a lifeform they understood as the unbloody equivalent of martyrdom, the willing sacrifice of one's life in witness to the Gospel. Extreme asceticism was integral to this form of life and was carried in somewhat modified form into the cenobitical (or community) form of the life that developed later.[9] Because desert monasticism fell outside the control of either ecclesiastical or imperial authority, it had a certain prophetic power in the strenuous debates over orthodoxy that engaged both Church and state throughout the period of the first ecumenical councils.[10]

The earliest meaning of Religious Life as consecrated virginity was significantly modified by the emergence of desert monasticism, and these modifications would have considerable influence in the subsequent development of the life. In this new form of the life, virginity, originally a mystical reality, came to be seen primarily as sexual renunciation, that is, as a form of self-control, and as a means toward contemplation. Although the eremitical form of monasticism did not survive as the dominant form of the life,[11] its effect on the understanding of Religious Life, in terms of flight from a world judged terminally corrupt, self-marginalization in relation to a compromised Church, extreme asceticism as integral to the life, and an the understanding of celibacy as primarily an ascetical practice, has been extensive. Many Christians became convinced that one could not live "first class" Christianity as an "ordinary" Christian, that is, "in the world." Religious Life came to be viewed as an elite form of the Christian life in opposition to Christian "secular" life, which was pervasively compromised.

C. The Church as Political Competitor: Secularization

The path from cultural cooptation of the Church by the empire to the medieval situation of competition between the Church and the secular order in the aftermath of the fall of the Roman Empire was, historically speaking, rather short. The sack of Rome in 476 CE signaled the end of the Roman Empire in the West and the inevitable decline and eventual disappearance of the culture of late antiquity. In other words, the world in which the Church was born and came to maturity was coming to an end. In the cultural and political chaos that ensued, the Church was the only institution with sufficient centralized power to deal with the situation. It exerted that power not only morally, but politically and militarily, in relation to the emerging local regimes which, in the ninth century under Charlemagne and the tenth century under Otto I, federated into the so-called Holy Roman Empire, which eventually included most of modern Europe.

The Church claimed supremacy in the spiritual sphere while acknowledging the legitimacy of secular rule in the temporal sphere. However, it also claimed that, in case of disagreement, the spiritual power was superior to the temporal. Secular sovereigns often resisted the Church's control and the Middle Ages saw centuries of Church-state struggles. At times the Church forced the state into compliance with the threat of excommunication of kings and nobles and the consequent liberation of their subjects from their jurisdiction, the use of interdict, and even the use of superior military might. At other times secular rulers enforced their claims to appoint compliant ecclesiastics and even went to war against popes and bishops. But, on balance, the Church controlled the Middle Ages which, in a certain sense, it had built. It was not until the emergence and consolidation of the nation-states in the wake of the Protestant Reformation in the sixteenth century that the balance of power shifted to the secular order.

The historical construct known as the Middle Ages extended from roughly 500 (i.e., the Fall of Rome) till roughly 1500 (i.e., the Protestant Reformation). The medieval period was the "golden age" of the Church as institution and it is hard to exaggerate the power of the synthesis that it represented. Under the aegis of the religious unity of Jewish monotheism within the overarching religious worldview and moral order of Christianity, the political and legal genius of Rome, the philosophical wisdom and aesthetic achievement of Greece, the mathematical and scientific originality of the Arab world, the military vigor of the so-called "barbarians," and the artistic finesse and commercial inventiveness of emerging national cultures on the continent created a cultural-social-economic-political-military-religious colossus that was a worthy successor to the Roman Empire.

Although life in the Middle Ages was often brutal and usually short, especially during plague, famine, and war (i.e., most of the time), and the poor, as always, carried the burden that the rich generated, there was a coherence to the medieval world that held things together in a self-evident hierarchy of being and power in the physical, intellectual, and spiritual orders. Nothing that has succeeded the medieval synthesis has approached its universality, and certainly the Church would never again have the power, authority, and influence that it did in the Middle Ages.

The power of the medieval Church was as thoroughly political, economic, and military as it was spiritual, if not more so.

While in one sense the culture of the Middle Ages was more pervasively Christian than any culture before or since, in another sense the Church became more secular than it had ever been or ever should be. The Church exercised enormous political leverage, making and breaking monarchs and sanctioning its universal legislation with threats of temporal ruin and eternal damnation. The Church was a massively wealthy landowner, a military force to be reckoned with, the controller of the newly emerging universities, the richest patron of the arts, and the arbiter not only of behavior but of what could be thought, written, read, or taught. The Church in the Middle Ages was not so much coopted by the world as it had been within the Roman Empire; it had, in a sense, *become the world* because temporal power operated to a large extent under ecclesiastical franchise. The Church of the Middle Ages was profoundly (although, of course, not exclusively) secular. It did not experience itself as having become something other than itself but as having achieved its true identity by subsuming the world into itself. There was no real difference between Church and world because the whole world was Christian, that is, "Christendom" (the ancient Far East was not yet in continental sights and the "new world" had not yet been "discovered").The question was which had transformed which? Was the whole world Christian or had Christianity become pervasively worldly? The answer remained ambiguous.

It is not surprising that the Middle Ages gave rise to new forms of Religious Life, first the basically feudal form of *cenobitic monasticism* (e.g., Benedictinism) and somewhat later the *conventual mendicant* form (e.g., Franciscanism), both of which embodied as well as responded to the ambiguities of the ecclesiastical situation. The mendicants did not flee into the desert. In a very real sense, there was no neutral or wilderness place to "go" since the whole known world was Christendom. Rather, following the lead of early medieval monasticism, which had moved from the desert into the rural areas of Europe, the mendicants set up a kind of Church-within-the Church, a spiritual desert as it were, but within the new urban settings and the surrounding countrysides. They dedicated themselves not only to conventual life (which was a kind of combination of eremitical spirit and cenobitic lifestyle) but also to preaching the Gospel as masters in the emerging universities, combatting heretics, and especially itinerant preaching among the poor. In other words, they introduced into the originally stable monastic tradition an early form of mobility.

This "mixed life" emerged as the earliest form and forerunner of later forms of apostolic Religious Life. It was institutionally restricted to men but an enormous number of women were attracted to the mendicant ideal and participated in it as prayer support in the enclosed "second orders" (e.g., women Franciscans or Dominicans) or as members of "third orders," "secular orders," or various kinds of confraternities. Members of these latter were not canonically Religious since that status, for women, was reserved to the cloistered and required the Profession of lifelong celibacy, but many of these groups were the forerunners of the apostolic Congregations that were finally recognized in 1900 as a genuine form of Religious Life. One of the most famous of the third-order mendicants was Catherine of Siena who is now a doctor of the Church.

In other words, both the cenobitic monastics and the mendicants operated on the assumption of the cultural hegemony of the Church and the self-evident need for all people to be practicing members of the only true religion, namely Catholicism. But they strove to live a kind of life—stable and enclosed monasticism or the mendicant *vita apostolica* (a kind of literal imitation of Jesus in his poverty and itineracy)—that departed radically from the worldliness of the institutional Church while adhering firmly to its spiritual message. Their monasteries and convents, at least in the vision of their founders, were communities of common life in which the members renounced wealth, eschewed the exercise of power in either the secular or the ecclesiastical domain, devoted themselves to prayer, asceticism, and study, and shared the fruits of their contemplation with others. They were not hermits; nor were they the kind of apostolic agents of the institution that clerical male Religious later became.

D. Church and State as "Perfect Societies": Isolation

The balance of power in the medieval struggle between Church and state began to shift as the Renaissance (beginning in Italy in the fourteenth century and lasting in various parts of Europe into the seventeenth) gave scholars independent access to knowledge that predated the medieval synthesis and was not under the complete control of the Church. The Protestant Reformation (in the sixteenth century) cracked the structural unity of the Roman ecclesiastical monopoly. The emergence and increasing consolidation of the European nation states, some of which followed their princes into Protestantism, subverted the Church's political control of the continent. The scientific revolution (beginning in the seventeenth century) began to challenge the hegemony of revelation as the sole source of true knowledge while subverting the claim of the hierarchy to be revelation's sole authoritative interpreter. In the following century, the Enlightenment enthroned reason where faith had reigned supreme, and modernity hovered on the historical horizon. While God might still be in "his heaven" the growing consensus on earth after the Renaissance was that "man was the measure of all things." The Church progressively lost its hegemony as medieval Christendom began to come apart. Increasingly the temporal order prevailed in the struggle for the minds and hearts of people and the Church retreated little by little into a kind of isolationism perhaps most powerfully symbolized by the pope becoming, by his own declaration, a "prisoner of the Vatican" in the nineteenth century.[12]

As the pope now lived on a tiny plot of land that the secular powers agreed to leave inviolate on condition that the Church not interfere in secular affairs, so the secular rulers increasingly divided up and assumed the powers and rights the medieval popes had once claimed. No longer could the Church execute those who questioned her doctrines, control what scientists could study and conclude, determine what books could be written and read, crown or depose monarchs, dictate policy to heads of state or government, or sanction civil legislation.

In largely Catholic countries, the Church retained considerable power to influence most of these areas, sometimes having actual powers under concordats or through provisions in treaties or Constitutions. And the popes continued to speak out on topics they deemed doctrinally, morally, or spiritually important. But their leverage in such matters, except among Catholics, depended more on the cogency of their arguments and the persuasiveness of their spiritual claims to divine backing than on their power to temporally or spiritually sanction disagreement. The Church could exercise real power only in regard to its own adherents and it could no longer enforce such adherence. It therefore continued to have enormous power in so-called Catholic countries (like Ireland or many Latin American countries) but relatively little in more pluralistic societies (like the United States) and virtually none in countries that had established Protestant churches (like Switzerland or Norway) or that were virtually non-Christian (like Japan). Church and state operated in their respective spheres, overlapping occasionally and either working out the overlap by various formal and informal arrangements or settling into a relatively permanent state of mutual opposition on certain matters.

This practical separation of Church and state was a *de facto* reality which the Church recognized at one level, admitting that the state was a "perfect society" in the temporal order as the Church was in the spiritual order. But at another level the Church did not accept in principle the separation of Church and state. It continued, right up to Vatican II, to maintain that Catholicism was the only true religion, that all people were called by God to be members of the Catholic Church, and that anyone who was not a member was, minimally, in a state of invincible ignorance and, maximally, in heresy, schism, or some form of sinful unbelief. If all people were actually Catholic the Church would have jurisdiction over all, but in fact it had jurisdiction only over its own members and that jurisdiction was limited to religious matters and sanctioned spiritually rather than physically, economically, legally, or militarily.

Part of the Church's response to its circumscribed situation in the modern context was the development of a vast institutional system, which both served its members and fostered their identification with the Church and their subordination to its leadership. Every Catholic was supposed to be a registered and practicing member of a parish within a diocese whose bishop was appointed by and directly accountable to the pope, who also claimed direct jurisdiction over every individual Catholic. A system of separate education institutionalized the catechesis of Catholic children. In some places like the United States, Canada, and many European countries, not only primary and secondary but often even university level secular education of Catholic youth took place in Catholic institutions. Catholic hospitals and funeral services, social service agencies, social and recreational clubs, relief organizations, and associations of all kinds proliferated to keep Catholics among their own as much as possible. Marriage outside the faith was not only frowned upon in theory but loaded with restrictions that made it extremely difficult in practice. Relationships between Catholics and even Protestants, to say nothing of non-Christians, were suspect when not forbidden.

The relation of Church to world, in short, was not so much one of struggle as of *isolation*. The Church and the world increasingly ran largely on separate tracks, coming into conflict over specific issues such as divorce or the legitimacy of a particular military operation, and with the Church speaking publicly, with uneven effect, on social and political issues that had implications for the Church and its members, for example, justice for workers or family life.

Again, it is not surprising that a new form of Religious Life emerged to further this separatist agenda, namely, *apostolic Congregations* devoted to education, health care, social service, and foreign missions. These new Congregations, especially those of women, drew on a complex history that dated back to the end of the Middle Ages, when women's Religious Life began its long struggle against the universal imposition on women Religious in the thirteenth century of papal enclosure.[13] It also drew on the non- or semi-monastic forms of men's lay and clerical Religious Orders such as the medieval hospital and military Orders (e.g., the Brothers of St. John of God) and the teaching Orders (e.g., the De La Salle Brothers). Many women's Congregations also looked for inspiration to the non-monastic clerical order (e.g., the Jesuits), who bridged the threshold between the medieval and modern periods, responding especially to the challenge of the Protestant Reformation in Europe and the need to evangelize the Far East and the newly discovered western continents. The "mixed life" of the medieval mendicants and early modern Brothers offered a model of non-cloistered, originally nonclerical, conventual lifestyle, while the "contemplation in action" ideal of clerical and missionary Orders offered a theological rationale and spirituality for a fully Religious, non-cloistered, active ministerial life which modified even conventual practices in favor of the apostolate.[14]

The works of these new apostolic Congregations of women (and some of men like the Christian Brothers and Marianists) were explicitly religious in nature and purpose and were exercised largely in institutions built and owned by the Congregations or by the Church, and operated exclusively by Church personnel who were, mainly, Brothers and Sisters and their occasional lay employees. Clerical Religious (e.g., Jesuits, Redemptorists, and Holy Cross) established networks of institutions of higher education. These Religious were committed to providing for Catholics an alternative to the essential services offered by the secular society around them. They intended to shelter their charges from contamination by the world, arm them to resist its seductions, prepare them to compete with it on its own level and to actively promote its conversion, and care for Catholics in all their spiritual and temporal needs from birth in a Catholic hospital to burial in a Catholic cemetery.

The institutional Church's marginalization and even isolation from the world helped spur the short-lived but significant development of "Catholic Action," a form of the "lay apostolate." Where clergy could not go and Religious did not feel called to go (namely, into the workplace, the secular universities, and the spheres of business and politics), lay or secular Catholics could go. The vision of men like Leo Suenens,[15] Canon Joseph Cardijn,[16] and Yves Congar[17] fired the movement to train lay Catholics to use their ordinary and daily involvement in the secular sphere as an instrument for the evangelization of the secular order. Although this vision motivated the institutional Church to begin to reach out through the laity to the secular sphere from which it had been largely isolated and marginalized throughout the modern period, we can see, in hindsight, serious flaws in this vision and its implementation.

For one thing, the lay apostolate in its Catholic Action form was not actually "lay" in the sense intended by its theological promoters, that is, nonhierarchical and nonclerical and genuinely secular in identity and location,[18] because it was defined as "participation by the laity in the apostolate of the Church's hierarchy."[19] Thus it was understood from its inception not so much as the assumption by the laity of their baptismal vocation to mission but as a kind of extension of the clerical and hierarchical ministry.[20] Furthermore, its agenda was, like that of foreign missionaries, essentially, even if unintentionally, imperialistic: namely, the Catholicizing of the secular order and the conversion of non-Catholics to the institutional Church.

It is therefore perhaps not surprising that the call of Vatican II to lay people to undertake their baptismal mission to the secular order has not really caught on. Laity in the Church have no real model for nonclerical ministry (except, of course, women's Religious Life which, as we will see, was viewed as a kind of second-class clergyhood). So, as many lay people have taken seriously their ministerial identity they have overwhelmingly sought positions in parishes and other explicitly clerical structures doing, as far as their nonordained status allows, basically sacrament-related or otherwise clerical ministries.

But what is significant for our purposes at this point is that the development of the lay apostolate helped to consolidate the understanding of the Church-world relationship that shaped modern apostolic Religious Life, especially that of women, up to Vatican II. Religious in this period understood themselves not as a prophetic element within the institutional Church but as the concentrated, even elite, embodiment, of the Church as institution. Hence, they understood themselves as the institution understood itself: as isolated, estranged, alienated from, indeed in opposition to "the world," which included everything that was not the institutional Church. The Church was related to the world, the *saeculum*, through its laity, that is, the "seculars" in the

Church. Clergy, Religious, and members of Catholic Action, were concerned almost exclusively with the Church *ad intra*, either tending to Catholics through Catholic institutions and services or attempting to convert non-Catholics to the institutional Church through home and foreign missions.

However, and significantly, while the Church defined "the world" as anything outside the Church, Religious defined "the world" as anything outside Religious Life. In other words, for Religious "the world" included secular Catholics (even the families of Religious themselves and their lay coworkers), as well as the non-Catholic world. The terms "the world" and "secular" became virtually synonymous and essentially pejorative. Unlike the consecrated virgins of the first centuries, modern Religious did not see themselves (nor were they seen) primarily as one form of life in the Church (like matrimony), sharing the Church's position toward the world outside the Church, but as an alternative to "ordinary" Christian life which was considered "worldly" or "secular" in relation to Religious Life. This was bound to raise an even greater challenge for Religious than for the rest of the Church when the Council turned to embrace the modern world.

E. The American Experiment: Separation of Church and State

The new development in Church-world relations in the modern period, a development not welcomed by the Church until Vatican II (and even then with considerable reserve), was the American experiment with the so-called "separation of Church and State." The new nation was founded by self-exiled refugees from England seeking autonomy from the established religion of Britain for the free exercise of their faith. After the Revolution in which the colonists won independence from the mother country, they added to the new nation's Constitution (ratified in 1788) ten amendments which came to be called the Bill of Rights,[21] the first of which forbid the government to establish any religion, to interfere with the practice of any religion, and implicitly, therefore, to favor one religion over another. However contorted the interpretation of this amendment has been in American jurisprudence, the basic principle that every individual is free to follow his or her own conscience in the matter of religious belief and practice was a radical departure philosophically, politically, and practically from anything that had preceded it.

For Catholics in America, who were a persecuted minority at the beginning of the country's history and continue to face discrimination in some places down to the present,[22] the First Amendment meant that, under the protection of the law of the land, they could freely practice their religion, educate their children in the faith, and participate as equals in the political, economic, and social life of the nation. To Catholic Church authority, however, the new doctrine of religious freedom was heretical. It appeared to some to be based on, or at least to imply, the theological presupposition that all religions were intrinsically equal, a sure incentive to religious relativism and indifferentism. It clearly violated the principle that "error has no rights" by according equal rights to "false religions."

In fact, the American provision for non-establishment of religion was not a theological position on the relative merits of religions. It was the expression of a political conviction that the state was not competent to make a judgment about the truth or falsity of any religion. The state's task was to protect the right of the citizen as a person to follow his or her own conscience as long as there was no overriding concern for the common good that demanded state intervention. The eventual acceptance of this stance by the Church came not in terms of the American political position on the separation of Church and state, but in Vatican II's biblically based recognition that freedom of conscience is a value superior even to the Church's claim to be the sole true religion.[23] If people have a God-given duty to follow their conscience (which they do), they must have a corresponding right to do so and it extends to the matter of religious or denominational affiliation.[24] Civil protection of the right to act on that conscience decision was therefore clearly justified, indeed necessary. So, the political principle of separation of Church and state came in the back door of the theological affirmation of freedom of conscience. This affirmation, though biblically buttressed, was due in no small part to the Church's experience of increasing religious pluralism over which it had no control even in formerly Catholic countries, and its minority and even persecuted status in many places. The Church could not claim the right of its members to freedom from religious persecution in places where it was a minority religion if it denied the same right to members of other religions in places where Catholics were a majority.[25] The Church might continue to claim it was the only true religion but it had to relinquish the claim that what it considered false had no rights. Error might not have rights but people, even if in error, do.

F. Vatican Council II: Solidarity

The same Council which, in *Dignitatis Humanae*, the "Declaration on Religious Liberty," recognized this right of conscience and its political implications also promulgated *Gaudium et Spes*, the "Pastoral Constitution on the Church in the Modern World,"[26] which declared the Church's solidarity with the very world with which it had had such a troubled relationship throughout the modern period, and that it had rejected more and more explicitly since the loss of the Papal States. That pastoral Constitution affirmed the legitimate autonomy of the secular order, and declared that the Church desired not only to abandon its stance of isolation and animosity toward the world but to share intimately in its concerns and destiny. The magnitude of the effect of this reversal of position on the world itself and the Church's relationship to it has probably not yet been fully appreciated. It marks, along with the affirmation of freedom of religion and the guarded and tentative recognition of religious pluralism as somehow, mysteriously, part of God's plan of salvation,[27] a really new orientation of the Church toward the world. The history of negativity toward the world (defensiveness, cooptation, competition and secularization, isolation and animosity) was now supplanted by a positive evaluation and an embrace of a kind of equality and *solidarity* that really had no large-scale precedent in the Church's experience, even in the Middle Ages.

The new attitude toward the world was indeed a breath of

fresh air for lay Catholics who lived and worked in the secular sphere. These Catholics, in practice, affirmed many of the values of the modern world, profited from its progress, and shared its ambitions even as they struggled to keep their religion out of conflict with the rest of their lives. The "Sunday Catholic" who had lived in two self-enclosed worlds could now be, in good conscience, a seven-day-a-week secular Catholic, and a seven-day-a-week Catholic secular. The term "secular" still had a faintly negative odor for most Catholics because "worldly" (its English equivalent) as a positive term was still new on Catholic tongues even decades after the Council. But whatever language is used, the affirmation of the world as the proper sphere for the living of one's faith, rather than a negative or even hostile environment in which one must somehow preserve one's faith against all odds, meant liberation and empowerment in relation to everyday life as a participant in one's culture and its history.

For Religious, however, who also rejoiced in the new attitude, the challenge of incorporating it into their lives has proved much more difficult than almost anything else they have faced in the wake of the Council. Historically, Religious Life has been virtually defined as "death to the world" and, since the exodus to the desert of the first hermits in the late third century, as "leaving the world" or "flight from the world," or "separation from the world." (Death to the world and flight from the world are not synonymous, as we will see later, but that fact was not clear to most Religious.) Religious were, virtually by definition, those who renounced secular life including marriage and family and the full participation, as individuals, in the economic and political spheres open to lay Catholics. How, then, were Religious to understand themselves in this new context in which world renunciation seems to have no justification? If it has no justification, does Religious Life itself differ in any significant way from that of committed secular Christians? And if it does not differ, what is the point of undertaking obligations that are not demanded by the Gospel?

These questions, which ushered many Religious out of Religious Life in the 1970s and 80s, still have not received a fully adequate and coherent theological response. The sincere affirmation of the world, the increased sense of solidarity with the laity, the resituation of many of the ministries of Religious in the primary structure and locale of lay Catholicism (namely, the parish) rather than in separate Catholic institutions run by Religious, the involvement of Religious in many of the political concerns and economic dealings that were once the exclusive province of the secular component of the Church (namely, the laity), the abandonment of the cloister and other monastic devices of separation from the world, the relativization of monastic common life in favor of a pluralism of forms of community, and even the exchange of the anachronistic habit for contemporary clothes have all signaled the appropriation by Religious of the new positive attitude of the Church toward the world. But they have not yet been accompanied by a new articulation of the understanding of the distinctiveness and significance of the new form of Religious Life that has emerged.

That distinctiveness and significance, it is clear, has something to do with the relation of Religious to the world and it is articulated in Profession of the vows of consecrated celibacy, evangelical poverty, and prophetic obedience. If we are to understand Religious Life in this new, world-affirming ecclesial context it is imperative to develop a sound, biblically based, coherent "theology of the world" that can both affirm the world's goodness and the solidarity of Religious with it and reappropriate in a new context whatever the tradition of "death to the world" has striven to articulate throughout the twenty centuries of Religious Life in the Church. Only within such a theoretical framework, which can coherently relate the world and Religious Life, can we begin to answer some of the questions about the meaning of poverty and obedience, the proper location and exercise of ministry, and how Religious can and should live their distinctive lifeform in the Church and world today.

III. Meaning of "World" in the New Testament

The preceding section intended to show that the Church, from its inception, has seen itself called out of, distinguished from, positioned against, in rivalry with, or missioned to "the world" which it somehow was not *of* or *in* or one *with*. In other words, whatever the actual relationship between the Church and world was in any particular era, that relationship was not one of identity. The Church was one thing; the world another. The Church saw itself as ending where the world begins, or vice versa. But it is abundantly clear that such a separation is neither possible nor historically verified. While the world can and has existed without the Church, the Church needs the world if it is to exist as a human and earthly reality. All who are members of the Church are simultaneously, in some sense, participants in the world, that is, in the created universe and in the human race. The two realities, Church and world, overlap, commingle, and reciprocally interpenetrate each other. Despite this evident fact, some degree of alienation from or rejection of the world, whether moderate or extreme, has been integral to the Church's self-understanding as the community of those whom God has called out of the world (the *ekklesia*) for the sake of the world. History shows that if and when the Church becomes too much of the world it is to some extent compromised and in need of purification or reformation.

Deep theological reflection on the world itself, not simply on Creation as the *source* of the world or on cosmology as the *Constitution* of the world but on the meaning of "world," has been seriously lacking until quite recently as the Church, throughout history, has positioned itself *ad hoc* in relation to whatever aspect or dimension of the world confronted or engaged it and then has reflected retrospectively on what its strategies and tactics implied. When the political situation was threatening the Church became defensive; when the Church was in a position of power it was assertive or even dominative. To the desert monastics the world was a moral threat to be fled; to the mendicants a potential paradise to be reclaimed; to the missionaries a challenge to conquer for Christ; to the enclosed monastics the object of prayer for its conversion. Whether the world was seen primarily in positive or negative terms, was embraced or rejected, emulated or despised, partnered or competed with, depended largely on the impact of the immediate sociohistorical situation on the ecclesiastical institution and its members.

Vatican II, following centuries of explicit world-rejection and condemnation, which was aimed especially at Enlightenment rationality, scientific progress, democracy, and modernity in general,[28] did an about-face in *Gaudium et Spes*, the "Pastoral Constitution on the Church in the Modern World." The Council's whole-hearted embrace of the world went well beyond the medieval synthesis and later Christian humanism. Whether or not this "turn to the world" was overly optimistic about human goodness or even naïvely short-sighted about the massive evils of contemporary culture (as some critics of the Council and others have contended), there is something profoundly valid in the conciliar move toward solidarity with the world which precludes any turning back. Instead, theologians and biblical scholars as well as Christians in the pew are challenged to raise explicitly the question, "What is the world: what does it mean; what is the Christian response to it; what do various states of life and vocations in the Church have to contribute to that response; what does this participation in the world offer to the Church; what are the dangers the world raises for the Church?" Religious, precisely because of their historical identification almost to the point of self-definition with world-denial, have a particularly high stake in this project.

Scripture, which the Council called the "soul of theology,"[29] is the nonnegotiable starting point for theological reflection on the world, both because of its foundational role in Christian self-articulation and because the New Testament itself is the source of much of the ambiguity about the meaning of the world and of the ambivalence of Christian attitudes toward it. Κόσμος (*kosmos*), the Greek term for "world," is extremely polyvalent. It has the potential to denote everything from the material universe to the present moral order.

Although "world" occurs in a number of the New Testament writings, especially the Pauline corpus, it is overwhelmingly, both theologically and numerically, a Johannine category. Significantly, it occurs 105 times in the Johannine corpus (seventy-eight times in the Gospel alone, which will be our primary focus), in contrast to fourteen times in the Synoptic Gospels combined, forty-eight times in the Pauline letters, and thirteen times in the Catholic Epistles. In other words, it occurs over a hundred times in the Johannine literature and only sixty-five times in the rest of the New Testament combined.[30] Analyzing the nuanced use of the term in John, then, will enable us to see how, from the beginning, Christianity understood that reality from which it distinguished itself. But, as we will see, that understanding was more a felt response to reality-as-experienced than the product of a clear, theological or philosophical analysis of that reality. Today we need a more critical discourse if we are to deal coherently with issues of world engagement raised by contemporary concerns about vocations in the Church and mission to the world.

By way of prolepsis, we will see that the term *kosmos* is not univocal but richly polyvalent in the New Testament in general and especially in the Fourth Gospel. Furthermore, the various meanings are not morally identical or even equivalent. They run from the divine to the demonic. John usually does not indicate, except by context, which meaning is in play. No doubt this helps explain why, in later centuries, the term "world," which is most often used negatively in the Gospel, has tended to be used univocally to mean evil or whatever is opposed to the Church or the Gospel. Consequently, we have to sample various texts in context in order to develop a theological typology of *kosmos* in the evangelist's writing. I will restrict myself to the Gospel because it provides ample material for the task at hand.[31]

A. The World: the Created Universe as Theater of Human History

The polysemous and even ambiguous meaning of the term *kosmos* appears the first time the term occurs in John's Gospel, in the Prologue:

> The true light which enlightens every human being was coming *into the world*. It was *in the world* and through it the *world* came to be, and the *world* did not know him.[32] He

came to his own and his own did not receive him. (1:9–11
[emphasis added; my translation])

Scholars differ about whether the first two sentences refer to
the role of the Word (the true light) in Creation or to the coming of the Incarnate Word, Jesus, into human history as the
Light of the World. But in either case, the world (which here
means the entire universe and not just planet Earth) which
came to be through the true light is obviously God's good Creation, and it is this world into which the true light shines in
both Creation and the Incarnation.[33] The ambiguity attaches to
the phrase, "the world did not know him." The meaning seems
to have glided first from the true light (neuter) to the True
Light (specified now as masculine) and from the world as the
created theater of human history to the human beings themselves whom the True Light came to enlighten and who did not
know him. Is this ignorance of the Light culpable, suggesting
that "the world" in verse 10b is somehow guilty or evil? The
phrasing seems to be in contrast to the following verse, "He
came to his own and his own did not receive him" in which "not
receiving" is clearly an act of choice. The world's "not knowing"
can and probably does mean simply incomprehension, the
general failure of humanity as a whole to recognize, to discern
the presence of God in and through Creation. In contrast, the
deliberate rejection of the True Light (the Word Incarnate) by
"his own," that is, by the religious leaders who were beneficiaries of the first covenant and who should have recognized him,
is clearly culpable.

Our first meaning of *kosmos*, then, is basically positive. The
world created by God is the universe as a whole,[34] which is a primary form of divine revelation.[35] But in the Gospel, the term
particularly refers to the earth, our world, as the created home
of humans and the theater of human history. This world as
divine Creation is ontologically good (cf. Gen 1:10, 18, 21, 25,
and esp. 31) and morally neutral. However, a second meaning
of *kosmos* is hinted at in this text, namely, the human race as a
whole, which appears morally poised between recognition and
nonrecognition of the Creator. Finally, we are alerted here by a

first hint that *kosmos* may have a negative meaning. There is a world that culpably rejects Jesus, one of its "own," who comes to them from God.

Other examples of the positive or neutral usage of the term *kosmos* are 16:21 in which Jesus speaks of the woman in labor who forgets her suffering when a child is born "into the world"; 16:28 where Jesus describes his mission in terms of coming from the Father "into the world" and then "leaving the world" and going to the Father; 17:11 in which Jesus says to God, "now I am no longer in the world" because he is on his way, through glorification, to the Father; 17:18 in which Jesus says of his disciples, "As you [Father] sent me into the world, so I sent them into the world." In all of these cases, the meaning seems to be that the world is the "place" or locus in which Jesus' own saving work as Incarnate Word occurs and in which that work continues through his disciples after his glorification. The meaning is essentially neutral. This is particularly clear in 17:15, where a contrast is explicitly drawn between the world and evil. Jesus says to God concerning his disciples, "I do not pray that you take them out of the world, but that you guard [or protect] them from evil [or from the Evil One]." The world and evil/Evil One are clearly not identical. Indeed, they are antagonists. The disciples do not need to be removed from or protected from the former but only from the latter. In short, the world, as Creation, is ontologically good and as the context of human history is morally neutral.

B. The World: The Human Race

A second meaning of *kosmos* in the Fourth Gospel is humanity or the human race. The most striking example of this usage is John 3:16–17:

> "For God so loved *the world* as to give the only Son that **everyone** believing in him [the Son] might not perish but might have eternal life. For God sent the Son into *the world* not that he [the Son] might judge *the world*, but that *the world* might be saved through him." [emphasis added; translation mine]

The context makes it clear that "the world" God loved is the whole human race to which belong those who are saved by believing in the Son ("**everyone** believing") as well as, by implication, those who reject that salvation by rejecting Jesus. The world which Jesus comes to save, which is destined to receive eternal life, is not the material universe—which is not a moral agent to be either saved or judged—but people who believe or refuse to believe. The designation of this object of God's love as "the world" emphasizes the universality of God's salvific will and Jesus' saving work which are not meant for Jews alone but for every human being which the True Light came into the world to enlighten. Notice how the first two meanings of world overlap in this text without clarification. The Son is sent "into the world" which most naturally means "into human history transpiring on this planet." But he comes "not to judge the world but to save it." This immediately suggests that the world into which the Son came was humanity itself.

Another example of this usage of *kosmos* to designate humanity is 12:46, the summary of the first part of the Gospel, which the evangelist puts on the lips of Jesus:

> "I have come into *the world* as light, that **everyone** believing in me may not remain in darkness. If **anyone** hears my words and does not keep them, I do not judge that person; for I came not to judge *the world* but that I might save *the world*." [emphasis added; my translation]

In this text we have the Creation/human history meaning (I came into the world as light) and then the universal human object of Jesus' saving work (everyone/anyone or the world as the human race). The "**everyone**" (πᾶς) who believes and the "**anyone**" (τις) who hears and does not keep Jesus' words makes the distinction between those who accept him and those who reject him, but "the world" includes both groups, that is, the whole of humanity, which Jesus came not to judge but to save. Humanity will be divided not on the basis of some divine exclusivist election—for God desires to save all and Jesus comes to carry out that universal salvific will of God—but on the basis of each person's choice to accept Jesus or reject him. "The world" in this second sense is fundamentally positive, denoting the human race as composed of moral subjects whose destiny will be determined by their own choice.

However, this distinction between those who accept salvation and those who reject it reveals a major bifurcation in this second meaning of *kosmos* as the human race. When used of humans beings in general, prior to their moral decision for or against the True Light, the term refers to humans in their natural state as distinct from the order of grace or what John calls "eternal life." Every human comes into the world as a creature of God, good by nature, created and destined to participate in the life of God, but not yet a child of God, divinized by grace. The natural human being must be born anew. This second birth requires not only God's salvific will but human choice and cooperation. The distinction between humanity's natural status and the divine status of those who actually become children of God through their free choice to share in Jesus' divine filiation is mediated in the Gospel by a network of terms referring to origin. *Whence* do Jesus, his disciples, his adversaries, his opponents come?

The major difference between Jesus and his adversaries on the issue of origin is not tied to geography, race, or religion. Rather, the latter place their confidence in their biological origin from Abraham which makes them, by blood, members of the covenant. Jesus, however, while acknowledging that Abraham was indeed beloved of God and the covenant promised to him is indeed valid, maintains that true descendence from Abraham comes not by physical birth, that is, from nature, but through faith. Only the Son, whose eternal origin in God Abraham rejoiced to see (cf. 8:31–59) and to whom Moses bore witness (cf. 5:46–47) can make them truly free, that is, alive with eternal life. Consequently, human beings as human, regardless of ethnicity or religion, are "of this world," children of their human parents. They are part of natural Creation, part of the world that came into being in the Word as the Creation that God saw as "very good," but they are not yet participants in divine life. They are, as Jesus says in chapter 8:34–38, still slaves in the divine household until the Son who alone dwells in the

Father's house by nature makes them free. Jesus came into the world precisely to offer "life in all its fullness" (cf. 10:10), that is, divine life, to those once born as human but called to a new birth as children of God.

Eternal life, which Jesus claims for himself, he comes to share with all who believe in him:

> But to as many as received him, he gave the power [that is, the capacity] to become children of God; to those believing in his name, who were born not of blood, nor of the will of the flesh, nor of the will of a male, but were born of God. (John 1:12–13 [my translation])

In the Fourth Gospel, therefore, those who believe in Jesus are not called "adopted children" (τεκνία) of God. They are, rather, τέκνα Θεοῦ (1:12), really children of God. They have become by grace what Jesus as Son is by nature. The language of birth is taken utterly seriously. It is not a physical birth but a spiritual birth making one really a child of God.

The primary text on this subject is the dialogue between Jesus and Nicodemus, a sincere Pharisee who comes to Jesus by night.[36] Nicodemus introduces the question of origins by his confident assertion that he knows *where* Jesus is from because of the signs Jesus does. Jesus, however, counters with the statement that Nicodemus does not, indeed cannot, really "know" the things of God because he is basing his conclusions (even correct ones) on purely human observation. Real spiritual seeing, salvific knowledge of God's revelation in Jesus, requires a new birth. When Nicodemus registers his incomprehension at this requirement, Jesus replies:

> "Amen, amen, I say to you, unless one is born of water and spirit s/he cannot enter into the reign of God. That having been born of the flesh [ἐκ τῆς σαρκὸς] is flesh and that having been born of the spirit [ἐκ τῦ πνεύματος] is spirit." (3:5–6 [my translation])

In other words, natural human capacities, the powers we have from our human origin as children of our parents, although good, are radically inadequate for comprehending the realities of "eternal life" or the "reign of God."[37] Good will, which Nicodemus certainly evinces, is not sufficient. The incapacity is not moral but ontological; it derives from Nicodemus's origin. Only that which is born of God can receive the things of God. Consequently, human beings, if they are to participate in eternal life, must be born twice, once in the water of human birth by which they become human (of the flesh), and then anew (of the Spirit) by which they become children of God, sisters and brothers of Jesus (cf. 20:17), partakers in divine life. Although the term "the world" is not used in this pericope, its equivalents, "of the flesh" in contrast to "of the spirit" and "earthly" in contrast to "heavenly," are. Jesus finally says to Nicodemus, who is totally befuddled by this talk of a new birth: "If I tell you about earthly things [τὰ ἐπίγεια] and you do not believe, how will you believe if I tell you of heavenly things [τά ἐπουράνια]?" (3:12). The contrast is between the natural order to which humans belong by their parental origin and which is ontologically good, and the order of divine life into which they enter only by being born of God, something that they are completely incapable of achieving by their own power. It is crucial to note, however, that natural in John does not mean evil. It means ontologically incapable of divinity.[38]

The same message is carried by the story of the Man Born Blind in John 9.[39] The Fourth Gospel does not seem to have the Pauline category of "original sin" as a situation of evil or even privation predisposing one to evil arising from human generation. The human is not tainted in origin. The "flesh," that is, natural humanity, is not evil or a source of evil. It is simply radically incapable of imparting divine life (cf. 6:63). The use throughout John of the language of generation is based on our human experience that beings generate within their own species: a plant does not generate an animal; an animal does not generate a human being; human parents do not generate a child of God. The human being, prior to birth from the Spirit, is not evil or sinful but simply naturally unable to see or participate in that which is beyond the reach of human capabilities, namely, the Reign of God, or divine life. The blindness from birth of the man in chapter 9, Jesus says, is not due to his sin or that of his parents (cf. 9:2–3). All humans come into this world, according to the Fourth Gospel, in a condition not of sinfulness but simply of congenital incapacity for the divine,[40] an inability to "see" a world which "No one has ever seen…[except for] the only God who is in the bosom of the Father" and who became incarnate in Jesus (cf. 1:18). They must be enlightened by Jesus, the one who has come into the world as True Light. This enlightenment is new life, divine filiation, being born of God, initiation into "eternal life." A new reality opens before the spiritual eyes of the one who has washed in the "Sent One" (cf. 9:6–7).

This same sense of *kosmos* as the natural order in contrast to the divine order into which we are initiated by the new birth in the Spirit occurs in John 17:16–17 when Jesus says of his disciples, "They are not of the world [ἐκ τοῦ κόσμου] as I am not of the world. Consecrate them in the truth; your word is truth." Again, the issue is origin. The identity of Jesus' disciples is not determined by their human birth (of this world) but by their participation in Jesus' life, their consecration in the truth which he, as Word of God, is. Thus his disciples are "in the world," that is, in human history as human beings, but not any longer "of the world," that is, deriving their identity purely from their human nature. The world they are no longer "of" is not evil; it is natural. Those born of God are not called to renounce or denounce the natural, much less to attempt to escape from it, but to be transformed in their very humanity by the divine life they now have. They are "in" the world but "of" God.

In short, this second meaning of *kosmos*, like the first, is ontologically good and morally ambivalent. The human race includes all people to whom God's universal salvific will extends in Jesus. The members of this human race, as human, are by origin (procreation) not morally evil or sinful. Rather, they are radically incapable by nature, by human origin, of participation in divine life. This situation is changed by the acceptance or rejection of the new birth. By the Spirit the originally natural human being is given a new divine origin that is participation by grace in the divine filiation Jesus enjoys by nature. This graced existence, Catholic theology has always maintained, does not negate or destroy human nature, but rather elevates it. This basically good human nature is also, however, capable of choosing to reject the Light and to align the human subject with the Evil One. It is this choice which leads us to the third meaning of *kosmos* which can be positive or negative. It is the negative meaning that has largely controlled Christian attitudes toward the world throughout history.

C. World: The Imaginative Construction of Reality

1. Presuppositions

We turn now to the most important, but also the most complex, use of the term *kosmos* in John and must begin by precluding certain confusions. First, the use of the term "the world" in John is similar to the use in that Gospel of the term "the Jews" and both have caused major misunderstandings throughout Christian history. Although "the Jews" (οἱ Ιουδαῖοι) is used both positively to refer to God's Chosen People (e.g., 4:22) and neutrally to refer to the ethnic/religious community of Israel and its practices and traditions (e.g., 4:9; 8:31; 19:40), by far the most frequent and vivid use of the term in John's Gospel is to refer to some of Jesus' contemporaries who culpably refused to accept him; indeed, sought to kill him (e.g., 10:31). In other words, the most characteristic use of the term "the Jews" in John is morally negative. This negative meaning is the most narrow in reference—probably referring almost exclusively to the small group of historical Jewish leaders, the Temple hierarchy, who participated in Jesus' execution—but is widely understood as referring to all Jews, both leaders and ordinary people, both those of Jesus' time and place and those of subsequent centuries everywhere in the world. Throughout Christian history there has been a strong tendency, whose apotheosis was the twentieth century Holocaust, to take this third and pejorative meaning of "the Jews" as the normative and definitive meaning and thus to characterize all Jews as deicides and thus as legitimate objects of Christian hatred and persecution.

The term "the world" (ὁ κόσμος) in John presents a parallel picture. We have just seen that virtually all reality, including the natural universe of which our finite planetary home is a part, and humanity considered universally and as natural but called to divine life, is essentially good and is referred to as "the world." Our attitude toward it should be positive, that is, grateful and loving. However, in the Gospel the term "the world" is used most strikingly to refer to a morally evil reality that opposes God's project for humanity and history. This evil reality is not a place, an object, or people. It is crucial, if we are to understand the world-rejection that has characterized Religious Life almost from its beginning and which has a valid role to play in Religious Life today, to understand what this negative reality is and how it is related to the world to which Religious are called in ministry. Only a nuanced understanding of world in this third sense, that is, as an imaginative reality-construction which can be either positive or negative, can ground an attitude toward the world which is sufficiently differentiated to inform the mission of Religious to the world and enable coherent choices by Religious about ministry and lifestyle.[41]

A second presupposition about the negative use of *kosmos* in John concerns the Evangelist's highly concentrated and personalized treatment of evil. Most of the New Testament speaks of Satan, demons, the devil(s), elements of this world, principalities that are sometimes good but often evil, spirits, Beelzebul, and so on, and Jesus in the Gospels confronts and defeats these spiritual agents of evil in their various embodiments and activities. John, however, seems to have concentrated his understanding of evil in a single malevolent agent, Satan, and a single decisive battle, the cross. It is significant that there is no account in John of Jesus' temptation by the devil in the desert at the beginning of his public life, nor of Jesus struggling with temptation in the Garden before his arrest. Nor does Jesus, in John, perform any exorcisms. And as we have already seen, John does not present humanity as somehow already in Satan's grip from birth. Rather, people are free to hear Jesus' word and thus receive eternal life or to reject it. This distinctive Johannine approach to evil can actually help us to determine the negative meaning of "world," but it requires a grasp of how John presents evil.

In the Fourth Gospel, Jesus is in mortal conflict with a spiritual agent called the "Ruler (or Prince) of this world" (ὁ ἄρχων τοῦ κόσμου τούτου).[42] Jesus calls him the devil (ὁ διάβολος), a liar (ψεύστης) and the father of lies, a murderer from the beginning (ἀνθρωποκτόνος ... ἀπ' ἀρχῆς).[43] Elsewhere he is called [the] Satan (ὁ σατανᾶς).[44] Jesus, in his paschal mystery, does battle with this evil agent, exposes his lie, destroys his murderous power over the human race, and passes definitive judgment on his regime.[45] Jesus promises to send the Paraclete who will convict "the world," which this agent generates, regarding sin, justice, and judgment (16:8–11). In his lifting up on the cross, Jesus will draw all people to himself (cf. 12:32), thus wresting them from the influence of the Ruler of this World. So "the world's hatred" of Jesus' disciples (cf. 15:17ff) is motivated by the fact that Jesus has already called them out of this evil regime, out of darkness into his own light.[46] The question, then, is what is the relationship between Satan and the evil world on the one hand, and humanity in general and Jesus' disciples in particular on the other?

In 17:9, at the Last Supper with his disciples, Jesus says to his Father, "I am praying for them [his disciples]; I do not pray for the world but for those you have given me." Obviously, Jesus is not excluding from his prayer either the world that is the good Creation of God and the context of human history, nor the human race for whom he is about to lay down his life. The specification of those for whom he prays as "those you have given me" might seem to suggest that there are some who have not been given to Jesus by God. In 6:39–40, 45, Jesus did speak of those whom the Father gives him as if there were others not given to him. But in fact, these texts affirm that all people are taught of God and it is God's will that they all will believe and have eternal life. Nevertheless, it seems clear from these texts and from the defection of Judas to which Jesus refers in 17:12 that Satan can claim one who willingly aligns him- or herself with him even though the salvific will of God is universal and Jesus, the Incarnation of that will in this world, excludes no one, for he is "the Savior of the world" (4:42). In other words, "the world" for whom Jesus does not pray is something other than the created universe or the human race. But it is intimately related to them, especially to the human race, and discerning that relationship is crucial to our purposes.

2. The world as imaginative reality construction

Theologians and biblical scholars in recent years have become acutely aware of the role that the imagination plays in understanding reality, especially ourselves, the world, and God.[46] These "limit concepts," which we tend to think of as referring to free-standing entities (my skin-encapsulated self; planet Earth swinging in space; a divine being in heaven) are actually neither free-standing nor entities. They are imaginative constructions (which does not mean fantasies) by means of which we participate in reality as a whole.

We also tend spontaneously, but inaccurately, to equate imagination with reproductive or synthetic mental functions. For example, I can "imagine," that is, mentally reproduce, my office while I am actually in my car; I can combine, or mentally synthesize, notions of past time and present travel and "imagine" traveling back to the Middle Ages. But the imagination with which we are concerned here is the constructive imagination, a much more powerful capacity than our ability to recall or combine. It is our capacity to construct reality, to create dynamic images through which we interpret and respond to reality not as a collection of fragments but as a complex whole composed of wholes.

The images of the constructive imagination are not mental drawings but tensive hermeneutical grids by which we "make meaning" of our extremely rich and multilayered experience. Because I am going to suggest that the "world" with which we are concerned in this volume, including the *good world* to which we are missioned, the *evil world* which we confront, and the *alternate world* which Religious Life constitutes, are imaginative constructs, it is worth our time and effort, at this point, to elaborate this concept of imaginative reality-construction, especially our world image, in more detail.

Five characteristics of "images" as products of the constructive imagination will help clarify the concept and thus help us grasp what we really mean by this third sense of "world" as imaginative reality construction. First, **the images of the constructive imagination are dynamic** rather than static. The image is the tensive cohesion by which the imagination construes as one, as a whole, that which is dispersed in experience. We might, for example, image the Church as hierarchical institution or as People of God on the way. Each of these images includes some dimensions of the reality we call Church and excludes others, emphasizes some features and relativizes others. Each image has implications for the structure and functioning of the Church, for what is important and what is peripheral, for what belonging means, who counts and how, and so on.

The three "master-images," that, in dynamic interrelationship, decisively control our participation in reality are the God-image, the self-image, and the world image, by which we construe the ultimate coordinates of reality rather than segments, aspects, or dimensions of reality. So, for example, we may say that a person lives in a "world of her own" meaning that, for her, reality as a whole is bounded by her own concerns which do not intersect meaningfully with those of others and are perhaps quite idiosyncratic. Or someone may say that when her mother died her "world fell apart." Her mother was the organizing center of reality for this person and the disappearance of this center left reality in tatters. New meaning, new connections, new ways of relating must now be found for all that became meaningless at the death. And if this does not happen this person will live not in "world," in a coherent whole, but in some kind of vacuum which fails to hold reality together.

Images are dynamic in that they are constantly being built up, modified, affected by experience, and also in that they affect feelings, attitudes, and behaviors. For example, women who live in a patriarchal world with its mandated dependencies, *a priori* limitations on expectations and achievement, and ontologically defined inferiority are controlled in important ways by this world-image and the structures and systems which incarnate it. Their self-image, God-image, projects, relationships, attitudes and so on are profoundly affected by this patriarchal world-construct. A patriarchal world image and Church image has had a profoundly distorting effect on how women Religious have understood their identity in the Church and their vocation to ministry. And the emergence of women Religious from that patriarchal world image into a feminist "world" has both energized these Religious and seriously disturbed the guardians of the older world, the patriarchal *status quo.*

Second, **images develop and operate hermeneutically**, that is, through and for interpretation. The emergence of an image which integrates a wide range of disparate experience is often signaled by an expression such as, "I am beginning to get the picture...." For example, "I am beginning to get the picture that promotion in this company is not possible for a woman." The imaginative construction, the image of "this company" as a gender-determined constructed "world" in which women are, by definition, inferior (rather than simply as a business that sells shoes), is *built up by the interpretation* of numerous experiences of relationships, behaviors, failed efforts, and so on.

But then the image *begins to control interpretation* of what is going on, and what is and is not possible in "this company." "This company" is not a property, a population, a program, a policy, a project, or a product. It is a complex imaginative construct built up through interpretations which finally unify a range of experience into a whole which is much more than the sum of its parts and which now enables the person to understand what cannot be identified materially, proved, or even perhaps clearly articulated. But, in fact, the person now understands the reality of the situation in which she is involved much better than the empiricist collecting written data, documented instances or clear cases of discrimination. She is able to "make sense" of what others may claim is perfectly legitimate, accidental, normal, or even non-existent. She is seeing "a whole" rather than a collection of parts and the whole enables her to understand the parts in a much more complete way.

Our world image, along with the self-image and the God-image, is a "limit reality" construct. It determines what we experience as "the real world." The poor may not be, for some people, part of their world or even part of "the world." The poor are simply an abstract category. Even someone whose world includes the poor, who cares deeply about the poor, may in fact think that trying to do something about poverty is pointless because "in the real world" the rich are never going to curtail their wants in terms of others' needs and the poor and their allies are never going to have the power to change this. So, the world image includes not only what is real, but also what is important and what is possible. Religious founders, impelled by a certain world image, namely, the Reign of God, were fired with an energy derived from the Spirit that negated the "realistic" impossibility of doing something about suffering and mobilized the Congregations they founded toward world transformation.

Third, **images can never be fully articulated and clearly thematized**. The image is not a mental drawing. Rather, inchoate realizations interact with reality in mutually modifying ways so that the "limit images" (God, self, world) are undergoing continual development. This is easy to recognize as our self-image undergoes minor and major changes because of the people and events that affect us. If asked at any point what our self-image involves we could talk for a very long time without beginning to say everything, even everything important, about who we really see ourselves to be.

The ongoing permutations of the God-image as we experience ourselves as finite beings in a world we do not control are the most important dynamic factors in growth in the spiritual life. Again, who could articulate clearly who God is for her or him?

The world image includes everything in one's experience as experienced from the standpoint of oneself as subject. Moment by moment new experiences, developments, people, challenges, insights, information, and so on are emerging in relation to oneself who is moment by moment changing in large and small ways in response to these influences. For example, the world image of most of us changed in a major way when the first spacecraft took humans out of the sphere of Earth's gravity. Our world now included outer space as a possible habitation. A parent's world image changes radically with the birth of her child. But even the thoughtless remark of a friend, a physical illness, or a disappointment alters our sense of "where" we are in reality.

There is no point at which one can name or even indicate everything that is included in one's image of "world," much less explain it clearly and comprehensively. But we can make qualitative statements like, "I live in a much richer world than I did before I knew Jane" or "His world is so rigid and narrow he is frightening." One reason ministry poses such problems for Religious today is that the world from which and to which we are sent has become so much larger, more complex, and more interrelated. We used to image this school or this hospital to which we went in the morning and from which we returned at night as the world to which or in which we ministered. And the convent which we left in the morning and to which we returned at night was a relatively stable reality construction whose contours and coordinates we knew and within which we knew how to function. The dimensions and features of the world to which we now need to respond are much harder to discern, identify clearly, describe, analyze, and therefore engage. And the world of the convent is no longer the monolithic reality it once was, if indeed it exists at all. One question we will eventually raise is whether, in any sense, Religious today live and minister in a distinctive world.

Fourth, **images operate simultaneously in relation to all three modes of time**: past, present, and future. Under the pressure of current experience the imagination can shake loose the seemingly fixed contents of *the past,* leading to reinterpretation of what one thought was definitive, for example, the personal choice of Religious Life. The imagination can reframe our *current* experience so that what once seemed clearly "wrong," for example, participation in a non-Christian religious practice begins to appear permissible or even desirable, or something which seemed of the essence of Religious Life, such as the habit, now appears nonessential. Many Religious have had to re-imagine the role of institutions in their corporate identity. Their motherhouse or novitiate, their schools or their hospitals, which are deeply embedded in their collective experience and thus constitutive of their world, are being sold, inhabited by nonmembers, converted to new uses. The world in which these institutions were symbols of identity and rocks of corporate stability is now a different world. And that can lead to the necessary re-imaging of *the future* of the Congregation itself.

A massive reconstruction of the world image took place for all Religious in the wake of Vatican II when the "convent world" which had been virtually a "total institution" suddenly (historically speaking) ceased to be a self-contained sociological entity and its denizens became participants in the very world that formerly had been excluded from their experience. Again, this raises the question of whether Religious have simply been swallowed up in the secular world or whether they are being challenged to reconceive their world as distinctive but in ways the earlier image could not comprehend.

Finally, **images, especially the limit reality constructs, are loaded with affect**. This is very obvious when we think of the self-image or the God-image. A positive or negative self-image can make the difference between happiness and suicide. There is probably nothing as important in the spiritual life than one's God-image, whether God is a just judge who misses nothing or a lover who misses nothing. The meaning of "nothing" is radically different in these two images, one of which is terrifying and paralyzing and the other life-giving and energizing. Likewise, our world image is not an intellectual or abstract construct. Whether we, like God, "so love the world" that we willingly give our lives for it or flee the world in hatred or fear depends largely on how we image it. This means how we interpret it, what we think it means. The world image of Religious in an earlier time was largely negative. Religious prayed fervently for the people, good and bad, who had to work out their salvation in a context that was, for all intents and purposes, a virtually constant "near occasion of sin." But they themselves ventured into that dangerous secular milieu only when necessary and after having taken appropriate precautions such as wearing clothes that made their social assimilation in most settings difficult to impossible, disguising personal identity as much as possible, restricting where and when they would appear "in public," traveling in protective company, rendering strict accounts of their extra-conventual activities, and so on. Furthermore, the world of the convent or monastery was so markedly different from that of the extra-conventual world that cross-fertilization as well as contamination were largely impossible. The fundamental question we are raising in this volume concerns both "worlds," that of Religious Life itself and that to which Religious are missioned.

3. World as reality construction in the New Testament

We are now in a position to use this understanding of "world" as imaginative construction of reality to understand the evil world that hates Jesus and his disciples and which, through his paschal mystery, he overcomes. We will also use it to understand the alternative construction, which Jesus calls "the Reign of God." Later we will be using it to talk about Religious Life as an "alternate world." But our question at this point concerns the evil world construction of the Prince of This World. Unlike "the world" of Creation and history, and "the world" which is the entire human race, "world" in the negative sense is not a place or a group of people. It cannot be located or separated from other reality. It is a construction of reality which has certain features and which permeates history, culture, human consciousness, institutions, systems, ideologies.

In the Synoptic Gospels' narratives of the temptations of Jesus (e.g., Luke 4:1–13), we see clearly the construction of and the clash of "worlds." Jesus, just baptized, is filled with the Holy Spirit and has heard God's voice claiming and proclaiming him as beloved son (cf. Luke 3:21–22). He is living vividly in the world of the Spirit when he is confronted by the Devil, who three times challenges Jesus' reality construction with a diabolical alternative. Satan projects reality as belonging not to God but to himself. He invites Jesus to enter into this construction of reality by claiming divine power as his own, turning from the worship of God, and cynically mocking God's promises. The organizing center of reality is at stake for Jesus: God or Satan. Choosing between worlds is not a matter of geography or ethnic belonging or religious identity. It is a choice about how reality is construed by him and for him.

It is possible, and some of Jesus' contemporaries had made such a choice, to be a religiously practicing Jew living in the very shadow of the Temple, and to be actually living in Satan's world. Jesus' controversies with his opponents in the Gospels are actually a clash of worlds. Is reality, in truth, a power structure or a place where the last are first? Is it a society of the blessed poor or of the powerful rich? Luke's presentation of the Beatitudes followed by the Woes (Luke 6:20–26) is actually a contrasting of these worlds according to the principle of dependence on God versus self-sufficiency.

The parables of Jesus in the Synoptic Gospels are narrative strategies for challenging his hearers to discern in what world they were choosing to live. The parable of the Prodigal Son opposes the world of "earning our way with God" to that of accepting divine life from God as gift. The parable of the Eleventh Hour Workers makes the same point. The parable of the Pharisee and the Publican in the temple shifts this same contrast into the moral sphere. The parable of the Good Samaritan, with its main characters a heretic on the one hand and clerics in the religious establishment on the other, makes especially clear the meaning of "world" as reality construction by the contrast it pictures between the world as Reign of God and the worlds of institutional religion and ethnic belonging. One can be a member in excellent standing in the world of family, ethnic group, religion, or society (like the priest and the Levite) and be actually living in a world in opposition to God. Conversely, one can be living in a world condemned as heretical (like the Samaritan) and be a true observer of the Law.

In John's Gospel, which has neither a list of Beatitudes nor parables, we see the same concentration that we noted above concerning John's presentation of Satan in contrast to the pervasive presence and activity of a host of evil spirits in the Synoptics. John's Jesus talks more abstractly but more trenchantly about "world." The contrast between "worlds" is presented not in parables in which we see the denizens of different worlds interacting but in terms drawn from the sphere of family and family resemblance. "World" is manifested in belonging. Only those who understand and interact with reality in a similar way live in the same world, are children of the one Parent whom Jesus calls his Father.

One of the major differences between Jesus and his opponents in the Fourth Gospel is that Jesus knows whence he comes, where he is, and whither he goes. Jesus comes from God, lives in God, and goes to God, whereas his opponents do not know either his origin and destiny or their own (cf. John 8:14). Jesus' opponents, who claim that they are descendants of Abraham (cf. 8:33), disciples of Moses (cf. 9:28–29), and children of God (cf. 8:41), repeatedly ask Jesus about his origins (e.g., 8:19), and accuse him of being a Samaritan, that is, a heretic (cf. 8:48), of being possessed by a demon, that is, evil (cf. 7:20 and 8:48), of being the product of fornication, that is, unclean (cf. 8:41), and of being a messianic imposter from Galilee rather than the true Messiah from Judea (cf.7:41–42). Jesus, on the other hand, claims to be from God (e.g., 8:18 and elsewhere) and accuses his opponents of being not true children of Abraham (cf. 8:49–51), not true disciples of Moses (cf. 5:45–46), not really children of God (cf. 8:42–47), but of being from the Devil who is a murderer and the father of lies (cf. 8:44). Jesus is from and lives in the "world" of God and his opponents are from and live in the "world" of the Evil One.

It is important, as we have already seen, to avoid any anti-Jewish interpretation of these passages, that is, to avoid literalizing "world" as race or ethnic group or religion. Jesus' accusation is not that his adversaries, *as Jews*, are children of the Devil. Jesus himself and virtually all of his disciples were Jews but not from Satan's world. Rather, precisely insofar as his opponents are *unfaithful* to their Jewish heritage as children of Abraham and disciples of Moses, insofar as they *deliberately refuse the truth* God is revealing to them in Jesus, they are of the Evil One. Their origin, and thus their identity, is not the covenant with Yahweh that creates the world of genuine Jewish faith, but their partnership with Satan.

Jesus' historical opponents were, of course, ethnically and religiously Jews, as he was, but the accusation of evil applies to anyone of any historical period, any religious faith, and any ethnic or racial origin who rejects the truth.[48] Most of the people who belonged to Jesus' "world" were Jews as were most of his opponents who belonged to Satan's world. And many non-Jewish people, down through history, would come from the "world" Jesus denounced. In other words, *where* one is from, one's "world of origin," is a pivotal question because it determines *who* one is. That "where" is a spatial metaphor for speaking about one's relationship with God, whether positive or negative, as the global context in which one sees, chooses, acts. In short, the originally "neutral" human condition of being born "of the flesh," being "of the earth," is determined freely by people who either do the truth and come to the Light or who align themselves with the Prince of This World, seek darkness because their deeds are evil, and become the agents of the evil world (cf. John 3:17–21), which is neither material nor geographical but moral. Consequently, another way of speaking of these "worlds" is light and darkness. Those who dwell in the light are Jesus' disciples; those who dwell in darkness belong to the Prince of This World.

A final text, 15:18, gives us another clue to the nature of this negative world. Jesus comforts his frightened disciples by saying, "If the world hates you, know that it has hated me before you." There is deadly, implacable enmity—not just intellectual or practical disagreement, but hatred—between Jesus' world and the evil world. The world in this text is not the created universe, the human history that is unfolding in that universe, nor humanity as a whole or any particular individual or group of people. It is a construction of reality which is in opposition to Jesus and his own and which can be incarnated in multifarious ways.

According to John, and the New Testament in general, the personal agent in whom this complex network of forces originates is Satan, the final enemy of God and Jesus, bent on the destruction of the world which is God's good Creation including the human race called to divine filiation. But Satan does not operate in the open and has so hidden his persona that most people in the Western world have trouble believing there is such an agent, much less recognizing him where he is operative. Satan's vision and agenda are incarnated in the systems of domination in all areas of human experience.[49] People are both enmeshed in the toils of this powerful, deadly, ubiquitous, and malicious collusion of forces for evil and they are agents of this evil in history through their participation in these structures.[50]

Satan's world cannot totally corrupt God's good Creation and it cannot finally take hold of any human being who does not freely surrender to it. The paschal mystery of Jesus sounded its death knell, but it will not be totally vanquished as long as history continues. Jesus taught his followers to pray that God's Reign would come on earth, that is, that the reality construction, the "world" of God, would become the reality construction characteristic of this world. The Synoptics call this divine reality construction the Reign of God; John calls it Eternal Life; Paul calls it Life in the Spirit. It is the world we come to know through the Gospel, the world of discipleship.

It is difficult for us to understand in the abstract what this "world" is. Because we never see or engage it except as embodied in some person, system, ideology, institution, and so on, we naturally tend to concretize it as a place, a people, a country, a group, a political party or social system or economic mechanism, something which we can identify and engage as if it were freestanding and clearly distinct from the "good world." However, this evil world pervades the natural and historical world in which we live, the good Creation of God and the struggling human beings who are torn between good and evil. Like the weeds among the wheat in Jesus' parable (see Matt 13:24–30) which cannot be uprooted without destroying the crop, the reign of Satan and the Reign of God are intimately intertwined in the field of this world which includes both. This is precisely why the struggle against the "world" is so fraught with ambiguity; so dangerous that some Christians have actually tried to escape it by physical isolation.

In summary, the metaphor of "world" when it is used negatively in John's Gospel refers to an imaginative construction of reality according to the coordinates of evil. In this evil "world" the negative values of greed, violence, domination, exploitation, hatred, infidelity, lies, and all their relations and progeny structure the relationships and behavior of its denizens, who rationalize these negative values in oppressive ideologies and incarnate them in social systems and structures which perpetuate the evil.

However, there is not a total and clear-cut and therefore easily recognizable "face" to this evil world. Economic systems that are structured for the advantage of the wealthy sometimes include provisions for the poor, even if only to keep them from annoying the rich, and may proceed under a rhetoric of free enterprise and respect for property which can be positive values. Political systems that are dominative and oppressive may also empower segments of the population. Wars may be waged and criminals executed by people convinced that these strategies promote justice and the defense of human rights. Religious systems based on sacralized power may actually offer, at times, consolation in suffering or strength for resistance in the crises of life. Patriarchal social structures may shore up an order that keeps chaos at bay.

If the mission of Religious to the negative world is to go beyond simply alleviating the suffering caused by the world or even praying from a safe distance for its conversion, discernment must come into play in ways not recognized in earlier times when needs, such as for education or health care, were easily recognized and efforts easily focused. The disciples of Jesus need to be able to see what is really going on, to tell what time it is and what it is time for, to be able to distinguish weeds from wheat in the same field, to know who is who in the clash of persons and nations. In short, they must be able to distinguish the agents, the timetables, and the dynamics of the Reign of God from those of "this [evil] world" so that they can foster the former and resist the latter.

There are, then, basically three meanings of *kosmos* in John (and in the New Testament generally). First, "world" means the ontologically good and morally neutral *natural universe*, Creation as cosmos, and it includes the earth, which is the locus of human action and the context in which history, both natural and human, unfolds.[51] World in this sense is essentially positive. It is the reality that God, at Creation, pronounced "good," indeed "very good." This is the world which contemporary ecotheology and ecospirituality are challenging Christians to rethink and reappropriate not as dominators but as participants. Later I will be suggesting that this world is not only not to be renounced by Religious but is to be affirmed, even cherished.

Second, "world" means *humanity* as **universally** created and loved by God not only as part of the natural universe but as specifically made in the image and likeness of God and called to divine life. But it also means humanity as **natural**, that is, as susceptible to grace but only by a new birth, an act of God by which the natural human being, cooperating with God, is divinized. Religious as moral subjects are part of this world. They have chosen definitively the new birth in Christ and as ministers are called to foster the free response of others to the offer of divine life in Christ.

Third, "world" has a systemic meaning as *an imaginative construction of reality* according to the principles either of the Gospel or of the Prince of This World. Evil is incarnated by individual and collective human agency in the political-economic-social-religious systems that organize reality, both natural and human, for the triumph of evil in human history. The Gospel presents Jesus' defeat of the Ruler of This World, namely, the paschal mystery, as the principle or source for the ultimate subversion of this evil world and the reorganization of all reality into the Reign of God. The victory of Christ over the evil world has been achieved in principle: "In the world you have affliction, but take courage, I have overcome the world" (John 16:33). But this victory must be realized historically, incarnated in the natural and human worlds that came good from the hand of God but are still controlled in many ways by the forces of evil, through the action and passion of human beings. Religious take part in this struggle in a particular way. The burden of this volume is to describe the specific contribution of Religious to this Gospel enterprise.

IV. Religious Life and the Meanings of "World"

A. Introduction

In this final section we will look, by way of anticipation of and background for the rest of this volume, at the relationship between Religious Life and each of the three meanings of *kosmos* discerned above: the world as created universe, as humanity, and as imaginative construction of reality. Because of the contemporary explosion of concern about the natural world[52] and the theological implications of this development for Christian faith it seems important to devote more extended attention to Religious Life in relation to this first meaning of the term. These reflections will provide background for much that follows and prevent the need for repetition in other places. The second and third meanings of *kosmos*, that is, the world as humanity and as imaginative construction of reality, will be treated much more briefly here since they are the focus of the rest of the book.

B. The World as Part of the Created Universe

The people of biblical times knew that there was more to the created universe than planet Earth and more to this world than humans. The psalms are filled with human wonder at the life-giving power of the sun, the nocturnal light of the moon, and the dazzling diversity of the stars (cf. Ps 19:1–5). Biblical peoples were awestruck by the power and beauty of the natural phenomena of earth: sky and sea, animals and plants, rivers and waterfalls, wind, rain, and snow (cf. Pss 104, 148). But we have to recognize that contemporary people have a vastly expanded sense of the universe, temporally, quantitatively and qualitatively. And in our postmodern context we are acutely aware of the ecological degradation of planet Earth by modern humanity's intellectual, industrial, and technological "developments" and of the seemingly minuscule place of Earth and humans in the vast temporal and spatial expanse of the universe.

Christianity as a religious tradition has a checkered record in relation to the natural world. On the one hand, unlike religions that regard the material as the enemy of the spiritual,

Christianity has valued and even exalted the natural world. Christians regularly proclaim their faith in God as the Creator of "all things seen and unseen." All creatures are called upon to bless the Lord and part of the solemn duty and great glory of human beings is to provide the voice and the language for Creation's praise of its Divine Source.

However, Christian tradition has also fostered a fear of Creation as a distraction or a seduction drawing people to itself rather than to their common Creator. Furthermore, the belief that humanity is the pinnacle of Creation has fostered a sense of entitlement, domination, and utilitarianism in relation to the nonhuman world which is often viewed as a limitless supply of resources for human projects. Humans, including Christians, have tended to see themselves not as stewards, much less as participants, in the natural world but as owners and sovereigns who could make whatever use they wanted of "lower" creatures.

The history of Religious Life in this regard is also ambiguous. The nature-reverencing ethos of Benedictinism or Franciscanism at their best has to be seen in relation to the extremism of certain ascetical traditions bordering on hatred of the world and the flesh. Even Francis, the ecstatic poet of the "Canticle of the Creatures," recognized toward the end of his life that he had abused his body in his pursuit of spiritual perfection.[53] And the history of spirituality, especially that of Religious, is replete with much more egregious examples than Francis.

The doctrines of Creation and Incarnation that lie at the heart of Christianity stand in judgment on these attitudes and practices of domination, violence, and rejection of the material universe. Today, a fascination with the "new cosmology" and an enthusiasm for "Creation spirituality" have led many Christians, including many Religious, toward a deep suspicion of biblical theology (thought to be at the root of world-denying attitudes) and an affirmation of a kind of neo-paganism that deifies the natural universe, views the "universe story" as the only believable sacred history or revelatory source, and is uncomfortable with a personal God who is "lord of all" and with any kind of religious tradition which seems less than all-inclusive in regard to religious/spiritual traditions, practices, and even ethical options.

Although this raises questions for any Christian, it obviously presents special challenges for Religious, whose life is a personal commitment to the triune God focused on a relationship with Jesus Christ to the exclusion of any other primary life commitment (to family, career, projects, etc.). This primary relationship is expressed in a vow of perpetual consecrated celibacy within the framework of Catholic Christian faith. Given this highly specific and explicit character of the lifeform, the attempt by some Religious to "look the other way" on this issue, to simply make the "universe story" rather than the biblical tradition as divinely revelatory as their orienting metanarrative, to resituate their spirituality in nature-based practices that make occasional gestures toward an impersonal cosmic spirit but avoid trinitarian or incarnational references, and to define their ministries as basically nondenominationally affiliated contributions to creating "a better world," cannot finally succeed. This issue will not simply go away if no one talks about it. Christian faith in its explicitly Catholic form is intrinsic to Religious Life and those entering this life today as well as those who have lived it for decades, if they are to embrace this life authentically, must finally integrate their contemporary sensibilities into their Religious commitment. If Catholic faith and its characteristic spirituality, which are at the heart of Religious Life, disappear from the personal or corporate horizon of its members the life itself will wither at its root, no matter how much good individuals may continue to do.

Recognizing that this turn toward nature and the universe, whatever its problematic implications for Christian faith, is not a frivolous fad but a genuine theological issue that deserves to be taken seriously is the first step in dealing with it. Like most real theological questions it arises from important insights and expresses real values. It demands a new way of looking at certain topics so that those insights can be validated and those values can be affirmed and pursued without, in the process, negating the validity of the Christian religious tradition and its centrality in Religious Life.

One important aspect of this topic, which is beyond the scope of these reflections on Religious in relation to the created universe, is the perceived disconnection for many postmoderns of religion from spirituality. For many people reverence for the earth and commitment to its care are part of an ecospirituality which has no explicit connection to any religious tradition (such as Christianity, Buddhism, etc.).[54] I have taken up this question of the relationship between religion and spirituality elsewhere[55] as have numerous other contemporary authors.[56] Here I want to deal with the theological issue of whether Christianity is compatible with, or even a positive resource for, a postmodern universe consciousness which can ground a full commitment to eco-responsibility. We will look at the two distinctive aspects of the Christian vision that have foundational importance for the relationship of humans to the created universe, namely, Creation itself and the Incarnation of the Word in Jesus.

1. The Distinctive Judaeo-Christian Vision: Creation

In recent years there has been a strong reaffirmation by many theologians of the importance of the Christian teaching on Creation and its implications for a "Creation-based spirituality."[57] Certainly not all would follow those "Creation theologians" who see a virtual contradiction between a "redemption theology" (which they see as radically negative and unfaithful to the Christian tradition) and a "Creation spirituality"[58] (which they see as affirming the "original blessing" and reflected in the authentic mystical tradition). Rather, many mainstream theologians are concerned for a better balance in both theology and spirituality between these two facets of God's action in the world, Creation, and redemption.[59]

An overemphasis on original sin, its sad legacy in human history, the power of concupiscence to divert people from God to creatures, the need for asceticism, self-denial, and penance have indeed tended, at least in certain historical periods, to promote a negative attitude toward created reality including material creation itself and the products of human invention. But such overemphasis does not negate the basic Christian belief that God is the source of all created reality and that it is good. The Manichean assertion that matter comes from an evil principle and is therefore the enemy of the spirit has always been considered heretical in Christian theology. Furthermore, Catholic theology from the time of the Reformation has resisted the teaching of predestination and the pessimistic conviction that human nature was corrupted, rather than weakened, through original sin. However, human experience, including our heightened awareness of human culpability in the degradation of the world, makes it naïve in the extreme to pretend that evil and the need for redemption is a figment of the negative imagination or a mere "blip" on an otherwise serene screen of peace and beauty.

Our interdependence with all of reality is not simply a fact of experience that is being urgently brought home to us by the fallout from the drastic degradation of the planet and its ecosystems that we are finally beginning to face. It is rooted in the revelation of the divine origin of all being in God's free creativity. Our own creativity and productivity, which has done so much good and so much harm to our planet and its inhabitants, is not an independent exercise of human sovereignty but is meant to be a participation in that divine creative work. Christian biblical faith and theology can and should be a rich resource for the involvement of all Christians, including Religious, in a Christian ecotheology and ecospirituality.[60] Any lingering attitudes or practices of world-rejection that are aimed at Creation must be definitively expunged from Religious Life. Responsible participation in Creation supplies adequate challenge to anyone serious about asceticism without recourse to gratuitous abuse of self or nature.

In summary, the doctrine of Creation—that all that exists came forth good from the hand of a loving God, is sustained in existence from one moment to the next by that same creative power, and is called finally to participate in a destiny of glory (cf. Rom 8:18–23)—provides a solid biblical and theological foundation for an appreciation of and commitment to the universe in all its beauty and bounty, its danger and endangerment. Many Religious, individually and as Congregations, have already come to recognize that participation and even leadership in the work of reversing ecologically destructive attitudes, policies, and practices and developing a new spirituality of sustainability firmly rooted in a theology of Creation is as critical in the twenty-first century as educating children or nursing the sick was at the time their Congregations were founded. Furthermore, this "green" commitment is integral to the commitment to justice and peace that most renewing Congregations made in the aftermath of the Council. Whatever we will finally conclude about Religious and the world it cannot imply any rejection of matter or nature and must imply full commitment to the flourishing of all that God has created.

2. The Distinctive Christian Vision: Incarnation

If the narrative of Creation in the Old Testament as it informs the theology of the New Testament supplies the basis for a fundamentally positive approach to the universe, the Resurrection, the bursting forth in the executed Jesus of the fullness of divine life and his return to his own as living and active, is the revelatory event that supplies the specifically different Christian "take" on all of reality including the natural world. Since Religious Life is a way of being Christian, not an alternative to Christianity, it is critical that the self-understanding of Religious be grounded in a clear perception of what, in the concrete, this Christian vision implies.[61]

Through their experience of the Risen Jesus, the first Christians came to believe that in him the fullness of divinity was present and manifest in their midst and accessible in their experience.[62] One of the most striking expressions of this conviction, arising from and rooted in Resurrection experience, is Thomas's response to the Risen Jesus' invitation to touch him, "My Lord and my God" (John 20:28). Jesus is, for Christians, what God is and means.[63] Ultimate reality, absolute mystery, in other words God, is encountered in Jesus. This faith in the Incarnation of God in Jesus, which is at the heart of Christian faith, has profound implications for the theology of the religious tradition we call Christianity and its characteristic spirituality. Two of these implications most dramatically and really distinguish the Christian faith perspective from that of other religious traditions and are directly relevant to our present concern: the relation of Religious to the world.

First, the mystery of the Incarnation reveals that divinity is not something exclusively transcendent, utterly different from humanity. **Divinity is both one with us and, indeed, one of us.** Second, our humanity, personal and corporate, divinized in Christ, is the **locus, the instrument, and the focus of God's salvific and liberating work** in this world. Each of these implications needs to be explored in some depth because both directly affect Religious Life as the living of Christian faith and spirituality in a particular and radical way. And both are relevant to the question of how Religious are related to the world understood as God's good Creation.

a. GOD IN JESUS IS ONE OF US

The *first overarching implication* of the Incarnation is that the fullness of divinity is encountered in Jesus. The foundational revelation event, the breakthrough of divine life in the Resurrection, is not primarily revelation *to* human beings but *in* a human being. The Incarnation means that God in Jesus has become human to give the power to become children of God to those who believe in him (cf. John 1:12–13). At no point before, in, or after his death is Jesus anything other than human. He is the human in whom God comes to us, but he was, is, and remains truly human. This has profound effects on Christianity as a religious worldview and on its spirituality.

The first effect of the Christian affirmation that God is one of us in Jesus has to do with the meaning of *history* in religious experience. In Jesus, God entered human history as a historical subject. Human history is the locus and context of salvation. Therefore, it is not the aim of the Christian to escape from history through nirvana or contemplative transcendence or flight from the world. Incarnation, even though it has been badly understood at times by Christians in general, including Religious, means not escape from but involvement in human history, in its process, its challenges, its successes and disasters, its destiny. Human history is not the prison or the nemesis of the Reign of God but its raw material, the "place" of its occurrence.

The Council, in the opening lines of the "Pastoral Constitution on the Church in the Modern World," correctly refocused our vision on the world that Catholics had rejected for centuries and on our historical task of world transformation. The Incarnation-rooted affirmation of the significance of history and the finality of Creation's process as transformation in Christ is one of the features which distinguishes Christianity from some other world religions in which history is viewed as a temporary stage through which humans pass on their way to timeless perfection, a tissue of illusions which we must transcend, or a distraction from concentration on the timeless essential. Therefore, the affirmation of the significance of history also distinguishes Christian Religious Life from some other, non-Christian forms of monasticism.[64] Involvement in history is not simply one option among others for the Christian Religious. It is intrinsic to our spirituality.

A second effect of our faith in the Incarnation is that *matter*, including our own bodies, is not seen as a prison from which the truly spiritual person must escape or as a hindrance which must be ruthlessly subordinated to spirit. As Teilhard de Chardin so vividly realized and eloquently articulated, matter is not opaque and inert, a weight on the spirit, but a luminous medium, shot through with divinity.[65] In the Resurrection the humanity of Jesus, including his body, was glorified, not dissolved. And that glorification reveals the potential, the destiny of the whole material universe, including our own very material humanity, which is groaning toward fulfillment (cf. Rom 8:19–23).

A third effect of the revelation of the humanity of God in Jesus, and the effect most important for our present question, is that *particularity* is infinitely precious. In the Christian worldview, the particular in not an illusion or even a mere instance of the universal. Christians do not seek God by abstracting from the concrete and the particular. Every pebble, every butterfly, every individual person with her or his absolutely unique fingerprint, every ethnic group and race, every religious tradition in all its specificity and distinctiveness is, like the particular individual Jesus of Nazareth, a locus of revelation. Differentiation does not divide or fuse, said de Chardin; it unites.[66] The Incarnation reveals that unity is not achieved by the loss of individuality through an homogenization of everything in undifferentiated uniformity, but through the unique validation of particularity in the genuine union of relationship. Friendship, that is, particular subjects in intimate relationship, not absorption, is the human ideal proposed by Jesus in his metaphor of mutual indwelling— his and ours, ours in each other and in God—which is modeled on the differentiated unity of the trinitarian God.[67]

The Incarnation, with its affirmation of irreducible particularity, has sometimes been a cause of scandal for Christians as well as incomprehension for participants in other religious traditions which view particularity as a kind of restriction or limitation, a worldly imprisonment from which, finally, the purified will be liberated. This "scandal of particularity" has taken on a heightened importance in the context of post-Newtonian cosmology. The new cosmology understands Earth and its denizens (human beings and other beings) within the context of an expanding universe whose history originated in a "big bang" which predated the emergence of our galaxy, solar system, and planet (to say nothing of humans and their religious traditions) by billions of years.[68] This understanding of the universe has significantly broadened our horizons. For many people, including some Religious, the Christian metanarrative, the "Jesus story" which centers history in the person of a unique, individual, particular human being, suddenly appears too small, too narrow, too anthropocentric in the face of this "universe story" which seems to provide a much more comprehensive framework for our self-understanding.[69]

The suspicion that the Christian story is too limited to be ultimately meaningful in light of contemporary science is exacerbated by the evidence of religious pluralism. Other religious traditions can no longer be dismissed as pseudo-religions, the credulous ignorance and superstition of the unevangelized. Moreover, if there is more than one path of salvation Christianity appears as not only temporally but also substantively extremely limited. One can be tempted to suspect that all religions are little more than minor "blips" on local screens and that the only "religion" worthy of the name is awe-struck reverence for the immensity of reality itself which can probably be explained, as some scientific theories do, without reference to the "god hypothesis."[70]

The relation of religion to post-Darwinian and post-Newtonian science is a major issue in contemporary theology which is being energetically addressed by both scientists and theologians.[71] Likewise, how the validity of other religious traditions can be understood in relation to the christological claims of the Christian tradition is a major item on the agenda of theologians.[72] Both topics, important as they are, are beyond the scope of our present discussion. However, I would like to suggest that there are essentially two ways, relevant to our concerns, of understanding the particularity of Jesus. One way, which leads inexorably to the conclusion that the Jesus story is substantively irrelevant for the scientifically and interreligiously enlightened contemporary person, is to *reduce* Jesus to his particularity as a first century Jewish male who lived a short life in one small country, was executed, and is now a figure of history whom we admire and even imitate but with whom we cannot relate personally and whom we must not universalize. If this is our vision of Jesus, one unaffected by the role of the Incarnation and the Resurrection in Christian revelation,[73] then Jesus is plainly too limited to be the object of genuine religious faith. He differs in no way from other moral paragons and charismatic religious leaders in human history.

But a second way of understanding the particularity of Jesus is to take utterly seriously the faith of the Church that *Jesus is the Wisdom of God incarnate.* The Wisdom literature of the Old Testament presents Holy Wisdom as the immanence of the transcendent God present (hidden or manifest) and active in all Creation.[74] Wisdom is the transcendent God creating, sustaining, indwelling, governing, and luring the universe to completion and wholeness.[75] Christian faith holds that this Wisdom, Holy Sophia, God presented in Scripture in feminine gestalt,[76] became incarnate in Jesus.[77] Jesus does not imprison or restrict or constrain God but focuses the infinity of Ultimate Reality, enabling us in our finitude to see, encounter, and relate to the invisible and transcendent mystery we call God. The God whom Jesus mediates is not only transcendent but also immanent in all reality, not one being alongside other beings or outside or inside the universe. God as Holy Wisdom is she who "reaches from end to end mightily and governs all things well" (Wis 8:1).

To say that Jesus focuses the reality of God as Holy Wisdom is somewhat analogous—and all analogies limp—to saying that Mozart focuses the transcendent beauty of music so that, in listening to this particular piece of music, composed by this particular (male, Western, young, white, eighteenth-century, European) artist, and played by this particular orchestra, on these particular instruments, we can actually experience real music in the concrete rather than fantasizing about the possibility of music in the abstract. It is somewhat analogous to saying that the relationship with one's particular, gendered, actual spouse focuses the unbounded reality of love that is universal in its being but can only be experienced in the concrete and particular. So, Jesus gives specific form to divinity. In him we know through our own human experience that God is life and love against whom death cannot prevail; that gender is not a defect in our humanity but rather a privileged way of being fully human; and that community beyond the boundaries of family and ethnicity, race and class is possible.

In Jesus, who was both a faithful Jew and a free Jew, we learn that fidelity within a particular religious tradition can open us to the infinite mystery of God that is mediated by all religious traditions even as the encounter with the infinite God in our own tradition can relativize the tyranny of religious institutions which have usurped the role of faith. The Christian experiences in Jesus not just the theoretical possibility that God could be present and active in the whole universe but the reality of divine Wisdom at work in the world.

Knowing Jesus progressively introduces the believing Christian into the Wisdom of God that Jesus incarnates. This Wisdom embraces, connects, and unites all that is. She opens us to, connects us with, not only the truth and beauty of our own tradition but also the whole spectrum of God's journey with diverse human communities. Just as belonging to a healthy family does not isolate a person in a private ghetto but enables her or him to enter confidently into ever expanding circles of relationship, so the particularity of the Christian tradition that is rooted in the particularity of Jesus is the matrix within which Christians participate in the whole of reality. Astonishment at the reaches of the universe, reverence for other religious traditions, the recognition of the value of every individual person, as well as the daily love affair with the natural world from its majestic mountains to the pebble on the seashore, from the towering redwood to the hidden grain of wheat, from the transparent beauty of water to the stars that differ from one another in glory (cf. 1 Cor 15:41), is part of the genius of Christianity. Our response to the particular is our worshipful response to divine revelation which is not general and abstract but vastly and minutely particular.

Other religious traditions bring to the table of interreligious dialogue other perspectives on Ultimate Mystery and the nature of reality. These perceptions and their implications can enrich the Christian vision without invalidating it or replacing it and Christians are slowly learning to value these contributions. But it is likewise the right and responsibility of Christians to bring our particular gift to the table, that is, to help keep the whole human family mindful of the fact that God is manifest in history, in matter, and in the particular. In other words, growing awareness of the universe story, increasing reverence for the natural world of which we are a part, active responsibility for sustaining the ecosphere that sustains us, and participation in interreligious dialogue can and should plunge us ever deeper into the mystery of God, immanent in Creation, as this mystery is revealed and encountered in Jesus, the Wisdom of God incarnate.

b. Our humanity is the locus of God's presence in the world

The *second overarching implication* of the Incarnation, that is, that the fullness of divinity is encountered in Jesus, is that for Christian faith our humanity, divinized by the life of the Risen Jesus, is the locus of God's presence and liberating work in the world, including our participation in the struggle to promote sustainability. The traditional theological language for this astounding affirmation is that the baptized are "the body of Christ." This is not a decorative figure of speech. It is a powerful semantic metaphor by which the Church expresses its faith that the baptized are the real, sensible, effective presence of Christ in this world. As J.A.T. Robinson put it:

> Paul uses the analogy of the human body to elucidate his teaching that Christians form Christ's body. But the analogy holds because they are in literal fact the risen organism of Christ's person in all its concrete reality.[78]

As Jesus' own historical body was the real symbolic presence of his person in first century Palestine, so his glorified body, which we are, is his real symbolic presence in the twenty-first century. In other words, this understanding of the "body of Christ" is not primarily an evocation of Paul's teaching on the interdependence of the baptized in the Christian community (cf. 1 Cor 12:12–13). It is, rather, the theology evoked in 1 Cor 6:15, 19: "Do you not know that your bodies are members of Christ?...Do you not know that your body is a temple of the Holy Spirit within you, whom you have from God and that you are not your own?" It is John's theology of the new temple, the new dwelling place of divine Wisdom, raised up in the Resurrection when the Spirit of Jesus is poured out on his disciples (cf. John 2:19–22).[79] It is the theology of the branches (cf. John 15:1–11) which bear the fruit of salvation through their participation in the life-giving vine.

In the Fourth Gospel Jesus prays to God on the night before his death, "Now I am no longer in the world but they [his disciples] are in the world" (John 17:11). The point is not that they are successors of a Jesus who is now absent or even nonexistent but that they are his new mode of presence. Jesus "goes away" in his earthly mode in order to "come" to them in the Resurrection and indwell them in the power of his Spirit (cf. 14:28). Jesus had just told his disciples that those who believe in him, namely, his disciples, would do his works and do even greater works than those he had done during his pre-Easter life (cf. John 14:12), that anyone who received the disciples received Jesus himself just as anyone receiving Jesus receives the One who sent him (cf. John 13:20).

During his pre-Easter career Jesus could say that a person's response to him was their response to God (cf. John 5:23), that anyone who saw him saw God (cf. John 14:9–10). Now, in his post-Easter Resurrection life he can say that the response of people to his disciples is their response to Jesus himself.[80] In short, just as Jesus is the presence of God in the world, so the disciples are the presence of Jesus in the world. In Jesus "all the fullness of the Godhead dwells bodily" (cf. Col 2:9), and in the Christian Jesus is present so that what is done to them is done to him and what they do is what he does.

Christians, including Religious, who really believe this and take seriously their identity as the Body of Christ who is Wisdom Incarnate and by his Resurrection alive and present in them and through them in the world know that they are always acting "*in persona Christi.*" This is not pious "acting as if" to motivate one to the practice of virtue. It is a reality that arises from baptismal union with the Risen Jesus who indwells them as Spirit. Christian faith in the Incarnation and the Resurrection does not necessarily make Christians do different things than non-Christians but it makes them do everything they do differently because they live not as mere human individuals but Christ lives in them (cf. Gal 2:20).

Consequently, Christian participation in the contemporary task of reversing ecological degradation and promoting sustainability, a work Christians share with others, is the work of Christ; Holy Wisdom at work in the world that is God's good Creation. Religious participate in this work specifically as Christians, bringing to it resources from their own charismatic traditions as well. One particular contribution Religious can make is to help keep the ecological commitment of Christians truly Christian by their deep knowledge of and explicit articulation of the rootedness of such commitment in the biblical soil of creation and Incarnation.

C. The World as Humanity

We turn now, very briefly, to the second meaning of *kosmos* that was discussed in section III above. The world that God so loved as to send the only Son is humanity as a whole, created as the crown of nature but called and destined for eternal life through the new birth in the Spirit. Consequently, in this brief section we raise the question of how Religious are related to the human race of which they are a part, both to the baptized who share the life of God in Christ and to all other people.

Again, the history of Religious Life on this topic is fraught with ambiguity. Thomas à Kempis's famous and oft-cited dictum, "As often as I went out among men [i.e., humans] I returned less of a man,"[81] epitomizes the ambivalence toward, if not the deep suspicion of, all human relationships outside the convent/monastery itself that has characterized Religious Life for centuries. The Gospel challenge to "hate" one's family (cf. Luke 14: 25) was often interpreted literally as a mandate for alienation even from parents and siblings.[82] Consecrated celibacy was often interpreted as a negative judgment on marriage which was seen as inferior to the Religious state[83] with the implication that married people were inferior to Religious, and that marriage was a distraction from single-hearted love of God (cf. 1 Cor 7:32–35). Even relationships within the Religious community itself were regarded as dangerous and formators devoted often exaggerated attention to warnings against "particular friendships."

On the other hand, virtually all Religious Rules proclaimed, explicitly or implicitly, that charity was the highest of the virtues. From the time of Benedict at least, Religious considered the obligation to welcome as Christ all who came to the Religious house as a hallmark of the life. And the model of love within the community itself was that of the first Christians as presented in Acts 4:32. Religious not only prayed for "the world" from the safety of their cloisters but ministerial Religious undertook lives of total, very hands on, dedication to the spiritual and corporal works of mercy which they often expanded beyond Christians or believers. Religious in missionary Orders left their home cultures, usually for the rest of their lives, to bring the Good News and its embodiment in the works of mercy to strangers in remote lands.

In the wake of the Council, most Congregations took seriously the solidarity with the human race that was proclaimed in *Gaudium et Spes.* Not all the actions that followed were prudent. Some Religious, as was noted in *Finding the Treasure,* virtually "returned home," rejoining their family of origin as the primary affective horizon of their lives. Some others became involved in relationships that led to serious problems in celibate commitment either heterosexual or homosexual. Some Religious became involved in relationships with other members or nonmembers that could be recognized as "coupling" even if the relationship was not explicitly sexual.

All of these situations are problematic from the standpoint of consecrated celibacy as well as community. Although there was considerable writing about the goodness of relationships, their importance for human maturity, the sanctity of sexuality and marriage, and the importance of cooperation with the laity and with non-Catholics in ministry, there was very little actual engagement of the theological or biblical bases for valid discernment in this area. On the one hand, Religious were encouraged to abandon attitudes to which they had been formed of elitism and alienation from others within and outside the community and, on the other hand, there was no alternate formation on which to rely.

It is past time to affirm unambiguously that for the Christian, Religious included, there can be no alternatives or exceptions to wholehearted love of neighbor. The second great commandment is part of the first and Religious Life does not suspend this commandment or modify its universality. The question, then, is how to integrate Religious Life into the practice of universal love rather than how to fit the love of neighbor into a sacralized institutional regime. In other words, Religious have to be formed in this area for discernment which takes appropriate account of the factors pertinent to their particular lifeform, including their ministerial responsibilities, their community life, their celibate commitment, their relationship with their families which changed but was not obliterated when they entered Religious Life, their own needs for mature relationships with people of both sexes, and so on.

For our purposes in this chapter, it would seem that two conclusions are paramount. First, the "world" that is the human race must be regarded by Religious (as by all Christians) as God regards it. Like Peter in Acts 11:1–18, Religious require a full conversion from any tendency, hanging over from "cloistered" formation and customs, to call "unclean" (or "worldly" or "secular" in a pejorative sense) those whom God created and loves, and that includes all people without exception.

Second, all that was said in the previous section about the implications of the Incarnation and Resurrection for the Christian attitude toward the world as the created universe applies *a fortiori* to the world as humanity. As we will have occasion to discuss in subsequent chapters, the ministry of Religious arises directly out of their participation in the mission of Jesus according to the charism of their own Institute. As members of Christ's body they act "*in persona Christi*" as they care for and work with the people God created and calls to eternal life. They may be doing work which could be perfectly valid without reference to Christ, such as healing, teaching, organizing, writing, counseling, and so on. But, in fact, they do not do it without reference to Christ. Nor do they act as independent agents but precisely in virtue of their incorporation into their Religious community.

In short, their baptismal identity specified by their Religious Profession is incarnated in loving response to the world as humanity, not in general or in the abstract or from a safe distance but in the specific and concrete relationships that are part of the real, historical life of the Religious. All that will be said about community, witness, and ministry flows from this principle. The scope of our concern for the human family is universal and its quality unreservedly positive.

D. The World as Reality Construction

We come finally to the one biblical meaning of "world" which is negative, namely, the world as the imaginative construction of reality according to the values and strategies of the

Prince of This World in opposition to the world-construction of the Reign of God. This evil world is the world to which Religious "die," an expression that will require careful analysis in succeeding chapters. This has always been the world Religious rejected, fled, left, abandoned—expressions which require reevaluation in light of contemporary understandings—as part of their total commitment to God in Christ.

Perhaps because of the flight to the desert of the third and fourth century hermits, which for a very long time was considered the "original" and therefore normative form of Religious Life, the world tended to be thought of as everything other than Religious Life itself. Thus, an exaggerated negativity toward the natural world and an extreme separation from non-Religious within and outside the Church seemed to be implied in the renunciation of the world. The real object of world renunciation was always the evil reality construction, not God's good Creation, either natural or human. But to some of our predecessors, lacking the sociological and theological tools for making some of these distinctions, the term "world" seemed to include everything but Religious Life itself and the renunciation tended to be universal and as total as possible.

Also affecting our current understanding of the evil world and the meaning of Religious renunciation of that world is our realization of the systemic character of evil, something our historical forebears could not have seen as we do today. The language of renouncing "Satan and all his works" refers primarily not to an individual evil agent and his particular acts. We are talking about a systemic reality construction that affects every aspect of human experience, whether political, economic, social, educational, or religious. It is all-pervasive and mingles evil with good in ways that make discernment and effective action very difficult.

Because the rest of this volume will be concerned with how Religious, from within an alternate world which they create, position themselves in relation to the evil reality construction of "world" I will merely state, at this point, the hypothesis underlying what will follow. As already mentioned, all the baptized are called to renounce the power that opposes God in this world and to live in such a way that the Reign of God not only structures their own personal lives but is fostered in this world by the way they live and what they do. Our question is, what specifies the way Religious live this common baptismal calling? What difference does the specification of baptismal commitment by Religious Profession make?

I will propose that Religious Profession is a paschal act by which Religious "die to the world" (the evil reality construction) and undertake to live the Resurrection in a radical way within history, prior to physical death, by creating and living within an "alternate world" which derives its coordinates exclusively from the Gospel. Living in and acting from this alternate world constitutes a prophetic lifeform in the Church that subverts the evil world in favor of the Reign of God. The means by which Religious create this alternate world are the vows that both witness to and ministerially effect the Reign of God as well as affecting the personal and communal spirituality of Religious.

Chapter Two
Naming the Harvesters:
Identity of Religious

I. Introduction and Transition

This volume, as has been said, is concerned with the relationship of Religious, individually and corporately, to their context, to the "field" in which the treasure of Religious Life has been "hidden" both as a leaven for transformation and as a no longer immediately recognizable lifeform struggling for new visibility and articulateness in a postmodern and postconciliar situation. In chapter 1 we turned our attention to the global term for that context, namely, "the world." Our purpose was to develop a nuanced, biblically based, theological understanding of the meaning of the term *kosmos* (world) in order to ground the diverse relationships Religious have with this polyvalent reality. We distinguished three very different meanings of the term: the world as the *created universe;* the world as *humanity;* and the world as *reality construction.*

The world as created universe denotes the entire cosmos, animate and inanimate, including humans and all other species. But for our purposes it refers especially to the cosmic environment as the theater of human history.

The world as humanity refers to the whole human race as the object of God's universal salvific love but also to humans as naturally mortal, in need of God's free gift if they are to participate in divine life, and morally responsible for the use of their freedom.

The world as reality construction is the image of reality that determines the attitudes, postures, and actions of human agents functioning within social, cultural, economic, political, religious, and other systems and institutions.

The world as reality construction, which is our primary concern, is simultaneously both the Reign of God in process of realization and the kingdom of the "Prince of This World," the agent of evil, actively bent on the destruction of God's good Creation, both human and other than human. Paul refers to this evil reality construction as the work of "principalities and powers," "world rulers of this present darkness," "evil spirits in the heavens" (see esp. Eph 6:12). Christians, with the rest of humanity, are involved in this struggle over the destiny of the cosmos and especially of the human race. Different people and groups participate in this struggle in different ways. In this chapter I will further the development of a theological framework for this volume on the mission of Religious by focusing on the other pole of the relationship, namely, Religious Life as a lifeform and Religious themselves, individually and corporately. In other words, after attending to the nature of the *field* to which Religious are missioned—the world—I want to concentrate now on the *harvesters* sent into that field—Religious and their life.

In what follows I am assuming the understanding of Religious Life that was developed in volumes 1 and 2, which I will briefly recall here. In volume 1 we looked at Religious Life, as it were, from the "outside," at its location and identity in the world and the Church. The life itself, I suggested, is sociologically a vast and diverse social movement in history, and the different Orders and Congregations are social movement organizations (or concretions of the movement in organized, institutionalized form) in various historical/cultural and ecclesial settings throughout history. Religious as individuals were looked at relationship to the anthropological archetype of the *monastic*, the psychological archetype of the *virgin*, and the sociological ideal type of the religious *virtuoso*.

We also studied Religious Life dynamically as a personal and communal enterprise, an integrated lifeform in a process of transformation. That transformation has been both actively undertaken by Religious themselves and passively undergone as painful purification in the postconciliar renewal efforts of the past forty years. The diversity of forms of Religious Life was analyzed in terms of the diversity of charisms giving rise to *stable monastic* and *mobile ministerial* forms of the life. And finally, we looked at the life as an ecclesial reality, both in relation to other elements and populations in the Church and as a lifeform. The dynamic interaction of contemplative immediacy to God and voluntary social marginality of Religious gives rise to the *prophetic character* of the life and its characteristic social strategy of selective participation.

In volume 2, we looked at Religious Life, as it were, from the "inside" at its internal structure as a personal lifelong commitment in response to a personally discerned vocation within the context of a particular community. The two constitutive and structuring relationships of the life, namely, the relationship to *Christ in perpetual consecrated celibacy* and the relationship to the *members within a community* life that forms the primary affective horizon of its members, were examined in detail.

In this third volume our primary concern is the interrelationship between Religious Life (corporately as a lifeform and as lived individually by the members) and the world to which they are missioned. Consequently, we need at this point to construct a more comprehensive biblical and theological model of Religious Life itself, concentrating on the life as an integrated totality within and in relation to the world in all three meanings of world that we have distinguished. In other words, we need to articulate a global theological phenomenology of Religious Life as mission.

In this chapter I will propose a three-stage, progressively specified identification of the life beginning with Religious Life as *religious*, that is, as a response to revelation; then as *Christian*, that is, as a paschal reality, a participation in the death-Resurrection mystery of Christ; and finally as *Religious*, that is, as a lifeform distinct from both clerical and lay life in the Church, This last distinction results from Profession and the living of the vows. I will suggest that through this particular way of specifying their baptismal commitment, Religious create an alternate world in which the Reign of God is realized in an exclusive and total way within the framework of history.

This creation of and self-situation within the Reign of God, lived exclusively and totally, is the position from which Religious participate in both promoting that Reign in the world and subverting the reality construction of the Evil One. Of course, Religious share with all the baptized this mission of promoting the Reign of God. But they live this mission in a particular way in virtue of their Profession of consecrated celibacy (which was considered in depth in volume 2), and of evangelical poverty and prophetic obedience, which I am treating as the vows of community and ministry. I hope that the theoretical framework established in this chapter will facilitate the work of the rest of the volume, namely, a full-scale exploration of the mission of Religious as it is realized not only in the personal quest for union with God and in the living of transcendent community life, but in the mission-based exercise of ministry.

The exploration of mission, then, will be organized around the other two vows of Religious Profession, evangelical poverty, which specifies the relationship and interaction of Religious with the economic dimension of the world, and prophetic obedience, which does the same in relationship to the political dimension. Each vow will be studied first in terms of its own nature as, respectively, the creation and living of the economics and the politics of the Reign of God in mission to the world. Second, each will be studied in terms of its realization in the transcendent community life characteristic of Religious Life. Finally, each will be studied in terms of its role in the quest for God, the unitive spirituality of Religious themselves.

II. Religious Life as a Religious Reality[1]

The relation of Religious to "the world"[2] understood as the struggle between opposing reality constructions (the Reign of God and the Kingdom of Satan) is not a self-initiated commitment of like-minded people to the creation of a better world. Religious are *consecrated and sent* into the world by Jesus as he was consecrated and sent by God (cf. John 17:17–19; 20:21). And as he came into the world by God's initiative to do the will of the One who sent him, that is, to mediate God's universal love for the world by his salvific death and Resurrection, so Religious are involved in the world struggle in virtue of divine mission. The paschal mystery of Jesus to which the Gospel bears witness, rather than any purely human utopian vision, provides the pattern for the world involvement of Religious. It specifies the end, the means and methods, the priorities, and the price of this involvement.

Because there are many people from many faith traditions (or none) who are committed to various projects to bring about a different or better world, Religious need a clear sense of identity and mission if they are to know where, when, with whom, and how they can effectively cooperate in such projects, as well as when the Christian specificity of their mission entails resistance to the vision, objectives, or methods of other people or groups. For example, Thomas Merton, a passionate participant in the peace movement during the Vietnam War, was faced with the painful necessity of repudiating the choice of symbolic protest by self-immolation of a highly motivated young Catholic Worker, Roger LaPorte, on November 9, 1965.[3] Merton's stance in this instance provoked major tensions with some of the people in the movement to whom he was closest. He also struggled with the challenge from some of his friends as well as his critics in various social justice enterprises to discern if or how his continued fidelity to his cloistered monastic lifeform, which kept him from physical participation in many peace activities, was a genuine contribution to the causes he espoused.[4] Discernment between good and evil and among goods, wise deployment of personnel and energy, and appropriate responses to ecclesiastical and civil authorities demand clarity about who Religious are and what their mission entails.

But before we can explore the specifically Christian nature of the life and mission of Religious we have to establish the character of the life itself as a specifically *religious* phenomenon and to do that adequately requires situating Christianity within the context of religion as a human phenomenon. In other words, Religious Life is a specific lifeform within a specific religion. While this was self-evident and unproblematic for anyone who entered Religious Life prior to the Council, today there is considerable confusion and contention around this affirmation that has serious implications for how Religious, individually and corporately, understand their identity and their mission to the world.

A. Whence the Question?

Several factors are contributing to the questioning of the religious and the specifically Catholic Christian character of Religious Life. Two of these arise from the contemporary context in which the Life is situated, namely, the postmodern ethos of secular culture and religious pluralism.

1. Postmodernism[5]

Postmodernism, the nebulous but powerful cultural challenger to the rationalistic and scientistic ethos of modernity, is characterized, among other features, by its theoretical and practical resistance to coherence.[6] It inclines us to recognize and even embrace the fragmentation of our experience and to be suspicious of any attempts to ground that experience in foundational truth about reality or to unify it within any overarching framework or "metanarrative." Christianity, however, like all of the world's great religions, is a coherent faith tradition that claims to be grounded in divine revelation. It presents itself in a metanarrative, an overarching and underlying story that reaches from Creation to the end of the world and into which the personal stories of the individual believers are supposed to fit.

It is hard to deny that some formulations of Christian foundational beliefs are scarcely credible and that the sometimes totalizing claims that Christianity has historically made for its universalistic story do appear imperialistic. Although a unitary worldview, whether religious (such as Christianity or Hinduism) or scientific (such as the "universe story"), is not necessarily totalitarian, it does have to be coherent, and that will entail certain inclusions which are intrinsically related to its truth claims and certain exclusions which are incompatible with those claims. In other words, a completely eclectic, idiosyncratic, and fragmented religious tradition is a contradiction in terms. Consequently, religious faith faces challenges in the postmodern context that neither the modern nor the medieval worldviews, both of which were unitary, presented.

2. Religious pluralism

As the increasing religious violence of our time is making very clear, the unitary and coherent character of religious worldviews can easily lead to absolute claims to truth and divine approval and even to a sense of mission to exterminate those who hold other views. Christianity has a long history of such absolutism. One of the most stimulating and challenging effects of the postconciliar renewal was the emergence of Catholics, including Religious, from an exclusively (and even militantly) Catholic context into a religiously pluralistic one. Such people no longer saw the Catholic Church as the only true religion and all other spiritual traditions as, at best, embodiments of invincible ignorance and, at worst, sinful structures of apostasy, heresy, or paganism.

As Religious mixed more frequently with spiritually mature and socially committed non-Catholics and even non-Christians, many began to relativize in theory and tone down in practice their specifically Catholic or even Christian identity and commitment. It did not seem to matter a great deal whether one served the poor or witnessed for peace as a Catholic or Presbyterian, a Buddhist or an agnostic as long as the poor were served and peace promoted. Non-specific religious rituals could bring people together for mutual support and renewal of motivation in ways that tradition-specific prayer sometimes could not. It often seemed more respectful of others and more conducive to cooperation to put aside sectarian labels which suggested divisive dogmatic positions and to affirm what all had in common, namely, a commitment to the vision of a better world.

Within Religious Congregations this more positive evaluation of other religious traditions and of spiritualities that are
not religiously based[7] raised a question that could hardly have
been imagined a few decades ago: is Catholic, or even Christian, faith and practice really the basis of Religious Life or even
essential to it? Perhaps, at least for some people in the community, the bond of unity in the Congregation is not a quest for
the triune God of Jesus Christ, nor a personal relationship with
Jesus articulated through perpetual Profession and/or commitment to the Reign of God expressed in the Gospel. Rather,
it is better expressed in the shared commitment of members to
a particular project (e.g., education, health care, peace making),
shared worldview (e.g., feminism or ecological sustainability),
common value or "charism" (e.g., mercy or truth), or even the
desire for utopian community with like-minded people and a
simple lifestyle.

Although this question was seldom raised explicitly in community deliberations, in some communities it has created an
unspoken culture of reticence about the explicitly religious
and Catholic character of the community and its mission. This
reticence was palpable in the tendency to focus on the objectives and means of ministry (on which there was a high level of
consensus that did not have to be expressed in religious terms)
rather than focus on ultimate motivation (concerning which
there was considerable diversity and which inevitably raised the
religious question). Increasingly spirituality, including participation in Catholic liturgy, tended to be seen as a private matter
discreetly left to the individual. There was a tendency to avoid
specifically Catholic or Christian expressions of faith such as
Eucharist or the reading of biblical texts in the celebration of
community rituals, to avoid mention of Jesus except as an outstanding figure in a long line of moral models, and to use para-
phrastic references to Ultimate Reality that did not entail
recognition of God as one, trinitarian, or personal. The "universe story," not as the context for but as an alternative to the
"Jesus story," was increasingly evoked.[8] In some communities,
these choices and behaviors manifested a growing uneasiness
with the seeming exclusivity and perhaps narrowness of the

Christian framework in general and with its normativity for the identity of Religious Life in particular.

Without doubt one of the major challenges facing theology today is the development of a valid and adequate theology of religions to replace the traditional dualistic understanding of Christianity as the "one true religion" in opposition to all other traditions regarded as materially false no matter how sincere their adherents.[9] Such a theology is a prerequisite, pre-sciently perceived by such late twentieth century figures as Bede Griffiths, Thomas Merton, and Raimon Panikkar, for the project of achieving a differentiated unity of religions that would valorize their diversity rather than homogenize them.[10] There are, and always have been, a variety of religious traditions, that is, coherent, faith-based worldviews that have shaped and supported the personal self-understanding, community life, and the quest for God of their participants. These traditions must be recognized as God-given paths of salvation for their participants and sources of spiritual wisdom for the whole-human family and not simply as "good-faith mistakes" of people ultimately called to Christianity.[11]

Furthermore, and prior to the achievement of theoretical clarity on this difficult question, experience has already demonstrated that there are theological or philosophical insights and spiritual practices in all of the great religions which can be shared by others without disrespectful "raiding" of the original tradition nor denaturing of the religious commitment of those who seek enrichment from traditions, Christian or non-Christian, not their own.[12] For example, many Catholics have learned much about discernment and the integration of faith and justice from Quakerism, about prayer from the theory and practice of Buddhist meditation or Hindu yoga, and about reverence for the nonhuman world from native peoples. Conversely, the Beatitudes have powerfully influenced reflection among non-Christians, for example, Gandhi, on such issues as nonviolence and distributive justice.

But, important as the development of a theology of religions is, and enriching as cross-traditional sharing can be, nothing is to be gained (and much can be lost) by collapsing the boundaries that give coherence and identity to each tradition. Distinction, as Teilhard de Chardin pointed out, is the basis of genuine, mutually enriching unity in diversity as opposed to an undifferentiated uniformity. Genuine religious traditions, including Christianity, are holistic, coherent, and specific and are not, and cannot be, essentially eclectic or syncretistic. Each Christian believer, in other words, cannot create some kind of personal spiritual synthesis that ignores what she or he finds problematic in the Christian tradition and incorporates whatever is found attractive or useful in other traditions. Or at least, the resulting "religion" will not be Christianity or Catholicism (nor some "new" super-religion) but an idiosyncratic spiritual experiment that belongs to no tradition, even if it satisfies the current needs of its author.[13]

In summary, the position I am proposing is that the core faith tradition of Christianity, including its Scripture, doctrine, morality, liturgy, and mission is constitutive of authentic Catholic Religious Life and spirituality. This entails not only a broad and deep knowledge (both theoretical and practical) of the Christian tradition but also the realization that some of what constitutes Christian faith is genuinely incompatible with some aspects of other traditions and vice versa. For example, the trinitarian character of God in the Christian tradition is really different from, and not just a different version of the non-personal ultimate reality of Buddhism, and the divinity of Jesus, which is not acceptable to Jews or Muslims, is basic to Christian faith. Hindu caste is not a possible embodiment of the Christian understanding of the human person in community who is made in the image and likeness of God nor is Marxism an acceptable version of the coming of the Reign of God for Christians. The recognition of real differences and even incompatibilities among religious (or quasi-religious) traditions does not negate either fruitful interreligious dialogue, mutually enriching sharing, both theoretical and practical, among their adherents, nor serious engagement with worldviews different from the Christian vision of reality. But it does mean that religious traditions, including Christianity, are not grab bags of interchangeable beliefs and practices but unified worldviews, and Catholic Religious Life is not simply an experiment in generic monasticism or utopian communitarianism but a specific lifeform within a particular faith tradition.

Once again, we must recognize that this is "a hard saying" for the postmodern sensibility which is highly intolerant of any exclusion, or necessary inclusion, in principle, whether of ideas, beliefs, practices, or people, in any sphere of life including religion. Nevertheless, ignoring the theoretical self-contradictoriness and practical impossibility of total inclusivity, as well as the vapidity of a vague religious identity that has no roots in a coherent tradition and no purchase on the future beyond the lifespan (or even current enthusiasms) of the individual or group that constructed it, will not make this problem go away.[14] If Religious Life is to continue to be the response to a distinctive vocation within the Church, and not an alternative to the Church, its Catholic identity has to be both claimed and valorized even as it strives to develop a truly open, interdenominationally and interreligiously sensitive worldview and a practice which affirms the solidarity in mission of Catholic Religious with all people of good will who espouse the same or compatible goals.

B. Catholic Christianity as a Religious Tradition

The meaning of Catholic Christian identity for Religious today, and what that identity implies for their life and ministry, has to be understood at a much deeper level than might have been necessary for people who undertook the life in preconciliar times. Probing this issue requires some background on the origins, nature, and function of religion in human experience, that is, what religions have in common, and attention to what differentiates religions from one another. Religious Life is not simply religious; it is specifically Christian and Catholic.

1. The origin and nature of religious traditions

Genuine religious traditions, in contradistinction from private religions or idiosyncratic spiritualities, do not originate in theory or as projections of personal needs. They originate in the experience of the powerful inbreaking of ultimate reality, of transcendent mystery, of what Rudolf Otto called "the numinous" or "the holy" (with or without personal overtones), into the life of an individual such as the Buddha, Moses, Jesus, or Mohammed, or into the history of a community (which seems to be the case in many primal religions).[15] This experience of being addressed or claimed or overwhelmed or transformed by ultimate reality is not self-induced even if, as Otto, William James, and others have recognized, there seems to be a human predisposition for the experience of the holy, and even if the subject actively prepares for it as did Gautama through meditation or Jesus through his Jewish upbringing and baptism and his fasting in the desert as an adult. The foundational experience[16] not only offers the subject a particular "take" on ultimate reality, for example, on God, but on all of reality in relation to the ultimate. The Buddha was not only personally transformed by his enlightenment but came to understand the nature of all reality and of the human condition and destiny in an original way. Jesus not only experienced himself as the Beloved Son of the one he came to call "Abba," he also understood all human beings as called to divine filiation, with its implications of universal equality as sisters and brothers of the same divine parent; freedom from human domination; vocation to eternal life; and mission to make that divine filiation universally available. In other words, these foundational religious experiences were not merely personal mystical experiences of union with ultimate reality, but also revelations of "how things are," the seed of a holistic, coherent, unified worldview that presented itself as divinely authenticated.

These radically transforming experiences of the inbreaking of the ultimate gave rise to religious traditions which were institutionalized as Buddhism, Judaism, Christianity, and so on. The institutionalization of religious tradition in cultural systems of belief, morality, cultic life, and practices of personal formation creates the possibility for other people to enter into and assimilate the religious worldview, including its implications about God and all of reality that were intimated, even if only inchoately, in the originating experience. Each religious tradition, because of the uniqueness of the originating encounter, understands ultimate reality in a particular way, as having certain properties, as being in a particular kind of relationship with the universe including humans, and as offering particular possibilities and making particular demands on believers.

The adherents of a genuine religious tradition do not think that the founding figure or group, the subject of the originating experience, invented (either in the sense of "made up" or of "found") the contents or dynamics of that experience and subsequently decided to offer it to, or to impose it upon, others. This, incidentally, is a major difference between the great world religions and, on the one hand, authentic primal religions which make no claim to universality on the one hand or, on the other, much "new age" or "experimental" religion in which fundamental tenets and practices are borrowed from various traditions, invented, or combined according to some personal insight or agenda of the founder or promoter.

Authentic religious tradition is founded on the belief that the originating experience was (God-)given. In theological terms, it belongs to the category of "revelation," God's free, self-communicating inbreaking to human experience.[17] Jewish monotheism, for Jews, is not an invention of Abraham or Moses but the only possible response to the way God is, revealed at least inchoately to Abraham and Moses, even though it took many years and much experience for the divine self-revelation in Israel's history to be worked out in Jewish faith as radical monotheism. In other words, the divine reality Moses encountered at the burning bush[18] really *is* "one" and that has consequences that are not compatible with polytheism. That Allah alone is God and Mohammed is his prophet is not, for Muslims, arguable. Muslims believe that it was revealed by Allah and incarnated in the Koran whose revision or relativization is unthinkable. And Jesus' experience of his own divine filiation and the consequent belief of Christians that in him they really encounter the living God is not merely a theological theory. It is, in the Christian framework, what God revealed in Jesus.

In short, the content of religious faith traditions derives from revelation experienced in the disclosive encounters in which they arose, whether the revelation is understood as coming from a divine subject or from the very nature of ultimate reality itself, whether it takes place in the experience of an individual subject or of a community, and whether it is a single event or an experience unfolding over time. This revelatory experience provides a framework for a holistic perception of reality as a whole, which, at least in its essentials, is coherent within itself and with the originating experience and which is not amenable to revision of its core commitments or a relativization of its foundational claims. This is not a matter of doctrinal rigidity or administrative control nor does it rule out development in beliefs or practice. It is a matter of faith responding to how things are perceived really to be.

This conviction of truth within religious traditions is the source not only of their power to form communities and to shape the lives of their participants but also of their dangerous propensity for intolerance, against which perpetual vigilance is required. But finally, one cannot be "a little bit Christian" or "moderately Muslim" any more than one can be "somewhat pregnant" or "relatively human." One either believes—that is, sees reality within this particular framework—or one does not. And believing is not an arbitrary choice among equal possibilities like choosing vegetarianism as a health measure. It is more like the nonnegotiable vegetarianism of the Hindu whose commitment to saving every sentient being sees the killing of any such being for any reason, including food, as actually evil.

Most people, at least until relatively recently, were born into a religious tradition, such as Christianity, and grew up being gradually initiated into the faith vision of that tradition through participation in its institutionalized life practice. Eventually, they either personally appropriated that faith tradition within which they developed a mature religious spirituality, drifted away from or rejected the faith into which they were born, or continued to externally practice within the institution while no longer actually participating in the faith tradition.

Today, many people grow up without such formative experiences of faith and may, at some point, begin searching for some framework of meaning in life and eventually find their way into participation in some faith tradition such as Catholic Christianity, which they finally embrace as their own. In other words, genuine religious faith cannot really be anything other than a free, personal response to what one actually perceives as true. Saying an adult "yes" to and within a religious tradition is mediated by, and often results from, a long process either of catechesis within the inherited tradition of one's family, or of searching and experimenting. But however one comes to faith, it is not an arbitrary choice among equal alternatives. It is a conviction, no matter how it is arrived at, that *this* is indeed the life-giving truth about God, oneself, others, and the world, and that life within this framework makes sense because reality actually is this way.

2. Religious faith as tradition, spirituality, and institution

Every religious (or quasi-religious) faith, that is, revelation-based "take" on the whole of reality, is a *wisdom tradition*.[19] It involves a coherent vision of reality, a way of acting in the world that responds appropriately to that vision, and ways of initiating people into that vision and way of life. Sociologists of religion speak of it as a cultural symbol system involving "creed, code, and cult" through which a community handles the major issues of individual and social life such as sexuality, kinship, property, power, birth, maturation, leadership, healing, and death in a way that appears divinely sanctioned; that is, self-evident and necessary.[20] Not just the great "world (or universalist) religions" such as Christianity, Judaism, Islam, Hinduism, but also native and tribal (i.e., local) religions are, at base, such wisdom traditions.

These wisdom traditions generate *spiritualities*, that is, ways of living the faith vision. Spirituality in this sense includes such common and behavioral elements as observance of the moral prescriptions of the tradition and participation in its public rituals. But spirituality also connotes both the internalization of the wisdom tradition and the individuality with which one appropriates it. So, a Catholic Christian not only believes what the Church believes, lives a moral life according to Catholic norms, and celebrates sacramentally in the Church community, but also is interiorly committed to the tradition and has developed a personal relationship with God in Christ within the ecclesial community. This personal spirituality may be simply that of an individual believing Catholic, or it may be shaped by that person's participation in some "spiritual family" within the Church, such as Benedictinism or the Charismatic movement, or some particular life situation, such as family, or pastoral responsibility as a cleric. It is only through the development of an authentic personal spirituality that one appropriates one's faith tradition as the shaping wisdom of one's life.

Religious wisdom traditions not only generate characteristic spirituality(ies) but also necessarily generate *institution(s)* which can stabilize the tradition, make it historically visible and socially functional, present it to potential members and the larger public, and initiate people into the life of the community. When most Catholics speak of "the Church" they usually mean not the community and its tradition but its institutional embodiment and often, even more restrictively, the Vatican which is one element of the institution. The identification of the tradition with its institutionalization is the source of serious problems when, as is virtually always the case, the institution is unfaithful to a greater or lesser degree to the wisdom tradition it is created to serve and becomes oppressive of the vibrant spirituality it exists to foster.

Institutionalization of religious tradition, in other words, is a very mixed blessing. It is sociologically necessary if the tradition is to maintain its identity, offer its riches to new members, initiate and form its members in the faith, guard the purity and assure the relevance of its teachings, promote the morality that these teachings imply, contribute its wisdom to the common human enterprise and so on. Just as the individual person acts through her or his body and the social groupings to which she or he belongs, so the faith tradition acts (not only, but importantly) through the institution. But just as a person cannot be reduced to her or his body without dying, so the Church cannot be reduced to or equated with the institution without becoming moribund.

An institution as old as the Catholic Church has not only deepened its original wisdom through the courage of its martyrs, the prayer of its mystics, the heroic virtue of its confessors, the reflection of its theologians, the ministrations of its pastors, the ministries of its members, and the everyday fidelity of its millions of ordinary "saints" down through the centuries, but has also experienced all kinds of institutional deformation. Routinized ritual more concerned with sacralizing class divisions than with divine worship or pastoral service, oppressive moral rigidity enforced through spiritual terror tactics, doctrinal narrowness and intolerance, scandalous abuses of power over the defenseless, clerical corruption, fiscal mismanagement, alignment with the rich and powerful, and the marginalization of the very people Jesus treated with preferential love, are only a few of the open sores on the body of the Church as institution. The scandal which such institutional evil causes is understandable and because it has become much more public in an age of investigative journalism which gives no quarter to claims of religious privilege, mass media that thrives on exposure of the scurrilous, and a much more sophisticated laity who are not easily hoodwinked or intimidated, it has shaken the faith of many people.

Even those who are quite capable of distinguishing between the wisdom tradition the Gospel has generated on the one hand and a corrupt institution on the other may find it virtually impossible to maintain a public affiliation with the latter. Many Religious today, precisely because of their commitment to the Gospel, are so alienated by the violence of the ecclesiastical institution that they cannot with integrity see themselves as public figures within it, and are tempted to have as little to do with it as possible even if they do not actually officially repudiate it or leave their Congregations.

This alienation on the part of some, perhaps many, individual Religious is part of the current tension over religious identity in many Congregations. And it is not unconnected with the issues of postmodernism's fragmentation and refusal of meta-narratives and the emergence of religious pluralism discussed above. The incoherence between the Gospel itself and the institution that often claims Gospel authority for hypocrisy and corruption demands selectivity on the part of people who belong to the tradition and can see the evils in its institutional embodiment. The more incoherence (and consequent selectivity) there is, the more fragmentary and uncompelling the unitary vision of the tradition appears to be. This internal breakup of coherence (what psychologists call "cognitive dissonance") is reinforced externally by the plurality of religious traditions which seem to have equal claims to theological validity and better institutional track records. In other words, these factors, individually and together, tend to relativize the religious tradition itself, and this undermines its characteristic spirituality and public practice. The strength of a unitary worldview is precisely its coherence, and the sense of self-evident truthfulness that this coherence generates. When the coherence seems to be radically subverted, when the "center does not hold," the entire enterprise is endangered.

Obviously, not all Religious (probably relatively few) are personally involved in these dilemmas to such a degree that their own Christian identity is endangered, but the problem is widespread enough that many Congregations are feeling its effects in arenas of liturgy, ministry locations and choices, personal prayer patterns, attempts to formulate mission statements or take public stands on the basis of Christian faith, and the formation of new candidates for Religious Life in the Congregation. This situation has direct implications for the major topic with which this volume is concerned, the relationship of Religious Life to the world. It is not an issue we can afford to circumvent, suppress, or try to finesse.

Religious Life, in other words, is a specifically Catholic lifeform within the Christian faith tradition, not a generically monastic or humanistically utopian experiment in community nor a permissive context for a variety of private "religions" or "spiritualities" put together by individual members from whatever sources seem to offer usable materials. This leads to the question with which this chapter is primarily concerned: the identity of Religious in mission to the world.

III. Religious Life as Christian

A. The Christian Originating Experience: Resurrection

Religious traditions, as we have seen, originate in revelatory experience from which emerge distinctive holistic and coherent visions of reality that appeal to the adherents of a particular tradition as true and ultimately meaningful. This unitary worldview or "take" on reality is the framework within which the believers interpret reality, including God, themselves, other people, and nonhuman creation. Such a framework does not have to be (and should not be) a closed system impervious to influence from other traditions with their distinctive worldviews. But it does have the character of a metanarrative, an overarching story or version of reality that has a certain consistency and coherence derived from the organizing power of the originating experience.[21]

The originating and nonnegotiable experience at the heart of Christian faith which grounds and shapes the Christian take on reality is resurrection, that of Jesus and our own. In what follows I will not attempt a full theological explication of the Resurrection[22] but will, instead, draw out of that theology what is relevant for our purposes, namely, how the Resurrection gave birth to and defined the meaning of Christianity and, within that new religious vision, gave rise to a distinctive lifeform, namely, Religious Life. We will then inquire into the implications of the mystery of Resurrection for the constitutive coordinates of Religious Life, namely, the celibate God-quest, transcendent community, and ministry.[23]

Christianity is the only religion that claims that its founder, who was a real historical person (i.e., not a mythological dying-rising god-figure), actually died and rose from the dead. It is crucial to understand that Christian faith in Jesus' Resurrection is not a belief that he was resuscitated, that is, returned to his pre-death condition. Jewish tradition knew of cases of resuscitation and the Gospels attribute a few such miracles to Jesus himself, but Jesus' followers never assimilated his Resurrection to those episodes. In fact, the account of the raising of Lazarus in John 11 makes a point of contrasting Lazarus's resuscitation to the Resurrection of Jesus which follows a short time later. Lazarus was resuscitated, that is, returned to his pre-death condition (see John 12:2), and the enemies of Jesus plotted to kill the resuscitated Lazarus (John 12:9–11), whom they obviously saw as still mortal.

Furthermore, the Resurrection does not mean that Jesus, although now personally dead, lives on in the memory or the imitative practice of his disciples. Rather, it means that Jesus' disciples had experiences of him after his human death that led them to claim that Jesus himself, in the full integrity of his personal humanity, was actually alive with an entirely new kind of life, was present among them and able to interact with them, and even that he now lived within them. Because of their experience of his indwelling, they claimed to be really his post-Easter body, the instrument of his presence in the world as our natural bodies are the instrument of our human presence in the world. They were not just imitating his earthly life in remembrance of him but actually carrying on his own action in the world, doing his work as he had done the work of God dwelling in him. The Risen Jesus is not just a revered memory or a moral model but an actual participant in the lives of his disciples, through whom he participates in the life of the world throughout all post-Easter time.[24]

The life of the Risen Jesus, as Paul explained to the Corinthians and the Gospels present narratively through the Easter recognition scenes,[25] is qualitatively different from his pre-Easter life. He now lives the absolute, eternal, and indestructible life of God, no longer subject to death nor bound by the conditions of space, time, and causality. But this life is fully personal, truly human as well as divine, because the Risen Jesus remains fully and truly human. This is the fullness of life that Jesus came to bring (cf. John 10:10) and that he now communicates to his disciples who, because they believe in him, will never die (cf. John 11:25–26). Jesus promised that after his death he would return to his disciples to share with them this eternal life, now freed from the limitations of earthly existence, which is his as glorified Son of God. They will live with his own life: "Because I live, you also will live" (John 14:19).

Although the Church has, in theory, always believed and preached this understanding of the Resurrection, it has often been obscured or even misunderstood theologically, liturgically, and especially in the spirituality of Christian believers. For many Christians, even those who joyfully sing "Alleluia" on Easter, the Resurrection of Jesus proclaimed in the Gospel is simply too good to be true. They cannot imagine such a thing happening in the real world, and so they believe something they can imagine, such as that Jesus, like any other human being who has died, is somehow "with God," in heaven (wherever or whatever that is), or perhaps reabsorbed into the cosmic process where he, like others of the deceased, have some influence on affairs in this world.[26] But for them, in any case, Jesus himself is gone even though his example and teaching remain to inspire those who look back on his life with faith. For such Christians, any kind of personal relationship with Jesus (such as that to which Christian mystics such as Teresa of Avila and Bernard of Clairvaux, among many, testify)[27] is in reality imaginative memory or even pious make-believe. God, transcendent (and perhaps non-personal) Spirit, is for them the only real focus of religious faith, and God is the same for all religions no matter what symbolic language they use to speak of this reality.

Of course, this position is not the authentic Resurrection faith of the Christian tradition any more than the practical unitarianism or naïve tritheism of many Catholics is authentic trinitarian faith. To cut Christian faith loose from the Resurrection is to sever it from its life-giving root and the source of its specific identity. And as we will see, it also invalidates the original impulse that gave rise to Religious Life and which remains the real basis of its spirituality whenever in history and wherever in the world it is lived.

Authentic Resurrection faith is the Christian conviction that in Jesus the hold of death on humanity was definitively broken. Jesus, born into the dispensation of mortality as all humans are, really experienced the death that is the lot of all. But he broke through death to new life which is God's own life lived now in his humanity. His Resurrection was not just his personal victory over death but the victory of all humanity (cf. Rom 6:5). In Jesus' Resurrection "death is swallowed up in victory" (cf. 1 Cor 15:54). A new humanity, no longer under the definitive rule of mortality, is inaugurated and those who are "in Christ" through baptism in his Spirit participate, even now, in that new and indestructible life. As Jesus says to Martha: "I am the resurrection and the life; the one[s] believing in me, even though [they] die will live and everyone living and believing in me never dies. Do you believe this?" (John 11:25–26 [my translation]). Jesus' final question is crucial. The Christian believes that death, which is inextricably related to sin or separation from God, has really lost its grip on the baptized, even during this earthly life as well as in the fearsome passage through physical death. This is not a promise of resuscitation at the end of time or of disembodied immortality in some realm outside of time. It is an assurance of eternal, that is, divine, life, possessed here and now, which will never be taken away and will be fully manifest after physical death.

For the first Christians, this entailed a radical revision of their Jewish eschatology or their Greek philosophical anthropology. It answered the ultimate human question posed by death as the universal destiny of human beings in an altogether new way. If death is no longer the end of human life as both Jews and Greeks believed—it must be remembered that neither Sheol (the Jewish version of the afterlife) nor the Elysian Fields (Greek immortality) was integral human life—then all the strategies which humans have developed to deal with death, to stave off the personal obliteration that death visits on the individual, became unnecessary.

Reproduction, by which one lived on through one's progeny, the building of political and social structures that would outlive their founders, the creation of immortal art and the elaboration of great philosophies whose beauty and truth are indestructible are *no longer necessary* as our only ways to deal with the finality of personal death. Human beings may indeed continue to do all these things precisely because they are valuable in themselves, but they can now do them *freely* rather than because they are necessary as the only available bulwark against permanent personal erasure from the land of the living. Hope against death now lies, not in strategies of human self-perpetuation but in the Resurrection of Jesus in which we share because we have died and risen with him in baptism.

> If we have died with Christ, we believe that we shall also live with him. For we know that Christ being raised from the dead will never die again; death no longer has dominion over him. The death he died he died to sin, once for all, but the life he lives he lives to God. So you also must consider yourselves dead to sin and alive to God in Christ Jesus. (Rom 6:8–11)

Certainly one implication of Resurrection faith that immediately emerged in the new Christian community was the joyful acceptance of *martyrdom* as total assimilation to Christ in his physical death and the new life to which it gave access. This Christian embrace of martyrdom was quite different from the heroic self-sacrifice of Jewish martyrs like the Maccabean brothers and their mother (cf. 2 Mac 7), who died in fidelity to Torah and expected from God a restoration of the bodies they had sacrificed. But as the early Church narratively presented martyrdom in the paradigmatic story of the death of Stephen (Acts 7:54–60), the Christian martyr is actually identified with Christ in his paschal mystery.

Ignatius of Antioch (d. in first decades of the second century) longed for martyrdom, writing to Christians who might try to weaken his resolve: "I am God's wheat, and I am ground by the teeth of wild beasts that I may be found pure bread [of Christ]" (*Epistle to the Romans* 4:1). The martyrdom of Polycarp of Smyrna in 155 was recounted by eyewitnesses in *The Encyclical Epistle of the Church at Smyrna, Concerning the Martyrdom of St. Polycarp:*

> Chapter xv: 1 And when he had uttered the Amen, and had finished his prayer, the men who superintended the fire kindled it. And a great flame breaking out, we, to whom it was given to see, saw a great wonder; for to this end also were we preserved, that we might announce what happened to the rest of mankind.

xv: 2 For the fire, assuming the form of a vault, like the sail of a vessel filled with the wind, defended the body of the martyr roundabout; and it was in the midst of the flame not like flesh burning, but like bread being baked, or like gold and silver glowing in the furnace. And we perceived such a sweet-smelling savor, as though from the breath of incense, or some other precious perfume.

The *Acts of Perpetua and Felicitas* chapter v.2 recounts the third-century martyrdom of a young slave woman:

Scarce had they finished their prayer, when Felicitas found herself in labor. She cried out under the violence of her pain. One of the guards asked her, if she could not bear the throes of childbirth without crying out, what she would do when exposed to the wild beasts. She answered: "It is I that suffer what I now suffer; but then there will be another in me that will suffer for me, because I shall suffer for him."

Death, no matter how real and horrendous, was radically different for the baptized. It was a passage in Christ to God in glory, a participation in the paschal mystery of Jesus.[28]

Within a couple decades of the Resurrection of Jesus, even during the period of the writing of the New Testament, some Christians drew out another possible implication of this new faith by developing a remarkable and original lifeform in the Church, the life of *consecrated virginity*.[29] It is important to realize that this new form of life arose concomitantly with the experience of the first martyrdoms. It was not, as has been suggested, a "white martyrdom" or voluntary ascetical substitute for bloody martyrdom once the period of persecution had waned.[30] It was, like martyrdom, seen as mystical participation in the paschal mystery of Jesus. The difference between the two forms of assimilation is that one took place in the experience of death and the other was realized as a way of life. Many consecrated virgins were also martyrs, but the Church recognized them as "virgins *and* martyrs," not as virgin martyrs, that is, as people doubly assimilated to the Risen Jesus and not as people who were martyred while they happened to be unmarried. Vir-

ginity was a free choice, not of an ascetical ideal but of a particular way of living their baptismal union with Christ.

The virgins made the radical choice to live the reality of the
Resurrection, which is characterized by neither marrying nor
giving in marriage (cf. Mark 12:25),[31] in a visible way *within* history and *before* death, not beyond history and after death as is
the case for all Christians. They chose not to marry, that is, not
to undertake their "species role" by founding or continuing a
family through procreation. There is no need to perpetuate
what is, in fact, imperishable, namely, eternal life in Christ.
Consecrated virginity was seen as the radicalizing of the baptismal assimilation to Christ, drawing out even within the
framework of history (i.e., before physical death) the full implication of that assimilation.

The lifeform of consecrated virginity was integrally Christian but also very distinctive within the Church. The fact that it
was most readily understood as "marriage to Christ," that is, as
an alternative to human marriage, well expressed the self-
understanding of the virgins. Theirs was a definitive, irrevoca-
ble choice that was self-evidently perpetual. It was not a choice
of ascetical death but of mystical life. In many cases, it actually
precipitated martyrdom precisely because it was a self-removal
by the virgin of her reproductive capacities from the economy
of family and empire. Early explanations of the life as "eschatological" or as "paradise regained," which are somewhat problematic today because they can suggest some kind of escape
from history, were attempts to express this Resurrection character of Religious Life. Today we would probably capture the
same reality more easily by language about the radicalization of
baptism. The earlier expressions, however, call attention to the
relation of the renunciation of procreation to the Resurrection
of Christ as the root of Religious Life.

The breaking of the absolute and necessary connection
between death and procreation as the remedy for death left a
Christian free to choose marriage and children, a choice
defended even by Paul, who apparently chose not to marry, as
completely legitimate and good (cf. 2 Cor 7:25–28; see also,
Heb 13:4). But it also left Christians free to give their whole

being and life, to the exclusion of any other primary life commitment such as that to spouse and family, to living their baptismal union with Christ as a lifeform within the concrete structures of human history. This new lifeform, arising immediately out of Resurrection faith, had no real antecedent in Judaism or in paganism and was the beginning of Religious Life that would develop in many ways throughout subsequent Christian history.

It is important to emphasize, however, that the Resurrection faith that gave rise to Religious Life is not different from the Resurrection faith of other Christians. All authentic Christian faith is participation in the paschal mystery of Jesus. What differs among Christians is not their faith but how they choose to live it, to incarnate it in the here of this world and the now of history. The choice not to marry for the sake of the Reign of God is the acceptance, Jesus says, of a particular charism offered to some of his disciples but not to all, to manifest, even within this world, within pre-death history, the totality of the demands of the Gospel and the power of the love of God to satisfy the human heart (cf. Matt 19:10–12). After the Resurrection of Jesus this motivation for celibacy, "for the sake of the Reign of God," became a christological motivation as the early Church came to understand that what Jesus called the Reign of God was actually inaugurated not only *by* Jesus but *in* Jesus. In other words, the choice of virginity for the sake of the Reign of God was a choice of total self-donation to the Risen Jesus in whom the Reign of God is present and active.

B. The Distinctive Christian Vision

As we saw in chapter 1, the distinctive Christian "take" on reality was defined by the affirmation of the Incarnation, the fullness of God's presence in the human being, Jesus of Nazareth. In this chapter we have identified the source of this affirmation in the originating Christian revelation experience, the Resurrection of Jesus from the dead. A whole new dimension is added to the Jewish revelation of God in Creation, in Torah, in Scripture. Jesus, alive, present, and active now becomes the center of the new Creation variously referred to in the New Testament as the Reign of God, eternal life, or life in the Spirit. This new Creation does not negate the original Creation nor does the gift of the New Law, that is, the Holy Spirit, negate Torah. The revelation in Christ does not nullify the Old Testament. But for the Christian all things are fulfilled—made new—in Christ.

The faith conviction that God is really and fully present in Jesus has ramifications for the Christian view of reality as a whole, that is, of the world understood as universe, as the human race in history, as a reality construction. If divinity is fully present in humanity, then Creation and Incarnation become a single unified divine salvific project, the fulfillment of Creation through divinization. The Incarnation is not a remedy, a "plan B" to repair a sin-damaged Creation. Transcendence and immanence are not mutually exclusive but mutually inhering. Universality is revealed in particularity, thus validating the particular as the medium of revelation. Eternity is present in history, which is destined for fruition rather than destruction. The material is suffused with spirit/Spirit. World, then, is not something from which the Christian seeks to escape but that which—in, with, and like Christ—the Christian embraces. But the Christian, baptized into Christ's paschal mystery in which death is the path to resurrection, is not a romantic optimist who denies the reality of sin and the power of evil. All Christians, including Religious, must be fully engaged in the struggle against the evil "world" and for the world as Reign of God.

IV. Religious Life as Specific Lifeform

Having looked at Religious Life as *religious*, that is, as a way of participating in a particular faith tradition which has a characteristic metanarrative that gives meaning to a particular way of believing and living, and then inquired into that particular faith tradition, namely, *Christianity*, within which Catholic Religious Life lives and moves, we are in a position to look at the life as a *specific lifeform* in the Catholic Christian religious tradition.

The point of this chapter is that Religious are not simply a group of like-minded people living and working together for a better world with an occasional reference to Jesus as memory or model. Religious Life, because it is *Christian*, is a way of living the life of the Risen Jesus in this world. The project of Religious is his project, the Reign of God. But *Religious* have chosen to incarnate this identity and project, which are characteristic of all Christian life, in a specific and distinctive lifeform in the Church. The defining coordinates of this lifeform are the celibate quest for God, transcendent or eschatological community, and ministry rooted in Profession and Congregational charism. All three of these coordinates are radically Christian but they specify a lifeform that is distinctive in relation to other vocations in the Church.

A. The Celibate God-Quest

The single-hearted quest for God is the mystical or unitive heart of Religious Life and affects all aspects of the life. This unitive dimension of the life is nurtured and experienced in its most concentrated form in contemplative prayer, which irradiates the whole of the life. Christian prayer, as Christian, is not an exercise in awareness, a practice of mindfulness, a centering of psychic energy, the cultivation of ego-transcendence, or a merging with nature. Any and all of these might be part of the life of any Christian, including Religious, and might serve various spiritual, psychological, and therapeutic purposes. But Christian prayer is essentially a *relationship with a person* who gradually becomes the affective center and effective motivation of one's life. Jesus Christ, alive, present, and active in the life of Christians and through them in the world is that center. Prayer, for the Christian, is about becoming who we are by baptism, namely, the body of Christ, his living and active presence in the world.

Religious share this vocation to contemplative prayer with all Christians, but their commitment in consecrated celibacy specifies their prayer as it does all aspects of their life. The choice to commit oneself to Christ to the exclusion of all other primary life commitments raises the stakes for Religious. The human heart abhors a vacuum. It was made to love, to give itself totally and freely and perpetually. Having left their family of origin in response to a vocation to participate in the itinerant prophetic mission of Jesus, and having chosen not to marry and found a family of their own, Religious need to find in their relationship with Christ the affective depth, totality, and effectiveness that will nurture their hearts to human and spiritual maturity.

Consecrated celibacy, as we saw in volume 2, gives a particular "shape" or character to the God-quest of Religious. There I spoke of it in terms drawn from the tradition of "nuptial or spousal spirituality" dating back to the earliest instances of Religious Life in the Church. Although the language and symbolism of this tradition may not speak to all Religious, some of whom experience Jesus in their lives primarily as friend or brother or coworker, and so on, the priority of the spousal tradition, quantitatively and qualitatively, in the history of Religious Life testifies to the defining importance of the exclusive commitment to Christ that characterizes the life of consecrated celibacy. The experience of Jesus in contemplative prayer, however it is symbolically mediated or metaphorically expressed by any particular individual, has a constitutive priority in Religious Life. Certainly some of the most outstanding women and men Religious throughout history, for example, Bernard of Clairvaux (1090–1153), Hildegard of Bingen (1098–1179), Francis (1181–1226) and Clare (1194–1253) of Assisi, Gertrude of Helfta (1256–1302), Meister Eckhart (1260–1328), Julian of Norwich (1342–1416), Catherine of Siena (1347–1380), Teresa of Avila (1515–1582), John of the Cross (1542–1591), and more recently Thérèse of Lisieux (1873–1897) and Edith Stein (1891–1942), among many others, have testified to a biblically based Jesus-mysticism of extraordinary theological depth, devoid of the sentimentality or unhealthy pseudo-sublimation that some contemporary Religious fear is intrinsic to this type of spirituality.[32] As a recent commentator on the writings of John of the Cross points out, the nuptial or marital imagery in the writings of John (and this could be said of most others who have shared this type of spirituality) is inspired by the biblical *Song of Songs* and makes his spirituality not an ascetical ascent to perfection, but a growth in relationship, a journey of love, in which God and the person seek each other as friends and lovers.[33]

Certainly no one would claim that Religious have any kind of monopoly on or superiority in the contemplative life. The mysterious union of people with God is the divine secret. But just as married people serious about their spirituality or single people committed to growth in the spiritual life need to plumb the implications of their state in life for their prayer life, so Religious need to ask how, specifically, their choice of consecrated celibacy as the form and context of their relational life affects and shapes their quest for God in prayer.

B. Transcendent Community

In volume 2 we explored at length the theological and spiritual distinctiveness of the form of Christian community that Religious undertake.[34] The Church is a historical realization in the world of the new kind of "family" Jesus inaugurated. This new family is not rooted in biology, that is, in physical kinship or ethnicity or any other kind of purely natural bond. Its bond is hearing the word of God and keeping it (cf. Luke 8:19–21). In other words, faith, not blood, is the foundation of this new social reality which came to be called Church (cf. Luke 11:27).[35]

Religious have chosen to incarnate this Christian community in a specific lifeform in the Church in which natural family (which retains its basic validity in the Christian dispensation), either that of origin or that which one might have founded had one married, plays no constitutive role. Religious come together with others whom they have not chosen and to whom they are not related by blood or other obligations, bound only by shared faith in and total self-gift to Christ, the Word incarnate, for the sake of the world.

Religious community is not a utopian commune created for the mutual advantage of its members. Nor is it a corporation for assuring their economic well-being, or a benevolent society devoted to good works. It is a non-patriarchal household of faith, a shared discipleship of equals, that not only fosters the contemplative quest for God and the ministry of its members but also witnesses in the world to the possibility that limited human beings can live the very life of the Trinity, the unity in diversity of totally disinterested and altruistic love among radically equal persons. Religious make a public lifeform of Jesus' prayer "that they may all be one. As you, Father, are in me and I am in you, may they also be in us" (John 17:22). But even that actual and visible living of the trinitarian life of God communicated to us in the Spirit is not the final goal of Religious community. Jesus' desire is that his disciples might be united in and by the oneness of God is "so that the world might believe" (John 17:21). Christian community, and in a distinctive way Religious community, is ultimately for the world.

First and foremost, then, Religious community is a *witness to what the world is called to become: a universal, transcendent, and inclusive community* no longer divided by family, tribe, race, ethnicity, religion, or class. This witness is given by Religious through their choice to live this type of community visibly, within the conditions of history. In a world in which family and other biologically, politically, and economically based principles of division still play a legitimate role, for Christians as for others, Religious community prophetically announces that all natural ties must finally be relativized by the unity to which the entire Creation is called. In this sense, Religious community, like other aspects of the life, has an eschatological character. It is a choice to live in the present that to which the Church is lured by the end time, to incarnate in history that which will be realized fully in eternity.

C. Ministry

Finally, the Christian character of Religious Life affects the ministry, both individual and corporate, of its members. People often raise the question of whether there is any real difference between what Religious do (teaching, nursing, social work, catechesis, research and writing, political involvement, and so on) and what participants in other religious traditions or even nonbelievers do in some of these areas. Christians may call their teaching in a public school ministry, but is there any real difference between what they are doing and what their non-Christian colleagues are doing? Hidden in this question is often an implicit fear of hierarchical dualism: is Christian ministry better than similar action undertaken by non-Christians? The answer to the first question, is there a *difference*: yes. The answer to the second question, is Christian ministry intrinsically *better* than comparable activity by non-Christians: no. Comparing any contribution to a better world to any other is pointless, and, in any case, beyond our competence since we cannot know the heart of other historical actors nor gauge the long-term effects of their efforts.

But there is a profound difference between Christian ministry and other forms of benevolent action. The difference derives from the fact that Christian ministry is not simply something a well-motivated person has decided to undertake. It is rooted in mission, in Jesus' sending of his disciples in the power of his Spirit to announce and help effect not just a better state of affairs in this world but what Jesus called "the Reign of God." This mission gives Gospel content, shape, modality, and priorities to the ministry of Christians, including Religious. The mission of Religious is further specified by their *Profession* and the *charism* of their Congregations, a topic we will investigate more fully later in this volume.

The mission of Religious, as Christian and specifically as Religious, gives rise to a plurality of ministries. Ministry, for the Religious, is neither a job nor a career (though, as we will see later, these features of contemporary work affect their ministry). Religious may change from one job through which they exercised a particular ministry to another, but both jobs are equally ministry. They may retire from a particular career in which their ministry has been exercised, but they never retire from ministry itself. Their ministry, as the expression of their Christian and Religious mission, whether in a high-profile profession, a poor barrio, or a retirement room in the infirmary, is participation in Jesus' work for the coming of the Reign of God in this world. It is, in other words, ongoing revelation among our contemporaries of who God is, what God desires for Creation, and how God is at work in the world. It is not only that the love of Christ impels us (cf. 22 Cor 5:14), but that, as Paul said, "It is no longer I who live but Christ lives in me" (Gal 2:20).

There may be no visible or external difference between the work a Religious does and that done by a non-Christian colleague, but there is an intrinsic difference because the Christian is not only doing an important work for the benefit of humanity but specifically promoting the Reign of God in this world. And two Christians, one a Religious and the other a lay person or a cleric, may be involved in the same Christian ministry but the Religious is acting not only as a Christian but also as a Religious. That is, she or he ministers in virtue not of ordination or hierarchical appointment but in virtue of Profession and specifically the vows of poverty and obedience, and in function of the particular charism of her or his Congregation. As we will see, this has important practical consequences for the discernment and actual exercise of ministry by Religious.

V. Religious Life as Alternate World

The primary purpose of this chapter has been to emphasize the fact and the significance of the *Christian* character of Religious Life in relation to the world, namely, its character as mission. In this final section I want to suggest, by way of brief prolepsis, how Religious Life as *Religious* undertakes this mission to the world. *My hypothesis is that the specifically Religious form of world engagement is precisely the creation of an alternate world,* which, as we will see, is done through the Profession of evangelical poverty (the economics of the Reign of God) and prophetic obedience (the politics of the Reign of God). The rest of this volume will be an unfolding of this hypothesis but here I want to adumbrate it as part of the theological framework for what will follow.

A. Religious Life as World

World, we have already said, is an imaginative reality construction. No two people live in exactly the same world, but people's individual worlds often overlap and merge so that they share a common world. For example, marriage merges the personal worlds of two people into the shared world of a new family in which they live and into which others can be incorporated. Religious Life is a shared world, a lifeform that a group of people construct, which is permanent, stable, visible, distinct, and into which others can be incorporated. In the recent past it was a "total institution" with its own sociological subculture. Today it is still a world, a reality construction with its own worldview, but it is no longer a total institution and its culture is primarily theological and spiritual rather than sociological. We have just identified its structuring coordinates as the celibate God-quest in contemplative prayer, transcendent or eschatological community which is shaped by the vows, and ministry rooted in Profession and shaped by the charism of the Congregation. Thus, Religious Life can be seen as a reality construction within which a group of people undertake a particular way of living the eschaton, the Resurrection-initiated Reign of God, within history, twenty-four hours a day and seven days a week, in a visible socioecclesial incarnation.

B. Constructing the Alternate World of Religious Life

A person enters the alternate world of Religious Life by Profession of the vows. As discussed in some detail in *Selling All*,[36] Profession is not simply a juridical assumption of supererogatory obligations. Rather, it is the public, solemn, and formal undertaking of a new life, or entrance into a new world. Like the profession of faithful, loving, and fruitful monogamy by two people entering the state of matrimony, Profession is the deepening and shaping of one's fundamental baptismal commitment by the choice of the state of life in which it will be lived.

The new life undertaken by the Religious involves a death, often described as "death to the world." This metaphor, for all its problems, captures something important. The human reality of physical death is a one-way street. No one returns on this road. Death is definitive, irreversible, total, visible, and public. The disappearance of the person through death is final. Bodily resurrection, which Christians believe is the other side of death, is not physical resuscitation. The life one enters through death is the indestructible eternal life of God, which is real but not visible, except in the case of Jesus, to anyone on earth prior to the eschaton.

Like Jesus' death, the death Christians die is death to sin, that is, to this "world," the evil reality construction in which all struggle prior to death. The new life they live, they live to God. Religious, by Profession, anticipate in their life in history, prior to physical death, this death to the "world" and life to God. They do this by undertaking life in a new world constructed by the vows. Consequently, to speak of Profession as "death to the 'world'" is to identify both what Religious renounce (Satan and his kingdom) and the mode of that renunciation (final, definitive, irreversible, and total through the undertaking of a particular and public way of life in the Church for the world). Profession is a one-way commitment to life in the Reign of God without compromise or attenuation for the rest of one's life.

However, it is important to emphasize once again that the alternate world Religious create is, first, *not a place or state where Religious go to escape the world of God's good Creation* including both the natural universe and the human race. Whatever may be true for non-Christian forms of monastic life, Christian Religious Life is rooted in Creation and Incarnation and thus animosity toward or escape from the world is not a Christian, much less a Religious, option.

Second, the alternate world of Religious Life is *not an escape from history* as the ongoing enterprise of the human race. Christian Religious Life is a participation in the project begun by Jesus Christ in his paschal mystery: the transformation of this world into the Reign of God which must be accomplished through the participation of his members in history. Therefore, Christian Religious cannot retire to their cloister, wish the world well, and devote themselves to peaceful self-cultivation. Like Jesus on the roads of Palestine they cannot rest until the earth is healed, the Good News has been preached to every creature, and justice reigns in the peaceable kingdom foretold in Isaiah 11:9.

Third, Religious Life as alternate world is *not a "lifestyle enclave"* in which like-minded people arrange to live with their own kind undisturbed by the challenges of social, political, and economic otherness. In the past Religious Life had developed a sociological subculture, a "cloister" (whether physical, cultural or legal) that largely protected its members from interaction with the rest of the human family, even other Catholics, except in the most structured circumstances, in which, presumably, no "contamination" was possible. Nothing in the life of Jesus suggests that this is what he was proposing to his disciples. On the contrary, the Reign of God that Jesus preached was a world in which prostitutes, tax collectors, women and children, the poor, the sick, the lame, the disreputable, the mentally ill, all the marginalized of society, were welcome as equals.

In short, the alternate world Religious create is not an escape from anything. It is not a defended sphere of life for the morally or spiritually superior or the religiously privileged. It is a prophetic challenge to the "world," to the evil reality construction of the Prince of This World, raised by the construction, in its very midst, of a way of life that is the polar opposite of that "world."

C. Describing the Alternate World

As has already been said, the alternate world of Religious Life is a paschal reality. Religious, by Profession, die to the "world" in a definitive act of disassociation from the reality construction of the Prince of This World. But, obviously, Religious must live in some world. They choose to live in the Reign of God. The construction of that world, which is not simply a vision of reality but also an institutional incarnation of that vision in the time and place in which they find themselves, is accomplished through the living of the vows.

The global vow of consecrated celibacy establishes the overall relational context of this new world: a particular and exclusive relationship to God in Jesus, a nonbiologically based transcendent community of those who hear the word of God and keep it, and a universal mission to all humanity modeled on the mission of Jesus from God. The day-to-day life of this contemplative community in mission is structured by the vows of poverty and obedience.

As we will see in part 2, the vow of poverty is a commitment to the living of an alternative economic system right within the "worldly" economic systems that have, over the course of history, oppressed and dehumanized the vast majority of people, the poor of this earth, for the benefit of the rich. We do not live in the peasant situation of the time of Jesus, in the class system of late antiquity, in the lord and serf system of feudalism, or in the horrors of the industrial revolution. Our challenges are market capitalism, globalization, technological oppression, international debt. But all the economic systems of the "world" have in common that they work for the rich and powerful against the poor and powerless. By the vow of poverty, Religious undertake to live an alternative economy in which no one is rich and no one is poor. This has a profound effect on their own relationship with God, their community life, their mission and ministry (the burden of chapter 6), and as a result on the witness they give in the world to the Reign of God.

Similarly, by the vow of obedience, which will be taken up in detail in part 3, Religious undertake to construct and live an alternate political system. Christianity was born in a political system of oppressive colonization. It has lived through systems of empire, feudalism, sovereign states, totalitarian regimes, dictatorships, and democracy. Different from each other as these systems were, they were all primarily structures of domination, based on hierarchy, in which the powerful control the disempowered for the advantage of the former. Religious, by their vow of obedience, undertake to create and live a different kind of political life in which there is no hierarchy, in which all participate as equals, where coercion is not the normal *modus operandi* of leaders and nor is heteronomous submission the way of the members. This new way of organizing power for the empowerment of all affects in radical ways the relationship of Religious with God, with one another in community, and with those they serve in ministry, and as a result gives prophetic witness to a new reality that is coming into being, the Reign of God in this world.

VI. Conclusion

In these first two chapters I have attempted to provide a biblically based theological framework for a reengagement with the fundamental question of the relationship between Religious and the world. The theoretical incoherence of the traditional approach to this issue which simultaneously proclaimed love of neighbor as central to Religious Life while regarding all contact with the world (including people) outside the convent or monastery as at least dangerous was exacerbated in practice by the conciliar reversal of the Church's stance toward the world. The presupposition of part 1 is that a new approach to the relationship between Religious Life and the world demands a reexamination of both poles of the relationship: the world on the one hand and Religious Life on the other.

World, which has tended to be understood in a univocal and unnuanced way as simply negative, had to be "parsed" into its very diverse meanings. Our examination yielded several biblical references for the term: God's good Creation including the entire universe but especially, for humans, our immediate planetary context which is the theater of human history; the human race as object of God's universal salvific will and individual human persons as moral subjects; and the reality construction which constitutes the imaginative world within which persons and groups live and move. All of these meanings are at least potentially positive. However, a subset of the third referent is the negative or evil world construction of the personal agent of evil whom Jesus called "the Prince of This World" and whom Paul refers to as "the principalities and powers." This evil "world" operates through systems and institutions that are created and sustained by human beings. It is the only appropriate object of rejection by Christians and therefore by Religious. A major difference between the understanding of this evil "world" by contemporary Religious and their predecessors is that the former are much more aware of the systemic and institutional character of "world." We are able to make the distinction between places, people, groups, and so on, and the systems in which they are involved, willingly or not, for good or for ill. And this enables us to realize that subverting "world" is much more complicated than attempting to convert individuals, pick up the pieces of the wreckage caused by evil, or encourage benevolence by the wealthy or powerful. We will attend to some of the implications of this realization in the chapters that follow.

Religious Life and the individuals and groups which live it was distinguished from its many possible analogs, for example, lifestyle enclaves; affinity groups devoted to particular good works such as feminism, peace, and sustainability; charismatic groups identified with particular values such as mercy; economic projects for the benefit of its members; solidarity groups; non-Christian monastic and humanitarian communities; political caucuses, and so on, by its specifically religious and Christian character.

As a religious lifeform, Religious Life is situated within a particular, revelation-based wisdom tradition, namely, Christianity. As Christian, Religious Life is rooted in the foundational revelation experience which gave rise to Christianity, namely, the Resurrection of Jesus. Consequently, the Incarnation, which became central to Christianity because of the Resurrection, is seen not as the competitor to the primal revelation of Creation but as the completion of Creation. Not only did all that exists come forth good from the creative will of God, but it came forth in the Word of God who became flesh in Jesus of Nazareth. The coming of God into Creation in Jesus laid bare the struggle at the heart of Creation between good and evil, a struggle played out in the ministry, Passion, and death of Jesus and the definitive but not fully realized triumph of good in the Resurrection.

Religious Life, like all Christian life, is shaped by this fundamental identity in Christ with its implications of the value of matter (including especially the flesh), the embrace of particularity, the treasuring of individuality, the reality and validity of history, and the call to universal unity and right relations among all creatures but especially within the human family. And finally, Religious Life is a particular form of Christian life in which some Christians, responding to a personal call to consecrated celibacy, undertake through their vows a unique paschal project of "death to the 'world'" and creation of an "alternate world" in which the eschaton, the Reign of God, is lived in a particular and concrete way in this world, in history, in a visible sociological incarnation.

The "unpacking" of this final point will take place as we now examine the relationship of Religious Life and individual Religious to the world in its many meanings. We will be constantly returning to the issues of the celibate quest for God, the living of transcendent community, and mission-based ministry rooted in Profession and charism as prophetic witness and action in relation to the world, which must be healed, sustained, promoted, and cherished and the Satanic "world" which must be subverted and finally overcome. The motivation and strength for this struggle is founded in Jesus' encouragement in the face of inevitable opposition: "In the world you face persecution. But take courage; I have conquered the world" [that is, the evil reality construction of Satan] (John 16:33).

Chapter Three
Naming the Task:
Mission to the World

I. Introduction

Having inquired into the meaning of "world" as the field into which Religious are sent and explored the distinctive character of Religious Life as an "alternate world" from which Religious enter that field in ministry, we turn now to the question of the nature of the engagement: the mission of Religious to the world. What is it that Religious are sent to do? How is it related to what other Christians are sent, by their baptism and specific vocations in the Church, to do? In other words, what is the mission of Religious and how is it distinctive? The purpose of this inquiry is certainly not to establish any kind of hierarchy among people, vocations, or ministries in the Church. This is not only impossible, but futile and counterproductive. Rather, the purpose is to help Religious clarify for themselves their own vocation to mission in the Church in order to facilitate individual and communal discernment about ministry, to strengthen their corporate and personal commitment to the ministry they undertake, and to understand the mutuality between their ministerial vocation and that of others in the common mission which springs from baptism.

II. Presuppositions and Implications

Three presuppositions will undergird our inquiry into the nature of the mission of Religious. First, mission is being used here in its properly *religious and specifically Christian sense.* Many institutions and business enterprises today formulate and publish "mission statements" which are actually self-initiated articulations of a self-chosen group identity and purpose. The institution or corporation which formulates its own mission is free to change that mission or even abandon it if it chooses to devote itself to some other project. But mission in the religious sense implies that one is *sent* by God and/or the believing community acting in God's name to do something that is antecedent to and prior in importance to one's own purposes. Jesus says that God consecrated him and sent him into the world specifically to give eternal life to all who believe in him (cf. John 3:16). He, in turn, consecrates and sends his disciples into the world (cf. John 17:17–19) to do the works that he does and even greater works (cf. John 14:12). As the Church began to grow, it chose some of its members—such as the Seven for the Jerusalem Church (cf. Acts 6:1–6), Peter and John for Samaria (cf. Acts 8:14), or Saul and Barnabas from Antioch for Asia Minor (cf. Acts 13:2–3)—publicly commissioned them for particular apostolic tasks, sent them, that is, missioned them, to carry out their charge, and expected the sent ones to be accountable for their fulfillment of the mission. All Christians, including Religious, as Vatican II insisted, participate by virtue of their baptism in the identity of Jesus—prophet, priest, and servant—and in his mission of establishing the Reign of God in this world.[1] Thus they are sent into the world to announce the Gospel in various ways. But Religious, as we will discuss later, are also sent into ministry by their Congregation on the basis of their Profession and according to the Congregational charism which includes its particular articulation of the common Christian mission.

A second presupposition is a partial response to the frequently asked question of whether there is any difference between what Christians call mission and ministry and the good work of other people of good will, whether religiously motivated or not, who are trying to make a positive difference in this world. In other words, is the rhetoric of the fostering of the Reign of God simply an in-house motivational device for Christians that has no theological substance or public significance? I am presupposing that Christian ministry is *not simply doing good in this world,* which is a mandate of our common humanity, and which does not necessarily flow from any particular faith commitment, although it may be shaped and strengthened by such. More importantly, however, doing good in this world does not demand an absolute preference of the good of others to one's own unto the laying down of one's life, which Jesus says is the internal form of the life of discipleship because it is patterned on his mission, which entailed the cross. The challenge to follow and imitate Jesus in ultimate self-sacrifice for the salvation of the world is not a personal decision to which certain individual Christians might feel called; it is integral to the mission of Christians. Consequently, it is integral to the mission of Religious. But because of the prophetic character of Religious Life in the Church, which was explored in some detail in *Finding the Treasure,*[2] the vocation of Religious to total self-sacrifice has particular characteristics which will be discussed later.

The third, and most important, presupposition has to do with the object on which Christian mission is focused. The evil against which Christians are struggling is not what philosophers call "natural evil," such as disasters like floods and earthquakes, sickness and accidents, or even natural death. Alleviating the suffering arising from these natural events is the legitimate object of benevolent action on the part of all human beings. But such suffering is part of what it means to be finite and, painful as it is, it is not something that humans can totally eradicate nor would its eradication solve the fundamental human problem.

The human predicament which is the object of Christian mission to the world is "moral evil," that is, *the evil caused by human choice, both individual and societal, both personal and systemic, arising from the "world,"* the evil reality construction that we identified in the last chapter as the Kingdom of Satan. Significantly, the Book of Genesis mythically presents the ultimate human predicament, namely, death, *not* as the natural end of human life or anything such as old age or sickness that leads to it. The first death recorded in Scripture is not that of Adam and Eve but the death of Abel (Gen 4:1–16) who was murdered by his brother. In other words, the human predicament begins not with "natural evil" (e.g., human death) but with something that "should not be" (fratricide), something contrary to and destructive of God's good Creation. The Book of Wisdom, as we will see, says even more explicitly that death was not intended by God but entered the world through the envy of the devil (Wis 2:24). We will have to explore what such language means, but its theological import is that that against which we struggle is not, ultimately, nature—even as "red in tooth and claw"[3]—but the deformation of Creation, including humanity, by the working out of the project of the Prince of This World.

That which was intended to be God's "peaceable kingdom" (Isa 11:1–9) and the fruitful context for those created in God's image and likeness, now deformed by the world as evil, must be called forth from its entanglement with evil by the Spirit of God which will renew the face of the earth (Ps 104:30). This was the focus of Jesus' mission and ministry (cf. Mark 1:14–15; Luke 4:16–21): to announce and inaugurate the Reign of God as *shalom*, well-being for all God's Creation. This is the mission to which all Jesus' disciples are called at baptism when they "renounce Satan and all his works"—that is, definitively disaffiliate from the reality construction of the Evil One—and are initiated into Christ, that is, commit themselves to promoting the Reign of God in this world. Different Christians, through their choices of state in life and ways of participating in the mission of the Church, shape their participation in this struggle in various ways. But no one, once baptized, can walk away from this project. Christian mission to the world is the vocation of all the baptized to participate in Jesus' salvific work. Christian ministry, whether individual or corporate, private or institutional, is a way in which that mission is carried out.

Two ways Christians have traditionally tried to handle this struggle against evil have come to appear inadequate today, even if legitimate and necessary. The first strategy, "flight from the world," consisted in disengaging as much as possible from the values, dynamics, and behaviors of the world (understood globally as everything outside the Church) and putting one's energy into living the Christian life as purely as possible within the ecclesial community. This strategy of separation was espoused most dramatically by the desert hermits in the third and fourth centuries. They physically fled the urban Church, which they felt was hopelessly compromised by its complicity with the secular Empire, and went out into the desert to do combat with the powers of evil and to seek God alone. This eremitical tactic was continued in one way or another throughout history, in both secular and Religious life in the Church, by the relative ghettoizing of secular Christians in opposition to the world and especially by various degrees of cloister for Religious. The "flight from the world" was not always geographical, but its primary tactic was separation or voluntary estrangement from, rather than engagement with, the world. Of course, one purpose of this separation was to foster, by prayer and example, the conversion of the world, but its primary purpose was to protect Christians from contagion by the world.

Another tactic for dealing with the world was to try to counteract its effects by "picking up the pieces" of the destructive work of evil. Christians were to care for the victims of the world: the sick, the poor, the orphaned, the imprisoned, the uneducated, the homeless, the violated, the exiled, the oppressed. This was the work of the whole Church and Religious often undertook one or another dimension of this work as the "special apostolate" of their Order. Again, this ameliorative activity, which was blessed by Jesus himself in the scene of the last judgment (cf. Matt 25:31–46), was Gospel-motivated and often highly effective, but it addressed the fallout, the effects, of evil, rather than its roots.

A genuinely new perspective on Christian mission to the world was introduced by the Council, which acknowledged that these responses, however necessary, well-intentioned, and even effective, are ultimately inadequate as individual approaches.[4] Both flight from the world and care for its victims, taken by themselves, express a kind of existential (even if unintended) despair of the world. Satan's dominion over the world which God so loved as to give the only Son is more or less accepted as "how things are." So we fix our eyes on the world to come, offering as much help as we can to the victims of evil as we make our way toward eternity.

The Gospels suggest that this was not Jesus' approach. He did not flee the world even though there were ways to do that in his time.[5] Furthermore, his miracles of healing, feeding, exorcising, even resuscitating the dead were something more and something other than palliatives for the fortunate few with whom he came in contact during his short ministry. Jesus really intended that God's Reign should come here on earth and within history as it is in heaven and understood his own mission as announcing the coming of the Reign and his ministry as inaugurating that Reign (cf. Luke 4:16–21). This implies that neither "flight from the world" nor "picking up the pieces," nor even both together is an adequate response on the part of the Church to evil. The mission of the Church to the world is determined and defined by how we understand the evil reality construction of world and how we think God, in Jesus, dealt with this situation. Christian mission and ministry as Christian, therefore, are not forms of humanitarian benevolence, but theological projects rooted in and continuing the mission and ministry of Jesus to subvert definitively the Kingdom of Satan and foster in this world the Reign of God. Consequently, our primary task at this point is to understand Christian mission and ministry as Christian. We will then be able to specify, briefly by way of anticipation at the end of this chapter, and in much greater detail in the rest of the book, what is specific and distinctive about the mission and ministry of Religious within this common mission.

III. The Christian Understanding of Evil: The Death That Should Not Be

In chapter 2 we discussed at length the centrality of the Resurrection of Jesus in Christian faith. Jesus, after his death by crucifixion and burial in a sealed tomb, returned to his disciples alive with an altogether new and indestructible life. The revelatory experience of Jesus' bodily (i.e., integrally human) Resurrection from the dead shapes the Christian understanding of reality, both of so-called natural evil, that is, the negative implications of creaturely finitude, and moral evil, that is, the implications of the demonic construction of reality. In chapter 2 we were primarily concerned with how the defeat of death (whether natural or violent) by the Resurrection affected the first Christians and their descendants in relationship to mortal life in this world. By removing the absolute conditioning of human choice by death which was misunderstood as the definitive end to meaningful human existence, the Resurrection freed the first Christians to confront their mortality, whether by natural or violent death, differently. Christians no longer saw death as the threat of final extinction and were therefore free to choose to live, even within history, as if death were not the absolutely determining reality which human experience, unenlightened by faith in the Resurrection, suggests that it is.[6] They could give their lives in witness to Jesus through martyrdom, and they could renounce perpetuating themselves by reproduction through the choice of consecrated celibacy, precisely because death, whether inflicted violently or allowed to have its natural consequences in childlessness, was not the end of life but the passage through the gates of death to the fullness of life that they had already experienced through faith in the Risen Jesus.

The story of the resuscitation of Lazarus in John 11 is the primary New Testament text exploring the subject of human death as the natural end of life and distinguishing it from the only death that is truly fatal for humans, eternal death. The text makes clear that Lazarus died of "natural causes," that is, of sickness (cf. John 11:3), not as a result of his sin or the violence of others. There is a telling exchange between Jesus and Martha of Bethany when Jesus arrives after the death of her brother, Lazarus. Martha says that Jesus, had he arrived sooner (which he could have done [11:5–6]), could have prevented Lazarus's death (11:21). She expresses the universal human desire to be spared natural death. Even though death is natural for all finite beings, it feels violent, not right, to those who suffer it or who are left behind. When death occurs we are tempted to think that God, who could have prevented it but for some mysterious reason chose not to, let us or our loved ones die. Death, even though natural, is a wrenching rupture of relationships precisely because only faith can assure us of the reality of divine life and thus the continuity of life through human death into the Resurrection.

Of course, the desire that death not occur is the desire for a miraculous suspension, in this particular case, of the natural implications of mortality. Jesus' reply to Martha, that Lazarus will rise, is actually a reinterpretation of natural death as real but relative because of the eternal life which Lazarus, a believer, already possesses. Mortality, Jesus says, is not absolute because one who lives and believes in Jesus never dies (cf. 11:26). Martha, however, is not consoled in the present by what she hears as a vague prediction about some future event.[7] "I know he will rise in the resurrection on the last day," she says. But who knows when the "last day" will be or what "rising" might mean? In human experience, death always seems to have the last word, or at least the only word that counts in the present.

Jesus, however, says in effect, "No, that is not what I mean." He is not promising "pie in the sky bye and bye." "I *am* the Resurrection and the Life," he says—right now—and "anyone who believes in me, even though they die, will live" (cf. 11:26). Then he asks her, and us, "Do you believe this?" The problem for Martha and for all later believers is that, even though one believes in Jesus, death seems utterly real and devastatingly final when it strikes down the living. Martha's brother is dead, four days in the tomb, and definitively beyond rescue because physical decomposition has set in (cf. 11:49). For Lazarus, who believed in Jesus and is now dead, what is this life that Jesus claims to be and of which he claims to be the source for all believers?

Clearly, Jesus is not speaking of immortality, either endless life in this world or the indestructibility of the disembodied soul in some extra-worldly realm. He is speaking of Lazarus's real participation in Jesus' own eternal life, a participation which is already being experienced by Lazarus but which Martha and all disciples can only know by faith.

This implies that Jesus' disciples, whose ministry is the continuation of Jesus' ministry in this world, are neither called to prevent or indefinitely retard natural human death nor to proclaim the immortality of the separated soul. What Christians have to offer to those to whom they minister must be, as Jesus offers Martha and us, access through faith to eternal life, a life that is qualitatively different from immortality in this world or beyond. Alleviatory ministries, if they do not mediate the reality of eternal life, as did Jesus' resuscitation of Lazarus as a symbolic revelation of the reality of divine life, may offer great temporal solace to their recipients, but they are not Christian ministry as Christian.

In this chapter, I want to pursue the significance of the Resurrection of Jesus not in regard to the natural evil of human death, which is already a huge challenge to hope in God, but in relation to Jesus' ultimate confrontation with moral evil which is even more challenging to faith and hope. Jesus' Resurrection was indeed the relativizing of mortality, which is natural but not ultimate, by the assurance of the bodily (i.e., integrally human) resurrection of the dead. But more importantly it was the definitive defeat of evil, which is not natural and which can, indeed, be ultimate. Christian ministry is primarily participation by his disciples in Jesus' victorious confrontation with the evil world, the reality construction of Satan.

A. The Revelation of Death as Evil

Mortality, as we have just seen, is part of what it means to be finite. Only a miracle could prevent a person from eventually dying. The idea that Adam and Eve (i.e., humans) would not have died had they not sinned is hardly credible unless we think that God could or would have ruled Creation by ongoing suspension of the laws of nature, because it is in the nature of created reality, which is not its own source of being, eventually to decompose. In sentient beings this decomposition is what we mean by natural death.

Most cultures, including Judaism, accepted death as natural and not morally evil or totally tragic. The biblical expression "to lie down with (or to be gathered to) one's ancestors" (e.g.,

2 Sam 7:12 and *passim*) expressed the sense that peaceful death at the end of "length of days" was a fulfillment of God's intent for the human being. Only if one died without posterity was natural death a genuine tragedy. (The Levirate law and various forms of surrogate procreation and adoption were strategies for coping with this tragic dimension of mortality.) Death was the natural termination of the life God had breathed into the person at birth and which returned to God with the person's last breath. This is not to say that death is not a source of suffering and grief. According to the Genesis narrative of Creation humans lost, by sin, the experience of their shared life with God, which would have made natural death some kind of transition from life to greater life rather than the fearsome rupture, the blind crossing from known life into mystery, that it is now. But death as the natural end of human life, for all its loss and pain, was nonetheless seen as part of God's plan for humans. Furthermore, even the violent or premature death of the evil person, as we will see shortly, was comprehensible as God's justice at work in the world.

But the violent or premature death of the just, the death that "should not be," presented a challenge to Israel's faith in a just and loving God. It posed a genuine moral conundrum because it violated the expectation that the faithful Israelite would fulfill his or her appointed length of days and leave behind posterity who would continue the deceased's participation in the Covenant community. How could they understand, as consistent with God's wisdom and power, that the just should not have the opportunity to reach old age, that is, fullness of days, and see the life of the family secured for generations to come? Or what were they to make of the death of the innocent poor person whose misery in this life led only to virtual non-life in Sheol in the next, that is, who, without fault, never had a chance at anything that could be called real life? What of the rape and murder of the virtuous wife whose shame followed her to the grave and dishonored her husband and children? What was to be said of all the cases in which the virtuous died violently while the violent lived in prosperity? Here we are not in the realm of nature taking its appointed course, of God's perhaps inscrutable but loving providence, or even of divine justice being meted out to the wicked. This was the triumph of evil, of that which "should not be." God's justice seemed to be defeated by human evil and the innocent were the victims whose unnatural deaths testified to that defeat. This was the struggle of Job, whose faith in God even as he experienced undeserved suffering eventually resulted in the resolution of his suffering by the restoration of his prosperity in this life before he died "old and full of years" having seen his descendants to the third generation (cf. Job 42:7–17).

The solution to Job's suffering, namely, superabundant restoration in this world, actually leaves the conundrum intact: how can a just and loving God underwrite the ultimate and final triumph of evil over good, of death over life? If all, just and unjust alike, finally go to Sheol, that place of endless shadows from which no one returns, what is the point of living justly in this life if that one and only life is full of misery and ends in premature or violent death? The wicked who seize the day to live happily in this life would seem, finally, to be the wiser.

A transition to the New Testament confrontation with the conundrum of unjust suffering is the Book of Wisdom, a late (c. 100 BCE or slightly later) Greek addition to the Hebrew Scriptures written by a diaspora Jew in the Hellenistic culture of Alexandria but within the religious worldview of Judaism.[8] This sage gives poetic expression to the distinction between natural death and death as evil that is crucial to our understanding of Christian mission as participation in Jesus' struggle against the death that "should not be." The sapiential text foreshadows the response to evil constituted by the paschal mystery.

> Court not death by your erring way of life
>> nor draw to yourselves destruction by the works of your hands.
> Because God did not make death,
>> nor does [God] rejoice in the destruction of the living,
> For [God] fashioned all things that they might have being;
>> and the creatures of the world are wholesome,
> And there is not a destructive drug among them
>> nor any domain of the nether world on earth,
> For justice is undying.

It was the wicked who with hands and words invited death,
  considered it a friend, and pined for it,
  and made a covenant with it
Because they deserve to be in its possession
                              (Wis 1:12–16 [translation mine])

For God formed [humanity] *to be imperishable*,
  the image of [God's] own nature [God] made [humanity].
But by the envy of the devil, death entered the world,
  and they who are in his possession experience it.
              (Wis 2:23–24 [translation mine and emphasis added])

In other words, according to the sage, God did not create evil. God created all things good. Therefore, insofar as death is evil it is not God's creation. Evil, including death as evil, is foreign to God's will and work, which are love and justice. But evil, whose primary result and manifestation is violent death, is real, and is mediated into human experience from a source (here identified as the devil) other than Creation but operating through Creation, that is, through or in "the world."

There are two intertwined realities in human experience, namely, God's originally intended world of love and justice, and a world of evil whose source is diabolical but which is made operative in the world through human choices. Physical death, in other words, after the fall, is an ambiguous reality. Insofar as it is the natural conclusion of human life in this world it is not truly evil, no matter how painful, because it is neither ultimate nor final. In that sense, it is not really "death" because death by definition is final. But insofar as it is evil it comes from the devil. So the sage is interested in the "death that should not be," the death that is brought into the world by "the envy of the devil" and is sought and experienced by those who share Satan's project.

After describing the folly of the unjust who figure that, since death is the final and ultimate extinction which comes for all regardless of their choices in this life, the "wisest" course for humans is to enjoy without scruple or restraint whatever they can get in this life by good means or bad (cf. Wis 1:16—2:9), the sage goes on to say:

> But the souls of the just are *in the hand of God,*
>   and no torment shall touch them.
> They seemed in the view of the foolish, to be dead;
>   and their passing away was thought an affliction
>   and their going forth from us, utter destruction.
> But *they are in peace*...their hope is full of immortality
>
> (Wis 3:1–4 [emphasis added])

Just before this assurance of the unquenchable life of the just, the text describes the plot of the wicked to condemn the just person to a shameful death and just after this assurance the sage discusses the various kinds of "unnatural" death which seem to mock divine goodness and justice: violence, childlessness, premature death. In other words, the Book of Wisdom distinguishes between the death of the just, even that which "should not be," and that of the wicked. The *just*, whether living in this world or deceased, *are alive* in the hand of God and the *wicked*, whether before or after natural death, *are dead* because they belong to the devil.

Although the Greek words "soul," "immortality," and "imperishable" (or "incorruptible") are used in these Wisdom texts, the context makes it clear that the discussion is not about the "immortal and imperishable soul," a separate spiritual (and thus naturally immortal) substance contained in the physical body and liberated from it at death such as Greek anthropology envisioned, but about the God-fearing person, the faithful Jew, who is with God after death, in contrast to the wicked person who suffers "utter destruction." The sage, who is thoroughly Jewish in theology, is talking about the fate of persons in their wholeness, not substances or components. It is persons in their integrity who are either "in the hand of God" or "in the possession of death." The Wisdom author was not particularly concerned with the "how" of these conditions but with the fact that the destiny of the evil person and that of the just are radically different and in both cases definitive.

This message is very close to that of Jesus in John 11. Death appears, in human experience, to be a single reality, the same experience for the just and the unjust. It appears to be the ultimate and final end of human life. But in fact, there is death and death. The death of the just person, like the wisdom hero and Lazarus, is real but relative and, therefore, not truly tragic. The death with which the Wisdom author and Jesus are concerned is not the natural effect of mortality. They are concerned with the final and definitive death that God did not create, which is not part of the natural order, a death which comes into the world from and by the action of Satan, and which is ultimate and irreversible.

The category introduced by this text is that of *death as the fruit and expression of evil.* The sage says that this evil death is invited by the wicked, whose absolute and final death is a result of their own moral choices. But it is also the death "that should not be" that the wicked impose on the defenseless. It is the violent death of the just, which is indeed evil, which seems to announce the triumph of the Evil One. This is why unjust death presents the conundrum that it does.

Jesus, in his ministry and especially by his crucifixion, enters into the death "which should not be." Satan, operating through the perversion of the persons, systems, and structures of the world, that is, the opponents of Jesus, the religious structures of first century institutional Judaism, and the political structures of imperial Rome, executed Jesus precisely because, by his life, his teaching, his saving acts of power, he announced and communicated eternal life. God had sent Jesus into the world because God loved the world and willed that humans not perish (i.e., die the final death) but have eternal life (cf. John 3:16). Jesus appropriated that mission as his own, to give life in all its fullness (cf. John 10:10). This divine life, lived personally and communally, is what the Synoptics call the Reign of God. By his direct confrontation with death as evil Jesus addresses the Satanic world, the Kingdom of the Prince of This world, and brings it to an end. Christian mission is the working out of this victory over the death "that should not be" between the time of the paschal mystery of Jesus and the consummation of the world.

In his Resurrection Jesus returned to his disciples, not as a resuscitated corpse doomed to die again, that is, still subject to a death whose reign continued, but as himself, radiantly and indestructibly alive with the very life of God which transfigures but does not abolish his human life. The experience of Jesus as risen transformed the consciousness of his disciples, illuminated their experience of God, themselves, the world, and human history with an entirely new understanding of life and death. They experienced themselves as sent by the Risen Lord to continue his mission.

Their mission, like his, was to confront death, not primarily natural mortality but the death "that should not be," the death that is the incarnation of evil. This death that is the work and manifestation of evil is both the fate of the unjust who freely refuse the offer of life and willingly choose death, and the fate visited upon the defenseless by the powerful. Whether chosen or inflicted, this is the suffering and death that alienates people from God, the former by their own choice, the latter because it seems to proclaim that God does not care, or that God is powerless against evil. In the end, death as evil proclaims that might makes right and therefore the "wise" will make their truce with evil, which has the final word, and the powerless will succumb to it because they have no choice. Christian mission is about the conversion of those seduced to evil and the liberation of those condemned by it.

Preaching Jesus' Gospel as the Good News of eternal life to those condemned to death, acting salvifically in Jesus' name, his disciples would "do even greater things" than the pre-Easter Jesus himself had done (cf. 14:12). Ministry, then, is essentially paschal in structure. It is not simply "doing good," or "making the best" of a damaged world, or "picking up the pieces" left in the wake of evil. It is the multitude of ways in which death as the final claim of moral evil, the death "that should not be," is conquered by divine life. The criterion of ministry as Christian is not whether something needs to be done but whether it gives eternal life to those who receive it.

B. The Nature of Death as Evil

To understand Christian mission as confrontation with death that was revealed as evil we need to explore the nature of that death, the source of its destructive power, and its confusing disguises in the world in which the Reign of God and the Kingdom of Satan are so intimately intertwined. Unless we understand the inner structure and dynamics of evil it will remain almost impossible to discern its presence and make the choices in regard to ministry that will most effectively counter-act it. I will turn again to the Gospel of John from which the Church draws the texts for its celebration of the paschal Triduum.

1. Jesus' violent death: Light, Love, Life

Jesus' death was not simply the natural end of his human life. It was the violent death that is the expression of evil. Con-sequently, if we are to understand Christian mission and min-istry as participation in that of Jesus who saved the world through his death and Resurrection, we have to answer the theological question: "Why did Jesus have to die as he did?" Would not his life of teaching and compassionate service have been sufficient for the salvation of humanity by providing a model of right relationship with God and neighbor? Why could he not have died peacefully, at the end of a long life, sur-rounded by family and friends? Of course, even the peaceful death of the good person, because of the rupture that it involves, is marked by suffering, not only for the person depart-ing but especially for those left behind. But the supreme conundrum is the death "that should not be" of which Jesus' crucifixion is a paradigmatic example.

John's Gospel tells us three important things about the vio-lent death of Jesus, which appeared to be the triumph of evil over God's infinite goodness that he represented. First, Jesus' death is not presented in John's Gospel as expiation for sin but **as revelation, light in the darkness of evil**. His death is not *keno-sis*, descent into annihilation, his being swallowed up by evil, but his glorification. It is the ultimate revelation of his identity and mission, of his relationship with God and with humanity. Furthermore, it is the glorification of God, the ultimate revela-tion of who God is in Godself and for humanity (cf. 17:1–5). If this is the case, we encounter God fully and finally in the passion and death of Jesus, that is, precisely in the death "that should not be."

Second, according to the Fourth Gospel, the motivation for Jesus' death was not appeasement. God is not presented in this Gospel as an infinitely offended deity who demanded the worst possible suffering of an infinite and innocent victim to assuage "his" wounded dignity. Rather, John's Gospel says that **the motivation for the Incarnation and, therefore, the Passion, was love**. "God so loved the world as to give the only Son" (John 3:16). Jesus in John is "God's Gift" (cf. 4:10), who is not a scapegoat bearing our sins or a victim paying a ransom for our release or a priest offering expiatory sacrifice. Jesus himself, sent by God's love, defines his own mission as love. "Greater love than this no one has than to lay down one's life for one's friends" (John 15:13 [translation mine]).

Jesus' violent death was not the reconciling of an avenging God with those whom God had rejected because of sin. It was a free act of love on Jesus' part, incarnating the infinite love of God, and it was done not for his enemies but for his friends (cf. 15:13–15). The violence in Jesus' paschal mystery is entirely demonic in its source and human in its execution. God, by contrast, is in this very same event the one who loves humanity so much as to enter, in Jesus, into the demonic sphere, to vanquish death by life. This same intimate intertwining of demonic evil and divine love in the same event continues to characterize the world that Jesus' disciples engage in ministry and in which they must discern what is of God and what is of evil, what is to be fostered and what subverted.

Third, the central struggle in John's Gospel is not defined primarily as the struggle between good and evil (although it is certainly that) but specifically as the **struggle between life and death**. Jesus did not come primarily to defeat evil in order to restore some kind of cosmic or ontological order to a damaged Creation. Rather, Jesus came primarily to give life, God's own life, in all its fullness (cf. 10:10), by giving the power to become children of God to all who believe in him (cf. 1:12–13). The life Jesus comes to give, which will cost him his own natural human life, is not immortality either as indefinite survival in this world or as a disembodied soul-life in some vague world outside of time. It is the indestructible and super-abundant life of the Trinity lived in our own bodily humanity right now and forever even as we pass through the gates of human mortality. Jesus, expiring on the cross, is glorified in the presence of God by the divine life that is revealed in his death. That life is revelatory precisely because, as we will see below, it is the very opposite of the fateful choice the Genesis myth attributes to humanity as the first sin.

2. The origin of death as evil

To gain some purchase on this mystery, to begin to understand why Jesus died as he did, we need to return to the root of the problem: the entrance of death as evil into the human situation which, by God's will at Creation, was never intended to include evil. The ancient Hebrews puzzled over the "why" of death, not just death as a natural termination of the human lifespan but death as that which "should not be."

The first death in Genesis, as already noted, is a murder. The real problem is not mortality; it is death as the incarnation of evil. To answer the question of how death as evil entered God's good Creation, they developed, under the inspiration of the Holy Spirit, a very profound myth of human origins (cf. Gen 2:4a—4:16).[9] This story is not a typescript of what happened in the first days of the universe story. It is a myth, a narrative attempt to account for our present experience of alienation from ourselves, each other, nonhuman creation, and God; of being in exile in this world; of being fiercely attached to life but under the sentence of a death which is not a serene passage from divine life under the conditions of mortality to eternal life with God, but a violent rupture of everything we hold dear. Even natural death, in the present dispensation, is marked by pain and suffering, but violent death is the paradigm of our human experience of death as evil.

The Hebrews who developed the myth that we call the story of Creation and the fall were people who believed that God was one, all powerful, and loving. God did not want any of God's creatures, especially humans, to suffer or die. Especially the innocent should not die and certainly not violently at each other's hands. The murder of Abel by Cain was the consequence of what their parents had done in the Garden. Somehow, the sacred author concluded, death as evil entered the world through the free choice of humans and humans must have been under the influence of something other than God when they made that fateful choice. What the biblical authors gave us is the story of "the fall" in Genesis 3, one of the most profound meditations in religious literature on the origins of the human predicament of death due to evil.

Throughout history Jews and Christians have been pondering the meaning of this myth, trying to understand the source of the tragic human situation in which we find ourselves. What did Adam and Eve, that is, humanity, do to bring about this unhappy state of affairs in which all humans desire life above all other goods and yet must die? Why do human beings even inflict death on one another? The myth of origins raises the crucial question: *What is basically wrong with us?*

The Bible's fundamental answer is that humanity sinned. But what was that sin? And why did it have such a catastrophic effect? One hypothesis is that the sin was **disobedience**. God set an arbitrary test for the first couple to see if they would obey God without question. They were free to eat of every tree in the Garden except one. As every child knows, it suffices to forbid something for that something to become irresistible. The human pair was tempted by the prohibition and ate of the tree and death, with a number of other forms of suffering leading to death, was the punishment. This hypothesis presents God as an arbitrary dictator whose basic concern is "his" own domination and control. And when challenged by human initiative this God is absolutely vengeful, expelling the couple from the Garden, blocking the way to the tree of life, condemning them to alienation from the land, from one another, from God. This is a woefully inadequate answer—unworthy of the God who created humanity out of love and in God's own image and likeness, and shallow on the subject of human responsibility.

A second hypothesis, based on the fact that the couple were tempted by a serpent who was a symbol of sexuality in the ancient Near East, is that the sin had something to do with **lust**, that is, with sexual disorder. This might account for the fact that the immediate result of the sin was shame over their nakedness and the distortion of the original relationship of equality between the man and the woman into a hierarchical relationship of domination and subordination. But it is hard to imagine what might have constituted sexual perversion when there were only two humans and God had specifically created them for each other.

A third hypothesis is that the sin was basically **pride or hubris**. The humans wanted to be like God. This is, in fact, what the tempter invites them to desire (Gen 3:4–5). "God," says Satan to the couple, "is jealous of divine power and does not want you to be like God. God wants you totally dependent on Godself for your very existence, therefore totally subordinate." An important German theologian and exegete who is also a depth psychologist, Eugen Drewermann, proposed a penetrating analysis of the story of the fall.[10] He affirmed that the temptation was indeed to try to become like God, but suggests that the motive was not pride. It was *fear*. The tempter woke humanity up to the fact of their creaturehood, that they did not create themselves and could not sustain themselves. They could go out of existence as easily as they came into existence, at the whim of an all-powerful and unaccountable Creator. Humans, says Drewermann, are basically terrified by ontological insecurity and the resulting existential dread, generated by the fact of their total dependence for their very being on a God over whom they had no leverage. This terror of their own creatureliness drove the humans to the desperate act of trying to seize divinity, trying to be like God, or more exactly, to become God—the source and guarantor of their own existence.

Paul, in his theology of Christ as the Last Adam, says that Jesus, although actually divine, did not consider divinity something to be grasped at or clung to, but rather embraced the human condition of creatureliness even unto death, and that is why the obedience of the Last Adam counteracted, healed, the disobedience of the first Adam (cf. Phil 2:6–11; Rom 5:19–21; and elsewhere).

Prior to Satan's intervention, according to the Genesis myth, the human couple lived in joyous freedom with a God who had created them out of love, desired their existence with infinite and unshakable desire, sustained them in every way, walked and talked with them in the intimacy of the garden. God was experienced as utterly trustworthy and loving. Humanity was absolutely secure in God's love. Satan awakens fear, insecurity, the suggestion that God is unreliable and thus that humans are not safe. Fear of an untrustworthy God, says Drewermann, is at the base of our human predicament. We experience ourselves as ephemeral creatures of a capricious God adrift in a dangerous world.

Actually, we have only to observe our individual and collective behavior to prove the truth of this analysis. We will give up even our most precious political and personal rights to leaders who claim that they alone can protect us from invaders, or terrorists, or criminals, or even each other. We justify preemptive attacks on anyone we fear might harm us even if they have not actually attempted to do so. We surrender even the sanctity of our consciences to religious officials who claim that they alone can interpret God's demands and only they can keep us safe from divine vengeance. Witness our unending concern about financial security, our early warning systems on our property, our hoarding of goods we do not need, our over-consuming against possible scarcity, our obsession with health and futile efforts to prolong life beyond all reasonable limits, our suspicion and fear of anyone who is different from us, of the stranger, of the poor or the ill or the marginal, of the immigrant who might take our job or challenge our way of life. Danger, disease, violence, scarcity, and death lurk around every corner threatening us with extinction.

Self-protection becomes an all-consuming preoccupation. We must supply for ourselves the security we cannot expect from a distant and unreliable God whom we project as, like us, preeminently concerned with "his" own prestige and power. Love can be demonstrated—as God did so lavishly for the first human pair—but love cannot be proved and without such apodictic proof humans, under demonic tutelage, decided that they could not trust God's love for them.

Drewermann says that our sense of cosmic aloneness in a dangerous universe is reflective of our fundamental suspicion that God, our Creator, is not trustworthy. God does not need us but we need God. So we are in a position of ultimate powerlessness, of total vulnerability. The ultimate hierarchy is the ontological inequality between God and humans. And this leads to our frantic efforts to defend ourselves against God, other people, natural disasters, or whatever threatens our existence. Of course, no matter what we do to protect ourselves, death eventually comes for each of us. Paradoxically, this is the one absolute certainty and absolute uncertainty of the human condition, revealing the self-contradictory nature of the human "solution" to creaturehood. We will certainly die. But when and how? And then what?

Every religious tradition, finally, has to come to grips with this question, has to say something coherent about death. There are many theories about what death means and what happens to us when we die. And whatever is proposed about the nature of death determines how we should live before death. If death is pure extinction, hedonism says, "Eat, drink, and be merry because once you die it is all over." Or the Stoic says, "Live nobly, create works of beauty and wisdom and power that will outlive you, and die with dignity so that you will be honored in memory and you will leave behind you a better world." If death means transmigration of our soul into another lifeform, then we should live so that our good karma will make our next life better than the present one. If death is simply our reabsorption, as non-personal elements, into the cosmos then we should be sure to do in this life everything that we really want to do because we will not pass this way again.

For Christianity's ancestor, Judaism, the worst thing about death was that, whatever one's personal fate, one could no longer participate in the covenant community. In Sheol no one remembers Yahweh and from the grave no one gives God praise, says the psalmist (cf. Ps 6:6 and elsewhere). So the only remedy against the pain of natural death was procreation.

One's children would inherit one's property, carry on the family name, and keep one alive in honored memory. One lived on in one's descendants so even those incapable of physically reproducing found methods of designating heirs so that they would not wholly die.

Christianity, born in the experience of the Resurrection of Jesus, interpreted death differently, indeed made a radical departure from its Jewish roots.[11] Jesus taught his followers that God had sent him to deal with the human predicament, to defeat death by initiating them into the indestructible life of God, not just as creatures (as Genesis suggests) but as children of the One who is the ultimate source of eternal life. In Jesus God responded to the original distrust, the existential fear, of the human being. God crossed the ontological divide between Creator and creature not just to visit or to reassure, but to share in humanity by becoming a human being. The terrifying inequality between Creator and creature was abolished by the Teacher and Lord who called his disciples "friends" (John 15:15). Those born of God through faith in that divine human being, Jesus, would share by gift the same life Jesus had by nature: God's own life. Humans would have by gift what they had tried to take by force, a life that could not die, could not be destroyed, even by the fearsome passage through the gates of human mortality.

Jesus' announcement of this incredible Good News meant that the ultimate threat, death, could no longer be wielded by the powerful to dominate the weak. Therefore, it was a lethal challenge to those whose power depended on their control of life and death. When Pilate threatened Jesus, "Do you not know that I have the power to release you, and the power to crucify you?" (19:10), he was claiming precisely that ultimate control, and Jesus repudiated it. Only God, Jesus says, has the power of life and death and God could be trusted absolutely to use it only for life.

Jesus posed the ultimate challenge to dominant earthly power. He challenged the religious leaders whose system of salvation by legal observance he undermined by the offer of utterly free salvation to those who opened their hearts to it by faith. He challenged the political system of providing safety in return for total subjection by assuring his hearers that God knew their every need, and could and would meet it. He challenged all systems of dominative power by creating a community of equals whose place was guaranteed not by wealth or status or family or talent or ethnicity but by divine filiation received through faith alone.

Both the religious hierarchy and the political leadership knew that Jesus, if he were believed, was announcing the end of their power regimes. The only recourse of his enemies was to discredit his claim by inflicting on him the very death he claimed to have disempowered, the death they claimed to control, the death "that should not be." They executed him to reassert that death, which they had the power to inflict, did indeed have the last word. If God could not save Jesus from death, and Jesus could not save himself, then the message that death was powerless was empty. Death was still the ultimate threat and it was still in the hands of the powerful.

The Resurrection was God's signature to the truth of Jesus' claims, the manifestation of infinite divine life in a human being, which Jesus had announced as God's gift to every person who chose to accept it. John's Gospel presents Jesus' death as revelation of the Human One (cf. John 19:5) who, in the very experience of the death our first parents sinned to avoid, trusted absolutely in the saving love of the Creator whom he recognized not as arbitrary power but as loving Parent. Jesus' total trust in God in the very experience of death destroyed death's power to alienate humans from God.

Throughout the theological history of the Church this Good News that Jesus proclaimed and established has been explained in many ways, some of them hardly credible today.[12] One, already mentioned, is the judicial explanation that God was infinitely offended by human sin and could only be mollified by the expiatory destruction of an infinite victim. So, God chose God's own Son as a substitute for sinful humanity and decreed that the Son be killed in the most horrible manner possible to satisfy the blood-thirst of divine justice. Jesus, in this scenario, took our place, suffered more intensely than any human has ever suffered and thus, by paying the required price, reopened the gates of heaven that were closed by God as punishment for the sin of the first couple. Most Christians probably learned some version of this theology of divine retribution in their catechesis.

Today we realize that this explanation is not only questionable theology but productive of a dangerous spirituality. It presents God, as some feminists have charged, as an absolute (male) monarch who is the ultimate child abuser. God punishes the innocent in the place of the guilty. And, in reality, nothing is done about our guilt. What is "solved" is God's rage, not our incapacity for love, our fear of a capricious and dangerous God. I want to offer a theology of Jesus' paschal mystery that I believe makes better sense of what happened on Calvary and therefore of what the Resurrection means.[13]

First, God did not will Jesus' death, much less kill him. God gave Jesus to humanity out of love for us, and Jesus shared totally in God's desire that we should have life. God "gave" the only Son, and Jesus "came" to give life. He was not God's surrogate victim but God's accomplice in salvation. Jesus' death was the result, not of God's demand for satisfaction, but of Jesus' life among us. Nor was his life simply a prelude to his death. His life was the *cause* of his death. This means that death was not the purpose of the Incarnation. Jesus did not "come to die." Jesus' public ministry began with his baptism when he signified his total solidarity with humanity and God affirmed that this human being was indeed the Beloved Son, a real human being who was vulnerable to death as we are, but who, unlike us, did not fear God as the untrustworthy and dangerous potentate who held the power of life and death over him. Jesus was the human being that God originally created, the one who joyfully called God "Abba," his beloved Parent whom he trusted with his whole being.

As soon as Jesus is baptized he goes into the desert where, as the last Adam, he confronts the one who had deceived Adam and Eve, or more exactly who deceives all of us who are the children of the mythical first humans. Satan attempts to seduce Jesus into existential fear. He challenges Jesus to put his security in something he could control—his power to produce for himself what he needed, even from stones; his ability to manipulate God by God's own promise to protect him—and, finally, to surrender himself into the power of Satan who promised him security and even the whole world. Jesus refuses all Satan's suggestions and banishes him, albeit temporarily, from his life (Luke 4:1–13). Jesus renounces Satan and all his works and all his pretenses and returns from the desert to begin his ministerial career, caring for his sisters and brothers, his fellow creatures, those who are called to be, like him, beloved children of God but who do not yet know it.

Jesus' message was that in him God's relationship to humanity was made manifest. He said that God is loving, faithful, and utterly trustworthy. God cares for everything God has made, but especially for the poor, the suffering, the sorrowing, the sick, the marginalized; the very people that the powerful of this world oppress and exploit. Jesus confronted every kind of death, not just natural mortality but the death caused by human evil. He healed the death of the senses in blindness and deafness; the death of the body in paralysis and atrophy and fever; social death by exclusion and marginalization because of gender or race or social status; economic death by poverty and debt; and especially religious and spiritual death by exclusion from worship because of sin or impurity. Jesus said, "God does not will or cause any of this and God can and will handle all of it. You are safe no matter what happens to you, because God counts every hair of your head and can supply every need and remedy every ill. All you have to do is accept God's saving love" (cf. Matt 5:36; Mark 10:30; Luke 12:7). Of course, this is a challenging "all" because it means abandoning self-sufficiency and entrusting oneself in total self-gift to God. It means surrendering one's invented self, the self that is supposedly "like God," in exchange for the true self made in the image and likeness of God. It is accepting, once and for all, that one is the free creature of an all-loving Creator rather than an ersatz "creator" who is the figment of our own delusion. God does not love us because we are good (or powerful or autonomous). God loves us because God is good and nothing we ever do, Jesus says, can make God not love us.

Jesus entered into death to act out what he had preached, that no matter what is done to us, even the imposition of violent death, we are secure in God's love. God can and will save us, even from the very worst evil that others can unleash on us. Jesus does not simply announce this to others. He puts it into practice when those evils are unleashed on him.

We do not know that Jesus' suffering was the worst ever suffered. That is not the point. Jesus suffered paradigmatically all the kinds of violent, humanly inflicted suffering to which we are vulnerable: the agony of physical torture, the psychological pain of betrayal and abandonment by his friends, the torment of mockery and loathing, and the failure of his life's work. He suffered fear so intense he sweated blood. He even suffered the spiritual desolation of feeling abandoned by God as his tormenters taunted him that God could not or would not come to his rescue.

Finally, Jesus underwent death, not natural death but precisely the death "that should not be." And in that extreme moment, as his life was ebbing from his body, he refused to despair of God or to embrace the dynamics of the world of Satan by hating his killers. He prayed for his executioners, loving them to the very end as he believed God loves every human being (cf. Luke 23:34). And he commended himself to God with his dying breath, going, as John's Gospel says, into the glory of his Father. Only at this moment when the Beloved Son had passed through every possible challenge to his utter trust in God and total solidarity with humanity, both the good and the evil, is what began in Genesis, God's work of Creation, really accomplished. Jesus says, "It is finished; it is consummated" (cf. John 19:20). Creation has achieved its goal in the absolute union of creature and Creator in indestructible trust and love.

The point of killing Jesus was to invalidate his message, to prove that what he taught about God was not true (cf. Luke 23:35–38). The authorities of temple and state had made it perfectly clear that God had abandoned the messenger to death. God could not come and take this messianic pretender down from the cross. And everyone except a few women disciples whose love was stronger than death, everyone including his other disciples, got the point. They went into hiding, knowing that all was over. Their hope for this new dispensation that Jesus had preached and seemed to have inaugurated through his teaching and healing ministry died on the cross, accursed by God (Deut 21:22–23), and was buried in a sealed tomb. Death was still, and finally, in control.

But soon after his death, when the disciples expected nothing but a return to the *status quo* of poverty, oppression, and death, Jesus appeared in their midst, undeniably himself, alive with an indescribable fullness of being and life, shining with divinity, still marked with his now glorious wounds. He had not, after all, been conquered by death. He was victorious not only over death but over the sin which was the cause of the death "that should not be." Jesus' absolute trust in the One he called his loving Parent was fully and radiantly justified.

But it is important to underscore two points: Jesus did not die a natural death and he did not "come back" to natural life. His life did not run its course to death, which is the natural fate of all mortals. He died prematurely and violently as a result of all the things that "should not be." He died of human hatred and injustice. In him all the powers of death struggled with God's infinite power to give life and his ravaged body and spirit were the battlefield of that struggle. When death had done all it could do, Jesus emerged fully alive. He did not take up another span of mortal existence as Lazarus did after his resuscitation. He entered definitively into the divine life of the Trinity. And in his return to his own he revealed to them that what he had said about God was utterly true. God can be trusted no matter what evil is unleashed on us. Life, not death, is the ultimate reality. And that life is, for us, precisely divinized human life. Jesus rose bodily, that is, humanly to divine life.

IV. Implications for Christian Mission and Ministry

Christian mission and ministry, which is a continuation of Jesus' mission, is not simply humanitarian benevolence. It is not even a religiously motivated effort to make the world a better place. The Christian understanding of what ministers are doing is different. Christians are trying to live into concrete existence in this world, that is, in the totality of Creation both human and nonhuman, the "world" which is the reality construction inaugurated by Jesus, namely, the Reign of God. This involves the final undoing of the reality construction of the Prince of This World, the Kingdom of Satan. These two worlds, as we have seen, are intimately intertwined in human history as well as in the hearts of human beings. It is this commingling of reality constructions that complicates the discernment, the decisions, and the actual practices of ministry. However, there are certain characteristics that are intrinsic to Christian mission and ministry.

First, Christian mission is a **global project**: the announcing and effecting in this world of the Reign of God. No matter how local, limited in scope, and particular in object the ministry of the individual Christian might be, it draws its meaning and significance from its participation in this global enterprise, which intends explicitly the ultimate integration in God of all reality. Whatever we know of Creation and whatever we come to know as our knowledge of the universe expands is included in the global intention of God, the flourishing of all Creation in wholeness and peace. Jesus lived and ministered in a tiny, colonized, poverty-stricken country for a brief few years. But his mission from God embraced every atom of Creation from the Big Bang to the eschaton, every human ever born or to be born. This global vision is the framework for discernment, deployment of resources, and actual ministry.

Second, this global mission is **universal** in its application. There is no one, no thing, no place, no enterprise that is excluded from the universal salvific will of God revealed in Jesus. From the Christian perspective, nothing is finally reprobate. Nothing is foreign to the concerns or the efforts of Christian ministry. Just as Jesus' ministry embraced not only the law-abiding but the sinners, the clean and the unclean, those who followed him and those who murdered him, Jews and Gentiles, women and men, the poor and the rich, humans whose hearts he calmed and nature whose storms he calmed, so Christian ministry extends to every creature. In the context of limited resources and personnel and of restrictions of all kinds, discernment is crucial and painful choices must be made. But it is not discernment about whether someone or something is worth our salvific commitment but about how best to do what we are sent to do, namely, to preach the Gospel to every creature.

Third, Christian mission has a very specific focus. Christians announce and effect the Reign of God specifically by their struggle against **moral evil**, the death "that should not be." The life they are called to mediate into this world is neither indefinite survival here nor immortality of the soul hereafter. It is eternal life, divine life, lived here and now and into eternity, which can be received only by those who choose to accept it.

This means that it must be presented and offered in a credible way. Evangelization, proclaiming the message of who God is and what God desires for humans and for the rest of Creation, is at the heart of Christian mission no matter in what particular ministry one is involved. Evangelization is not about converting people to a particular denomination, or even a particular religion, much less about selling eternal security for temporal subjection. It is about announcing the Gospel, the Good News that God the creator is totally trustworthy in life and in death, and all powerful against the threats of those who would control and oppress physically, socially, economically, politically, or ecclesiastically. God is the one who knows our every need before we voice it (Matt 6:8) and out of whose hand no one can snatch us (John 10:29–30).

It is not absolutely necessary that those who hear the Gospel recognize it as Christian. But it is absolutely necessary that those who preach it know whence it comes and what it is about. How this Good News can be preached today in the complexity of modern society and its institutions, in a multireligious and multicultural context, requires study as well as creativity and cooperation with partners within and outside denominational and religious boundaries. But it is crucial that Christian ministry not devolve into an effort to alleviate suffering for its own sake or even a purely political struggle for just institutions and systems. Ministry is not about "picking up the pieces" or even about changing the systems which create the pieces. It is about the eradication of the root cause of suffering in this world and the mediation into this world of the absolute love of God poured forth in Jesus' paschal mystery.

This means that the focus of Christian ministry is the "principalities and powers" which create the evils of poverty, exile, homelessness, educational disempowerment, environmental devastation, and all the forms of "the death that should not be" in order to consolidate the domination of those who claim to have the power of life and death over the oppressed. No one objects to people giving aid to the suffering, especially if they do it person-by-person rather than institutionally and if the handouts are not accompanied by analysis and exposure of the violent dynamics at work in causing the suffering in the first place. What unleashes the violence of the oppressors is the threat to their construction of reality. Christian ministry, by, for whom, and how it operates, exposes and challenges this reality construction. Christians ministering in the name of Jesus, because they are subverting the world that opposes the Reign of God, can expect to share his fate and for the same reason. Conflict, persecution, and even death are not anomalies in Christian mission and ministry. They are witnesses to the Christian character of the mission.

Finally, Christian mission is not exclusively the work of the Church (community or institution) in relation to the extra-ecclesial world. As we saw in chapter 1, the evil world is very much within the Church as well as outside of it. And conversely, much that reflects and embodies the Gospel, whether knowingly and explicitly or implicitly and substantially, is outside the perimeters of the institutional Church. As Jesus said when his disciples were upset that someone "not…in our company" was casting out demons in Jesus' name, "…whoever is not against you is for you" (Luke 9:49–50). Consequently, Christian ministry is **often to the Church** itself, where it encounters the same dynamics of violence, dishonesty, abuse of power, and oppression that it encounters in the rest of the world. Ministry to the

Church, which is especially the work of Religious because of the prophetic nature of their vocation,[14] is especially fraught with danger and suffering precisely because of the investment of the ministers in the Church which is their spiritual home and should be the primary source of social support in their ministry. As the biblical prophets exemplify and Jesus testified, it is always easier to call to conversion groups of which one is not a part. "A prophet has no honor in the prophet's own country" (John 4:44).

In summary, the specifically Christian character of Christian ministry derives from the mission in which it is grounded. That mission is participation in the mission Jesus accepted from God in the Incarnation and fulfilled in his paschal mystery. The Christian character of ministry is not a narrow or parochial focus best kept private as the Christian participates with non-believers and believers from other faith traditions in the work of improving the world. It is precisely what Christians bring to the enterprise that they share with these fellow workers. Ministry, especially the nonclerical prophetic ministry of Religious, is not, or should not be, about narrow dogmatism, proselytizing, or imposing ecclesiastical requirements or sanctions. Rather, it involves a particular kind of comprehension of reality and analysis of the struggle in which the human family is involved, a particular genre of resources for addressing the challenges, a particular kind of relational basis for engaging in the struggle, a particular source of strength for commitment and perseverance, and the renunciation of certain strategies and tactics which might be humanly effective but are incompatible with the nonviolence and universalism of the Gospel. Christian ministry is rooted not in the espousal of a cause, however lofty, but in a relationship with a Person and identification with his divine vision that the Gospels call the Reign of God.

V. The Distinctiveness of the Mission and Ministry of Religious

Devoting most of this chapter to a consideration of the *Christian* character of mission and ministry arises from the fact that the mission and ministry of Religious is not substantially different from that of all the baptized. Nevertheless, there is a specificity to the mission and ministry of Religious which is important for their own self-understanding and discernment and which marks out their engagement in the common work of the Church's members.

A literary analogy may help us to reflect on the differences among Christian states of life, especially in relation to the subject of ministry. A newspaper article, poem, painting, song, or eulogy could each be used to testify to the same event, such as a fatal fire. Each genre has potentialities for making some elements of the event more striking or salient even as it constrains what can be said about other aspects. A newspaper article, for example, will be long on facts and perhaps short on the emotion carried by a poem or the loss expressed in the eulogy. A painting or photograph, because it does not use words, has a nondiscursive immediacy that can appeal directly to the viewer's sensibilities, but because it does not speak in words, its message may be less available to people who did not know the person who perished in the fire. All states of life in the Church witness to the same reality, the paschal mystery of Jesus. And they all entail participation in his mission of proclaiming and bringing about the Reign of God through some form of ministry. That is the common Christian vocation. But each state in life, such as matrimony or Religious Life, also raises to striking visibility certain aspects of the paschal mystery while being less suited to express other aspects as clearly. And the specific ministries through which the Reign of God is promoted by people in different states of life may be different or done differently.

The "genre" of Religious Life draws its specific power from the fact of being a lifeform constituted by a perpetual commitment to Christ in consecrated celibacy, evangelical poverty, and prophetic obedience lived in community and expressed in explicitly religious ministry within the Church. By way of anticipation of the two parts to follow, I will indicate here, very briefly, how the "genre" of Religious Life gives a unique shape to the participation by Religious in the common Christian vocation to mission and ministry.

Religious Life, at its root, is an embodiment in a particular, concrete, historical lifeform of Resurrection faith. By choosing not to marry and procreate but to pour all the life-giving energy of one's being into seeking first and only the Reign of God, Religious declare in the most radical and public way possible that humans do not have to take remedies against death. Death has no power over the faithful Christian. But Religious witness to this in a striking way by stating existentially that they do not need descendants or works or reputation or anything else to insure that they do not disappear in death. At death, believers pass definitively into life. Religious choose to live only that Resurrection life, in time and history before death as well as in the passage through death. By focusing their affectivity on Christ to the exclusion of any other primary life commitment, Religious make ministry, that is, the service of Christ in the members of his Body, not part of what they do in this world but the totality. The first great commandment and the second coincide not only in theological fact but also in actual practice.

By choosing not to pursue wealth, the all-consuming passion of human beings striving to shore up their existence by providing security for themselves, Religious confidently live in the "insecurity" of total trust in the God who is utterly trustworthy. What Religious have they share rather than save or hoard for their own individual or corporate protection. What they do not have they do not covet. Not only greed but even private ownership is not necessary for the one who is totally safe in the infinite love of the utterly faithful God. The result of this approach to material goods, as we will see in much greater detail in part 2, is a community in which all contribute according to ability and all receive according to need. Working to redistribute the goods of this world for the benefit of all is the natural and logical expression of the open-handedness of those who do not have to take care of themselves. Evangelical poverty is a substitution of a total economic interdependence for the anxious concern for taking care of "number one," and its overflow is ministry to the disadvantaged pursued not for gain but for love.

By a vow to obey only God, a commitment to discern at all times and in all circumstances God's will and way in this world,

Religious individually and corporately confront the power structures of Satan's world with the calm but definitive refusal to submit through fear to those who claim the power of life and death. With their lives they declare, "The Lord your God shall you worship and God only shall you serve" (Luke 4:8); "We must obey God rather than humans" (Acts 5:29). Those who really believe that no power on earth can either make us secure or put us out of existence, that no one has "power of life and death" over us, can pursue the truth and promote the good without hedging their bets or toning down what might be offensive to the powers, either secular or ecclesiastical. Risking death for the sake of Reign of God is possible precisely because death has no power over them. Martyrdom in its physical realization may not be the fate of every Religious but all Religious should be living and ministering in such a way that martyrdom, physical or in other forms, is a logical result of how they live and what they do.

Because Religious choose not just to live personally a life that renounces Satan and all his works and seeks first the Reign of God but also to come together to create a visible lifeform in the Church and world that makes the Reign of God concrete as a social reality in history, they live a prophetic witness on a day-to-day basis. It is out of this Resurrection-based corporate lifeform, that is, the Religious community, that Religious minister. Consequently, the immediate "sending agency" for the Religious is neither her own choice nor the ecclesiastical authorities but the Congregation, and the determining criterion of particular ministries is the charism of the Congregation.

Religious Life is a distinct, not superior, lifeform in the Church. It is different from but not an alternative to the Christian life that Religious share with all the baptized. It is my suspicion that if Religious Life is to reappropriate its ministerial identity in the context of the new millennium it will not be by inventing new works or establishing new institutions, although both of these might be done. It will not be by returning to the physical visibility of habits or the sociological visibility of large group living. It will not be by finding a way to concentrate its personnel in a few common works such as a school or a hospital clearly labeled with the Congregational name or logo.

Rather, reappropriation of its ministerial identity will take place through a contemplative renewal of the Gospel vision that gave rise to Religious Life in the first place.[15] The first Religious, the consecrated virgins of the first century, were responding to the Resurrection with their whole beings. Indestructible Life had so possessed them that death was no longer significant. Sharing that divine life with others is the natural, and urgent, expression of that Resurrection experience and the inner form of ministry. How Religious share Resurrection life is a practical matter that requires ongoing discernment and that will change depending on personnel, resources, time, place, and context. But only those for whom Jesus' mission, "I have come that they may have life and have it to the full" (John 10:10), has become their own mission will finally be able to mediate the specifically Christian Gospel to our violent and suffering world.

Part Two

Evangelical Poverty
The Economics of the Reign of God

Chapter Four
A Biblical Approach to Poverty

I. Introduction and Transition

In part 2 we will begin to explore the nature and dynamics of
the alternate world Religious create by their Profession of the
vows. Our first task will be an examination of the vow of
poverty. In this chapter, after describing the major challenge of
defining evangelical poverty in the contemporary context, we
will try to discern the meaning of poverty in Scripture. In chapter 5 we will explore how evangelical poverty, as the economics
of the Reign of God, contributes to the creation of the alternate world both within the Religious community itself and,
through the community's prophetic ministry, in the world. In
chapter 6 we will discuss the spirituality of Religious poverty in
its unitive, communitarian, and ministerial dimensions for
those who undertake, by Profession, to create, live in, and minister from this alternate world today.

II. The Conundrum and Impasse
of Evangelical Poverty

Few Religious who made Profession prior to Vatican II can
be unaware of and untroubled by the stark differences between
what they understood by the vow of poverty made decades ago
and what they are living today. But probably even fewer would
want to revive the former, no matter how confusing and unsettling the present situation is. Poverty may have been the sim-

plest, though not necessarily the easiest, of the vows to practice in "the good old days." Its practice was minutely spelled out in terms of common life which governed what the Religious was to wear, eat, use, buy, or spend. Permission was the mechanism that guarded the personal practice of poverty. It meant that the Religious could acquire, have, keep, use, or dispose of material goods only with the permission of the superior. Although Religious were responsible for asking only necessary and legitimate permissions, real responsibility for the substantive decisions in regard to the use of material goods rested with the superior. Thus, in general, a sincere Religious who lived the common life and was exact about obtaining permissions could be certain that she was practicing her vow.

No one would pretend that there were not Religious who circumvented their obligations under the vow of poverty. Some solicited, received, and kept gifts from family or friends without permission, manipulated superiors into allowing independent use of patrimony, persuaded secular friends and relatives to supply what they knew they should not ask of or would not obtain from the community, hoarded all kinds of things against a "rainy day," or even engaged in business transactions that were in clear violation of the vow such as acquiring real estate, taking out personal insurance policies or appropriating retirement benefits for personal use. But such cases were not the rule. Nor were they "gray areas" caused by misunderstanding. Religious were well instructed, prior to Profession, on the obligations of the vow of poverty and the collective culture of the "total institution" insured general conformity to expectations.

Whatever ascetical value practices of the common life had, they also conduced, even in the best-case scenario, to a certain immaturity in the economic sphere. The exaggerations that appeared in the early stages of adaptation when Religious were allowed to make some autonomous decisions about clothes, personal care, entertainment, travel, food and drink, revealed that the suspension of all financial responsibility from their late teens until they were forty or fifty years old economically infantilized many Religious who were mature, responsible adults in other areas of their lives.

Once the conciliar renewal began, the movement from small personal budgets that were little more than a strictly regulated adolescent's allowance to the use of personal checking accounts and credit cards, receiving paychecks, handling contracts, and administering large personal and professional budgets was extremely rapid. Use of a community car regulated by permissions, charts, and keys, common dwellings that were furnished and maintained by unseen agents, the dispensing of identical clothing from common stores, and so on, rapidly gave way to a high level of individuality in these areas and others.

The changes came too quickly for Congregations to prepare or plan for them. For example, it could become necessary for fifteen Sisters in the local convent to find other ministries when the parochial school where they had taught and lived together was closed on short notice. Often the new ministries required only one person and therefore necessitated an individual dwelling, a car for her own use, perhaps a different kind of wardrobe, a certain autonomy in regard to living expenses. In situations like this, superiors and Congregations often just registered uncontrolled changes rather than identifying and choosing among real options.

Some Congregations tried to incorporate the changes into their documents, thereby giving the appearance that what was happening was what should be happening. Other Congregations did not try to "legislate" what was developing but focused on making the necessary financial mechanisms work for individuals and the community while applying what brakes they could to excesses. Unfortunately, these braking actions often succeeded only in inconveniencing responsible members while the "operators" took advantage of the situation, creating in some communities a climate of mutual suspicion, jealousy, and above all silence and even secrecy around all issues of money. Some Religious got into financial difficulties, such as credit card debt, that they could not handle, and sometimes community leaders were caught on the horns of a pastoral dilemma: force an issue and lose the Sister or look the other way as practices developed that were obviously incompatible with a vow of poverty and deleterious to any meaningful understanding of community life.

However, not all of the postconciliar changes in the way Religious dealt with material goods, and probably not the most important ones, were negative. Quite the contrary. Many Religious very quickly grew up from adolescent dependents into economically responsible adults who now knew how much things cost and where they came from. They became aware of how their personal choices affected the poor in their own society and elsewhere. Congregations learned how to use responsible investments as leverage in the struggle for social justice. Individuals learned what it meant to take a realistic role in the fragile financial operations of their Congregations in a time of ministerial upheaval in the Church and meteoric financial developments in the secular sphere. New ministries among the materially poor opened their eyes to the protected and even privileged condition Religious have long enjoyed, and continue to enjoy, in regard to education, travel, health care, and the daily requirements of clothing, food, and shelter.

The issue of poverty, which had been largely a matter of standardized exterior practices of asking permission and observing a traditional, collective frugality, rooted in a personal interior spirituality of detachment and asceticism, took on a very public and intensely critical character. Religious, no longer sheltered in the total institution of convent life and institutional ministry, came to see the widespread poverty of the majority of the world's people against the enormous wealth concentrated in the hands of a tiny minority of first world magnates as humanly obscene and religiously scandalous. Ministry to the materially-deprived rather than to the middle or upper classes who could pay for their services in Catholic schools and hospitals, direct hands-on work to alleviate the effects of deprivation rather than what in hindsight seemed to be "white glove" intellectual and spiritual ministries to the already-privileged, physical presence among the materially poor rather than the provision of services to those who could travel to obtain them rose to the top of the agenda as Congregations discussed what Religious should be thinking about, planning for, and doing ministerially in the new situation. Rhetoric often outstripped behavior,[1] but Religious were becoming, individually and corporately, much more aware of the economic situation in general and of the excruciating poverty of so many millions of people at home and abroad. Something had to change. Poverty was moving to the center of reflection on Religious Life.

But the sheer enormity and complexity of the situation, the up-close contact with daily tragedy of the most personal kind, and the healthy embrace of a more adult personal lifestyle generated a great deal of confusion and even guilt in individual Religious and in Congregations. On the one hand, they asked, was it authentic to protest against poverty while enjoying the "good life" of the first world middle class? On the other hand, what effect, realistically, would driving an unsafe car, subverting one's influence by appearing inappropriately dressed at a professional meeting, coming home at night to a dangerous inner-city environment, or even becoming a vegetarian have on the poverty of millions of people? How could personal practices of simplicity or even austerity affect social systems? And how could one change or even authentically advocate for the change of social systems of which one was the daily beneficiary? Did it make sense for someone with a doctorate in economics or political science to resign from her university position to work in a Latin American barrio? But, conversely, did it make sense to teach economic theory or political science to those who could afford a university education when people in the Latin American barrio were dying from the effects of first world economic and political policies? How could Religious talk about justice and the alleviation of poverty when they jetted around the world to attend the conferences discussing the problem of poverty, stayed in "moderate" hotels where one room had more amenities than whole villages in Africa, worked on computers which cost more than the annual income of many third world families, and conducted ministerial business over dinners in restaurants that wasted more food in one night than some inner-city families ate in a month?

Religious, intensely conscious of the conflicts between their relatively secure and well-furnished lives and the real material poverty of the majority of the world's peoples, were deeply concerned about the Profession of poverty which they could hardly believe was not laughable, if not insulting, to people who struggled daily with dehumanizing destitution. This is what I mean by the "conundrum of poverty": this situation of perceived incoherence between the Profession of poverty and the life of relative comfort that most Religious live and which, they know, they do not really want to exchange for a life of destitution. The "impasse" is the paralysis, both theoretical and practical, both personal and Congregational, in the face of this conundrum.

Virtually every effort to deal with the issue, whether by Congregational divestment of corporate holdings, relocating ministries from middle-class to lower-class settings, changing the vocabulary of "poverty" to "simplicity of life" or "solidarity with the poor," or simply attempting to curtail personal expenditures, presents real and intractable problems.

One problem is the non-reception by those who are really poor of the well-meaning efforts of those who are not actually materially destitute. Another is the internal conflict of the Religious who is deeply concerned about the destitute but also knows that she does not want to live that way and sincerely believes that neither she nor anyone else is called to do so if they have a choice.

There are community conflicts, expressed or implied, when some individuals or groups who have made certain choices for solidarity with the poor are perceived, sometimes quite accurately, as sitting in judgment on their more "lax" companions who are not convinced that these choices are relevant to the real problems or that their own first world ministries are any less important to the Reign of God than inner-city or third world ones.

The danger of a kind of self-serving "conspicuous deprivation" which is patronizing of the poor and, even if unconsciously, hypocritical, is not purely hypothetical. And, of course, there is the even more serious problem of those few in the community who simply refuse to take the whole issue seriously and would rather give themselves to "spiritual" pursuits that allow them to keep their hands clean and eyes averted while living the life of the well-off, aesthetically cultivated, socially well-connected single person in first world society.

Religious cannot indefinitely defer dealing with this conundrum and trying to find a way forward out of this impasse if the poverty they vow is to be meaningful in their own lives and a prophetic contribution to the coming of the Reign of God. A first step in this endeavor is to achieve some clarity about what we really mean (and do not mean) by evangelical, that is, Gospel, poverty. Only on this basis can we ask how evangelical poverty is related to material destitution, injustice, and oppression on the one hand and to frugality, simplicity, solidarity, and poverty of spirit on the other. Achieving a clearer understanding of the meaning of poverty requires looking honestly at our experience of this reality, and then bringing the resources of Scripture and tradition as well as the relevant secular sciences to bear on that experience, remembering that for Religious, evangelical poverty is both individual and corporate, both mystical and prophetic, both personal and ministerial.

III. The Meaning of Evangelical Poverty

As we noted in regard to the term "world," some terms are so traditional, venerable, and commonly used that those discussing the topic assume that they all share the same understandings. Only when discussion breaks down in misunderstanding or incoherence does it become obvious that the terms themselves need reexamination. Poverty, especially in discussions among Religious, is surely such a term.

A. What Evangelical Poverty *Does Not Mean*: Absolute Voluntary Material Destitution

Although poverty, in its first and most obvious sense, has to do with the lack of the material goods necessary for physical survival—edible food, clean water, breathable air, adequate clothing and shelter, available and effective health care—it is clear that there is no such thing as living in *absolute* poverty.

Total lack of any one of the necessary material goods results in death. So poverty is always quantitatively relative, denoting a position on the spectrum running from death on one end to luxury on the other end. The materially poor are closer to the death end; the rich are closer to the luxury end. Anyone who embraces poverty voluntarily chooses to move closer to the death end of the spectrum but obviously must stop before reaching it because death is not a valid human or spiritual objective.[2] The fact that the non-voluntarily poor never seek to move closer to the death end of the spectrum bears reflection. Is even the pursuit of poverty a luxury of the privileged? This raises a further question, as we will see in a moment: is poverty as voluntary not a contradiction in terms?

Poverty is not only quantitatively relative; it is also qualitatively relative to historical-cultural setting. According to the poverty guidelines updated periodically by the United States Department of Health and Human Services, a single person living in the United States in 2010 with an annual income below $10,890 was living in poverty.[3] However, such a sum would be untold wealth in much of the third world. A computer is considered standard equipment, not a luxury, for a first world university student. But even a primary education, with or without access to a computer, to say nothing of a university education, would not be "standard" in many parts of the world. In other words, there is no meaningful way to establish, in absolute material terms, what constitutes poverty or wealth.

For Religious, poverty is also relative to ministerial context and content. Some ministries, even in very poor settings, may require a car, electronic equipment, expensive medical supplies, and educated personnel. Others, including some carried on in relatively affluent suburban settings, may require only patient presence and a listening ear. Again, the attempt to establish absolute standards on the basis of which to compare one ministry to another is pointless and counterproductive.

Not only can real poverty, especially if it means destitution, not be absolute; it can also rarely and only with considerable qualification actually be *voluntary*. Not having a choice is of the essence of real poverty. The person who can choose to be poor usually can also choose not to be. Furthermore, the interior resources of spirit for handling material deprivation that are available to one who has had access to intellectual, aesthetic, cultural, and spiritual formation is an inalienable wealth not available to the truly destitute. One can choose not to have or not to use even what is necessary and this might be a heroic act of solidarity with the poor. But as long as one does not have to choose this lack in the first place and is able subsequently to reverse the choice, one is not truly poor in the way the involuntarily poor are.

When chosen poverty becomes irreversible the person has become by necessity, that is, involuntarily poor, and therefore truly poor. Like Jesus, who though divine by nature voluntarily became human and therefore irreversibly mortal, which led to his murder, some Religious actually do come to share irreversibly in the condition of poverty, even unto death, of those to whom they minister. When, in the late nineteenth century, St. Damien de Veuster, SS.CC., contracted the leprosy of the people he had voluntarily gone to the island of Molokai to serve and therefore could no longer leave the island on which he died, he had indeed become one of them unto death. Notre Dame Sister Dorothy Stang so identified with the people whom she went to serve that she became a Brazilian citizen. This made her vulnerable to the violence that led to her martyrdom in 2005. These are only two examples of those who have truly embraced irreversible solidarity with the involuntarily destitute. But insofar as the poverty Religious vow is voluntary it cannot be strictly equated with the involuntary poverty that leads to death. Death may be the price of what is freely chosen but destitution leading to death is not the object of the choice.

The problem that voluntariness introduces into Religious poverty was articulated clearly and bluntly by Rosemary Radford Ruether writing to Thomas Merton, who had mentioned his experience of not having running water in his hermitage in the woods as an experience of poverty in solidarity with his poor Kentucky neighbors:

> In actuality you only share the external appearances of economic deprivation with the poor hillsman who has no run-

ning water....But actually there is nothing in common
between you and them for the simple reason that they have
to be there, and you don't. You can dress up and walk into a
hotel, and they won't throw you out. You have the knowledge and skill to handle the larger world of our society, and
that is precisely what they lack. No one would confuse a
Catholic Worker type with a real ghetto person, and no one
would really confuse you with a real impoverished hillbilly.
You may identify with them, but they do not identify with
you. The reason is that you can never share the culture of
poverty, the deprivation of outlook, and because you don't
share this, however much you may ape the external circumstances of poverty, your culture marks you off as a member
of the possessing class.[4]

Merton responds, admitting Ruether's point ("obviously I
am not one of the hillbillies" [p.84]) and goes on to describe
quite accurately the conundrum of acknowledging poverty as
an eschatological sign and being unable, because of the class
structure of society, to practice real material poverty as a voluntary way of life while living in a first world culture. He frankly
concludes that "I don't see any way out...we have to start [dis-
cussing poverty] with the very sobering realization that voluntary poverty, in the context of our society, cannot be anything
but phony in so far as we are identified with the top layer of
people anyway, like it or not."[5]

The conundrum Merton acknowledges is that insofar as
poverty is voluntary it is, in a sense, not really poverty. But I
think there is an alternative to concluding that voluntary
poverty is therefore "phony," which would reduce the vow of
Religious to play-acting. Voluntary poverty as the object of a
vow is "phony" if there is only one valid and honest definition
of poverty, namely, involuntary material destitution. In other
words, the problem of how the evangelical poverty Religious
vow can be relative, voluntary, and also absolutely authentic lies
in how we understand poverty.

The fact that the evangelical poverty Religious vow cannot
be absolute destitution (because this means death) nor voluntary destitution (because this is a contradiction in terms) sug-

gests that poverty and destitution are not synonymous at all. Evangelical poverty does not mean the irremediable lack of the material goods necessary for survival and, *a fortiori*, the degradation of one's humanity that grinding want, what Simone Weil called "affliction," can and often does cause.[6] In fact, to deliberately seek such destitution would be contrary to God's creative will for humanity and would do nothing to ameliorate the situation of the truly destitute.

Many Religious Congregations at the time of their founding or in other difficult periods of their history were actually involuntarily destitute. Members died from tuberculosis and other diseases directly related to exposure to harsh climate conditions and the lack of adequate nourishment, clean water, sanitary facilities, and health care. Congregations have tended to idealize these times of want and even institutionalize some of the practices that developed under such circumstances. But, in fact, none of these groups wanted to remain in the situation of destitution. They wanted to preserve the heroic idealism and courage, the virtues of trust in providence, frugality, inventiveness, and sharing to which hard times had challenged them. But they did everything possible to finally achieve a decent level of well-being for their members and those to whom they ministered and to institutionalize the procedures which would assure reasonable well-being in the future. Destitution has not been, in actual practice, an objective of Religious poverty. Nevertheless, the idealization of the time of poverty as a "golden age" of Religious fervor suggests that there is something about material deprivation, about tending toward the death pole of the spectrum of possession rather than toward the luxury pole, that is integral to the spirituality of Religious.

One of the root causes of the unanalyzed malaise of Religious around the issue of poverty is precisely this deep ambivalence about the moral status of poverty. On the one hand, if poverty calls forth a beatitude for its victims, "Blessed are you poor" (see Luke 6:20), should not the dedicated Christian seek to be actually poor? If Jesus was so poor that he had nowhere to lay his head (see Luke 9:58) and was sometimes so ministerially burdened that he had no time even to eat (see Mark 3:20), should Religious live in decent housing with three meals a day provided? Is it not hypocritical of Religious to make a vow of poverty and then live in moderate circumstances in which they do not want for the necessities of life and even have access to such "luxuries" as education, travel, and modern technological equipment?

On the other hand, poverty is clearly a bane in the existence of the poor and much Religious ministry is aimed at its abolition. Adding themselves to the number of the destitute in this world is hardly a promotion of the Reign of God in which, Scripture says, there should to be no poor (see Deut 15:4 and Acts 4:34). Religious feel challenged to opt for a life in physical solidarity with the poor and yet realize that their ministries, including those to the materially poor, require the use of resources that the poor do not have. And if truth be told, most Religious do not really want to live in a situation of destitution where most of their time and energy is devoted to physical survival.

This energy-sapping ambivalence and nagging "bad conscience" suggests, perhaps, that it is time to declare once and for all that destitution is, in itself, an unqualified evil. No human being should lack what is necessary for decent living. Poverty in the sense of absolute, involuntary material destitution is degrading and dehumanizing. It destroys the spirit as well as the body. Gustavo Gutierrez, that tireless champion of the poor and enemy of poverty, has starkly defined poverty as early, unnecessary, and anonymous death. Real material poverty brings its victims to the death end of the spectrum of possession, usually long before they would die of natural causes, and when they do die—of malnutrition, exposure, preventable or curable disease, or poverty-generated violence— their deaths are invisible to all but their immediate companions who know that the same fate will soon claim them as well. Not only do the poor lack the material necessities of life, but because of that lack they are also voiceless and without leverage in the economic, social, and cultural systems which victimize them. Religious need to unambiguously condemn absolute and involuntary destitution, its causes and its effects, and commit themselves unreservedly to its abolition. What they abhor for others they should not choose for themselves. But what, then, does the vow of evangelical poverty intend?

B. What Evangelical Poverty *Does* Mean: Living the Economics of the Reign of God

The positive values of the evangelical poverty that Religious voluntarily undertake by vow, such as community-sustaining frugality and equity of access to community resources, simplicity of life, moderation in the use of material goods, unselfish sharing in community life, responsible work, financial accountability, detachment, and solidarity with the poor, are not equivalent to or an imitation of material destitution.

In the first place, these practices are voluntary and, as we have just seen, it is of the essence of destitution that it deprives its victims of choice concerning the use of material goods. Second, unlike the poverty that renders its victims powerless under oppression, none of these practices is disempowering, depriving the Religious of influence or voice within the social system of Religious Life. On the contrary, a Religious remarkable for an open-handed and non-possessive approach to material goods is usually more influential in the community than the flashy consumer or the selfish hoarder. Finally, unlike destitution, these attitudes and practices do not move one toward the death pole of the possession continuum. If anything, they are healthier ways to live than their alternatives. They promote a balanced and non-obsessive lifestyle that frees mind, heart, and body for participation in the very things the poor are denied by material want, such as aesthetic enrichment, contemplation, friendship, and meaning in life. Indeed, they equip the Religious for the struggle to abolish destitution.

Profession of evangelical poverty commits the Religious to attitudes and practices which promote and express what the Gospel calls "poverty of spirit." But Religious are suspicious of talk about "poverty of spirit" precisely because they know that these attitudes and practices are *not* destitution or a movement toward destitution. They fear a genteel and disincarnate "spiritualization" of what others suffer in brutal reality. But rather than disdain these attitudes and practices as superficial, contrast them with "real" poverty, or abandon the language of poverty in favor of such terms as "simplicity" or "sharing" (which are at least equally vague), I would suggest that we need to recognize that these values and their attendant practices are integral to a genuine and demanding attempt to live the economics of the Reign of God among themselves in the "alternate world" they attempt to create, live in, and minister from as they struggle to incarnate that Reign in the field of this world.

Evangelical poverty is not simply destitution undertaken for good motives any more than consecrated celibacy is merely making the best of involuntary singleness. Evangelical poverty is neither devotion to destitution nor an escape from "real" poverty into an ethereal romanticism. Rather, these values are constitutive of the poverty to which Jesus called his disciples and on account of which he declared them "blessed." It is also integral to the abolition of destitution defined as involuntary material want. Evangelical poverty, like the poverty of Jesus and the disciples he called to join him in his itinerant ministry, is a commitment, by the witness of our life and the practice of our ministry, to bringing "good news to the poor." The only news that is good for the poor is that their poverty is at an end, that is, that the Reign of God is emerging in this world.

In short, neither the poverty Religious choose for themselves nor that which they are committed to abolishing from the lives of others is simply economic destitution. Our question is the following: what does the maldistribution or lack of economic resources, and conversely the access to material well-being for all people, mean in the plan of God for humanity and the world and how does/can Religious Life reflect and participate in that divine design? Realistic answers to these questions must be sought, first of all, in Scripture. Jesus is the model and teacher of evangelical poverty. But before examining the New Testament data on poverty we must inquire into the conception of poverty that informed Jesus himself, that is, the Old Testament attitude toward and teaching about poverty that shaped Jesus' own spirituality.

IV. The Old Testament on Poverty and the Poor

Reflection on poverty and the poor is pervasive in the Old Testament and provides a rich context for understanding what Jesus, who was formed in the spirituality of the Hebrew Scriptures, modeled and taught on this subject.[7] By characterizing even very briefly the Old Testament material on poverty we can identify almost every aspect of the subject that needs to be taken into account for our project of reflecting on the meaning of evangelical poverty in contemporary Religious Life.

But, rich as the Old Testament material is, the diverse nature of this material and the relative dearth of specific historical and sociological information about the actual events that underlie that material require us to handle it carefully. The topic of poverty moves kaleidoscopically within the biblical text and the sorting of the actual referents of the material falls well beyond the scope of this book or our purposes in this section. The point of the present section is to gather and highlight *three major themes* that contributed to the worldview of Jesus We will explore these themes by selective examination of *five major collections of Old Testament material,* namely, the primary history (the creation myths and the liberation narrative), the saga of the monarchy and the prophets, and the wisdom tradition in relation to two different contexts.

Different strands of Old Testament reflection on goods and their lack and on poverty and oppression appear in different bodies and genres of literature. Some of the material is "placed" narratively and quasi-historically/geographically to construct the plausible story line of Israel's experience of liberation and response to this divine initiative, while other materials, whose contexts are obscure, are grouped more thematically. But our concern is not with the circumstances that gave rise to these texts but with the theology and spirituality related to evangelical poverty discernible in this wide-ranging story of Israel's adventure with God.

The five sets of diverse and complex materials we will be considering, which were probably edited around the mid-first millennium BCE, were no doubt gathered from older material.[8]

From them emerge the three themes that concern us. First, material creation, which God has lavishly provided, is good. Second, poverty, whose prime analogue is economic neediness and wretchedness, is a negative condition, not a value. In other words, there is no biblical warrant for denigrating Creation on the one hand or idealizing poverty on the other. Third, and emerging from the first two, both the experience of enjoying God's bounty and the enduring of hardship and poverty show us that God's people were able to and often did develop a profound disposition of dependence on God that became central to Jesus' teaching on poverty. This attitude, developed below, is what I, following many other scholars, refer to as "Anawim"[9] spirituality.

A. Poverty and Plenty in the *Primary History* and in the *Prophets*

In this section we will be examining the first three of the five sets of material. The primary history includes the Creation myths and the epic saga of the Exodus, desert journeying, and entrance into the Promised Land. This is followed by the tales of the monarchy and its critical counterpart, the prophets.

1. Creation myths

Any discussion of poverty and wealth, that is, of human relationship to material goods, must begin with an understanding of material goods themselves. Where do they come from? What is their moral status? How are humans (who are also but not only material beings) related to them? The foundational Judeo- Christian thinking on these questions is embedded preeminently in the accounts of Creation in the Hebrew Scriptures.

As is well known, there are two accounts of Creation in Genesis. The first Creation account (Gen 1:1—2:4), which derives from what has been called the priestly tradition and is therefore probably the later of the two accounts,[10] presents us with a serene and hierarchically ordered universe brought forth in stately sequence by God's all-powerful word. Creatures positioned above and below, the higher and the lower, the greater and the lesser, are all ordered to each other in peaceful tranquility. Culminating their orderly arrangement is the human being, the crown of God's creative work, made in God's own image and likeness, who is to participate in God's own benevolent dominion over all the rest of Creation as well as in divine responsibility to care for it. Even the subordination, as food, of the plants to the animals and the animals to the humans seems natural and devoid of violence.

From this account we draw the characteristically Israelite understanding of material reality. Israel attributed all things to the one God who was uniquely good. Israel's God, unlike the deities of some of its neighbors, has no evil counterpart or rival. Nor is Creation, as in some of the cosmogonies of surrounding peoples, the result of some heavenly or cosmic struggle. There is no difference, in terms of origin, between matter and spirit, human and nonhuman. Although only the human is made in God's image and likeness, God's final evaluation of "*all* the work that God had done" was that all of it "was *very good*" (see Gen. 1:31 [emphasis added]).

The second Creation account (Gen 2:4b—4:26), probably a much earlier tradition, is much more anthropomorphic and anthropocentric than the first account. Humans, rather than being called forth from nothing by the almighty word of God, are modeled out of the clay of the earth and enlivened by God's breath. God's Creation is still presented as good but this account ruminates upon how evil entered this good Creation. There is still no "other god" in opposition to Yahweh, no coeternal principle of evil, and no heavenly battle from which creatures emerged marked with the sign of original violence. But one of God's own good creatures, the serpent, rises up in opposition to God and leads the man and the woman into rebellion.

From this account of Creation we draw another characteristically Israelite assumption about the relationship of humanity to the rest of the created universe. Humans are part of Creation, made from the very stuff of the earth. Their primary task is not to dominate or lord it over Creation but to care for it, to tend it, to enable it to flourish. And they are dependent upon it as it is dependent upon them.

This second account is highly realistic about the disorder that mars Creation. Whereas the first account presents us with a seamless and unchanging order, a universe of singing spheres with humans called to add the lyrics to the cosmic hymn of praise, the second account recognizes that from the beginning there were fissures in the structure of Creation. Although the second account does not introduce the issue of suffering and violence until after the "fall," which involves some alienation of the humans from God, it is not hard to imagine that, even if humans had not been part of the story, fertile lands would have become arid and earthquakes would have swallowed whole ecosystems. Volcanoes would have erupted; lightning strikes would have ignited devastating forest fires; species would have become extinct. Bloody battles for geographical or sexual dominance and food would have split the animal kingdom. But such "natural evil," which is intrinsic to a finite universe, is different from the kind of evil introduced by the free choice of the human creatures.[11] Part and parcel of the biblical understanding of reality is that humans, the crowning achievement of God's good Creation, the beneficiaries of God's creative bounty, could and did at times choose to relate to Creation, to material goods, in sinful ways. And sin has consequences that unfold in the history of humanity and the planet.

Although the primordial relationship between humans and the rest of material creation is positive by virtue of divine origin, it has been so often perverted by human aggression and exploitation as people have struggled with each other over possession of that which was given by God to all,[12] that Creation itself has often appeared to be the problem. Material goods themselves have often been seen as a threat to morality and holiness, as competing with God for human allegiance. In the history of Christian spirituality, extreme asceticism was sometimes based on hatred of the world (e.g., in Manichaeism), ontological dualism in which matter was denigrated in favor of spirit (e.g., in Gnosticism), and other forms of abhorrence and rejection of Creation. And those members of the human family who seemed closest to materiality, especially women who were more deeply involved in the processes of procreation through pregnancy and childbirth, were stigmatized as threats to men who were deemed more spiritual. Indeed, the antagonism between the sexes, male domination of women and nature, is presented in the second Creation account as originating in the sin of the first humans, which distorted the relation not only of humans to God but their relations with nonhuman creation and with each other.

In short, the theology of Creation in the Old Testament grounds a positive, participatory, nonexploitative relationship of humans to material goods. God intended human beings to have what they needed and provided for them with wisdom and care. Creatures as such are not God's competitors for the devotion of human beings. They are neither intrinsically evil nor temptations to infidelity. Rather, humans share with the rest of creation a relation of joyful dependence on an all-good God and mutual interdependence among themselves. They are commissioned to participate in God's special responsibility for their fellow creatures.

Only when human beings overreach the boundaries God has set, when they become greedy and proprietorial, does their relationship to material goods, as well as to one another, become distorted. Unproductive labor and scarcity leading to competition, conflict, and even murder are the result of a disordered relationship to God's freely given bounty. Taken together and in concert with various other materials in the Old Testament where Creation is discussed, such as Isaiah 40 *ff.*, these texts affirm that Creation is good, God-given, and amply adequate for the needs of all. Distortions arise from human actions that are not intended by God.

2. The liberation narrative

The Bible begins the long narrative of Israel as a people with a story set in the second millennium BCE. Due to a famine in Canaan, the family of Jacob, grandson of Abraham and Sarah, journeyed to Egypt in search of food and pasture and was soon enslaved by the Egyptian state. The misery of the Hebrews under Egyptian domination was not due to laziness or vice. They were the victims of oppression, of injustice wreaked upon them by a ruler against whose power they were helpless. In their poverty and oppression they cried to the God of their ancestors Abraham, Isaac, and Jacob. Narratives, intertwined throughout Exodus to Numbers, tell the story of God's redemption of the people through the leadership of Moses who obtained their release from Egypt, led them through the desert to Mount Sinai, and mediated the covenant between Yahweh and Israel which was eventually expressed in the Law or Torah recorded in the Book of Deuteronomy. This story of exile, enslavement, liberation, desert sojourn, covenant, and entry into the land was constructed much later by the survivors of the Babylonian exile, most plausibly on the basis of legends and stories remembered and retold over centuries. This redemption/liberation strand of theology and spirituality complements and invites dialogue with the Creation strand.[13]

The foundation saga of the Exodus is well known to readers of the Bible. After their escape from Egypt where they had experienced physical, economic, and social oppression by their Egyptian overlords, the Hebrews spent "forty years," that is, a long and formative period, in the desert wilderness, a place not only of danger and physical privation but also of immediacy to the natural world. The desert wandering was a time to which the prophets Hosea and Jeremiah would later point as a time of challenge to spiritual growth. Two features of Israel's desert experience are especially important for our appreciation of poverty in the context of weakness. First, lack of resources can foster either dependence on God in hope or rebellion against God in despair. Second, lack of possessions can be the economic basis for a particular type of community life that is rarely possible in an economy of private property.

The Book of Exodus recounts how the Hebrews began to rebel against Yahweh and Moses almost as soon as they were out of Egypt. They were now homeless itinerants in a dangerous wilderness. At least in Egypt they had lived indoors and had food and water enough to sustain them. Now they complained about lack of the basic material necessities of life. God responded to their cries by providing daily bread, manna from heaven, which could not be stored (and therefore could not be hoarded, bought and sold for profit, or monopolized and rationed for power by the upper class), but which could be confidently expected day by day from a provident God who gave sustenance to all alike. When the sojourners were parched, God provided sweet water from rancid springs and abundant water springing miraculously from a rock to slake the people's thirst. Their clothes somehow remained wearable and they were well rid of the jewelry and trinkets they had given Aaron to build a golden calf to worship in place of Yahweh and in the absence of Moses.

In the desert, with no fixed abode, no controllable source of food and water, no land to own or till, and little institutionalized leadership, the Israelites had the opportunity to experience themselves as a community of equals. Aside from gender (Israel was always a patriarchal society), the primary source of social stratification and the related inequalities of resources and power is private ownership. Where there is disparity in property there will almost inevitably be disparity in power. During the time of the desert wandering there was a simplicity to the social relationships among the people that lent itself to later idealization.[14] During the wilderness trek, the people were possessionless. Whatever befell the individuals in the tribe of wanderers affected all of them. They were a large "family" holding in common everything that enabled them to stay alive. Even Moses and Aaron could not have survived without the people any more than the people could have found their way without their leaders. People played different roles in the community but these were not, for the most part, roles of domination and subordination.

Obviously, the story of the desert sojourn is an idealized epic account written long after the events it purports to recount. Like foundational epics of every people this one articulates recalled experiences and tradition (available only in the form of oft-told tales) whose meaning was so profound it definitively shaped the identity and destiny of a people. Israel's story of the desert sojourn portrayed them as people who responded to their poverty sometimes by grateful and confident dependence on God and sometimes by rebellion against God and Moses, singing praises to the God of their salvation or murmuring and complaining about their material want. When the sojourners were faithful and obedient, trusting God and Moses, they made their way, not without difficulty, but with well-founded confidence, toward the future God had promised. When they were petulant, angry, rebellious, idolatrous, and disobedient they suffered all manner of physical problems but especially confusion, inability to deal with their enemies, and internal dissension and violence. And they lived a community life in the desert that Israel would later recognize as the social and political ideal that God had in mind for the tribes of Yahweh.

When they eventually arrived and settled in the land promised them, they faced new challenges, which they met in various ways. The egalitarian ideals reflected in the Book of Deuteronomy were in tension with the realities of the neighborhood in which they settled. Deuteronomy's vision that Yahweh's people should live from their own experience of having been poor and oppressed in Egypt and liberated by God clashed with the demands of living amid powerful empires hungry for resources. But before turning to that part of the tradition we can draw some conclusions from what we have seen so far.

From the long story of Israel's liberation two kinds of poverty emerge. The poverty of the Hebrew slaves in Egypt was definitely regarded as an evil from which God rescued them. It was neither the result of their immorality nor primarily (much less exclusively) economic. The poverty suffered in Egypt, although it certainly involved material want, was primarily a sociological condition. Lack of the necessary material goods for a decent life was the consequence of oppression and injustice. The poverty from which God rescued them, and which they were to banish from their midst once they were settled in the land of promise, was of human making. The remedy for this kind of poverty was social justice.

The second kind of poverty, however, was the possessionlessness of the desert community. It was a difficult, but not an evil, condition. Rather, if freely embraced and lived in community, this lack could ground the kind of loving trust in God that should be typical of this people who claimed the status of being dearer to God than all other peoples of the earth and a kind of community of equals that was generally unknown among their neighbors. When Yahweh heard the cry of the poor and led them out of "that house of bondage" into the freedom of the promised land they found true prosperity, not abundant or excessive wealth created by human effort, but a universally shared adequate well-being and dignity that was a gift of God. Before there was a name for it, the Anawim, the "poor of Yahweh," had emerged in the desert. The task of the people was to ensure that this God-given freedom and well-being was not undermined by human evil. Even when their disobedience merited just punishment God provided remedies that allowed the disheveled band of survivors to reach the promised land. The desert experience was a long schooling in dependence on Yahweh as the people oscillated between obedience and rebellion learning that the former led to life and the latter to death, offering later readers a wealth of material to ponder.

3. Monarchy and the prophets

The Old Testament seems clear that the voice of prophecy emerged within the establishment of the monarchy, as though the choice to establish a more politically, socially, and economically stratified nation called for critique from the more egalitarian worldview represented by the desert tradition reflected in Deuteronomy. The portion of the Old Testament called the "Former Prophets" or the "Deuteronomistic History" (Joshua, Judges, Ruth, I and II Samuel, and I and II Kings) tells the tragic story of Israel from the settling of the Promised Land to the loss of the land in the fall of Israel to Assyria (in the 7th c. BCE) and Judah to Babylon (in the 6th c. BCE).[15]

The story begins with great hope. God sets before the people a land flowing with milk and honey which they are to have as long as they remain faithful to Yahweh by keeping the Covenant.[16] Essentially, as we have seen, this people was to be a "classless" society in which each family had a fair share of the land from which to produce what was needed for life. But this situation was gradually subverted by the greed of the powerful who, under increasing pressure from foreign imperial forces, expropriated the lands of the vulnerable creating a vast under-class of indebted poor. With the rise of the monarchy the general population was driven deeper into debt by the taxation necessary to support the court and maintain minimum independence from encroaching imperial powers, and by the unjust practices of those who lent at usury and bribed the judges on whom the poor had to depend for redress.

What today would be called a "capitalist" or commodity economy replaced the agrarian one. Cash crops on amalgamated land replaced the subsistence farming that allowed all to live decently. And in the wake of this concentration of wealth in the hands of the few came debt-slavery and widespread poverty, even destitution. The Deuteronomic ideal, "there will...be no one in need among you" (Deut 15:4) was forgotten. The egalitarian society had become a class society of "haves" and "have nots."

Beginning in the ninth century BCE, a series of prophets, spokespersons for Yahweh, rose up to speak the word of the Lord to an increasingly corrupt leadership. Both the "former prophets" (appearing in the books of Samuel and Kings) and the great writing prophets of the 8th to the 6th centuries BCE, Isaiah (740–701 BCE), Jeremiah (626–586 BCE), and Ezekiel (593–571 BCE), who foresaw and foretold the coming disaster of defeat and deportation, identified its cause as social injustice rooted in idolatry and reliance upon foreign sponsors, and described conditions under which God's people could flourish once again.

Numerous minor prophets, such as Hosea, Amos, and Micah, made similar critiques of injustice and envisioned the day when justice would again flourish in God's land for God's people—and indeed, for their neighbors. All of the prophets excoriated the rich and powerful for crimes of extortion, expropriation of the land of the poor, lending at exorbitant usury, debt-enslavement, corruption of the legal system through bribery, unjust judgment and refusal of redress of grievances to the poor, and luxurious living in the court and among the wealthy that was paid for by the misery of the destitute. Such evil was masked by ostentatious fasts, exorbitant sacrifices, and opulent temple ritual, which was itself mocked by the idolatrous worship of pagan gods to which the leaders turned a blind eye. Infidelity to the very heart of the covenant, that is, loyalty to Yahweh and solidarity as the People of God, cried to heaven for vengeance and the fall of the monarchy in both kingdoms was, according to the prophets, God's answer to ubiquitous iniquity.

Poverty during the monarchy and the ministry of the prophets was certainly an economic reality. Most of the people lived at subsistence level or in grinding material want. Even more, though, poverty was sociological. Economic oppression meant degradation, dehumanization, powerlessness, hopelessness; misery of spirit as much as of body. Wealth, in this situation, was not the moderate well-being of the wise but the self-absorbed, greedy, ostentatious luxury that disgusted Yahweh, who abhorred their alliances with pagan powers, their meaningless feasts, soulless sacrifices, and toe-tapping Sabbath observance as they waited for the opening bell of another week of dishonesty in the market place and violence against the poor.

For a few there was prosperity and plenty, an ever-rising standard of living that left most of the population behind, and military security built on alliances with pagan powers. But underneath festered the desperation of the poor, whose cry came to the ear of God as had that of the Egyptian slaves under Pharaoh centuries before. The northern kingdom, the first to fall, would never regain its identity or power, and the southern kingdom would be restored only partially amid confusion and division that would never be fully resolved. The storyline becomes obscure shortly after the return from exile, but the people live under colonial rule almost continuously until the second temple was finally destroyed in 70 CE and the Jewish people were proscribed from the land.

B. Post-Exilic *Wisdom* Spirituality

In this section we will examine the final two sets of Old Testament materials which are relevant to our inquiry. Since the actual historical circumstances of return from the exile in Babylon are difficult to follow after the first phase of resettlement in Jerusalem and are, in any case, not directly relevant to our purposes, we turn to consider Old Testament material that is presented without explicit narrative context. Called "Wisdom" or "the Writings" (Job, Psalms, Proverbs, Ecclesiastes, Song of Songs, Wisdom, Sirach) this body of life-experience and reflection upon it probably shares much (though not all) of its characteristics with Israel's contemporary neighbors. Scholars assume that most of this material was, in fact, gathered and edited in the period after the exile, and so it seems later than some of the material we have examined so far. However, it also includes some older material as well.

This sapiential material is diverse in genres and diffuse in its ruminations on ordinary life. Our interest is in two sets of material that are intermingled in the Wisdom corpus, one arising from and reflecting a context of ethical order and the other the context of ethical disorder. Assembling and preserving this biblical tradition was costly and required great scholarship. Therefore, it can be presumed that it addressed the needs and reflected the values of its elite sponsors. But the Wisdom literature was not completely divorced from the concerns of ordinary people. The common-sense sayings of the Book of Proverbs and the heartfelt prayers of Psalms, for example, emerge from and sustain a broad spectrum of people.

Israel's wisdom tradition, like that of its neighbors, was "this-worldly" in focus. Wisdom was a quest, as the Old Testament scholar Roland Murphy put it, for the good life in the here and now characterized by prosperity, length of days, and honor or prestige.[17] The good life, however, as Israel understood it, was not totally a matter of economic success nor was it exclusively intrahistorical. In Israel, Torah was the ultimate wisdom and the keeping of Torah, which proceeded from fear of or reverence for the Lord, was the path to life. Life itself included not only the span of one's lifetime and continuation in one's progeny, but also, by the time Wisdom of Solomon was written (possibly as late as the first century BCE) a conviction that

> ...the righteous live forever,
> and their reward is with the Lord;
> the Most High takes care of them.

Therefore they will receive a glorious crown
and a beautiful diadem from the hand of the Lord

(Wis 5:15–16)

From the sapiential tradition we can derive two points of view, relevant to our understanding of poverty and riches, which need to balance each other.

1. Wisdom as the serenity of ethical order

In general, biblical Wisdom literature recognized that both excessive wealth and dire poverty were threats to the good life. In Proverbs the sage prays:

Two things I ask of you....
 Remove far from me falsehood and lying;
 give me neither poverty nor riches;
 feed me with the food that I need,
or I shall be full, and deny you
 and say, "Who is the Lord?"
or I shall be poor, and steal,
 and profane the name of my God

(Prov 30:7–9 [emphasis added])

This sapiential emphasis on moderation, justice, order, and generosity as the proper approach to material goods and on economic well-being as the natural condition of those who fear God and live according to Torah represents a significant strand of Old Testament reflection on the subject of poverty and wealth, providing an important ingredient for our reflection on evangelical poverty.

This strand of Wisdom literature reflects the basic understanding of prosperity as the natural consequence of virtue but also suggests that poverty is the consequence of vice, especially of laziness and folly. The wise live well and long and can perhaps anticipate some kind of blessed afterlife, but those who give themselves over to folly will suffer in this life, die in disgrace, and be cut off forever from the God of the living. The good choose life and prosperity; the evil choose death and destitution.

It is not difficult to move from a belief that the good are prosperous because they do good and the evil choose their own fate

by their espousal of evil to assessing the hearts of humans from
the circumstances of their lives. Such a move is open to misunderstanding and misjudgment. But the sages recognized that
poverty was sometimes the undeserved burden of people who,
for one reason or another, were simply unfortunate, and therefore that there was an obligation incumbent on the prosperous
to care for the innocent poor through generous almsgiving.

However, within this basically positive strand of wisdom we
find the enigma of the suffering of the just and the prosperity of
the wicked, which are explored at length and great depth. The
Book of Job, for example, depicts a holy man whose way before
the Lord was the epitome of wisdom expressed especially in his
care for the poor. But Job suffered what only the wicked and
foolish should suffer. Through suffering he achieves a wisdom
that goes beyond natural insight into total trusting faith in a God
whose ways are not our ways. Job is, by the end of his experience,
a quintessential representative of the Anawim.

The Wisdom hero in the Wisdom of Solomon 2–5 is another
figure of the persecuted innocent whose fate and ultimate destiny call into question a simplistic equation of virtue with material prosperity. But he, like Job, is an exception to the generally
optimistic theology of the wisdom tradition in which goodness
leads to material prosperity and evil to destitution. Both Job
and the Wisdom hero offer us access to the second, more complex and nuanced insight of the Old Testament sapiential literature on the vicissitudes of poverty.

2. Anawim spirituality in the context of ethical disorder
Anawim spirituality, which developed most explicitly during
the post-exilic period, brought another meaning of poverty
into prominence. Its roots are old, extending back to the
prophets, who themselves drew it from the exodus and desert
experience. It is heard in the prophets who address the postexilic situation of relative powerlessness and oppression and it
is embodied especially in the psalms.[18] This poverty comes to be
seen, not primarily as economic or sociological, but as predominantly religious and spiritual in meaning.

The Anawim, the "poor of Yahweh" or the "remnant of

Israel," were a minority who had been purified by suffering and were waiting faithfully for the messianic deliverance of Israel in eschatological times. These people were, in most cases, economically poor. They were also sociologically oppressed and politically voiceless, lacking recourse and redress in a society that had no room for them or their prophetically nurtured eschatological dreams. But it was not simply material destitution nor sociological oppression that distinguished the Anawim. Rather, it was their spirituality, their confident looking to God alone in their suffering as they faithfully awaited the redemption of Israel.[19]

This Anawim spirituality which had a powerful influence on the spirituality of poverty developed in the New Testament, especially in the teaching of Jesus, was "rediscovered" by biblical scholarship in the second half of the twentieth century.[20] The texts that reflect this spirituality, particularly the psalms, draw a sharp contrast between sinners and the pious, who are spoken of metaphorically in terms of riches and poverty respectively. Numerous psalms picture the powerful or rich as righteous in their own estimation while they viewed the weak as poor and sinful. Anawim spirituality suggests that in God's eyes, however, the real sinners are the powerful (rich) who oppress the weak (poor) while the truly pious or righteous are those who struggle to be faithful to Torah and depend for their salvation neither on the powerful in society nor on their own righteousness but on God alone. They are described by Jesus in the parable of the Pharisee (the rich man) and the publican (the poor one) who go up to the temple to pray in Luke 18:10–14.

"Poor" in this context, then, is not exclusively a literal economic or sociological category. "Poor" has become a religious category.[21] It characterizes the humble, those who seek justice, who truly keep God's law not only by external observance but by inward fidelity, who are open to God and trust God with all their hearts. Rather than being a negative economic or sociological condition (even if, in fact, the Anawim were materially poor), poverty had become a metaphor and a positive synonym for the disposition of the faithful, the pious, and the lowly whose only hope is in God. Their spirituality, though born in suffering and oppression, was conceived, as we will see, as not necessarily incompatible with a more comfortable situation.[22]

This last point is important. The spirituality of the Anawim has affinities with the Creation and sapiential traditions in which economic poverty is not God's plan, is indeed an evil, but in which wealth was not to be the focus of one's concern or the locus of one's hope. It also had deep affinities with the Exodus/Sinai tradition in which actual poverty, but not degrading destitution nor class oppression, could foster absolute trust in God in those who had nowhere else to look. As we will see, in the New Testament Jesus addressed his call to conversion to both the economically rich and the economically poor, to the oppressors and the oppressed. And he practiced and preached an Anawim spirituality that is not incompatible with economic well-being and also is not always and automatically characteristic of the economically poor or even the sociologically oppressed. Poverty of spirit, Anawim spirituality, is not determined by one's economic or social condition; it is a freely chosen posture before God that is open to anyone who has ears to hear. As A. George says,

> ...the experience of concrete, material, and especially social poverty seems to have led the people of the Old Testament to submit themselves humbly into the hands of God and to trust his grace. It is, strictly speaking, not an idealization of poverty, since this was never for them a value in itself. But poverty *did* have an indisputable religious richness for them: it called them to open themselves to God and prepared them to receive both the demands and the gifts of Jesus.[23]

In the New Testament the ideal "poor one" is Jesus himself who, born in a stable, living the life of itinerant ministry, and dying naked on the cross, commends himself trustingly into the hands of God. Anawim spirituality, as we will see, has played a determining role in the meaning of poverty throughout the history of Religious Life.

V. From the Old Testament to the New Testament

Old Testament material on poverty and the poor is focused for the Christian in the person, mission, and message of Jesus. On the subject of poverty there is considerable continuity between the two testaments, but there is also significant discontinuity which has important implications for Christians in general and Religious in particular. The Old Testament, as we have seen, was composed over a period of hundreds of years by people whose access to their subject matter, in most cases, was primarily in the form of ancient traditions, stories, law codes, myths, and rituals. The New Testament, by contrast, was composed in less than a hundred years by people who, for the most part, either participated in the events about which they wrote or had some direct access to the generation that did. Furthermore, the New Testament is clearly focused on a single individual, Jesus of Nazareth, who lived a short life in a single small country and who was proclaimed as the Christ in the wake of his paschal mystery, whereas the Old Testament is the story of a people's gradual growth into Yahwistic monotheism through an adventure with a God whom they came to know in their historical experiences which ranged over many centuries, lands, ethnic groups, and religions.

The New Testament, therefore, provides a perspective on poverty deriving from the practice and preaching of Jesus who, though formed in the Jewish tradition, reinterpreted, developed, and focused that tradition in original ways. This should warn us against the tendency that sometimes appears in liberationist literature to construct a contemporary theology and spirituality of poverty almost exclusively in terms of the Old Testament, especially the Exodus and the prophets. While this tradition is important, even constitutive, of the ideal of poverty that Religious embrace as Christians, that ideal is quintessentially shaped by the New Testament.

Different as the two testaments are, they share one trait in regard to their treatments of poverty that is particularly important for our project: namely, that poverty is an intrinsically relative term, both quantitatively and qualitatively. "Poor and rich" or "poverty and wealth" are merismatic extremes, which include the whole human race and the economic situation of every member of it. Everyone is somewhere on the spectrum between the two extremes of death at one pole and luxury at the other. But what constitutes poverty in one setting might be wealth in another. And what one person would experience as severe poverty, such as want of adequate food and shelter, might be relatively insignificant to someone experiencing dehumanizing racial oppression, life-threatening illness, sexual abuse, emotional despair, spiritual desolation, or social isolation. This intrinsic quantitative and qualitative relativity of poverty leads to its being defined differently depending on the *context* in which it is experienced and *who* is speaking about it.

As we have seen, in the Old Testament there was great variety in the understandings of poverty. The poverty of the Hebrews in captivity in Egypt, which was both economic want and sociological oppression, was very different from their poverty in the desert, which was still material and perhaps even more extreme than what they had experienced in Egypt. However, the desert experience gave rise not only to complaining but also to a religious meaning of poverty that eventually came to be called "Anawim" spirituality and was idealized by later writers such as Jeremiah and Hosea and is powerfully expressed in the Wisdom literature, especially in many of the psalms (e.g., Ps 25, 35, 40, 68, 74, 87, 113, 147, and elsewhere). We also saw that the prophets' passionate condemnation of the economic and sociological poverty that the wealthy and powerful wreaked upon the vulnerable during the monarchical period was quite different from the sages' condemnation of an economic poverty brought on by laziness and folly.

Although the temporal and geographical scope of the New Testament is much more restrained than that of the Old Testament we have to expect to find there also a variety of understandings of poverty and the poor, wealth and the rich, depending on context and speaker. For example, eschatological urgency gave rise in Jewish Palestine to Jesus' disconcerting demands for total self-dispossession that find virtually no place in Paul's preaching in the more cosmopolitan and largely Gentile context of mid-first century Asia Minor.

In what follows we will examine the diverse approaches to poverty in the New Testament focusing on our purpose, namely, to gather the biblical resources for a contemporary approach to evangelical poverty for Religious in a first world context. I will organize the material under two unequal headings: the *imitatio Christi* or imitation of Christ and the *sequela Christi* or following of Christ. In other words, we will first inquire into Jesus' own relationship to material goods which is the model for Christians in general and Religious in particular in their personal use or renunciation of such goods. Then we will look at how the Gospels on the one hand and Acts and the Pauline literature on the other present the reception of Jesus' teaching on poverty and riches as a norm for the following of Christ by post-paschal disciples in various situations. It is hoped that this effort will allow us to discern the heart of Jesus' teaching on poverty which provides the framework for the practice of evangelical poverty in Religious Life.

VI. The Imitatio Christi: Jesus and Material Goods

Before looking at the teaching of Jesus on the subject of poverty and the appropriation by his disciples of this teaching it is important to see what we can derive from the Gospel materials about Jesus himself in relation to material goods.

A. Jesus' "Ontological" Poverty

Jesus is often presented in spiritual literature as the "poor man" *par excellence*, born naked in a stable and executed naked on a cross. This important "spiritual inclusio," however, is a technique for interpreting Jesus' life in terms of Anawim spirituality rather than a description of his actual experience of material poverty throughout his pre-paschal life.[24] The infancy narrative in Luke is a *midrash* designed to present Jesus' parents as members of the Anawim, the "poor and lowly remnant of Israel," who awaited the eschatological salvation promised by the prophets and prayed for in the psalms, and to present Jesus himself as the fulfillment of that promise.[25]

Jesus' death on the cross was the culmination of the *kenosis* (self-emptying) in which the Word of God, by becoming human, impoverished himself by assuming the limitations of a creature, even though he was by nature divine, in order that we, human by nature, might be enriched by the gift of divine life (cf. 2 Cor 8–9; Phil 2:5–8).[26] In other words, we are here in the realm of theological exposition of the meaning of the Incarnation rather than in the sphere of Jesus' historical experience of relationship to material goods. Obviously, no one can "imitate" the Incarnation itself but this "ontological poverty" of the Word-made-flesh should motivate us, Paul says, to cultivate the same *mind* or *attitude* or *disposition* in ourselves that Christ had in laying aside the prerogatives of divinity for our sakes (cf. Phil 2:5–8). So, we need to see how Jesus himself related to material goods and what he taught about that relationship. As we will see, poverty is absolutely central to his life and teaching but it may not mean exactly what we are tempted to imagine.

B. Jesus' Pre-Easter Life Situation

Jesus was born in a patriarchal agrarian society in which wealth was based, traditionally, on land ownership passed from father to son. Jesus' own father Joseph, however, was an artisan rather than a landowner so he would have been considered, technically, "poor," that is, dependent. His livelihood derived not from his own land but from work done for others. However, as an artisan skilled in a trade that was in constant demand, Joseph was probably better equipped to maintain a home and provide for a family than many small landowners who were at the mercy of adverse weather cycles, poor land, tax collectors, and land-hungry aristocrats. Joseph would have had sufficient work during the period of Jesus' childhood in Galilee to support his family in moderate comfort and it seems unlikely that, had there been a dearth of work, Jesus would have learned his father's trade and probably practiced it during his youth and most of his adult life. In other words, if Jesus had lived in the hellenistic Diaspora he would have been considered, as an artisan, middle class rather than poor. And even in Palestine he was actually better off economically than the peasants whom he would later lead.[27]

Jesus, in leaving his primary family of origin, not founding a secondary family of his own, and undertaking an itinerant ministry of preaching, teaching, healing, and exorcising, became, by his own choice rather than by necessity, "poor." He was voluntarily poor rather than lacking choice as was the case for most of the poor to whom he preached. Furthermore, Jesus clearly was not an ascetic like John the Baptist (cf. Mark 2:18–20). He did not choose a kind of extreme renunciation that would result in a daily experience of neediness and want. Jesus was, in short, not indigent. He was supported by wealthy women disciples (and perhaps others); he had affluent friends who invited him into their homes; and we are never told that Jesus or his disciples were reduced to begging or experienced persistent hunger[28] or other forms of destitution. This leaves us with the question of what Jesus' freely chosen lifestyle meant.

What we do know from the Gospels about Jesus' actual relation to material goods can probably be summed up under four headings. First, he was an *itinerant*. He had no fixed abode, no place in this world to call his own. This was a free choice on Jesus' part since he could well have remained in his home in Nazareth (where his relatives obviously thought he belonged [see Mark 3:21 and 31–35]), joined a stabile community such as the Essenes at Qumran, or founded a home of his own. Jesus' choice of itinerancy was related to his mission from God, to announce the Gospel to all of Israel (cf. Luke 4:42–44). In the material insecurity of having "nowhere to lay his head" (Matt 8:20), he lived the confidence he preached in the infinite providence of God, his "Abba," who provides for the birds of the air and lilies of the field (see Luke 12:22–34).

Second, Jesus and his disciples shared a *common purse*. Apparently it had enough in it to tempt Judas to steal from it. And, significantly, Judas's appropriation of common funds was considered stealing (cf. John 12:6), which suggests that he was the "treasurer" of the community's goods, not an independent financial agent. In other words, economic common life was a constitutive part of the missionary lifestyle of Jesus and his itinerant band of disciples.

Third, we certainly get the impression that life in this band was *simple but not destitute.* Jesus and his disciples were able to afford preparation for the Passover meal in a large, furnished guest room (cf. Luke 22:7–13). At the Last Supper, when Jesus tells Judas to leave quickly, the other disciples think he has been sent to buy something for the feast (cf. John 13:29). So, they had at least moderate purchasing power and apparently it was not unusual for them to use it, even to render a celebration more enjoyable and festive. Furthermore, Jesus and his disciples seemed able to dine in the houses of even wealthy friends or acquaintances without causing the embarrassment that the presence of the disreputable would. And Jesus expected to be treated like an honored guest, that is, as an equal of his host, not as a "charity case" or some kind of exotic social misfit invited to satisfy the curiosity of the upper class. He noticed, and objected to, the lack of such ordinary courtesies as being offered water to wash his feet and being greeted with a kiss of welcome (Luke 7:36–47).

Fourth, Jesus and his companions *gave alms.* When Jesus sent Judas from the Last Supper, his disciples thought Judas was to give something to the poor (cf. John 13:29). So almsgiving must have been a common practice in the group. But Jesus was not an absolutist or extremist on this subject. When some of the disciples objected to a lavish expenditure on Jesus himself by a woman disciple, Jesus defended her, accepting her action as appropriate under the circumstances even though it diverted a fairly large sum of money from almsgiving (cf. John 12:1–8 and parallels).

In short, the picture we get of Jesus' own relation to material goods is that he had enough of this world's goods to live simply. He was not destitute or a beggar. Nor did he aspire to be such or to imitate those who lacked the necessary resources for life. Jesus was not a practitioner nor a proponent of what we, today, would call "real" (that is, involuntary) or extreme, material poverty, that is, indigence or destitution. Rather, he came to announce to the poor the good news that God has heard their cry and that in Jesus their poverty was coming to an end.[29]

C. Jesus' Practice of Voluntary Poverty

This still leaves the question of why Jesus chose a life of celibate itinerancy, which, in his patriarchal and agrarian culture, was a choice of poverty even though not of economic destitution. It clearly had to do with his prophetic mission which he claimed in terms of the passage from Isaiah 61:1–3, the passage he quoted in the synagogue of Nazareth at the outset of his ministry: "The Spirit of the Lord is upon me, because he has anointed me to proclaim good news to the poor...." (cf. Luke 4:18–21). His practice shows the priority he gave to the materially destitute, the large crowds of impoverished peasants who followed him. But his ministry included equally many whose poverty was not economic but physical, spiritual, psychological, social, or educational such as the people whose mental and physical diseases he cured, the sinners he forgave, the social outcasts he embraced, and the religious leaders with whom he debated the interpretation and practice of the Law.

Social scientific work on the New Testament is coming to a consensus on describing the ministry of Jesus as the galvanizing of a mass movement of peasants in first century Palestine.[30] These 'am ha'arez, or "people of the land," who were impoverished by civil and religious taxation, politically oppressed by Roman occupation, and despised by the religious elite for their illiteracy and incapacity in regard to the Law, were enlivened by Jesus' proclamation that the eschatological reversal of fortunes prophesied by second and third Isaiah was at hand. Indeed, in Jesus himself who expelled demons, multiplied food for the hungry, cured physical and mental diseases, and even raised the dead, God's saving power was at work. In him, the Reign of God was at hand (cf. Mark 1:14–15).

Jesus' solidarity with the poor, to whom he was sent to preach this good news, involved a voluntary self-identification with them, which an increasing number of exegetes view less as an act of sympathy or imitation and more as a strategy for bringing about the change he was announcing. Various schol-

ars have proposed different understandings of just how Jesus'
practice of voluntary poverty in celibate itinerancy advanced
his program of inaugurating the new world which he called the
Reign of God. While none of these suggestions can claim certitude, they illustrate ways in which we can understand Jesus'
practice of voluntary poverty not as a canonization or advocacy
of destitution but as part of a program to abolish it.

For example, one New Testament scholar has persuasively
argued that Jesus' own choice to renounce the economic security of family and to walk away from his trade which would have
supported him, as well as his requiring this same renunciation
of his itinerant band of chosen disciples, was motivated by his
intention to form a new kinship group, based not on blood or
property but on faith. This new community would be led first
by Jesus and, after his death, by these disciples whom he had
formed by their sharing of his life and practice .[31] This new
"family" of faith was the nucleus of the new world, the Reign of
God, that Jesus was inaugurating.

Another New Testament scholar, C. J. Gil Arbiol explains
Jesus' lifestyle in terms of the sociological strategy of self-
stigmatization. "According to the sociology of deviation, self-
stigmatization is the process through which a charismatic
individual sets out to assume a social stigma and reevaluate it
positively in order to build an alternative to that situation...."[32]
The powerful in society stigmatize certain characteristics such
as poverty, lack of powerful family connections, gender, race,
sexual orientation, and so on making those characterized by
these features "guilty" of them. The oppression of the stigmatized and the ascendancy of those free of the stigma are thus
legitimated and the oppressive hierarchical social structure
based on this stratification is consolidated. When the charismatic leader of the oppressed assumes the stigma as a kind of
"badge of honor" the stigma is transvalued and the social stratification based on it is subverted. We see Jesus using this strategy
in assuming the despised role of the servant in the footwashing, thus transvaluing servitude into friendship.[33]

Jesus, as charismatic leader of a mass movement of poor
peasants, assumed the social stigma of poverty and revealed

that their poverty, for which the elite reproached and despised them, was precisely what made them dear to God who hears the cries of the poor, who puts down the mighty from their thrones and exalts the lowly, who fills the hungry with good things and sends the rich away empty. But the poor are dear to God not because poverty is a good thing or even because the poor are more virtuous than other people but because God's justice is affronted by the oppression of the defenseless and God's mercy reaches out to those who have no one, even themselves, to depend on but God. The economically and even spiritually rich, on the other hand, who in their self-sufficiency feel no real need of God, are rejected. The paradigm of this contrast is the parable of the rich (and virtuous) Pharisee and the poor (and sinful) publican who went up to the temple to pray (see Luke 18:10–14).

Jesus preached and inaugurated by his own practice the coming of a new order, the construction of an alternate world, the inbreaking of the Reign of God. In that alternate world the poor would be welcomed, honored, placed at table with the rich and powerful, even preferred to their oppressors who were now admitted only as fellow guests advised to choose the lowest place, sharing the open table fellowship which Jesus inaugurated. Jesus' solidarity with the poor, his freely chosen condition of being without family or independently owned material resources, was not a strategy for spreading poverty but for reversing the social evaluation of those who were poor and thus giving them ingress into the Reign he was establishing. In his own life and practice Jesus broke the hold of the most powerful mechanisms of social control in his society, namely, family and wealth. He established another kind of *kinship*, the new family of those who hear the word of God and keep it. He established another *basis for well-being in this world*, shared community in divine life expressed in shared economic well-being. This new belonging, new access to both material and social *shalom*, was an announcement of good news to the poor who are welcomed into a new world, the Reign of God, where they are no longer ostracized, oppressed, and anonymous but valued siblings of Jesus, children of God in a new family of faith.

The importance of these exegetical experiments in interpreting the meaning of Jesus' choice to renounce family and economic security, that is, to become voluntarily poor, is that they focus our attention on the nature of and the motivation for voluntary poverty. Jesus did not have to be family-less, homeless, economically poor. He chose poverty, not because it is good in itself or superior to other situations in life. Rather, voluntary poverty was a missionary strategy for furthering the Reign of God.

D. Conclusions on Jesus' Practice of Poverty

The foregoing examination of how the pre-Easter Jesus actually lived sheds considerable light on how Christians in general and Religious in particular are called to live in imitation of him. The *imitatio Christi* is not a literal mimicking of the particulars of Jesus' pre-Easter life but a deep appropriation of what he was actually doing and his motivation for doing it.

First, although we cannot literally imitate Jesus' *kenosis*, that is, his laying aside the prerogatives of divinity and pitching his tent as a human among us, we can "let this mind be in [us] that was also in Christ Jesus" by *renouncing any attitudes or practices of superiority* by which one believer would attempt to take precedence over another on the basis of birth, wealth, office, or any other title. The community which Jesus founded is a discipleship of equals in which the first is last and servant of all.

Second, Jesus, like his Old Testament forebears, notably the wisdom teachers, and unlike some of his contemporaries, such as John the Baptist, lived a simple life that was not marked by extreme material deprivation. As we will see, he placed an original stamp on this moderate stance toward material goods by radicalizing the Old Testament exhortation to sharing, by insisting on the extreme danger that wealth poses to the total dedication to God demanded by the first commandment, and by requiring an absolute detachment from material goods expressed in the renunciation of anything which is an impediment to whole-hearted discipleship. Sharing was institutionalized in Israel (the sabbatical year, the jubilee year, the right of the poor to glean, almsgiving to the poor) in order that there might be no poor among the people (see Deut 15:4). But Jesus developed *a lifestyle of total sharing* that included the homelessness and dependency of celibate itinerancy; the giving and receiving of alms; sharing of a common purse with his disciples. This practice was not aimed only at the prevention of poverty but at the establishing of a new kind of community based solely on hearing the word of God and keeping it.

In sum, Jesus' choice of voluntary poverty, that is, of celibate itinerancy and its resulting lack of material security, was not an imitiation of the desperately poor nor a canonization of poverty as destitution. It was a choice of solidarity with the poor that was motivated by his mission to announce the good news that poverty was at an end. It was a ministerial strategy for abolishing poverty, not a way of promoting or idealizing it. The strategy was aimed at the inauguration of the Reign of God in which all would be united in a new family not based on blood, and would share in a new and abundant life that was not based on material wealth.

All Christians are called to this poverty of Gospel equality and open sharing which announces and fosters the Reign of God. Religious make a free choice to build together an actual sociological lifeform, namely, the Religious community, that incorporates radical equality among themselves and those to whom they minister, real celibate itinerancy (renunciation of family and home), common purse (total economic interdependence), and non-accumulation of either personal or corporate wealth. In other words, they create, in the actual historical situation of the earthly present, a sociological lifeform that is the "alternate world," the Reign of God that Jesus preached and lived with his first disciples. This enterprise is not the only way to live the *imitatio Christi* and is not necessarily a better way. It is the way to which some disciples today, like some disciples of Jesus' time such as Peter or Mary Magdalene, are called. Others, like Mary and Martha of Bethany or Jesus' own parents, are called to build homes and found families. There are a variety of ways to incarnate, sociologically, Jesus' life of total and grateful dependence on God, generosity expressed in free sharing of gifts received, and humble participation in a shared humanity. These different ways give different kinds of witness in the Church and world.

What is of paramount importance is that the *imitatio Christi*, for all Christians, involves an approach to material goods modeled on and motivated by the practice of Jesus.

VII. *The* Sequela Christi*:*
Discipleship and Material Goods

A. Methodological Presuppositions

The rapidity with which the original circle of Jesus' Palestinian followers became a widespread religious movement in the Hellenistic world and beyond creates several problems in interpreting Jesus' teaching on poverty.

1. Who are the disciples Jesus addresses?

A first question is, *whom* is Jesus addressing in any given pericope? Are his words meant only for the/an inner circle of itinerant followers of his own lifetime (e.g., the ones called "the disciples," "the apostles," the "twelve disciples" or simply "the twelve," "the seventy," the larger circle of women and men followers in John)? Or does the term include his special friends (e.g., Martha and Mary, Peter, James and John, Mary Magdalene), whether itinerants or householders? Does it include the "large crowds" in general or only those in the crowds who would eventually remain faithful? Does it include the 120 gathered on Pentecost, or later Christians who had never known the pre-Easter Jesus (e.g., Cornelius whom Peter converted, the first deacons in Jerusalem, Paul and his co-apostles, Paul's communities, or present-day Christians)?

The second problem is a corollary. *To whom does Jesus' teaching*, especially his more absolute and extreme demands, *apply?* Is a given demand, such as to hate one's parents, siblings, and children (see Luke 14:26) or to sell all one possesses and give the proceeds to the poor (see Luke 18:22) in order to be Jesus' disciple, meant only for the original itinerant band, for all Jesus' hearers, for some special class of later followers (e.g., Religious), for all Christians of all time? Does it apply only in special circumstances or always and everywhere? Is it a hyperbolic challenge or a literal condition of discipleship?

2. What did Jesus actually teach?

Our task of discerning Jesus' teaching on poverty is further complicated by the fact that none of the New Testament material simply recounts what actually happened during Jesus' life and ministry. All of it is suffused with post-Resurrection faith and theological interpretation which took place, as we will see, in particular communities whose particular circumstances led to shaping the Jesus material in particular ways, emphasizing some aspects of his teaching and practice and muting other aspects. Consequently, we are never dealing purely and simply with "what Jesus said" or "what Jesus taught." We are dealing with *Jesus' teaching as received and interpreted in particular circumstances by certain elements of the Jesus Movement.*

3. How does Jesus' teaching apply to later believers?

Finally, the New Testament material is not simply the record of the first few generations of Christians to which we can look for distant models which may or may not be relevant to our own situation. The New Testament is part of the canonical Scripture of the Christian community. The Church believes and claims that what we find in the New Testament documents is *relevant for all Christians of all time.* But we are not first century Palestinians or Hellenistic converts so we have the task of figuring out how this material is relevant to us. Fundamentalists solve this problem by refusing to acknowledge it. Everything in the text, in their view, is to be taken literally "at face value." For all kinds of reasons this apparently simple and honest approach is manifestly inadequate but finding an alternative which neither eviscerates the "hard sayings" as pure hyperbole nor "walks away" in despair in the face of their seemingly impossible demands requires serious effort.

B. The Three Stages of the Jesus Movement

The Jesus Movement unfolded in three stages in two very different sociocultural and economic contexts. In these three stages, which followed each other very rapidly and at times overlapped, Jesus' teaching on family and riches had to be adapted quickly to new situations. We will first sketch briefly these three stages and the way the teaching of Jesus was presented in each and from this material we will attempt to synthesize the teaching of Jesus on the relationship between Christians and material goods that is relevant for all disciples down through the ages and which Religious are called to incarnate in a particular way in the Church.

1. The first disciples of the pre-Easter Jesus

During his public ministry in Palestine in the second to third decades of the first century Jesus had disciples, students who listened to his teaching. However, unlike the rabbis of his time who taught their disciples interpretation of the Law, Jesus (who was not officially a rabbi although he was recognized as a teacher) apprenticed his disciples to himself by forming them into a community and proposing to them an original and authoritative teaching that was validated by deeds of power (cf. Mark 1:22, 27; Matt 7:29; Luke 4:36). This group of disciples was not coterminous or synonymous with "the crowds" which followed Jesus with enthusiasm at one point and abandoned him at another. They were a restricted group whom Jesus invited and challenged to a demanding attachment to himself and embrace of his way of life as well as unconditional acceptance of his teaching. This restricted group of disciples included, at least, men (the twelve and others), women who traveled with him and provided material support for the group (cf. Luke 8:1–3), and another group that Luke tells us numbered seventy and which New Testament scholars have plausibly suggested included both men and women, some of whom may have been married couples, but who, in any case, were sent out in pairs preparing the way for Jesus himself (cf. Luke 10:1, 17).

However, Jesus also had some disciples who were not part of the itinerant band but clearly belonged to Jesus' chosen followership, such as Mary and Martha of Bethany and, according to John, their brother Lazarus (see Luke 10:38–42; John 11 and 12:1–8), the royal official whose child Jesus healed and who, with his whole household, became a believer (see John 4: 53),

Zacchaeus (see Luke 19:1–10), the healed Gerasene demonic (see Mark 5:1–20), Nicodemus and Joseph of Arimathea (see Matt 27:57; John 19:38–42), and others.

It must be remembered that the evangelists, on the one hand, were constrained by the literary form of Gospel (i.e., an account of the life of Jesus) to present all their material as having occurred in the lifetime of the pre-Easter Jesus and the time of his Easter appearances but, on the other hand, were writing for diverse communities formed after the historical lifetime of Jesus. Consequently, they use the term "disciple" for those who were surely part of Jesus' original group but they also seem to include in the term others who would be more typical of post-Easter followers, presenting them literarily as part of the original group. The presence of householders, for example, as well as itinerants in the group of disciples was certainly more characteristic of later Christianity[34] but their presentation as contemporaries of Jesus (which some undoubtedly were) actually captures well the fact that the first and later disciples, itinerants and householders, are equally disciples of Jesus. Priority in time is not priority in discipleship and discipleship is compatible with many forms of life.

The Gospels present two types of teachings of the pre-Easter Jesus on the subject of relation to the goods of this world, especially family and possessions. One type seems to call his disciples to the kind of Anawim-sapiential spirituality Jesus himself exemplified in his daily life: detachment, total and joyful dependence on God, gratitude, generous sharing, simplicity and moderation. The second type is a "radical" or "extreme" demand for total renunciation of personal possession of goods and of family and the carrying of one's cross unto death, again exemplified by Jesus who left home, family, and trade, and finally surrendered his life to fulfill his mission.

The Gospels also suggest that the demands of discipleship can be met in different life situations. Some disciples shared Jesus' itinerant life of evangelizing ministry and others, equally disciples, remained in their ordinary life situations. Two tax collectors, Levi and Zacchaeus, illustrate this diversity. Levi was called to literally abandon all and follow Jesus as a member of the itinerant missionary band (Luke 5:27–32; Mark 2:13–17). Zacchaeus (Luke 19:1–10) remained in his ordinary life as a tax collector but, after being encountered and called by Jesus, totally reordered his relationship to material goods in terms of justice, generosity, and hospitality. The fact that Jesus accepted the hospitality of both and shared table fellowship with both identifies both as disciples, one called to literally abandon all and follow the itinerant Jesus, the other to relate to material goods in a new way. It is important that the Zacchaeus story occurs only in Luke who, as we will see, has the most "extreme" text on the requirement for *all* who would be disciples of Jesus to hate family, renounce all they possess, and carry the cross unto death (cf. Luke 14:25–35). If Zacchaeus is a disciple, and he clearly is, he must be fulfilling these "radical" demands and he is doing it without literally abandoning home, possessions, and occupation.

2. The first generation of disciples in Palestine

The peasant mass movement Jesus galvanized dispersed abruptly and permanently at the crucifixion. Like other messiahs and messianic movements of the time, Jesus had been executed and his movement apparently had come to nothing. It was too dangerous to appear to be his followers. But Jesus' inner circle of disciples, scattered on Good Friday, quickly regrouped. We are told that Jesus appeared to them a number of times in the days after Easter, "not to all the people but to us who were chosen by God as witnesses." These are the ones "who ate and drank with him after he rose from the dead" (Acts 10:41). When the Holy Spirit descends upon this original group of disciples at Pentecost it is clear that it is neither restricted to the Twelve or the seventy (Judas' replacement, Matthias, is chosen by lot from this group of those who had been with Jesus throughout his ministerial life [see Acts 1:21–26]), or to men (Jesus' mother and other women are explicitly mentioned as part of the group [Acts 1:14]), but it was definitely not a "large crowd" or an indiscriminate group of anonymous hangers-on. It was made up of those, approximately 120 we are told in Acts 1:15, who had been disciples of the pre-Easter Jesus (cf. Acts 2:21–22) and who would now carry on and lead not the mass peasant movement which had disbanded but the work of announcing the Reign of God which Jesus had inaugurated. The Risen Jesus commissioned them to bear witness to him and make disciples of all nations, baptize, forgive sin, form community (cf. Matt 28:16–20; Mark 16:15–18; Luke 24:44–49; John 20:19–23).

The disciples of the pre-Easter Jesus, now filled with the Holy Spirit, are the nucleus of the first generation of disciples in the Church. Their work began immediately with Peter's Pentecost address to a crowd made up of Jews from Palestine as well as Jews and God-fearers from the Diaspora who had come to Jerusalem for the feasts (Acts 1:14–35).[35] About three thousand people were immediately baptized (Acts 2:41), becoming disciples who, in many cases, had never known the pre-Easter Jesus.

Acts goes on to describe the life of this first generation of post-paschal disciples (Acts 1:43–47). Luke is undoubtedly giving an idealized picture of Christian beginnings, constructed by a non-witness many years later, since it is scarcely plausible that all the newly baptized from all over the known world simply relocated instantly to Jerusalem, learned a common language, and set up housekeeping in the environs of the temple. But he describes the Jerusalem community in order to summarize the essential ingredients of Christian life: fidelity to the apostolic teaching (especially concerning the Resurrection), community (one heart and soul), Eucharist, prayer, and a spirit of joyful gratitude expressed in generosity and hospitality. Their attitude toward material goods is basic to their new way of life: "they had all things in common" (2:44–45; 4:32–37), dispossessing themselves willingly so that all would have what they needed. The issue of dispossession, then, reoccurs in this second stage of the Jesus Movement. But the motive for dispossession, the well-being of the community, assimilates this first, stable community to the kind of discipleship exemplified by Zacchaeus, Martha and Mary, and others of Jesus' non-itinerant disciples rather than to the literal abandonment of family and goods of the missionary band.

However, the Acts of the Apostles and the letters of Paul also present numerous examples of missionary discipleship, that of the Twelve, Stephen, Philip, and eventually Paul, Andronicus and Junia, Aquila and Priscilla, and others, that does call for a literal leaving of home and/or family, and material possessions, like that of Jesus' original itinerant group.

3. The disciples in the wider world

Within a couple decades of Jesus' death and Resurrection the Christian Movement had spread well beyond Palestine into the Jewish Diaspora in the far-flung Roman Empire and had begun to attract not only Jews but also Gentiles whose acceptance into the Christian community as full-fledged, first-class disciples who were not required to convert first to Judaism Paul successfully championed. The story of the internationalization of Christianity is available to us primarily in the second half of Acts (chapters 13 to 28) and the Letters of Paul.

Paul personally bridges the three stages of the post-paschal Jesus Movement because he himself never knew the pre-Easter Jesus but was assimilated to the first disciples by an appearance of the Risen Jesus on the road to Damascus. He knew and related to the original Jerusalem community under the leadership of James. And he carried the Gospel to people who not only did not know the pre-Easter Jesus but were not, like the Jerusalem community, raised in the Mosaic tradition.

This new type of Christian disciple, Gentile by birth, familiar with Hellenistic philosophical traditions about human nature and the good life (both political and ethical), and converted to Christianity by a post-first generation apostle is the prototype of most of today's Christians. "Disciple" by this time has a much wider application than it did in the first or even the second stage of the Jesus Movement. And the relationship of Christians to material goods was understood quite differently by different types of disciples in different cultural settings. Nevertheless, all disciples, no matter where or when they became part of the new community, looked to the teachings of Jesus for guidance in this matter.

In trying to grasp what discipleship, particularly in relation to material goods, had come to mean by this time we also have to attend to the fact that at least two of the Gospels (Mark and

Luke) as well as the letters of Paul were very likely composed in and for communities that were not exclusively or even primarily Jewish and most of whose members could not have known the pre-Easter Jesus. In particular, for our purposes, Luke, writing in Syrian Antioch in the eighties, almost certainly was dealing with a predominantly second- (or even third-) generation Gentile Christian community that included many who were economically well off, a situation Luke had to address in the light of Jesus' teaching on renunciation and on Anawim spirituality.

In other words, the Gospels themselves give us not simply what Jesus taught about the relationship of disciples to material goods but the interpretation of Jesus' teaching for later disciples in a wide variety of contexts: Jewish and Gentile, rural and urban, secure and persecuted, poor and prosperous. For our purposes Paul and Luke, both of whom were dealing primarily with Gentiles who were not rural peasants or Jerusalem Jews but hellenized city-dwellers in Asia Minor and Europe, are particularly instructive.

a. Paul

It is completely beyond the scope of this chapter to give even a brief sketch of Pauline theology and spirituality.[36] The primary reason for this brief consideration of Paul's approach to material goods is that he demonstrates how deeply the preaching of the Gospel on a subject like poverty is affected by *who* is preaching it and the *context* in which it is being preached. After noting how pervasive the concern with renunciation of family and possessions is in the canonical Gospels and the strong emphasis on the economic basis and expression of common life in the first part of Acts it is remarkable to note that the term "poor" is almost absent from Paul's extensive writings. He seems very little concerned with economic issues and nowhere suggests that leaving home and family and renouncing material possessions are requisite for, or even particularly conducive to, discipleship.[37] Furthermore, he makes no mention of common life and quite clearly expected his converts to continue in the condition in which they were when they became Christian (see 1 Cor 7:20). That would seem to have included their family condition and their occupational or business involvement. In other words, Paul's writings alert us to the fact that Jesus' teaching regarding poverty needs to be interpreted in various contexts and not literalized into an absolute material blueprint for all disciples in all settings.

Three reasons help to account for Paul's relative non-attention to a theme which seems so central in the Synoptic Gospels. First, *Paul did not know the pre-Easter Jesus* and Paul's ministry predated the formation of the canonical Gospels. He had little knowledge of and shows little interest in the life of Jesus in his Palestinian career which is the context for Jesus' teaching on poverty. Paul draws his version of the Gospel primarily from his conversion experience on the road to Damascus. This experience of the glorified Christ Paul learned to interpret in terms of the emerging tradition (baptismal formulas, credal confessions, christological vocabulary, messianic biblical interpretations, etc.) that was developing in the early Church. Consequently, he focuses almost exclusively on the paschal mystery (the death and Resurrection) of Jesus into which Christians are baptized.

To be baptized into Christ's death is to die to sin, and to rise with Christ is to live the transformed life of those who, as a new Creation, already share in the life of God. Paul draws out the implications for faith and morality of this incorporation into Christ placing particular emphasis on the community of love that flows necessarily from becoming a member in the body of Christ. Even the monetary collection for the Jerusalem community (discussed at length in 2 Corinthians 8 and mentioned elsewhere, such as in Romans 15:25–27) to which Paul devoted considerable effort seems to have had less to do with alleviating economic distress than with cementing the bonds of charity between his Gentile converts and the Jewish "mother church" in Palestine.[38]

Second, the people to whom Paul's missionary activity was directed were not the impoverished and oppressed peasants to whom the pre-Easter Jesus preached. *Most of Paul's converts were not materially deprived.* Indeed, the "Jews of the Diaspora and their proselytes, to whom the preaching of Paul was addressed

...were heads of businesses, commercial people, and well-off artisans."[39] Unlike Jesus, Paul was not galvanizing a mass movement by announcing good news to the poor and subverting an unjust and violent socioreligious system in which the vast majority were victims of oppression. Paul, therefore, felt little need to change the social structures of the societies to which he brought the Gospel. The salvific work of Jesus reaches every person as s/he is, whether that person is Jew or Gentile, rich or poor, slave or free, male or female.[40] Consequently, becoming a Christian did not entail changing one's social condition, basic relationships, or state of life.

Third, Paul was *preaching primarily to Hellenists* whose philosophical (mainly Stoic and Cynic) presuppositions would not have disposed them to understand or respond to a spirituality of voluntary poverty. Although Paul christianized the philosophical attitudes toward material goods of his converts in terms of the mystery of Christ who became poor in order to enrich us (cf. 2 Cor 8:9) he did not attempt to substitute another approach, such as self-deprivation or renunciation, for those attitudes. Indeed, such a spirituality would have been foreign to Paul himself who was a hellenized Jew.

Within the Greek philosophical framework economic well-being was part of the ideal of happiness. However, a virtuous person within that framework should be detached from, that is, not dependent upon possessions but able, like Paul, to maintain one's equilibrium and dignity among changing external conditions (cf. Phil 4:11–14). Paul christianized this philosophical ethics by claiming that his own *autarkeia*, that is, autonomy, was not human self-sufficiency but the conviction that he could do all things in Christ who strengthened him (cf. Phil 4:13). Paul, although he recognized the legitimacy of an apostle's being supported by those to whom one ministered, refused payment for his own apostolic service since he considered himself a "slave of Christ" (Gal 1:10) who received his wages only from his Master. Therefore, he worked as a tentmaker to support himself and not burden those to whom he preached the Gospel (cf. 1 Cor 4:12; 9). He also insisted that every person should provide for himself and be equipped to aid those in need by honest work (cf. Eph 4:28; 2 Thess 3:6–12).[41]

In short, Paul, unlike Jesus in the Synoptic Gospels, does not propose much less demand voluntary self-dispossession as a condition or even an ideal of discipleship. And, unlike the Jerusalem community extolled in Acts, Paul's communities are not encouraged to develop any kind of community of goods or to organize a system of charitable care for the economically needy although they are encouraged to share their resources when this is needed. This striking difference between Jesus and Paul has to alert us to the necessity of very careful interpretation of the Gospel ideal of poverty that Religious profess by vow.

b. LUKE

We turn finally to Luke's Gospel. It is almost certainly the latest of the Synoptics and dates, at the earliest, from the late first century. It was written in and for a predominantly Gentile community. Luke is especially useful for our purposes because this Gospel brings together virtually all the themes so far discussed and because Luke's community, more than the other New Testament communities, resembles in many respects the contemporary first world situation within which Religious are trying to conceptualize and practice evangelical poverty today. Specifically, Luke's community was class-stratified, comprised it seems of a small minority of wealthy people and a large majority of poor. It was a community struggling with issues of inclusiveness specifically of Gentiles and Jews (and perhaps some Samaritans), women, the poor, the lame, the diseased, the outcasts. It was a community trying to reinterpret its mission in light of the seeming failure of God's promises to Israel in Jesus which the fall of the Jerusalem temple had seemed to seal and a parousia that was delayed indefinitely. Finally, Luke's Gospel reflects a relationship with the Old Testament and the emerging New Testament that is not unlike the contemporary Christian challenge of maintaining continuity with the originating Gospel revelation while trying to reinterpret the tradition for new situations.

Luke's presentation of our subject has two strands which are paradoxical when juxtaposed but the paradox is highly enlightening. On the one hand, he presents the starkest, most radical version in any of the Gospels of Jesus' demands for *total renunciation of family and possessions.* On the other hand, he offers instruction on the *right use of possessions* which implies that many in his community who were truly disciples did not abandon family and possessions.

A parable which occurs only in Luke, that of the Rich Man and Lazarus (Luke 16:19–31), provides a way into the first strand of Luke's project: *stark warning of his community about the danger of wealth.* It begins with a description of the two characters. The Rich Man is at the luxury end of the spectrum of possession: living in a gated house, dressed in the latest style and richest fabrics, feasting sumptuously every day, and honorably buried when he dies. Lazarus is at the death end of the spectrum: homeless, covered with sores under rags that expose his wounds to the dogs, starving for some crumbs from the Rich Man's table, and finally anonymous (the text implies) in death. The issue starkly set out is the divide between the extravagantly wealthy and the desperately poor.

Next we witness an after-death scene between Lazarus, now peacefully reclining in Abraham's bosom, and the Rich Man suffering in Hades that dramatizes the eschatological resolution for which the Old Testament remnant, the Anawim, waited in hope and which Jesus evokes during his ministry as the imminent coming of the Reign of God. This new world will be characterized by the "great reversal." Those who were self-sufficient in their riches in this life will be poor forever while the poor and suffering who, in this life, could look only to God for salvation will be richly satisfied in the world to come. This is Mary's message in the Magnificat (Luke 2:46–55): the proud powerful will be abased and the vulnerable lowly lifted up; the hungry will be filled and the rich sent empty away. It is the message Jesus preaches in the Lukan Sermon on the Plain in which he fills out the meaning of his vocational statement in the synagogue of Nazareth: that he has been sent to bring good news to the poor, release to the captives, sight to the blind, and freedom to the oppressed (Luke 4:18–19). Unlike Matthew, Luke balances the Beatitudes of this sermon with the Woes: blessed are you who are poor, hungry, weeping, hated and defamed, but woe to you who are rich, full, laughing, valued and praised because the former will receive their reward in the Reign of God while the latter have had their reward. Thus Abraham says, in response to the Rich Man's pleas for relief, "Child, remember that during your lifetime you received your good things, and Lazarus in like manner evil things: but now he is comforted here, and you are in agony" (16:25). And furthermore, says Abraham, the new situation is definitive. It cannot be reversed because it results from the Rich Man's free choice.

Interestingly, the Rich Man is not accused of actively oppressing or mistreating Lazarus in life. But when the Rich Man asks Abraham to send Lazarus to warn his brothers it is clear that there is something they could do, and therefore something he himself could have done, to avoid his fate. What? Is the implication that they should become impoverished beggars? That is hardly compatible with Jesus' message that God is acting to abolish the poverty of the poor, not to spread it, nor Abraham's naming of Lazarus's poverty as "evil." The fault of the Rich Man is not that he was rich but that being rich made him blind to the plight of the poor. Lazarus sat at his gate day after day and the Rich Man did not see himself obliged to do anything about the situation. He had not made Lazarus poor so poverty and the poor, he apparently concluded, were not his problem.

We are once more in the spiritual framework of the Anawim. Wealth leads naturally, if not inevitably, to self-sufficiency and self-absorption which blinds the rich to their need for God and their obligation to the poor. Poverty, by contrast, leads naturally, though not inevitably, to dependence on God because there is no one else to help and the pious poor, the true Anawim, refuse to believe that God has finally abandoned them. Their hope is occasioned by poverty but it is grounded in faith. By its very presentation of the characters—the Rich Man has no name because he is identified with his possessions, and Lazarus' name means "God helps"—the text suggests this contrast between the spiritual effects of wealth and of poverty. It is made explicit when the Rich Man pleads that if someone from the dead would go to his brothers they would repent but Abraham, the father of faith, says that if they will not listen to Moses and the prophets they will not respond "even if someone rises from the dead."

Here the connection between the Old Testament and the New becomes clear. In the Old Testament Moses in the Law decreed that there were to be no poor in Israel (cf. Deut 15:4) because those who had wealth should share it with the poor, and the prophets excoriated the oppression of the poor by the rich. This should have told the Rich Man (and his brothers) what was required (justice and generosity) and what was forbidden (greed and oppression). But if they had ignored this biblical preparation they would not be able to grasp the significance of the one who "rose from the dead" in fulfillment of the Law and the prophets. The Risen Jesus, in Luke, will explain his own death (as the ultimate Poor One of Yahweh) and Resurrection (the great reversal) to the Emmaus disciples (Luke 24: 27) precisely in terms of their fulfillment of the Law and the prophets.

Numerous other passages in Luke explore the dangers of wealth. In Luke 8:14, in the parable of the Sower, Luke describes the unreceptiveness to the Word (the seed) of the wealthy because they are choked by the "cares and riches and pleasures of life."

In Luke 12:13–21, we have a series of situations in which the issue of possessions is raised. It begins with Jesus refusing to arbitrate a dispute over inheritance between two brothers, not because Jesus is unconcerned about justice but because he is more deeply concerned with the issue of greed and covetousness which can divide families and communities and which cannot be healed by arbitration but only by conversion.[42] The dispute leads Jesus directly into another warning about riches: "Take care! Be on your guard against all kinds of greed: for one's life does not consist in the abundance of possessions" (12:15).

This is followed immediately by a parable (12:16–21) about a Rich Fool who, having an unusually good crop one year, decides to tear down his barns and build bigger ones to store his "stuff." His utter confidence in his "ample wealth" prompts him to "relax, eat, drink, and be merry." But God says, "You fool!" You will die tonight and you cannot take it with you. The problem, once again, is not that the man is rich. It is that he is a fool. "The fool says in his heart there is no God" (Ps 14:1) because his wealth, which he thinks is his own rather than God's gift to him, makes him think he is in charge of his own destiny. Jesus concludes, "So it is with those who store up treasures for themselves but are not rich toward God."[43]

The consummation of Luke's presentation of Jesus' teaching on the dangers of wealth comes in 18:24–30, the logion on the "needle's eye." This is the conclusion of Luke's version of the story carried by all three Synoptics of a rich (young) man (ruler) who comes to Jesus to ask what he must do to inherit eternal life. (We will return to this story shortly in relation to the differing vocations in the Christian community.) But in Luke, when the ruler turns away from Jesus' invitation to "sell all" and follow him, Jesus says "How hard it is for those who have wealth to enter the kingdom of God! Indeed, it is easier for a camel to go through the eye of a needle than for someone who is rich to enter the kingdom of God." The image (not the content) is typical Gospel hyperbole, designed to shock the hearers into attention. His alarmed hearers ask, "Then who can be saved?" Does wealth, purely and simply, bar one from eternal life? Jesus replies, "What is impossible for mortals is possible for God." He seems to be saying, as Pilgrim puts it, that "riches represent such a barrier, they are so tough for the human will to let go, that it is indeed a miracle when a rich person lets go and becomes a disciple."[44]

Luke ends this section by pointing, through Peter's response, to the first disciples of Jesus as examples of the kind of renunciation of material goods that is required for discipleship. Peter says, "Look, we have left our homes [or all things, or all our possessions—τὰ ἴδια] and followed you" and Jesus replies that those who have left all will "get back very much more in this age, and in the age to come eternal life" (cf. Luke 18:28–30). This can hardly be a promise that, like Job, those who give up home and possessions will receive back more of the same in this life. That would simply nullify their renunciation. What Luke envisions as the result of forsaking reliance on family or on personal wealth is the kind of community life he describes in Acts 4. The ideal Jerusalem community was made up of those who sold all in order to hold all things in common, to have no poor in their midst, and to live a life of joyful dependence on God. Jesus is saying that there is a form of life, even before death, that is not based on personal ownership and is very much more blessed.

Even though Luke seems to have shifted from expectation of an immanent apocalyptic parousia to concern for the life of discipleship in the present, he presents Jesus as warning his disciples to be prepared for the sudden return of the Son of Man. He frames the warning in terms that clearly refer to the dangers of wealth: "Be on guard so that your hearts are not weighed down with dissipation and drunkenness and the worries of this life [classical temptations of wealth], and that day catch you unexpectedly" (Luke 21:34).

Another story gives access to the second strand of Lukan reflection on our topic: *the right use of material goods*. Only Luke recounts the encounter between Jesus and Zacchaeus (Luke 19:1–9). Zacchaeus is a chief tax collector which means he was the major operative in an essentially corrupt business in which he enriched himself by oppressing the poor, usually through underlings who did the actual collecting of taxes. He was both a sinner and rich. He was, however, drawn to Jesus whom he so desired to see that he climbed a tree to get a good view as Jesus entered Jericho. Jesus commanded him to come down "for I must stay at your house today." Readers of Luke will recognize the "must" (δεῖ) as a marker of divine necessity, the unfolding of salvation history. Zacchaeus is delighted but Jesus' detractors immediately "grumble" because he is going to dwell with a sinner, and especially one who sins against his own people. All the problematic pieces are on the table: a sinner who is Jewish but working for the Gentiles, the scandalized righteous, ill-gotten goods, the defrauded poor. Luke pulls it all together for his purpose of instructing the wealthy in his Gentile community about discipleship and material goods.

Zacchaeus enters the story as a sinful but eager inquirer and finishes as a disciple. In order for this transformation to take place two things are required. The first is the encounter between Zacchaeus's openness and Jesus' call. The second is Zacchaeus's conversion expressed in a reordering of his relationship to wealth through restitution (four-fold!) of all he has gained through fraud and generous giving (half his goods!) to the poor. Zacchaeus is not asked to and does not give up his home or his job. He is a different kind of disciple from Peter who says he has left home, father, and fishing boat to follow Jesus in his itinerant ministry. Zacchaeus invites Jesus into his home and straightens out his business dealings through honesty and almsgiving. Jesus, who comes "to seek out and save the lost" (19:10), declares this converted extortioner of his own people a "son of Abraham" (19:9), that is, a true Jew.

Luke actually presents a whole series of episodes, sayings, parables, example stories, and exhortations which illustrate how people of means can and should make a right use of their wealth, thereby living their discipleship just as fully as those who literally abandon all. At the base of this teaching is the parable in Luke 16:1–13 which many people find very disconcerting, that of the "Dishonest Steward."

This steward, either caught mismanaging his master's affairs or the victim of calumny to that effect designed to get him fired, is given notice. He promptly lowers the sum of the debts a number of people owed his master in order to "make friends" who can aid him once he is out of a job. And Jesus, through the lord in the story, approves of this "prudent" or wise tactic. We are not told that the Lord approved the original dishonesty. The man was being fired for that. But exegetes tend to see what the steward waived as either the "overcharge" on the debts by which the steward was lining his own pockets as he collected the debt principal for his master[45] or as the usury the master was imposing on his debtors and that the man had been willingly collecting for him.[46] In either case, the steward is no longer enriching himself at the expense of his master's debtors, that is, making enemies by Mammon, but was now making friends, creating community, by his use of "the Mammon of unrighteousness."

The crux of the story, for our purposes, is what Jesus calls "the Mammon of iniquity." New Testament scholar Douglas Oakman analyzes the term etymologically and linguistically and concludes:

> The linguistic evidence points to Mammon as signifying wealth collected in the bank, or the storehouse, or the treasury: wealth which then becomes the object of trust for the powerful-wealthy to the exclusion of God and neighbor. More importantly, Mammon is based in a system that exploits the many for the benefit of the few. To serve Mammon is to be alone in one's self-sufficiency; to serve God is to have concern for others and to practice reciprocity.[47]

Wealth, when it becomes the source of one's security, has become one's god. "Where your treasure is, there will your heart be also" (Luke 12:34; Matt 6:21). Love of this idol alienates the person from God and isolates her or him from the neighbor. The principle for the right use of material goods, in short, is not necessarily abandoning them literally but refusing to let them become one's "treasure."

Some people may be personally called to total abandonment of their possessions. For some, for whom money is like drink to the alcoholic, total renunciation may be the only way to free themselves from the idolatry of wealth. But for everyone the spirituality of the Anawim, of detachment and dependence on God alone, and community solidarity which equalizes well-being through generosity and sharing is the only Christian approach to material goods. That which is usually the result of injustice and an impediment to discipleship, "the Mammon of iniquity," must become the means of doing good, the way in which one honors the only true God and promotes the good of the neighbor. The steward in the story used Mammon to establish bonds of community, and in that he, in contrast to the "fool" (ἄφρων) who built bigger barns to hoard his goods, acted wisely (φρόνιμος) in regard to the wealth over which he had some control.

Following from this basic principle, that there is a right use of wealth, Luke provides numerous examples of how to do this. He frequently, in both the Gospel (e.g., 12:33) and Acts (e.g., 10:2; 24:17), exhorts to almsgiving or the distribution of one's goods to the poor. Christians are to lend freely (Luke 6:27–36) and to give abundantly, even more than is asked (Luke 6:37–38). They are to welcome to their table the poor, the uninvited, the socially marginalized, rather than their friends or the rich who can reciprocate (Luke 14:7–24).

Finally, Luke alone has Jesus tell the parable of the Good Samaritan (Luke 10:29–37) in response to the question of a lawyer about whom he should regard as his neighbor, that is, as one who has a claim on his love. The "love command," to love God with all one's being, to love one's neighbor as oneself, and even to love one's enemies, is identified by all scholars as the center of the Gospel. But the Lukan Jesus concretizes this by showing how one who is despised as an apostate, that is, a loathed Samaritan, fulfills this command by reaching out extravagantly not only to a stranger but even to his enemy, a Jew. The Samaritan places his time, his energy, his reputation, perhaps even his safety if his act were observed, and his wealth completely at the service of this stranger-enemy, while the victim's co-religionists passed by on the other side of the street. The lawyer who had challenged Jesus correctly identifies the neighbor as "the one who showed mercy" as God shows mercy. Jesus' emphatic, "Go and do likewise" sums up his teaching not only about love as the distinguishing characteristic of a disciple but about how wealth is to be incorporated into such discipleship.

To briefly summarize, Luke, writing to a community of second- or third-generation hellenistic Gentile Christians which includes both wealthy and poor, directs much of what he has to say about discipleship and material goods to the economically secure members of his community. Luke presents Jesus' demands for total renunciation of home, family, profession, and possessions as addressed to all disciples: "…none of you can become my disciple if you do not give up all your possessions" (Luke 14:35). However, Luke clearly recognizes that many disciples will be householders like Martha and Mary

(Luke 10:38–42) and have stable professions like Zacchaeus (Luke 19:1–10), and therefore necessarily will own and use material goods. Luke uses the renunciation material from the life of the pre-Easter Jesus and his itinerant disciples to articulate in the starkest possible way that the real demands of discipleship for complete detachment from all that would impede the disciple's relationship to Christ, love of neighbor, participation in the community, and dedication to the Reign of God is not a purely theoretical or optional ideal but the absolutely nonnegotiable condition of discipleship for every Christian. Any attachment to , that is, any worship of, material goods, no matter how seemingly legitimate or innocuous, becomes an impediment to discipleship which demands the worship of God alone.

C. Discipleship, Poverty, and the "States of Life"

Having investigated the New Testament materials on poverty we now have to raise the question of whether Jesus' teaching on the subject of the relationship of disciples to material goods applies to all disciples, or to all disciples in the same way. In other words, are there aspects of this teaching that are mandatory for all and other aspects to which only a few are called? If the latter is the case, are there "levels" or "classses" of discipleship? In the history of Christian spirituality it has been proposed, for example, that Religious are called literally to leave all, including family, home, and possessions whereas such demands are impossible for lay Christians to observe and therefore must be regarded not as commandments of Jesus but as "counsels" reserved for the "perfect."

Any adequate theology of the evangelical poverty that Religious undertake by vow must take a position on this question. If there is nothing specific about the poverty Religious profess, there is no point to the vow. But if Religious are called to a response to the Gospel to which other Christians are not called we are once again involved in the kind of spiritual elitism, the two-tiered discipleship, that Vatican II disavowed when it taught that all Christians are called to one and the same holiness.[48] By way of anticipation, I will suggest in what follows that

Jesus' entire teaching on the relationship of disciples to material goods is applicable to all his disciples equally but that
because discipleship is incarnated in a variety of equal but distinct states of life and life circumstances the concrete practice
of these teachings will vary considerably. Our task will be to see
how, in fact, an unconditional commitment to Jesus' teaching
is possible in different forms of discipleship in order, in the following two chapters, to investigate the specific meaning of
poverty in the Religious state of life in its distinctive corporate
and individual realizations.

It seems clear from the Gospels, as we have already seen, that
Jesus, even in his pre-Easter life, had different kinds (not
degrees) of disciples. Some whom he called to go about with
him in his itinerant ministry, including the twelve and a group
of women (see Luke 8:1–3), apparently the seventy (see Luke
10:1, 17), and by implication some others, like Bartimaeus (see
Mark 10:52), were required to share his homeless lifestyle in service of the proclamation of the Reign of God specifically as
"good news to the poor." Others, like the householders Mary
and Martha of Bethany, the tax collector Zacchaeus, the Royal
Official in John 4 whose whole household became believers, or
the cured demoniac of Gerasa were also, and equally, called to
discipleship but they were called not to abandon family and possessions but to use their God-given material gifts to promote
Jesus' work through hospitality, generosity, justice, and witness.

After the Resurrection, although there were some disciples
like Paul and the Twelve who were called to abandon all and
devote themselves exclusively to the preaching of the Gospel
(cf. Acts 6:2), the new community, both in Judea and in the
Diaspora, among both Jews and Gentiles, immediately incorporated many people (whom the New Testament often calls collectively "the saints")[49] who were married and employed and who
exercised their discipleship in the context of their everyday
lives. Furthermore, there were full time pastoral ministers such
as presbyters (possibly both male and female), deacons (male
and female), overseers or bishops (cf. Eph. 4:1–16) in the earliest churches who were resident rather than itinerant ministers,
usually married, who hosted the community in worship as well

as leading it in life and mission. As Elisabeth Schüssler Fiorenza demonstrated in her major work, *In Memory of Her*,[50] the early Church, while its members exercised many charisms in a variety of functions, was a discipleship of equals. This is the picture we get from the Acts of the Apostles' description of the early community and also from Paul's teaching on the Church as the Body of Christ whose many members are equally important but whose functions are various (e.g., 1 Cor. 13).

The early Church, therefore, had to interpret Jesus' teaching on the relationship of disciples to material goods for a much more diverse community living in a much wider variety of sociocultural contexts than the original small contingent of disciples that Jesus recruited in the peasant context of first-century Palestine. This transposition of the teaching on poverty into a new key was accomplished in the Gospels by applying the texts on literal renunciation which were originally directed only to the itinerant disciples who were called to share the self-stigmatizing lifestyle of the pre-Easter Jesus to all disciples as the nonnegotiable standard, and then recognizing that this absolute interior detachment and renunciation could be lived in a variety of ways. The absolute demand for renunciation, in other words, was radicalized through interiorization which could be expressed in a variety of outward deeds.

This process of radicalization by interiorization had its model in Jesus' own teaching about the Law. In Matthew's Sermon on the Mount Jesus radicalizes the behavioral demands of the Decalogue itself. He says, "You have heard....but I say to you" (cf. Matt 5:17–47). In each instance he takes a behavioral prescription of the Law ("you have heard"), such as not to murder, commit adultery, swear false oaths, or retaliate disproportionately for an offense, and insists ("but I say to you") that it is not enough to carry out the behavior commanded. The prohibition of murder proceeds from an interior renunciation of anger; fidelity in marriage expresses the interior faithfulness of the heart which does not entertain even lustful thoughts; reverence for God makes not just false oaths but all swearing of oaths unlawful; moderation in retaliation must arise from love of one's persecutors which tends to the renunciation of all retaliation. It is important to note that—contrary to what we spontaneously think—the interior disposition is more, not less, demanding than the exterior behavior. This section in Matthew concludes with "Be perfect therefore as your heavenly Father is perfect."

All Jesus' disciples are called to this perfection. This interiorization is not a false "spiritualization" or "idealization" of the demands of the Law. Jesus did not come to abolish the Law but to fulfill it (cf. Matt 5:17). The fulfillment of the Law is realized first interiorly in one's attitudes, choices, desires which must then come to expression in whatever outward behavior is called for in the circumstances. If one's heart is right, right actions must follow. So, the Gospel teaching on poverty says, on the one hand, that all Christians, poor and rich alike, and in whatever condition or state of life, are called to total interior renunciation of, that is, detachment from all material goods. The disciples' "treasure" is Christ and that is where their hearts must be. Christ will not share his absolute claim on the heart with Mammon, the god of wealth or wealth as god. Whether one is called to literally abandon one's material goods for the sake of Christ and the Gospel or to use them prudently and generously to promote the Reign of God, no one can be Jesus' disciple if she or he is attached to anything, that is, does not renounce all things.

One way to approach the apparent dilemma of absolute Gospel demands made on all but incarnated literally by only a few is to focus on the text which has most often been invoked (erroneously I will argue) as the foundation of the "precepts and counsels" position, namely, that of the rich (young) man (Matt 19:16–22, 23–30 and its parallels in Mark 10:17–31 and Luke 18:18–23, 24–30). This pericope is of particular interest to us here because it concerns precisely the voluntary renunciation of wealth.

Many years ago New Testament scholar Simon Légasse took on the apparent dilemma of this passage in relation to Religious Life in his doctoral dissertation.[51] Légasse argued, as I have throughout this chapter, that the call of the rich young man, though it appears in the Gospel as a single episode from the life of the pre-Easter Jesus, must be read in two contexts or through two lenses. The first, the *historical context*, is that of the pre-Easter Jesus teaching his original disciples in first century Palestine. In this context, Jesus called this man to join his immediate circle of homeless, itinerant disciples, a call which was not addressed to all who were Jesus' disciples even during his lifetime. For example, the cured Gerasene demoniac (Mark 5:1–20) was not allowed by Jesus to go with him, presumably because his witness was needed in his local situation from which Jesus and his band were barred by the townspeople while the healed blind man, Bartimaeus, was allowed to go with him (Mark 10:46–52). Mary Magdalene went about with Jesus (Luke 8:1–3) but Martha and Mary of Bethany did not, perhaps because their ability to provide Jesus with a safe and welcoming environment during his strenuous and dangerous ministry was a more valuable contribution to the mission and one which they, as householders, were uniquely able to supply (cf. John 12:1–8). In other words, discipleship, during the lifetime of Jesus or afterward, is not equivalent to membership in the itinerant band. Nor was or is the latter a superior form of discipleship. However, it is the form to which this inquirer, the rich young man, was called by Jesus. His problem was his failure to respond to *his* vocation, not to some general requirement.

This historical context, however, is not the context in which we find the text on the call of the rich man now. The second context is *the Gospel* itself. The evangelists have universalized the episode and made it paradigmatic of the call to discipleship whenever and wherever it occurs. Matthew's version of the call of the rich man is the most pertinent for our purposes because it seems to make a distinction between keeping the commandments which is "good" and selling all and following Jesus which is "perfect." Furthermore, Jesus seems to say that the latter is only necessary *if* the rich man wants to be perfect, suggesting that this is a supererogatory work which he was free to accept (and become perfect) or reject (and still be good). Légasse argues, rightly in my opinion, that none of the above surface reading is valid.

According to Légasse, who has studied this pericope in the context of its parallels in Mark and Luke (which we cannot go into here), Matthew has recast the Markan original to make the story universally applicable and to draw the reader into the story as a participant. We, the readers, are the "someone" (εἷς) inquiring of Jesus "What good must I do to have eternal life?" The dialogue then proceeds in three stages.

First, Jesus insists that the "good" consists in the fulfillment of the will of God who alone is good. This will is already revealed in the Law which Jesus recalls for the questioner. Second, Jesus interprets the decalogue by adding the second great commandment, "You shall love your neighbor as yourself" from Leviticus 19:18.[52] In other words, for the Christian, doing "good" means keeping the Law (which Jesus did not come to abolish) as interpreted (fulfilled) by Jesus by his emphasis on the second commandment as equal to the first (cf. Matt 22:34–39).

The third stage of the teaching begins in v. 20 where the questioner claims to have kept all these precepts and then asks, "What do I still lack?" Jesus does not, as we would expect, reassure the man that if he has kept the Law he has done all that is required. Rather, he says that "if he wishes to be perfect" he must sell all, give to the poor, and come follow him. Everything hinges on the meaning of perfect. As Légasse points out, "perfect" in Matthew (the only evangelist to use the term) must be understood as it was understood in Jewish teaching, not in contrast to but as synonymous with "good."[53] God alone is "good" (Matt 19:17), that is, perfect, and Jesus' disciples are called to be perfect as God is perfect (cf. Matt 5:48). Jesus' challenge, "if you would be perfect," means "if you want to have eternal life" (which is what the man, in 19:16, came to Jesus to seek), not "if you wish to be better than you are required to be." Jesus is not proposing a counsel, an option, in contrast with an obligation. To will to have eternal life is to will to be perfect, that is, to do God's will, or to be like God who alone is good. The only time in the New Testament that "perfect" expresses superiority to something less good

is when the final and heavenly state of salvation is compared to the present, earthly state (1 Cor 13:10, Ph 3:12) or when "perfection" designates the normal Christian life, in con-

> trast to an immaturity which we are...called to outgrow (1 Cor 14:20; Col 1:28).[54]

If this is the case, it would seem that Matthew (with his source in Mark) makes abandoning all one's goods an absolute requirement for a perfection which is obligatory for all. Légasse, with other New Testament scholars, puts this requirement in the context of Jesus' teaching, immediately following this pericope, on the dangers of riches. For humans, being rich is so formidable an obstacle to salvation ("Then who can be saved?" his disciples ask in alarm) that only with God is it possible (cf. Matt 19:25–26). Riches fall in the category of "scandal" like the eye or the hand or the foot that one must be prepared to pluck out or sever if it presents an impediment to that unreserved following of Christ which is required for discipleship (cf. Matt 5:29–30; Mark 9:43–47). These "extreme" demands of Jesus are uttered in the context of the eschatological urgency of the early Church in which following Jesus did present the very real possibility of martyrdom. Only one who is disposed to abandon all, family, wealth, one's bodily members, even life itself, can be a disciple. But the demand is not limited to the first century context. Anything that stands in the way of any disciple's total devotion to God and following of Christ is to be abandoned, rejected, immediately and absolutely renounced.

The close of the pericope makes clear that for this man riches was indeed *the* impediment to his following of Christ. He had kept the commandments of the second tablet of the Law pertaining to love of neighbor—you shall not murder, commit adultery, steal, bear false witness, dishonor parents. This man's problem was the first great commandment, to love God alone with his whole heart and mind and soul and strength. His heart was captive to his possessions. Jesus has put his finger on the man's "imperfection," the "lack" in his apparently sincere desire for eternal life that had led to his keeping the commandments all his life. That which keeps him from being "good," that is, "perfect" is his captivity to Mammon. He went away grieving because he had many possessions that he obviously was not prepared to surrender in order to follow Jesus. Matthew has moved "following Jesus" beyond the context of membership in the pre-Easter Jesus' itinerant band and is clearly, by the context he assigns, applying it to all disciples of all time regardless of state of life or situation. The "extremism" of the Gospel demands is not an invitation to eviscerate them, making them impractical and inapplicable theoretical "ideals" appropriate only to a distant time and place or some elite group. Rather, the radicalism of the demands universalizes them by the very requirement it imposes to interpret them in ever-new contexts and incarnate them in different practices and situations.

As we will see in the next two chapters, Religious choose to incarnate this radical detachment from riches, which is equally incumbent on all disciples, in a particular lifeform which is not a "better" or "superior" way of following Christ but which is distinctive and, as such, gives a particular kind of witness in the Church and to the world of the challenge posed to all disciples, to renounce all to follow Christ.

VIII. Summary and Conclusion: Scripture on Material Goods and Poverty

We are now in a position to synthesize the array of resources which constitute a scriptural basis for the evangelical poverty Religious vow in preparation for inquiring into the corporate and individual living of that vow in the next two chapters.

A. The Old Testament Background

Jesus, who is the exemplar and teacher of evangelical poverty, must be understood both in continuity with the Old Testament which shaped his own spirituality and as original in relation to it. We saw that the Old Testament witnesses to at least three fundamental themes pertinent to our topic. First, **Creation is fundamentally good**. Material goods and prosperity are a gift of God, necessary for human life, which human beings who are made in God's image and likeness should accept with gratitude and joy and use responsibly. Indeed, humans are partners with God in caring for the whole of Creation and assuring the well-being of all in the community.

Second, **poverty is always evil**. When economic poverty resulting from misfortune deprives some people, especially members of one's own community, of what they need others must come to their aid with compassion and generosity for there should be no one in want among God's people. Sociological poverty, the oppression of the weak by the powerful, is injustice that God hates and will punish severely as the prophets proclaimed. The wise person, however, one who truly follows Torah, knows that inordinate love of wealth that leads easily to forgetting God and mistreating one's neighbor is as dangerous as abject poverty, which causes despair and alienation from God. Consequently, moderation, contentment with sufficiency, responsibility, justice, generosity, and hospitality should mark the behavior of the true Israelite, the wise person.

Third, whether one is well-off or impoverished, one's interior disposition in regard to material well-being is more important than one's external situation or behavior. The Old Testament offers no ideal of poverty as such for in itself poverty is always regarded as an evil to be avoided or remedied. But in its presentation of the Anawim, the pious poor of Yahweh who will form the faithful remnant of Israel among whom the Messiah will finally establish the Reign of God, the Old Testament suggests that even poverty can, if borne faithfully, promote spiritual growth. **The spirituality of the Anawim is characterized by a total openness to and trust in God.** One might say that the "poor of Yahweh" are those who never lose touch with God's providence in the Creation story, with God's liberating action in the Exodus and gift of the land, with the Covenant and Torah. Whether enjoying prosperity or suffering want, they are the truly wise. They know that God alone is the source of all good and intends good for them; that God hears their cry when they are in distress as well as their confident praise in all circumstances. God is their creator, their liberator, their protector and their only desire.

Jesus is quintessentially the "poor one of Yahweh," totally dependent on God throughout his life and clinging to God in the extremity of death. In him the promised Reign of God which he is anointed to preach as good news to the poor has actually arrived.

B. The Gospel *Novum*: No One Can Serve Two Masters

Jesus lived the Old Testament ethos of grateful and joyful acceptance of God's good Creation, of solidarity with the oppressed and prophetic resistance to injustice, of sapiential moderation in the use of material goods, of Anawim spirituality even unto death. But he also had a highly original insight into the nature and dynamics of wealth that led to his preaching of an ideal of poverty that we do not find in the Old Testament. Whereas the primary (though not exclusive) concern in the Old Testament was how material goods mediated the practice of the second great commandment, that is, love of and justice toward the neighbor, Jesus was equally concerned with the role of wealth in the practice of the first commandment, that is, the absolute and total love of God above all things. Jesus was acutely aware of the potential of Mammon, that is, of accumulated wealth in whatever form, to pervert the human heart and to subvert the relationship of the person to God. Jesus' teachings on the subject of wealth are pervasive in the Gospels and virtually all of that teaching is devoted to warning his followers about the dangers of wealth.

The basis of his teaching was the principle: "No one can serve two masters. Either [s]he will hate the one and love the other, or [s]he will be devoted to the one and despise the other. You cannot serve both God and Money" (Matt 6:24; par. Luke 16:13).[55] "Money" or "wealth" in this saying is the translation of "Mammon" (μαμωνᾶ), which is quasi-personified as a god.[56] Wealth, Jesus says, is not just a morally neutral means for accomplishing human purposes which might be evil or good. There is no good Mammon, no "Mammon of Justice." Mammon is wealth specifically as God's competitor for the human heart. Love of money is idolatry (cf. 1 Titus 6:10; Heb 13:5). It is totally incompatible with love of God.

When the texts on this subject are read in light of each other they reveal a subtle and profound analysis of the dynamics of human desire. Jesus speaks of desire, of trust, of ambition, of striving, and of all of these in terms of "treasure." Treasure is not simply what we have or use; it is what we love. Our treasure, whether God, another person, pleasure, reputation, status, or wealth, is that in which we trust, what we count on, where we place our security. It is the ultimate source of our happiness. If our treasure is threatened we are threatened. Our treasure is that for which we will sacrifice other, indeed all other, goods. Jesus warns that wealth is the primary contender for the role of "treasure" in human lives, mobilizing the dynamics by which we enthrone as god something other than God. "Where your treasure is, there your heart will be also" (Matt 6:21; Luke 12:34) appears precisely as the conclusion to the warning against storing up earthly treasure in Matthew and the exhortation to sell what you have and give alms in Luke.

The Beatitudes and their corresponding Woes in Luke's Gospel make absolutely explicit this opposition between God and Mammon: "Blessed are you who are poor, for yours is the Reign of God.... Woe to you who are rich, for you have received your consolation" (cf. Luke 6: 20, 24). All three Synoptics contain the shocking dominical logion, "It is easier for a camel to go through the eye of a needle, than for the rich to enter into the kingdom of God" (Mark 10:25; Matt 19:24; Luke 18:25). All three texts have πλούσιον (the) "rich," rather than "someone who is rich"; that is, someone who happens to have wealth. Wealth defines "the rich." It is who s/he is. Something like a divine miracle, Jesus says, making possible by God's intervention what is impossible to humans, is required to break the hold of money on the heart of its owner. Wealth, Jesus suggests, is not what we own but what owns us. Furthermore, people do not usually become rich by accident. The commitment of time and effort expended to make money, the insensitivity to others' needs as one pursues financial gain, and even the almost inevitable injustice involved in acquiring wealth, are an entangling and absorbing preoccupation that almost always, Jesus implies, corrupts the person morally and takes God's place in the person's life.

In light of this analysis it is not difficult to see why Jesus calls for absolute renunciation of wealth, which, against the background of the Old Testament, is a Gospel *novum*. Whether one possesses much or little the attachment of the heart to "the bird in the hand" of resources under our control rather than to the uncontrollable "bird in the bush" of God's providence subverts trust in God and is almost certain to imprison the soul. John of the Cross gave classic expression to this insight when he said that it matters little whether a bird is tethered by a cord or a golden thread; it is not free.[57] Total renunciation, that is, the complete detachment that disposes one effectively to abandon everything, if that is necessary, for the sake of God, is required of all disciples in relation to all material goods. In this sense, Matthew's "Blessed are the poor in spirit" captures the full scope of the challenge even better than Luke's "Blessed are you [who are actually] poor" because of the universality of Matthew's version and the fact that it proposes a permanently valid spiritual disposition rather than describing a material state of affairs that should end. Poverty of spirit, total detachment from material goods, is demanded of the poor as well as of the rich; of those with much and those with little. It applies to all possessions, regardless of the source or the nature of one's wealth.

C. The Principle of Discernment: Trust vs. Anxiety

Jesus, ever the physician of the soul, apparently knew how easy it is for human beings to assure themselves that they are really not interiorly attached to their belongings and therefore in no need of actual self-dispossession in order to be "poor in spirit." Both Matthew (6:25–34) and Luke (12:22–35) record a discourse of Jesus about anxiety and trust that supplies a principle of discernment for anyone tempted to such evasive self-confidence. The passage is familiar. Jesus tells his disciples not to worry, not to be anxious or preoccupied, about their life or about what sustains it (food, drink, clothes) for three reasons.

First, **worry is useless** because humans have no control over life itself. This was demonstrated by the example of the Lukan Rich Fool in the immediately preceding passage whose planning and striving, "building bigger barns," in anticipation of a life of leisure came to naught when he suddenly died. If life itself is not under human control it is pointless to worry about what supposedly sustains that life.

Second, there is **no need to worry** because God is a loving Parent who knows that his/her children need material supports for their lives and is able and eager to supply those needs. If God is solicitous for nonhuman creatures, for birds and flowers, how much more concerned is the divine Parent for God's human children. This, however, is only reassuring if one actually believes and hopes unconditionally in God.

Third, **anxiety about material possessions is characteristic of pagans**, not of children of God and disciples of Jesus. The concern of the disciples, the single eye, should be focused on the Reign of God, which demands all their solicitude, all their effort. If they are concerned about the things of God, God who knows their needs will provide for them more abundantly than they could provide for themselves.

Luke ends this discourse with the "treasure and heart" logion whereas in Matthew the logion precedes the discourse. But the point is the same. The litmus test of attachment is anxiety. True detachment is recognized in the trust that generates a profound sense of security not based in self-sufficiency, in having enough, but in God. Jesus himself is the ultimate model of this trust in God against all temptation to idolatry. His public life begins in the desert where he chooses God over food, power, and prestige (see Luke 4:1–12; Matt 4:1–11) which are presented precisely as the temptations to idolatry offered by the Prince of This World, and it ends on the cross where he prays, when stripped of everything, "Father, into your hands I commend my spirit" (Luke 24:36).

D. Love of God and Love of Neighbor: Poverty and Community

This chapter has attempted to ground the understanding and practice of evangelical poverty in contemporary Religious Life in the Christian Scriptures. Although we have certainly not exhausted the topic of poverty and wealth in the Bible, it should have become clear that the topic is pervasive in the sacred text. And, in both testaments, the lens which focuses the issue of the human relationship with material goods is the suffering of the poor.

Although God's Creation is bountiful and God's intention is the well-being of all creatures, the prevailing situation of most people in most periods of human history is poverty. Whatever evangelical poverty is about, it must be somehow a response to this situation. In the next two chapters I will suggest how Religious Life, as corporate enterprise and as personal spiritual project, constitutes such a response. Religious have always been concerned with caring for the poor, whatever form of poverty they suffer. This concern has been facilitated by their own frugality in the use of material goods and exercised through their ministries. In other words, the coincidence of the first and second great commandments has been, in practice, the primary motivation of ministerial Religious Life. But we are now, perhaps, in a position to bring this insight, that love of God and love of neighbor are two sides of one coin, into a little sharper focus in terms of poverty.

In the Old Testament the emphasis fell predominantly on justice, which was the bulwark of the people against economic and sociological poverty. In the New Testament the emphasis shifts in a subtle but crucial way from justice to community. Or more exactly, justice is subsumed in an ideal of community. Israel was a community of blood to begin with and therefore caring for all members, especially the poor or needy, was a self-evident obligation in justice. However, Jesus formed around himself a new people, a New Israel that was not bound together in any natural way. From the very beginning this group of disciples understood themselves as a new kind of "family," united not by blood or ethnicity or Law or shared enterprise. Faith in Jesus, crucified, risen, and present in their midst, bound them together. They were those who "heard the word of God and kept it." In this community there were to be not only no poor but no divisions, no hierarchy, no less or more honorable members. No one was to be excluded, marginalized, considered a stranger or unclean. This vision of community was the context within which the new Christians understood Jesus' teaching and practice and committed themselves to following him on the way and promoting what he called the Reign of God.

The community Jesus founded was one without classes based on power, status, privilege, wealth, gender, race, talent, or any other "possession." But rather than trying to achieve equality by raising everyone to the level of the most highly placed, this community would achieve equality by the willing abasement of everyone. Jesus' disciples were to "seek the lowest place" (cf. Luke 14:10), to seek to be the "servant of all" in imitation of the one who was among them as one who served (cf. Mark 9:35; Matt 20:27; 23:11; Luke 22:24–27; John 13:1–15). This totally new ideal of community at the "bottom" rather than striving for the "top" was rooted in God's *kenosis* in Jesus. God in Jesus laid aside the prerogatives of divinity in order to become one with, equal to, his brothers and sisters. They in turn are to have his mind in them, laying aside all claims to superiority in order to become one in the community he called into being.

The role of possessions, always a primary mediator of human relationships, was critical in this new community. It is here that we see the continuity and the newness of Jesus' teaching in relation to his Jewish background. Both the first and the second great commandments, Jesus said, require that his disciples "renounce all their possessions." First, they are to love the Lord their God *with their whole being.* God alone is to be their treasure, the lodestone of their hearts. Consequently, Mammon—possessions of any kind to which one is attached—has to be completely and definitively dethroned. "Renouncing all" is the nonnegotiable requirement of discipleship because nothing may compete with God.

Second, they are to love their neighbors *as themselves.* Those who have renounced all are radically equal among themselves in their empty-handedness, their non-possession. Behaviorally, this means sharing, the holding of all things in common which Luke says characterized the first community in Jerusalem. As we have seen, this is not necessarily incarnated in a community living under one roof and literally sharing a common purse. It is often expressed in free almsgiving to those in need, in hospitality that excludes no one, in reciprocal sharing of time, talent, and resources, and in mutual service unto the laying down of one's life for one's friends, that is, for those to whom the disciples relate, as Jesus related to them (cf. John 15:15). The point is that "no one considers anything her/his own" but all see themselves as stewards of God's good gifts intended for all. Poverty of spirit, in other words, in the Christian context is not an obligation in justice, an ascetical challenge, or a philosophical ideal. *It is the root of community life* among the people who have become "family," not by blood or ethnicity or any other ties except those of faith and love. The community so formed is the place of the emergence in this world of the Reign of God.

Chapter Five
Evangelical Poverty

An Alternate Approach to Goods and Possession

I. Transition and Introduction

As we turn our attention explicitly to the second vow, evangelical poverty, which I will discuss in terms of the construction of the alternate world of the Reign of God, it may be helpful to consolidate what has been established so far. First, in part 1, chapter 1 of this volume we looked carefully at the meaning of "world" and saw that in Scripture this term is highly polyvalent. The world that God created through the Word includes not only the natural universe but the human race which God so loved as to give the Word made flesh for its salvation. This world came forth from the creative hand of God who declared it "very good." But this originally good Creation is shaped throughout history by humanity into "world" in another sense, namely, the imaginative construction of reality either according to the coordinates of the divine plan into the Reign of God, a peaceable community of justice and love, or according to the coordinates of the Kingdom of Satan,[1] a destructive regime of hatred, violence, and greed.

These two diametrically opposed projects are intimately intertwined in human history and difficult to distinguish, much less separate. Jesus described this situation in the allegory of the weeds among the wheat (Matt 13:24–31; 36–43):

"The Reign of God is like a householder who sowed good seed in his field. While everyone was asleep his enemy came and sowed weeds all through the wheat....The slaves of the householder came to him and said, 'Master, did you not sow good seed in your field? Where have the weeds come from?' He answered, 'An enemy has done this.' His slaves said to him, 'Do you want us to go and pull them up?' He replied, 'No, if you pull up the weeds you might uproot the wheat along with them....'"

His disciples approached him and said, "Explain to us the parable of the weeds in the field." He said..."The one who sows good seed is the Son of Man, the field is the world, the good seed the children of the kingdom. The weeds are the children of the evil one, and the enemy who sows them is the devil. The harvest is the end of the age..." [my translation].

Although the allegory is somewhat elliptical in its one-to-one correspondences, the basic message is clear. The field is the world in the basically good sense described above. It is a fertile field that will produce according to what is sown in it. There are two "sowers," two agents at work in the field. One, Jesus, sows good seed and the other, the devil, sows bad seed. The former seed produces wheat and the latter weeds: respectively, the children of God and the children of Satan.

For our purposes, the important point is that the two kinds of seed grow together and any purist attempt to simply eliminate the evil will inevitably eliminate also much that is good. Until the "end of the age," the two will be necessarily intertwined. Thus, the work of believers will be not to achieve a swift and definitive victory of good over evil but to constantly discern what to foster and what to subvert and how to do this. It is the "children" of light or of darkness who will be the forces for good or for evil in the field of this world. Both the Reign of God and the Kingdom of the Evil One are simultaneously at work in and through the institutional structures and systems of human history, which influence and are influenced by the moral choices of human beings as individuals and as groups.

The role of all people of good will is to make this world a fit-

ting home for all creatures by the progressive advance of good
and subversion of evil. Christians see this as promotion of the
coming of the Reign of God and the final defeat of Satan's
kingdom. For Christians this is a "paschal project," rooted in
the Resurrection of Jesus who, seemingly destroyed by Satan's
evil power in the crucifixion, rose to new and indestructible life
which will finally be shared with all God's good Creation.

This project of life emerging from death is the establishment
in this world of the values and priorities built into reality by
Creation and Incarnation including the affirmation of history,
materiality, and particularity as we saw in chapter 1. The flourishing of Creation including the participation of all humans in
the eternal life of God is the divine intention to which Christians commit themselves when, in baptism, they renounce
Satan and all his works, die with Christ to the dynamics of the
evil reality construction we call "sin," and rise with him to new,
divine life. Thus all Christians (in union with all people of
good will but in a particular way, that is, within the framework
of the paschal mystery of Christ, as we saw in chapter 3) are missioned by God to participate in Jesus' work of defeating evil
and bringing to fruition God's good Creation, including
humanity.

Second, in chapter 2 of part 1 we looked specifically at the
identity of Religious who participate in the mission of all Christians but in a distinctive way. By the choice of *lifelong consecrated
celibacy* in response to a personally discerned, charismatic vocation, they have chosen to give themselves to God in the Risen
Christ to the exclusion of any other primary life commitment
such as marriage and family.

This essentially unitive or mystical vocation to the celibate
God-quest, which involves the choice not to focus their affectivity primarily on an individual human being, family, work, or
project, involves Religious in a particular way in that new family
Jesus founded, which is based not in biological, social, economic, political, or other human relationships, but in faith.
The primary, immediate affective context of the Religious is
the "kinship without fathers" (cf. Luke 8:21) of those who hear
the word of God and keep it (cf. Luke 8:19–21; 11:27–28). So

from the beginning, Religious have formed communities reflective of this transcendent and all-embracing relationship. *Transcendent community*, whether lived in its eremitical or cenobitical form, flows directly from the celibate commitment.

Third, in chapter 3 of part 1 we discussed how Religious, because of their life choice of celibate consecration, also appropriate in a distinctive way the mission to the world into which all Christians are inaugurated by baptism. For Religious, *full-time and universal ecclesial ministry* is their characteristic expression of that mission. It is specified, as we will see later, by the charism of the particular Congregation to which the Religious belongs, but it begins with Profession and ends with death embracing the totality of their time, gifts, life-energy, and commitment. It is specifically and explicitly Christian, a preaching of the Gospel to all creatures.

In volume 2 of *Religious Life in a New Millennium: Selling All* I explored the first two of these characteristics, namely, consecrated celibacy and transcendent community, as the constitutive relational coordinates of Religious Life. In this volume, we are concerned specifically with the third, namely, *mission to and ministry in the world*. Parts 2 and 3 of this volume are concerned with evangelical poverty and prophetic obedience as, respectively, the economics and the politics of the "alternate world" that Religious create through the Profession of the vows. In other words, consecrated celibacy and the transcendent community it grounds bring into existence a new context for baptismal life, but how that life is lived, day to day, and how it gives rise to a particular approach to ministry is still to be explored.

In the previous chapter, we explored the biblical data on poverty that will inform this and the following chapter on evangelical poverty as the economics of the "alternate world" of Religious Life and the spirituality of those who inhabit that world. In light of Scripture it is clear that the vow of evangelical poverty that Religious make must be clearly distinguished from destitution or the involuntary lack of the material resources necessary for a genuinely human life. Indeed, evangelical poverty involves a commitment to the abolition of material destitution, which is an evil not intended by God and inimical to human dignity. On the other hand, Scripture supplies rich resources for developing a spirituality of poverty as an original Gospel approach to material goods, which, in turn, has implications, both for the community and the individual Religious within it and, through their ministry, for the world.

In this chapter, we will explore the corporate dimension of Religious poverty, that is, how poverty structures the Religious community itself as a distinctive lifeform in the Church, governs its functioning in relationship to material goods, and influences its mission and ministry. In other words, we will be looking at how evangelical poverty, corporately embraced, helps create the "alternate world" within which Religious live and from which they minister. The role of evangelical poverty in the personal transformation of the Religious as an individual will be the subject of the final chapter of this part.[2]

II. Creating the Alternate World

All Christians are involved in the struggle for "world" inaugurated by the life, death, and Resurrection of Jesus in which the victory of God over Satan was realized. Jesus' paschal mystery is the principle of the Christian enterprise. It establishes definitively that eternal life comes through death, not through death as a natural biological process but through the death "that should not be" which results from the refusal to integrate one's life into the reality construction of Satan. It is the death that Jesus accepted in principle when he refused to "fall down and worship" Satan in exchange for position and power in Satan's world.

Jesus did not die a natural death. He was executed because he subverted the oppressive political, economic, social, and religious systems of his society by preaching good news to the poor and opening his table fellowship to all, especially to those whom the religious and political authorities excluded. The followers of Jesus continue to risk and accept death in their effort to realize in this world the Reign of God which Jesus announced, the discipleship of equals in which all are welcome and cared for, and in which all flourish. Until the Reign of God is realized on earth as it is in heaven, until all Creation, and especially human beings, can experience the infinite *shalom* of God, the struggle between the Prince of This World and the true Prince of Peace will be waged in and by the followers of Jesus in collaboration with all people of good will. However, as we discussed in chapter 3, different members of the glorified Christ, living in different states of life or lifeforms, participate in this struggle in different ways. Our question, then, is what is the distinctive way Religious participate in this enterprise?

A. Profession as Creation of the Alternate World

By way of anticipatory summary, *Religious participate in the struggle for the Reign of God by creating, living in, and ministering from an "alternate world."* Again, this world is not a geographical place, an institution, or a specific group of people. "World" is a particular reality construction, a complex, global interpretation of reality within which we coordinate our thinking, feeling, choosing, acting. Specifically, the imaginative construction of reality, the world, is primarily a certain way of understanding, organizing, and operating within and upon the basic coordinates of all human life: namely material goods, power, and sexuality. Material goods which we humans relate to in terms of *possession*, power which we exercise through *freedom*, and sexuality which we construct and express through *relationship* are, in their interaction, the "raw material" which humans shape into "world," as they work out their destinies, personal and corporate, in history.

The distinctiveness of Religious Life as a lifeform arises from the members' public, lifelong commitment by Profession of the vows to a characteristic approach to these three coordinates of "world," relationship (through consecrated celibacy), material goods (through evangelical poverty), power (through prophetic obedience). This approach creates a particular, concrete, twenty-four hours a day, seven days a week sociological reality that is a realization of the Reign of God. In other words, by Profession Religious create a "world" that is fundamentally Christian, that is, a paschal reality, in uncompromising opposition to the world-construction of Satan. But it is also distinctive in relation to the ways other Christians, for example, married people, single people, or clerics organize their Christian lives to foster the Reign of God.

Recalling the discussion of the subject in *Selling All*,[3] Profession is the formal, solemn, and public act by which individuals, through their total, exclusive self-commitment to Christ, integrate the totality of their personal life into the reality construction that began in the charismatic vision of a founder or foundress and has been lived into reality by generations of Religious within a particular Congregation. By their personal and corporate living of the vows Religious create the distinctive and characteristic lifeform, the alternate world, by which they participate with Christians called to other states of life in the Church's mission of witnessing to and realizing the Reign of God in this world.

Religious Profession had been understood in modern times, especially since the 1917 Code of Canon Law,[4] within a highly juridical framework as the assumption of narrowly defined supererogatory obligations. In reality, Profession is not primarily about obligations or practices even though it entails such. Profession is a global life commitment. Like marriage, which inaugurates a shared lifeform of monogamous self-donation between spouses and primary commitment to their relationship and to their children, Profession is an orientation of one's whole person, life, and history, through choices made in relation to material goods, power, and personal, sexually expressed relationships, within the context of the transcendent community toward the realization, by particular means, of the Reign of God in this world. It is a specification of their baptismal[5] commitment, the commitment by which all Christians renounce Satan and all his works (i.e., die to sin) and choose to live as disciples of Jesus and participants in his mission. The specification of that baptismal commitment which Religious make by Profession is a total self-gift, not merely a restriction on specific behaviors in arcane arenas of a medieval lifestyle.

The vows, no matter which ones are made in particular Congregations,[6] are Gospel-based global metaphors for the stance

Religious take toward the fundamental coordinates of human existence, that is, relationships, material goods, and power. It is through these performative metaphors that Religious imagine and construct the living parable of Religious Life as alternate world. Like Jesus' parables, which often began with, "The Reign of God is like…," the vows not only describe but narratively generate a different world, not just a different way of living in this world.[7] The world of Jesus' parables is the Reign of God. Christians in different states of life give particular shape to their participation in this new world. In this chapter we are concerned with how Religious, through the vow of evangelical poverty, try to tell this story into reality, to generate a particular and distinctive version of the Reign of God and offer it in and through the Church as a real possibility, a future full of hope, to the world in which they live.

B. Characteristics of the Alternate World: Utopianism and World Involvement

Two characteristics of the alternate world that Religious construct are particularly important today. First, the world-construction of Religious has always been frankly **utopian**, an attempt to incarnate in a concrete lifeform a religious and spiritual ideal which is largely at odds with contemporary culture. But in earlier times utopian projects, whether religious, political, or social, were easier to understand because most people lived in relatively unified and stable social units such as family, parish, neighborhood, school, or workplace for which some ideal image existed. Any contemporary utopian project, however, is particularly challenged by the homogenization of life styles and expectations generated by globalization and by postmodernism's suspicion of all unitary projects and metanarratives.[8] In other words, constructing a "lifeform," let alone a utopian one, is a highly suspect project in the contemporary context. Religious Life as a state of life or a lifeform, especially one undertaken by perpetual commitment, does not "make sense" to most of our contemporaries as it once did even to those who disagreed with the specific values around which the life was organized. Hence, Religious have more need now than in the past to know and to be able to articulate what they are doing and why.

Second, in the aftermath of the Council the "total institution" model of Religious Life had to be and was deconstructed[9] in favor of the **full involvement in the human enterprise** that the Council recognized as the vocation of the Church and therefore of Religious.[10] Today, Religious are no longer protected by the isolation of their lifeform from the mainstream of society and culture. They are faced with the gravity, scope, and difficulty of constructing and living this ideal or utopian lifeform within the larger society. Consequently, Religious are challenged to rearticulate the nature of their venture and to commit themselves explicitly to pursuing it in the very midst of this ambiguous situation within human history, in cultures and social settings which are structured to a large extent by the satanic dynamics of sexual exploitation, economic oppression, and political domination, locked in mortal struggle, armed with initiatives (religious and nonreligious) that promote right relationships among all God's creatures.

III. Structure and Dynamics of the Alternate Economic World

At the beginning of chapter 4, I discussed the conundrum and impasse experienced by contemporary Religious in relation to the vow of poverty. As noted, one of the causes of this malaise is that the lives of Religious often seem very similar, materially, to that of many living in first world culture. Religious have adequate housing, drive modest but safe cars, receive pay checks for their work, eat decent meals, handle credit cards and bank accounts in their own names, go to films and museums and take vacations, and dress appropriately for their environment and work. They live within a budget, but so do most middle-class people. And erstwhile practices such as asking permissions for small objects or picayune sums of money now seem almost quaint. More strenuous efforts at solidarity with the poor such as fasting, vegetarianism, volunteering in shelters and soup kitchens, or living among the materially disadvantaged are choices by Congregations or personal choices of individual Religious rather than obligations of the life itself.

In short, Religious Life does not seem to differ significantly from that of people who do not make a vow of poverty. If poverty is purely an interior disposition (as "poverty of spirit" is sometimes misunderstood to mean), why make it the object of a vow, since the first beatitude calls all Christians to such a disposition? What prophetic valence does the evangelical poverty of Religious have? And how can it be considered constitutive (with consecrated celibacy, prophetic obedience, transcendent community, and corporate ministry) of an "alternate world"?

As we saw in chapter 4, the poverty Religious vow is not destitution, either absolute or voluntary, nor the disempowerment and even death that destitution entails. Rather Religious vow Gospel or evangelical poverty. I find Dorothee Soëlle's term, *possessionlessness*,[11] an apt descriptive name for this freely chosen condition that is a positive response to Jesus' challenge to the rich man who had kept all the commandments: "You lack one thing; go, sell what you own, and give the money to the poor...and then come, follow me" (Mark 10:21). Dispossess yourself entirely, Jesus says, and join me in my homeless, itinerant lifestyle of preaching good news to the poor and doing God's saving works in the world. The model of Religious poverty is not the poor of our inner cities or the destitute on the streets of Calcutta but the band of disciples who followed Jesus. However, we also are not seeking to mimic a first-century lifestyle.[12] Nor are we seeking some timeless formula for the practice of poverty which will be equally applicable in all cultural settings. We are trying to discern what following Jesus in possessionlessness means today, especially for Religious in economically richer contexts.[13]

It is important to insist, here and for all that follows, that the poverty we are talking about is real possessionlessness, not merely simplicity of lifestyle, sharing, self-control, responsibility in the use of material goods, or even solidarity with the materially poor, although all of these should be part of our practice of the vow. This is why I have argued in other contexts for retaining the term "poverty." To be really without possessions is to be poor. On the other hand, if we are not really without possessions, then we should probably name differently whatever particular practice or attitude we do intend to embrace. So, we begin by asking what it means to be literally without possessions. How can we accomplish that? What effect does it have? In other words, what is possessionlessness and what is its prophetic valence?

A. The Object of the Vow of Poverty: Material Goods

Poverty, obviously, has something to do with material goods, things that Jesus implies can be owned, sold, given away. We are in the domain of that which can be possessed as property, that which we can have as our own, and that which if possessed by one person cannot be simultaneously possessed by another. Material goods are the primary (although not the only or ultimate) object of evangelical poverty. We might speak about status, reputation, knowledge, love, and so on, as "possessions" but this is an analogous use of the term because spiritual goods cannot be actually owned as private property. It is important to keep our focus on the primary analogate, material reality, lest our speculations become diffuse and falsely "spiritualized"; that is, purely theoretical.

B. Handling Material Goods: Economy

The composite of materials, attitudes, behaviors, policies, and so on governing the handling of material goods in a society constitutes what we call its economy. There are different ways to organize these elements. We can talk about a barter economy, an industrial economy, a technological economy, a service economy, a capitalist economy, a global economy, and so on. But these political-economic systems are the epiphenomena of deeper dynamics. Lewis Hyde, a startlingly original and profound cultural analyst of our day, in his oft-reprinted book *The Gift*,[14] says that there are essentially two kinds of economies: those based on *having* and those based on *being*, that is, commodity economies and gift economies.

1. The commodity economy: the primacy of having

In an economy of having, material realities are looked upon and evaluated as **commodities** to be acquired for private use. First world capitalist-market economy, probably the most completely commodified economy in Western history, manifests the salient features of an economy of having.[15] In such an economy the primary objective of economic activity is *acquisition*, that is, taking as much of the available goods as possible out of circulation into private ownership.[16] This includes not only food, clothes, real property, and money, but even the sources of raw materials and the means of production. Land, water, seeds, minerals, factories, and businesses and all that these may be used to produce are the legitimate objects of acquisition and that which they produce becomes, through money paid for them, a "second generation" of private property.

Basic to the primary objective of acquisition is the *right to private property*, which is considered as natural and as inviolable as the right to life.[17] Indeed it is more sacred than the right to life in some societies in which one can justifiably kill a person in defense of one's property. The right to life of the robber or even the trespasser is secondary to the right of the owner to protect his or her material property.

In a commodity economy the *good life* is primarily a function of what one has. Luxury for its own sake, having more or better than one needs, is an index of well-being. But perhaps more importantly, *status* in a commodity economy depends on what one possesses. Wealth is a public statement of one's worth. Often the primary indicator of a person's identity and worth is the earning power of their occupation or their family financial background.[18] The rich are important and powerful; the middle class are in the business of becoming rich(er); the poor are unimportant except as a nuisance factor, a drain on the prosperity of the rich.

The commodity economy is *radically individualistic*. The ideal is to be economically independent and therefore always able to take care of "oneself and one's own" without depending on others and, often, no matter what happens to others. Even though in fact a commodity economy entails tremendous real (though hidden) dependence—which is clearly demonstrated by a power failure which disrupts every element of a society from top to bottom, or by a fluctuation in the market which can bankrupt a millionaire overnight—the illusory conviction of complete independence is sedulously cultivated.[19] No one wants to ask for help, even in adverse circumstances completely beyond one's control, because need is a primary indicator of weakness and inferiority. People want to have not only their own home on their own land but their own entertainment center, sports facilities, a car for each member of the household, and even an independent fallout shelter stocked with emergency supplies. The denizens of the commodity economy oscillate between extensive real dependence and a cultivated illusion of independence. What they fear most of all is interdependence with its implications of relationship and mutual responsibility.

A commodity economy, because of its material character, is *zero-sum based.* There is only so much; what one person has another cannot have and vice versa. Consequently, each must defend what s/he has lest s/he become poorer as the other becomes richer. Defense of one's possessions, or the effort to acquire what another possesses that one needs or wants, leads to competition, and almost inevitably to interpersonal conflict or international war.

A commodity economy, in other words, is always an economy of *scarcity.* No matter how much there is, even when the glut overflows into endless landfills and things cannot be disposed of quickly enough to make room for the latest versions, there is always the possibility that there will not be enough. Consequently, hoarding "against a rainy day" requires acquiring what one does not need now and may never need but theoretically might need at some future time. Insatiable greed and its behavioral manifestation in rampant consumerism masquerades as prudence and foresight, although at times (e.g., during the Reagan era in the United States) it has been frankly lauded and recommended as an admirable trait. The market economy depends on incessant economic growth, which in turn depends on generating pseudo-needs and programming obsolescence into products that will have to be replaced long before they are worn out.

The hallmark of the commodity economy is that possessions own their owners. Having has overtaken being as the criterion of genuine humanity. Such an economy, based on the self-contradictory premise that material reality can be expanded indefinitely without self-destructing, is a tiger whose tail one cannot release because letting go is at least as dangerous as hanging on.

2. The gift economy: the primacy of being

In contrast to the commodity economy is the gift economy, in which being has priority over having. In an economy of being material realities are looked upon primarily as **gifts**, first as that which one has freely received from God, community, family, or benefactors, and then as that which one can share or give away. Even today some primal and tribal societies operate much more as gift economies than commodity economies. Communism as well as many other utopian experiments in community have tried to establish gift economies and many of these experiments have failed precisely because of the economic implications of their attempts at community. In a few cases, such as among the Amish,[20] the success of the community model has been extraordinary and has evoked wonder if not imitation in the surrounding society.

In a gift economy members of the community use goods but do not own them, or, if they do own such things as their dwelling, tools, clothing, and such, they possess only what is necessary and *no one possesses as private property the resources that everyone needs,* such as land, air, water, food, and shelter. To hoard more than one needs or attempt to take possession of the common goods is obscene and socially despised, especially when other members of the community are in need.

Therefore, *mutuality and interdependence* rather than complete independence is the preferred way of relating. In other words, the gift economy is primarily *communitarian* rather than individualistic. As long as the community has what is necessary everyone in the community will be cared for. Each person's well-being affects everyone else's, so members of the community have no need to defend their possessions against the predation of other members. The door can be left unlocked and the keys in the car. Going to war within the community over goods does not make sense.

Scarcity may well be a concern in a gift economy and most such societies have experienced cycles of serious want. But *scarcity is a communal concern* rather than a private disgrace. Everyone has a right to what s/he needs and no one has a right to more than s/he needs. *Greed is disgraceful and hoarding is dishonorable.* Furthermore, such a society is basically economically egalitarian. No one has a markedly lower standard of living because s/he cannot earn or produce, even though all are expected to work for the common good. And no one has a markedly higher standard of living because of what s/he can produce. What one does not need is meant to be shared.

Status in such a society is based on who one is, not on what one has. One's primary contribution to the society is oneself and only secondarily what one can do or produce. Thus children, who are by definition nonproducers, are precious and to be cared for by the society as a whole, and elders who have contributed to the community over many years, especially if they are wise and generous, are honored well beyond the time when they can produce, defend, or even actively lead the community.

The hallmark of a community of gift is that material goods are means to communal ends and those ends are not derived from the economy. Material well-being is important in any society but in a gift economy it is not the *raison d'être* of individual or social life. Material goods are in service of life lived in relationship, not vice versa.

In summary, the basic contrast between a commodity and a gift economy is in how material goods are viewed and thus in the economic activity which governs and mediates relationships in the community. In an economy of having the fundamental economic activity is acquiring, that is, taking goods out of circulation into private ownership. In an economy of being the basic economic activity is contributing to the common good. Material goods are like blood in the social body. As long as they are kept in circulation, the whole social body is nourished. When they pool up in one place, the deprived parts begin to wither and die and the place of accumulation becomes swollen and dysfunctional. In other words, these two kinds of economies are not intrinsically equal. The choice of one or the other tilts the society toward the reality construction of the Reign of God or toward that of the Prince of This World.

C. The Gospel Ideal of the Human Relation to Material Goods

A little reflection suggests that the Gospel ideal of the human relation to material goods is essentially that of a gift economy rather than a commodity economy. First world market capitalism and analogous systems are commodity economies. In other words, from the economic standpoint the Reign of God is a gift economy and the reigning economic system of the context in which first world Religious live is much closer to the reality construction of the Prince of This World. However, a blanket condemnation of the reigning economic system of the first world or the people who participate in it would violate the observations already made: namely, that the values of the Reign of God and of the Kingdom of Satan are intimately intertwined in the field of this world in which "wheat" and "weeds" cannot be apodictically identified and separated. Furthermore, such a condemnation would suggest that no one living willingly in this economic system is struggling against its deleterious features and effects, or that no Christian could live the Gospel in this context.

As we saw in chapter 4 in relation to Luke's community and the Pauline communities, there are Christian ways to live in this world without either forming an alternate community or surrendering to the pursuit of Mammon that Jesus condemned. However, it is clear enough that the operative priorities, predominant motives, and ordinary procedures of first world economy as a system are based on acquisition. Private property interests rather than the common good are more likely to drive its political decisions and financial operations. The world to which Religious "die" by Profession, whose economy they reject definitively by the vow of poverty, is precisely the economic system based on the primacy of having and the commitment to an ever-expanding economy in which the rich get richer and the poor get poorer, in practice if not necessarily in principle.[21] The world Religious espouse is the communitarian, relationship-based economy of gift. The way they choose to live this commitment, by the creation of and living in an alternate economic world rather than by resistance to the commodity economy from within the world, makes the life itself a distinct reality in the Church.[22]

An important Gospel passage makes it strikingly clear that the world that is the Reign of God is governed by different economic priorities than is the commodity economy. Probably the Gospel parable that makes its economically secure hearers most uncomfortable, even angry, is the parable of the Eleventh Hour Workers in Matthew 20:1–16. What most upsets people is that the vineyard owner, who seems to represent God, pays the workers he sent into his vineyard at 5:00 p.m. the same amount he pays those who have worked since dawn, bearing the burden of the day's heat. And he does not just discreetly slip the 5:00 p.m. shift a little something extra under the table because he feels sorry for them. He lines everyone up in reverse order to the time of their hiring so that the dawn workers will see that the evening workers are getting exactly the same as they are, that all are getting the same pay no matter how long they have worked.

It is important to note what they are all paid: a "day's wage," or enough to live. The dawn workers did not receive more nor the evening workers less than they needed. What each is given is what each needs. Goods are distributed according to need, not according to "merit." The vineyard owner is the God who makes rain fall on the just and the unjust, who gives what we need, not what we earn or deserve, and who commands us to do likewise (cf. Matt 5:45).

When the early workers complain that this is unjust the vineyard owner replies specifically in terms of gift. "Am I not allowed to do what I choose with what belongs to me? Or are you envious because I am *generous*?" (Matt 20:15 [emphasis added]). The workers, says the owner, are talking about justice, but humans have no claim on God in justice because everything they have is God's gift, including their being, life, strength to work, and the task in which they are engaged. That every human have enough to sustain life is not only a matter of divine justice but more importantly of divine gift. The world God created is one in which all creatures are meant to flourish. God does not say that work is unimportant, nor that commutative justice is irrelevant. Adam was commissioned to work from the day of his creation (cf. Gen 2:15). The vineyard owner does not want anyone standing around idle, even for the last hour of the workday (cf. Matt 20:6–7). He sends everyone into the field to do as much as they are able to do in the time they have. But we humans do not earn our way with God nor does God value us because of what we have or produce. People have a right to what they need to live, regardless of their capacity to work. We cooperate with God in producing what everyone needs so that everyone, the first and the last, will receive from God what they need whether they are able to do much or little, provided they make the contribution they can.[23]

It is hard to imagine a more radical subversion of first world economic wisdom than this uncoupling of the right to survival from earning power and its attachment to divine gift. God intends that all people, no matter when or even if they entered the "work force" or how much they can or do contribute, have both "what is just" (i.e., what they need) and "divine generosity." The equation of divine justice with divine gift is a basic subversion of our "you get what you earn" and "you pay your way" economics.

IV. Living in the Alternate World: Community and Ministry in a Gift Economy

Religious Life, if it is really an alternate world whose economy is in stark contrast to, rather than being a modestly pious reflection of, the capitalist market economy, must be founded in and function from deep convictions and real historical choices derived from the Gospel. American films about convent life which now appear somewhat naïve often reflected a perception that can be instructive of Religious as living in a "different world."

In these movies hardened mobsters, shamed by ethereally wise nuns, returned their ill-gotten goods; selfish business tycoons generously endowed the local Catholic grade school; the mercenary bishop yielded to Mother Superior's trust in divine providence which produced the needed funds just in time to bail the parish out of debt and keep the school open; and everything ended happily for all concerned. The message was that a faith-approach to material goods actually worked, even in a hard-nosed commodity economy. These movies made good Catholic theater because, in fact, the real nuns who were the models for the film characters actually lived lives that were economically very different from those of their contemporaries. They actually did appear, certainly to Catholics but also to others, to have a proper estimation of the real but non-ultimate importance of money and its appropriate role in promoting good rather than evil, and to be right about the true focus of trust in the face of adversity: God rather than Mammon.

This perception of Religious as people living in a different economic world was based on what the ordinary Catholic knew of convent life. Religious survived on "wages" that were actually low-grade allowances and included no health insurance or retirement benefits. Somehow, they not only survived in active ministry but also educated their newer members and cared for their elderly. They lived without complaint in whatever housing was provided for them. They worked, usually at least six days a week, often carrying "extra" ministries such as tutoring or giving private lessons to supplement the community's meager income, and they usually (unlike their clerical counterparts) did not only their own domestic tasks of cleaning, cooking, and laundry in the convent, but often the janitorial and business work of the school or hospital as well. They depended on free-will contributions of everything from dental services to repair work in the convent and accepted gratefully the yield of canned goods collections, bake sales, Christmas donations, and in-kind "tuition" from poorer families. They were never seen at "worldly" entertainment such as movies or restaurants where money might be "wasted" on nonessentials like recreation. And, of course, their uniform dress obviated any need for expenditures on personal appearance.

For all kinds of socioeconomic and religious reasons this system of ministry by Religious to basically Catholic clienteles worked. It was even spiced by a certain hand-to-mouth excitement factor that looked more romantic than it really was. It was not hard to believe that, economically, Religious lived in "another world" from that of ordinary people, a world in which total dependence on God combined with plucky ingenuity somehow made ends meet in a way that seldom seemed to work in the "real world" of ordinary people facing doctor's bills, mortgages, children in trouble, and lost jobs.

In the wake of the Council, a number of mutually interacting factors drastically changed this scene. The sudden decline in numbers of Religious, the closing of many Catholic institutions, the entrance of Catholic laity into the mainstream of American life with the resulting dispersal of Catholics from ethnically based parishes and dependence on Catholic institutions and services, among other factors, made this highly-unusual economic system that had sustained Religious Orders and their institutions for decades completely unworkable.

Parishes could no longer afford to maintain a convent built for twenty Religious teaching in the parish grade school for three Religious, none of whom was working full time in the parish. Nor could the three who now traveled daily from the parish to full-time ministries elsewhere maintain the twenty-room convent in their "spare time." Religious now needed employment that would support at least themselves and, it was hoped, help support the Congregation and its un- or under-funded elderly or ill members. They now needed to pay for food, medical services, professional development, clothes, housing, transportation and other necessities that could no longer be obtained through the former system of minimized needs, massive overwork, contributed services, free will offerings, and barter.

The *Bells of Saint Mary's* economic system was no longer workable, but its very-understandable replacement by Religious as paid workers in various religious and secular forms of employment has raised, for both Religious and laity, a new question: what difference does a vow of poverty now make? Jokes about Religious making the vow and other people living it are only partly facetious and often mask a mild resentment of the claims Religious make about their life which seems, at least economically, to be more like that of their neighbors than different. In fact, Religious are frequently better educated than other people, especially women, of their background, travel more extensively, and seem to have the resources such as clothes, cars, computers, and decent living quarters that many people in our society lack. Such comparisons, although superficial at best and substantively invalid when examined closely, do challenge Religious to go much deeper in their self-understanding as well as in the way they present their life to others, not in order to justify it or themselves but to release its full prophetic power in the world.

Evangelical poverty, as we will see, does indeed have very real and profound implications, both behavioral and spiritual, for the community dimension of Religious Life as well as for the mission and ministry of Religious. It also, as a particular appropriation of the poverty of spirit extolled by the first beatitude, has implications for their personal spiritual life. Our concern in this chapter is with the first two dimensions: community and ministry which both contribute to the influence of Religious Life in the transformation of society. The third, the role of poverty in the spiritual life of Religious as individuals, will be the topic of the next chapter.

A. Community in the Alternate Economic World

1. Possessionlessness and total interdependence

a. DIVESTMENT

Religious Life begins, economically, with a *total material self-divestment*. Just before Profession, the novice disposes definitively of the administration, use, and revenue (formerly called *usufruct*) of all her personal property (formerly called patrimony); declares that, even if she should leave Religious Life, she will never claim to have earned anything that the Congregation would then owe her; and makes a will that disposes at her death of anything she now owns or which might have been added to her personal property during her life by inheritance or gift. Henceforth, although there are prudent provisions in Canon Law protecting the personal property of Religious,[24] the understanding embodied in these legal arrangements is that the professed Religious will have no further role in the handling of any personal property and no independent access to it or anything it might generate.[25] She can acquire nothing in her own name since anything she acquires as a member of the Institute belongs to the Institute. Anything she receives in her own name, for example, inheritance from relatives, must be handled the same way property owned prior to Profession is handled. In short, she has no independent access to private property, nor can she exercise independent control over even that property that is held in her name by another, either by the Congregation or by someone else.

This public, legal self-divestment is as dramatic in content and intent (though not in staging!) as Francis's stripping off the rich clothes his father had given him and renouncing his inheritance before the bishop in the piazza of Assisi. In one radical act the new Religious becomes effectively possessionless.[26] Thus, a person entering Religious Life from a wealthy family or after building up significant savings has no more access to money or anything it can buy, to real estate, to health or retirement benefits, to any source of funds for education, travel, entertainment, or even as a capacity for gift-giving than a person who enters young, from a poor family, without earnings or savings or connections of any kind.

b. Lifelong mutuality and interdependence

The effect of this initial act of self-divestment by which all members of the community become possessionless is the creation of a community of economic equals who pledge themselves to a *lifelong mutuality and interdependence* in regard to everything that materially sustains and affects life. This community, however middle class it may look to outsiders, is firmly based in an alternate economy, namely a radical economy of gift, in which private ownership of property, which is the lifeblood of a commodity economy, plays no role at all. All that the Religious will have or use for the rest of her life will come to her from the community and everything that she produces or acquires will belong to the community. She will share the well-being of the community in times of prosperity but also its experience of scarcity, debt, or even penury in times of want. Her use of material goods—her housing, transportation, clothing, food, spiritual and educational opportunities, recreation, travel, and everything else that requires monetary support—will be determined by the common arrangements of the Congregation governed by its Constitutions, policies, and customs as administered by Congregational leadership.

Ideally (and there are always struggles to maintain ideals) the determinations made about how any individual in the community receives and uses common resources are not affected by any of the usual sources of economic leverage that operate in secular society. No one in the community has more because she produces more or receives less because she is less able to contribute. A retired member in the infirmary has no less access to health care than a member who is a university president or a major officer in a health care network. Everyone receives according to need and contributes according to ability, whether that contribution is a six-figure salary or the daily prayer and suffering of a ninety-year-old retiree. This, not the uniformity of collective life in the "total institution," is what "common life" means at its most fundamental level.

The contemporary challenges to the actual living of this egalitarian common life of complete economic interdependence and mutuality, that is, to the actual functioning of the Religious community as an economy of gift, arise from the changed circumstances that have individualized many aspects of day-to-day living in postconciliar Congregations. Within the preconciliar total institution model of community in which common life entailed life under the same roof, material uniformity in dress and food, identical ministry, and so on, dependence was the primary behavioral expression of the economy of gift. Everyone contributed to the community everything she earned and received from the community, through permissions and distributions by authority, everything she needed. Indeed, these were the only procedures available for the handling of material goods.

In the immediate postconciliar period, the dissolution of the total institution model of community sometimes gave rise to a fierce spirit of *independence*. Some of this reaction was short-lived and immature experimentation with newfound personal autonomy. However, some of it was not only actually illegal but also seriously subversive of the common life in the gift economy. Ways of generating funds for personal use without consultation with (to say nothing of approval by) Congregational leadership ran from independent use of patrimony and gifts to diverting earnings to personal single-signer bank accounts or secret "slush funds"; running up debt on credit cards that were sometimes not authorized by the Congregation to various kinds of gambling; acquiring real property through clandestine deals with family members or friends to appropriation of retirement benefits, and so on.

Issues that had never been dealt with in preconciliar formation because they were, in effect, practically inoperative suddenly began to surface in the attitudes and behaviors of some Religious. Congregations faced the attitudinal and behavioral fallout of these unaddressed repressed issues, such as financial insecurity and anxiety of members about their personal future and that of the Congregation expressed in attempts to secure independent sources of livelihood; the status attached to spending power; the immature over-dependence and the equally adolescent acting-out of total independence; mistrust, secrecy, and furtiveness in financial dealings with leadership; power dynamics galvanized in those who wielded "the power of the purse" and unresolved authority issues in those on whom it was exercised; scrupulous and fearful, usually resentful, penny-pinching by those who needed to make an external "them" responsible for their own uncertainty and guilt around money; the financial implications of professional hierarchy; choices of recreation and diversion by people who had not participated in normal adult relaxation since they were teenagers; and so on.

Many Religious, individually and as Congregations, have begun to acknowledge and address the issues around money that had simply never surfaced explicitly in preconciliar days when Religious in general had little personal or unsupervised access to or use of it. New policies and procedures that take *realistic account of the fact of individualization* in both ministry and lifestyle have been developed to promote appropriate diversity and individuality while minimizing the privatization that subverts the gift economy.

Congregations have struggled to make their financial affairs as *transparent* as possible in order to rectify both immature ignorance and irresponsibility on the part of members about the real financial challenges facing the Congregation, and the power of secrecy wielded in the past by some superiors. Transparency at the Congregational level, it is hoped, will encourage trust and transparency among the members.

Most importantly, Religious are seeing the necessity of a serious *spiritual transformation* (about which more will be said in the next chapter). Religious, both those who entered before money became a personal issue for most members and those entering today, need to examine deeply the meaning of material goods, and especially money, in human experience in general and in capitalist culture in particular, in order to discern what is going on in their own hearts. Money is the primary motivator in the world that Religious share with the rest of humanity. Especially in capitalist contexts it defines the identity, status, power, rights of participation, privileges, and even the survival of persons who are, in practice if not in principle, subordinate to money in virtually every sphere of life.

The pursuit of wealth controls the imagination of people in economically rich countries from their earliest years. It has sunk deep roots in the consciousness of those who enter Religious Life today long before they reach the novitiate. As children and adolescents, these candidates have owned and spent on a scale undreamt of by any preadult cohort in Western history. Few of them are entering as adolescents who have never worked, saved, or owned, but rather usually as economic adults with significant holdings. They have experienced material ownership as the primary determiner of identity and personal worth. Thus, a profound spiritual conversion is necessary if they are to embrace a gift economy which most of them have never seen in action or perhaps even imagined.

Simply telling the candidate that certain behaviors such as accounting for all expenditures are expected of members is totally inadequate if she does not understand the radical difference between the basic principles of the commodity economy she is leaving and the gift economy she is embracing. If she is not both challenged and assisted to interiorize the Gospel values that underlie the latter she will see financial policies as disciplinary regulations or control mechanisms rather than as the expressions of a radically evangelical approach to material goods. Formation to evangelical poverty, in other words, demands at least as much time and effort as was once devoted to explaining permissions and common work. But most important is the spiritual growth into evangelical poverty of spirit (which we will take up in the next chapter) that will enable the new Religious to enter fully into the reality of the gift economy.

If Religious Life is to be an alternate world in which money does not have the absolutely dominant role it does in the world at large, if it is to witness to the possibility of another way of living together in which resources are for people rather than vice-versa and dignity and rights are nonnegotiable features of shared existence rather than rewards reserved for the wealthy, then the gift economy must be understood, spiritually appropriated, and freely embraced in practice by all the members. This demands the kind of prayerful individual and communal study, discussion, and discernment that postconciliar Religious have devoted to other issues such as identity and ministry, feminist and ecological commitment, and social justice involvement. What Religious *are*, individually and corporately, is at least as important for the world as what they *do*. It is hard to imagine an area in which the witness of the Gospel is more important for the transformation of society into the Reign of God than that of material goods, especially money.

2. Responsibility in the gift economy

One of the salient and admirable characteristics of preconciliar Religious, especially perhaps women Religious, was personal responsibility. The system of preconciliar common life made it difficult if not impossible for an irresponsible individual to survive. Tasks were apportioned in such a way that everyone knew who was responsible for what and daily, even minute-by-minute supervision assured that everything assigned, whether cleaning the stairs or balancing the books or administering the school or hospital, was in fact done. And usually it was done well.

Such individual responsibility exercised by all members in the corporate enterprise was both an exercise of and a witness to the common life in a gift economy in which all contribute according to ability. Needless to say, not all members were equally reflective about the significance of what they were doing in fulfilling assignments of various kinds but because responsibilities were assigned in terms of obedience, most members understood them as intrinsic to the spirituality of the life. And because most Religious never saw any earnings produced by their work, and there was no relationship between what a person did and what she received in the community, most Religious probably did not think of responsibility in terms of the vow of poverty. However, if the economy of gift is the root of the common life of mutual interdependence then a person's contribution to the community's survival and flourishing belongs at least as much to the sphere of poverty as to that of obedience.

As ministries and living situations have become more individualized, responsibility for the common life necessarily is often subordinated in practice to responsibility for oneself, one's personal environment, and one's work. But the gift economy cannot exist in reality unless everyone in the community is personally invested in its well-being. Unlike the mainstream commodity economy, which operates on the principle that if everyone takes care of "number one" all will be taken care of, the gift economy says that if no one gives absolute priority to "number one" all will be cared for.

In a community of mutuality and interdependence, personal responsibility for the corporate enterprise cannot be replaced by a bureaucratic structure that assigns responsibility solely to officers and staff while the membership is occupied elsewhere in private pursuits. On the other hand, it is simply no longer possible to have all members present, as they once were around the refectory table or in the community room, for first-person communication about daily life and ministry. In this respect, Religious Life today is not unlike modern family life, which requires organization, scheduling, apportioning of responsibilities, and mutual accountability. But, although the logistics may be more complicated, corporate responsibility touches upon all the dimensions of the life. Our concern here is with the aspects that are related directly to the vow of evangelical poverty as the basis of common life in a gift economy. Consequently, we will look at two areas of concern: financial responsibility and accountability.

a. FINANCIAL RESPONSIBILITY: LIVING THE COMMON LIFE

One of the paradoxes of financial responsibility is that on the one hand it is expressed in a variety of exterior procedures yet on the other hand it is much more fundamentally concerned with interior dispositions and attitudes than with routines and behaviors. A person can be a model of fulfilling Congregational financial requirements to the letter and yet be in a fundamentally adversarial relationship with the Congregation and its leadership on the subject of money and even in a perpetual state of distrustful resistance to or rebellion against the implications of the vow in her life. And some people whose financial affairs are in a rather continuous state of unintentional disarray are peacefully and profoundly living a spirituality of poverty in a freely embraced common life. Once again, spirituality cannot be reduced to practices.

Although poverty from the standpoint of finances (by which I mean the actual handling of material goods, especially money) can legitimately be approached from numerous angles, I will propose a particular, simplified approach to the topic in hopes of stimulating more nuanced personal and corporate reflection on the subject.

Responsibility has to do with answering, responding, to an "other." To whom and how and for what purpose do we respond when it comes to material goods? I would suggest two practical questions by which to discover our operative answer to this basic question. First, is the community the *primary and real context* of our economic life and behavior? Second, in our attitudes and actions, who *really owns* the things, especially money, about which we normally use the adjective "my," as in "my salary" or "my car"?

There is probably wider variation among Congregations on the subject of material goods than on any other. Canon Law repeatedly consigns issues concerning use of material goods to "particular law," that is, to the provisions in the Constitutions and customs of the particular Institute. Some Congregations, for example, provide no discretionary funds to individual members while others allow a small budget to cover daily needs and others authorize control of rather large amounts of money, the use of credit cards, bank accounts, and so on because of the variety and complexity of members' ministries. So, the major issue is not specific policies and resulting behaviors but basic attitudes that flow from the fundamental possessionlessness undertaken by the vow of evangelical poverty.

The gift economy expressing itself in the economic common life of Religious is based on the assumption that the primary "other" to whom the Religious responds or relates concerning material goods is the Congregation of which she is a vowed member. The person entering Religious Life leaves her primary family, that is, her family of origin, which ceases to be responsible for her. If she is already financially independent she leaves her job or occupation which has provided her support and which she may have used to help support her primary family. As we have already observed, at Profession she divests herself of the administration, use, and revenue of anything she possesses and makes a valid will for the disposal of any property that remains in her name when she dies. In short, she transfers to the Congregation responsibility for everything that pertains to her material support and well-being.[27] And she commits to the Congregation anything and everything which she will acquire as a member or over which she will have any kind of control for the rest of her life. This free choice to be totally without possessions in a community of gift, which the rich man in the Gospel who was challenged to "leave all" to follow Jesus was unable to make, establishes the total mutual economic involvement of the member with the Congregation. This choice, made by every member, is the very foundation of the economy of gift, which makes the Religious community economically an alternate world.

Some Religious today, perhaps because there was no preparation for the dissolution of the total institution model of Religious Life which had previously left few areas of financial discretion to individual members, have drifted into, or deliberately chosen, modifications of this radical economic interdependence. Some have made their blood relatives participants in their economic lives in ways that subvert their primary relationship to the Congregation. They encourage relatives to supply houses, vacations, recreation, cars, money, clothes, and other goods, especially if the Religious feels the community could not or would not provide them. Relatives underwrite loans, make substantial gifts that are not reported to or authorized by the Congregation, and assume responsibility for the health decisions, care, education, travel, ministry location and other elements of the life of the Religious. Others have turned to friends, colleagues, or other non-relatives for similar support.

Obviously, such arrangements make the Religious, to a greater or lesser degree, a financially independent agent in relation to the Congregation and subvert the common life by giving different members different degrees of access to material resources. The egalitarian community based on shared possessionlessness becomes a class society based on property. This real inequality can encourage others in the community to find ways to keep pace with those who have opted out of the common life. In other words, the dynamics of the commodity economy, that is, competition and individualism, begin to replace the dynamics of sharing characteristic of the gift economy. Once a member has effectively ceased to regard the community as her primary economic context, it can be extremely difficult for Congregational leaders to challenge this development.

The second basic question is who really owns what the Religious handles? Most Congregations long ago abandoned the monastic custom of avoiding the use of the first person singular possessive pronoun, a practice designed to keep the commonality of ownership visible even as individuals made use of goods that, in fact, only they used. Religious do not refer to "our" room or "our" pen or even "our" computer. But, in fact, the real owner of anything the Religious earns, handles, or uses is the Congregation. Religious do not own in their own name.[28]

But conversations about money within some Congregations can reveal that this is not necessarily a universally shared understanding among members. For example, do earning members talk about "transfers" of their salaries or other income to the Congregation (implying that they are the conduit of funds which they do not own) or of "donations" or "contributions" to the Congregation (implying that they are owners in a position to give or withhold)? In other words, do earning members think that they are supporting the Congregation rather than that they, like all other members, are supported by the Congregation? How do ministerially active members feel about the care of aged and infirm members and how do the latter experience their own position in the community? Are they regarded as a financial drain on earners or as full and equal participants in an economy of gift and the corporate ministry it supports? Do members think that they have the right to receive in their own name the retirement benefits that accumulated during their years of employment and especially to decide without consultation how to use those monies?

An ethos of proprietorship among members of a Religious Congregation subverts the common life and therefore the gift economy that it expresses. Quite simply, no matter how it is explained or justified, ownership creates inequality in the community by establishing a class hierarchy based on wealth. The Religious who effectively owns a house and a car over which she exercises complete dominion; disposes freely of a large salary

254 • BUYING THE FIELD

or pension which enables her to dress elegantly, take expensive vacations, cultivate a wealthy social cohort, take advantage of whatever educational and cultural opportunities she chooses; and who "donates" as she sees fit and reports when and how and what she chooses is not in the same community with the one who lives according to Congregational financial guidelines, transfers all income to the Congregation through the budgeting and reporting systems that apply to all members, recognizes the right of other members to use what she does not need, and discerns the details of her financial dealings with appropriate Congregational leaders. The history of Religious Life demonstrates conclusively that wherever and whenever Orders have become corporately wealthy or privatization of wealth among the members has become common the life itself has been subverted and the choice is reformation or death. This is a history lesson contemporary Religious cannot afford to ignore.

b. ACCOUNTABILITY: PERSONAL AND CORPORATE CONVERSION

How these two questions about participation and proprietorship are answered manifests fairly reliably whether a Religious participates in the common life expressive of the economy of gift, or functions within a commodity economy of which independent ownership is the distinguishing characteristic. Accountability is the expression in action of economic and financial responsibility. If, as Religious, we really do not own anything, do not have independent use of material goods, if everything really belongs to the community no matter which member produced it or uses it at a given time, then Religious are accountable for what they earn, receive, and use.

Transparency and trusting communications between a member and Congregational leaders about financial matters is a hallmark of free participation in the common life. The mechanisms of such communication differ widely among Congregations, but some are fairly common across Congregational lines, such as budgeting, using a centralized banking system and/or Congregational access to local bank accounts, keeping financial durable power of attorney up to date, and discernment about major expenditures, accounting, regular transfer of income, and so on. These are not just inconveniences but the recognition in practice that since one does not own anything the Congregation has rightful access to all that one administers in its name. And since the Congregation's resources must be equitably available to all members these resources must be known and corporately managed.

Accounting for earnings as well as substantial gifts in money or kind acknowledges that whatever one acquires, one acquires as a member of the Congregation and for the community. For example, requesting necessary permissions, following Congregational guidelines about housing, travel, and other major expenses, registering vehicles or credit cards as requested, are some of the ways in which the Religious not only accepts responsibility for the Congregation's overall finances but also acknowledges repeatedly and in relationship to all that she uses the fact of her possessionlessness. Accountability can be experienced as annoyance or intrusion; or it can be a way the Religious honors her belonging to the community and witnesses to herself and to others that membership is meaningful and has a real and even daily impact on her life.

Some Congregations today are beginning to ask themselves what kinds of patterns have developed in the community (perhaps almost accidentally while everyone was attending to more urgent matters) concerning gifts, patrimony, real estate, extra earnings, and so on. To what extent have practices of dependence on family or other nonmembers for both financial support and life decisions developed to fill policy vacuums as older procedures became irrelevant and new ones were not yet in place? As Congregations have gained experience in these matters, they have seen the need to address more explicitly and intentionally what it means to live the vow of poverty in reality. And fortunately, today, that wisdom tends to be shared among communities.

However, some, perhaps many, Congregations have experienced that individually and corporately we as Religious still carry from our overly dependent pasts as well as from our capitalist and competitive societal context some psychological and spiritual baggage in the area of finances. Suspicion, secrecy, and resentment on the one hand and extravagance or individualism on the other call for genuine conversion of heart and not just better policies and procedures. As human beings and people who have grown up in a capitalist commodity economy we continue to struggle with the greed, competitiveness, and proprietorship which express the existential insecurity of the children of Adam and Eve. We will examine this aspect of the issue in the next chapter on the spirituality of poverty.

Personal conversion and corporate renewal concerning the vow of poverty is not primarily about obligations in Canon Law but rather about the reality of what Religious claim to be doing with their lives; their identity as Religious and their belonging to one another in mutuality and interdependence; and the prophetic potential of the economics of the Reign of God that Religious undertake to live in the alternate world they create by Profession. Coming together in a community of equals as people who have chosen to respond literally to Jesus' challenge to "renounce all," to become truly possessionless in order to participate in his reality construction of this world within our time in history, is to offer an alternate vision of the human condition and its possibilities. In other words, it is prophecy embodied.

B. Ministry in the Alternate Economic World

If the kind of community life Religious live is the embodiment of the economy of gift as a prophetic witness to the Reign of God, ministry is the prophetic action through which this life of discipleship is mediated into the historical situation. Ministry, as it is carried out by Religious in "apostolic Congregations,"[29] is the gift economy at work in the world specifically through the Church as the Body of Christ. It is the way that Religious attempt to subvert the evil reality construction of the "principalities and powers" and foster the Reign of God not only in themselves and in the alternate world of the Religious community, but in the world itself. The peculiarity of the form of Religious Life that developed in the post-Reformation era (since the sixteenth century) is precisely that active engagement in the world through service of the neighbor is constitutive of the life and not simply the overflow of the pursuit of personal holiness.

Few aspects of Religious Life have been more conflictually affected by the conciliar renewal on the one hand and the cultural upheavals of postmodernity on the other than ministry. The stress arises from a number of factors, but the one which will occupy us in this section is the disruption of the connection between ministry and the economic life of ministerial Congregations especially as that has been experienced by women Religious in economically developed countries.

It seems to me that if Religious Life, especially that of ministerial Congregations, is to remain coherent for its own members and be able to make some sense to those outside, it is crucial to clarify for ourselves how our ministry is and is not related to material goods and how both are related to the Gospel. If Religious allow themselves, individually and corporately, to get so caught up in the scramble for financial survival in a ruthless market economy or so preoccupied with meeting economic emergencies that they lose sight of why they are Religious in the first place, ministry, which is intrinsic to their life, could be fatally subverted. This is not a purely imaginary worst-case scenario when the challenge to make ends meet is probably more severe now than it has been, for most ministerial Congregations, since their foundations.

In what follows I will be making two very different kinds of observations and suggestions. From within my own areas of competence, I will discuss scriptural, theological, and historical data which in my judgment are critical to a revisioning of the corporate dimensions of evangelical poverty as the economic root of the alternate world Religious create, live in, and minister from as community. I hope that, whether my suggestions are accepted or contested, the issues they raise will be taken seriously as critical for ongoing renewal in this area.

In addition, I will make some practical observations and suggestions, which I offer as examples of imaginative experiments. In this area I claim no more competence or authority than any other Religious who is living through and is confronted by the economic and financial challenges of our time and far less competence than the financial agents in Congregations who specialize in these matters. Some of my strategic or tactical observations may be well wide of the mark and some suggestions economically or financially naïve or impractical. In that case, I invite the reader to improve on them, taking from this text only a sense of urgency and commitment to envisioning new solutions and a conviction that, whatever strategies we develop, they must be rooted in sound biblically based theology and spirituality rather than in a sense of emergency or even panic in the face of economic challenges.

1. New Testament data on ministry and its support

As we have already seen in chapter 3, Religious ministry is not just "doing good" or "making a difference" in the world. It is not simply benevolent action baptized by Christian rhetoric. It is, first of all, *Christian* (and therefore explicitly religious rather than purely humanitarian) which specifies it in terms of its object, namely, the mediation into this world of Jesus' Resurrection life and the promotion in this world of the Reign of God. Second, it is *Religious*. This ministry emanates from and is an expression of the alternate world which Religious create by Profession and live in as community in mission. Economically, this world is radically different from the commodity economy of having. It is, as we have just seen, a community of gift rooted in the commitment of every member to accept Jesus' invitation to "renounce all that you have," that is, to be without possessions in this world, and to "come follow me."

Consequently, by its very nature the ministry of Religious cannot be reduced to and must not be understood within the secular category of gainful employment even if, in fact, the Religious is paid for what s/he does. Religious ministry is not a sacralized job. It is rooted in the Gospel that it serves. The fundamental principles of ministry for Religious are expressed in the missionary exhortation of Jesus to his itinerant followers in Matthew 10:1–10 and its close parallel in Luke 10:1–12.[30] Jesus sent them (the twelve or the seventy) out with this charge:

> "As you go, *proclaim the good news,* 'The kingdom of heaven has come near.' Cure the sick, raise the dead, cleanse the

lepers, cast out demons. *You received without payment; give without payment.* Take no gold, or silver, or copper in your belts, no bag for your journey, or two tunics, or sandals, or a staff; for the laborers deserve their food." (Matt 10:7–10 [emphasis added])

Two principles emerge from this text, which distinguish ministry from a job. First, the purpose of ministry is the fostering of the Reign of God: "Proclaim the good news, 'The kingdom of heaven has come near.'" Second, ministry is not motivated by the desire or intention to make money (even the money necessary for livelihood) but by the mission to preach the Gospel freely: "give without payment."

The *directly evangelical purpose* of ministry means that the private intention of the worker is not what distinguishes ministry from a job. Rather, the very nature of the work as preaching the Gospel, specifically through the service of the neighbor, qualifies it as ministry. A Religious who takes a position because it pays well even though there is no discernible ministerial reason for doing this work might describe her job (e.g., as a receptionist in a business office) as her "ministry" because, at least in her private intention, she is doing some good in this world (e.g., showing kindness to her coworkers and clients). Without denying that one can do good in any situation—and one would hope any Christian would be trying to make her or his environment a better place—it remains a fact that this work is not directly evangelical, that is, fostering the Reign of God through service of the neighbor. This business enterprise to which she is contributing directly is not about serving the needs of others but, as a corporate agent in the commodity economy, it exists to make money for those who have a stake in it, including its employees. In other words, the primary purpose of this "ministry" is not to preach the Gospel but to earn a salary. Unfortunately, financial exigency has led some Congregations to encourage or even require that the work of members be salaried, even if that means that the work is not directly evangelical.

Proclaiming the Gospel that the Reign of God is at hand is exemplified in the text by certain works: "cure the sick, raise the dead, cleanse the lepers, cast out demons." This list is illustrative, not exhaustive. It could have included the works Jesus refers to in the Last Judgment scene in Matthew 25 such as clothing the naked or visiting the imprisoned, or the "varieties of service" that Paul lists in 1 Corinthians 12:4–11, or any of the spiritual or corporal works of mercy. An exhaustive list would certainly include teaching, pastoral care, social justice involvement, leadership and many other directly ministerial activities. But the illustrations given are not simply "good works" in general. They are ciphers for the subversion of all the causes, forms, and results of the "death that should not be" which is the mark of the evil world construction that ministers of the Gospel are committed to subverting.

Wherever suffering, exclusion, violence, and death are being overcome the Reign of God is arriving. Jesus, opening the eyes of the blind, causing the paralyzed to walk, feeding the hungry in the wilderness, and consoling the bereaved, was bringing about the Reign of God in the world even as he announced it. Thus the ministry to which he commissions his band of full-time itinerant disciples is not just to do something useful with a pure intention, or even to "pick up the pieces" left in the wake of evil. They are missioned to announce, through their struggle with the effects of violence and greed, that the news is good. God's Reign is near. Proclaiming the Gospel and effecting the Reign of God are the same thing in two modes, in word and in deed. This insight is central to the charism of ministerial Religious Life.

The second distinguishing characteristic of ministry in contrast to a job is that *ministry is to be free*, that is, making money is not its motivation. Jesus enunciates the ministerial implications of the gift economy when he says, "As a free gift (δωρεάν) you received, so freely give." That this "free giving" refers specifically to ministering not motivated by pay is clear from what follows. Ministers of the Gospel are not to take precautions about their support, about making a living, because they have a right to expect that their needs will be adequately met if they are faithful to preaching the Gospel. In other words, the economy of gift in which everything is received freely from God overflows in the free sharing of God's gift, not only with those with whom one shares life in community, but also with those whom one serves in ministry. To minister freely is an implication of the gift economy as is community based in possessionlessness.

When profit is not the motive for ministry those served by Religious are not humiliated by their neediness, denied service because they cannot afford it, or alienated by the doling out, from a position of economic or social superiority, of hand-outs that emphasize and consolidate the dependence of the poor on their benefactors. In other words, the free ministry of Religious announces and effects the Reign of God in which all are welcome, all are cared for, the last are first at the table, and Resurrection life has ended the reign of the "death that should not be." The very existence of the national Retirement Fund for Religious, which helps Religious Congregations meet the retirement needs of their members[31] whose lifelong ministries did not generate the benefits that accrued to most paid workers, testifies to the fact that ministerial Religious, at least those in the developed world in the past two centuries, have not structured their ministries around their own needs but around those of the people they served. Rather than feeling shame at what could be interpreted as economic naïveté and lack of foresight, or panic at the financial vulnerability which has resulted from this choice to minister without "due" compensation, their experience of insecurity should assure Religious of the validity of what they have traditionally done in ministry. They have preached the Gospel freely.

By contrast, it is salutary to note that in ecclesiastical situations where ministry has taken on the character of paid employment, corruption and dysfunction have often followed. When the Church has resorted to selling indulgences or relics or Mass intentions, to giving ecclesiastical positions to those who could pay for them, to charging for sacraments or preaching, or in other ways made ministry a commodity, the results have seldom been good. Even today, the financial scandals plaguing parishes and dioceses and even the Vatican testify eloquently to the corrupting influence of the commodity economy on ministry, which, by nature, should belong to the economy of gift.

The issue of pay for work is further complicated for women Religious, especially in capitalist cultures, by the fact that women's work has been and still is seriously undervalued and underpaid, that women are paid less for the same work than men, and by the fact that if some women, such as Religious, work for less than they "are worth" they can undercut the legitimate demands of women in general for fair and equitable compensation. Thus, part of the motivation in some Congregations for insisting that Sisters be paid what their educational qualifications, experience, and job performance "is worth" is a commitment to structural reform of compensation structures for women.

This issue requires careful case-by-case discernment. Insistence on just compensation by Religious ministering in institutional settings, such as hospitals or universities, which have pay scales applicable to all employees in a particular category, is reasonable and necessary, both as a strategy for promoting equal rights for women and minorities and because their salaries are helping to support their communities and their under-compensated ministries. But ministries which can only function if subsidized by the Congregation, such as inner-city shelters or schools for at-risk children, should not be forfeited because the minister is not making money. It is precisely such ministries that should have priority among Religious as they did for Jesus and his disciples. Preference for the poor is constitutive of ministry.

If a Congregation is going to espouse a ministerial ideal that determines ministry by need rather than by recompense there must be a conscious effort, in initial and ongoing formation, to deconstruct any tendency among Religious to hierarchize ministries in the Congregation in terms of salary. A high-earning member is not more valuable as a person or as a minister than one whose ministry earns less or is even being subsidized because the Congregation is committed to presence and service among those who cannot afford to pay for what they need. Few secular tendencies are more destructive of community and ministry than succumbing to the culture's valuation of people by their salaries. This is an insidious temptation among Religious and can take all kinds of forms from covert "advertising" of salary differentials to more affluent "lifestyles" which higher earners affect.

Lower earners who project a "conspicuous deprivation" (as if because of their commitment to the poor they have less than their "richer" fellow members who, by implication, are less committed to the poor) can also perpetrate violations of common life. The Religious community can remain a classless society, a discipleship of equals, only if everyone really believes that every member of the Congregation is possessionless and that every member's ministry is "free," that is, not chosen or pursued to make money, and therefore that the economy of the Congregation is a gift economy in which everything is held in common, all members have equal access to all resources, and none have economic priority. This is a serious spiritual challenge for Religious who live every day of their lives immersed in a capitalist commodity culture in which wealth is the primary determinant of status and access to power.

The problems arising today from the effort to adhere to the two Gospel principles, that ministry is about preaching the Gospel and that it is not for sale, are enormous. We can be tempted, as with the text on total dispossession which undergirded the preceding reflection on the community of gift, to treat the text on ministry as gift as a hyperbolic articulation of an impracticable ideal. But before making that move, I would suggest that we look at what the New Testament itself suggests about the livelihood of ministers if ministry itself should not be price-tagged yet ministers have a right to what they need.

As we saw in chapter 4, Jesus and his itinerant followers did not live in penury, much less destitution. Although there is no comprehensive discussion of how they handled the issues of economic survival there are a number of hints. John 12:6 and 13:29 refer to a *common purse* in the community, a way of maximizing the benefits of whatever resources were available. Jesus and his friends also *accepted the hospitality*, including lodging and food, of others that they were not in a position to return in kind (e.g., Luke 10:38–42; Mark 1:29; John 12:1–8). Luke tells us that

Jesus was *supported by wealthy benefactors,* especially women who went about in his company as did his male disciples (Luke 8:2–3). In addition, Jesus seemed to call the disciples in his itinerant band away from their regular employments such as fishing (cf. Mark 1:16–20) or tax collecting (cf. Matt 9:9) which would have impeded full-time accompaniment of him in ministry. When he sends them out on their first missionary ventures he specifically tells them to travel lightly and not to charge for their ministry but to accept what was offered them.

The Acts of the Apostles tells us that the earliest Christian communities also had various ways of handling economic necessities. The first Jerusalem community is described as sharing all their possessions (Acts 2:44–47), that is, as having realized, at least for a time, the Deuteronomic ideal of having "not a needy person among them" (cf. Deut 15:1–5).[32] The new Christians, we are told, sold their property to create *a common fund* which supported not only the members of the community but the community's ministers as well (cf. Acts 4:32–37).[33] Religious communities have always seen this experiment in common life as the model of their own community life as a gift economy.

From the beginning there were two kinds of ministers in the Christian communities. Some were itinerant apostles or prophets, such as Paul, some of the twelve, Barnabas, Philip, Andronicus and Junia (perhaps a husband and wife apostolic team), whose task was to carry the Gospel message to new frontiers and establish or foster new communities of believers. Others were resident ministers, such as James (cf. Acts 15:13), Timothy (e.g., 2 Tim 1:1–3), Phoebe (cf. Rom 16:1), and Aquilla and Priscilla (cf. Acts 18:26), who presided over the life and worship of the established communities, catechized converts, taught the baptized, and oversaw the care of the needy. These stabile ministers were supported by the communities in which they served.

In the case of the itinerant apostles, however, we see at least two models of ministerial support. Paul tells us that at times he was *supported in ministry by the members of communities he served* (cf. 2 Cor 11:8) and that he, like other apostles, indeed had a right to such support (cf. 1 Cor 9:1–12). But he also sometimes chose to use his craft as a tentmaker (cf. Acts 18:3), that is, *to support himself by his secular work*, so that he would not have to put any financial burden on those he evangelized. He wanted to preach the Gospel freely so that it would be freely received. However, although his tentmaking supported the minister, Paul never seems to have considered tent-making itself a ministry. Apparently the earliest apostles took seriously Jesus' challenge: to minister by preaching the Gospel, not to charge for their ministry, and to confidently expect that their basic needs would be met in one way or another.

This biblical data, sketchy as it is, offers several suggestions about the relationship between ministry and the financial support of ministers. First, the *attitude toward material goods* in relation to ministry is the same as it is in relation to community: complete detachment from wealth, frugal use of what is necessary, interdependence, and a basic willingness to suffer scarcity and insecurity when necessary. While it is clear that adequate material goods are necessary for the support of ministers and their ministries (and in many cases ministry itself is a way of redistributing material goods which, in the commodity economy, tend to be concentrated in the hands of the wealthy), ministry is not motivated by profit-making.

Second, there are *a variety of ways* in which adequate resources for the support of ministers and their ministries might be obtained: accepting economic assistance from donors and handling funds prudently especially through sharing within the community; support from the communities served to the extent that they are able to do so; and engaging in secular employment that supports the ministry provided the gainful employment does not interfere with the ministry and is not viewed as or substituted for ministry itself.

I am not proposing that we can or should imitate literally the economic strategies that worked in the first century (although some of them could spark our imaginations). But we can draw from these texts "permission" for Religious to be creative and diverse in seeking ways to support themselves and their ministries today. Although there is a powerful cultural imperative in capitalist economies to support oneself by one's work, never to need, ask for, or accept assistance, and to stockpile money so as never to be in want, there is no evangelical blueprint which prescribes salaried work by every minister, ownership of profitable institutions, or building up financial "cushions" as the only paths to economic survival in ministerial Congregations.

2. Distinguishing between work and ministry
Equipped with some basic New Testament data on the nature of ministry and on the relationship of material goods to ministry, we turn now to a critical distinction which can easily be obscured by the economic emergencies that ministerial Religious Congregations have faced in the postconciliar period. Work (equated with gainful employment) and ministry have become virtually interchangeable in relation to financial support for the individual and for the community. This equation has obscured, or at least veiled, the nature of ministry as the proclamation of the Gospel as well as its essentially gratuitous character. Congregations continue to struggle seriously with this situation through divestment of holdings, magnanimous sharing of scarce Congregational resources with those outside the Congregation, heroic efforts to support increasing populations of aging and ill members, and careful investment strategies. But sometimes these efforts are not based on a clear rationale which would coordinate them in coherent patterns and policies.

a. Two models of work and ministry: monasticism and mendicancy

Hannah Arendt, the brilliant twentieth-century philosopher, in her classic work, *The Human Condition*, distinguishes among labor, work, and action.[34] **Labor** is our basic involvement in the metabolic cycle of nature by which we assure the survival of ourselves and the species. It transpires in the sphere of the necessary and requires primarily physical strength. Futility and therefore exhaustion is built into labor because what is done, such as housekeeping, planting and reaping, must forever be redone for the sake of survival. Laboring inserts a person into nature in a way that emphasizes human dependence and fragility. **Work** is our creation of an "artificial" world which outlasts the worker. It is the sphere of the useful and the beautiful. Work requires creativity but also the willingness to destroy some of nature in order to create what is beyond nature, such as to cut down trees in order to build houses or to make paper. But it results in a human world into which new humans can be born and in which they can survive. Work, unlike labor, does not simply exhaust the person in the struggle to survive, but also ennobles and frees. **Action** is the generation of the unity of the human race out of the plurality of unique persons. It is the sphere of the political and requires education, speech, and all the ways that humans can cooperate to create community. Action is, in a sense, that kind of behavior to which humans as humans are called and by which they transcend both nature and productivity to bring about the religious and the social well-being of the race.

In classical antiquity labor was the activity of slaves; work the activity of craftspeople (including artists and teachers); action the activity of the free person. This "division of activity" lasted well into the Middle Ages with slaves laboring just to stay alive or keep others alive, craftspeople earning their living by their skill, and rulers enjoying the freedom that wealth afforded. But Christianity on the one hand and the emergence of a money economy on the other would gradually change this situation. Religious Life was both an agent and a patient of this change.

The two forms of Religious Life which immediately preceded the emergence of the apostolic form that has given rise since the Council to the mobile ministerial form, namely, medieval monasticism and the mendicant life that developed in the later Middle Ages, highly prized work, which they did not distinguish sharply from labor. Work had three interrelated functions. First it was an **intrinsic element in the spiritual life** itself. Benedict wanted all the members of the community to work as assiduously as they prayed. Whether their "work" was actually labor (e.g., cooking or farming or drawing water) or work (e.g., building the monastery church or copying manuscripts), this engagement was first of all participation in God's plan for humans. Through work, the monastic entered willingly, through a long pedagogy, into the right relationship of humility with God, the neighbor, and him- or herself. Second, their work contributed to the **support of the community**, not by earning money but by directly producing, refining, and distributing all that was needed for its life. And third, work overflowed in various kinds of **service of the neighbor**, that is, of the people who lived around the monastery and profited from its economic stability, from the medical, agricultural, and other kinds of practical wisdom of the monks, as well as from the liturgical, spiritual, and educational resources of the monastery. Although the charity and hospitality practiced by the monks was a kind of preaching of the Gospel by action it was not a deliberate undertaking of active ministry. In Benedict's view any work was appropriate for a monk as long as there was a need for it and it did not interfere with the life of prayer and community. Any work could be for the glory of God, the good of the community, or a service to others, fulfilling both the first and second great commandments. In the monastic framework, however, work was paradigmatically **labor**, part of the interior formation of the monk through patience, peacefulness, long-suffering, recollection, constant prayer, and humble submission to the exigencies of creaturehood in dependence on God alone.

The mendicant movement represented both continuity with monasticism and a radical innovation, particularly in regard to work and ministry. The ideal of Francis, Dominic, and later mendicant founders was the "apostolic life" by which they meant the closest possible (indeed virtually literal) following of Jesus in his itinerant life of proclaiming the Good News. Rather than building stabile monasteries the mendicants lived together in "convents" (gathering places) or even individually in caves or huts from which they came together for community functions and from which they went out, like Jesus, to preach the Gospel in the rural countryside and the newly developing cities as well as to heretics and to students in the new universities. They aspired to imitate Jesus' own poverty by owning nothing personally and even, in some cases, owning nothing corporately. They took seriously the assurance that the preacher deserves support and so, besides laboring with their hands to provide for themselves what they could, they primarily depended on alms (hence their name, "mendicants" or beggars) from the believers in what was still Christendom.

The mendicants differed primarily from their monastic predecessors in the centrality they assigned to ministry. Thus ministerial mobility replaced monastic stability; work/labor no longer had its triple finality of sanctification, support, and charity but support had to be found for the one ministry of freely preaching the Gospel. Preaching, whether explicitly by word or through acts of service to Christ in the neighbor, was the one deliberately chosen work and ministry itself became a principal means of sanctification. Mendicants certainly labored, in Arendt's sense of the word, but their primary concern was **work**, whether intellectual or artistic or caritative, understood as ministry.

b. A NEW MODEL: APOSTOLIC CONGREGATIONS

The mendicant lifeform, as is easily seen, foreshadows in many ways the lifeform of the apostolic Congregations which emerged in the aftermath of the Protestant Reformation and whose period of ascendancy was the eighteenth to mid-twentieth centuries. However, as these new communities of Sisters and Brothers struggled to define themselves as both Religious who were not enclosed and ministers who were not clerics, they attempted to combine both the monastic and the mendicant ideals as well as the apostolic motivation and practice of the clerical Orders. Even women in the mendicant movement in the high Middle Ages and afterward were bound by monastic cloister and did not participate in the itinerant life and public proclamation of the Gospel of the male mendicants. The new apostolic lifeform as it was lived by the large majority who were women embraced the monastic life as fully as possible while committing its members to the fully apostolic life of the male mendicants. This braiding of lifeforms had interesting results.

Although these new Religious understood their life to have a twofold end, that is, the sanctification of the Religious herself and the service of the neighbor through specific "apostolates," in fact, the first was seen as primary and the latter as secondary.

Teaching, nursing, or social service was the overflow of the love of God in the love of neighbor expressed through direct service to Christ in his members. This commitment to fulfilling the first great commandment through the second was the ideal of the mendicant "mixed life" which Thomas Aquinas claimed was superior to the purely contemplative life, as illuminating is superior to merely shining.

The concrete result, in the life of apostolic Religious, was a combination of the monastic approach to service as an over-flow of the single-hearted quest for God and the mendicant approach to apostolic work as intrinsic to Religious Life itself. These women and men *were* Religious; the apostolate was what they *did* as an expression of who they were. So important was the apostolate, however, that they were sometimes willing (as in the case of the Daughters of Charity) to forego status as Religious in order to continue to minister. At other times (as in the case of the Ursulines) ministry was curtailed to maintain ecclesiastical identity as Religious.

Nevertheless, the ministries of apostolic Religious were actually more deliberately selected, organized, and pursued (even professionally) than were the various and changing occupations of monks which were always fit into a horarium of prayer and work-in-general that had unquestioned priority. As in the monasteries, so in the convents of apostolic Religious bells were rung and exercises performed according to a strict horarium. But the apostolic Religious figured out how to organize the monastic practices so that the apostolate, to which they gave most of the day and prime energy, would not be unduly disrupted. And like the mendicants, they responded with alacrity, even when they lacked personnel and economic resources, to more and more calls to take the Gospel into new fields of endeavor. Somehow, as long as they were ministering in exclusively or primarily Catholic settings, funds were obtained to support them and their works.

Government structures in these new Congregations borrowed both the familial rhetoric and ethos of the monasteries and the efficiency in ministry of the post-Tridentine male clerical Orders to which many of these women's Congregations owed their founding inspiration. Mobility, a heritage from the mendicants and the clerical Orders, was prized as a primary mark of a true apostolic Religious. Community life had all the uniformity of the most tightly structured monastery but superiors and members were moved about on short notice and often at great distances, making their relationships among themselves more mendicant-conventual than monastic-familial.

In short, life in preconciliar apostolic Congregations of women Religious and most Orders of Brothers was a hybrid of the monastic and mendicant lifeforms with a strong influence flowing into it from the male clerical Orders founded in the aftermath of the Protestant Reformation with their highly ecclesiastical identification, institutional setting, and missionary focus. Although this can be seen clearly only in hindsight and in the context of the late twentieth-century development of structural approaches to ministry, ministerial Religious were beginning to focus not on labor or on work but on **action**, that is, on the transformation of persons and society through structural change. Labor remained an important element in their shared life and spirituality and most of their ministry would be classified, in Arendt's terms, as work. But they were beginning to conceive of ministry less in terms of alleviating the results of injustice and more in terms of eradicating its causes. As we will see in the next chapter, this has important implications for a spirituality of ministry.

3. Redefining the relation of work to ministry in apostolic Congregations

Shortly before Vatican II it began to be ever more clear to many apostolic Religious, individually and as Congregations, that ministry was not simply a secondary end, an overflow in charitable activity of their monastic love of God, but rather absolutely central to their vocation and identity.[35] They were not monastics who exercised an apostolate but ministerial Religious. Ministry was their love of God incarnated in love of neighbor. They did not have a twofold end; their end was love of God and neighbor which coincided. Ministry was becoming, in their self-understanding, not something they *did* to express who they were but was intrinsic to who they *were*. The tension between their monastic practices and their ministerial commitments became increasingly acute.

This resulted, under pressures from the hierarchy, in the "new theology" that would inspire the Council and the Religious themselves in the lifestyle reforms that followed the Council. Medieval monastic clothes, cloistered dwellings, daily horaria, monastic ascetical practices, and government structures were largely abandoned, while the mendicant focus on preaching the Gospel became more and more central. But ministerial Religious were not mendicants either. Nor did they have the ecclesiastical position of clerical Religious. Probably no one could have foreseen the financial disruption of this life-form that would result from such a radical redefinition of the relationship of its members to ministry. Apostolic Congregations of women had been an anomaly in the 1600s when the Church had no model for women's Religious Life that was not cloistered or for ecclesial ministry that was not clerical.[36] They were even more so in the mid-1900s when there was no economic model for Religious Life of this type in a secularizing culture and market economy.

Prior to the conciliar reform of Religious Life, apostolic Congregations, especially in the first world, had evolved a system of economic support (briefly described at the beginning of section IV above) that was unique in relation to their monastic and mendicant predecessors. It was actually a system of alms and barter that looked like a system of self-support through work and which, in the later 1800s, became more and more institutionalized. Institutionalization, in many cases, made the ministries at least partially self-supporting, which helped foster the impression that their ministry was supporting the Religious. The flaw in this view was revealed by the sudden (within a decade or two) dissolution of many of these institutions in a large number of Congregations and the "loss" of others through transfers to lay boards, mergers, and closings. This has precipitated the economic crisis with which these Congregations are now contending.

We need not discuss here why, historically, the Religious who came to the new world to serve the Catholic minority moved so rapidly from small, often hand-to-mouth, fledgling operations on the western frontiers or in the emerging cities to the foundation of hospitals, the opening of social service agencies, and the establishment of the largest private school system in the world including primary and secondary schools, special education facilities, colleges and universities. There is little question that the Religious were responding to enormous needs with the type of efficiency that characterized American enterprises during the industrial revolution when hand-based methods of production gave way to machine-based methods and small enterprises were swallowed up in huge factories. The industrial revolution, it should be noted, was at its height at precisely the time (mid-1700s through the 1800s) that apostolic Congregations were transforming from small, *ad hoc* ministerial enterprises into large institutional ones.

But the context for the development of these institutions, in most cases, was a largely ghettoized, ethnically based, clerically run Catholicism. From birth in a Catholic hospital through education in Catholic schools to marriage to a Catholic spouse and eventual burial in a Catholic cemetery, the immigrant Catholics lived religiously and often socially within the boundaries of their parishes and dioceses. Within these tight-knit religiously and ethnically based communities, the Sisters had a privileged place and role as transmitters of the faith, role models and mentors, supports if not extensions of the clergy, and "special" incarnations of Catholic faith, identity, spirituality, and behavior. They were, for the most part, prodigiously hard working and self-sacrificial as well as totally committed, and their value to the Catholic communities in which they served was social, psychological, and professional as well as spiritual. To many people, in and outside Catholicism, the "good Sisters" rather than the clergy were the real public face of the Catholic Church.

These Catholic communities were actually the major source of the material support of the Religious, both financially and in terms of personnel. However, this support was generally not in the form of fair pay for work or compensation for services rendered. For example, although the "salaries" of the Sisters teaching in the school might be in reality token "stipends" totally inadequate for the support of the Religious or the school, much less the Congregation, the parish might supply housing for the Sisters and maintenance for the school itself while parishioners donated a car and gas, medical services, and financial advice, and conducted an annual round of collections in kind, benefits, and gifts that, together, kept the ministerial institutions and their Religious personnel financially solvent, as well as supplying large numbers of recruits whose contributed service in the institutions obviated the need to pay lay salaries.

Even as the ministries became more institutionalized, the Religious were running and staffing them. It appeared that this system of organized almsgiving, efficient barter, contributed services, and so on was actually a system of earning; that is, of payment for services rendered. But it was a system that could work only as long as the Catholic community was intact as a virtual ghetto and needed and wanted the presence and ministry of the Religious. The system was neither monastic (in which the Religious community sustained itself through the internal labor/work of its members) nor mendicant (in which the itinerant ministers were supported by the alms of those to whom they ministered by their work). Furthermore, it was not part of the capitalistic economy in which one is paid adequately for goods produced or services rendered and pays one's way out of the proceeds of that work. But there was a shared misperception that ministry (the preaching of the Gospel through word and service) was identical with the work (as gainful employment in the market economy) of the Religious who seemed to be supporting themselves (by earning what they needed and paying as they went).

As their highly visible and valued ministries of teaching, health care, or social service developed, Congregations were progressively institutionalizing them according to the pattern of parallel secular institutions that they needed to emulate in order to hold their Catholic clientele and provide competitive services. Thus, Catholic institutions owned or operated by Religious both influenced and were influenced by their secular peer institutions. Increasingly, Catholic institutions had to meet secular accrediting standards, match secular standards in facilities and salaries, and shape their policies and procedures according to secular models and laws.[37] At the same time, the ministerial motivation of the Religious often made the services of these institutions qualitatively superior so that they challenged the standards of service of their secular peers.

The election of a Catholic (John F. Kennedy) as president of the United States in 1960 symbolized the mainstreaming of Catholics in American society and the beginning of the end of this originally immigrant Church, its ghetto culture, and the unique economic system that had sustained the parallel track of Catholic services. Furthermore, Religious were experiencing a "placelessness" in the conciliar reenvisioning of ecclesial ministry as almost exclusively the work of clergy and laity within diocesan structures such as the parish.[38] The exciting conciliar theology of ministry as world oriented rather than exclusively Church oriented energized Religious in their growing conviction that they were not simply the job corps of the hierarchy or professionals in habits (i.e., religiously motivated workers) but ministers in the Church and to the world in virtue of their baptism and their Religious consecration (i.e., actors involved in structural change and development toward the Reign of God).

At the same time, as opportunities for lay women in the secular professions as well as in Church ministry increased dramatically, and the number of children in Catholic families as well as young people in the population at large decreased dramatically, there was a precipitous decline in the number of young women and men entering Religious Congregations. Consequently, as their economic base eroded, their personnel declined in numbers and increased in age and it became more and more difficult for Congregations to sustain their institutions. They began to raise serious practical and theological questions about these institutionalized apostolates.

Practically, it became clear that the progress of these institutions toward ever-greater financial stability and professional success, which had seemed inevitable in the 1940s and 1950s, was illusory. Sustaining them became almost impossible in many cases. Theologically, many Congregations began to realize the extent to which they were so tied to the financial and personnel demands of these institutions (which in many cases they could not meet) that they no longer had the ministerial mobility, that is, the psychological as well as physical flexibility, to go where they were needed and find new ways to proclaim the Gospel to the poor in this postconciliar Church and post-modern world.

A double bind was rapidly developing whose contours and dimensions were becoming increasingly clear by the 1980s. Large institutions were often an impediment to ministry understood as a preaching of the Gospel in situations of the greatest need, such as among the materially poor or through social justice involvement. But losing the institutions, whether by outright sale, by turning them over to lay boards, or by merging them with other religious or secular enterprises, meant losing whatever revenue they had provided, losing the public visibility that was a source of new recruits as well as financial contributions, and losing the sense of corporate mission that having most members of the Congregation living and working together promoted. If owning and operating large institutions (e.g., schools and hospitals) was a threat to ministry (flexibility, creativity, and mobility), withdrawing from these institutions was a threat to the ministers (their support, their visibility, their corporate identity). Institutionalization that had, at one time, seemed the self-evident way forward in ministry was beginning to appear as a complication and a paradox.[39]

The foregoing is a generalized and inadequate sketch of the situation and does not take account of the diversity between health care and educational apostolates, the variety of ways of sustaining institutions without hamstringing Congregations, and the interaction of factors such as personnel, finances, religious demographics in the first world, patterns of Catholic living, and so on. But I hope it is sufficiently descriptive to ground the suggestions for reflection in the next section. *The point is that a crisis had developed because of the identity in practice of ministry with work, work with gainful employment, and gainful employment with the economic support of Religious Congregations.* The veil that obscured the important distinctions among these realities was the thoroughgoing institutionalization of ministry within the preconciliar Catholic ghetto which created the impression that ministry was what made Religious self-supporting.

4. Current situation

Let me recall the distinction made above between work and ministry. Basically, all active ministry[40] is work in some sense, but not all work is ministry. Ministry refers to proclaiming the Gospel by doing the works (curing the sick, exorcizing, feeding the hungry, teaching, etc.) of liberation from evil that announces and promotes the Reign of God. One of the reasons postconciliar Religious began to prefer to talk about their mission and ministry rather than their apostolates is that the latter term tended to connote specific institutionalized "works" (e.g., schools or hospitals) whereas ministry placed the emphasis on the mission of preaching the Gospel and the flexibility of means (various ministries) through which that mission was accomplished.

Historically, as we have already seen, work as an element in Religious Life has had three different meanings, only one of which has to do with financial support. Work can be an activity **intrinsic to the spirituality** of the Religious, which we will discuss, in the next chapter. It can also **support** the community by providing what it needs to live. This can take the form of internal service such as farming to grow the monastery's food or cooking that food to feed the community, or gainful employment such as administering the Congregation's hospital. And work **can be ministry**, such as teaching or caring for the sick in or outside the convent.

The problem, as I have tried to present it, arises from the identification in some cases of work-as-support with work-as-ministry. If, as we saw in the section on Gospel principles, ministry is by nature free, then "earning one's living" by ministering is highly susceptible to misunderstanding. I am suggesting in this chapter that such misunderstanding has been common in the past when, in a sense, the confusion was relatively benign because the ministerial aspect had a clear priority for the individual and the Congregation as all members ministered in

Congregational institutions. Today, because of the financial stress afflicting many Congregations, the confusion is much more problematic and at least in some cases actually subordinates ministerial commitment to earning capacity.

Because of the misperception discussed above that Religious in institutional ministries were actually "earning their living" by the works (teaching, nursing, etc.) which they did as apostolates in their institutions, there is a tendency in some communities today to feel that every individual member should be "supporting herself" at least and ideally making enough money to help support the Congregation. This can easily lead to the scenario described above in which someone takes a job (gainful employment) and attempts to "baptize" it into a ministry by personal intention or motive. I have been trying to argue that, in reality, Religious, even in institutionalized ministries that did generate some revenue, were not actually supporting themselves. By their apostolates, they were involved in a unique economic system that worked under certain sociological conditions but that largely disappeared with the mainstreaming of the once self-contained immigrant Catholic community. But even if they had been supporting themselves or their Congregations, the equation of ministry with gainful employment would be theologically problematic.

The present situation finds Congregations struggling with day-to-day solvency and, sometimes, major debt, and trying to support ever-increasing numbers of aged and infirm members with the income of ever fewer "earners." This situation can generate high levels of anxiety and discouragement bordering on despair about the viability of the Congregation and its corporate ministry if not of Religious Life itself. Or it can offer a challenge to reenvision and appropriate anew the real meaning and role of ministry in Religious Life, which might provide the foundation of a different approach to the very real financial problems Congregations face. I would like to make a few suggestions about the second possibility. I am risking taking positions on some of the "hot button" questions in hopes of stimulating some thought and discussion about these "elephants in the living room" which we tend to talk around, not because I think I have workable answers to the problems.

It seems to me that the first challenge Religious Congregations face today is to achieve corporate clarity about the nature of ministry as it is presented in the New Testament and as it flows from the theology of Religious Life as an alternate world whose economy is one of gift rather than commodity. Ministry, as has been noted, has two biblical features that seem to be nonnegotiable.

First, *ministry is directly evangelical in intent.* It is explicit participation in Jesus' mission of preaching the Gospel to every creature. The nature of Religious Life as an alternate world, an incarnation as a historical lifeform of the Reign of God, involves a commitment to prophetic witness to and promotion of that Reign. Consequently, it is not the case that anything and everything done with a good intention or that produces some good effect is ministry, and *a fortiori*, Religious ministry.

The second feature, again flowing directly from Jesus' commissioning of his disciples and from the nature of Religious Life as a gift economy, is that ministry is not for sale. *Ministry is not a commodity but a gift.* It is not a way of taking care of oneself (the individual or the Congregation) by generating income but a way of enriching others. In the case of ministry, it is enrichment of others by the effective announcement of the Good News that the Reign of God is at hand.

Consequently, the first question that has to be asked when a Congregation discerns about its involvement in, continuation of, or support for a project or activity proposed as part of its corporate ministry is the same as the question that should be asked of an individual member who is discerning her/his ministry outside the framework of a Congregational institutional commitment. How through this activity (i.e., project, enterprise, etc.) will we/you promote the Reign of God? If there is no direct connection between what is being proposed and the proclamation of the Gospel, no matter how much revenue it might produce, it should not be pursued because it is not ministry.

This suggests that, given the current situation in both the

postconciliar Church and postmodern culture, communities probably need to have some serious discussions about how, today, we should understand "proclaiming the Gospel" and "promoting the Reign of God." Such questions had self-evident answers when, for example, the goal of the American hierarchy into which Religious were integrated, was "every Catholic child in a Catholic school." But if today most Catholic children are in public schools, and if a Gospel vision of ministry is not limited to Catholics, where and how can and should teaching, as ministry, occur? And is all teaching, no matter where, to whom, what, or under what conditions it takes place, ministry?

Ministry, I have argued, is Christian, that is, explicitly religious, by nature. Its purpose is to proclaim the Gospel, the liberating message of Jesus Christ. Today we need to inquire anew how Religious are to understand the relationship between their ministries and the Church. Are nonreligious projects which, though good and useful in themselves, have no reference to God, Jesus, the Gospel, or the ecclesial community, that is, no explicitly Christian identity, no methods or procedures which are normed by the Gospel or which model a Gospel way of life, actually a way of proclaiming the Gospel? Is any promotion of worthwhile objectives equivalent to promoting the Reign of God? Or does the Reign of God, the reality construction Jesus proposed in opposition to the reality construction of the Evil One, have a distinctive shape, coordinates, and content? And if the latter, what are they? Is helping IBM increase its quarterly profits ministry if it earns money for the Congregation? Is tutoring disadvantaged children in an inner-city school or caring for people living with HIV/AIDS ministry even if the pay is minimal or nonexistent? Are these (working for IBM or tutoring disadvantaged children) the contemporary equivalents of the works that Jesus sent the twelve or the seventy out to do?

Jesus challenged Zacchaeus to change the way he did his secular task of tax collecting. But he did not associate Zacchaeus with his band of itinerant ministers. Zacchaeus was called to be a good tax collector, but not to ministry. However, when Jesus called Levi to join that ministerial band he required Levi to leave the job of tax collecting behind to devote himself full-time to

Jesus' project. No doubt Jesus and his disciples could have used the income from Matthew's tax collecting or Peter's fishing. But they were not called to be tax collectors or fishermen with a good intention; they were called to ministry. What position should Religious, individually and corporately, take when genuine ministry which does not earn significantly (or at all) competes with a lucrative job that has no ministerial meaning?

The second question, it seems, is *what does it mean to minister freely*? Does this mean that Religious should simply donate their services without compensation or should allow themselves to be poorly compensated for the work they do as ministry when funds to pay for it are available? And if so, how are they to survive? It might be freeing to begin by recalling our challenge to the unspoken presupposition that often lies behind these questions, namely, that apostolic Religious have in the past been able to and, in fact, did support themselves by their apostolic work and therefore they should do so today. I have tried to show that ministerial Religious, in contrast to monastics who lived in an economically self-sufficient feudal lifeform, never have earned their living in the sense of supporting themselves. Institutionalization disguised this fact by making some apostolates (e.g., schools) look like their secular, moneymaking counterparts. Circumstances today, especially the de-institutionalization and individualization of ministry, simply reveal what has always been the case, that full time ministry, especially to the people who most need it, often will not support even the minister much less the Congregation. Ministry is certainly laborious work, but most often not in the sense of gainful employment adequate for the support of the minister or the community. Ministerial Religious have usually had to find ways to support their ministries rather than their ministries supporting them. The question is not how to overcome this situation, which actually seems to mark what we do as ministry rather than a job, but how to integrate this situation into our vision of Gospel mission and our practice of ministry.

Several facts, some of which have already been discussed at length, frame our substantive question: what does it mean to minister freely? First, Religious obviously require sufficient resources to live simply but decently, and the example of Jesus, as well as the approach to material goods of both Testaments, supports this. Second, first world culture does not support the kinds of work that Religious do as ministry. It will pay tens of millions of dollars to baseball players or movie stars but refuses to mandate a living wage for hard working parents in unskilled jobs or offer a salary sufficient to support professionals in education or health care. Third, even if (*per impossibile*) many or most of the active ministers in the average Religious Congregation earned six-figure salaries, their combined income could not support the community, liquidate debts, educate members, care for the aged and infirm, or underwrite nonpaying ministries. In short, Religious need resources to live, individually and corporately, if they are to minister at all, and those resources will not come primarily or adequately from the work they do as ministry. The conclusion is that support must come from elsewhere in a way that does not remove most of the members from ministry to the poor and the marginalized; the very people Jesus preferred and to whom he sent his disciples.

The freedom that, according to the Gospel, must characterize ministry, like the possessionlessness that characterizes community in the gift economy, is primarily a way of relating to material goods. The question is not how much a person is paid for the work s/he does in ministry but how pay (whether adequate or not) affects the choice of ministry, to whom one ministers, and how.

The Religious who is the CEO of a large hospital may be paid a salary that exceeds by tens of thousands of dollars the amount budgeted for the president of her Congregation who receives no "salary" at all. An inner-city community organizer whose minimal stipend has to be augmented by the Congregation to cover her living expenses, the ninety-year-old retired Sister in the infirmary whose needs are totally met by the Congregation, the fairly well-paid college professor, the spiritual director who is well remunerated by certain wealthy people but asks nothing of those who cannot afford spiritual assistance, and the hospice worker whose pay is minimally just are equally ministers. The point is not how much they "make" or do not make but the fact that they and the

Congregation are discerning and making choices not on the basis of how much each position pays but how each form of service promotes the Reign of God by proclaiming the Gospel in accord with the charism of the Congregation.

Most of these ministers are making some money; some are making nothing; and some are making a great deal. But they are all ministering freely because none of them is conditioning her ministry on the capacity of the receiver to pay. None of them is working for profit. The hospice worker would not accept a much more lucrative offer to model designer clothes. Nor would the community organizer abandon his ministry if the already-meager funding dried up entirely. But the college president will negotiate for the best salary she can command and the spiritual director will willingly accept compensation from those who can afford it. The hospital CEO does not budget for luxuries nor feel superior to the Congregational president and the retiree praying for the community does not feel ashamed of her need. In other words, to minister freely does not necessarily mean to receive no remuneration for one's work. Jesus' saying on ministering freely includes the assurance, "…for the worker deserves his [her] wages," which means support (Luke 10:7). Ministry is not necessarily volunteer work. But it is undertaken to proclaim the Gospel by serving those in need, not to generate income.

If this Gospel principle of ministry as gift is firmly in place and we are realistic about both the needs of ministers and their Congregations for support and the hard facts regarding remuneration in a first world context for service to the most needy, the conclusion seems to be that, like Jesus and the first Christian communities, today's Religious have to be as creative as were our founders in generating the resources necessary to support our members and our ministries. In the gift economy, this is a corporate challenge, not an individual problem. If those whose ministries are well compensated transfer everything they do not need and no one excuses her or himself from the obligation to work as long and hard as s/he is able the common purse will distribute resources according to need. And that purse will be part of a creative plan to generate funds for life and ministry. But such creative plans need to be developed with focused intention and political and social sophistication.

In fact, many Congregations have made great strides in this area. Sophisticated development offices with multiple coordinated projects and structures of contribution are actively inviting generous donors into financial partnership with Religious in ministry. Wise investments can generate far more than salaries ever did or could. Intercongregational ministries, individual Religious sharing ministerial gifts across Congregational lines, shared use of facilities, and shared national collections maximize personal and monetary resources for all participants. Religious, both individual ministers seeking support for their own ministries and Congregations as such, are learning to find and obtain grants, including those earmarked for financial development.

In other words, Religious have discovered that there is money available in the richest countries in the world to meet the needs that ministry addresses, but it is concentrated in the hands of the wealthy. Helping to redistribute it from the bank accounts of the wealthiest to the outstretched hands of the poorest via the ministries of Religious and others is not begging. It is a ministry in itself. But these tactics need to be coordinated into overall strategies, communicated effectively to all members of the community, and affirmed not as stopgap or emergency measures to get the Congregation "out of the woods" but as the appropriate way to finance ministry to the neediest in a capitalistic economy.

The foregoing tactics might be supplemented by others that might seem a little less immediately self-validating. Might a Religious, like Paul making tents, work part time in a secular job to support her non- or low-paying ministry? Might one Religious work at such a job to support another member ministering to those unable to pay as, in the past, some Religious did manual labor in the convent or hospital to enable others to nurse or teach? In these cases, works that are not ministries as such become the ministry of support. This is not a case of "baptizing" a job by good intentions but of ministering through participation in the ministry of another. If such arrangements were adopted by a Congregation today, care would have to be taken not to reestablish social class distinctions within the community on the basis of type of work or earning power.

I am suggesting that, in the last three decades, the basic understanding of work-as-ministry has undergone piecemeal reformulation among ministerial Religious in response to financial crises that have appeared to be due to changes in the work-as-support system. An unreflective identification of the two aspects of work arose out of the nearly total institutionalization of the ministries of Religious in the nineteenth and early twentieth centuries, which created the impression that ministry was supporting the Religious even as it served the needy. As the economic system that supported this misidentification came apart, Religious faced rising costs, increasing debt, declining membership, and increasing age and illness of members. This has created a situation in which the Gospel nature of ministry as a proclamation of the Gospel freely offered has been obscured by financial emergencies. The experience gained through living with these crises and meeting these emergencies needs to be imaginatively integrated into a theology of Religious Life as an alternate economic world created by the vow of evangelical poverty. Out of this alternate world Religious minister, that is, they freely proclaim and promote the Reign of God.

The current situation can be seen as the death knell of a once viable lifeform (as some proponents of a return to preconciliar Religious Life are gleefully predicting) or as a call to Religious as individuals and in community to embrace scarcity with the confidence in providence that has characterized virtually every Religious foundation. This "simplicity of the dove" does not preclude the "wisdom of the serpent" as Religious affirm the biblical ideal of having sufficient resources so that they are not preoccupied by want but not enough to become self-sufficient and independent before God. Corporate Anawim spirituality in a capitalist environment calls for an organized, purposeful, creative approach to generating material support for ministry and ministers. But it also calls us to keep our vision clear of dollar signs that obscure our Gospel motivation.

V. Summary and Conclusions

This chapter has been an examination of the economics of the alternate world which Religious create through Profession of the vow of evangelical poverty, live in as a community of those who possess nothing, and out of which they freely proclaim the Gospel in ministry to those in need. In creating this alternate world they attempt to be a historical incarnation of the imaginative reality construction of Jesus in opposition to the reality construction of the Prince of This World. The economic system of this alternate world I have described as a gift economy of being in contrast to the commodity economy of having. The Gospel way of dealing with material goods not as things to be acquired but as resources to be shared is the economic foundation for the community life of Religious as well as for their ministry. It is a prophetic lifeform in the Church for the sake of the world.

Chapter Six
Poverty of Spirit in the Quest for God

I. Transition and Introduction

Each of the vows Religious profess has at least three mutually interactive dimensions: the communitarian, the ministerial, and the unitive. In the last chapter we investigated how the communitarian and ministerial dimensions of the vow of evangelical poverty help create and foster the alternate world of Religious Life structured by the gift economy of the Reign of God rather than the commodity economy of the world in which we live. In this chapter we will focus on the unitive dimension of the vow of poverty, that is, on how the vow of evangelical poverty functions, or can function, in the personal spirituality of the individual Religious to foster the quest for God which is the very purpose of the life.

Let us begin by briefly recalling the conclusions from the exploration in chapter 4 of the biblical data on poverty. As we saw, both testaments agree that poverty is a polyvalent term that can refer to economic destitution (material want), sociological oppression (injustice), or a religious disposition of total reliance on God (Anawim spirituality). The first, when it is not caused by folly or laziness, is a physical evil that is not willed by God and is to be relieved, to the extent possible, by the efforts of the poor themselves and especially by the practice of justice and generous sharing by those who are better off. The second is the result of moral evil by the oppressor and it demands conversion and restitution. The third is a religious disposition that renders "the poor one" especially precious in the sight of God. It can be precipitated by material want or oppression, but it need not be. A rich person can be a true "poor one of Yahweh" and a poor person can be estranged from God and neighbor by anger, greed, and envy. Anawim spirituality or poverty of spirit is our concern in this chapter.

A. The Gospel *Novum* in Regard to Poverty: Renouncing All

As we have seen, the *novum* of the New Testament in regard to poverty, introduced by the example and teaching of Jesus, is the call to "renounce all" in order to follow him. This unequivocal demand of Jesus is directed equally to all his disciples, both to the itinerant band who went about with him sharing his full time ministry to the Reign of God (as do ministerial Religious today) and to those who were householders raising families and employed in secular tasks (as were most of Jesus' disciples in New Testament times, in the early Church, and throughout Christian history to our own day). This demand for total renunciation is neither a pure ideal that can be dismissed as hyperbole nor a completely impossible literal demand which would make virtually all Jesus' disciples spiritual failures. Jesus' demand that his followers "renounce all," like what follows, "take up your cross," is to be taken utterly seriously, though not necessarily literally. And it will be incarnated differently by different disciples living in different life situations. Not all will take up their cross by literally undergoing physical crucifixion; but none are exempt from facing the consequences, sometimes severe, of following Jesus in a world still under the influence of the Evil One.[1] Not every disciple will renounce all by literal possessionlessness like the members of the first Jerusalem community or Religious who make a vow of evangelical poverty; but no disciple is exempt from complete detachment from possessions even if or while one participates in the commodity economy.

The principle of the Gospel *novum* of renouncing all is "No one can serve two masters. Either he will hate the one and love the other, or he will be devoted to the one and despise the other.

You cannot serve God and mammon" (Matt 6:24; cf. Luke 16:13). Mammon, as we saw, is not wealth as such but possessions that have become one's "treasure," an idol or a false god, a master who commands the love and service due to God alone. But, though wealth is not necessarily Mammon, it is so difficult for humans to be detached from wealth, especially when it accumulates, that Jesus compares this feat to a camel going through the eye of a needle, something that is impossible for humans who can accomplish it only though the power of God.

Since virtually all disciples will necessarily possess and use money and even those with a vow of poverty will use it at least corporately, we need a principle of discernment, a way to tell whether our relationship to material goods is actually one of total detachment that leaves God as sole master in our lives, or whether we are really serving another master, Mammon. As we saw, Jesus supplied such a criterion, trust that overcomes anxiety:

> "...I tell you, do not worry about your life, what you will eat or what you will drink, or about your body, what you will wear.... Look at the birds of the air; they neither sow nor reap nor gather into barns, and yet your heavenly Father feeds them. Are you not of more value than they? And can any of you by worrying add a single hour to your span of life? ...you of little faith...it is the Gentiles who strive for these things; and indeed your heavenly Father knows that you need all these things. But strive first for the kingdom of God and his righteousness, and all these things will be given you as well. So do not worry about tomorrow...." (Matt 6:25–34)

In this passage Jesus says that anxiety about material goods or even life itself, as well as the conviction that we can achieve security in regard to these matters by working or worrying, is the sign of "little faith."

B. The Distinctiveness the Gospel *Novum* in Religious Life

In chapter 5 we explored the most important implications, at the corporate or community level, of undertaking to "renounce all" by a perpetual vow of evangelical poverty. Religious through their Profession of vows create an alternate world, an actual sociological realization in history of a lifeform in which the economic system of the Reign of God, the gift economy, is constitutive of their community life and ministry. However, their commitment to this new reality goes beyond the purely human ideal of gift economies, not only by the fact that the commitment is lifelong, but by the literal and complete self-divestment by all members through which they enter into this community of life. This divestment creates the life of total economic interdependence in which all contribute everything to and receive everything from the "common purse." Economic common life, as we saw, entails not only actual possessionlessness of each member but the attitudes and behaviors which make the common life both genuinely egalitarian and life-sustaining for all even as it supports the full time ministerial commitment of the Congregation.

We explored in some detail the effect of the perpetual vow of poverty on the ministry of Religious. Like those Jesus called into his itinerant band, Religious undertake full-time commitment to the preaching of the Good News. And like Jesus' first disciples missioned to announce the Reign of God, Religious do not carry on this ministry *as* gainful employment (even if, in fact, it helps support them and the Congregation). Rather, as those who have freely received, they are committed to freely give.

We looked realistically at some of the current potentially anxiety-producing results of trying to fulfill this Gospel charge outside the economically self-contained context of the enclosed medieval monastery and in a culture that is not as disposed to almsgiving as was medieval Christendom. The economic system in which ministerial Religious functioned prior to the Council and which was never really a commodity-based system of earning their way by services rendered, but rather a unique system of interdependence between Religious and the Catholic subcultures they served, fell apart in the mid-twentieth century due to sociocultural factors in late modernity over which Religious had no control. Combined with the decline in numbers of personnel, this created the economic crisis many Religious

Congregations are facing today. Nevertheless, while these difficulties are very real and have to be met with the creative ingenuity and the trust in God that Jesus preached and that motivated and sustained the founders of many of these Religious Congregations, they must not be allowed to compromise either the commitment of Religious to ministry or the freedom with which they exercise it.

II. The Meaning of Poverty of Spirit in Christian Spirituality

Individual Religious, by embracing complete possessionlessness on the day of Profession, not only enter into the community life of the alternate economic world and commit themselves to participation in its ministry, but they also lay the foundation for a personal spirituality of evangelical poverty whose goal is union with Jesus in his total self-gift to God in the Spirit for the salvation of the world. However, becoming in fact the "poor ones of God" following the poor Jesus, a task heroically undertaken in the original commitment, demands a lifetime of fidelity through challenges and failures and ongoing conversion. Different Religious families have elaborated diverse spiritualities of poverty, stressing voluntary material renunciation, community sharing, simplicity of lifestyle, generosity, solidarity with the materially poor, and other aspects of the virtue. My aim in this chapter is not to catalogue or describe these approaches or champion any one emphasis or form over any other in the practice of poverty. Rather, I want to get to the roots of evangelical poverty which generate whatever concrete practices are espoused in particular traditions of spirituality.

As a foundation for "unpacking" this unitive dimension of the spirituality of evangelical poverty I propose that we examine the ideal of poverty as it is formulated in the New Testament, namely, the first Beatitude. Both Matthew and Luke present Jesus proclaiming the *blessedness of the truly poor*. The similarity and the differences between the two versions are mutually illuminating.

A. The Beatitude of the Poor

Some contemporary Christians, including some New Testament scholars, in their concern to be realistic about the Christian project of evangelical poverty, prefer Luke's version of the Beatitude, "Blessed are you who are poor, for yours is the kingdom of God" (6:20) to Matthew's, "Blessed are the poor in spirit, for theirs is the kingdom of heaven" (5:3).[2] Except for the reverential use of "heaven" (a euphemism for the divine name) in Matthew's text, the major difference between the two formulations is Matthew's qualification, "in spirit," which can appear to be an idealization or "spiritualizing" of the harsh reality of real material poverty. The scriptural background developed in chapter 4 suggests that such is not the case. Luke's "poor" and Matthew's "poor in spirit" are identical in meaning and the Beatitude is addressed equally to all disciples regardless of their economic situation or state of life. Both evangelists are evoking the same religious/spiritual meaning of poverty, that is, "Anawim spirituality," the spirituality Jesus modeled in his relationship of total dependence on and confidence in the one he called "Abba,"[3] and the spirituality to which their vow of poverty calls Religious. This becomes clear as we compare the two accounts on three points: audience, context, and the theme of the great reversal.

First, each of the evangelists presents Jesus as addressing a particular audience. In Luke Jesus directly *exhorts* his hearers in the second person as *you* poor, you who hunger, you who mourn, you who are persecuted. In Matthew Jesus *teaches* his disciples in the third person, speaking about *those who* are poor in spirit.

The Lukan Jesus is presented as addressing a mixed audience composed of "his [i.e., Jesus'] disciples" and a crowd of "people" (presumably inquirers or potential disciples) from all over Judea, Tyre, and Sidon. In effect, this audience reflects Luke's community. The composition of this community is a subject of some controversy among exegetes, but a reliable position is represented by Lukan scholar Robert Karris who says that the third evangelist was writing in the early 90s to a predominantly Gentile-Christian audience located in pluralistic Syrian Antioch.[4] Many of these Gentile converts were well to do, the materially comfortable people whom Luke, throughout the Gospel, exhorts to generous sharing and social inclusiveness toward other members of the community who were economically poor, disabled, blind, sick, or marginalized in some other way. Such inclusiveness would have presented a serious challenge to the well-off in a Hellenistic-Gentile context. Nevertheless, it is hardly conceivable that Luke was dividing his community into the materially poor who are blessed and the economically affluent who are not.

Jesus' words in the Lukan sermon on the plain are addressed to a particular "you," that is, all who are listening to him, who must understand his words as addressed to themselves. All of them, wealthy and poor alike, are either the *truly poor* of the first Beatitude or "the rich" of the first Woe. Jesus is certainly not exhorting anyone to become materially destitute, hungry, or miserable. He is assuring those who are materially poor that they are dear to God, as were the Anawim of old, if indeed they cast all their care upon the One who hears the cries of those in distress. But he is simultaneously, and by the same words, challenging the well-off to that same Anawim poverty which is absolutely requisite for participation in the Reign of God. If, because of their confidence in their material wealth, they are not among these "poor" who are blessed, then the first Woe, "Woe to you who are rich," applies to them, not because they *have* money but because it is, in their case, *Mammon*. In other words, "the poor" is a spiritual category which includes the materially disadvantaged who trust in God for help and the well-off who know that their riches are neither their own nor their source of security but who look to God for the latter even as they reach out in effective solidarity to their suffering sisters and brothers. Luke's Gospel seems to suggest that there were more economically secure than desperately poor people in his community and that he is more concerned with their wise and generous use of their goods than with the patient suffering of the materially poor, since the plight of the latter could and should be relieved by the generosity of the former. The materially rich becoming spiritually poor would go far toward solving the economic problems of the materially poor.

In Matthew Jesus is not directly exhorting a "you" but teaching his disciples about the "kingdom of heaven" to which they all are called. Matthew's community, for whom this Gospel was written, consisted predominantly of Jewish converts to Christianity who saw themselves as reconstituted Israel.[5] The first and most basic characteristic of one who participates in this renewed People of God is the poverty of the Anawim who awaited in suffering hope God's vindication which arrived in Jesus. The kingdom, now as in the Old Testament, belongs to the "poor of Yahweh." Whatever a person's economic situation, the poverty to which they are called is that total openness to and dependence on God that characterized the Anawim. Matthew's first Beatitude, therefore, makes this explicit, "Blessed are the poor *in spirit*." One is not congratulated, declared blessed, simply because one is indigent. Poverty may be a more propitious platform from which to become the spiritually "poor one" precisely because it is difficult (though not impossible) to reject God when there is no place else to turn. Riches, on the other hand, are an occupational hazard (but not necessarily an impediment) for the believer because riches tend to blind one to one's need of God.

So the Matthean and Lukan Beatitudes carry the same message differently expressed because of the different rhetorical contexts and audiences. Those who are *truly poor* (whatever their material situation in life) are declared blessed. Because their hope is in God, not in anything of this world, their trust cannot be confounded. They are already and will be participants in the Reign of God.

Second, the context of persecution was common to both communities. Both evangelists probably used the so-called "sayings source" (Q)[6] for the three Beatitudes, namely, the blessing or congratulations of the poor, the mourning, and the hungering, which form the core of the passage in each Gospel. Both evangelists end the Beatitudes with the blessing on those who, like the prophets of old (and the prophet Jesus), are persecuted. This concluding Beatitude is actually an expanded summary and explicitation of the preceding ones and gives a clue to the real meaning of why the suffering are being "congratulated." It is not because they are, *in fact*, being oppressed but because of *why* they are being oppressed, that is, "for the sake of justice" in Matthew and "on account of the Son of Man" in Luke. They are blessed not because they are persecuted but because in the persecution that comes upon them because of their discipleship they rely totally on the One in whom they believe and steadfastly bear witness to their faith and hope despite physical and social suffering.

Persecution because of one's Christian commitment was, in fact, very likely to be a mark of a follower of Jesus in the first century. Opposition came from both the synagogue, which, especially after the fall of the Jerusalem temple, was becoming much less tolerant of sectarian or dissenting positions in the Jewish community, and from the Roman Empire which increasingly experienced the new Christian movement as politically and socially subversive. Persecution fell upon both poor and well-off Christians. But it left them all, whatever their class or status, hungry for justice and filled with sorrow, challenged to meekness and peacemaking in the face of violence and rejection. The "poor of Yahweh" stood fast in persecution because, like Stephen who is presented in Acts as a model of this poverty even though he was brilliant, well educated, eloquent, probably affluent, and certainly influential, [7] they were convinced that God in Jesus could and would save them.

Third, both versions of the Beatitudes presume the dynamic of "the great reversal." On the day of the Lord the poor will receive the kingdom, the mourning will rejoice, the hungering will be satisfied, the persecuted will be vindicated. And Luke intensifies this dynamic by the "Woes" (vss. 24–26) in which it is evoked in reverse: woe to you who are rich, well-fed, rejoicing, respected by all because you will experience the opposite. In the Reign of God things will be very different from what, in this world, appears to be the case.

We need to recall here our discussion of "world" in part 1. Two regimes are opposed to each other in the course of history: the Kingdom of Satan and the Reign of God. In these two

reality constructions, which are simultaneous and coterminous, the weeds and the wheat grow together in the field of this
world. Because the Reign of God is like a mustard seed or a bit
of yeast in a mass of dough, it is much less visible, seemingly
much less powerful than Satan's Kingdom, which is evidently
in the ascendancy. The denizens of that kingdom are those
who, in Walter Brueggemann's words, share the "royal imagination."[8] So, they are rich, well fed, filled with laughter, well
treated by the powerful. But the citizens of the Reign of God,
those who are energized by the "prophetic imagination," are
the poor, the hungry and thirsty, the mourning, the outcasts,
the downtrodden, and the persecuted. The Beatitudes congrat-
ulate these "losers" because, in the great reversal that is surely
coming when the "poor ones of Yahweh" will be vindicated,
they will be those Mary sang of in the "Magnificat" who will
receive God's mercy, be raised up, and be filled with good
things while the powerful and the well-fed will be rejected and
sent away empty (Luke 1:46–55).

In summary, both evangelists present Jesus as declaring
"blessed" those who are **truly poor**. In both Matthew and Luke,
the concluding Beatitude of those who are persecuted for the
sake of justice, that is, for Jesus' sake, clearly indicates that it is
not material conditions, whether material poverty or economic
wealth, that justify the congratulations offered to those who are
poor. Rather, they are congratulated because, as the truly poor,
the Anawim of God, they belong to the Reign of God. If they
are materially poor their disadvantaged condition in this world
is the manifestation of which (or whose) side they have chosen.
If they are well off their non-identification with the wealthy and
powerful, their solidarity with the disadvantaged, their dependence on God alone manifests the same disposition. This
choice, to cling to God alone in the face of the pressure,
whether coming from need or from the temptation to align
oneself with the *status quo* of Satan's regime or both, qualifies
them as the Anawim, waiting in hope for divine vindication. In
Johannine terms, if they were of this world, the world would
love its own. But since they are not of this world, as Jesus was
not of this world, the world hates them (see John 15:18–19).

B. The Implications for Religious of their Christian Vocation to Poverty of Spirit

The point of the foregoing is that Jesus' challenge to poverty of spirit, that is, to *true poverty*, is neither a "watering down" of the challenge to embrace real material hardship nor an invitation to an elite group to embrace voluntary destitution. Like the demand to "renounce all" it is a requirement for all Christians, for all who would participate in the Reign of God. When Jesus said that unless we receive the Reign of God as a little child we cannot enter it (see Mark 10:15 and parallels), he was not romanticizing the innocence of youth. The child, totally dependent on others for survival, is the concrete image of the one who, as Jesus says in John 15:5, can do nothing apart from him. The poor in spirit are those who know this and embrace this condition of total openness to and dependence on God. They alone are capable of receiving that which is inaccessible to unaided human efforts.

Religious share with all Christians this nonnegotiable condition for participation in the Reign of God. While their way of becoming poor in spirit is distinctive, the substance of the response is identical for all Christians. Religious, by their vow of poverty, undertake with and in their Congregation the construction of an alternate world rooted in the complete material self-divestment of every member. As we saw in the last chapter, the resulting economy of gift that characterizes this alternate world shapes their community life of total economic interdependence and their full-time, lifelong ministry of freely proclaiming the Reign of God. But it also is the root of their personal spirituality, the living of poverty of spirit both as members of the community and as individuals.

1. Corporate poverty of spirit[9]

Corporately, the Religious community in which vowed evangelical poverty is a reality will manifest in its life and mission its foundational choice for God and against Mammon. Religious Life, by choice, is neither a guarantee of financial security nor a money-making enterprise. Neither security nor profit brought the members together nor does it sustain their unity. But survival issues can easily pressure a Congregation into an obsession with money that subverts both community and ministry and compromises the fundamental commitment of the group to seeking first the Reign of God trusting that everything else that is really needed will be provided by their heavenly Parent.

Using the principle of discernment supplied by Jesus, a community can know whether poverty of spirit reigns among them by whether trust or anxiety is the climate of their life together and their corporate ministry. Today, the motives for anxiety and insecurity, if not outright panic, are multiple and urgent. This situation can easily provoke Congregations to responses typical of those whom Jesus described as sharing the anxiety of the "pagans" who do not know the God who cares more for them than for many sparrows. In the last chapter we looked at some of the moves that desperation about security can elicit. The point of looking honestly at this "elephant in the living room" was to challenge ourselves as communities to acknowledge the scope of the problem while refusing to succumb to solutions that would undermine the life itself such as foregoing the preaching of the Gospel in favor of paying jobs or putting price tags on our ministries that put them out of reach of those who most need them.

On the other hand, the community cannot sit in chapel expecting a financial windfall to eliminate debt and pay the bills. Congregations are challenged to put all necessary energy and creativity into dealing with their financial problems without permitting the anxiety over what "we will eat or wear or how we will sustain our lives" to subvert their prayer, community, and ministry.

While this is a struggle for each individual Religious, it is also a communal struggle. Anxiety, to say nothing of panic, is contagious. Even a few members' hoarding, nonaccountability, irresponsibility, selfishness, "outsourcing" of personal security, despair or laziness can demoralize others and create a self-fulfilling prophecy of doom. Conversely, prayerfulness, joy, confidence in others, willing restriction of wants, communal participation in efforts to find solutions, trust in and support of leadership, and commitment to contributing as well and as long as possible support corporate trust in the God who can and will provide for those whose poverty of spirit acknowledges only one sufficient Source of all good things.

2. Personal poverty of spirit

Before we turn to the topic of the deep spiritual roots of poverty and what it might look like in the ascetical practice, personal ministerial spirituality, and prayer life of the individual Religious in the contemporary context, I want to dwell for a moment on why the individual living of the vow of poverty has become a very different project in the postconciliar context than it was forty years ago. In my experience of Congregations in general, this is not due to laxity on the part of individuals or a general loss of fervor among Religious. It is the result of a radically changed context from that in which preconciliar Religious were formed in and vowed poverty.

Each individual Religious on the day of Profession undertook by vow a life rooted in complete dispossession. This not only created the basis and framework for a particular and distinctive incarnation of poverty of spirit and situated that project in the corporate context of a particular Congregation, but also inaugurated a lifelong project of becoming personally poor in spirit, truly poor, in imitation of Jesus, the poor one of God. This personal project will continue until the Religious breathes her life into the hands of God at death.

However, when most Religious alive today entered their communities the personal practice of poverty had been routinized and even mechanized by uniform practice over decades if not centuries within an essentially monastic form of enclosed, collective common life. There was little room, and not much need, for individual initiative or originality in the understanding or practice of the vow. This is not to say that individuals did not differ in generosity or even inventiveness in this area but, in general, everyone knew what was required in the Congregation, how to fulfill those requirements, and how to recover from failure. The fundamentally monastic form of common life and the system of permissions regulated virtually everything pertaining to the personal relation of the Religious to material goods.

The enormous changes in community life and ministry in the wake of the Council, especially the individualization of many aspects of life that had been basically collective in the past, so altered the rules of the game in the area of poverty that very few of the externals one had learned in initial formation were any longer applicable. Nor, given the speed and extensiveness of the changes, was there time or the necessary experience to develop alternative approaches. In many Congregations *ad hoc* solutions to novel and urgent problems in regard to housing, furnishings, equipment, reeducation for new ministries, communication, travel, transportation, the handling of money, and so on became precedents or even policies before they had even been discussed and, when such procedures did not work for the next person, new ones had to be invented.

Religious have been, for good and less-good reasons, extremely reticent to discuss money or its handling among themselves because they have not developed a common understanding that creates ground rules for behavior. What might seem absolutely necessary or at least defensible to one person might be shocking to someone else. The overall result of this largely unregulated development and the idiosyncrasies it has spawned has led some Religious to a *de facto*, if not theoretical, conclusion that the personal practice of poverty is simply a relic of a bygone age, the vestige of a spirituality obsessively focused on minutiae in an enclosed situation of economic immaturity. For some, evangelical poverty as a dimension of personal Religious spirituality has become a nonfunctional category. They do the best they can under the circumstances, without assuming others will understand what they are choosing or that they could, or need to, explain it.

Many highly motivated and zealous Religious have resituated their real concerns about poverty from the realm of personal practice to that of ministry. Solidarity with the economically deprived, ministry to those who are oppressed by capitalist market economies or the politics in poor countries, volunteer work in soup kitchens and thrift shops, participation in literacy programs and shelters for women and children, and projects like Habitat for Humanity or America's Second Harvest provide an opportunity for hands-on commitment to the materially poor without the necessity of pretending that one is poor oneself when, in fact, one's basic needs are adequately met. Others have turned to involvement in systemic change toward social justice as the most effective way to struggle against the causes of poverty. But sometimes these Religious do not see much connection between their commitment to the alleviation and eventual abolition of material poverty among the oppressed and the role of a personal spirituality of poverty in their own lives. This is the issue to which we now turn: what role does evangelical poverty play in the personal spiritual life of the individual Religious?

III. Desire and Poverty in the Spiritual Life

A. Locating the Problem: The Ambiguity of Desire

Even a cursory knowledge of the world's wisdom traditions, both philosophical and religious, suffices to establish that possessions, especially when abundant, are seen almost universally as a danger to the spiritual life. The danger is both personal and social. It is not the possession or lack of material goods as such that is problematic but, from the personal standpoint, it is the *craving* which a perceived or actual lack of goods induces and the *dissipation and luxury* that a surfeit of goods produces that impede the spiritual project. And from the social standpoint, possession of material goods is *divisive*.[10] As we saw in chapter 3 in relation to the origin of the evil against which Christian mission struggles, mimetic desire results in envy, covetousness, greed, selfishness, hoarding, and even violence. As the first letter to Timothy says, "…the love of money is the root of all evils, and some people in their desire for it have strayed from the faith" (1 Tim 6:10; translation is NAB).

All the great wisdom traditions have wrestled with the baffling paradox that humans cannot live at all without material goods but seem unable to live well with them. Humans, apparently, are the only animals who egregiously overeat, become addicted to substances they know will harm them, misuse sex, turn necessary storing into useless hoarding, deify money, and fight over goods that neither party really needs. Why do we humans become the willing slaves of what has been given to us to promote our well-being? Why are we possessed by our possessions? Why do we subordinate our aspirations for our highest values and noblest ideals to a base compulsion to possess? Many wisdom traditions have come to the same conclusion, namely, that at the root of all this dysfunction is desire. On the one hand, desire is what moves us to survive, to propagate, to achieve, to relate, to learn, to love, even to seek God. On the other hand, desire is a dynamic that seems intrinsically disordered.

The dynamics of desire, and the need to control if not eliminate it, has led many wisdom traditions to propose, at least for its "virtuosi,"[11] strenuous, even extreme, forms of asceticism in regard to food and drink, clothing, shelter, sleep, sex, speech, money, and the possession of personal property. Christian Religious Life, however, is both similar in some respects to spiritual virtuosity in other traditions and different in important ways precisely because it is Christian.

Christianity, based in the Incarnation of the Word of God and the sacramentalism to which the Incarnation gives rise, has been both less and more absolute in its approach to material goods. On the one hand, as we discussed at some length in chapter 1, Christianity affirms the goodness of all Creation and therefore the legitimacy of loving and using material goods that are meant, as Teilhard de Chardin made us aware, to be integrated by humans into the cosmic liturgy in praise of the Creator. On the other hand, as we saw in the last section, Jesus demands the renunciation of all things by those who wish to follow him.

Scripture seems to suggest that the reconciliation of these apparent opposites lies in the meaning of "renouncing all." Total detachment from everything insofar as anything impedes complete self-gift to and dependence on God is required of all disciples even though not all are called to incarnate this renunciation in the complete self-divestment which Religious undertake through the vow of evangelical poverty. And complete self-divestment by Religious is not an espousal of destitution but a renunciation of ownership in an economy of gift that is intended on the one hand to abolish the negative fallout from proprietorship and on the other to materially support all members of the community while enabling them to preach the Gospel freely.

B. Analyzing the Problem: Creaturehood

As background for an exploration of the role of evangelical poverty in the ordering of desire in Religious Life let me recall several points that have been developed previously. First, in the Christian context, neither material goods as such nor their possession and use are considered intrinsically evil. Second, desire, as a movement of the person toward the perceived good, is an absolutely necessary and fundamentally positive dynamic of the spiritual life. Therefore, third, the purpose of asceticism in the Christian spiritual life, including the practice of evangelical poverty, is not the eradication of desire but its ordering and education leading to the gradual integration of the person as the free and empowered subject of union with God.[12] Fourth, poverty as a condition of the spiritual life is not equivalent to material destitution nor necessarily fostered by it.

In chapter 3, I described briefly the astute analysis of the Genesis narrative of the fall by the German Scripture scholar and depth psychologist, Eugen Drewermann. The reader will recall that Drewermann was not proposing some kind of historical examination of "what happened at the beginning of human history" but was using the theological myth of the fall to explore in depth the human predicament as we continue to experience it even today. He examined the classical positions on the motivations of our mythical first parents in the fatal choice that we call original sin, and he rejected these classical theories in favor of the explanation that the fundamental motivation for the "sin" that alienated humans from themselves, each other, nonhuman creation, and God was not disobedience, pride, or lust, but fear.

As the pinnacle of Creation, human beings made in God's own image and likeness were gifted from the beginning with all that they needed for personal and species survival and flourishing: each other as equal partners in life, love, and work; responsibility for meaningful participation in God's own creative activity; intimacy with God in loving familiarity. Into this paradisiacal situation the serpent insinuated the diabolical suspicion that the God who had so lavishly endowed the human being was untrustworthy and therefore dangerous.

In the mythical scenario, Adam and Eve through the suggestion of the serpent became explicitly conscious of their creaturehood, that they were not the source of their own being and therefore not in control of it. Rather, God had called them forth from nothingness in an excess of love. God, the serpent suggested, could recall that gift. Unless the human couple could somehow secure possession of divinity itself, could become "like God" (recall, they were created in the image and likeness of God; they possessed by gift what they felt they lacked) in self-sufficient being, they lived under the sword of Damocles of annihilation.

The serpent persuaded them that eating of the tree of the knowledge of good and evil, far from bringing death as God, jealously protecting "his" superiority, had fallaciously warned, would give them ontological independence from a capricious, malevolent Creator who could reduce them, at will, to the nothingness from which they came. Thus, concludes Drewermann, the motivation for the original sin, the self-chosen alienation of humans from their all-loving Creator, was ontological insecurity in the face of nonexistence giving rise to existential dread of nonbeing. The choice was not between obedience and disobedience to some arbitrary "test" of subordination to an absolute divine tyrant but between acceptance and nonacceptance of *existence as gift*.

This interpretation sheds considerable light on a number of New Testament texts we have already considered in relation to poverty. For example, Jesus' sayings that we must receive the Reign of God "as a little child," or that without him we "can do nothing," can be, and often are, read as moral exhortations to an attitude of trust in or reliance on God. While this interpretation is certainly valid, these texts take on much greater depth if they are seen as actually evoking, and inviting us to embrace, our ontological contingency, our very real total dependence on God not only for all that we have, but for all that we are. In John, Jesus is even more radical. Not only can we not do anything good or salvific unless we remain in Jesus as a branch in the vine; we can do nothing at all. Cut off from him we are not only barren, we wither and die (see John 15:5–6). When Jesus points out that we cannot, by worrying about it, add an inch to our height or a moment to our life he is saying that we are indeed simply nonexistent unless called into being, moment by moment, by our Creator.

The ontological dependence of humans on God is not, as the serpent tempted Adam and Eve to believe, a threat God holds over creatures to compel their obedient submission. Drewermann says that this interpretation of the creaturely condition as one of subordination to a divine despot who, if provoked, can cut the fine thread of being itself is precisely the root of the violent God-image that has distorted the human relationship with God "from the foundation of the world."[13] The issue is not submission to a dangerous deity. It is the acceptance of the absolute and radical giftedness of being itself.

God created Adam and Eve (that is, humans) out of love, an infinite love that could not have been motivated by anything the creatures had to offer since prior to their creation they were not. In other words, it was unconditional, originating love that communicated being to what did not even exist, that drew into being out of nothingness creatures whom God created solely in order to love them. They had nothing to offer God except what God had bestowed on them. Again, a biblical text we examined in relation to ministry, "Freely have you received, so freely give," takes on deeper meaning in this context. It is not simply that ministers should share with those in need without expecting pay. Rather, in experiencing their very being as divine gift ministers reach out to foster, promote, and enable the very being of those to whom they are sent, particularly by announcing to them the good news that they are called and gifted to participate in the Reign of God.

Human beings, the Genesis myth suggests, find the fact that God needs nothing from creatures but created them only in order to gift them with divine life simply "too good to be true." Absolutely unconditional love is nearly impossible to imagine, much less believe. Human experience, even in the best of circumstances, rarely if ever offers us totally gratuitous love which nothing we can do would or could subvert. Perhaps the closest we come to experiencing such love is the love of a parent for an infant before it is even capable of returning or refusing that love. This may account for Jesus' preference for the parent-child metaphor for divine love, his experience of his human relationship to God as "Abba."

But human love, even at its best, is a faint image of the ontological self-giving of the Creator-God. Furthermore, human beings have a deep-seated fear of such a totally gratuitous, "unmotivated" love, suspecting that it is as unreliable as our own. We seem to need always to control love by having something to offer that the other needs, some way of reciprocating in kind so that no debts pile up, some protection against the devastation the other could wreak if, for some reason, he or she rejected us. We tend to suspect anyone who gives, who loves "for no reason at all." Our suspicion is that they are manipulating or dominating us by giving what we cannot repay, killing us with a kindness that reduces us to inert patients of another's action.

We might speak here, with reverence, of "God's dilemma." God could only create us out of nothing because that is what Creation is, by definition. But to create us out of nothing was to love "outside the box" of our human experience. It was to invite us to accept a love that "has no reason at all" arising from our own being, to believe that this love is not a subtle means of controlling us but a gift given in sheer unconditional gratuity. But, alas, as God made humans in God's own image and likeness, humans immediately constructed God in our likeness. What we seldom if ever experience in our own limited loving we cannot imagine of God. So we have attributed to God the self-interestedness (God made us to give "him" glory), the dominative power (we must submit to God's commands even if they seem contrary to our good), even the bloodthirsty vindictiveness (God's wrath demands the expiation of the Son slain in our place) that so often characterize our relationships among ourselves.

We might say that God's dilemma is how to convince us that none of this is true, that God is not "like that," or, more exactly, "like us." John's Gospel tells us that "God so *loved* the world as to *give* the only Son so that all who believe in him may not perish but may have eternal life" (John 3:16). In other words, the whole purpose of the Incarnation was not to supply a substitute victim to appease God's wrath but to reveal God's love as totally self-giving, even unto the "death that should not be" at our hands, and even to those who have refused that love. There is simply nothing God will not do, give, be to convince us that in God there is no wrath, that God is purely love, and that all God wants from us is that we accept that love which will enable us to love ourselves, our neighbor, our world, and God.

C. Solving the Problem

Many of the writers in the Christian spiritual tradition who have taken the most radical positions on the centrality of poverty in the spiritual life, such as Meister Eckhart, Catherine of Siena, Francis and Clare of Asissi, and John of the Cross, have treated the subject in this ontological framework. Exploring the relationship of these two loci, creaturehood as the "problem" and the Incarnation as God's "solution" will take our analysis of evangelical poverty to a deeper level than can humanistic or even religious considerations. At root, possessions are not simply encumbrances or constraints on the human project which wise people know they must control. And detachment is not merely the exercise of such control. Possessions become a problem when they are seen consciously or unconsciously as the solution to the problem of ontological insecurity, as a bulwark against the existential terror of nonexistence. Poverty is the courageous and resolute facing of this terror and abandonment of this protective strategy.

1. The deceptive human solution: property

As I have been trying to show, following Drewermann's lead, the human predicament, that is, what is fundamentally "wrong" with us (which is what the doctrine of original sin attempts to explicate) is that we were created by God "out of nothing," which induces in us a radical sense of existential precariousness. Because there is no foundation in ourselves for our very being, no basis under our own control, we experience ourselves in ongoing, imminent danger of falling back into the nothingness from we emerged. Our existence is totally rooted in God who creates us moment-by-moment out of sheer gratuitous love. We are not beings who *receive* a gift. Our being *is* itself totally gift. To accept our very being as gift should be boundless joy in unshakeable security, but humans find this acceptance incredibly difficult because there is nothing really analogous to such total unselfishness in our experience of human relationships. Such love is revelation in the absolute sense of the word. And revelation itself is utterly gratuitous, something over which we can exercise no control, which we cannot extract by force or verify as trustworthy.

In other words, our ontological condition is one that we can interpret as absolute gift or as radical existential threat. If we opt for the first the experience is freedom, security, joy, the most notable characteristics of those saints whose embrace of poverty is most radical. If we opt for the latter, the experience is insecurity, threat, anxious need for self-protection against an inscrutable Power who controls us absolutely and over whom we have no control. The doctrine of original sin is a recognition that the human race in its entirety starts out enmeshed in the experience of insecurity and fear, and to get out of the toils of that situation requires divine assistance that God freely offered in Jesus.[14] We are born into the situation of being "camels" called to "pass through the eye of the needle" of total detachment, something impossible to humans but possible to God.

The human entanglement in existential terror and distrust generates the acquisitive and proprietary approach to material (and other kinds of) goods. The paradox that we cannot live without material goods nor, it would seem, live well with them, is rooted in this ontological fragility experienced as existential danger. Few people think in terms of existential insecurity but all the limited needs we experience, the threats to our comfort or well-being that arise moment by moment in our dependence on what is other than ourselves, are rooted in that deeper need to exist. We need to eat, drink, wear clothes, be sheltered, and so on, in order to stay alive. Jesus himself acknowledged this need, but his solution to it was not "So store up more and more goods lest you perish." Rather, he assured us that our heavenly Father knows that we need all these things and can be trusted to care for human beings at least as effectively as for the birds of the air and the flowers of the field.

But to have any certainty about the timely availability of these nonnegotiable supports to our existence human beings feel the need to secure them as "my own." This attitude falsifies the situation on every level. The drive to own is the single greatest threat to the human solidarity that in fact would offer even some purely created protection against individualized danger. Furthermore, property under our control is ineffective as a bulwark against the danger of extinction because even the richest person, like the fool in the Gospel who built bigger barns to protect his abundant crop so that he could finally relax in the security of his possessions, has no real protection against death or disaster which can come from any direction at any time. (The global economic meltdown of 2009 was a shocking testimony to the illusory character of the security generated by the free market system that was widely believed to be virtually invulnerable.) But the saddest aspect of the situation is that the danger against which we build such elaborate defenses is an illusion because death is not really extinction but passage through mortality to even more abundant life. The temptation of the fool, whether in the Gospel or today, is to absolutize the bulwark (possessions) because we have mistakenly absolutized the danger (physical death).

Unless something intervenes in the ordinary socialization all humans undergo, security achieved and administered by oneself through the acquisition of property and the wielding of superior physical might gradually becomes an all-consuming obsession. Acquiring more and more money (and thus what money can buy) is the market economy version of this obsession on the personal level. Militarily achieved defense against all comers, actual and potential, is the social version. At root, acquisition by personal activity is the polar opposite of the reception of gifts to support the gift of life, which is the human experience of the gift of existence. It is an attempt to achieve by means completely unsuited to the desired end an ontological independence, a security that is, even in principle, unattainable. It is a fool's enterprise, as Jesus repeatedly taught, but it is universal in its appeal and seemingly self-evidently necessary, and it can be subverted only by a deliberate decision to confront it and to cease to be its slave.

2. The effective divine solution: Incarnation

The Incarnation is God's response to the human problem of ontological insecurity. In order to convince us of God's absolute fidelity and trustworthiness, of the foundation of our security in God's love rather than in anything which we can own or control, God in Jesus took on the very source of our insecurity, that is, creaturehood with its inbuilt liability to death.[15]

Most of the writers in the Christian tradition who have attended with preference to the issue of poverty in the spiritual life have centered their reflections in the mysteries of the Incarnation and the Passion, the crib and the cross of Jesus, rather than on his public life or teaching. They have turned to the two experiences in which Jesus did not have the power of initiative but was utterly subject to forces of extinction beyond his control. These two foci are the "places" of the deepest human experience of fragility and insecurity: birth and death.

God came to us as a newborn infant, utterly defenseless in an indifferent world, totally dependent on his not particularly powerful human parents for physical survival, threatened by homelessness, lack of protection against the elements, and the murderous designs of a ruthless king. Whatever the actual circumstances of Jesus' birth, the infancy narratives[16] symbolically present him as subject to all the dangers that birth into this world represents for the human being. At the end of his life he was conquered by superior physical, political, and religious power and delivered over to the last enemy, death. His friends and followers, with the exception of a few courageous and loving women, deserted him; God seemed to have abandoned him; he was humanly powerless to save himself. The threat of imminent annihilation became the intimate personal experience of God-become-human.

Rather than struggle physically, bargain with his executioners, or have recourse to any other tactic to achieve salvation or security on human terms, Jesus handed himself over confidently into the hands of God whom he trusted completely despite all the material evidence that God had abandoned him and that the powers of this world had won. The Resurrection was the manifestation that Jesus' confidence in the security he found only in God was indeed well founded. It is crucial for Christian faith that this was not playacting. In Jesus, amazing as this is, God accepted to experience creaturehood "even unto death," which is the ultimate claim of nothingness through which every human creature must pass. The early Church, dazzled by this mystery of divine solidarity in creaturely vulnerability, expressed it in the remarkable hymn in Philippians 2:5–11:

> Let the same mind be in you that was in Christ Jesus,
> who, though he was in the form of God,
> did not regard equality with God as something to be exploited,
> but emptied himself, taking the form of a slave, being born in
>   human likeness.
> And being found in human form,
> he humbled himself and became obedient to the point of death—
> even death on a cross.
> Therefore God also highly exalted him
> and gave him the name that is above every name,
> so that at the name of Jesus every knee should bend,
> in heaven, and on earth and under the earth,
> and every tongue should confess that Jesus Christ is Lord,
> to the glory of God the Father.

The exhortation, "Let this mind be in you," does not mean merely to model our attitudes or behavior on Jesus' humility and obedience. It means to take the same existential stance toward our creaturehood, our ontological fragility, that Jesus had toward his. Unlike Adam and Eve who tried to secure their existence, which was not even threatened, against possible betrayal by a dangerous Creator, Jesus, the last Adam (who is divine by nature) makes no effort to secure himself against the destruction which was actually being wrought upon him as a human being, because he trusts completely in the one he called "Abba."

D. Conclusion: The Role of Poverty in Christian Spirituality

As we have seen, most of the world's wisdom traditions, both philosophical and religious, have recognized the problematic role of possessions, and especially the desire for possessions, in the spiritual life. Although there is general consensus that desire for material things is potentially distracting and stultifying and that it can easily become addictive and even enslaving, the analysis of desire as the root of the problem and therefore the solutions proposed for handling it vary considerably among traditions, running the gamut from detachment and moderation to extreme asceticism and even self-affliction.

I have suggested that the Christian analysis of the problem of desire is conditioned in one way by the essentially positive evaluation of material goods that is rooted in Creation. It is conditioned in another way, and more radically, by the role of the Incarnation in relation to Creation. From a Christian standpoint, possession becomes problematic when it is exercised as a defense against creaturehood experienced, consciously or not, as an ontological vulnerability to annihilation. What needs to be rectified, at root, is this misunderstanding of Creation. Creaturehood is not a condition of servitude to a dangerous God but an unconditional gift of God who freely and out of love drew creatures out of nothingness, not to hold them hostage to an arbitrary divine will, but to incorporate them into divine life. Human resistance to belief in Creation as gift, according to Drewermann, is rooted not so much in disobedience as in the fear arising from our inability to conceive of something in God that has no real analogue in our human experience; that is, totally unconditional love.

The divine pedagogy designed to make it possible for humans to imagine and accept the gift of divine creative love is the Incarnation. In Jesus God became poor, even unto dispossession of life itself, in order that humans might accept that in God they are divinely rich. God's *kenosis*, God's self-emptying in Jesus, was the self-dispossession of divinity that revealed the riches of the gift of being. By assuming creaturehood and living it as gift, Jesus exposed the lie of Satan, namely, that God is dangerous and creaturehood is ultimate vulnerability. Through his life and teaching, up to and including his death and Resurrection, Jesus modeled for his disciples the grateful and joyful acceptance of total dependence on a God who can be trusted, and in the outpouring of his Spirit he empowered them to live this gift.

In chapter 4 we examined Jesus' practice of poverty and what it means for his disciples to imitate and follow him. All disciples are called to this spirituality of poverty which, as we saw, is less about extreme renunciation (much less hatred) of material goods than about the total detachment from anything that competes with God in the desire of the creature, the total renunciation of any "defense" of the creature against the love of God. We also looked at the difference that particular vocation and form of discipleship introduces into the practice of the common Christian vocation to poverty of spirit.

Ministerial Religious probably find the closest Gospel analogue to their vocation and lifeform in the itinerant disciples who traveled about with the homeless Jesus announcing the Reign of God on a full-time basis. These disciples were called to leave family, home, and secular employment, and not to found a secondary family of their own. They were to hold all things in common, live from the shared purse, apprentice themselves exclusively to Jesus on a twenty-four-hours-a-day basis, and have no other life's work than the proclamation of the Gospel. This is a different form of discipleship from that of stabile householders, disciples who marry, found and raise families, own property, and support themselves by gainful employment. Therefore, it behooves us to inquire into the role of evangelical poverty in the distinctive personal spirituality that Religious try to live in the context of a commodity economy which is, in many ways, inimical to their project.

IV. Desire and Poverty in Religious Life: Asceticism

So far, we have explored the issue of desire, its root in crea-turehood, and its profound ambiguity. By their perpetual Pro-fession of evangelical poverty Religious attempt to confront the challenge Jesus offers his followers: to renounce completely the fear-inspired attempt to protect ourselves against our onto-logical fragility and to become the "little children" to whom God offers eternal life. Religious construct an alternate world in which the economy of the Reign of God based on complete self-divestment and possessionlessness, and lived in a commu-nity of total economic interdependence, opposes Satan's world construction based on greed and competition for a limited supply of goods in an attempt to "become like God." But the Profession of evangelical poverty does not end the struggle between the deeply felt need to fill the ontological "hole" of creaturehood and the desire of the Religious to open her or himself without reserve to the infinite love of a creator God who is all-giving Abba. This struggle begins in earnest for the Religious in initial formation, is definitively embraced by Pro-fession of poverty, and continues throughout her or his Reli-gious Life working itself out in a life of personal asceticism, ministry, and contemplative prayer.

A. Perverted Desire: A Tale of Two Sons

One of Jesus' parables (Luke 15:11–32), often called "The Parable of the Prodigal Son," is a profound exploration of the dynamics of perverted desire in the spiritual life. The parable is most often invoked to present the younger son, the Prodigal, as a model of youthful sin and sincere repentance while the older son is the negative type of human refusal to participate in divine generosity. Most of us like to think of ourselves as the younger son, coming to our senses, repenting of our folly, and basking in a glorious welcome home by our loving God. And most of us prefer not to think about the elder son who lurks in our hearts resenting the lazy and the selfish who seem to "get away with murder" while we slave dutifully without receiving the appreciation we deserve. But there is more to this story than meets the eye.[17] One reason the parables often fail to "work" in our spiritual lives is that familiarity with the ending leads us to identify with the wrong characters. In this parable there is no "ending": rather, this "never-ending story" poses exactly the right questions about possessions and desire. In effect, in this story there is no hero with whom to identify.

Both sons are primarily concerned with taking care of themselves, achieving a security they can control. As we find out from his reaction to the celebration for the returned younger son, the elder son is really working to earn pride of place in his Father's good graces, which will eventually assure his inheritance. The younger son, of course, could not even wait for the old man to die but demanded his inheritance and severed the bond of dependence the elder son was cultivating. There is little to choose between earning security by obsequious dependence and seizing it by brazen independence. In fact, neither son was able to accept in grateful joy his sharing in the life of his father who, like God with Adam and Eve, freely offered him everything he could possibly need or want.

According to the parable, the younger son, reduced to destitution in the "far country" which is struck with famine, "comes to his senses." But the reader should note, he does not really repent of anything. He acknowledges that he has "sinned" but we do not hear from him any heartfelt remorse for having shamed and wounded his father. There is a huge difference between admitting that one is objectively wrong (especially when it is evident by its consequences) and being genuinely sorry for what one has done. Even a jury in possession of a signed confession will look for some signs of genuine remorse in the convicted. Conversion does not begin with the admission of guilt, especially when there is no way to disguise it. It begins in heartfelt sorrow, not that one has been caught or will be punished, but at the harm one has done, especially to the innocent.

The younger son "came to his senses" in the realization that he was in a mess from which he could not extricate himself. His father's servants have all they need and he is starving. So the issue is how to get renewed access to the paternal wealth. Pro-

jecting his own small-mindedness on his father he is sure that
playing the "son" card will not work, so he plans his abject confession, admitting he has sinned, and even prescribing his own
penance, which will, he hopes, at least assure him of economic
support. "Make me as one of your hired servants," that is, able
to work for food, which he could not do in the "far country"
where "no one gave him anything."

The father ignores this self-centered and indeed self-serving
confession. He overwhelms the miscreant with the love that
preceded, accompanied, and now follows the sin because it is a
love completely focused on the one he sees not as a sinner but
only as his son who was lost and is found, was dead and is now
alive. He is found by his father's love; he is alive because he is
home, no matter whether love or hunger has lured him.

The son might have been overwhelmed at a welcome he did
not expect (but should have if he had any real knowledge of his
father) but he has yet to be converted. He is still calculating
how to take care of himself, how to earn his way to the security
he had tried unsuccessfully to seize. What still eludes him is
what it means to be the child of such a parent. As Jesus says to
his disciples when they are jockeying for position in his Reign,
"Unless you *be converted* and become a little child, you cannot
enter the kingdom of heaven." The human predicament is that
we are born fake "adults"; we have to become real children.
That is the process of reeducating desire from the need to possess to the capacity to receive.

The elder son, returning from the fields where he is earning
his father's approval and the recompense he is sure he deserves,
is enraged when he learns what the rejoicing is all about. He has
done everything he was asked to do while his profligate brother
was wasting not only their father's wealth but also part of the
principal on which his own inheritance would be based. This
son too is immune to his father's feelings, unable to grasp the
latter's joy and relief at having his younger son home safe. His
greed and envy burst out in the comparison he makes between
his own unflagging service and his brother's rebellion. But he
convicts himself with his own words: All these years I have *slaved*
(δουλεύω) for you; I have never transgressed a single *command*

(ἐντολήν). And you have never given me anything like what you are lavishing on this arrogant and worthless *son of yours* (ὁ υἱός σου). Like the angry mother who says to her husband, "Do you know what *your* son did today?" the elder son never refers to the younger as his brother, only as his "your son."

The issue for the elder son is, as it was for the younger, creating a bulwark against dependence, establishing a controllable source of security that will outlast the father. But the elder son's behavior reveals two other features of the perverted desire to be the guarantor of one's own being. First, it is the attitude not of a son but of a slave who is not working with his father in a common project but rather is keeping commands so as to have a right to be recompensed accordingly and not have to accept anything as gift. Second, the effect of insecurity and perverted desire is competition and the hatred it engenders. Like Cain slaying his brother because he is jealous of God's love for Abel, the elder brother cannot abide the father's love for his brother. There is only so much (love, money, inheritance) to go around and what one gets the other does not.

This scene is a classic case of what René Girard called "mimetic desire" which begets rivalry, hatred, and eventually violence. The elder son wants to make the father in his image rather than accepting the challenge to become truly "like God" in openhanded generosity toward those who deserve it least. "Deserving" is not in God's vocabulary any more than is "revenge." These belong to the tit-for-tat language of the existentially threatened, whose only assurance that they are safe is a system they can control. This elder son is just as alienated from his father as is his wayward brother. He is, by his own admission, a slave, not a son. In fact, he is less than a slave. He is already the hired hand his younger brother asks to become!

The Father's answer is so simple. "My child [τέκνον], you are always with me and all I have is yours." To the father his child is always a child, never a competitor or a servant. True security consists in the "being with," the contemplative union that the mystics describe as sharing in God's very life. This is the object of true desire, but for these two sons tangled up in perverted desire it is a long way off. As the Father says to his elder son, all that God has is ours, not by law or as recompense or by seizure, but because as Paul says, "He who did not spare his own Son...will he not also give us all things with him?" (Rom 8:32). The Incarnation is God's answer to our existential fear.

The parable ends without a resolution. We do not know whether the father's lavish love finally converts the younger son from greed to love, or whether the simple assurance of the father's boundless love finally relaxes the desperate grasp for security of the elder son. The point is that only we can resolve the story as we recognize both sons in our own hearts, discern our own futile strategies, no matter how finely disguised, for guaranteeing our security, dismantle our defenses against a "dangerous" God, undergo the conversion by which we surrender our manipulative dependence and our blatant independence and open our hearts in joyful acceptance of our creaturehood which, finally, is our divine childhood. We do not find the true model of sonship in this parable. The true Child is Jesus, the Beloved, who says to his Abba, "Everything I have belongs to you, and everything you have belongs to me" (John 17:10; translation is from the NET).

B. The Purification of Desire: Asceticism

The path toward true spiritual childhood, toward the purification of desire, lies through a long ascetical process of "letting go" which will go on throughout the spiritual life but which ought to be undertaken in focused seriousness in the formation process of the candidate for Religious Life. This person arrives from a world of greed, possessiveness, envy, and "me-first" consumerism into a community based on shared and freely chosen possessionlessness lived in the common life of total economic interdependence. S/he begins to live in the gift economy of the Reign of God according to the particular charism and spirit of her or his Congregation. The transformation of distorted desire into the ardent desire for union with God that is the purpose of Religious Life requires strenuous and focused effort. This effort begins in the recognition and acknowledgement of what we are up against.

As we have seen, Eugen Drewermann, in his analysis of the

fall scene in Genesis as an exploration of the human predicament, postulated that ontological dread perverted the loving desire of the human creatures for union with their Creator into a compulsive desire to defend themselves against a dangerous and untrustworthy God. Self-gift in response to unconditional love was twisted into anxious greed for self-sufficiency.

René Girard, in a complementary analysis, explains perverted desire in terms of competitive imitation, or what he calls "mimetic desire."[18] Mimesis, or imitation, is not intrinsically or necessarily perverse. The desire to be like God was implanted in us by God's own Creation of humanity in the divine image. But, says Girard, we actually learn to desire not by imitating God but by imitating the desires of others. *I* begin to want what the *other* values. As my desire more and more coincides with that of the other the object desired by both is obscured by the mounting rivalry between us. Mimesis becomes first acquisitive, then competitive and conflictual, and finally violent. As one of Girard's disciples explains, mimetic desire is contagious and escalating, as the fashion industry, the arms race, the stock and real estate markets, and advertising in general demonstrate. We become psychologically incapable of enjoying the intrinsic value of anything. Value derives from the need to have what the other has or wants.[19]

In short, Drewermann unveils the *root* of perverted desire, namely, the ontological terror of the creature in the face of its own contingency, and Girard describes the *dynamics* of perverted desire as conflictual mimesis through which the creature attempts to assuage that ontological fear by acquiring what it learns is valuable because another desires it.

These modern theorists are underwriting what Scripture, the mystical tradition, and theology all recognize: that acquisitiveness is a perversion of true desire. The hunger and thirst of the human heart is insatiable because that which it needs, namely being itself, is infinite. The insatiability of true desire is the source of a kind of delightful suffering, the never-ending, ever-deepening desire for God which, the mystics tell us, will not cease (even though it will no longer be painful) even on the other side of death.[20] But the insatiability of true desire for

320 BUYING THE FIELD

God is perverted into an insatiable desire for material, psychological, or social goods that we hope will fill the ontological void. This is the source of the futile restlessness of heart that Augustine so famously described: "You have made us for yourself, O God, and our hearts are restless until they rest in you."[21]

When the dynamics of acquisitive desire are triggered by the existential insecurity of finitude they generate deep feelings of vulnerability, worthlessness, and danger. These powerful feelings of insecurity can take over a person's life so that s/he cannot live for even a short time without certain anxiety-reducing objects. This is the essence of addiction, an extremely prevalent disorder of modern culture to which Religious Life itself is not immune.

We usually think of addiction in terms of substances such as nicotine, alcohol, or drugs, which create physical dependency. But certain behaviors such as compulsive gambling, eating (or not eating), shopping, watching television, listening to mind-numbing sound, sexual stimulation, playing computer games, or even exercising can cause equally powerful psychological dependency. All addictions have in common that gratifying them temporarily assuages the gnawing emptiness and anxiety. But it takes ever-increasing doses of the gratifying substance or behavior to calm the anxiety and still the craving. And the guilt and worthlessness this gratification produces leads deeper into the addiction.

Addiction, which assuages the inner demons of desire, is not the only testimony to the destructive role of perverted desire in modern life. We are obsessed with "security" from outside threats such as terrorism, crime, immigration, or simply difference. Billions of dollars that could be spent on solving society's real problems such as hunger and disease are spent on police state surveillance in public and private places, indiscriminate searches of persons and property, and electronic data-gathering about innocent people who just might be or become a threat. Increasingly violent border patrols are militarizing historically peaceful boundaries. Gates and guards and dogs and sirens "protect" the rich against the poor or even the "other."

And this mounting paranoia meets with general acceptance by otherwise sensible people.

But a few outlaw acts, even major ones like the September 11, 2001, terrorist attacks in the United States, could not possibly generate the level and extent of fear on which unscrupulous politicians play for power if those fear mongers were not tapping into a deep sense of vulnerability in ordinary people. These same people, if they stop to think, know that a hurricane or earthquake, a slip off a curb or down the stairs, a tainted piece of fish, a rogue wave on the beach, a falling piece of equipment, or a flu virus could end their life at any moment of any day. Indeed, a heart attack is far more likely than a terrorist attack.

In other words, there is no such thing as safety or security in the sense of absolute, or even relative, invulnerability. Death is a heartbeat away for every mortal, no matter how well guarded, powerful, or wealthy one may be. Why, then, do relatively remote possibilities move people to surrender their most cherished rights as persons and citizens in exchange for a "protection" that is, finally, completely unreliable because it is quite simply impossible? Fear of the unknown danger taps in to the reservoir of existential insecurity that creatures, beings not in control of their own existence, experience without knowing what it is or how it works. Material and behavioral "things," seem to offer some protection and our need for them grows in proportion to the perceived threat.

Faith in God as the only source of security leads Religious to make a different and radical choice in regard to material goods. But, as experience so well demonstrates, this originating act, the vow of evangelical poverty, does not eradicate once and for all the problem of acquisitive desire any more than a vow of consecrated celibacy obliterates all the challenges arising from the need for human intimacy.

Every Religious, therefore, is challenged to develop a personal practice of evangelical poverty which, if it is to be more than an external correctness within a mandated Congregational framework, must progressively come to grips with the deep existential roots of perverted desire. This practice springs from the vow but is shaped by one's personal history, particular circumstances, and growing human and spiritual maturity. Such a practice can no longer be acquired by observing common regulations such as asking permission for every item used or having only those items approved for all members, if it ever was. In other words, contrary to what some—Religious themselves as well as secular observers—have suggested, namely, that in renewed Congregations the vow of poverty has lost its relevance in the personal life of individual Religious, poverty as personal practice is more demanding now than it ever was and more critical in the quest for God.

As we have observed more than once, if we start with possessions themselves, asking what a serious personal practice of poverty requires, we are likely to end in a quagmire of contradictions and guilt-producing conundrums. Is vegetarianism the proper choice for a "poor" Religious? What types of clothes are appropriate? How much should one spend on vacation? Is it more "poor" to shop in thrift stores than department stores? Should a Religious pay for spiritual direction or a retreat that many ordinary Christians cannot afford? Is eating in a good restaurant, attending the theater or a baseball game, contrary to poverty? Should a Religious have a computer for her own use? Or a car? And on and on.

By focusing attention away from particular things and specific behaviors in relation to them such as buying, paying, or using, I want to get to the more fundamental and crucial issue of the education of desire. Jesus focused the question about possessions in precisely these terms when he said, "Where your treasure is, there your heart will be also" (Matt 6:21). John of the Cross expressed the same idea differently by saying that it matters little if one is held captive by a thick chain or a thin cord. The issue is not so much *what* binds us as that it *binds* us. If desire is rightly ordered, then the choices which flow from that desire as we handle material goods will be rightly ordered. So, our real question is, how is desire reeducated?

Every spiritual tradition, including Christianity, has recognized the indispensability of fasting in any serious spiritual program. Indeed, "fasting" is a kind of metonymy for ascetical practice in regard to material goods in general. It is a kind of pedagogy of desire by abstinence. Fasting, however, has multiple meanings and operates differently in different traditions. Fasting in the Christian context is not exclusively, perhaps not even primarily, about restricting the intake of food and drink, and its purpose is not asceticism for its own sake or even for the sake of self-control. Fasting is about desire. Because food is absolutely essential to life our need for it is real, continuous, and urgent. Furthermore, the sensual pleasure it affords not only motivates us to eat to sustain life but also makes us experience nourishment itself as a bulwark against the gnawing insecurity of creaturely contingency. We even speak of "comfort food" precisely because eating meets a psychological need that is often more urgent than physical hunger. Fasting, by which we deliberately renounce food and drink, is paradigmatic for a whole range of renunciations that are voluntary; directed toward real, imperious desires; touch our sense of existential insecurity; and have consequences that are both painful and potentially transformative.

In this paradigmatic sense, "fasting" is freely renouncing something that is **good** in itself, that we **desire**, and which is **available** to us. Therefore, since renunciation of the available and desirable good cannot be absolute or universal, fasting has to begin by identifying what, among good, desired, and available objects, a particular person is called to renounce. In other words, fasting as spiritual practice is not just indiscriminate self-denial arising from a generalized suspicion that the material as such is somehow evil or that pleasure itself is always dangerous. Rather, the discernment in which true Christian fasting is grounded involves carefully tracking our felt desires into the deep lair where the ravenous beast of existential insecurity lurks in order to confront and tame that beast.[22] Christian spiritual literature often portrays the spiritual life, especially that of Religious, as a desert confrontation where fasting enables the spiritual person to recognize, struggle with, and finally overcome the wild beasts of desire. Jesus' own public life began with such a desert encounter in which his physical, psychological, and even spiritual needs were manipulated by the Evil One to entice him to take into his own hands his own life and vocation.

Religious make a collective and personal statement that acquisitive and conflictual desire is not the appropriate, healthy, or ultimately successful way for humans to relate to material goods and they undertake a life that incarnates and models an alternative approach. By dispossessing themselves completely and setting out to follow Jesus in his itinerant ministry of announcing the Reign of God, which is diametrically opposed to the kingdom of Mammon, they are not just shrewdly exchanging the (very uncertain) possibility of becoming independently wealthy by competition in the market place for the moderate (but reliable) security of life in a total institution. In other words, Religious Life is not a way of handling existential insecurity by lowered expectations and displaced economic responsibility.

Religious "renounce all" because they really believe that only in God can their souls be at rest, and that from God alone comes their hope and their salvation (cf. Ps 62:1–2 and elsewhere). In the love of Jesus and participation in his mission, the deepest desires of their heart will be satisfied. By anchoring their hearts in God alone, Religious are claiming to know what their treasure is and where it lies. They do not need to be anxious, whether their communities are enjoying relative prosperity or suffering economic hardship. And they have no need to possess as their own even that which they use. The classical term in the history of spirituality for this sublimation of existential insecurity is detachment. And we have already seen that this seems to have been what Jesus meant by the poverty of spirit to which all believers are called but which takes the particular form of itinerant common life for some disciples.

This ideal of ever-deepening detachment arising from true security in God is not attained by thinking about it or even believing in it, but by ongoing practice. I want to suggest some possible ways of practicing poverty through "fasting" today, not because I think they are the only or best or even necessary ways, but as examples that might invite us to reflection about a practical personal spirituality of poverty for our time.

Religious Life in the commodity culture, in renewed Congregations that no longer operate as total institutions, obviously cannot be lived meaningfully as it was in preconciliar times. But, if anything, the profound spiritual challenge of facing the radical insecurity of creaturehood with absolute trust in a loving Creator is a more daunting project today than it was when Religious were relatively insulated within an economically stable lifeform from both the threats of a volatile market and the mass media's insistence that consumerism is the only answer.

Fasting, in the sense we are discussing here, is a practice of poverty calculated to expose and gradually neutralize existential insecurity even as it fosters and nourishes trust in God. As a practice that is not restricted to food and drink but is directed toward the education of desire, fasting might be understood as the voluntary renunciation of whatever challenges the ideal of real detachment, whatever taps into our anxiety and stimulates the desire for what we do not really need. It need not involve conspicuous practices or absolute prohibitions about particular objects such as clothes, types of food, use of equipment, travel, recreation, or other things over which Religious often agonize. It might be as simple (but difficult) as turning off the television when there is nothing worth watching, stopping a few bites short of satiety or declining a second drink, closing a novel in order to get the sleep needed for the next day's work, accepting patiently a foodless cross-country flight or non-reclining airplane seat, resisting the impulse to buy something just because one saw it in the catalogue or to "graze" up and down store aisles or through malls when there is nothing one actually needs, turning off a computer game in order to get back to work, not asking for the return of something lent to another, using up leftovers in the office, kitchen, or bathroom, and making the effort to recycle rather than throwing things away. It might be not spending inordinate time and energy selecting clothes for an event, not buying "more" car, computer, phone, television, or other services or equipment than one needs just to have the "state of the art," not replacing the still serviceable by the "top of the line."

Many such renunciations, which attract no attention, do not feed our complacency, and do not impede our work or threaten our health, can constitute an ongoing practice of "fasting" that gradually subverts acquisitive desire and repeatedly recenters our hearts on the One who alone can satisfy them. The more often we let go the more capable of letting go we become. Being capable of letting go, even unto the figurative or literal laying down of our life itself if that is called for, is the definition of detachment, of the poverty of spirit Jesus proposed to his disciples.

Developing an inner disposition to "fast" rather than consume can gradually refine one's ability to discern wisely in some of the areas that pose dilemmas for Religious today. Rather than either despairing of the possibility of any coherent approach to poverty or trying to arrive once and for all at *the* right formula which would be applicable in all circumstances, fasting can become a habit of paying attention to what is going on within us as we face choices. Rather than deciding never to eat meat, never to buy new clothes, not to have cable or high speed Internet service, an answering machine or a cell phone, or not to use a car, genuine detachment would foster an interior freedom that allows one to be honestly and peacefully flexible in diverse circumstances which might call for very different decisions about the same objects and behaviors.

One might, for example, not buy meat for oneself or choose it when there are options but also not embarrass or inconvenience a host by refusing what is served. The relevant question might be whether having or not having certain means of communication makes one more or less available to those one is called to serve. Does not-driving preserve natural resources or simply displace the burden of time and money on those who end up providing one's transportation? In other words, rather than simply yielding spontaneously to all attractions or establishing nonnegotiable rules for all situations, one could be cultivating an interior freedom from both the need to acquire and consume and the need to conform to an imperious ideal image of oneself as "poor" or to appear as poor to those whose approval or censure plays too great a role in our life. This seems to have been the practice of Jesus, who could fast for forty days and pray all night but also graciously accept dinner invitations from the well-to-do and enjoy eating and drinking enough to be criticized as a glutton and wine bibber.

Such freedom of spirit would make one ever more responsive in community and ministry while educating desire toward the one thing necessary. Paul gave one of the best descriptions of the fruit of such fasting, namely genuine detachment, in Philippians 4:11–13:

> ...I have learned to be content with whatever I have. I know what it is to have little, and I know what it is to have plenty. In any and all circumstances I have learned the secret of being well-fed and of going hungry, of having plenty and of being in need. I can do all things through him who strengthens me.

But Paul's motivation was not ascetical performance. He wanted to be "all things to all people, that I might by all means save some. I do it all for the sake of the Gospel...." (1 Cor 9:22–23).

The disciplined life of a detached Religious that attracts no attention by conspicuous deprivation or ostentatious asceticism can give a powerful prophetic witness in our obsessively consuming society. In the Gospel, avarice (the insatiable desire for wealth for its own sake), greed (the desire for more than one needs), covetousness (mimetic desire for another's possessions), and luxury (the condition of habitual excess), which are earmarks of capitalist culture, were clearly and repeatedly condemned by Jesus. However, his condemnation of "riches" (meaning attachment to material goods) was not some arbitrary behavioral standard reflecting the virtue of moderation in classical Greek culture of the first century. Nor was the vow of poverty invented by Religious founders as a form of economic control. The perversion of desire which evangelical poverty seeks to eradicate is rooted in the primordial rejection of creaturehood, of that "spiritual childhood" which prepares us for entrance into the Reign of God.

The perversion of desire alienates human beings from their Creator, estranges them in fear and suspicion from one another, fosters the rivalry that leads directly to violence, and stultifies the spirit by over-indulgence and addiction. The practice of poverty through asceticism, a "fasting" that leads to genuine detachment, not only constantly subverts the perversions of desire in the Religious herself but models for others a way of living in this consumption-driven world which actively creates an atmosphere of peaceful community in a sharing of goods. As Teresa of Avila famously said, this has nothing to do with pusillanimity. Rather, real detachment from possessions manifested in peacefulness, openhanded generosity, equanimity in situations of inconvenience or want, lack of anxiety or worry, the ability to celebrate joyfully and mourn authentically, and restraint and gratitude in the use of goods all bespeak an unshakable interior security in the God who keeps count of every hair of our heads so that we do not have to obsess about them.

V. Poverty and Work in Religious Life: Ministry

Ministerial Religious, like most other adults in non-poor societies, spend most of their waking life working. Work in the life of a Religious, therefore, must not be simply a way of funding a spiritual life which is carried on "after hours" as a kind of luxury. Rather, work is integral to the spirituality of Religious. In the last chapter I explored *work as ministry* in an effort to show that ministry should not be reduced to or equated with work understood primarily as gainful employment. Now I want to look at *ministry as work* in order to argue that work as a human activity is not simply a way to support ourselves and our ministries but is actually integral to the spirituality of the minister.

Commodity culture suggests that the primary, if not only, purpose of work in human life is the production and acquisition of money. Religious, however, do not work to become rich but to promote the Reign of God in the world. And, in any case, as we have seen, the work they do for the transformation of persons and society is not likely to produce very much money. If it does, Religious will either lower the cost of their service to the poor or fold the excess back into their ministries. In other words, evangelical poverty understood as radical detachment from material goods has always influenced the work Religious do and how they do it. Our question here is how ministry specifically as work functions in the spirituality of Religious today.

A. Biblical Resources on Work

The Genesis narrative of human origins presents work, like desire, as an ambiguous reality. Intended as a divine gift by which humans share in God's creativity, work was perverted by sin into labor experienced as drudgery. And indeed this ambiguity has marked the relation of humanity to work throughout human history. On the one hand, the suffering of being unemployed or unable to work testifies to the positive significance work has in human experience. On the other hand, millions suffer in meaningless drudgery that does not sustain them or their families.

According to the first Creation account in Genesis 1:1—2:3, God created humanity in God's own image, male and female, and gave them a double charge: to reproduce and to "have dominion over" the earth. This "dominion" is not divine permission for humans to exploit nonhuman creation for pleasure and profit but the charge to participate in the "work" of God (see Gen 2:2–3) by caring for the Creation that God produced. The religious institution of the Sabbath is rooted in and witnesses to this understanding of work as human participation in divine activity.

In the more anthropomorphic second account of Creation in Genesis 2:4b–25, work comes into more explicit focus. God created the heavens and the earth and planted a garden on the earth. But the garden required ongoing cultivation so God created the earth-creature (*ha-adam*) to till the soil and care for the animals. God then differentiated the earth-creature into male and female thereby creating the possibility of human procreation, the primordial way by which humans participate in God's own creative activity.

Both accounts, separately and together, present work at its origin as a gift and a privilege. But, according to Genesis, the alienation of humanity from God by original sin negatively affected this dimension of human experience. Work became burdensome labor: the woman's painful struggle in giving birth and the man's sweaty struggle to wrest their livelihood from the resistant soil. The character of work as painful (labor) derives, according to Scripture, not from the intrinsic character of work as God intended it, but from the sinful perversion of God's good Creation through sin.

Once again, we have to remember that the Genesis myth is not a videotape of what happened to our ancestors "back then." It is a theological exploration through narrative of the present predicament of humanity. On the one hand, humans need and want to work. It is as natural to them as eating or breathing. By work they achieve identity, build their uniquely human world, create and sustain community, and bring to life the progeny who are their bulwark against extinction. On the other hand, labor is often dehumanizing and futile, sometimes barely preferable to death itself. Humans oscillate between the joy of achievement (work) and the suffering of drudgery (labor), both of which are included in the notion of work.

In the last chapter, in relation to the economic systems of monasticism, mendicancy, and ministerial Religious Life, I briefly sketched Hannah Arendt's analysis of labor, work, and action. We need to recall that distinction, with some expansion, for our concerns in this section with the role of ministry as work in the spirituality of Religious. These three terms (labor, work, and action) overlap in daily usage, and most of what Religious do as ministry, while it is usually called "work," also involves both labor and action; this helps account for its ambiguous character. Ministry as work is often difficult, repetitive, and seemingly futile, that is, laborious, but it is also creative and productive, that is, constitutive of the human world. And that human world, in the context of ministry, is intended to participate in the Reign of God. Ministry is fatiguing and monotonous as well as absorbing and exciting and it is oriented toward the transcendence we call salvation. It is this ambiguous character that makes work a sphere of spiritual development that calls for attention and practice, discernment and commitment.

Religious Life, from its beginnings in the context of classical antiquity, involved an understanding of and an attitude toward work itself that was quite original. As we saw in the last chapter, the first virgins, the desert hermits, the medieval monks, and mendicants recognized the role of work not only as the **material support** of the Religious themselves (which it certainly was) and as **service of the neighbor** (which was an expression of love of God), but also as **spiritual practice** which occupied the hands so that the spirit would be free to focus on the prayerful quest for God. Work, especially as part of the monastic form of Religious Life, was one phase of a kind of spiritual respiration, the rhythmic "inhalation and exhalation" of "*orare et laborare.*"

Although the role of work was somewhat different in the desert, in the monastery, and in the mendicant community, one's Religious Life was often described as a "return to Paradise" in which work was not drudgery but participation in God's creativity. The Religious lived as Adam and Eve in the Garden before the sin that led to the curse of labor. But, of course, there was no historical or geographical Paradise to which to "return." The Paradise the Religious were "recreating" was actually eschatological, not behind them in prehistory but ahead of them in the Reign of God. It was to be "reclaimed" by being achieved. The balanced monastic life, by its non-rebellious acceptance of labor, its creative engagement in work, and its peaceful action of ongoing liturgical praise and community life was bringing into existence in the burdensome context of pre-industrial culture the Paradise in which humans live in harmony with, rather than struggle against, nature, other creatures, one another, and God. The monastery or convent was intended to be Creation "restored" to its pristine nature, that is, life lived as God intended humans to live. The bell ringing regularly to call the Religious from work to prayer and back to work created a rhythm that precluded both anxious preoccupation and distracted sloth.

Those who entered Religious Life prior to the mid-twentieth century will recognize much of this "unworldly" ethos of work in the preconciliar convent routine with its balanced, if strenuous, horarium of work and prayer. All shared in the labor and work of maintaining the community and carrying on the apostolate while being generally detached from concern with money, success, or career. It would be sheer romanticism to maintain that there was no laziness and shirking, no ambition and competition, no overwork or scrupulous compulsiveness among Religious. But the ideals were clear and commonly espoused. Work was neither an extracurricular activity nor the primary purpose of the life. It was part of the spirituality of Religious as were prayer and community life.

However, two major changes in this basic approach to work, both labor to sustain the community and shared ministry, occurred beginning in the mid-twentieth century. First, ministerial Religious were slowly developing a theology of Religious Life in which ministry as the work Religious do was seen not simply as the "overflow" of a basically contemplative life or as a "secondary end" subordinate to the "primary end" of personal holiness, but as intrinsic to and constitutive of their life. Second, as we saw in the last chapter, their relationship to ministry as work was radically disrupted by the individualization of ministry and the anxiety about financial survival introduced by the changes in Church and world that followed the Council.

If the Genesis myth tended to illuminate the theology and spirituality of work characteristic of medieval and, to a large extent, modern approaches to Religious Life the contemporary approach to ministerial Religious Life with its theology of ministry and its highly individualized approach might find further resources for its spirituality in the New Testament. The Gospel of John is a particularly rich resource for exploring the originality of the Christian theological understanding of work, while the Synoptics and Paul address quite directly some of the spiritual issues raised by the new understanding of the life characteristic of ministerial Congregations.

John uses the noun ἔργον ("work") in the singular and the plural, and the verb ἐργάζεσθαι ("to work") with its near synonym ποιεῖν ("to do" or "accomplish" or "bring about") more often than any of the other Gospels. In the Fourth Gospel it is usually employed in a clearly theological sense in which "work" (in the singular) usually refers to God's project in Creation which Jesus is missioned to accomplish through the "work(s)" (usually in the plural), which constitute his ministry and later that of his disciples.

Often missed in this Gospel is the overarching schema of Jesus' "finishing" God's work of Creation. Genesis 2:1–2 says "on the seventh day God *finished the work* that he had done [emphasis added]." But in John 5, Jesus calls attention to the fact that Jewish interpretation of Genesis recognized that the work of God was not completely finished by the first act of Creation. People continued to be born and to die on the Sabbath, so God was continuing to do the specifically divine "work" of giving life and executing judgment and thus the Sabbath was not absolute. When Jesus healed a paralyzed man at the Pool of Bethzatha in Jerusalem on the Sabbath the Jewish authorities questioned this violation of the Sabbath rest. Unlike the Synoptic Jesus who justified his Sabbath healings by the priority of humans over laws and his own lordship over the Sabbath (see Matt 12:1–14 and parallels), the Johannine Jesus replies, "My Father is still working, and I also am working" (see 5:17). His accusers understood very well the implications of this response and took up stones to execute him for blasphemy "because he was not only breaking the Sabbath, but was also calling God his own Father, thereby making himself equal to God" (John 5:17–18).

Jesus was claiming in act what he frequently claimed in word, namely, that the "works" that he did (such as curing the paralytic), were the manifestation of his one "work" which the Father had shown him, committed to him, and empowered him to bring to completion (see John 5:19–24). He says explicitly, "I can do nothing on my own. As I hear, I judge" (5:30), and "[t]he works that the Father has given me to complete, the very works that I am doing, testify on my behalf that the Father has sent me" (5:36).

The works, both his signs and his words, were Jesus' completion of God's one work of Creation by the salvation of the world through the giving of eternal life to all who believe. When his disciples returned to the well of Samaria after Jesus had conversed with the woman and she had gone into the town to call her fellow townspeople to him, Jesus said to them, "My food is to do the will of the one who sent me and to finish his work [singular]" (John 4:34). At the Last Supper Jesus "reported" to his Father in prayer, "I glorified you on earth by finishing the work [singular] that you gave me to do" (17:4). At the moment of his death he finally claimed, "It is finished." What God began on the first day of Creation is now truly accomplished and Jesus can "hand over his Spirit" for the life of the world (see 19:30). The Great Sabbath finally announces the completion in principle of God's work.

In John there is a marked and explicit "succession" in the great work begun by God. The Father commits his still "unfinished" creative work to Jesus and Jesus hands on to his disciples the task of mediating the fruits of the work he accomplished on Calvary to the world. God so *loved the world* as to desire its salvation. Jesus comes into the world, *loving* his own unto the laying down of his life for them. And he commissions his disciples to *love* one another as he has loved them, so that the world will know that God has sent Jesus and loves them as he loves Jesus (see John 17:23). Before his death Jesus promised his disciples that the "works [plural] I do, you also will do, and greater than these will you do" (14:12). In his Resurrection Jesus returned to his own and commissioned them to continue his work of taking away the sin (singular) of the world (see 1:29) by forgiving the sins (plural) of those who enter the ecclesial community (see 20:23). He is explicit: "As the Father has sent me, so I send you" (20:21).

In this succession there is both continuity and discontinuity. Jesus takes away the sin (singular) of the world and his disciples forgive the sins (plural) of those they attract into the community. Taking away the sin of the world is the work of Jesus whose works his disciples will now do. This entire dynamic is rooted in the fact that Jesus is the unique Son of God who gives his disciples the power to become children of God. This succession takes place in an "already but not yet" eschatological framework. Jesus has overcome the world and broken the power of Satan (see John 16:17), but his disciples will continue to face persecution in and from the world where Satan is still active (see 15:18–25).

This succession schema roots the works of Jesus' disciples in

Jesus' own works, which in turn are rooted in the one work of God which began in Creation, was committed to Jesus who brought it to completion in the paschal mystery, but which is still to be made fully effective in the world through the works of his disciples throughout history. This is the theological basis of a spirituality of ministry as work. When Jesus' disciples preach, teach, heal, comfort the sorrowful and the dying, and do all the other works by which they announce the Gospel, they are not just doing humanitarian service baptized by a good intention, much less simply earning a living or keeping themselves occupied. They are participating in Jesus' own work of saving the world. Thus, the primary point of what they do, like that of Jesus' signs of enlightening the blind, healing the paralyzed, feeding the hungry, raising the dead, is not simply alleviating human misery but announcing effectively the gift of eternal life. Work as ministry is essentially preaching the Gospel of the Reign of God. Those disciples, such as Religious, who devote themselves completely to ministry as their full-time work over the whole of their lifetime are taking on the work of Jesus by doing his works. What Religious have come to see in a new way in recent decades is that this work of Jesus is not what Arendt would call "work," that is, bringing about the specifically human world through making, but, more precisely, what she would call "action," though understood in the light of the Gospel not simply as the humanization of the world but as the structural transformation of persons and society into the Reign of God.

There are a number of passages in the Synoptic Gospels that focus our attention on the spirituality of work, not so much on its intrinsic theology as participation in the creative work of God and the salvific work of Jesus, but on the religious experience of disciples in ministry. Much of that material occurs in the parables. In this section, however, I want to focus not on the parables but on the narrative material in the Gospels and Paul, in order to address two topics that pertain directly to work as we experience it in ministry. I am selecting narratives I find particularly illuminative, though others could serve the same purpose.

Two passages from the historical narrative of the Gospels, namely, Mark 1–4 which describes the intense activity of Jesus and his disciples, and the Martha and Mary episode in Luke 10:38–42 in which Jesus seems to denigrate active service in relation to contemplation, throw light on the first topic: **the tension between work and prayer** which many full time ministers experience acutely, especially today when the balance is not maintained by a monastic horarium allotting, at least externally, adequate time for each.

Most vividly in Mark, especially in chapters 1 to 4, we get a picture of a whirlwind ministry in which both Jesus and his disciples appear massively "overworked." After an already intense day of teaching and exorcism, Jesus went out to a crowd described as "the whole city" of Capernaum, bringing him their sick and possessed (1:32–34). His early morning prayer the next day was interrupted by his seemingly frantic disciples announcing, "Everyone is searching for you." Jesus responded not by claiming his right to some time to himself, but rather that he and they had to take the message to even more towns throughout Galilee where he preached in their synagogues and cast out demons (1:35–39).

In chapter 2, he is so mobbed by the crowds that a paralytic had to be lowered through the roof to get Jesus' attention (Mark 2:1–12). As he went toward the sea, "the whole crowd gathered around him" (2:13). He is pursued even into a private dinner party by officials badgering him with questions designed to trap him in speech (2:15–17). In chapter 3, Jesus is so pursued by the people that he tells his disciples to have a boat "ready for him because of the crowd, so that they would not crush him" (3:9). Even when he was at home "the crowd came together again, so that [Jesus and his disciples] could not even eat" (3:20). His family thought he was out of his mind, so overwhelming was the scene. We see Jesus so exhausted that he is sound asleep in a boat in the middle of a violent storm at sea that panicked his disciples (4:38).

As the Gospel continues, Jesus is rejected in his hometown. His precursor and perhaps mentor, John the Baptist, is martyred. In short, from the moment his ministry begins Jesus faces incessant and escalating demands for help, ever-increasing crowds pressing upon him day and night, lack of time for solitude and personal prayer, the menace of hostile religious authorities, family misunderstanding, rejection, political threats, extreme fatigue, no time even for regular meals or ordinary recreation with friends. The Markan picture of Jesus at work makes the challenges of even the most "overworked" minister today look leisurely by comparison!

But in Luke we have another presentation of Jesus' attitude toward ministry as work: the well-known and incessantly disputed scene of Jesus at dinner in the house of Martha and Mary (Luke 10:38–42). The history of commentary on this passage has often presented it as a judgment on the hierarchy of states of life: Martha represents the inferior life of active service and Mary represents the superior life of passive contemplation. Jesus apparently canonizes the latter at the expense of the former. Actually *Jesus* does not compare or contrast the sisters or their activities; Martha does. Jesus does not criticize Martha's work, but her anxiety, especially about Mary's nonparticipation in it. The question is, what is Jesus saying about work and prayer?

Interestingly, the medieval Dominican theologian, Meister Eckhart (1260–1328), who was a high mystic by any account as well as an indefatigable teacher, preacher, writer, Religious superior, and formator, turned the traditional interpretation on its head. According to Eckhart , Jesus is telling Martha that she should not be anxious and troubled at her sister's spiritual immaturity. Given the sincerity of Mary's commitment to Jesus, which was a basic choice of the "better part," she would eventually grow beyond her ministerial inactivity and realize that genuine devotion to Jesus leads necessarily into διακονία, the serving or ministry that Martha represents and which is not inimical but intrinsic to contemplative attention. Eckhart says that being both Mary, that is, a "virgin" (a contemplative) and Martha, a fruitful "wife" (an active minister), is superior to being a newly married bride[23] immaturely infatuated with the relationship.

In this interpretation Eckhart follows his slightly older contemporary, Thomas Aquinas (1225–1274), who taught that the "mixed life" of ministry and contemplation was superior to a purely contemplative life because it is better to "illuminate" or enlighten by handing on the fruits of contemplation to others through active ministry than merely to "shine" or be enlightened in silent prayer.

The same message is expressed by Jesus who comes in vision to Catherine of Siena and commands her to leave the much-loved cell in which she had spent three years in solitude and contemplation. Rooted now in that contemplative formation, Catherine undertakes, at Jesus' command, an extraordinary public ministry in ecclesiastical and secular politics, administration, health care, spiritual direction, and writing which ends only with her death.[24]

However, as Bernard McGinn points out in his commentary on Eckhart's theology,[25] the point of Eckhart's passage is not to contrast states of life or even practices in the spiritual life. The point is that active involvement in the service of the neighbor which announces the Reign of God is absolutely necessary for sanctity, not as some kind of concession to those incapable of sustained prayer but as a fulfillment of the second great commandment which is one with the first. We fulfill our God-given mission when we are so deeply rooted by prayer in God, in the "ground" of our being, that our work is truly spiritually fruitful rather than simply human philanthropy. For this to be the case, according to Eckhart, work must have three characteristics: it must be orderly, discriminating, and insightful. A person who has arrived at this state is capable of prodigious work in the midst of the concerns and troubles of the world without becoming harried or dissipated, something earlier mystics under neo-platonic influence had held to be impossible [26] In short, the model of human sanctity is Jesus himself who was indefatigable in his ministry, which led to his martyrdom, and who was always doing the work of his Father in whom he was totally grounded. Just as Jesus in the Gospels does not appear deprived or haggard in his ascetical life, he does not appear frenetic or frantic in his ministry. As he says in John, "I do always the will of the one who sent me" because "I and the Father are one."

This does not solve the ongoing practical problem all committed ministers, including Religious, face: how to achieve a spiritually healthy balance between strenuous work and deepening prayer. Achieving this balance calls for prudent handling of time and energy, attention to living situation, ongoing nourishment through spiritual reading, formation in Scripture and theology, appropriate times of withdrawal, use of spiritual direction, friendship, and all the other means the Religious should have incorporated into her or his life during formation but which need to be adapted once s/he is no longer in that protected environment.

The principle, however, is clear: "Taking care of ourselves" or "protecting ourselves or our privacy" is not the prime task of the Religious. That is not how Jesus lived. Nor can we simply put prayer on hold until there is nothing else that is urgent, claiming that "our work is our prayer." That also is not how Jesus lived and leads more or less quickly to ungrounded work and no prayer. Only when ministry and prayer become one, an integration achieved over a lifetime not of watching ourselves perform in either sphere but of attending always to God and always to the neighbor, will we arrive at the end able to say with Jesus, "It is finished."

Many of the greatest saints—Origen, Augustine, Benedict, Francis of Asissi, Catherine of Siena, Julian of Norwich, Angela Merici, Teresa of Avila, Ignatius of Loyola, John of the Cross, Alphonsus Liguori, John Vianney, Madeleine Sophie Barat, Louise de Marillac, Damien of Molokai, down to those of our own day like Oscar Romero and Mother Teresa—were characterized by what many would call incredible "overwork" in ministry and by lives of such intense prayer that they all qualify as mystics.

A second problematic topic in a contemporary spirituality of ministerial work that can be illuminated by the example of Jesus and Paul, is **availability and mobility**, which are two sides of a single coin: namely, detachment, which is another name for the poverty of spirit Jesus required of his followers. Availability is openness to the other, and in this context especially to the needs of the other. It demands that one's own needs, concerns, projects, relationships, desires are held sufficiently lightly that the needs of others can be heard. Mobility is the response, the willing self-displacement that is required in order to meet the need discerned. It is the willingness to move, geographically, intellectually, emotionally, professionally, relationally, occupationally, or in any of numerous other ways, to meet the needs of the neighbor who is to be loved with one and the same love with which we love God.

Jesus in the Gospels responded to an incredible number and diversity of needs, which often demanded that he move swiftly from place to place. He did not choose membership in the Qumran monastic community (where scholars have suggested he may have spent some time before deciding on his itinerant ministerial vocation). He did not marry and settle down in a permanent relationship. He had no fixed abode, not even a place to lay his head. He called his circle of full-time companions to leave home and family and regular employment and share his itinerant lifestyle; to travel lightly and be prepared to be accepted or rejected but never discouraged.

Paul was obviously driven by the same missionary urgency to preach the Gospel everywhere. Before the first Gospels were written Paul was already responding to Jesus' Great Commission, "Go into all the world and proclaim the good news to the whole creation" (Mark 16:15; cf. Matt 28:19).

However, Jesus and Paul together suggest that availability and mobility can be realized in diverse ways. Jesus never left his homeland, which was a very small country that he could traverse on foot in a matter of days. Paul, by contrast, was a "world traveler" (although the world of his time was the Mediterranean basin), who traveled on land and sea throughout the Middle East, Asia Minor, northern Africa, and Mediterranean Europe, who dealt with people of many cultures, and who finally died a martyr's death far from home.

Not all Religious are called to a life of incessant physical displacement, and no one can judge anyone's ministerial commitment but her or his own. But all Religious are challenged to remain truly detached from "home" and "family," both literally and figuratively. The desire to settle down, to circumscribe one's life with the familiar (people, place, patterns, projects), is natural, perhaps especially so for women, and it becomes more urgently attractive as people get older.

Ministerial Religious in preconciliar days were moved about so frequently that one person might serve on ten, twenty, or even more different missions in a lifetime. Today Religious, who are usually not moved by authorities, are pressured by many factors, some beyond their control, to find a livable situation and simply stay put. The issue is not necessarily geographical location. Some missionaries have generously given a lifetime of service to the people of a single location where their deep familiarity with the culture and knowledge of the language makes their ministry particularly effective. Some Professions espoused as ministry require relative permanence because of the way they are institutionalized. But some Religious have placed such high priority on proximity to family or friends or even community, to a particular relationship, to cultural familiarity, comfortable physical surroundings, peace and quiet, or even the path of least resistance that they no longer hear the call to put out into the deep, to go into the whole world, that helped steer them to ministerial Religious Life in the first place. While some Religious have courageously retooled more than once to meet new needs, some others have settled for a succession of "odd jobs" that keep them busy but that leave them mostly free to pursue their own interests.

Availability and mobility are rooted in and expressions of evangelical poverty, the detachment from one's own needs and projects and interests that allows one to hear the cry of the poor, and the detachment from property and people that allows one to move when and where new needs announce themselves and to courageously reconstruct one's life in response to ministerial challenges. Mobility can take many forms but it always means stretching beyond the familiar or the comfortable and confronting the challenges of the new and the untried. Only the Religious her- or himself knows whether s/he still has an ear tuned to the "Come follow me," the "Go into the whole world" or whether s/he has, in effect, opted out of ministry in favor of comfort and security.

B. Work and Evangelical Poverty in the Contemporary Context

As long as Religious participated in the institutional apostolates of their Congregations they were assigned specific tasks in a larger enterprise that was usually rooted in some way in their charism, governed by the Constitutions, and carried out under the direct control of Congregational and ecclesiastical authority. Often, the Congregation had received its specific ministry(ies) from its founder, who had been inspired by God to meet particular needs and the members shared in a sociology of knowledge that both gave a basic coherence to the common project and the work the individual did within that project, and grounded a sense of communal and personal efficacy in mission.

The individualization of ministry in the wake of the Council shifted the burden of discernment, both about what ministry to undertake and where and how to pursue it, from the Congregation to the individual Religious in consultation with the leaders of the Congregation. She no longer had the daily experience of working with dozens or even hundreds of others who all assumed, as she did, that this was indeed what God called them to do, usually because the work had been committed to them or approved for them by ecclesiastical authority. The loss of the institutional base and context erased the measuring lines that had made a certain apostolic effectiveness encouragingly visible. In the days of institutionalized Congregational apostolates one knew how many of the school's students had gone on to college, how many of the hospital's patients had recovered or died well, how many parentless children had been placed in good homes. One could see how many new institutions the Congregation had opened and how many new candidates had joined the ranks of its workers.

As Religious fanned out to tackle myriad new challenges in inner cities, in poor barrios, in educational systems not owned by the Congregation, in parishes, spirituality centers, secular social service agencies and community health care facilities, in the peace movement, the political sphere, and through social activism, they were at first filled with the excitement of the unfamiliar challenges and the sense of addressing much more directly the major obstacles to the Reign of God from which they had been somewhat buffered by the institutional settings of preconciliar shared apostolates. More "on their own" in discerning the needs and in developing responses, they were stretched and expanded personally and ministerially. However, after more than forty years of this confrontation with the intractable evils of poverty, oppression, injustice, violence, ecclesiastical obstructionism, and governmental indifference, with the unavailability of funds for even the most urgent and obvious needs, with their own waning physical energies, with loneliness and isolation among colleagues of good will whose motivations were sometimes incompatible or at least simply different from their own, many Religious have found themselves dealing with temptations that did not surface so readily in the institutional apostolates of yesteryear.

These struggles usually lie somewhere on a spectrum that runs from surrender to despair at one end to crushing overwork at the other. What they all have in common is a growing realization that our best efforts are not getting the job done. Unnecessary illness and premature death are no less prevalent. World poverty is increasing rather than decreasing. Education is less affordable and less available than ever and its quality more questionable. Injustice is compounded by massive corruption in high places, both secular and ecclesiastical. War is ever-more ubiquitous and in many cases there is not even a credible pretense that it is motivated by just causes or is capable of bringing about anything other than greater concentration of power and wealth in the hands of the few at the expense of the oppressed and hopeless poor. The unavoidable question today is, what are we really accomplishing? Is the Gospel making any difference? Does preaching it make any sense? And even, is preaching the Gospel really what we are doing as we anxiously weigh salaries against need?

If one answers these questions in the negative despair is hard to avoid. This can take the form of a kind of resignation that amounts to "Why keep trying?" Why should we put in sixteen-hour days often seven days a week and deny ourselves most of the good things of at least a middle-class lifestyle, when whether we do so or not very little changes and seldom for the better? Without making explicit decisions to back out, some Religious have just found a way to withdraw into a relatively comfortable and undemanding middle-class situation in which they keep decently busy at respectable occupations eight hours a day, bring in an acceptable salary, and devote the rest of their time to pursuits that are personally enriching.

Every Congregation today seems to be dealing with at least a few members who are chronically "unemployed" or perpetually "in transition" because there is nothing that really engages their energies, or at least nothing on which they want to expend their energy. There are others who move from one form of "retooling" to another without ever seriously undertaking the successive forms of ministry for which they "prepare." In the absence of the momentum of large Congregational apostolates that carried the Religious, ministerial zeal has to be deeply rooted in Gospel soil to survive, much less thrive, in the massively discouraging realization that one is not winning the battle against evil. The Reign of God is no more evident today than it was when most of us started.[27] Unless one is profoundly identified with Jesus whose public ministry had no institutional support and was opposed by both the religious institution and the state, whose followers were fickle and undependable, and whose work ended in his Passion and death and the dispersal of his followers, Resurrection hope in the mission to which we are committed becomes insubstantial.

Most Religious, as far as I can observe, are closer to the other end of the spectrum from despair. They are working, often well beyond "retirement age," far more than forty-hour weeks, in ministries that are often physically demanding and psychically draining. They may be running political programs, doing community organizing, serving in clinics, teaching or tutoring, serving in underdeveloped areas of this country or abroad, counseling in prisons, doing hospice work, heading catechetical programs, leading parishes with ineffective, oppressive, or no clergy, exercising leadership in Congregations burdened by debt, doing retreat or spiritual direction on a shoestring budget, fund-raising, doing social work in homes or agencies, providing legal advocacy, or doing so-called "volunteer" work in all kinds of programs that are often understaffed and underpaid. They are pitting ever-increasing efforts against ever-mounting odds and asking more of themselves than seems reasonable by any standard. The question is, when is this generosity and zeal rooted in the Gospel and ready to go "even unto death" for the sake of the Reign of God, and when is it compulsive overwork that does not know how to stop and is rooted in the inability to accept that achieving peace, justice, universal literacy, good parish communities, health care for all, prison reform, an end to poverty and oppression and violence, decent housing for everyone, and so on, is not in one's power to achieve?

The spiritual problem at the root of both quiet despair of our work and furious overwork that will not take less than success for an answer, and much that lies between them, might be called "the heresy of efficient causality." Human beings, perhaps especially those who are most altruistic, disciplined, and highly motivated, tend naturally to think that if they do the right thing well enough with sufficient commitment and energy they will achieve the desired result. If one attends class and studies hard one will graduate. The loyal and productive employee will be promoted. The athlete who trains assiduously will win. For most people, including committed Christians who participate in various ways in ministry, significant portions of their lives do fall into the logic of "effort normally brings success." If they raise their children well, fulfill their employment duties assiduously, save prudently, are faithful to their relationships and so on they can reasonably expect at least some success that is visibly attributable to their efforts.

However, such human projects and the work God entrusted to Jesus and to which full time ministers devote all of their life's energy are qualitatively different. Ministry is not a human enterprise. Our efforts are not, and cannot be, proportionate to the task. Therefore, ministry, especially when it is a full-time investment of one's whole life, is engagement in an enterprise which will not succeed in our lifetime. This great work has been accomplished by the death of Jesus, that is, by his utter human failure against the evil he confronted. On the cross the world, Satan's kingdom, apparently triumphed. But, as Jesus said to his disciples, it was a pyrrhic victory in which the apparent victor perished.

The Resurrection was the definitive sign that when evil has done all it can do, life springs forth more abundantly than ever because hatred has not been able to extinguish love. Jesus' accomplishment of the salvation of the world and the Resurrection in which it consists are still matters of faith, not vision. What we see now, what we participate in through our human experience, is Jesus' acceptance into his own being, his own experience, of human evil "unto death," the "death that should not be."

Jesus told his disciples, in numerous and varied ways, in direct discourse and parable, that their work would not succeed by human standards. He told them (see especially the Last Discourses in John 13–17) that the world would hate and persecute them as it had him, that is, unto death. They are not the vine but the branches that cannot bear fruit of themselves. They are not the master but the "unprofitable servants" whose best work is never enough. They are workers in, not the owner of, the vineyard. They will never succeed in pulling up all the weeds but must continue to cultivate the wheat even as the weeds entangle the harvest. As Jesus could do nothing except what he saw the Father doing, so Jesus' disciples can do nothing except what they see him doing. They saw his best efforts end in betrayal and crucifixion. The servant is not above the master but finds her or his blessedness in being like the master (see John 15:20).

The conviction that what we do in ministry should succeed, that we are the efficient causes of salvation at least in our small corner of the vineyard, is the fundamental possessiveness that drives uncentered overwork and produces discouraged despair. It must, finally, be surrendered in the embrace of the poverty of the cross.[28] When Catherine of Siena, that prodigiously effective minister who accomplished more in thirty-three years than most people can in twice that time, said to God, "You are the one who is; I am she who is not," she was acknowledging, with profound spiritual joy, her existential poverty as a creature and her ministerial poverty as a branch in the true vine.[29]

The minister who is rooted in this poverty of being and doing does not despair precisely because s/he does not expect to succeed in human terms but is fully confident that God in Jesus has overcome the world and this victory, the Resurrection, will appear when God reveals it. Her role is to actualize that salvation in whatever ways Jesus calls and allows her to do. S/he is not called to "save the world" but to announce, "today salvation has come to this house." And s/he announces that Good News with every concrete act of loving service, through all of the spiritual and corporal works of mercy that are so many idioms by which to speak a word of courage to the weary and downtrodden.

On the other hand, the minister rooted in existential poverty, no matter how hard or long she works, will not be pathologically overworked because s/he is not frantically trying to bring about results that continue to elude her or him. She is doing all she can, as well as she can, as long as she can, even unto death but her final word is not a cry of failure and frustration but a peaceful, "Now you may dismiss your servant," and "Into your hands I commend my spirit." When we look at the great "workers in the vineyard," at Paul who evangelized the known world in less than two decades, Teresa of Avila who refounded an order in the midst of the Inquisition, Catherine of Siena who had influenced all Europe by her death at the age of thirty-three, Alphonsus Liguori who worked into his nineties "without wasting a minute of time," or Mother Teresa of Calcutta whose ministry could not even be contained by the enormous subcontinent of India, we realize that there is a massive difference between working even unto death in and with Christ and working oneself to death in the stubborn conviction that one can and must and will succeed.

Once again, spiritual poverty reveals its true face as detachment; detachment from self as effective and from results as measurable. But detachment is neither resigned passivity nor a pseudo-spiritualization of failure. It is an integral part, the dimension of poverty, in a spirituality of ministry as work.[30]

VI. Poverty and Prayer in Religious Life: Passive Purification

The sober conclusions of the last section lead directly to the final dimension of a spirituality of evangelical poverty, that is, poverty of spirit, that I want to consider in this chapter, namely, growth in prayer. Obviously, much that supported, if not carried, Religious in preconciliar days is no longer part of the life as it is lived in ministerial Congregations today. The collective form of community life in the total institution, the economic and social security of ministering in the Catholic ghetto, and the relatively assured "success" of Congregational apostolates in established institutions are, to a large extent, gone. For some people this is the very definition of the demise of Religious Life itself. They cannot imagine authentic Religious Life that does not look like and function in an essentially monastic form.

For most who have ridden out the last forty years of change, that is not the only possible conclusion. What they do know is that the spirituality of ministerial Religious Life which is necessarily more individualized today demands a more mature approach to the reality of community, a different and more selfless commitment to ministry, and above all a profound commitment to prayer as experienced union with Jesus who is the center of their life. These developments are absolutely necessary if the life is to be meaningful, ministry effective, and community real and rich in the very changed cultural and ecclesial situation of the twenty-first century postmodern world. Individualization can easily become deadly individualism if community is not rooted in the common life that emerges not from physical proximity under the same roof in the total institution but from economic interdependence that expresses itself in the economics of the Reign of God; if the spirituality of evangelical poverty is not nourished by ongoing ascetical practice and expressed in the commitment to ministry as the work of announcing effectively the Reign of God in this world. But none of this will be possible without the effective commitment to prayer that is the heart of the life.

It is probably much clearer to Religious living today than it might have been when regular prescribed prayers said at provided times with supportive companions in aesthetically conducive settings was the norm, that prayer must grow or die and that the primary responsibility for their life of union with Christ rests primarily with the individual Religious. Prayer is not formulas to be recited or rites to be performed, even if some formulas are used and some rituals celebrated. Prayer is the life of relationship that is at the heart of Religious Life. That relationship must be nourished by time in solitude and in communal worship; by *lectio divina* of Scripture and other serious and challenging spiritual literature; by ongoing theological and nontheological reflection leading one into new insights into God, self, and world; by silent communion in which the mystery of God is welcomed into the wordless intimacy of love and God's love is poured forth in us as divine affirmation, energy, courage, and peace. Only from the ongoing experience of a life of prayer, a life shared on a moment-to-moment basis, in good times and bad, with the One to whom one's life is totally given can today's Religious remain centered, focused, fearless, committed, and able to continue unto death in the quest for God and the coming of God's Reign which is the very essence of Religious Life.

In volume 1 of this work, *Religious Life in a New Millennium,* I devoted two chapters to John of the Cross' presentation of the Dark Night experience as possibly illuminating of the corporate experience of ministerial Religious in the postconciliar years. A review of chapters 5 and 6 of *Finding the Treasure* and the accompanying appendix briefly summarizing John's theory might be helpful in engaging this final section on poverty of spirit and prayer.

Here I am concerned with the passive Dark Night, the final stage of interior purification of the individual person. Most students of John of the Cross seem to agree that not everyone experiences, psychologically, what John describes (which is undoubtedly based on his own experience), but his work has become a classic resource on this subject because, no matter how a person experiences it subjectively, the purification effected by the Dark Night has to occur, in one way or another, if a person is to come to that union with God toward which all prayer life aims.[31] There is only so much we can do in the spiritual life (and indeed it is a great deal), but at some point God must "finish" the work because, in the end, it is God who freely gives Godself to us on God's terms, not we who attain to God on our terms.

As people mature in the spiritual life they will face developmental challenges in the life of prayer just as they do in physical and psychological growth. And just as human development is usually laid out in terms of infancy, childhood, adolescence, and maturity with different theories refining this pattern in different ways, the spiritual path is usually laid out in terms of the purgative, illuminative, and unitive ways, again with all manner of refinements and variations according to different authors. Not everyone reaches human maturity and not everyone, apparently, attains spiritual maturity. But no one reaches maturity without passing by way of the preceding stages, even though some people mature much more rapidly (or more slowly) than others, spend different amounts of time in different phases, relapse (or revisit) stages of development already more or less negotiated, and experience various phases in more complex and differentiated ways than others. Consequently, we can talk about spiritual maturity and the developmental demands it places on people without denying that individuals differ widely, experientially, in how they negotiate these passages.

While active purification, increasing illumination, and growing union are always interlacing and overlapping over the span of the spiritual life, it is normal for the early stages of the life to be marked by more strenuous efforts on the part of the person who has a sense of urgency about growing in relationship with God and a capacity for initiative and self-direction in the matter. The earliest stages of the spiritual life of a committed Religious, which usually today begin well before she or he enters the novitiate but are intensified during formation, are marked by strenuous efforts to deal with the personal obstacles to prayer, to growth in virtue, to becoming a committed member of the community and an effective minister. Usually the person has an invigorating sense of making progress in the spiritual life, despite failures, including deepening in their relationship with God.

At some point, the activity in the spiritual life of the person appears to be less effective. They "plateau" in an experience of relative proficiency in the life of prayer, virtue, community, ministry but they may have a vague sense that there is something lacking. It might be an experience of prolonged darkness or aridity in prayer that cannot be "jump started" by previously successful methods; discouragement or "marking time" in ministry which remains relatively effective but is no longer energizing in the same way; greater consciousness of inability to handle certain temptations or addictions; or boredom or lack of energy for life that might feel like depression or burnout. Something begins to announce to the person that there is more to the spiritual life than they seem able to access. Their efforts in prayer, retreats, and spiritual direction to move forward seem futile. However successful and accomplished they look to others, and actually are, they know that something is arrested. They hear the call to something beyond where they are but also know they cannot answer. This sense of paralysis can begin to prepare a person for the interior work that only God can accomplish.

Whether the next phase of the spiritual life is dramatic and devastating or relatively mild, incessant over long periods of time or intermittently intense, short or prolonged, accompanied by severe physical or psychological trauma and disruption or not, the process and purpose are the same. The person is being detached by God's action from the deeply rooted self-centered ego, what the post-Freudian psychologist Karen Horney[32] called "the ideal self," the self-proprietorship of the subject which is an impediment to God's full possession of the person. Only the radical poverty of spirit that no longer wants to or can control one's own spiritual life, that has stopped "calling the shots" or running the program or determining the goals and has surrendered completely to God's initiative in profound existential realization of one's nothingness in relation to God's allness, can finally receive the gift God so wants to give, full union with Godself in Christ. Apparently, even Jesus, who certainly was as totally open to God as a human being can possibly be, seemed to pass through some final stripping of the spirit in his experience of abandonment on the cross.

The prayer of union is the goal to which the spiritual life is directed and it is the deep wellspring of the selflessness toward which ministerial Religious Life must grow and hopefully finally embody. This prayer is characterized by profound poverty of spirit, total detachment from the ego that frees the true self for full union with God. The asceticism by which we progressively neutralize through detachment the fierce desire to be our own source of being and the growth in ministerial self-donation through the work of proclaiming and fostering the Reign of God in this world are phases or dimensions of development in the life with God which must be completed, finally, by God's own action in the passive purification to which fidelity in the life of prayer opens us. Poverty of spirit actualized by unitive love is the purpose and the final realization of the vow of evangelical poverty.

Part Three

Prophetic Obedience
The Politics of the Reign of God

Chapter Seven
Remodeling Authority and Obedience

I. Introduction

Few aspects of Religious Life have changed more radically and dramatictally, especially among first world women Religious in ministerial Congregations, [1] than the understanding and practice of the vow of obedience. In pre-renewal Religious Life, from the moment Religious arose in response to the bell which they regarded as the "voice of God" until they retired in response to the same bell, they saw virtually their every act as an exercise of obedience to Constitution, customs book, horarium, assignment, or the directives of superiors. Today Religious do not sacralize the alarm clock. Their schedules are set according to individual professional and personal commitments. The Constitutions contain few if any detailed directives about specific practices. Congregational leaders do not busy themselves with the details of members' daily lives nor make unilateral decisions about their living situations, finances, or ministries. So sweeping has been the change in the practice of obedience in Religious Life that some, both inside and outside the life, have concluded that obedience, for all intents and purposes, has simply "withered away." It is ritually professed in deference to the ancient custom of the triple vow formula but seems to have no real influence on the daily life of the Religious.

The difference between what Religious understood by, and practiced as, obedience in preconciliar days and how they live this vow today may be one of the clearest indications of the theme I have been developing over the three volumes of this series, namely, that postconciliar Religious, especially first world women Religious in non-enclosed Congregations, have birthed a really new form of Religious Life which is not simply an updated version of the "apostolic Religious Life" officially approved in 1900. Contemporary Religious have not just modified certain external practices of poverty and obedience but have developed a really new understanding, a new theology and spirituality of the vows that is both substantially continuous and significantly discontinuous with previous understandings.

To briefly recall what has been said on this subject in previous chapters and will be described and focused in much greater detail in the fourth part of this chapter, preconciliar apostolic Religious Life was a hybrid lifeform in which Religious lived as monastics at home within the "total institution"— the above description of obedience in a preconciliar context illustrates this point—but carried out external "apostolates" such as administering and staffing Catholic institutions. These apostolates were exercised exclusively within the context of the institutional Church to support, sustain, and implement the ministerial projects of the hierarchy. In hindsight, it is clear that, even before the Council's call for renewal, strains had begun to develop between the hierarchy's understanding of Religious as a dedicated "work force" within Catholic institutions and the evolving self-understanding of many Religious Congregations as charismatically grounded communities who had a legitimate right to self-determination in regard to their lives and ministries.[2]

The major difference between the collective, ecclesiastically located and controlled institutional apostolates of preconciliar apostolic Congregations and the more individualized and often noninstitutionally situated ministries of many Religious today is that the latter often are not expansions or adjuncts of the Church's ordained ministry, connected to parish and diocese. Rather, as we will see in greater detail following, these ministries are directly in the service of world transformation as it is evoked in *Gaudium et Spes*. Religious are cultivating the "wheat" (not just Catholic wheat) even as they struggle to subvert the "weeds" (not all of which are outside the Church) in the one "field," which is this world.

Religious do not come from their own monastic world to labor in an ecclesiastical plot in which they do not live. Rather, they are living and working in the one field of God's good Creation, which is constructed in various ways. They are *being* the alternate world of the Reign of God right in the midst of the reality construction of the Prince of This World. This world-insertion, flowing directly from the conciliar resituation of the Church itself in, with, and for the world after centuries of world-rejection, is the most influential factor in the transformation of Religious Life that we have been experiencing. It is largely responsible for the deconstruction of the total institution version of Religious Life (at least in those Congregations which have participated in this renewal), but more importantly it is the reason for the new understanding of ministry that has led to a new interpretation of the vows of poverty and obedience.

In this part 3 of the present volume, I am going to argue that, as we saw in regard to evangelical poverty, prophetic obedience has not "withered away" or become inoperative in ministerial Religious Life. If anything, it has become more deeply integral to the life. But, for at least three reasons, it does need to be newly articulated. First, we are living in a postmodern culture in which authority and therefore obedience are understood very differently from the way they were when most Religious alive today entered. Clarity about what we can appreciate and appropriate from this new sociocultural situation and what requires prophetic criticism and challenge is crucial. Second, some people in the Church, both laity and hierarchy, have not yet really grasped the effects of the Conciliar renewal in ministerial Religious Life. The tensions between official understandings of contemporary Religious Life as a slightly modified version of the preconciliar form and the emerging self-understanding of deeply renewed ministerial Congregations often surface in terms of authority and obedience. Consequently, it is vitally important for individual Religious and Congregations to develop a language by which to clarify what they are doing and why. Third, Religious as individuals and as communities are carrying a good deal of psychological, sociological, and political "baggage" from the whole history of Religious Life that needs to be reexamined. There are treasures in this shared history, some of which need to be refurbished with contemporary theological and spiritual resources and appropriated anew. But there is also much that is outmoded or was from its inception more rooted in secular theory and practice, and sometimes more in very inadequate theology than in the Gospel, which needs to be replaced with contemporary resources more compatible with Religious Life.

As we proceed I will occasionally modify the term *obedience*, as I modified the terms *celibacy* and *poverty*, in order to keep us mindful that the object of the vows is not equivalent to what these terms denote in a secular context. *Consecrated* celibacy is not merely the condition of being unmarried but the particular way Religious handle one of the three major coordinates of human existence, that is, sexuality and relationship. *Evangelical* poverty does not mean material deprivation or even simple living but the particular way Religious deal with another coordinate of the human project, that is, material goods and ownership. Likewise, *prophetic* obedience is the way Religious choose to handle the third major coordinate of human life, that is, freedom and power.

The vow of prophetic obedience is integral to the project of ministerial Religious Life, to creating and sustaining in this ambiguous world, in this field of wheat and weeds, the alternate world that is the Reign of God lived on a full-time basis over the whole of one's life. Prophetic obedience is the politics of the Reign of God, just as evangelical poverty is its economics and consecrated celibacy the source of its social incarnation in transcendent community. This alternate world is the Gospel reality construction *in* which the members live and *from* which they minister. Ministry is no longer seen as a secondary end (the salvation of souls) overflowing from the primary end (the sanctification of the Religious). Rather, the first commandment to love God with one's whole being is incarnated in the fulfillment of the second commandment to love and serve the neighbor. Religious choose to do this, and only this, with the whole of their lives.

As ministerial Religious Life has emerged from its semi-monastic self-understanding the healthy individuality resulting from the demise of the total institution deconstructed the collectivist understanding of community. As we saw in the last chapter, that deconstruction has radically affected how Religious understand economic common life. From the uniformity of living under one roof, wearing identical clothing, eating at a single table, and so on, common life has become a radical embrace of shared possessionlessness. The changed understanding of their life has also affected how Religious understand and practice obedience. Rather than seeing obedience as everyone doing the same thing, preferably at the same time, in the same place, and in the same way, according to the detailed prescriptions of Rule and superiors, it is increasingly seen as ongoing individual and corporate discernment of and fidelity to the will of God for the promotion of the Reign of God in the time and place in which we live.

Religious obedience, in this light, is a *prophetic* enterprise of mediating the three-pronged encounter of God (mediated through the Christian tradition), the People of God (as leaven within the wider human race), and culture (in this time and place).[3] Like the prophet Moses, who mediated the encounter of the Hebrew people with the God of their ancestors in the time of the Exodus, Religious today must both model in their community life and facilitate by their ministry the discernment of and response to the call of God to their contemporaries in the postconciliar Church and postmodern world. This is not an "apostolate from above" of those with some kind of special access to God's will announcing it to ordinary (or even benighted) people. It is primarily a matter of "being among the people as one who serves," as one who struggles alongside her or his sisters and brothers to discern and do the will of God in this very complex world. Like the prophet Jesus, Religious in ministry will both share the condition and the fate of those to whom they are missioned and with them struggle to make the Reign of God more real in this world. Ministerial Religious have chosen to have no other primary life commitment, no other "voice" in their ears, than that of God's people and the God they serve. Thus, contemplation which attunes them to God, and social marginality which places them in solidarity with the poor and oppressed, condition their discernment and shape their work.

If we are to reappropriate the deep meaning of the vow of prophetic obedience, and articulate it in this new key, we must first situate this project in terms of the three interrelated contexts in which it is unfolding: the changed *sociocultural understanding* of authority and obedience in the postmodern world; the current *ecclesiastical context* within which ministerial Religious Life is struggling for self-definition and appropriate autonomy; and the *psychological, sociological, and political legacy* of Religious Life itself which needs to become conscious so that it can be appropriately handled.

II. Contradictions in the Sociocultural Understanding of Authority

The majority of people in Religious Life today entered from family or school contexts in which parental authority (direct or through agents acting *in loco parentis*) was, at least in theory, largely unquestioned. Transferring obedience from parents to superiors exercising their authority within the familial ethos of semi-monastic Religious Life was a natural move. Today, not only is parental authority itself relativized in many ways, but most candidates enter their Congregations as fully emancipated adults coming from contexts such as employment or graduate school, where unquestioning obedience to any personal authority figure is virtually unimaginable.

Not only is authority itself regarded as intrinsically relative, but post-Freudian psychology, which permeates the first world *Zeitgeist*, leads most moderns to see human development as taking place over the entire life span rather than terminating at the end of adolescence. Therefore, healthy maturation involves a continual expansion and deepening of personal autonomy toward full "individuation."[4] This basic conviction about lifelong personal development reflects and is complemented by the worldwide sociopolitical movements toward liberation from all forms of oppression. Together these cultural currents have shifted the burden of proof to anyone promoting submission or conformity that restricts individual rights and self-expression.

In light of such developments, any presentation to candidates for Religious Life of a theology and spirituality of obedience has to take account of a completely changed cultural understanding and evaluation of authority. There is very little, if any, cultural support for an *a priori* presumption in favor of uncritical submission to superiors. The bumper sticker admonitions to "Question [all] Authority" and "Just Do It" are much more self-evidently rational to moderns than the previously easily accepted injunctions to "keep the Rule and the Rule will keep you" or to "just do as you are told" by those in authority. Most of us would probably agree that, despite its susceptibility to distortion and the fact that it makes any formation in obedience much more challenging today than it was in times past, this is a healthy development.

However, this widely shared commitment to ongoing growth in personal autonomy through the exercise of critical judgment and personal responsibility is culturally subverted by other and contrary currents in contemporary society. Since the Holocaust, which most candidates today cannot personally remember, very disturbing data continue to appear about the capacity of modern people for the very kind of destructive "blind obedience" that led to the massacre of millions of people by the Nazis in the 1930s and 40s.

In the early 1960s a PhD student in psychology, Stanley Milgram, carried out a series of experiments at Yale University to answer a question that arose during the 1961 trial for crimes against humanity of Adolf Eichmann, who was found guilty of mass murder of Jews during the Nazi regime. Milgram's research question was whether Eichmann, who was just following the orders of his military superiors, was really guilty (i.e., responsible and accountable) for what he did as "the architect of the Holocaust."[5] In other words, can or does obedience to legally constituted authority lead people to do objectively immoral actions for which they feel (and perhaps have) no subjective responsibility?

In Milgram's famous experiments,[6] volunteers were enlisted to participate as "teachers" in a "laboratory test" of the effect of punishment on learning. These "teachers" were instructed to administer increasingly powerful electric shocks, beginning at fifteen volts, to volunteer "learners" (actually actors) who gave the wrong answers to test questions. Even after the "learners," seated behind a curtain out of sight of the "teachers," began to cry out for mercy, "Ultimately 65% of all the 'teachers' punished the 'learners' to the maximum 450 volts [supposedly enough to seriously harm or even kill them]. And none of the subjects [i.e., 'teachers'] stopped before reaching [at least] 300 volts." Needless to say, this "Eichmann response" was shocking at the time.

Milgram died in 1984 but his experiments have been repeated, with legally mandated modifications, at intervals since the 1960s, with alarmingly consistent results. The *New York Times* of February 7, 2008, reported on two new academic papers, one by a doctoral student at Ohio State University and one by a professor at Santa Clara University, reporting that in modified replications of Milgram's experiment the results were fundamentally the same as the 1960s results. Careful analyses of these results establish that a large majority (two-thirds) of the ordinary, moral, non-sadistic participants in these experiments, who had nothing personal against their victims, were willing to do serious violence to anonymous others if commanded to do so by someone they considered to be an authority, especially if the authority assured them that he, not they, was responsible for the results.

Milgram made deliberate connections between his experiment and the gassing of millions by Nazi subordinates on the orders of military superiors. And the most recent interest in the Milgram experiments followed the exposé of the torture by American military personnel of Iraqi prisoners at Abu Ghraib prison. The explanation and excuse offered for these new war crimes, once again, was in terms of "just following orders." In other words, "blind obedience," disturbingly similar to what was once inculcated in novices who were taught to obey without question not only reasonable and moral commands but even (or especially) those that appeared unreasonable or somehow wrong. They were assured that "even if the superior erred in commanding, the subject never erred in obeying." Of course, there was always the caveat, "unless the action commanded is sinful."[7] But, as the Milgram and later experiments showed, it was precisely the conviction that the person in authority knew more than the one obeying, would not be commanding something immoral, and took full responsibility for the command and its results that made the "torturers" willing to suspend their own moral judgment in deference to the superior's. Some of the "teachers" were clearly anxious about what they were doing. Nevertheless, they continued to pull the switch when commanded by the "lawful superior" to do so. Religious, especially those who were young and inexperienced, who were conditioned to vest unlimited confidence in their superiors, and who had a significant interest in not being dismissed for disobedience, have often been incapable of making a quick and decisive judgment that their superiors were commanding something sinful much less to summon the courage to resist.[8] Furthermore, something does not have to be sinful to be wrong and therefore not to be done.

No matter what might have been said for blind obedience in the past, the Holocaust (and later events like the massacres at My Lai and El Mozote, and the torturing at Abu Ghraib and Guantánamo) should establish unequivocally that blind obedience cannot be proposed or defended today, no matter how it is explained or qualified.[9] To obey blindly, no matter who is commanding, is to abdicate one's moral responsibility. That is never a viable option. No one who has reached the age of moral responsibility can blamelessly substitute another person's conscience for his or her own. "Doing what I was told" without making a judgment that it is the right thing to do, or at least that it is not wrong, is immoral in itself, to say nothing about the morality of what is done. This conviction is just as important in formation for Religious obedience as the disposition to obey lawful authority.

Rethinking the vow of obedience as a prophetic commitment to moving our world away from the politics of Satan's kingdom toward the politics of the Reign of God has to take account of this paradoxical sociocultural context in which, on the one hand, traditional notions of obedience owed to natural or designated superiors is everywhere questioned and relativized, if not simply dismissed, while, on the other hand, blind obedience to experts in the academy, the military, business, medicine, or government is very widely accepted and practiced. If Religious obedience is to be prophetic today, it has to find a way to criticize, challenge, and propose effective alternatives to both a false autonomy that rejects all authority and a "blind obedience" that abandons all moral responsibility before the will of those in power. Formation for such obedience in today's sociocultural context requires the development in candidates of an uncommon moral maturity in judgment and action.

III. Conflicts in the Ecclesiastical Context of Religious Life

Religious living in the second decade of the twenty-first century are contending not only with an ambiguous secular context that challenges any Gospel understanding of obedience, but within a highly stressful ecclesiastical context in which the meaning and practice of obedience is frequently a flash point. Clashes between Church authorities and ministerial Religious, both individuals and Congregations, have been rather frequent and often traumatic over the past fifty years and there is little reason to think that this pattern will change significantly any time soon. Religious are struggling to live in this situation with integrity while striving for nonviolent engagement and eventual mutual understanding. Crucial to this difficult process is theological clarity about the emerging form of their

Religious Life and a growing ability to articulate their experience and their convictions clearly and convincingly.

Ministerial Religious Life as it has continued to emerge since the Council has all the features that have marked "new forms of Religious Life"[10] (e.g., cenobitic monasticism, mendicant life, clerical Orders, Congregations of apostolic life, etc.) within the two-thousand-year history of this charismatic lifeform in the Church. It continues to have much in common with the apostolic form of the life that was born at the beginning of the modern period (c. 1600s), was finally approved by the Church in 1900, and remained normative for non-enclosed Congregations until the 1970s. However, the emerging form involves enough that is really new that we should not be surprised if Church authority views this development with some misgivings, as it has historically viewed most innovation in Religious Life, especially among women. The Vatican does have a certain responsibility to protect consecrated life as a charism in the Church. This responsibility, however, has often (though not always, as Vatican II demonstrated) been exercised by way of obstruction or repression[11] rooted in a deep suspicion of anything new (which even popes like John XXIII have deplored).

It took more than three hundred years for the institutional Church to finally recognize what the People of God who were being served by them knew very well, namely, that vowed women who "went out" of their cloisters to serve God's people were truly Religious. This apostolic form of Religious Life, although "radically" new in respect to the exercise of an active external apostolate by vowed women, was not a clean break from its mendicant predecessor, nor is the development which we are witnessing today, which I have been calling "mobile ministerial Religious Life," a clean break from its predecessor, "Congregations devoted to works of the apostolate." There is continuity in what is constitutive of Religious Life, namely, total commitment to God in Jesus Christ in a stable lifeform established through lifelong commitment by public Profession of the evangelical counsels lived in community and mission. But there is discontinuity as well arising primarily from a new understanding, springing directly from the Council,[12] of mission and ministry in and to the world. This new understanding has had major implications for the living of community life and the vows, as did the undertaking of active apostolates for the earliest apostolic Congregations.

From today's perspective, it is increasingly clear that traditional apostolic Religious Life, from which this new form is gradually becoming distinct, even though its members exercised apostolates outside the cloister, remained a monastic and even "semi-cloistered" form of Religious Life. Within the convent, the life retained the government structure, habit, horarium, practice of the vows, prayer life, form of community life, and spirituality of the enclosed monastery. Indeed, the habit was a kind of "portable cloister" which kept the Religious, even when outside the convent for apostolic work, as separated from the culture and the people with whom she interacted as possible. And she was seldom outside the actual convent environment for very long, and virtually never alone.

Furthermore, the apostolates of these Religious were directly ecclesiastical. They were extensions of the ministry of the hierarchy, which entrusted them to Congregations (not to individual Religious), and they were virtually totally subject to the hierarchy's control. A major development in the general theology of ministry, which has affected not only the laity but also Religious, occurred when Vatican II recognized that the "apostolate of the laity" (meaning, in this case, the non-ordained secular baptized)[13] arises from their baptism and confirmation, not, as previously taught, from its participation in the apostolate of the hierarchy.[14] This realization that ministry was not the sole prerogative of the ordained was the seed (which took some time to germinate) of the new understanding of ministry that is galvanizing ministerial Religious Life.

Even in the almost exclusively clerical/hierarchical model of apostolate prior to the Council, struggles between Religious Congregations and bishops were not unknown or uncommon. The establishment of "exemption" for Congregations of pontifical right was an early attempt to guarantee some measure of autonomy to these Congregations, especially in regard to their internal affairs including decisions about if and when they would assign their members to work in particular dioceses or apostolates. This right to self-determination, limited though it was, was often circumvented by the local hierarchy. And diocesan communities did not have even the protection of exemption.

The resistance of many bishops to the Sister Formation Movement[15] in the United States as late as the 1950s, because it involved superiors taking some Religious temporarily out of institutional apostolates for purposes of personal and professional formation, testified to the severe limitations in practice on the exercise of any right of Religious Congregations to self-determination in the apostolate. The apostolic Congregation was, in the view of the hierarchy, basically a "job corps" to be used for the works of the institutional Church.

The rapid changes that conciliar renewal introduced into this picture caused understandable alarm among many in the hierarchy. First, virtually overnight (in ecclesiastical time) the "monastic-at-home" aspect of the life, which was key to clerical control of women whose service was vital to the apostolate of the local churches, disappeared. The struggle over the habit was not incidental. Its demise effectively symbolized the end of enclosure, a development that was integral to a new approach to ministry.

The devastating attack by Cardinal McIntyre of Los Angeles on the Immaculate Heart of Mary Congregation based in his archdiocese was probably the most dramatic example of a hierarchical attempt to crush this development. The documents of the 1967 Renewal Chapter of the California IHMs are remarkable for their clear expression, at that very early date, of what in fact has been gradually implemented in most ministerial Congregations over the past forty years. The immediate object of the cardinal's ire was precisely the modification of the internal monastic life of the Congregation (habit, horarium, freedom of movement outside the convent, government structure), the control of which he saw as critical to his control of the Sisters and of their apostolate. The Sisters realized that what was really at stake was not the externals of monastic life but the profound reenvisioning of ministry which led them to "insist on the latitude to serve, to work, to decide according to their own lights."[16] Cardinal McIntyre attempted to reinstate the monastic dimension of their life by edict and to impose his will in regard to their ministry. Finally in 1970, with the backing of the Vatican, he forced them to choose between "obedience" to him in regard to these matters and Religious Life itself.[17] This episode helped raise to visibility for all Religious who were actively pursuing renewal the relationship between the self-understanding of ministerial Religious and the issue of obedience, even though the process of dealing with this issue would take another three decades to mature.

Vatican attempts to get Sisters in general back into the monastic mode peaked in 1983 with the publication by SCRSI of the document "Essential Elements in the Church's Teaching on Religious Life as Applied to Institutes Dedicated to Works of the Apostolate."[18] Fortunately, this regressive document was never officially promulgated since even the Vatican personnel responsible for its formulation could not muster the required number of signatories. The document caused much angst and stirred up considerable controversy among Religious but it finally withered away when, in fact, most Congregations neither promulgated it nor attempted to enforce it.[19]

An enormous amount of progress in renewal occurred between the 1960s and the 1980s. Despite the continued tension with the Vatican and many in the hierarchy, Religious were supported in their renewal process by courageous men like Archbishop John R. Quinn of San Francisco[20] and other bishops who deeply respected and appreciated women Religious and their ministry in the Church. The twenty-plus years since "Essential Elements" has seen steady progress in the development of ministerial Religious Life and a growing recognition by more forward-looking members of both laity and hierarchy of the validity and value of this form of Religious Life.[21]

Such appreciation, however, is far from universal and as the renewal has continued the retrenchment from Vatican II has deepened, and the suspicion of and resistance to renewal has intensified in some quarters. Many in renewed Congregations suspect that the favoritism shown in recent decades by the Vatican office for Religious, CICLSAL, toward the minority of communities (represented in the United States not by LCWR but by CMSWR) which have maintained the more traditional form of the life is a less overt attempt to establish the "apostolic Congregation form" as *de facto* normative for all non-enclosed Religious.[22]

The current terrain of Religious Life is, in short, very complex and contested and likely to remain so for some time. In relation to the mandated renewal of Religious Life, some Congregations, supported by some members of the hierarchy and laity, are in considerable tension with Vatican II (implicitly in practice though not usually explicitly in word) and are engaged in a clearly restorationist agenda.[23] These are not my concern here. Likewise, a plethora of new communities of consecrated life have been founded that are not Religious Congregations but have incorporated some features of Religious, often monastic, Life.[24] These communities are postconciliar developments that have the advantage of "starting from scratch" as opposed to renewing or developing a "new form" of something that has existed for centuries.[25] These new communities, also, are not my concern here.

On the spectrum of the renewal of canonical Religious Life mandated by the Council there are some Congregations which were guided primarily if not exclusively by *Perfectae Caritatis* ("Decree on the Up-to-Date Renewal of Religious Life")[26] and its implementing documents. They see their renewal primarily as an *aggiornamento* (or updating) based on *ressourcement*, that is, spiritual deepening through renewed recourse to Scripture and return to their founding charisms. They are firmly committed to maintaining intact the traditional form of apostolic Religious Life with both its monastic community character and its institutional ecclesiastical apostolates. Most have made those adjustments to modern life suggested by the Council such as eliminating anachronistic practices and customs that are unhealthy for members or make the life appear simply odd, and assuring appropriate professional formation of their members for their apostolates. Members of these Congregations usually wear modified habits, live together under local superiors in designated houses/convents which are now often less strictly cloistered and more homelike, follow a more flexible horarium, collaborate more closely with laity than previously, and so on. In short, they are quite recognizably the preconciliar form of Religious Life carefully updated in a number of ways.

At the other end of the renewal spectrum are Congregations which have been guided by *Perfectae Caritatis* read primarily through the lenses of *Gaudium et Spes* ("Pastoral Constitution on the Church in the Modern World") and *Lumen Gentium* ("Dogmatic Constitution on the Church").[27] They moved rather quickly through a brief period of updating but soon realized that they were being called into a much deeper transformation in response to their sense of participating through Profession in the Council's call for the Church to be in, with, and for the world. This response has involved dismantling the "total institution" of monasticism-at-home and the development of their ministries of world transformation in more individualized and de-institutionalized ways. Their commitment is much less to collective apostolic works that care for the members of the Church or draw non-Catholics into it and much more to the transformation of Church and society toward the Reign of God.

These Congregations are necessarily involved in more experimental projects since there is no model for this way of being Religious, especially for women. They are increasingly recognizable, not by special clothing, identifiable separate dwellings, or similarity of their lifestyle to preconciliar Religious Life, but by where they are found, the stances they take individually and corporately in relation to issues in Church and society, and the explicitly Gospel (rather than strictly ecclesiastical) character of their involvements.[28] These ministries are shaped less by institutions than by what I have called "the alternate world" which the Congregation constructs through the Profession and living of the vows and from which it ministers. Reciprocally, these new ministerial commitments have implications for the living of the vows, community, lifestyle choices, governance, relations with the hierarchy, and so on that are increasingly, though not yet entirely, clear.

Between these two ends of the spectrum is a wide swathe of overlap. Some traditional communities are much closer to the newer communities than to the most traditional and vice versa.

More importantly, few communities are "purely" one or the other and virtually all have some of their members who are in tension with the majority position. A more humane and simplified approach to transfer of Religious from one Congregation to another has allowed many Religious to migrate into communities that are healthier for them.

However, both some Religious communities themselves and some of the hierarchy are less than comfortable with this situation. Some traditional apostolic communities that feel threatened by what they regard as "radical" changes level charges of "worldliness" or "infidelity" at ministerial communities. And some ministerial communities regard more traditional apostolic communities as fearful, rigid, and unresponsive to the challenges of the Council and the signs of the times. Such mutual recrimination is unwarranted and counterproductive, to say nothing of unevangelical. No one should object to a Congregation continuing in the form of Religious Life it lived prior to the Council provided it has implemented the updating required by Vatican II[29] and has done so, as the Council required, by a sufficiently communitarian process. On the other hand, history testifies that Religious Life is a broad and deep movement in the Church within which new forms have emerged that both embody the basic constituents of the life and embody them in a very new way. Benedictine monasticism did not go out of existence when the mendicant form of the life emerged. Nor was the mendicant movement the final and definitive form of the life. Ministerial Religious Life is not a displacement or replacement of apostolic Religious Life, but it is a new and different form of the life.

The hierarchy in general, and the Vatican, are not watching this ferment in Religious Life from the sidelines and are not all of one mind about what is happening. There seems, however, to be a clear official preponderance since at least the beginning of the reign of John Paul II in favor of more conservative, even restorationist, approaches to everything in the Church: theology, liturgy, mission, clergy formation, and so on. Religious Life is no exception. However, one must question whether it is helpful to play the newer form of the life off against the older form with intimations that the latter is more faithful to the charism of Religious Life, or even the only form that is faithful. Besides inciting rivalry and lack of charity, this tactic runs the risk of quenching the Spirit in regard to a life-form that is, after all, not part of the hierarchical structure of the Church but is precisely a charismatic phenomenon which develops under the breath of the Spirit rather than according to prescriptions of law.[30] Newness, creativity, risk-taking, and courageous embrace of challenge are characteristic of the work of the Spirit. Nothing is born full-grown. Growth, however, is fostered more by acceptance and patience than by condemnation or suspicion. Gamaliel is still a voice of wisdom: "if this...undertaking is of [humans], it will fail; but if it is of God, you will not be able to overthrow [it]. You might even be found opposing God!" (Acts 5:38–39).

Even while this struggle over the monastic character of Religious Life *ad intra* has been underway, more far-reaching changes were occurring in ministerial Congregations concerning the "apostolate" *ad extra*. The theological reflection of renewal-minded Religious, even before the Council, was leading them toward the conviction that they were not simply monastics in Congregations "dedicated to the works of the apostolate" as the title of "Essential Elements," quoting the language used in approving such Institutes in 1900, defined them. Nor were their ministries a participation in the ministry of the ordained who delegated certain works to Religious Congregations as it did to groups within the "lay apostolate" movement. Rather, ministry was intrinsic to their vocation as Religious. It was definitive of their personal vocation and identity and integral to their spiritual lives.

Many, including probably many Religious themselves, at first saw the de-institutionalizing and individualizing of their ministries and the resulting diversification in lifestyle as due primarily to such external factors as the decline in personnel and economic resources that was the product of many factors in the late twentieth-century capitalist world, over which Religious had no control. However, they soon began to realize that they were coming to understand ministry itself in a new way. The surrounding situation may have been a precipitating factor in some developments—as is often the case in the work of the Spirit—but even if it were possible to return to an earlier form of collective institutionalized apostolate, it is doubtful that ministerial Religious would choose to do so. What has changed is, primarily, their theology of mission and ministry and their spirituality as ministerial Religious.

As lay people began to internalize Vatican II's teaching that they are integrated into the mission of the Church and called to ministry by Christ himself by virtue of their baptism and confirmation[31] (not integrated into the mission of the hierarchy by invitation, permission, or delegation of the latter), so Religious in ministerial Congregations were realizing that their call to ministry was rooted in these sacraments of initiation as radicalized and specified by Profession. Religious discern with and are assigned to their ministries by the leaders of their Religious Congregations, in virtue of their vow of obedience, according to their own Constitutions, inspired by the charism of their Congregations.

Discerning where and how Religious should minister, therefore, was increasingly seen to be the task of the Congregation and its members. In some cases, it soon became apparent that sustaining large institutions such as schools and hospitals, which the laity were increasingly able and eager to handle, actually was hampering the ability of Religious to respond creatively to the urgent needs they were beginning to discern in a rapidly changing Church and world. There was need for their presence to and advocacy for the poor, deprived children, the elderly, and abused women; participation in the struggle for social justice; peacemaking; direct spiritual ministry; prison, hospital, and hospice chaplaincy and social work; promotion of the arts; engagement in the religious and secular academies including teaching, research, and writing especially in theology; promotion of ecumenism and participation in interreligious dialogue; influence among business, professional, and political agents; supervisory and organizational work in relief efforts at home and abroad, and so on.

In short, Religious' vision of themselves as ministers, and of their ministry of preaching the Gospel in the Church and world as the expression of their identity as Religious, was diverging sharply from the earlier view of their Religious Congregations as an essentially cloistered work force available to staff ecclesiastical institutions caring for Catholic clientele, especially children and the ill and aged. The ever-stronger note in the choice of ministries has been transformation from within rather than replacement of religious or secular institutions that were already addressing such needs and the initiation of transformative projects where they are lacking. Increasingly, although not exclusively, priority is being given to the liminal or marginal spaces where the institutional Church has been unable or unwilling to go.

In summary, the salient characteristics of a new form of Religious Life are becoming clearer. First, *ad intra*, ministerial Religious Congregations have not merely updated their essentially monastic life. They have ceased to be a monastic/semi-cloistered lifeform. Their members remain committed, vowed Religious but they are not cloistered, totally or partially, at home or abroad, attitudinally or behaviorally. Canon Law simply has no explicit categories for this reality because it did not exist when the Code was promulgated. However, the Revised Code has broadened its terminology regarding almost all the constitutive features of Religious Life and remanded most of the specification of these constituents to the proper law of the Institute. This makes the recognition of these new understandings much easier today than was, for example, the acceptance of the abandonment of choral recitation of the office by the Jesuits in the sixteenth century or the emergence from papal cloister by sixteenth- and seventeenth-century apostolic women Religious.

Second, *ad extra*, these ministerial Religious Congregations are no longer "apostolic" in the sense of being extensions of the clergy or hierarchy whose diocesan concerns and sphere of operations once defined the meaning of mission for the Congregation. Rather the vocation of the Congregation and of its members is intrinsically ministerial, arising from the Congregation's founding charism as it has developed throughout its history. Their ministerial identity does not come from ordination, their own or that of clergy or hierarchy into whose apostolate they were once subsumed. They do not minister as agents of the ecclesiastical institution (much less as "mini" or "substitute" clergy) but in virtue of Profession by which they belong not to the hierarchical structure of the Church but to its life and holiness. In other words, they are ministerial Religious, public persons in the Church because of their vows, but not clerics or delegates of clerics. Canon Law has no categories for this reality either. But fortunately, the Law says little about the nature or operation of the ministries of Religious who are not clerics and this leaves considerable room for development.

The explicit description of and legislation for this form of mobile ministerial Religious Life, which is Religious but not monastic, and ministerial but not ordained nor dependent on the ordained, is primarily in Constitutions and other documents of Congregations (i.e., in "proper law) rather than explicitly in Canon Law. However, because those Constitutions, once approved, are implied in the Code which recognizes the proper law of Institutes, this proper legislation is canonical, thus launching this new form of Religious Life in the Church with at least minimal official acceptance and recognition. This fortunate legal situation does not mean, however, that all Church authorities really understand the life or like what is transpiring.

This lack of understanding alone would suffice to explain much of the tension between Religious on the one hand and some diocesan officials on the other. The latter are not only being challenged to relinquish much of their control of a corps of workers that they had more or less "owned" in the past, but they also have understandable and often legitimate concerns about the effect of this development on the availability and good order of ministry in their dioceses. The ability of some of the hierarchy to appreciate the important extension of the Church's mission through these Religious is sometimes obscured by their concern over the decline in their numbers and their relocation in noninstitutional ministries; that is, about the diminishment of the work force available for ecclesiastical projects.

Furthermore, some hierarchical authorities have been slow to recognize values women Religious have come to consider nonnegotiable, for example, the real equality of baptized persons regardless of office, the equality of women with men and their right to self-determination, dialogue rather than edict or coercion as the preferred way of dealing with differences. The joint document *Mutuae Relationes* ("Directives for Mutual Relations Between Bishops and Religious in the Church") published in 1978[32] was a tacit recognition that, like it or not, the unilateral dominative relationship of bishops to Religious is a thing of the past. Bishops can no longer simply command and expect Religious to submit. The "Conclusion" of the document begins: "Dialog and collaboration are already a reality on various levels. There is no doubt, however, that they have to be developed further...." That development continues to be a rocky road.

Given that, on the one hand, the bishop is the highest ecclesiastical authority in the local Church as institution and therefore ultimately responsible for orderly and effective exercise of ministry, and on the other hand, that Religious minister in virtue of their own charismatic identity but often in the same geographical areas and even to the same clientele as diocesan ministers, collaboration is both necessary and probably not attainable in a definitive fashion that would solve problems once and for all. Ongoing negotiation is unavoidable. Outmoded hierarchical habits are bound to reassert themselves at times. And Religious need to remember that while they do not minister *by* hierarchical permission but in virtue of baptism, confirmation, and Profession, they do, nevertheless, minister *with* the ordained and laity and *in* the local Church. Smooth collaboration calls for a sometimes-sacrificial cooperation from both sides. One would hope both hierarchy and Religious are learning.

Underneath much misunderstanding is a still-unresolved tension, if not disagreement, about the reality and extent of the right to self-determination on the part of Religious Congregations. There is tension in Canon Law itself between the affirmation of the right of Congregations to legitimate autonomy of life and governance (e.g., Canon 586) and the claim of hierarchical authority to the right to interpret the counsels and direct their practice (see Canon 576).[33] The hierarchy tends to argue from law to life whereas Religious, today, tend to argue from life to law.[34] Once a lifeform (or some new form of it) has been lived into existence and tested by its fruits it can be codified in law to help members test their ongoing experience against their originating charism and to provide a pattern for similar enterprises. But it seems premature to use the law to delegitimate, *a priori*, new developments, which by definition are not explicit in the law because they did not exist when the law was codified.

No one needs permission to do something good. The presumption ought to be the right to self-determination of a Congregation in regard to both its life and ministry unless there are clear, serious, public reasons for hierarchical intervention. There are major advantages to both the Religious Congregation and the institutional Church[35] in the latter's public recognition (approval) of such groups but recognition should not be used to intimidate, control, or deform the charism of a Congregation for the sake of legal clarity or institutional efficiency. As we will see in the next part of this chapter, there are understandable historical reasons for the tendency to subordinate Religious Congregations to hierarchical control, but those reasons belong to the past and it seems time to reenvision these relationships.

Meanwhile it is encouraging that development in this area is noticeable if not rapid or consistent. The current Code of Canon Law (1983), it should be gratefully acknowledged, is actually light years ahead of Cardinal McIntyre or "Essential Elements," to say nothing of the 1917 Code. And a few times in recent history when Congregational authorities have respectfully declined to carry out hierarchical directives that were contrary to the community's self-understanding, charism, tradition, or Constitutions, or in violation of the conscience of members, the Vatican has tacitly acknowledged their right to self-determination by not forcing the issue. This may be a long ways from the open respect and trusting acceptance Religious, especially women, so ardently desire. But Religious need to remember that it took 400 years laced with excommunications, interdictions, suppressions, and psychological or even physical coercion for apostolic Religious Life to attain full recognition in the Church. At least grudging recognition in practice of renewed ministerial Religious Life has been forthcoming in a little more than four decades.

As we try to articulate what the vow of prophetic obedience can and should mean in the life of Religious today we will have to take account of the still tension-ridden ecclesiastical context in which we find ourselves. The understanding of Religious obedience still held by some (but by no means all) ecclesiastical authorities is largely incompatible with that which has emerged among ministerial Religious. Although it is extremely painful and discouraging for Religious, who have given their lives to the Church and serve it on a full-time basis and who within living memory were its favorite daughters and sons, to face disapproval and even oppression from those who should be their confreres in mission, this cannot be allowed to retard the evolution of the lifeform itself, the emergence of new forms within it, and a vital theology of prophetic obedience that is coherent and motivating for Religious in a new millennium. Suffering is the seal of authenticity of what is born under the sign of the paschal mystery.

IV. Ambiguities in the Historical Legacy of Religious Life

Besides the contradictory sociocultural approach to authority in first world society and the tension-ridden ecclesiastical context in which ministerial Religious Life is emerging, contemporary Religious have to contend with the ambiguities of the historical legacy of their lifeform itself. Obedience is not a disembodied Platonic form. It is essentially a relational reality operative within an actual community. Therefore, the way community is imaged at any particular time and within any particular form of Religious Life shapes the understanding of obedience.

When new forms of Religious Life come into existence they do not simply "start from scratch." The predecessor forms continue to influence the new form which transforms and carries forward what is compatible with its emerging self-understanding, always including what is constitutive of Religious Life itself, but abandons, sometimes rapidly and sometimes gradually, what no longer fits.

Preconciliar apostolic Religious Life carried forward and incorporated models of community, ministry, and political organization from its own historical predecessors, especially the **familial model** that emerged in the fifth century in early monasticism, the **military model** born in the Middle Ages, and the **monarchical model**, of early modernity. Because apostolic Congregations were monastic at home, involved in institutionalized apostolic works outside the convent, and part of a highly clericalized, Rome-oriented premodern Catholicism, these different models of community and obedience, which were never totally compatible with each other, were able to function in different dimensions of the lives of the members without coming into serious conflict with each other most of the time. While each model contributed certain positive elements to the way apostolic Religious understood community and therefore obedience, each also had limitations. These limitations have become more apparent in ministerial Religious Life precisely because these models do not work as well in the new form as they did in the past.

In speaking of "models" of community and the theology of obedience, I am borrowing the hermeneutical technique proposed by the late ecclesiologist, Avery Dulles, in his *Models of the Church*.[36] Dulles showed that the Church could be "read" through a variety of hermeneutical, that is, interpretive, lenses or "models." Each model highlighted certain features, relationships, problems, and potentials of the Church even as it muted other features. By mapping such models as "institution" or "People of God" onto the immensely complex and dynamic whole that is the Church, Dulles helped people to see that the Church was not a collection of elements which could be assembled in only one way, such as, laity and clergy assembled hierarchically. Rather, the Church is a unified totality that could be variously conceived from different perspectives or for different purposes.

In using this interpretive technique it is crucial to remember that models are heuristic devices, that is, tools for interpretation and discovery. The heuristic model is not an ideal pattern, like a role model, to which the reality should or must conform. Therefore, models do not function as criteria of adequacy. A heuristic model also is not a scale model, like an architectural mock-up of a proposed building, which has a one-to-one correspondence to the reality. Therefore, there is not a structural and functional identity between reality and model. Rather, the hermeneutical model *in its wholeness* is somewhat like the reality being studied *in its wholeness* and, therefore, can help us see what tends to be invisible when we look at the reality through other models. For example, seeing the Church as God's "pilgrim people" can help us see the dynamic and "*in via*" character of the Church, which, when our model is "hierarchical institution," we tend to see as a "finished," stable, unchangeable organization. The longer a social reality has been in existence, the more "invisible" the dynamics operative within it tend to be. By using a variety of models we can bring these dynamics into view and be better equipped to analyze, criticize, and make enlightened choices about our present and future as communities.

Although extremely helpful, therefore, models must be handled with care. The reality being studied, in our case Religious community and the understanding of obedience within it, has priority. Models can instruct not only by likeness but also by contrast. There is always more to the reality than any one model can illuminate. By "reading" Religious Life through three social models —family, military, and monarchy—with their implied theories and practices of authority and obedience we can see both the potential and the limitations of these understandings and how they are operative today. This, in turn, can suggest what can and cannot be carried forward into contemporary ministerial Religious Life.

Each of the three models emerged in particular historical and ecclesiastical contexts and each has had a certain priority within a particular form of Religious Life. The familial model achieved ascendency in cenobitic monasticism (e.g., Benedictinism) which was the dominant form of Religious Life from the fifth century until the emergence of the mendicant form in the Middle Ages.[37] The military model was prominent from the turn of the millennium (c. 1000) when the military Orders (e.g., the Knights Templar) were founded to fight the Church's wars on various fronts. It was subsumed, with modifications, into the clerical apostolic Orders and Congregations (e.g., Jesuits and Redemptorists) in the modern period. This modified military model combined with the political model of the divine right monarchy that was the predominant form of secular political organization at the time. The universal Church, although theologically not a monarchy, had become politically such, thus lending a religious legitimation to monarchy and a monarchical character to ecclesiastical organization.[38]

Apostolic Congregations, especially of women, from their emergence in the late sixteenth century until Vatican II when some of them began the evolution into ministerial Congregations, were a complex amalgamation of earlier forms of Religious Life. Not surprisingly, several models of community and obedience were intermingled in this mixed form. At risk of oversimplification one could say that the relational dimension of the apostolic Congregation as **community** was governed primarily by a familial model; the apostolic dimension of the community as **Congregation** was much influenced by a quasi-military model; the juridical or ecclesiastical dimension of the Congregation as **Institute**[39] corresponded to a large extent to the operative political model of the hierarchical Church, namely, monarchy.[40] There was much blending of models and spiritualities during this long history, but we can get a helpful picture of apostolic (especially nonclerical) Religious communities on the eve of the Council by exploring them through the interpretive lenses of these three models. This background will highlight how the ministerial form that is emerging today differs from its predecessor form.

A. The Familial Model

Cenobitic or communitarian Religious Life emerged in the west from the desert hermit form under the spiritual and organizational genius of Benedict of Nursia (480–547) in the fifth and sixth centuries. He conceived of the monastic community as a spiritual family with the abbot as father and the monks as brothers.[41] The monastery was a socially self-contained, economically self-sufficient unit of feudal society. It was enclosed and stabile, that is, the monks remained (ideally, at least) in the monastery of Profession until death and their entire life of prayer and work unfolded within it. This stabile and enclosed context fostered the development of the face-to-face, long-standing relationships between the abbot and his sons and among the brother monks that sociologists call "primary group relations" and which are characteristic of healthy families. The affective ethos, exercise of discipline, methods of decision making, sharing of responsibilities, education and formation of newer members, and care of the elderly and infirm could all be understood as the functions of a large but close-knit family in which love had priority but order was maintained.

For many reasons, this form of Religious Life was eminently well suited to the feudal historical and ecclesiastical context of the Middle Ages, especially the early period from 500–1000. Although it has survived to our own day, and even flourished, monasticism was succeeded by other forms of Religious Life called forth by succeeding historical and social contexts and ecclesiastical needs. In later forms of Religious Life, particularly the military, mendicant, and clerical apostolic forms, the familial model of community was much less appropriate. In fact, in these more apostolically oriented communities the term "brother" became a status marker of inferiority rather than an expression of radical equality while "father" was primarily a title of clerical eminence. Paternal governance yielded to more hierarchical patterns better suited for the effective deployment of personnel and to the establishment and running of institutions. Abbots (the term means "father") were replaced by priors, superiors, or even generals, and brothers were seen less as confreres and more as subjects or even servants.

Women Religious, during this long development, remained cloistered (therefore, stabile and enclosed), and consequently were much more able to retain a familial understanding of their essentially domestic communities. Even as class distinctions characteristic of later medieval society (which were hardly compatible with the family ideal) infiltrated the cloister, the rhetoric and much of the ethos of the familial model continued to operate. Superiors were still called "mother" (unless all the choir Religious became "mothers" like clerical "fathers") and the Sisters were equal siblings (unless that term was reserved for "lay Sisters" who were inferior to choir Religious). One need only read Teresa of Avila, the sixteenth-century reformer of cloistered Carmelite life, on the subject of class distinctions in a community meant to be a sisterhood to realize the strains on the familial model by the time apostolic Religious Life was emerging.

As members of later apostolic Congregations were moved about, sometimes very often, in service of their apostolic works, the stability that was the foundation for the primary-type relationships in the cloistered monastery was attenuated. The filial understanding of obedience which could develop in the stabile monastery between the abbot/abbess (who remained in office for many years if not for life) and the monk/nun (who remained in the same monastery over a lifetime) was still the ideal espoused and inculcated in the members of mobile apostolic communities. But it was difficult to practice such an ideal when the superior or the subject was likely to be moved the next year, or their positions reversed. Furthermore, unequal status relations were introduced into the apostolic community by the fact that members who were "equal" as Religious—only the superior was "superior"—were in positions of superiority and inferiority in relation to each other in their work lives. And as many or most Religious, at least in developed countries, became educated professionals, the medieval deference to the superior as the only person in the community knowledgeable enough to command was undermined. In sociological reality, most twentieth-century Congregations and even local houses were bound together at least as much by the apostolate they exercised together as by familial relationships. This is not to say that sisterly or brotherly love did not exist, but the *esprit de corps* of Congregations was more the camaraderie of people engaged in a highly motivating common enterprise based in a common spiritual life.

If this historical picture is to help us in rethinking obedience in community for our own time, and especially as it is developing in ministerial Congregations today, we need to appreciate the potential and the problems of the familial model. The potential derives from Scripture's presentation of Jesus' initiation of a new type of family, the household or kinship of God, which supplanted the natural family for believers. The problems arise from a failure to realize just how different from the natural family this new spiritual kinship really is.

In the Old Testament, Yahweh called the Hebrews to be God's special people. Although this people shared much blood kinship, it was not blood but the covenantal bond of the people with God that made the Hebrews (later the Jews) God's family. In the New Testament, Jesus radically transformed this already religiously based relationship by founding a new "family" or kinship[42] which, unlike the patriarchal family of the Jewish community, is not rooted in blood relationship at all but only in shared faith.

This new family, Jesus says, is composed of those who "hear the word of God and keep it" (see Luke 8:21 and 11:28 and Mark 3:35). Furthermore, this family has no "fathers" or any other kind of patriarchal authority figures: "But you are not to be called rabbi, for you have one teacher, and you are all brothers and sisters.[43] And do not call anyone on earth your father, for you have one Father, who is in heaven. Neither be called leaders,[44] for you have one leader, the Christ" (Matt 23:8–10, my translation). God alone, the sole source of the divine life shared by the members of this family, is "parent." It is interesting that Benedict's Rule does not say that the Abbot takes the place of God, but of Christ who is actually not our father but our elder brother.[45] And it is not the Abbot alone in whom the monks are to recognize Christ. They are to see Christ in each other, in guests, in the sick. In other words, Benedict's familial model was fundamentally fraternal rather than patriarchal despite the important role assigned the Abbot.[46]

The paternal metaphor for God is derived from Jesus' patriarchy-subverting[47] use of the term "*abba*" in his own filial relation to God which he came into the world to share with us: "to all who received him, who believed in his name, he gave power to become children of God" (John 1:12). Birth into this new family or household of God is not by physical procreation as Nicodemus mistakenly assumed (see John 3:4) but by "water and the Holy Spirit." The children of God who are thus born "not of blood, nor of the will of the flesh, nor of the will of a male, but of God" (John 1:13, my translation of ἀνδρὸς) are not human infants but Christians who share in Jesus' relationship to God ("my Father [who is now] your Father;" John 20:17, my translation) and, because they are Jesus' brothers or sisters, they are spiritually siblings of all other believers.

This new sociospiritual reality which eventually came to be called "Church" was not, therefore, a sacralization of the natural biological family with its relational patterns of patriarchal dominance and subordination. On the contrary, Jesus definitively relativized natural kinship in favor of the much deeper spiritual bonds of shared divine life.[48] The fundamental spiritual relationship among Christians as Christians, regardless of age, blood relationship, or position, is fraternity/sorority, oriented toward friendship, which is essentially a relationship of equality.[49] Jesus further specified this relationship as being one of mutual service (see John 13:1–20) in imitation of himself, the greatest of all who is among his sisters and brothers as one who serves: "the greatest among you must become like the youngest, and the leader like one who serves" (Luke 22:26–27).

"Religious community is a family" is, therefore, a metaphor. This means that it is profoundly true but not literal. The power and truthfulness of metaphorical language depends on keeping the affirmation (the "is") and the implied negation (the "is not") in tension.[50] So it is equally important to realize that "Religious community is not a family." The obedience of members, no matter how we are to understand it and no what matter the age of the parties, is not the submission of children to parents.

Religious community is not the primary family (the family of origin) nor the secondary family (the family one founds). Unlike a natural family in which distinctions in authority and power are innate or ontological, the Christian community is fundamentally a discipleship of equals. Any distinctions in the Religious community, no matter how necessary and important, are and remain provisional and relative. As baptism unites the Christian community, Profession unites the members of the Religious community in a real though not biological family, a household of faith and love.

There are many illuminating positive analogies between the natural family (primary or secondary) and the Religious community, but each analogy comes with an "is not." First, in regard to the primary family, there is analogy but not identity. Whereas people do not get to select their primary family, their natural parents or siblings or ancestors, Religious do freely select their community. However, the community they freely enter already has a particular charismatic identity and a particular history and the one who enters has no control over who was, is now, or may become a member.

So, just as members of a natural family must learn to love the family into which they are born, Religious must learn to love the members of the community they have chosen. They cannot partner exclusively with one or several members and must not exclude anyone. Given that this spiritual family is more numerous and more diverse than a natural family and that the supernatural virtue of charity rather than the natural bond of blood is the foundation of unity, genuine love in a Religious community can be a striking witness to the Gospel's power to overcome all human divisions. In this transcendent community, without natural foundation in blood relationship, Jesus' disciples are recognized by the love they have for one another (see John 13:35).[51]

Second, there is an analogy but not identity between the freely founded secondary family and the Religious community one enters by Profession. In both cases, the secondary family becomes the person's primary affective horizon. Like people who commit themselves to each other for life by marriage and place themselves and all they have in common, Religious commit themselves and all their personal resources to the community and depend on the community for all they need. The primary personal responsibility of its members is to and for the community whose requirements have a prior claim on its members' time and energy, even in relation to family of origin and personal friends. The Religious for whom family of origin remains, or becomes as she ages, her primary affective context—that is, the Religious who really lives "at home" (meaning with her relatives) and visits the community when necessary or convenient—has not really "entered" or has, in effect, actually "left." As in marriage, the freely chosen adult relationship inaugurated by lifelong vows has affective priority.

But, unlike a marriage in which each partner commits irrevocably to the other and the marriage is constituted by that mutual commitment, no member of the Religious community entered, or would leave, because of any other member. Thus, consecrated celibacy by which Christ becomes the affective center of the life of the Religious to the exclusion of any other primary life commitment relativizes community in an important way. One is a member of the community because one is a Religious, not the other way around. This is a very important difference from marriage, which prospective members need to understand, particularly today and especially in mobile ministerial Congregations. If candidates come to Religious Life seeking affectively what they had (or missed) in the family of origin or could have had in a secondary family by marriage they are going to have unrealistic relational expectations of a community which does not and should not revolve around them. Religious community is a unique and very challenging kind of social entity.

Third, the Religious community, like (and unlike) a family, involves not only the relationships of the members to each other but, through each other's noncommunity relationships, establishes a wide range of connections outside the Congregation. Many people and groups (such as the blood relatives and friends of other members, employees, benefactors, co-ministers and those to whom members minister) become part of the metaphorical "extended family" of the Religious community. Other people are attracted by the Congregation's charism and want to formalize some kind of spiritual or ministerial relationship with the Congregation as associates, oblates, volunteers in mission, prayer partners, and so on. These and many other relationships extend the community the way nonmember relationships extend a natural family. Numbers, geographical mobility, diversity among the members themselves, and the absence of blood ties among members makes maintaining porous, but effective, boundaries more challenging for Religious communities than for the nuclear family. But the community is neither a natural family defined by blood, nor an amorphous collection of people without identity or boundaries.

Finally, because Profession engages Religious for life, they usually pass through some of their youth, all of their adulthood, and their old age as members. Generations in a natural family are constituted by different age-related and blood-based relationships. But in the Religious community there are no parents or grandparents, no children, no "retirees" from mission. There are stages of formation and initiation into membership which take place whether the candidate is young and inexperienced or not, and some members do become mentors and wisdom figures, but such figures may be much younger than those they mentor. Such roles do not "come with the territory" and are not necessarily permanent or definitive of one's position in the Religious family. All the Professed in the community are basically in the same "spiritual generation," with the same rights and responsibilities in community conditioned only by their own ability to participate. It is a challenge to act on this realization while taking appropriate account of differences in experience, the diminishments of age, the discrepancies of abilities, and so on. But again, the Religious community, unlike the natural family, is a community of equal disciples whose primary relationship is to the One to whom they each have given their lives. All other relationships of spiritual fraternity/sorority and friendship radiate out from that one.

The New Testament does not present the new family Jesus inaugurated as exhaustively familial. Although all believers are called to fraternity/sorority in relation to Jesus and to one another as children of the same divine parent, the sibling relationship is not the culmination of community relationships. The ultimate relational goal of Religious community life is friendship among these spiritual siblings, who are like the grown children in a natural family except that they have freely chosen each other in the act of choosing the celibate relationship to Jesus as the central affective reality of their lives. Jesus set the pattern for the sibling relationship's orientation toward friendship when he said to his own disciples, "I do not call you servants any longer... but I have called you friends, because I have made known to you everything that I have heard from my Father" (John 15:15). Friendship is the highest form of celibate community love and a powerful resource for ministry toward which Religious community life is oriented.[52]

In summary, it is profoundly true to say that the Religious community, as community, *is* a family. Permanent commitment to one another, shared identity, warm and loving relationships of sisterhood or brotherhood oriented ideally toward friendship, willing mutual forgiveness and encouragement, active care and shared responsibility especially in hard times, solidarity, and much else derives from the fact that these people have chosen to be together for life sharing a common history, charism, spirituality, ministry, and ultimate goal.

But, it is also true that the Religious community *is not* a family. The metaphor of family supplies a hermeneutical model that illuminates many of the relational dynamics of community life. The natural family, however, is not an ideal model which Religious community should mimic, much less a scale model to be replicated in magnified detail. When this reservation is not kept in mind newer members can be infantilized and older members can become entitled tyrants. Members can compete childishly for the attention and approval of superiors or indulge in adolescent acting out in rebellion against authority. Religious Life is not a substitute for the primary family we leave when we enter nor a consolation prize for the secondary family we sacrifice by deciding not to marry. Consecrated celibacy is the interior form of a new relational life rooted in the Gospel invitation to a kinship in faith and love, which should flower in friendship and bear fruit in ministry. Healthy community life is one of the fruits of living that commitment generously and without illusions.

Some of the developments within community life within ministerial Religious Life since the Council, and especially the practice of obedience, seem to be direct expressions of this deepened and more nuanced understanding of how members of the community are and are not related to each other. One of the earliest and most decisive moves in renewing communities after the Council was to dismantle the patriarchal authority structures which had developed during the period when the monastic model of Religious Life was giving way to other forms while the rhetoric of the familial model remained dominant. The move was away from dependency relationships and toward adult-to-adult relationships among all members.

The inflated social status markers of superiors were de-escalated. Many communities abandoned "superior-subject" terminology and titles such as "Mother Superior." And Sisters or Brothers began to use each other's baptismal names rather than titles in all but strictly formal situations. This was not reflective of a repudiation of Religious identity or a loss of mutual respect but simply a more natural and appropriate way for Christian siblings and friends who are essentially equals to relate to one another.

Secrecy, which always generates dominative power, gave way to transparency as leaders realized that members had a right to know what concerned them personally and what was happening in the Congregation for which all members are co-responsible. Team models of leadership emerged at the higher levels while local superiors tended to disappear as unnecessary in most small communities. Mutual discernment increasingly replaced unilateral assignments in ministry. Grievance and appeal processes were established to handle more difficult situations in which right was not immediately apparent and could no longer be established by *fiat*. In general, consultation among equals replaced the "mother/father knows best" approach. Ministerial Religious have been living into an understanding of relationships within their communities modeled on Jesus' discipleship of equals in a spiritual family of adults in which there is no parent except God and Jesus is brother, friend, and model of all.

B. The Military Model

From the eleventh to the fifteenth century, war and religion, closely intertwined, were the primary preoccupations of Europe, and of the Church which had replaced the Roman Empire as the primary locus of social, political, and military power. A number of military Orders (e.g., the Knights Templar) were founded to defend the Holy Land and its pilgrims, to fight in the Crusades, to suppress heretics, to defend the pope, and so on. Even in the period of the ascendency of the military Orders there was widespread ambivalence at all levels about people dedicating themselves to God through bloodshed, even when the blood in question was that of "infidels" and "heretics," enemies of God and the Church. But even the great Cistercian, St. Bernard of Clairvaux (1090–1153), widely regarded during his own lifetime as the holiest man in Europe, preached a Crusade and defended this military form of Religious Life.

While we might think that the very idea of pursuing holiness by violence is bizarre we are perhaps not so far removed from the medieval ideal of the dedicated Christian warrior as we think. Most Christians today, including most officials of the Church, are not pacifists, nor does the Church propose pacifism as the only acceptable Christian position.[53] In fact, until very recently, Catholics were urged to participate in their country's "just" warfare, especially against such evils as Nazism and Communism. Many Christians are far more addicted to war, more willing to declare it just because we think God is on our side and the enemy is evil, and more able to excuse massive unnecessary carnage as "collateral damage" in just wars than would be compatible with any serious reading of the Gospel. The military itself, from the highest ranks to the lowest, is filled with good Christians who carry their Bibles into battle.

My concern, however, is not with military Orders or the military commitments of Christians, but with the military mystique that is a powerful source of metaphors and images as well as of processes and behaviors in many Religious Congregations, especially since the emergence in the sixteenth century of clerical apostolic Orders (e.g., the Society of Jesus). Many of the apostolic Congregations of Sisters and Brothers which began to appear in the sixteenth century and became the dominant form of Religious Life from the nineteenth century until the present, were founded or influenced by members of the clerical Orders who passed on to them a *quasi-* or at least metaphorically military understanding of both the spiritual life and ministry. This ethos powerfully influenced the understanding of community life and the practice of obedience.

Like the family model, the military model has deep biblical roots. The Old Testament is filled with wars whose occurrences and outcomes are related directly to Israel's relationship with the God they often imaged as a divine warrior protecting them in battle against their earthly foes. Personal and social suffering, especially in the Psalms, is frequently interpreted through images and metaphors drawn from battle. The rhetoric of warfare supplies a vivid vocabulary for praying for salvation from spiritual or physical enemies and calling down divine destruction upon them. From Genesis to Revelation, the human enterprise is commonly presented as a great war, a struggle of good against evil, of God and God's friends against a powerful spiritual foe and his minions.[54]

Jesus inaugurated his public life in a programmatic confrontation with this evil force whom he vanquished, nonviolently but decisively, and expelled from his life "for a time" (Luke 4:13, NAB translation).[55] Jesus then went about announcing the Reign of God, the alternative to Satan's kingdom, and bringing that Reign into being through words and deeds of power. The struggle intensified until, in the Passion, Satan seemed to take final control and Jesus was struck down in death. But the Resurrection revealed that God, in Jesus, has definitively triumphed. Nevertheless, as Jesus told his disciples on the eve of his Passion (see John 15:18–21; 16:1–4), they must be prepared for this struggle to continue. Jesus has indeed "overcome the world" (John 16:33) but every generation of believers till the end of time will have to make that victory real in ever-new situations. Not only is the believer's participation in this project often presented as a battle to the death with the forces of Satan, but also the personal spiritual life of the believer unfolds on an interior battlefield.

As early as Easter night the community of Jesus' disciples was found huddling behind closed doors for fear that they would suffer Jesus' fate (see John 20:19). Persecution broke out against them almost immediately and leaders and followers were martyred (Acts 7–8, 12:2, and elsewhere). The devil was depicted as a "roaring lion" seeking to devour the early converts (1 Pet 5:8). And Paul warned the community at Ephesus to

> ...put on the whole armor of God, that you may be able to stand against the wiles of the devil. For we are not contending against flesh and blood, but against the principalities, against the powers, against the world rulers of this present darkness, against the spiritual hosts of wickedness in the heavenly places. (Eph 6:11–12)

In short, the history of the Church in the world and the spiritual life of the individual disciple striving for holiness have been experienced, described, and interpreted in terms drawn very often from the rhetorical reservoir of military images, symbolism, and metaphors. It should not surprise us, then, if Religious who choose to devote their whole lives to striving for personal union with God and fostering the Reign of God in this world should have recourse to the military model to imagine their lives and work. The validity of seeing themselves as soldiers in the army of Christ fighting the forces of evil on the battlefields of this world and in their own hearts would seem to be both biblically and experientially self-evident. This is so natural that the spiritual life as warfare can cease to function as a metaphor and be seen as, in fact, reality itself.

As he did with the biological family, however, Jesus radically transformed the military analogy for Christian life. Most Christians are as blind to this transformation as they are to Jesus' subversion of the patriarchal family in favor of a spiritual kinship of equal disciples in a community without fathers. Intrinsic to the notion of war is violence. One fights to win and one wins by destroying the enemy. So the first act of war is to construct the adversary as enemy and the enemy as evil. The evil of the enemy justifies, indeed necessitates, "good" violence, which is used to defeat bad violence. The "good violence" evokes retaliation and the endless cycle of ever more widespread violence is set in motion. Contemporary theologians, following the lead of the French scholar René Girard who has elaborated a brilliant theory on the cultural importance and destructiveness of sacred violence, are beginning to realize that the shackling of Christian soteriology (the theology of salvation) to the cycle of human violence has deeply distorted our God-image and our understanding of God's salvific work in Christ and actually made Christianity, in many ways, an accomplice in the very evil Jesus came to overcome.[56]

Jesus, as we will see in more detail below, infused into the toxic cycle of human violence, which the Bible traces back to the first murder, an entirely new antidote. He faced and subverted the endemic human conundrum of violence in a divinely original way and taught his followers to undertake the same project. The Magna Carta of the Jesus Movement, namely, the Sermon on the Mount and especially the Beatitudes (see Matt 6), proposes nonviolence rather than warfare as the way to deal with evil. Jesus does not tell his followers to take up arms against their adversaries, to exterminate their enemies, to abolish evil from the face of the earth by any means they can muster. Rather, he exhorts them to face suffering with meekness, to be willing to mourn themselves rather than make others mourn, to make peace rather than wage war, to remain single-hearted in their commitment to God rather than dissipate their forces in vengeance, and above all to expect and accept persecution for the sake of justice rather than returning evil for evil. They are to love, not kill, their enemies (see Matt 5:44; Luke 6:27, 35). Jesus repudiated violence and therefore war as a way to peace. The challenge for Christian spirituality is how to affirm this teaching in theory and in practice without exalting victimhood, empowering evil, or exhorting the oppressed to collude with their oppressors in their own victimization.

Jesus not only preached the renunciation of violence and war. He willingly accepted to bear virtually every type of outrage which would seem to justify vengeance while refusing to use violence to defend himself or allow his followers to take up arms in his defense (see, e.g., Matt 26:52; John 18:11, 36). Jesus definitively subverted the military solution to evil by effecting salvation as the innocent, free, self-giving, and forgiving victim.[57] He was indeed a king, but from another realm where there is no violence because it is the truth alone that sets one free (see John 18:36–38). He is a king crowned with thorns and reigning from a cross.

The first Christians, beginning with the protomartyr Stephen, realized that discipleship of this Savior implied the renunciation of violence, even to save one's own life. They refused to take up arms to defend themselves or the Empire. They were willing to die rather than kill. But the pacifism of the first Christian centuries was eroded, as the Church became, by the fourth century, more a privileged agent of, than a challenge to, the Roman Empire.

Christians became soldiers and, though the medieval Church tried to "civilize" war by codes of chivalry and the enactment of the "truce of God" (precursors of contemporary rules for *jus ad bellum* and *jus in bello*), the Church itself became increasingly militarized as it defended itself against Islam and the "barbarians" from without and heresies from within. It elaborated a theological theory of "just war," preached and supported Crusades, and established regional and universal Inquisitions which resorted to savage torture and gruesome executions of "heretics" with frightening frequency. Churchmen, starting with the pope, had troops at their command. Weapons and warriors were blessed. The life of the soldier became a noble Christian calling.

While some of the worst examples of ecclesiastical violence, at least of the physical kind, have been renounced by the Church in modern times, it has not returned to its pacifist roots, theoretically or in practice, and the mythology of war retains its powerful hold on the Christian imagination. Religious today, especially women, might be tempted to think that this mythology is not part of their personal or Congregational experience. However, when a sociologist in the 1980s pointed out that Religious Life shared with prisons and the military the sociological characteristics of the "total institution," that should have caused more self-reflection than it did.[58]

In fact, a number of major changes embraced by some Congregations and strenuously resisted by others in the wake of the Council were actually calculated, consciously or unconsciously, to undermine the effects of the military model on individual and community life. The diametrically opposite reaction by different Congregations to such things as choice of ordinary dress, abolition of titles, grades, and ranks, institution of collegial leadership, and de-institutionalization of ministries reflects the ambiguous character of such quasi-military elements of Religious Life as uniforms, hierarchy and role-definition, chains of command, and regimental organization. Depending on one's point of view such elements can be seen as highly effective tools in the "war against evil" or as a cooptation of Religious into a violent framework by the very forces one is opposing. What these elements really mean and effect, as well as their ambiguity, becomes clear when we examine them in the light of the military model.

The military uniform (which is not equivalent to the strictly utilitarian required dress of McDonald's cashiers or flight attendants) is essential to military identity, as the habit, a sacralized uniform, was once thought to be essential to Religious Life. The military or Religious uniform, including usually a distinctive hair-dressing ("buzz cut," tonsure, head shaving, etc.) that cannot be removed at will, and a complete, elaborate outfit specified in every detail, meticulously maintained according to strict regulations, and worn whenever one is in public, both marks the wearer off from the rest of society and reduces individual identity within the unit to a minimum. At the same time, the distinctive dress establishes a total, common identity that manifests the purpose and status, the required code of conduct, and the duties and responsibilities of the wearer.

The uniform also makes the wearer visible at all times to superiors, comrades, and the public. This visibility not only identifies the wearer to colleagues and strangers and even protects her/him from real or metaphorical "friendly fire," but is also a major control mechanism for superiors who can always know where the uniformed person is and what s/he is doing, which, in turn, discourages any delinquent or even independent activity on the part of the person in uniform. The uniform strictly limits the kinds of interactions or relationships that nonuniformed people can initiate with the one in uniform and vice versa. For some Religious this was a protection from situations they found difficult or burdensome; for others it was a major impediment to the kinds of personal and ministerial relationships to which they felt called. At the same time, the uniform permits and enables certain behaviors that the non-uniformed may be restricted from performing. The habited Religious, for example, may have access, denied to "seculars," to prisoners or patients, and the uniformed soldier can take charge in an emergency in which "civilians" must establish their competence or credentials.

Unlike prisoners or draftees, those who freely choose to enter the military or Religious Life often experience investiture in their distinctive dress as a mark of achievement, a sign of dedication, an assimilation to comrades who share their commitment, and a continual challenge to live up to their calling. They welcome the status the uniform confers on them, are proud to be distinguished from those who do not belong to the chosen band, and willingly exchange much of their personal liberty and identity for regulated participation in the identity of an elite group. Religious who entered before the Council certainly knew this experience from the day of their clothing through receiving whatever insignia (different colored veil, ring, cross, etc.) marked final incorporation into the Congregation. Not only did the habit mark them off from the laity but also from other Religious, just as the army uniform not only distinguishes the soldier from civilians but also from members of the other branches of the service. Interestingly, most Religious who ceased to wear the habit began to see themselves primarily as Religious sharing a commitment with all Religious rather than as rivals of members of other Congregations for status and reputation, geographical dominance, apostolic works, candidates, or episcopal preference.

In the heated discussions about the habit in the early years of renewal, all these positive and negative considerations were exhaustively discussed. Most Religious, on both sides of the habit issue, were probably unaware of the degree to which they were actually struggling over the validity of the "total institution," and specifically military, model of the Religious Congregation. For some Religious the habit signified publicly their commitment to Christ, their involvement in institutional ecclesiastical apostolates, and their privileged status in the Church. For others, removing it was a way of lowering barriers in non-institutional ministries, surrendering elite status and privilege within and outside the Church, dismantling control mechanisms among themselves and in relation to others, and risking commitment in situations in which only their person and competence, rather than their institutional identity, made them credible.

This ongoing discussion embodies changing understandings of ministry on the part of the majority of first world (and increasingly other) women Religious. From a preconciliar understanding of themselves as living their Religious Life "apart" in the convent and "going out" to bring salvation to those "in the world" they are beginning to understand themselves as being simply "among their sisters and brothers as one who serves." In other words, the "two ends" of Religious Life, namely, the fulfillment of the first great commandment of total love of God, which overflowed into the fulfillment of the second in apostolic service, were becoming "one end."

Renewing Congregations were reading *Perfectae Caritatis* through the lenses of *Gaudium et Spes* on the very new relation of the Church to the world and *Lumen Gentium* on the Church as the People of God, rather than reading *Perfectae Caritatis*, as it were, "on its own" as an exhortation to internal spiritual renewal with appropriate updating of lifestyle. Merely modifying the habit is the equivalent of the army replacing the "doughboy" uniform of World War I with the crisper uniform of today; the dynamics of relation to the nonuniformed and within the ranks of the uniformed do not really change. By contrast, laying aside the habit altogether expresses a profound change in worldview and the embrace of a new understanding of and dynamic in ministry. Even before many Religious were able to articulate this, everyone with any symbolic sensitivity knew that it was simply not true that "it really doesn't matter what you wear." As any soldier can testify, being in mufti is more a change of life than a change of clothes. If ministry is not a war and the Religious Congregation is not an army, does one need a uniform?

A second feature of the military model that throws considerable light on Religious community and the understanding of obedience that it implies is the structuring of the military as a rigid hierarchy by means of title, class, and rank. Position in the outfit, marked by honorary titles and distinctive insignia, is the reward for outstanding performance of duty in strict conformity to requirements. Yet, status markers tend to reduce the person to role or function and strictly limit creativity within it. One is not rewarded for performing "above one's rank" or taking initiative about how one's assigned duty is to be fulfilled. One is rewarded for doing perfectly exactly what one's rank and orders demand.

The abolition of distinctions between lay and choir Religious, the dropping of titles such as "Reverend Mother" and gestures of deference as she walked by or into the room, the waning importance of "rank" based on order of entrance into the novitiate, free mingling of people in formation with professed members and of ordinary members with those in office, represented a fairly wide-ranging dismantling of the hierarchical structure in Religious Congregations. They were the equivalent of the enlisted person freely entering the officers club, failure to spring to attention or snap a salute when a superior officer approached, or wearing more or fewer bars or stripes than one's rank prescribed or one's performance merited.

The army would be in chaos in short order if its strict hierarchical structure were threatened by a relational spontaneity expressed in the familiar use of first names and if a prompt "Yes, sir" gave way to a lively discussion of alternative ways to handle the situation. Chaos, of course, is exactly what many fear will happen (or think has already happened) in Religious Congregations in which the quasi-military system of rank and title has largely disappeared. But if the internal order in a Religious Congregation is not, and never should have been, that of a total institution or military hierarchy, then the disappearance of these dynamics may be no loss at all, but gain. This is the testimony of Religious who have lived in "demilitarized" communities for several decades and who assure Church authorities and the laity in general that good order still prevails.

Closely related to this de-hierarchizing have been changes in leadership models and therefore in the understanding of obedience. Few things were more unsettling for Vatican authorities than the rapid move in ministerial Congregations toward collegial leadership, that is, leadership by a team of equals operating through dialogue and consensus rather than by a single general superior in whom supreme authority was individually vested and who governed by command. Consultation, as long as it was initiated from above and not binding on the "supreme moderator" except in a few juridically specified cases, was fine, but not shared authority or leadership. Military effectiveness depends on a strict chain of command in which one person is supreme at each level, orders flow only downward, and accountability only upward. Each unit has only one top officer and privates do not give orders to sergeants or captains explain themselves to lieutenants.

Even more alarming to some institutional officials was the natural transition in many ministerial Congregations to local houses without superiors. If there is no single supreme authority there is no one to hold accountable if things are not functioning properly, no one to whom to report violations and culprits, no one with authority to impose sanctions as needed, no one to settle disputes, and no way for higher authorities to effectively relay orders to the rank and file and have them enforced at the local level. In other words, the kind of control that is vital to military order and effectiveness and which seemed self-evidently necessary in preconciliar Religious Life was seriously threatened when the chain of command gave way to a circular table around which people gathered to contribute according to their competence rather than their rank, and by right of belonging rather than by permission. Again, the testimony of Religious in Congregations which are governed collegially rather than militarily is that this is not only much closer to the Gospel's vision of government in Jesus' community but that, even humanly, shared wisdom is actually more effective than hierarchical command for both individual spiritual development and ministry.

Finally, the individualization and de-institutionalization of ministries that began to replace the assigning of large groups of Religious from the same Congregation to a delegated apostolate under the ultimate control of the hierarchy broke the "company"[59] or "battalion" pattern in which Religious as the "shock troops" in the ecclesiastical army were deployed more on the basis of what needed to be done than on the basis of their competence to do it or affinity for it.[60] This was not due merely to the fact that there were fewer Religious to assign and that the ones on the scene were necessarily working with more lay people than fellow Religious and were not always "in charge." Rather, leaders of Religious Congregations had begun to listen to their members in a process of mutual discernment to discover where a Religious felt called by God to be and what s/he felt called to do. Spiritual writer and novelist Frederick Buechner beautifully remarked, "The kind of work God usually calls you to is the kind of work (a) that you need most to do and (b) that the world most needs to have done…the place God calls you to is the place where your deep gladness and the world's deep hunger meet."[61] That implies almost by definition that, if Religious really attend to their true call within the framework of their Congregational membership, not all members of a Congregation or even large groups of them will be doing the same thing in the same place virtually all the time. Only when the group as group, like the army, has a single definable objective which takes absolute precedence over personal gifts or interests is it effective to send a squadron of appropriate size to get the job done and to expect every individual to submerge his or her personal gifts or limitations in the group effort. In preconciliar days Religious were often assigned to community works more on the basis of what needed to be done than on the basis of their competence to do it or affinity for it, much less their interest or desire. This was not necessarily callous disregard for the individual but an understanding of the quasi-military way individuals were related to the group and its projects.

As Religious began to discern those places, often on the margins of society or outside ecclesiastical institutions, where the Gospel urgently needed to be preached, they increasingly found themselves ministering with members of other Congregations, with laity or ordained, with Catholics or non-Catholics, or individually rather than with a houseful of members of their own Congregation. This, of course, led to diversity of living situations which some feared would destroy "community" defined as a Congregationally exclusive group life under a single roof. It was the equivalent of members of the regiment not living in the barracks and eating in the mess hall.

Those engaged in these new ministries and living situations, however, were beginning to understand that the corporateness of the Congregation's mission is realized in the incarnation of its charism in each of these diverse ministries rather than in the uniformity of works undertaken. And community life is realized in the quality of relationships, shared charism, mutual responsibility and support, accountability, new ways of being together and corporately creating their future, all firmly based in the "common life" which is not a matter of shared space but is achieved by the perpetual commitment to shared possession-lessness with all the risks that that involves. In other words, they were seeing themselves more like Jesus' disciples sent out two by two to announce the Good News (see Mark 6:7), or Paul setting sail alone for new missions and making connections where he could, than as an ecclesiastical army with a clearly defined project like the Crusaders of the Middle Ages dispatched to destroy the infidels and retake the Holy Land.

There is no doubt that the quasi-military structure and dynamics of preconciliar Religious Life generated clear corporate identity and secure role definition, high visibility, intense commitment and *esprit de corps*, remarkable efficiency in the deployment and use of personnel, smooth integration of the hierarchically organized Congregation into the hierarchical structure of the ecclesiastical institution. Some of the persecution of women Religious by non-Catholics in the early days of

American history, as well as recourse to women Religious by beleaguered Catholics, was due, without doubt, to the recognition by non-Catholics and Catholic laity alike that women Religious, even more than the clergy, were the public face of the Church militant.

But the military model which was the pattern of the preconciliar form of apostolic Religious Life was rooted in an understanding of the Church and of its relation to the world which was actually contrary to the ecclesiology and missiology which emerged from the Council.[62] The understanding of the world as the enemy of the Reign of God, the sphere of sin to be avoided, rejected, and eventually either converted or destroyed was actually abandoned by *Gaudium et Spes*. The Council declared the Church's solidarity with the world and its peoples, its respect for and eagerness to participate in the adventure of modernity, its compassionate embrace of all that was suffering and limited in human experience.[63] This radical shift in understanding left Religious, who had for centuries constructed their identity in opposition to a world that was the very incarnation of Satan's kingdom, with the huge challenge to reenvision themselves as in, with, and for (though not of) the world which God so loved. The military model of Religious Life was ill-suited to ministry in this world with which the Church was no longer at war.

Unlike the familial model which has shaped the affective dimension of Religious community and the exercise of obedience within it and which can be purified of the distortions of patriarchal family structure and functioning, the quasi-military or total institution model which has shaped the understanding and practice of the ministerial dimension of the life is difficult and perhaps impossible to reconcile with the kind of Religious Life that is emerging in ministerial Congregations. As we will see, Religious obedience, especially as expressed in ministry, is prophetic witness to the Reign of God, not the quasi-military basis of effectiveness in conquering the evil world. And the community life that nourishes the ministerial commitment is not that of a total institution, the "barracks" from which the troops emerge for spiritual battle and to which they return to recuperate for the next assault. It is a social and spiritual union of minds and hearts of adult believers corporately witnessing to the Gospel among themselves, in the Church, and to the world.

The very idea of "military" requires an imaginative construction of some "other" (e.g., the world) as an adversary or opponent: the "other" nation, gang, team, church, and so on. The "other" must be collective, different from the group constructing it, and viewed negatively in some way so that the objective of the "military" unit can be understood as some kind of "victory," such as domination, extermination, defeat, conversion, and so on. Although it is not strictly necessary that the opponent be constructed as "the enemy," military action is more focused and passionate if it is. An enemy is, by contrast to the "good" self, obviously evil and deserving of defeat. Defining the regimes of the countries we want to "liberate" (i.e., make useful for us) as the "Axes of Evil" legitimates virtually anything done in pursuit of that objective, including destroying the country itself.

The Church, and Religious Life in particular, for centuries has constructed "the world" as the enemy fighting under its commander in chief, Satan, against the Reign of God. Negatively, Religious avoided the world as much as possible. Even fellow Christians and their own families were held at arm's length. Not infrequently, Religious participated actively through their apostolates in the battles against the secular threat in the form of forbidden movies, indexed books, non-Catholic organizations, mixed marriages, public schools, or ecumenical dialogue. In this enterprise, the military model with its identifying uniform, hierarchy of title and rank, one-way chain of command, submersion of the individual in the collective, definition by role, deployment by units, and especially its high profile identity, *esprit de corps*, unquestioning commitment to a common ideal and goal and the group's methods of pursuing them, and shared conviction of rightness and nobility were all part of a coherent and effective self-understanding and battle plan. So far, the military model works well to illuminate the self-understanding, the structure and the function of apostolic Religious Life as part of the defense of the Church in its war against God's enemies.

But once we raise the question of whether the imaginative construction of the world as opponent, the *evil enemy* that is always at war against God and the Church, is valid or compatible with the Gospel, the military model is open to critique. As with the familial model, the Gospel is very provocative on this subject. As we noted above, at the very outset of his ministry Jesus confronted Satan as the personal opponent of his messianic work and that confrontation continued through his ministry of exorcisms, forgiving sins, and freeing people's consciences from religious and political oppression until the final confrontation in which he surrendered his life into the hands of those who hated him.

Jesus formed around himself a band of companions in his work of liberation but he did not raise an army. Indeed, he is explicit that he could have done so, either a heavenly legion from God (see Matt 26:53) or an earthly one of his followers (see John 18:36), but he freely chose not to. He forbade his followers to take up weapons in his defense (see Matt 26:51–52; Luke 22:49–51; John 18:10–11). Jesus refused to fight those who defined him as their enemy. He never defined them as his enemy but prayed for them even as he died at their hands (Luke 23:34). He commanded his followers to "love your enemies, do good to those who hate you, bless those who curse you, pray for those who abuse you" (Luke 6:27–28)—in other words to have no enemies because the enemy, by definition, is precisely the person you do not love.

In short, although Jesus and his ministry *constellated* enmity among those who viewed him as a threat, he himself regarded no one, even his opponents, as enemies. This is extremely important for those who will engage genuine evil massed against them and those they serve but who must not become violent themselves in the process.

The Gospels speak in many ways about this constellation of enmity among Jesus' opponents. Even the infancy narratives, through *midrash* and typology, predict that Jesus will be a cause of division and violence. In Luke 2:34, when Jesus' parents bring the infant to the temple, "Simeon blessed them and said to his mother Mary, 'This child is destined for the falling and the rising of many in Israel, and to be a sign that will be opposed.'" They had already experienced, in the coming to the

Child's manger of the shepherds who were among the lowest of social outcasts, the "rising" of the oppressed (see Luke 2:8–18). Later they would witness the "falling" of the law-abiding religionists of their town as their friends and neighbors rejected Jesus as a false prophet and tried to kill him (see Luke 4:28–29). In Matthew's infancy narrative as well (see 2:2–18), we read of the "rising" of Gentile scholars from the east to seek Jesus in response to a heavenly sign and the "falling" of Herod, the king of the Jews, who murdered all the male children under two in his effort to destroy Jesus. Before the Child can even speak people are taking sides for and against him.

The adult Jesus, in Luke 12:51–53 (par. Matt 10:34–37), proclaims:

> "Do you think that I have come to bring peace to the earth? No, I tell you, but rather division! From now on five in one household will be divided, three against two and two against three; they will be divided: father against son and son against father, mother against daughter and daughter against mother, mother-in-law against her daughter-in-law and daughter-in-law against mother-in-law."

In John, Jesus frequently says that he has come for judgment (κρίσις); that is, to precipitate a crisis or reveal a division among his hearers (e.g., John 3:9, 5:30, 8:16, 12:31). Jesus predicts that because of him the temple will be destroyed (see Luke 13:34–35). It is not that Jesus actively desires or creates division or murder among his contemporaries but that his very presence, his prophetic message and ministry, provokes a crisis situation which forces people to take sides. When he says that anyone who is not with him is against him (Matt 12:30; Luke 11:23) he is saying that neutrality in the face of God's plan for the salvation of the world is not an option. His message about God, especially God's universal salvific will, is not one possibility among many. It is not a choice between eating meat or eating vegetables, but between eating or not eating. His hearers understood that their choice was to open themselves to God's salvation or to die in their sins (see John 8:24). Thus, their desire to kill the one who announced this.

But Jesus himself never counsels nor practices violence. He banished Satan from his presence at the temptation in the desert (see Matt 4:10) but he did not annihilate him. He tells his disciples at the Last Supper, in John, that the "ruler of this world" will be cast out, has no power over him, and is judged (see John 12:31, 14:30, 16:11) and that they should be at peace because he, Jesus, has "overcome the world" (16:33). Jesus talks of struggle, of enmity directed at himself and his disciples, of a successful outcome of his work despite opposition. But nowhere, even when he used language we might consider "war-like" does Jesus actually talk of making war, leading his troops into battle, wreaking vengeance, or destroying his enemies.

The most dramatic and convincing evidence that Jesus does not understand himself as a warrior king or his followers as an army or his project as a war or this world as a battlefield is his willing acceptance of death at the hands of those who have made him their enemy rather than violently resisting them. The One who counsels meekness (see Matt 5:5) is meek and humble of heart (see Matt 11:29), and suffers violence because he will not inflict it. Although he has many who declare themselves his enemies, many who are indeed opponents or adversaries, and who are somehow under the sway of Satan, a personal agent who sees Jesus as mortal enemy, Jesus himself has no enemies. The follower of Calvary's victim can have no enemies either.

This brings us back to the military model's dependence on the construction of the opponent as enemy/evil. When John's Gospel says, "God so loved *the world* as to give the only Son" (see 3:16), "world" is singular and inclusive. It refers to God's good Creation and the whole human race. I think this is where the parable of the weeds and wheat comes back into play. It is that one world, that one field, which responds in various ways to the good seed (the Word of God) sown in it by Jesus or the evil seed sown by the devil. The reason we harvesters (read: ministers) cannot pull up the weeds is that doing so would also uproot the wheat, and the distinction among weeds and wheat will be made by themselves, not by God. God gave the only Son so that *all* who believe, that is, all who choose to accept God's offer of salva-

tion—and we do not know how that will take place in the case of
any person—may be saved. If there are branches at the end cast
into the fire it will be those that are already, by their own choice
(their alienation from the vine), dead (see John 15:5–6).

Contemporary ministerial Religious, as we discussed at some
length in part 1, have been feeling their way, under the influence of the Council leading them deeper into Scripture, into a
whole new understanding of "the world" and therefore of what
ministry in and to the world means and how being Religious
with, in, and for the world shapes that ministry. To begin with,
they are not constructing the world as evil/enemy in opposition to God, over against which they can construct a different,
separate, good, and enclosed world of Church or convent.
Rather, they are constructing world as a complex possibility of
becoming/being the Reign of God or choosing to be/become
the Kingdom of Satan.

The two possibilities are inherent in the single reality. Religious are part of that reality; they have bought (or bought
shares in) that field which is the only field there is. In the midst
of that field they are first of all creating and living in and ministering from an "alternate world" which is not a separate place
or a closed group of people. They are "being the change they
desire" as Gandhi advocated, right in the midst of the very
ambiguous reality that is certainly, in many respects, very much
under the sway of the Prince of This World. By being the Reign
of God, individually and corporately as a Congregation, in the
only world there is they are simultaneously fostering the
growth of the wheat and trying to cut off the evil resources
(greed, violence, injustice, etc.) that nourish the weeds.

This helps explain the increasing de-institutionalization of
the ministries of these Religious. Although carried out in and
from the Church they are often not institutionalized ecclesiastical "works" done by Catholics for Catholics. Ministries such as
nonviolent peacemaking, justice ministry in cities and prisons,
work against poverty and racism, fostering of personal spiritual
growth through chaplaincies, spiritual direction, or retreat
work, commitment to ecological sustainability that heals the
divisions over resources among humans and the conflict

between humans and the rest of Creation, empowerment of the oppressed, especially women and the poor, interreligious dialogue, research and writing, artistic creation and many other ministries are an explicit prophetic proclamation of the Gospel to the world, both in the visible institutional Church and outside of it, in the heart of society and at its margins.

This activity, however vigorous and assertive, is neither defensive nor aggressive. It is, like Jesus' ministry, prophetic. It is not warfare, spiritual or political. The military model is not very illuminating of this type of life and ministry, which nevertheless does involve exhausting struggle. There is no question that there are opponents committed to sabotaging this ministry and even destroying the ministers. Persecution, from society or even the institutional Church is never lacking. But ministerial Religious, increasingly, are renouncing violence in all its forms as a tactic because they do not construct their opponents as the enemy even when they must deal with them as adversaries. The preferred option is for dialogue, negotiation, persuasion, nonviolent resistance when necessary, but always in the service of promoting free inward conversion rather than coercive imposition. When all these fail the choice is to suffer violence rather than inflict it.

As ministerial Religious Congregations try to articulate and organize their new approach to world, ministry, and Religious Life, they are realizing that they are not simply a relational reality, that is, people bound together in a community of love and support. They are a Congregation, an identifiable sociological entity in the Church and the world. The Congregation is a corporate reality that has an inside and an outside, an identity as Catholic Christian, as Religious, as carrier of a particular tradition and charism, as a social body whose members are bound together for life not only affectively in community but effectively in ministry. Its members are in this together in a way that other participants in the extended community (e.g., volunteers or associates or co-ministers) are not.

The Congregation is distinct from but not a rival of any other group in the Church or society that is committed to (some of) the same ideals. Partnership whenever possible, not competition, is the preferred model. To some, who want Religious Life to be clearly marked off from other forms of life inside and outside the Church, this seems to be a compromise of status or identity. But the response to this elitism or monopolizing of good will must be, like Jesus' when his disciples wanted to prevent someone "not in our company" from casting out demons, "...whoever is not against you is for you" (Luke 9:50).

In summary, the military model, although long operative in the self-understanding of Religious, is not appropriate for the kind of ministry rooted in the Gospel and articulated by Vatican II. Enmity, violence, vengeance, all the structures and behaviors that turn disciples of the nonviolent Jesus into warriors, must be definitively laid aside. Religious obedience has nothing to do with obeying orders, especially blindly. It has to do, as in the life of Jesus, with "doing always the will of the One who sends us." A vital sense of corporateness, *esprit de corps*, commitment, especially in relation to the Congregation's ministry, which, in the past, was inculcated by means of this quasi-military self-understanding, is an important value, but there are ways to achieve it without recourse to a system that has an inbred bent toward violence.

C. The Monarchical Model

The familial model has illuminated, both by similarity and contrast, the relational aspect of Religious Life as community and the military model has, primarily by contrast, helped us understand the ministerial aspect of the community as Congregation. But a third important aspect of Religious Life is the canonical or juridical aspect of the Congregation as Institute.

The juridical aspect of Religious Life, especially in the modern period, has been understood primarily in light of the political model of **monarchy**. The monarchical model has long controlled the ecclesiastical imagination of most people in the Western Church because it has been, practically if not theologically,[64] the paradigmatic organizational model of the universal Church from the Middle Ages until Vatican II. For a number of reasons, biblical and theological, political and sociological, the monarchical model is losing its hold on the imagination of ministerial Religious as well as of an increasing proportion of lay people in the Church. Its decline is being vigorously resisted by the hierarchical institution, and by some laity whose faith is heavily invested in a monarchical papacy as virtually identical with "the Church." The point of entry of the hierarchy's challenge to Religious on this point is "obedience," specifically obedience in virtue of the vow to authority outside the Institute. Therefore, it is imperative for Religious to understand this model, where it comes from, how it developed, how it functions, why it is problematic, and what is emerging as an alternative.

We do not have the space, and I do not have the competence, to trace the gradual transformation of the small Jesus-community gathered in Jerusalem in the mid-first century to receive the Pentecostal gift of the Holy Spirit (see Acts 1–2) into a worldwide monarchy which is physically headquartered in the Vatican city-state.[65] But a brief summary overview can supply a sufficiently clear picture to ground reflection and choices in this matter.

For purposes of clarity it is important to distinguish among the Holy See, the Vatican City State, the papacy, and the Roman Curia. They are not the same thing and their running together in the minds of many Catholics can cause serious confusion. The *Holy See* is the episcopal jurisdiction of the Bishop of Rome who eventually became the sole patriarch in the Western Church or the pope. *Vatican City* is a sovereign state, which was founded by concordat in 1929 to assure the pope and the Church a geographical base after the annexation of the vast Papal States by the kingdom of Italy in 1870. The Vatican was not to be understood as the successor or remnant of the Papal States (which ceased to exist) but as a new political entity. It is a theocracy about 110 acres in size. Its nine hundred or so permanent residents are subjects of the pope who is the head of state and government. The *papacy* is the office of the pope whose jurisdiction as pope extends far beyond the Diocese of Rome to the whole Catholic world. The pope exercises this jurisdiction through the *Roman Curia,* which is a vast network of offices running various dimensions of the worldwide

Church. When people talk about "The Vatican" they are usually not talking about the city-state nor the pope as Bishop of Rome but about the ecclesiastical/political entity, operations, and delegated authority of the Roman Curia, that is, the administration through which the papacy is exercised.

The Curia, as the papacy's administration, has been repeatedly identified, by those inside and outside the Catholic community, as the primary obstacle to a genuine biblically and theologically grounded organizational renewal of the Roman Catholic Church which, many believe, is a *sine qua non* for the reunification of the Christian churches.[66] Because the Curia actually runs the institutional Church, no one, even well-intentioned popes, seems to have any idea how to reform it.[67] But in effect the Curia so controls the exercise of the episcopacy in every local church as to render the bishops in practice, despite the explicit teaching to the contrary of Vatican II, little more than vicars of the pope.[68]

The Christian community began as a Jewish sect and only gradually became distinct from its matrix.[69] Its members believed the Risen Jesus to be the only Lord and therefore refused to recognize the Roman Emperor as divine. As a result, they suffered a succession of persecutions, differing in length and severity, at the hands of the Roman Empire. However, within a couple centuries the Church had won more than a hearing in the imperial court. By edict of the Emperor Constantine in 313, Christianity became one of the Empire's tolerated religions. In 380 Theodosius I made Catholic Christianity the official religion of the Empire. As the Church passed from being the object of imperial persecution to being an agent of the Empire the process of assimilation of the spiritual and religious authority of Church leaders to the secular model of royalty was underway.

In the social and political chaos that followed the fall of the Roman Empire to the "barbarians" (traditionally dated to 476), the only political power widespread and strong enough to maintain some unity and stability in the west was the Church. It became increasingly powerful until, by the high Middle Ages, it was the preeminent political as well as religious power in

Europe. As the Church's political influence increased the assertion of papal authority and power, not only in relation to episcopal sees or individual Christians, but also in relation to the emerging political units and their rulers, increased apace. Divine right monarchy, in which one ruler holds full executive, legislative, and judicial power believed to be conferred by God and symbolized by religious anointing, became the paradigmatic form of government as the various political groupings in Europe and the British Isles struggled, along historical, ethnic, linguistic, and religious lines, toward what would become, in the nineteenth century, a continent of sovereign states.

But one monarch, the pope, claimed authority over all monarchs because his authority was spiritual as well as temporal and theirs, though divinely sanctioned, was only temporal. Boniface VIII (pope from 1294–1303) was the high point of the medieval escalation of papal power. He actually claimed absolute power over the whole world, not only religious but temporal. (Fortunately, he met considerable opposition in his attempts to exercise this overreach.) But this development of the papacy had been well under way since the East-West Schism (which originated long before the date 1054 usually given for the definitive break), after which there remained, in effect, only one patriarchate in the West, namely, that of Rome.[70] For all practical purposes the communion of churches in the West was taken over by the papacy and became "a universal Church under a universal primate." The pope, who had been regarded as the Vicar of Peter, now assumed exclusive right to the title Vicar of Christ, which had originally been the title of the individual bishops in relation to their own dioceses.[71]

The development of the papacy, then, ran from the pastoral service of unity in the New Testament with Peter as a first among equals in the apostolic college to a *de facto* divine right monarchy by 1870. Vatican I (1869–1870) reaffirmed the dogma of papal primacy including the pope's ordinary, immediate, and episcopal (i.e., sacramental) jurisdiction, not subject to any other power, over every church, bishop, and individual believer. If this trajectory toward absolute papal primacy culminated in 1870, it did not cease to be discussed, debated, reaffirmed, questioned, and challenged right through Vatican II. Furthermore, at different times in the long trajectory leading to this understanding of papal supremacy strong cases had been made for the recognition of councils as superior or at least equal in authority to the pope, for regular councils to help in the governance of the Church, and for the recognition of the ordinary (not delegated) authority of bishops in their own dioceses.[72] The last was strongly affirmed by Vatican II but has been very hard to implement, especially since the retrenchment toward papal supremacy that began shortly after the Council with the ascendency of John Paul II and is vigorously fostered by the Curia. Finally, although not identical with papal primacy, papal infallibility, which was defined (not without considerable contestation) in *Pastor Aeternus* at Vatican I, is tightly linked to the primacy of the pope, giving him, in principle, a control over minds and consciences that serves to make him, in the understanding of many, if not most, Catholics, the lone supreme personal regulator of faith and life of all Catholics.

Ecclesiologists such as Patrick Granfield and Richard McBrien[73] correctly point out that, strictly speaking, the pope is not a monarch in the usual political sense because his status, although it includes the fullness of executive, legislative, and judicial authority (the normal definition of a monarch) is not hereditary but elective. And he is not, strictly speaking, an absolute monarch because there are spiritual limits (from Scripture and tradition) to what he can lawfully do. The pope, for example, could not abolish the sacraments or remove books from the Bible. But in a sense, as far as ordinary believers are concerned, these are technicalities. In effect, once elected (and the electors could not be less representative of those the pope will rule), the pope is supreme in all matters affecting the religious life of the baptized, from the youngest child to the highest-ranking bishop. He is not answerable in any way to any power or authority on earth and all, including his fellow bishops, are answerable to him. And he claims this power as divinely instituted. In other words, he responds very well to the accepted definition of an absolute divine right monarch for life.

Our interest here, however, is not with the definition of the pope's status, the biblical or theological validity of the claims that are made for or by the pope, the way the papal office is actually exercised, or the adequacy of the understanding of these matters by ordinary Catholics. It is with the conviction, which has profoundly shaped the imagination of Catholics and in particular of Religious, that monarchy is the divinely established and therefore only possible legitimate form of government in the Church. From this conviction it follows naturally that all units of the Church (dioceses, parishes, Religious Congregations, etc.) are not only subject to the pope in every ecclesial or ecclesiastical matter, but should reflect this monarchical structure internally. The bishop is the sole ruler at the diocesan level, the pastor at the parish level, the general superior in the Religious Congregation. Consultation might have its purposes but finally there is one supreme decider at each level who has all authority and is accountable only upward but not laterally or downward.[74]

Historical and social developments in the Church and the secular arena, as well as biblical and theological studies over the past three centuries, have begun to undermine this monolithic imaginative paradigm. We cannot even begin to trace this history, but I will mention several illustrative developments that suggest that the monarchical model not only cannot be traced back to Scripture, but also is losing its hold on the Catholic imagination (although it is incessantly rearticulated by the hierarchy and remains deeply entrenched in the more fundamentalist elements in the Church).

Probably the most well-articulated contestation of papal supremacy was the conciliarist movement that was precipitated by the corruption of the Avignon Papacy (1305–1377) among other things. Many theologians at the time were convinced that the Church needed to be able to call a pope to account for flagrant abuse of his office, dereliction of duty, or false teaching. This position, with many nuances and variations as it was argued from the thirteenth through the fifteenth century, basically held that a council was superior to the pope and that infallibility was a characteristic of the whole Church, not a personal prerogative of the pope.

This position, called conciliarism,[75] was condemned at the Fifth Lateran Council (1512–1517) and the eruption of the Protestant Reformation (1515) focused attention elsewhere. But the basic concerns that the conciliarists articulated have surfaced again and again in ecclesiological reflection. Contemporary theology, both leading up to and since Vatican II, has continued to stress many conciliarist themes, such as the nature of the Church as a community of equal disciples in a communion of local churches, the necessity for the papacy and episcopacy to function within the Church rather than from above it, and the collegial nature of the episcopacy within which the pope is the "first among equals" rather than a monarch in relation to vassals. The basis for these concerns is the New Testament which provides very little, if any, support for a monarchical model of the Church or such an understanding of the Petrine ministry; theology which supplies excellent arguments for a Church whose leaders, like Jesus, renounce power in favor of service; and the political common sense that warns that "absolute power corrupts absolutely."[76]

By the mid 1500s it was beginning to be clear that, whatever the theoretical claims to universal temporal and spiritual authority of the pope might be, he was, *de facto*, no longer a universal sovereign. Both Orthodox and Protestants remained Christian but were no longer Roman Catholic, thus breaking the hegemonic equation of the two terms. And because of the wide-ranging voyages of exploration in the sixteenth and seventeenth centuries which had "discovered" the Americas, the so-called orient, and Africa below the Mediterranean coast, it was also clear that not only was there a monotheistic religion besides Judaism that was not Christian, namely, Islam, but also that there were many religions which had no links at all to the monotheism of the Abrahamic tradition. The pope might be the absolute monarch of Western Catholic Christians but any claims to universal jurisdiction, temporal or spiritual, were counterfactual.

At the same time, in the fifteenth to the eighteenth centuries, the Renaissance, the Scientific Revolution, and the Enlightenment challenged the authority of the Catholic Church to determine by fiat what was true and to be believed. There were other criteria of truth besides ecclesiastical authority, such as reason, scientific investigation, and experience, and despite the efforts of the Inquisition the Church's absolute authority in the realm of knowledge had been definitively undermined.

By the late nineteenth century the Catholic Church as Christendom was over. Europe had reorganized itself into a collection of nation-states in many of which some form of Protestantism was the established religion, and the Church, shorn of the Papal States, was not a major player in this new political game. Any claim by the Church to authority in temporal matters in the secular sphere was otiose and its spiritual authority was limited to Catholic countries in which, as the French Revolution made clear, it could not be enforced politically or militarily.

At the same time, an interesting experience was brewing in the new world where Catholics found themselves a minority in a Christian population that had established a form of government which forbid the establishment of any religion at all. The papal Church had no categories for such a situation and would not, until the Second Vatican Council, come to terms with the fact that people had a God-given right to follow their consciences in the matter of religion. American Catholics were launched on a journey to full participation in their society which would gradually bring to maturity in the Church a theology of religious tolerance.[77] Effectively, if not explicitly, the authority of the papacy was now defined as the influence of the Church in the spiritual and religious (not necessarily political) life of people who freely choose to be Catholics.[78] This was about as far away as the papacy could possibly get from an enforceable claim to absolute spiritual and temporal sovereignty enforceable by legal or religious sanctions over everyone in the world.

Finally, in the twentieth century a wide range of liberationist movements has emerged which are rooted in experiences of social and political oppression and are nourished by religious, philosophical, and psychological theories of personhood and the freedom intrinsic to it. These movements have all contributed to a critical analysis of authority and power that could not have been imagined in the Middle Ages or even in early modernity. Increasingly, no claim to divinely sanctioned authority is immune from criticism.

Vatican II left in place, side by side with a new (actually ancient) ecclesiology of the Church as the People of God and the episcopacy as the seat of a biblically based collegial government in the Church, the hierarchical theology of the ontological difference between clergy and laity[79] and the claims of supreme authority and power for the pope.[80] The convoluted bureaucracy that is the Curia, the medieval processes of appointing bishops and suppressing theological diversity, and papal pomp rivaled only by the British monarchy in the Western world are still in place, but the divine right monarchy is moribund. It is not, however, likely to "go gentle into that good night."[81]

Monarchy itself is constituted by the claim that there is an ontological difference between the monarch and his (or her) subjects. This difference can be "blue blood," that is, the royal status inherited by birth. But in the Church, status is thought to be constituted by ordination.[82] Vatican II reaffirmed the teaching which continues to resist any coherent theological explanation, that the common priesthood of the faithful and that of the ministerial priesthood, by virtue of ordination, "differ essentially and not only in degree."[83] The Council reaffirmed that the bishop is ordained, not merely appointed like a pastor or "created" like a cardinal, and that he is not simply a vicar or legate of the pope. Rather he has the fullness of the priesthood in relation to the lower clergy. And of course, the pope is supreme in relation to the bishops among whom he is supposed to be the first within a college of equals but is, in fact, a ruler over them.

Despite the profound shaping, especially in the modern period, of the self-understanding of Religious by the monarchical model, the attempt to "map" the monarchical model onto Religious Life reveals the radical divergence between the two. As the Council taught, Religious are not part of the hierarchical structure of the Church where the monarchical paradigm is lodged. Canon Law picked up the teaching of *Lumen Gentium* 43, and the commentary on Canon 574 states that Religious Life "neither belongs to the hierarchical ordering of the

Church, nor is it an intermediate level between the clerical and lay state. Rather, consecrated life reflects the prophetic nature of the Church and enjoys a certain freedom and autonomy."

The monarchical appearance of the pre-renewal Religious Institute was, in a number of ways, very deceptive. First, the superior was not ordained (i.e., divinely and irreversibly altered) but simply elected by her/his peers, not for life but for a (usually short) limited term after which s/he returned to the "ranks" as one "subject" among the rest with no residual authority, rank, or power.[84] Furthermore, even the highest superior could be deposed and replaced by ecclesiastical authority.[85] In other words, s/he possessed no inalienable power or authority, no ontological distinction from her or his fellow Religious, nor was the authority conferred by election in any sense absolute or inviolable.

Second, when the general Chapter was in session the Chapter, not the superior, was the highest authority in the Institute. In other words, the highest executive power and the highest legislative power were separate, with the former subject to the latter. Even the judicial power of the general superior was limited by the requirement that there be witnesses when s/he commanded in virtue of the vow or put the dismissal process in operation. Monarchy is defined by the concentration of all three powers in the hands of a single individual and absolute monarchy by the ability to exercise these powers without accountability to outside agencies. Neither criterion is verified in the Religious Institute.

Third, although the general superior had "ordinary" authority (authority in virtue of office rather than by delegation) s/he actually had to have the deliberative vote of her council for major internal matters such as the admission of novices to vows, and had to refer all major external decisions, for example, alienation of the Institute's property beyond a certain amount or the dismissal of a member, to higher ecclesiastical authority (the bishop or the Vatican).

In short, the highest superior in a Religious Institute was not only elected by her/his peers but was limited by length of term, by constitutional parameters, by separation of powers, and by subjection to higher authority. Nothing characteristic of monarchy, much less absolute monarchy was verified even for the highest officeholder in the Institute, let alone for her or his appointees or delegates at the lower levels of government. Some Religious superiors may have operated autocratically or even dictatorially and the average Religious probably knew little about forms of government or limitations on authority or power, but in fact the government of the Religious Institute as such, unless it had ordained members, did not reflect in any significant way the monarchical model operative in the institutional Church.

Patriarchy (rule by powerful males) and ordination (the so-called "ontological difference" between ordained and non-ordained) are the basis of ecclesiastical monarchy. Women's and Brothers' Institutes had neither of these bases interior to the order. Brothers' Orders were somewhat more autonomous than those of women because they were, at least, male, but they were also subordinate to ordained authority and power. The lack of monarchical power in the nonclerical Institute is clearly highlighted by comparison with Institutes that have both lay and clerical members. Brothers in such Institutes are always in a subordinate position, often deprived of active and virtually always of passive voice, and often not participants in deliberative bodies. Clerical Orders with nonclerical members are rigidly class societies in which mobility between classes is ordinarily impossible and never in a downward direction (ordained to Brother). By contrast, in women's and Brothers' Institutes class structure is always provisional, more a practical fiction than reality. At the end of Vatican II there was little problem abolishing the distinction between lay and choir Sisters because, in fact, there was no basis except custom for the distinction in the first place (although there were reasons).[86]

This basically non-monarchical character of Religious Institutes in the absence of gender (patriarchal) and ontological (clerical) distinctions among members makes the Institute intrinsically egalitarian. The Constitutions and Canon Law may establish certain offices but these are legal provisions for good government rather than intrinsic inequalities among members. This provides a natural and organizational foundation for a discipleship of equals, a familial kinship of those united only by faith and love who have come together freely to love God and serve the world God so loved.

It is not surprising that as Religious, especially women, internalized the theology and especially the ethos of Vatican II the external trappings of monarchy in their communities, which had no basis in Scripture, no theological justification, and only juridical rather than ontological basis in Congregational organization, swiftly gave way to more egalitarian relationships and collegial government structures. Lay Sisters became full and equal members. "Superiors" became Congregational Leaders or Presidents or Prioresses.[87] Team leadership replaced one-person rule. Elected representative bodies, senates, or councils which had actual policy-making authority rather than purely advisory functions became part of Congregational government. Grievance procedures were put in place to facilitate nonhierarchical rather than judicial or authoritarian conflict resolution. The Religious elected to leadership began to operate as co-discerners with the Sisters/Brothers who were accountable to them. Leadership personnel abandoned the trappings and social distance of royalty and moved much more easily among their Sisters or Brothers as one who serves. It was much easier to reintegrate them into the community at the end of their terms.

For decades the Vatican has been uncomfortable with many of these developments and regularly warned that chaos was imminent but, in fact, a new order was emerging which was fairly smoothly integrated into Canon Law under the rubric of "particular or proper law." However, the therapy of the imagination, learning to function non-monarchically, has involved much trial and error. No one in the Church was used to this type of government and traditionalists feared the specter of "democracy" which, in their minds, could only mean the end of all authority.

Although deeply influenced by democratic sensibilities and making wise use of some democratic mechanisms, the form of government that has emerged in ministerial Religious Institutes is actually collegial rather than democratic. Consensus is much preferred to voting and is often achieved before even necessary votes are taken.[88] Majorities do not "take over" and silence the opposition or reverse the achievements of preceding administrations; rather, continual efforts are made to incorporate the best of all positions. Representation is not about establishing controlling influence over processes or policies but about making sure that all voices are heard. Total participation assemblies are structured not to determine which group gets its way for the next term but to participate in ongoing common education and formation toward a shared preferred future. Most Congregations probably still have quite a way to go to work out how to implement these ideals. But the point is that the ideal is not a better monarchy but a more evangelical form of government.

Collegial government is fairly well established in most ministerial Congregations at this point and the approved proper law of Institutes reflects this development. What had been a condition of disempowerment and domination when Congregations imagined themselves as mini-monarchies reflecting the monarchical structure of the universal Church, diocese, and parish, but without any real power in that system, was actually the condition of possibility for establishing in the Church a prophetic form of community life that incarnates the discipleship of equals that the Gospel proposes and the collegial form of government that the early Church developed and that Vatican II reaffirmed. This is the proximate context for the concept and practice of obedience that we will explore in the following chapter.

V. The Challenge: Remodeling Religious Obedience

The purpose of this chapter has been to describe and analyze, not exhaustively but I hope adequately, the very complex and challenging context within which contemporary first world Religious have been re-imagining the obedience they profess and live. This re-imagining must become clear and articulate if it is to be life-giving for themselves and prophetically effective in Church and world.

This chapter began with a selective look at the first world sociocultural context in which authority is widely dismissed as irrelevant by an excessively individualistic liberalism and blind obedience is fiercely clung to by a terrified fundamentalism prepared to kill or die, metaphorically if not literally, to avoid personal responsibility. I also tried to look unflinchingly at the tense ecclesial-ecclesiastical context in which a renewed theology of authority and obedience which is founded in the conciliar ethos, contemporary understandings of the human person, and ministerial responsibility is in frequent and often traumatic conflict with a restorationist, patriarchal understanding of authority in certain segments of the institutional Church. Finally, by means of various models, I tried to explore the imagination shaping the personal and communal experience of authority and obedience of Religious themselves. Each of these models, the familial, the military, and the monarchical, offers resources, both by contrast and by conformity, for the development of a theology and spirituality of prophetic obedience for our times.

There is no doubt that what Religious today mean by obedience is quite different from what most who entered in the preconciliar era were taught about this vow. In that era obedience was understood as unquestioning submission of mind, will, and execution to a religiously sanctioned and virtually absolute authority exercised by "superiors" of various kinds: Rule, horarium, superiors at various levels, the clergy, bishops, pope, or more vaguely "Rome" or the "Vatican." Such submission was understood as a response to God's will which these superiors expressed with near infallibility. Religious, of course, were not mindless robots. Most could recognize that some rules were at least pointless if not counterproductive and some superiors were unintelligent, self-serving, or even tyrannical. But these blemishes were aberrations in a system that was thought to be essentially sound, divinely sanctioned and therefore conducive—even when it demanded profound self-abnegation—to a life of obedience to God's will which was a sure path to salvation and holiness.

When in the process of renewal Religious ceased to live (or believe in) this automatic, if not mechanical, "theology" of blind obedience, it seemed to many people that obedience had become a moribund concept. The less said about it the better. But many Religious concerned about the integrity of their life and commitment, as well as some hierarchs trying to protect their power and stem the loss of their compliant work force, were uneasy with the theological vacuum created by the demise of the traditional notion of obedience. Actually, that vacuum was gradually filling with the resources for a rethinking of this dimension of Religious Life but living into its articulation has taken decades. Our task in the next two chapters will be to reconsider the notion of obedience "from the ground up" but with the intention of showing not only the newness of the contemporary understanding but also the continuity between what Religious in renewed Congregations have come to understand about authority and obedience and what Religious traditionally intended by their vow of obedience.

A vibrant theology of prophetic obedience might be the most urgent contribution Religious Life has to offer in our seriously dysfunctional Church and society, which swing between the anarchy of unrestrained individualism and the repression of totalitarian power structures. Obedience, well understood and generously practiced, spans the social gap between individual and community, between personal initiative and cooperation, between childish dependence and solipsistic independence. Prophetic obedience is another form of the responsibility we discussed in relation to economic possessionlessness (evangelical poverty) and the single-minded quest for God (consecrated celibacy). It is the third constitutive dimension of the lifeform, "the alternate world," within which Religious live and from which they commit themselves totally to the mission of world-transformation.

Chapter Eight
Prophetic Obedience

An Alternate Approach to
Freedom and Power

I. Introduction

A. The Prophetic Importance of Religious Obedience Today

Against the background of the preceding chapter the importance and urgency of a biblical, theological, and historical reexamination of obedience is clear to anyone involved with Religious Life, from within or without. The practice and understanding of obedience in Religious Life has changed so dramatically in the past forty years that some people think the vow itself is either in desperate peril or simply no longer relevant. For these people, the practice of obedience in Religious Life seems to have "withered away" as Religious community life has become increasingly collegial and the ministries of Religious increasingly individualized, determined by mutual discernment.

And yet, as the last chapter suggested, whether in secular society or in the Church, few features of contemporary experience are in more need of rethinking and reform—and thus of the prophetic witness that genuine obedience in Religious Life can offer on this subject—than the political issues of power, freedom, and authority with which this vow is concerned. Abuse of power, misuse of authority, coercion and intimidation in restraint of freedom—all of these buttressed with theologically faulty and psychologically unhealthy concepts of "obedience"—are rampant, in the Church as well as in societies both democratic and totalitarian. At the same time, socially dysfunctional and politically dangerous individualism, which rejects all organization of society for the common good, has become a threat to the very foundations of Western civilization.

In the last chapter we examined in some detail three very ambiguous aspects of the current context in which Religious are attempting to re-imagine, rearticulate, and reappropriate the reality of prophetic obedience and develop a more adequate understanding of the theory and practice of their vow: the excessively individualistic **culture of the first world** which paradoxically dismisses claims of authority in one's personal life while submitting mindlessly to fads, "expert" opinion, and manipulation; **ecclesiastical tension** between the preconciliar model of obedience as total submission within a Church understood as a divine right monarchy and the conciliar model of Religious Life as a prophetic vocation within the Church as People of God; and **ambiguous imaginative models**—familial, military, and monarchical—that have long controlled its self-understanding and its theology and practice and continue to be interactively operative. In addition, I want to mention three important historical factors that have fundamentally and—one can hope—irreversibly changed the moral, political, and religious landscape within which postmodern people (including Religious) think about obedience today.

B. Historical Factors Influencing the Renewal of the Theology of Obedience

All three factors signal, whether one likes it or not, that "blind obedience" is not one (perhaps outmoded) way of understanding the virtue of obedience but is a theological and moral contradiction in terms which must be definitively and finally rejected. Blind obedience, no matter how carefully qualified, cannot be salvaged. These factors are the moral obscenity of the Nazi Holocaust, the political evolution which came to expression in the democratic revolutions of the eighteenth and nineteenth centuries, and the transformation of consciousness in and through the liberation movements in the twentieth century.

As pointed out in the last chapter, the theological notion of "blind obedience" as a, if not *the*, Christian virtue has been definitively subverted by the horror of the **Nazi Holocaust** in which millions of people were exterminated by subordinates who denied responsibility for the mass murders they perpetrated on the grounds that they were "just following orders" of higher authority. Whatever the term "blind obedience" denoted prior to World War II, the claim that total abdication of one's freedom and responsibility to the commands of another human being can or does constitute the fulfilling of the will of God is morally repulsive no matter what office the one commanding holds or how the command is qualified.

Post–World War II political theologians such as Protestant Dorothee Soëlle and Catholic Johann Baptist Metz, in their personal and professional struggles to understand and repudiate the dynamics which engulfed their nation in cooperation with Hitler's genocidal "final solution," located much of the blame for this unspeakable evil in the theology of blind obedience as a Christian virtue. Soëlle goes so far as to say that, over the course of history, absolute obedience to authority had effectively replaced charity as the pinnacle and glory of Christian moral and spiritual life.[1] As philosopher Hannah Arendt chillingly proposed, the architects of the Third Reich's atrocities were not madmen whom we can consign to oblivion as terrible aberrations of nature, but "good Christians" whose moral compass had become so stuck on blind obedience that they marched confidently and resolutely into the wasteland of inhumanity convinced that they were doing God's will.[2]

But even prior to the horrors of the Nazi regime, historico-political forces were already at work in the world that would sooner or later have called the classical notion of blind obedience into question. The French and American revolutions in the eighteenth century undermined the foundation of absolute obedience by delegitimizing the notion of absolute authority. They replaced the understanding of a divinely instituted ontological superiority of some people to others (e.g., parent to child, king to subject, cleric to lay, and master to servant) with an affirmation of the God-given, ontological, and inalienable equality and dignity of every "man." Of course, it took a couple of centuries for the citizens of these new democracies to realize, even in word (and it is still not incorporated into practice in many spheres), that "man" means "human being," which includes people of color, women, children, the elderly and sick, handicapped, homosexually oriented people, and so on. But the basic affirmation of God-given human equality has undermined the ontological foundations and political legitimation of absolute authority and therefore of absolute obedience just as the Holocaust had destroyed the moral claim to blind obedience.

In our own time, **liberation movements** in general and feminism in particular have provided a social and theological analysis of patriarchy that has subverted the religious foundations of the classical understanding of authority and obedience. Liberation theologies in Latin America and Asia and more recently anticolonialism in Africa have been particularly concerned with the structures of class oppression based on wealth and caste. In the United States, South Africa, and other countries civil rights movements have targeted racial and ethnic oppression. Although developments in Muslim cultures are distinctive, the cry for personal liberty and respect for human rights is gathering momentum in the Middle East.

The most universal liberationist movement, operative now in virtually every corner of the world, is feminism, which has identified and analyzed patriarchy as intrinsically oppressive. Patriarchy refers to the ideology (theoretical and practical) of "natural" superiority and hence self-evidently justified rule of powerful men over women (and "feminized others" of both genders). Feminism claims that patriarchy is the archetypal, root, and quintessential paradigm of unjust oppressive power structures (or "domination systems") no matter who constructs them or on what basis.[3]

Secular feminism, while recognizing the negative contribution of religion to patriarchy, has been primarily concerned with striking the shackles of women in family and society in quest of economic and political equality. However, religious feminism has gone beyond these intrahistorical issues. The religious analysis of patriarchy by biblical scholars, theologians, and Church historians has challenged the patriarchal theology, structures, and practice of the institutional Church as contrary to divine revelation in general and to the will of Christ specifically. Hierarchy understood as sacralized patriarchy (and there are other non-patriarchal ways of understanding hierarchy) is not just socially and ecclesially dysfunctional. It is sinful.[4]

This increasingly strong and widespread position has provoked repeated attempts by the ecclesiastical hierarchy to protect and reinforce its power over women by appeals to the "divine will" revealed in the "natural order" and in the "tradition" of Church teaching.[5] The claim to absolute and blind obedience based on the ontological superiority of the ordained to the nonordained, coupled with the affirmation of divinely sanctioned total exclusion of women from ordination, is a transparent attempt to subjugate women absolutely and in perpetuity to male "authority," that is, male-dominant power. The Vatican understanding of Religious obedience, especially that of female Religious to male clerics, based on patriarchal theology that women Religious (with the majority of the Church at least in the first world, both male and female) repudiate as anti biblical and theologically baseless, is in serious tension with the understanding of the vow developing among Religious themselves. This tension can only deepen as the theoretical foundations of patriarchy continue to erode under the scrutiny of the secular and sacred sciences, the experience of believers, and the practice of modern society while women increasingly claim their God-given status as adult children of God.

In short, and by way of conclusion, from even this very brief survey of recent historical, cultural, theological, and ecclesial developments undermining classical understandings of obedience in general and Religious obedience in particular, if the obedience vowed by Religious is to have a genuinely unitive function in their spiritual lives, foster Gospel living in the "alternate world" of Religious Life, and offer a prophetic witness to the Reign of God in the world through their ministry, it must be radically rethought. The idea that obedience means that one person commands, thereby expressing the will of God, and everyone else in the community does as she or he is commanded, thereby fulfilling the will of God, has been revealed as antihuman, antimodern, antifeminist, and especially anti-Gospel. Despite its history, "blind obedience," no matter how it is understood or explained, is no longer a viable category.

C. In Search of an Alternative

In this chapter and the next I want to reexamine Religious obedience within the mystical-prophetic understanding of Religious Life I have been developing in this volume. Religious Life, I have suggested, is a concrete, sociohistorical lifeform that intends not just to promote, but also to realize the Reign of God in this world in a particular way. It is, in other words, an "alternate world" that Religious construct, live in, and minister from, and it is in ongoing opposition to the Kingdom of Satan. In the three chapters that compose part 2, we saw what this means in relation to the economic dimension of human life, how Religious by their vow of evangelical poverty construct and live the "economy of the Reign of God" right in the midst of the world in which Satan's Kingdom is also active. In this part we are concerned with the political dimension of human life and how Religious, by their vow of prophetic obedience, construct and live the "politics of the Reign of God" in this same context of struggle between the Reign of God and the Kingdom of Satan.

Throughout this volume and its two predecessors, I have spoken of each of the vows as having mystical (or unitive), relational (or communitarian), and prophetic (or ministerial) dimensions. In this chapter we will look at the role of obedience in community and ministry and in the next chapter at its role in the spirituality or mystical life of Religious. However, though speaking of the "vow" of obedience, I want to recall what has been said repeatedly: the vows are not primarily discrete acts by which Religious assume a set of limited, juridical, and supererogatory obligations. Rather, like marriage vows by which the couple constructs the new socioreligious reality of family, Religious Profession initiates the person into a permanent, unified relational lifeform. Consecrated celibacy, evangelical poverty, and prophetic obedience are the constitutive coordinates of this lifeform of the single-hearted quest for God, lived in transcendent community, and world-transforming mission.

Finally, we need to say a preliminary word about what it means to qualify the practice of Religious obedience as "prophetic." Essentially, prophecy is bearing public witness to God and the Reign of God in the concrete historical context of a particular place and time. In other words, it is not a timeless teaching about an abstract theory of the Reign of God in general. Prophecy is always a response to the "signs of the times," the problems and issues that challenge believers to live and proclaim the Gospel in the here and now. Moses was sent to lead the Hebrews out of bondage in Egypt, through the desert, to the mountain of God. Mary was called to bear, raise, follow, and accompany to death the one in whom God entered our history as a human being. Jesus preached the Good News of liberation from oppression to the poor of first-century Palestine struggling under the double domination of the Roman Empire and the religious hierarchy of Jerusalem. Religious in every age are called to live the life of Jesus' itinerant band of disciples, those he chose and called to leave all things and to go about with him on a full-time basis participating in his ministry of teaching, healing, liberating, and exorcising, and to continue that ministry after his Resurrection. That will always mean responding with the Word of God to the real challenges of a particular sociocultural-religious context.

There are two ways in which Religious carry on this prophetic vocation. Their life as a whole, in which they live the relationship pattern, the economics, and the politics of the Reign of God in the alternate world they construct, bears witness to the Gospel in and to the cultural context in which they live. Therefore, Religious Life in every age, and in every culture, will be different and specific to its sociohistorical context. There is no such thing as "Religious Life" in the abstract, a kind of platonic essence that is dropped down into successive historical milieux requiring only minor adjustments. The flight of the hermits to the desert in the fourth century was a prophetic response to the over-conformity of the Church to its imperial context and the construction of cenobitic monasticism a couple centuries later was a prophetic response to feudalism. The form of apostolic Religious Life that arose in response to the ghetto Catholicism of the immigrant Church in America in the mid-1800s to the mid-1900s is not the form required by the postmodern, globalized context of the twenty-first century. Therefore, developing and living their life in and for their own times is in and of itself a form of prophetic witness by Religious. It is this aspect of prophecy that we will be considering in the third section of this chapter, that is, obedience in **community**.

A second way in which Religious exercise prophetic obedience is through their **ministry**. As we will see, this is a stressful, conflict-ridden, active participation in the sociohistorical context of their times. This aspect of prophetic obedience is especially evident today when the ministry of Religious is often highly individualized and diverse, rather than institutionalized and collective. Prophetic figures such as the women martyrs of El Salvador or Teresa Kane, Joan Chittister, or Roy Bourgeois are not simply participants in a prophetic community but also highly visible individuals in open conflict with the domination systems of their societies and the institutional Church. Like Jesus in conflict with the religious authorities of his day, they are not simply witnessing by the fact of living personally and communally their commitment to nonviolence and liberation, but are also announcing the Gospel in word and deed, speaking truth to power in the public arena. This second aspect of prophetic obedience will be taken up in the fourth section of this chapter on ministry. But before considering obedience in community and in ministry we need to explore obedience itself as the politics of the Reign of God.

II. Prophetic Obedience in the Alternate World: The Politics of the Reign of God

A. The Structure of Prophetic Obedience

In part 2 of this volume, I proposed that evangelical poverty was the "economics of the Reign of God" which Religious incarnate in the "alternate world" they create. I want to use the

same process to talk about the structure of prophetic obedience as the "politics of the Reign of God," and then to make
explicit how all the aspects of what we mean by "politics" are
modified by this understanding.

Politics refers to all the features of a society's organization of
power. The politics of the Reign of God is a politics of freedom
based on equality and interdependence, in contrast to a politics of domination and individualism. As the economy of gift
leads to common life in which all contribute according to ability and receive according to need, so the politics of freedom
produces an interdependent community of equal disciples
who mutually exercise authority and obedience in service of
the common good. And, as the economics of the Reign of God
not only fosters the community life of its participants but witnesses to and promotes the development of the kind of community Jesus formed among his itinerant band of disciples and
commissioned them to promote in the world, so the politics of
the Reign of God not only creates an egalitarian and interdependent community among its members but witnesses to and
promotes Gospel community in the world.

We noted in the section on the economics of the Reign of
God that although there are more or less acceptable ways in
which a commodity economy can function, Religious create an
alternate world in which private property is renounced completely in favor of economic common life and they thereby
offer continuous, existential witness in the concrete conditions
of this world to the priority of the common good over individual wealth. The same is true of politics. An unequal exercise of
power, for example, in a limited monarchy or constitutional
democracy, or an espousal of individual rights that is not excessively individualistic, can be compatible with the common good,
or at least more compatible with the Gospel than a thoroughgoing domination system, such as absolute monarchy, dictatorship,
totalitarianism, or fascism, or the radical individualism that
denies any responsibility of the person for the common good.
But Religious create an alternate world in which the complete
renunciation of individualism goes so far as to make mutual
obedience the preferred dynamic of its political life and thus

radical egalitarianism a concrete sociocultural witness to the inner life of the Trinity and the form of community life Jesus founded.

In other words, Religious Life involves a radical stance in regard to wealth and power, namely, the complete renunciation of all private property and of all forms of individualism and hierarchy and the embrace of common life and the common good in shared possessionlessness and interdependent equality. That is why Religious make vows of poverty and obedience and why we need to qualify these terms, to call attention not only to the radicalism of this faith-based choice but also to its root in the Gospel.

Just as Religious celibacy is not simply a moral living of a condition of being unmarried for whatever reason, and poverty is not just a matter of asceticism or detachment in relation to material goods, so obedience is not merely doing what one is told when authority is legitimately exercised. Consecrated celibacy, evangelical poverty, and prophetic obedience are not supererogatory or extreme versions of ordinary human conditions but the radical choices by which Religious create an alternate world in which relationships, material goods, and power are handled in a qualitatively different way than they are in ordinary secular life, even in a legitimate, virtuous, deeply Christian secular life. This is the source of their prophetic power and thus it is crucial for Religious to understand what they are doing when they profess these vows.

B. The Terminology of Prophetic Obedience

In order to understand better what the Profession of prophetic obedience involves, it will be helpful to parse with some nuance the often overlapped and confused meanings of the terms that cluster around the topic of obedience: "power," "authority," and "freedom."

1. Meanings of power

"Power" in relation to the vow of obedience, like "material goods" in relation to the vow of poverty, constitutes the "what," the subject matter that Religious attempt, by vow, to incorporate into the lifeform they undertake by Profession. Like material goods, which are intrinsically ambiguous because humans cannot seem to live well with them but are unable to live at all without them, power is a very ambiguous category. Women, especially feminist women, are often leery of the very word. They have so often been the objects of the abuse of power that they can yearn for a world without power and deny that they have any interest in possessing or using power. But power as such (like material resources) is not only morally neutral; it is ubiquitous and absolutely necessary. Power is simply the capacity to *move*, that is, to *influence* oneself or something/one else physically or spiritually. Power is an intrinsic property of life itself, a manifestation of the immanent principle of self-movement, self-creation, and self-determination that characterizes living, as opposed to inanimate reality.

Power can be *coercive* when one is moved against one's will, either physically, such as in rape, or morally, such as by being forced to swear to something in which one does not believe. Coercive power, that is "power over," is rarely innocent or neutral. It is almost always in service of abusive power, as we will see shortly. (As we will explore below, however, coercion, even if necessary or legitimate, is not an exercise of authority. It is, on the contrary, the solution to which we have recourse when authority fails. Coercion is the admission of the breakdown of authority. The two concepts, coercion and authority, even though they both refer to power, must be kept distinct.)

Power, however, can be *empowering*, physically or spiritually. An adult can use physical power to carry a child up the stairs; the teacher uses intellectual power to enlighten her students. Power as assistance, that is, "power for," is what we bring to bear most often in ministry precisely to empower those who are in some way weak or disempowered.

Finally, power can be *persuasive*. This is the area in which we are primarily interested. Persuasive power is what we call **authority**, that is, the right to be heard and heeded, a right that places a claim on the hearer for some kind of appropriate response. Authority in its primary and strongest sense is the rightly exercised intellectual, moral, or spiritual influence of

one person on another person. By extension we can speak of
the authority of things, such as facts, literature, laws, customs,
and so on that legitimately claim a response from people.
Authority as "persuasive power" is discussed in the next section.

Religious Life involves many "privileged mediations" of
God's will that have genuine persuasive power in this sense.
(We will take up in greater detail the issue of the structure of
privileged mediations in chapter 9.) The Rule, Chapter enact-
ments, even the order of a house or community customs and
prayers can be invested with this kind of authority. But we need
to remember that these mediations exist for humans, to facilitate the exercise of genuine freedom, not vice versa. These
privileged mediations have persuasive power because the community has conferred authority on them, not because they are
somehow directly commanded by or willed by God. We will
return in a moment to this issue of conferred authority within a
structure of privileged mediations of the will of God.

2. Meanings of "authority" as persuasive power

Because we have been conditioned by those who have a vested
interest in domination to not make such distinctions we have a
tendency to reduce "authority" to coercive power. In other
words, we see a person as "having authority over us" if they can
force us to do something, especially against our will. This is precisely what I am trying to call into question. Coercion, the exercise of "power over" another against their will, is not authority.
One might, because one is in a position of public authority and
therefore in some way responsible for the common good, be
reduced to the exercise of coercion to prevent a greater evil. But
coercion, even if legitimate, testifies to the failure of authority,
rather than to its effectiveness. Persuasive power, that is, real
authority, may be external, evidential, or relational.

a. EXTERNAL AUTHORITY

The least important kind of authority is purely external. A
train schedule, a traffic light, or a price tag are authoritative
because they make a claim to recognition and response. But
that is because they are the codified conclusions to processes

by which we finally organize certain mundane aspects of life so that we do not have to incessantly repeat the organizational processes. We organize a number of aspects of Religious Life this way, for example, by agreeing on a schedule (in monastic terms, an horarium), setting dates for meetings (such as formally convening a Chapter), establishing processes for carrying on Congregational business, and so on.

Even though we once assimilated such arrangements to the personal authority of the superior or the written authority of the Rule and talked about them all as expressions of the "will of God," the time has come to recognize that these arrangements have, in themselves, no intrinsic authority. There is nothing intrinsically authoritative or divinely sanctioned about a meeting date or a budget form. This is not to say that such arrangements have no importance, can be ignored at will by community members, or have no role in the ongoing life of obedience to God that Religious undertake. It is to say that God did not choose June for Chapter or reveal that the annual retreat should last eight days. There is more to be said about how these arrangements function in the lived experience of obedience, precisely because they facilitate the mutual cooperation in the community that is correctly called obedience, but for now, I want to relativize them in favor of more intrinsic forms of authority.

b. EVIDENTIAL AUTHORITY

As the term suggests, and unlike external authority, evidential authority places a claim on us by its very nature. First, there are things that are *self-evident* and any refusal of appropriate response is self-destructive. If I live in a society that operates, mathematically, in base ten, refusing to recognize that two plus two equals four will lead to major problems when I try to balance my checkbook and could lead to a jail term if I apply my idiosyncratic arithmetic to my bill paying. In base ten, two plus two is self-evidently four.

Such things as a person's basic right to physical integrity, and therefore the obligation of other people, whether or not they are in positions of authority, not to deliberately and unnecessarily injure the person, are also self-evident. The tortures of the Inquisition were intrinsically wrong even though the perpetrators, at least in some cases, were probably ignorant of this. The same intrinsic claim must be recognized in relation to the individual's right to integrity of conscience. No one has the right to demand internal submission to something a person sees as false or evil. Although the Church did not officially recognize this fact until Vatican II, it was always self-evident; that is, it is not a conclusion of an argument even when argument is needed to make its self-evident truth available to some people. Freedom of conscience, like physical integrity, is not a privilege; it has an intrinsic right to respect.[6]

The kind of evidential authority with which we deal most often—and this is very important for a group of people who live according to a written law like a Rule or constitutions—is *conferred authority*, which is intrinsic but not self-evident. To take an example of conferred authority from the world of scholarship: some years ago, a scholar claimed that an ossuary or bone container he had discovered was that of James, the brother of the Lord, based on the apparent date of the ossuary and the inscription on its side. However, New Testament scholars did not just conclude that this ossuary was authentic because the man who discovered it said it was. They tested the actual age, worked to discern the character of the inscription, and so on. In the end, scholars decided that the ossuary was a fake. But had they satisfied all their test questions in the affirmative, they would have "conferred" authority on the ossuary, and it would have exercised evidential authority in succeeding New Testament scholarship. If later it were discovered that there was reason to doubt the original conclusion of authenticity the conferred evidential authority would be weakened, and if it were shown that there were more reasons to doubt than to accept its authenticity it would probably lose all authority. If, finally, it were shown to be a fraud, its authority would be revoked. In other words, when something is not *self*-evident the relevant community *confers* its evidential authority.

There is a strong tendency, however, for people to believe and claim that human, conferred authority is actually based on some self-evident, even divine, guarantee. Human beings seem to have a kind of Cartesian reflex that demands absolute certainty as the only valid basis for recognizing true authority, that is, a real "claim to be heard and heeded." Thus, in times past, this type of claim was often made for Religious Rules and constitutions and was the basis of such axioms as "Keep the Rule and the Rule will keep you." The Rule was God's will, and obedience to it—even when some prescriptions were rather clearly time-bound, of dubious value, or even genuinely problematic—was an absolute guarantee that one was obeying God's will.

This assumption was demythologized in the wake of the Council, when committees of quite ordinary people who were well known to their contemporaries revised or even rewrote foundational documents of the Congregation, and ordinary members of the Congregation voted on their acceptance. This obvious human authorship and approval precipitated a crisis of authority in many Congregations. The documents seemed to lose their sacred character as divinely authored and therefore their "real," that is, *self*-evident authority. People simply did not know how to assign real, sacred authority to documents whose authority was obviously conferred by humans. Just as biblical fundamentalists cannot entertain the real human authorship of Scripture since that would render Scripture nonauthoritative, magisterial fundamentalists cannot accept the established fact that some teachings of the magisterium, such as that unbaptized babies are definitively deprived of the beatific vision, have been simply wrong. That would undermine the absolute certainty they need to ascribe to all teachings of the magisterium if the latter is to have any real authority.

c. RELATIONAL AUTHORITY

The most important kind of authority is relational authority. This is the kind of authority that characterizes people and is exercised among themselves. It is the primary type of authority exercised in Religious Congregations. Again, failure to make distinctions between this kind of authority and other kinds, and among different forms of relational authority, makes it very difficult to rethink in contemporary terms the vow of Religious obedience. And some people, for example, some ecclesiastical officials who have vested interests in keeping authority identified with coercive power (especially their own), do not want nuanced distinctions in this area to be understood by those they want to control. Let me distinguish at least three kinds of relational authority, remembering our general definition of genuine authority as the right to be heard and heeded, that is, to place a claim on another to attend to what one is saying or requesting and to expect the hearer to respond appropriately.

First, we might identify *natural* or *quasi-natural* relational authority, such as that of a parent in relation to a minor child or of a teacher to a student. Because the parent is naturally responsible for the well-being of the child she or he has the authority, the claim on the child, that that responsibility entails. Someone acting *in loco parentis*, like a childcare professional or a primary school teacher, might share by extension in that natural authority. In other words, responsibility implies the authority necessary to fulfill the responsibility.

In times past it was generally assumed that nobility, because of their "blue blood" (i.e., ontological superiority by birth), had natural authority over commoners; that males, because of their superior gender, had natural authority over females; that whites, because of their racial superiority, had natural authority over people of color; that clerics, because of their sacramental superiority, had (super)natural authority over the laity; and so on. In all of these cases, the basis of the claimed "natural authority" was not responsibility (as in the case of the parent) but some kind of ontological superiority.

We need to raise to visibility, reexamine, and question the assumption that the authority (actually power) structures into which we have been born or socialized in society, the Church, and the Congregation rest on ontologically based hierarchical distinctions between superiors and inferiors. If the basic affirmation of ontological equality among all people is true, then no one except God is ontologically "superior" to any human being. The basic significance of the Incarnation is that God laid aside that claim by choosing equality with us. All intra-human "superiority" is, at best, relative, provisional, and constructed. What God does not claim, humans certainly cannot and must not claim.

A second kind of relational authority might be called *dialogical*. This is the right to be heard and heeded that arises when one speaks the truth in love within a relationship. In other words, the quality of the relationship itself calls for dialogical engagement, for listening, taking seriously, and responding in good faith to the other. Spouses have this kind of mutual authority in their marital relationship. A husband or wife does not have to listen to the judgment of the grocery clerk about the possible relocation of their family, but they do have to listen to and respond to each other. Even a minor child, in the family relationship, has a certain authority, a right to be heard and heeded at least in matters that concern the child's well-being. Whether or not a spouse's or child's wishes or suggestions can finally be followed, the right to be listened to and taken seriously is intrinsic to the relationship. The claim placed on the one addressed to listen, consider, respond is what we call authority; the proper response to that claim, namely, hearing, heeding, and responding appropriately (not necessarily compliance or submission) is obedience.

A kind of dialogical authority that is very important in Religious Life is that of friendship, the basic peer relationship among members of a Congregation that understands itself as a discipleship of equals united by love. If the Congregation is, as I have suggested a number of times, a community of persons vowed to a shared life based on common love of Christ, then members have a right to speak the truth to one another in love and each member has an obligation to hear and heed, that is, to listen to fellow members and to respond appropriately.

Sometimes this peer authority (a notion that can be traced back to the Rule of St. Benedict, who urged all members of the community to be obedient to one another) will be exercised in the context of personal friendship, when, for example, one Sister or Brother contributes to the ministerial discernment of another. But peer authority is always operative in corporate Congregational affairs. This does not mean a member simply does whatever another, or the group, or even the majority suggests, but she or he does not dismiss or ignore their intervention. Contributions to Congregational deliberation are not just "someone's opinion." To neglect to participate in the Congregation's processes of discernment and decision making, to refuse to really listen to the others in the Congregation and take their input seriously, and to fail to implement the decisions at which the community arrives whether or not the leader articulates them or they are written down, and whether or not one's own position has prevailed, is to fail in the obedience that one has vowed within the community. (This, incidentally, is one of the major differences between vowed members of a Congregation and oblates, volunteers, associates, etc. The members vow obedience. Obedient participation in the corporate exercise of authority is not optional for them as it is for nonmembers, even those formally united with the Congregation in some way.)

A third kind of relational authority is *office authority*, which is conferred on a person by appointment or election and is ideally exercised as part of pastoral care and leadership in the community. This is not (as with conferred evidential authority) about certifying the objective quality of the person. Whether or not one considers the elected official compatible or even competent one is obliged to recognize and respond to her/his authority. A community as community, by whatever processes it has determined, confers a particular kind of authority on its leaders that other members of the community in their dialogical relationships do not exercise. During the time they are in office, these leaders have the authority of office, the right to be heard and heeded precisely as leaders in matters pertaining to the common good, which can include the regulation of the attitudes and actions of individual members. Nevertheless, office authority is relational, which means it functions mutually, reciprocally, with the authority of the members. Both leaders and members exercise both authority and obedience, though not in the same way, within the context of the community as a discipleship of equals.

Therefore, recognizing the claim of an officeholder to be heard and heeded is not necessarily (despite a long tradition to the contrary) an *a priori* commitment to do immediately and without question what is suggested or even commanded. The leader places a claim on the other member to listen and the member must have an *a priori* disposition to cooperate with the leader, to heed and respond positively. Only such a disposition on the part of all the members can fully empower the office holder in her role of leadership and obviate the need for recourse to coercion. But, in some cases, genuine obedience (which we must still discuss) requires that the member introduce other considerations or hesitations that might call for adjustment of the original request or command or even its withdrawal. In the most extreme case, it might require the member to respectfully and conscientiously decline to comply with the request, a choice a truly authoritative leader should, in obedience, respect, even if some other action then needs to be taken.

A priori resistance—refusal to listen and consider, refusal to honestly and openly enter into the necessary dialogue to arrive at that which is both conducive to the common good and possible for the individual—is genuinely incompatible with obedience to office authority. Stubborn insistence on one's own position even when no principle is involved is a failure in obedience. Of course, this assumes a responsible exercise of authority by the officeholder. Dictatorial, to say nothing of fascist, domination is not an exercise of authority but of coercive power and it may be that resistance is both justified and necessary, precisely for the common good.

By qualifying the right of officeholders or community leaders to be heard and heeded, that is, their claim on members for the response to authority that we call obedience, by the obligation of the leaders to attend to the contribution of members, including their hesitations or conscientious objections to certain authoritative interventions of the leader, we are saying that neither authority nor obedience in the Religious community are unilateral. The "superior" does not exercise only authority and the "subject" only obedience. Rather the community leader and the member are engaged in a two-way, mutual and reciprocal transaction in which both exercise, in different ways and from different bases, both authority and obedience.

In matters within the purview of office, the presumption favors the leader, not because of some ontologically based superiority or dictatorial right to "call all the shots," but because of her special responsibility in the community for the common good. The exercise of authority is asymmetrical because the responsibility is diverse. However, both authority and obedience are required of equals as humans, as Christians, as vowed members of the Congregation. Diversity of responsibilities is not hierarchy of power and cooperation is not submission to heteronomous control. Modeling a truly Christian, adult, noncoercive, effective mutuality of authority and obedience can be a genuinely prophetic contribution of Religious Life to society and especially to the institutional Church, which so often forces believers to choose between infantile submission and "leaving the Church."

Recourse to outright coercion might sometimes (one would hope very rarely) be necessary. For example, if a member is flagrantly and publicly violating her vows, giving public scandal (although intelligent and respectful dissent is rarely scandalous despite what some ecclesiastical officials assert), compromising the Congregation's reputation or financial well-being, damaging other people in ministry, and so on, and more dialogical intervention is not effective, the demand for conformity might be necessary, even backed by the threat of sanctions. In other words, coercion becomes necessary when the situation is truly serious and authority properly exercised has proved ineffective. Genuine authority can only be exercised when genuine obedience is also operative. When the situation of mutual authority and obedience breaks down, coercion may be the only alternative to serious damage to individuals, the community, or the wider society. Nevertheless, women Religious in renewed Congregations are, rightly in my opinion, very hesitant to invoke this option of coercion except as an absolute last resort.

As a result of this unwillingness on the part of Congregational leaders to resort to coercive power over their fellow Religious, there are frequent conflicts about members and their ministries between women Religious leaders and ecclesiastical officeholders who tend to use threat and coercion as a first option and to expect other officeholders in the Church—in what they see as a "chain of command"—to enforce their positions. Congregational leaders, however, in exercising the office authority they have in virtue of election according to the constitutions, are not part of the hierarchical "chain of command." They have no more obligation than other members of the Church to enforce the will of agents outside the Congregation. Even though ecclesiastical authorities "certify" their elections, these ecclesiastical officeholders do not "confer" their authority. Just as a baptized and sacramentally married parent has no obligation to send her child to the parish school, and the family has no obligation to worship in one parish rather than another (as was once thought obligatory), so Religious superiors are not subject to ecclesiastical officers in the internal governance of their Congregations. Religious vows are made to God, not to the hierarchy, and Religious leaders derive their legitimate authority from the constitutions, not from the permission of ecclesiastical officeholders. The naïve assumption that ecclesiastical officials have some kind of universal authority to govern the nonordained in any and all matters even remotely related to their faith is without biblical or theological basis and needs to be firmly resisted lest authority degenerate into harassment or dictatorship. Only recognizing and respecting diverse spheres of authority will foster appropriate, mutually respectful relationships of different agents in the Church.

In summary, we have placed relational authority in the category of persuasive power or influence that consists in the right to be heard and heeded. This right arises from relationships that may be natural, dialogical, or constructed by the conferral of authority on an officeholder. Relational authority in the Religious Congregation, that which is exercised among the persons who make up the community, both peer relationships and the relationship between leaders and other members, works within and according to the authority framework of the constitutions upon which the members have conferred authority, which has been ratified by the appropriate ecclesiastical authorities, and which provides for leadership, processes of discernment, methods of decision making, ways of resolving conflicts, and so on in the community.

Although this fact is often obscured by the (invalid) assimilation of the Religious community to the hierarchical structure of the institutional Church, the Religious community is not a hierarchical structure but an egalitarian one. Its egalitarianism is not a secular political, one-person-one-vote democracy, but an incarnation of the discipleship of equals that Jesus formed around himself. Jesus never assumed a position of superiority over his disciples. In fact, he went to extraordinary and dramatic lengths to make clear that he was "among them as one who served," as one who "has washed your feet," precisely in order to manifest to them what the relationship among them should be. Furthermore, Jesus never coerced his disciples, even Judas.

While some people, especially some ecclesiastical officials, think that egalitarian organization is a recipe for social chaos, and others, especially some traditionalists inside and outside Religious Life, think that a noncoercive community is a contradiction in terms and a surrender to sinful egotism, both the Gospel and the lived experience of renewed Congregations has shown that such communities are biblically, theologically, psychologically, and ministerially more coherent and cohesive than their hierarchically organized predecessors.

Egalitarian Religious community is a prophetic witness to the dialogical authority that God exercises in relation to humans. The community of interdependent equal persons is the human image of the triune God who is a community of equal persons sharing unity of life and love. The authority in such a Religious community is the analogue of the authority of God, who never coerces human beings but invites us and enables us to become what we are created to be; who lures us in freedom toward ever-deeper love.

Defective theology has often presented divine power as coercive because God is self-evidently ontologically superior to humans and unbound by any considerations except God's own unfettered will. To the impoverished imagination of authoritarian personalities, this can only mean that God is, by right, a divine dictator whose inscrutable will is unaccountable and irresistible and who will punish with eternal damnation any challenge to "his" overwhelming power. In fact, God who created us in freedom always respects it. It is we who project onto God our own corrupt power agendas. In other words, the root of the misunderstanding of authority and obedience is, in the last analysis, a distorted God-image, a topic to which we will return in the next chapter.

3. Meanings of Freedom

This brings us directly to the third major concept that has to be explored if we are to develop a Gospel-based understanding of prophetic obedience, namely, freedom. This is a topic to which volumes have been devoted by philosophers, political scientists, psychologists, and saints. We cannot go into these discussions in detail, but, because genuine obedience has to be an exercise of, not a suppression or surrender of freedom, we need a nuanced adult appreciation of this category.

God created humans intelligent and free. We are not within our rights to renounce our God-given freedom any more than we may immobilize our intelligence or terminate our life. God not only does not demand the suppression of our human faculties, God is not pleased or honored by the rejection or renunciation of these gifts. We must exercise our intelligence and freedom, the faculties by which God impressed God's own image and likeness into our humanity, to our dying breath. Obedience is always and only something we do with our freedom, not a way of abolishing it or escaping from it or "sacrificing" it.

Freedom, philosophers tell us, has three valid meanings: spontaneity, choice (or what we call "free will"), and love.

a. SPONTANEITY

Spontaneity is the response of an organism to a stimulus. It is instinctual and nonrational and often protective of the organism. If you throw something at me I will spontaneously dodge the projectile. But, as experience teaches us, spontaneity in humans is often the enemy of our best selves. Someone once said that she was on a "seafood diet," meaning "If I see food, I eat it." She was joking, of course, but we all experience the spontaneous, and imperious, movements of both appetite and aversion. Part of spiritual and moral and even human maturity is learning to regulate our spontaneity in relation to the moral good but also in relation to social conventions, the needs of other people, our personal obligations, and so on.

One of the purposes of the novitiate, sometimes in the past unfortunately pursued with excessive zeal, was to teach the novices to control their spontaneity in favor of virtue. However, a healthy person needs to keep alive a capacity for genuine spontaneity, the ability to respond to persons, situations, and opportunities, as well as dangers, without being paralyzed by fear, analysis, caution, or suspicion. Laughter is the Creator's seal of approval on spontaneity. One cannot fake real laughter, totally suppress it, nor plan it. It erupts when the ludicrous or preposterous occurs announcing the irreducible difference between the divine and the human. The important thing is to realize that we can be enslaved and even destroyed by spontaneity rather than liberated or protected by it. The person who cannot resist the impulses to buy, eat or drink, gamble, have sex, or explode in rage is addicted. And addiction is not freedom but slavery.

b. LIBERTY OF CHOICE

Liberty of choice is what most people mean by free will. It is our capacity for self-determination. It emerges at a very young age in the child's triumphant "no" to a parental directive. Our "yes" or "no" can bear on options across the whole range of reality, physical, moral, intellectual, social, spiritual. Choice is intrinsic to and expressive of our freedom and it is what most people regard as the epitome of freedom. Commitment is the ultimate exercise of free choice which, paradoxically, ends free choice in regard to the object of commitment and places the commitment in the sphere of true freedom or love.

Religious exercised freedom of choice when they entered Religious Life and eventually made Profession. Church law and Religious constitutions are very clear about the requirement that Religious Profession, to be valid, must be freely chosen. Freedom of choice is the human power by which we cooperate with God in becoming holy and with one another in building community and ministering to a broken world. But it is also the source of all the moral evil in the world from schoolyard bullying to terrorism, from rape and murder to the Holocaust. The capacity of the human for evil is awesome and terrifying and the real struggle of the human adventure is the effort to promote the triumph of good over evil in our own lives and in the world. The struggle between the Reign of God and the Kingdom of Satan is a struggle between free wills.

The paradox of free will, of choice, is that often we do not seem able to use it the way we choose. St. Paul lamented that the good he wanted to do he did not do and the evil he repudiated he ended up doing (see Rom 7:14–25). This universal human experience has challenged philosophers, psychologists, and theologians throughout history. Why, if we are really free, can we not manage to choose the good that we desire? Most thinkers agree that we really cannot choose evil as such. We choose the apparent good, but we are often mistaken about, or even culpably blind to, what is really good. Often we are caught between two goods, each of which is good under a different aspect, or two evils that seem equally bad, and we have to make a choice about relative values that are not entirely clear. Learning to reason morally and choose virtuously is a lifetime challenge. Would that as much energy in the novitiates of former times had been devoted to teaching new Religious how to discern and choose well as was devoted to teaching them to submit blindly.

Wise choice demands discernment that is not a mechanical process of lining up alternatives, doing some kind of moral arithmetic, and going with the column that has the most positives or the fewest negatives. It is a moral and spiritual habit or stance which attunes a person to God's will, helps one learn to listen to and for God in all the ordinary affairs of daily life and in the major decisions that one faces. (These topics will be taken up in chapters 9 and 10.) The act of discernment is the expression of this habit of discernment, and one who has not developed the habit will be hard pressed to act wisely in a conflictual or confusing moral dilemma.

Wise people try to build into their lives processes and attitudes that foster discernment so that in critical situations, when they are under the greatest stress, they do not have to "start from scratch." Societies codify some of these conclusions so that "following the rules" becomes not mechanistic routine but a short cut to choosing solutions that experience has shown to be usually prudent. For example, slowing down when the traffic light turns amber has a presumptive priority over stepping on the accelerator because a few seconds saved is not worth a deadly accident, and that realization has been institutionalized in amber lights. Only a hormone-addled adolescent thinks a traffic light is an affront to personal freedom and a challenge to prove that "rules are made to be broken." Societies, large and small, develop systems of aids to good judgment that reasonable people appreciate and respect.

Religious have developed a very sophisticated and complex network of processes for the guidance and strengthening of liberty toward the good. The Rule, the constitutions, the customs, relationship patterns in community, interactions with leaders, accountability procedures, as well as personal practices of prayer, spiritual direction, retreats, and so on are all meant to guide and support our liberty in discerning and doing God's will. Consequently, these realities form what might be called a "structure of privileged mediations of God's will," in our lives. When they function as they should they are powerful aids to the fruitful use of liberty, not to its suppression or renunciation. They are rightly regarded as "expressions of God's will," not because God is making explicit rules to govern our behavior down to its minutest details but because God's will for us is our growth in love, and that growth includes our daily choices and actions as well as major decisions. We will have more to say about the structure of privileged mediations when we examine the role of formation in the spirituality of obedience in chapter 10.

The problem with these mediations of God's will arises when we short-circuit these supports of liberty by equating them, purely and simply, with God's will imposed materially and woodenly on an unquestioning "subject." It is not always better to obey even when the superior is right, much less when he or she is wrong, and sometimes the Rule should not be kept, even if it is, strictly speaking, actually possible to do so. Reclaiming our human and spiritual liberty within Religious Life, which Religious have been in the process of doing since the Council, should not mean abolishing or repudiating all the means of discernment and guides to prudent action that have been built up over centuries of the living of Religious Life, but rather re-appropriating them as dynamic and flexible helps, and developing a freedom in peacefully deciding when and how they are or are not helpful. A level of obedience to authoritative structures and dynamics should operate in the lives of individual Religious and of the community as a whole, not as a behavioral straightjacket turning members into robots or clones and community life into a military exercise, but as a shared wisdom which is gradually internalized by formation and practice. Religious Life is a *life* and it should and does propose with authority a *way of living.*

c. Freedom as Love

Finally, the ultimate good of the human will is freedom in the full sense of the word. It cannot be reduced to either spontaneity or the exercise of free choice. Real freedom is the effective orientation of the human being to the good. In other words, it is love in action. Freedom is a participation in God's self-identity as infinite goodness, self-giving love. If we were really free we would plummet into the abyss of God's life and love like a boulder seeking the floor of the ocean. We would fly like a perfectly aimed arrow into the heart of God. Our spontaneity would be a glorious song of love and our free will would be subsumed in love like a fish in the life-giving water that flows through it. But, alas, we are not truly free. We struggle with our vices, our addictions, our selfishness, our blindness. We constantly exercise our free will in the service of our real freedom but rarely with total success.

However, all Religious began Religious Life in an act of true freedom at the moment of Profession when they offered themselves in unrestricted, unqualified self-gift to God in love. Probably none of us was perfectly free at that moment from all the less than perfect motivations we were blind to at the time, but our desire was to exercise not just a limited and reversible act of free choice but to activate the very depths of our beings in total self-gift, in true freedom. As Margaret Farley says, commitment, the ultimate act of free choice, intends to give a future to our love.[7] At the moment of Profession we oriented our whole life to God, forever. In a sense, Religious Life is a lifelong attempt to live into that original act in every dimension of our persons, in all our relationships, through everything we do until we finally arrive in God where we will be utterly free.

Obedience, then, is not a sacrifice, a suppression, or a surrender of our freedom but the effort to maximize it by disciplining our spontaneity, educating and forming our free will toward love, and growing gradually in the ability to love God and neighbor with our whole being. Recognizing that growth in love of God consists in union with the will of God (another term we must reexamine in chapter 10), Religious have undertaken a lifeform in which a whole gradated structure of privileged mediations of God's will operates to facilitate discernment of that will and support the efforts of members to fulfill it not only in their personal lives but in community life and ministerial involvement.

To reduce obedience to "doing what one is told" or "keeping the Rule" is to flatten out and trivialize a major dimension of Religious Life. Such a jejune understanding or practice of obedience infantilizes the Religious, mechanizes the life, and encourages rigidity in the members and tyranny in leaders. Unfortunately, as some Religious in the last few decades have recognized that this understanding of obedience that they were taught in formation is counterproductive, they have simply marginalized obedience or even repudiated it in their lives in favor of a personal exercise of liberty, of free choice, that does not recognize any real authority in the Congregation, whether of peers, persons in office, or other privileged mediations of God's will. They have traded an infantilizing dependence for an individualistic and isolating adolescent independence rather than growing into a mature interdependence in which the authority-obedience transaction is an exercise of mutual power striving for freedom. I am suggesting that a much more productive approach would be to deepen our understanding of obedience so that it can function as a Gospel-based exercise of true freedom.

III. Living the Politics of the Reign of God: Prophetic Obedience in Community

Although Religious obedience is vowed to God, not to any human being in or outside the Congregation, it is practiced in the social context of community, the Religious community first and then the larger Church community. The latter context will be considered in the next section in relation to prophetic obedience in ministry which is the primary locus of interaction between Religious and ecclesiastical authority. Here our attention will be focused on obedience in the Religious community itself. Living the politics of the Reign of God in Religious community offers ongoing prophetic witness in the Church and in the world.

A. Contrasting Religious Community with Secular Social Organization

1. Equality vs. hierarchy

Religious obedience, we have just seen, is a mutual exercise of authority and obedience in which persuasive power (authority) appeals to freedom (choice in love) for a response (obedience) which promotes the common good. This dynamic of mutual authority and obedience operates in various ways in different spheres: between peers in the community; between those in office and the other members of the community; in the community as a whole pursuing their life and mission. But it is never unilateral (one person commanding and the other submitting) nor an imposition of coercive power of a "superior" on powerless "subjects." It is a mutual, reciprocal, and free transaction between committed adults.

Obedience is actualized in the Congregation considered, first, as a community; that is, as a social reality modeled on the itinerant band of disciples whom Jesus called to live with him on a continual basis, to accompany him in his ministry, and to continue that ministry after his Resurrection. Therefore, we need to examine, from the standpoint of the organization of power (i.e., politics), what kind of community Jesus formed and Religious now construct in imitation of that first community, and how it contrasts with the understanding of sociopolitical organization in secular society, and unfortunately often in the institutional Church in which it is situated.

As we have seen, in modern Western society, power in general, including authority, is almost always understood hierarchically. No matter how considerately it is exercised, hierarchical power is virtually always coercive to some extent, because the subordinate must submit to the hierarchically superior power. The threat of enforcement, therefore, lies behind virtually all such exercises of authority because in a hierarchical relationship people frequently are not free to move out of the relationship. Participation in hierarchically organized social systems is generally not voluntary but "natural" (e.g., in the family) or "necessary" (e.g., in the state).

The coercive exercise of hierarchical power, at least in non-fascist social organizations, has two functions. First, hierarchical authority armed with coercive power is seen as necessary for the common good; the only way to maintain order in a group of individuals with diverse aims and projects and to get things done efficiently and effectively. Someone has to have the final say. The operating assumption is that people cannot be left to their own devices because they are less able, less committed, less virtuous, less divinely inspired, and so on, than those who are appointed by God or society to control them. Second, hierarchical authority and its attendant coercive power is exercised when the social structure is under some kind of threat, for the good of the problematic individual her or himself and for the good of those whom he or she influences. Thus lawbreakers are arrested, students expelled, books censored, theologians silenced, ministries closed down, and so on, for the protection of the offenders and of those they would lead astray.

This is not to deny that in both secular society (at least in nontotalitarian regimes) and the Church efforts are made to encourage willing cooperation and participation and to recognize the input of citizens, the rights of the oppressed, and the dignity of the People of God. But it is to say that in a hierarchically organized power structure any participation by the subordinates tends to be seen as a privilege accorded by those who hold power to those who do not, rather than as the right of free and equal people because, in fact, the people are not equal. Coercion, whether psychological, moral, spiritual, or physical is always an option in the repertoire of the hierarchs who regard it as an ordinary means of assuring the common and individual good. The threat of sanctions is intrinsic to the exercise of authority as "power over."

2. Religious community: a different approach to social organization
Religious Life starts from a different premise because it is essentially and only a voluntary society of equals. First, unlike most other major social structures such as the family, the secular political system, or the institutional Church, Religious Life is not a "natural" or "necessary" society. It is not "natural" because no one is born into it and it is not "necessary" because no one has to enter it or remain in it for survival in this life or salvation in the next. Thus people come into the social system of Religious Life as free subjects of personal power which the institution does not confer on them or control. Religious decide freely to join with other members of the Congregation in order to maximize their personal power by integrating it into the Congregation's exercise of power to create the community itself, to assist others through ministry, and to influence through persuasion the structures of society and the Church.

Second, Religious Life as a social entity is radically egalitarian. There are no children in Religious Life so there is no intrinsic or natural age-based, parental superiority. There is no gender dichotomy as basis for superiority in the celibate Congregation. Nobility and reputation of any kind is renounced upon entrance. (That was one of the purposes of suppressing personal names and taking new ones that relate each individual to the communion of saints in the equality of grace rather than to the family of origin and ancestral privilege or even to one's previous secular identity and achievements.) The surrender of all financial resources upon entrance erases class distinctions. And for Sisters and Brothers there is no ecclesiastical inequality based on ordination, which would make some members ontologically or ecclesiastically superior to others in the community.

In short, Religious Life is intrinsically, that is, by its very nature, a voluntary, egalitarian network of Gospel-based relationships in which power is not organized hierarchically and therefore cannot normally be exercised coercively. Of course, those Religious old enough to remember the life as it was lived in the preconciliar era will immediately say, "That's not how the Congregation understood itself or how I experienced it when I entered." In preconciliar times, candidates gave up all personal power and submitted themselves, by vow as they understood it, within a hierarchical power structure operated by nonaccountable superiors who were plenipotentiary stand-ins for ecclesiastical monarchs. I am suggesting that this was a fundamental misunderstanding of Religious Life and therefore that the postconciliar renewal was not the invention of something brand new but the retrieval of the Life as it originated in the first century before it was subsumed into the increasingly hierarchized structure of the Church as institution.

It is very important for Religious, especially women, to become aware of how their life devolved from a free, vocation-based choice made by adults who felt called to an exclusive love of Jesus Christ and commitment to his work of bringing about the Reign of God in this world into a hierarchical power structure. Recall the brief overview of the history of the Church from community of disciples to absolute monarchy in the previous chapter. Religious Life followed and mirrored the development of the institutional Church, which was born as a discipleship of equals gathered around the Risen Jesus, and quickly evolved into the official religion of the Roman Empire upon which it modeled itself institutionally.[8] The Church has never really extricated itself from that secular political model. Vatican II attempted a reform of this development, a return to

the sources that called the Church back to a Gospel understanding of itself, but this transformation was resisted by the
Vatican power elite during the Council and by the Curia ever
since. The contradictions between the two models are written
into the documents themselves[9] and the last two pontificates
have been devoted to a restorationist program that has kept
the conciliar insights into the nature of the Church as community from bearing fruit, theologically or organizationally. Faith
in the Holy Spirit grounds the hope that eventually the renewal
called for and initiated by the Council will take hold, but at the
moment the monarchists are still fairly firmly in control, at
least at the institutional level.

B. Factors Calling Religious to a Different Approach

A number of factors characteristic of the late twentieth and
now the early twenty-first century have led Religious, especially
women, to existentially challenge this historical evolution of
the Church from the original community of equal disciples
into a hierarchical power structure. They have undertaken a
theologically based sociological transformation of their own
life which involves a reappropriation of the original genius of
Religious Life as a voluntary society of equal disciples.

Some of these factors are ecclesial, and others originated in
the secular order. Still other factors are experiential arising
from the actual living of Religious Life since the Council. Biblical and theological resources have been foundational in understanding what was happening and enabling Religious to
articulate and claim these developments not as social tinkering
or interesting experiments in individualism but as Gospel-
based renewal. But as the institutional Church has sunk back
into its monarchical past, Religious Life has carried forward its
appropriation of biblical and conciliar egalitarianism. The tension between the two developments is not surprising but the
better we understand it the less likely we are to be thrown off
course by reassertions of "power over" masquerading as genuine "authority."

One clear indication that a profound transformation of
women's Religious Life as social entity is indeed occurring is

the aggressive and threatening scrutiny of their life and ministry by the Vatican in recent times.[10] Religious, particularly women, have been under suspicion precisely because they have emerged, especially in first world countries, as empowering "carriers" of the conciliar vision of Church as community of equal disciples and thus as a primary challenge to the monarchical ecclesiology which Vatican II challenged but which is increasingly invoked by the hierarchy.

1. Ecclesial, cultural, and experiential factors

Certainly the major *ecclesial* factor encouraging women Religious to rethink the nature of their community life and the role of obedience within it was the Council itself. As we saw in the last chapter, by valorizing a number of models of Church, especially that of the pilgrim People of God understood as the Body of Christ in and for the world, the Council relativized the historically absolutized institutional model of monarchy. The People of God model introduced notions of baptismal equality, universal participation, collegiality and subsidiarity, shared stewardship of personal as well as material resources, the reciprocal and mutual responsibility of leaders and members, freedom of conscience, and so on. This gave Catholics in general permission to think outside the monarchical box, and women Religious were better prepared theologically, experientially, and organizationally than almost any other segment of the Church to exercise that permission. The community life of contemporary Religious, especially women, is a developing Incarnation of the new ecclesiology.

As has already been mentioned, the emergence of secular *feminism* probably has been the most important cultural factor in the questioning by Religious of dominative hierarchical structures. Feminism's critique of patriarchy as an ideology of domination sacralized by Christian hierarchy and undergirding sexism in family, society, and Church supplied a theoretical basis for the social revolution in women's Congregations from total, blind, and unquestioning dependence on the "fathers" (and their mother-delegates) toward a claim to legitimate self-determination. This claim is actually Gospel-based but it could hardly have found voice so quickly or so clearly without the foundational support of the feminist analysis.[11]

At the same time the involvement of Congregations in developments taking place in the fields of *psychology and sociology* were leading Religious to question the infantilizing primary family model of Religious community life and its implied mother-child relationship between superiors and subjects. Claiming their identity as a community of adults in mission was a surprisingly rapid and radical development that has taken place in less than four decades but that is clearly irreversible. Because leaders in women's Religious Congregations do not regard their fellow Religious as "subjects" (much less children) they do not fit well in the "chain of command" model of authority and obedience that the ecclesiastical hierarchy constantly evokes. As we will see, this is not merely a diversity of sociological models but a theological conflict because Religious, in fact, are not part of the hierarchical structure of the institution.

Finally, the *ministerial experience* of Religious themselves in the immediate postconciliar period furthered reflection on community as social organism rather than ecclesiastical army. As the numbers and financial resources of Congregations declined, they were less able to staff and run huge institutions. The military model of obedience that had been so efficient in training large numbers of recruits, deploying regiments of workers, and maintaining a clear chain of command that ran upward from local to provincial to general superiors and on up to hierarchical legitimators of these women officeholders, seemed less and less appropriate to the kinds of ministries in which Congregations were increasingly involved. It was much more difficult to treat one or two people like expendable foot soldiers in a battalion than it had been to handle in that way hundreds of troops for whom there were ready replacements in the barracks.

Members began to have faces and personalities and not just "name, rank and serial number." This, of course, led to a greater awareness of the giftedness of the individual persons who make up the Congregation and the need to affirm, develop, and capitalize on their gifts. In other words, the increasing recognition of the real power of each member was not a source of fear on the part of leaders or of competition among the members but of mutual appreciation of shared riches in an increasingly interdependent and egalitarian community. While the hierarchy was lamenting the loss of a free labor force for the staffing of institutions, Religious were moving into the role Cardinal Léon Suenens envisioned for them in his ground-breaking conciliar-era treatise, *The Nun in the Modern World*.[12] Religious were beginning to exercise ministerial influence in many areas of modern society in which the Gospel needs to be proclaimed.

In short, an amazing confluence of influences coming from Church, society, and lived experience, only a few of which have been mentioned here, has moved women Religious faster than any other element in the Church toward a new understanding of power, authority, and freedom.

2. Biblical and theological resources

An explosion of theoretical resources for a renewed under-standing of Religious Life supported and validated these devel-opments in the understanding of community, and therefore of authority and obedience. During this period a number of women Religious for the first time since the Middle Ages received first-class educations to the doctoral level in theology and biblical studies. They were studying with, and studying the works of, the major theologians of the Council, and many of these Religious scholars were also feminists. As they have looked at the foundational materials of Christianity and its his-torical and theological development over the past 2000 years, they have been able to undergird, biblically and theologically, the Council-inspired movement away from monarchical eccle-siology with its military and familial overlay toward an under-standing of Church as a community of equal disciples in mission to the world. Although it would take us too far afield to pursue this topic in detail, once again I will point out some directions for further thought and discussion.

a. BIBLICAL RESOURCES

Women scholars working in New Testament began to see the Gospels as consisting of more than Matthew 16:18, the Petrine text upon which the whole top-heavy hierarchical structure of the institutional Church has been constructed.[13] They called attention to Jesus' repudiation of dominative understandings of ecclesial leadership in Matthew 23 where Jesus warns his disciples that his Church is not to be modeled on the hierarchical structures of Jewish or pagan religiopolitical institutions but rooted in the basic equality of sisters and brothers who have only one parent, God, and one teacher, Jesus. They interpreted the footwashing scene in John 13 as Jesus' call to all his disciples, no matter what their station in the Church, to relate to one another in mutual service among friends. These scholars looked at how the early Church is presented in the Acts of the Apostles 4, namely, as a voluntary community united by one heart and one soul which expressed its love in an equality of life and ministry founded on mutual interdependence and an openhearted and openhanded sharing of resources. They studied Paul's presentation of the Church in Romans 12 and 1 Corinthians 12 as a unified body in which no member was solely "in charge" or able to dispense with others.

The Christian community, biblical scholars were discovering, was a community of the gifted, that is, a community of Spirit-empowered equal disciples whose corporate power was available for life and mission. The gifts of all were equally needed and valued. It was not an aristocracy of the rich and powerful appointed by Christ to dominate their inferiors. Feminist biblical scholars moved steadily toward an affirmation that the Jesus Movement was, at its inception, a discipleship of equals, and that this in itself was a prophetic announcement of the coming of the Reign of God. Historically, this original and originating ecclesiology was soon submerged in the patriarchal retrenchment that was in the ascendency by the late second century. But we now recognize and can name the perversions for what they are and reclaim the New Testament basis and legitimation for a new understanding of what it means to be a

Christian community and not just a group of Christians in an essentially *worldly* (i.e., dominative) sociopolitical order.

b. Theological resources

Women theologians have brought new reflection to bear on the mystery of the Trinity which is the ultimate foundation for a society of mutual interdependence in full equality of persons.[14] Moral theologians have reexamined our understanding of conscience, moral agency, and responsibility, which cannot be alienated by oneself or dominated by others, and which therefore makes all human beings fundamentally equal in the impartial love and justice of God.[15] Church historians have exposed the very human roots of political developments in the Church that have nothing to do with the Gospel and everything to do with the machinations of power.[16] Ecclesiologists and sacramental theologians have investigated, and found wanting, the arguments against the full inclusion of women in ministry and the system of sacramental dependence manufactured by a clerical elite to protect its own monopoly of power.[17]

In short, the understanding of obedience within the framework of a monarchical ecclesiology has been undermined by developments from within and from outside the Church. A new understanding of what it might mean to be a community of the Reign of God has been authenticated by the experience of women Religious themselves, and has been increasingly legitimated, even mandated, by solid research in the areas of biblical studies and theology.

What, then, does an understanding of the Religious Congregation as a voluntary society of equal disciples called together by their personal commitment to Jesus in transcendent community mean for a rethinking of the vow of obedience in Religious Life? Perhaps the first thing that must be said is that no secular political model can supply an appropriate ecclesiology. To adopt such models is precisely to render the Church *worldly* in the pejorative sense of unredeemed secularity. The Church is not an Empire, a divine-right monarchy, a constitutional democracy, a republic, a military dictatorship, a totalitarian state, a fascist regime, a laissez-faire capitalist economic power structure, or any other type of purely secular government.

The fact that the institutional Church has tried many of these models, especially the authoritarian ones, and has almost hysterically repudiated others, especially those with egalitarian potential, does not change the fact that Jesus did not come to establish another form of secular government. He came to establish a community of equal disciples whose bond of unity would be their faith in and love for him rising out of the new life in his Spirit that they received from his open side on the cross. This fact gives us the right and the responsibility as Religious to search for and build a type of Christian community that is original and prophetic, not only in the midst of the world of the "principalities and powers," but even in the midst of the institutional Church itself that has in many ways adopted or succumbed to the models of the world.

Religious Life, if is to be true to itself, must be a communitarian lifeform that is fundamentally egalitarian and interdependent rather than hierarchical and individualistic. It is not egalitarian in the political sense of modern one-person-one-vote democracy but in the trinitarian sense of interpersonal mutuality. Power, in such a lifeform, is a resource to be shared within the community and with others through ministry. It is not the possession of some, unavailable to others. Dialogue, the mutuality of authority and obedience exercised in and for freedom, is the mode in which power is exercised in such a community. All in the community speak with authority, that is, with the right to be heard and heeded; and all in the community are called to obey, that is, to respond appropriately to what the Spirit is saying through the community's discourse. By the vow of obedience one assumes one's place as an equal adult at the circular table of community discernment and dialogue and commits oneself to stay at the table, no matter what, as the community works out anew, from day to day, how to be together in community and in ministry.

Congregations who understand themselves as such communities of egalitarian interdependence will continue to evolve structures and procedures, human and revisable, for carrying on their community life and ministry in orderly and effective ways and each of the members will be responsible for implementing these decisions, when convenient and inconvenient, when one's suggestions have prevailed and when they have not. These Congregations will call forth leaders who exercise office authority through pastoral care for the members, articulation of shared vision, service to the common good, and facilitation of shared ministry and to whom the members respond in free obedience whether the leader as a person is congenial or not.

Congregations will make corporate choices about their presence in the Church and the world and commit themselves to living those choices. Members will call themselves and each other to account when that is necessary and put their corporate power into the support of their members and their ministries. And all of this will flow from a constantly cultivated attitude and practice of personal and corporate discernment, the ongoing effort to stay prophetically attuned to the will of God, that is, to God's purposes for the world that God so loved as to give the only Son. All of this is what it means to practice the vow of obedience in community today, to live the politics of the Reign of God in the alternate world constituted by the Profession of the vows.

If Religious can actually live this alternate model of biblically based sociopolitical life as a community of equals right in the midst of a Church enmeshed in hierarchical ideology and a world structured by a diabolical abuse of power by the mighty against the weak, they will be offering a prophetic witness to the real possibility of living the Reign of God in history. This model of Religious Life can give the lie to the contention that individualism, competition, domination, repression, coercion are the only way order can be maintained, the only way the real world can work. It can demonstrate that power is not a zero-sum commodity that gives its possessors the right to control the disempowered but that power is a shared resource that is a participation in God's capacity to create, to do good, and to foster the flourishing of all Creation. By being together as a community of equals in obedience ultimately to God alone, Religious will preach that Jesus, not the Prince of This World or his political or ecclesiastical minions, defined us when he said, "I no longer call you servants, but I have called you friends" and "you are to love one another as I have loved you," unto the laying down of your life (see John 15:13–15).

IV. Living the Politics of the Reign of God: Prophetic Obedience in Ministry

A. The Meaning of Prophecy[18]

Prophecy is one form (not the only one) of the ministry of the Word to which Jesus missioned his itinerant band of disciples, the men and women like Simon Peter and Mary Magdalene, whom he called to leave all things, accompany him continuously in his work of proclaiming the Good News in first-century Palestine, and continue this work even to the ends of the earth after the Resurrection. The life and ministry of this band of disciples, as we have seen, is the biblical model of Religious Life. Ministerial Religious live this prophetic vocation not only in the community of equal disciples sharing both material resources and power, but also in ministry which is intrinsic to their life, as it was to Jesus'. Prophecy as ministry has particular characteristics which distinguish it from other ministries of the Word such as evangelization, teaching, and catechesis, although these other ministries can be the context of prophetic ministry and thus be prophetic themselves.

Prophecy, whose ultimate expression is martyrdom, is not primarily or even essentially about foretelling the future, predicting chronologically subsequent events. It is *bearing witness* to God and God's Reign in the *concrete and particular circumstances* of the cultural and ecclesial setting in which it occurs. The prophet mediates a three-way encounter between God, God's people, and the sociocultural context. Thus prophecy is not the teaching of abstract truths, formation in the faith, application of laws, or interpretation of texts (although it might include one or another of these at times and any of these can be exercised prophetically). It is about the discernment of God's will in complex and ambiguous situations where answers often are not clear-cut but decision and action cannot be deferred. Furthermore, prophecy is often a response to situations of injustice and oppression, especially to what have been called "structures of sin."[19]

The prophet, in other words, is telling the absolute future of God, the Reign of God, into the present, bringing the word of God to bear in the here and now. To do this the prophet must both share the situation and experience of the people to whom he or she is sent, and also cultivate a continuous presence to God that is deeply attentive and courageously faithful to the divine will. However, the prophet neither "channels" God from some superior perspective of divine wisdom unavailable to his or her contemporaries, nor "accommodates" the word of God to the *status quo* in which they and the prophet are enmeshed. Rather the prophet in some sense must both "become" the Word he or she is charged to speak and, at the same time, achieve a certain kind of "marginality" or detachment that enables her or him to discern between the cause of God and the "world" under Satan's influence. This transformation into God and refusal of complicity with the evil world enable the prophet to read "the signs of the times" and have the courage to speak truth to power while offering hope to the oppressed. The prophet, therefore, is always both in solidarity with the people and something of an outsider: critically marginal in relation to the power structures of the culture; and challenging to her or his contemporaries, both oppressors and oppressed. The prophet, like Jesus, is in constant danger from the elites, both religious and secular.

New Testament scholar Marcus Borg describes Jesus' cultivation of these two prophetic characteristics in terms of "mysticism" and "detachment."[20] First, Jesus' prophetic vocation was rooted in and expressive of his *mystical life*, the intense contemplative prayer life that the Gospels present as the root and source of his *experiential knowledge of God*. Jesus not only took part in Jewish vocal prayer and liturgy (e.g., see Luke 4:16; Matt 26:17), he spent long periods—whole nights (Luke 6:12), hours before dawn (Mark 1:35), times of decision making (Luke 6:12–13) and anguish (see Mark 14:32–42), and, at least once, "forty days"—in prayer to God (see Mark 1:13 and pars.). Jesus not only knew about God; he *knew God* intimately. He experienced God as his "Abba" (Mark 14:36), his loving parent, from whom he drew his own identity, and whose project was his own. In John's Gospel Jesus speaks of being "one" with God (John 10:30) whose words he speaks and whose works he does (see John 14:10).

Second, Jesus the prophet, deeply immersed in the life and world of the people of Israel to whom he was sent, also needed to be free, *uncompromised by* the forces and dynamics, the "structures of sin," the influence of the "Evil One," which distorted the world called to be the Reign of God. Contemporary New Testament scholars have made us much more aware of the world in which Jesus lived and how like, in one way, it is to the world in which Christians live today. It was a world structured by closely intertwined economic, political, social, and religious domination systems. A "domination system"[21] is a two-tiered structure in which a few people (the rich, the politically powerful, the religious authorities) oppress the vast majority of the people for the benefit of the oppressors. Those in the oppressor class "bind burdens too heavy to carry, place them on the shoulders of the oppressed, and refuse to lift a finger to help them" as Jesus said of the Jerusalem hierarchy (see Matt 23:4). Because they draw their power from the domination system, they have a vested interest in keeping those structures, the *status quo*, in place.

The prophet, in the language of biblical scholar Walter Wink, is called to name, unmask, and engage these powers in the cause of the liberation of the oppressed. This is the meaning of what has been called taking "the option for the poor."[22] To do so, the prophet needs to be free of, uncompromised by, these systems. Of course, not everyone who has wealth or power is necessarily enslaved by it, but the more one is involved in these systems the more likely one is be implicated in their domination. Jesus, by his choice of celibacy, homelessness, possessionlessness, and nonparticipation in the hierarchical structure of institutional Judaism, was singularly uninvolved in, and thus uncompromised by, the domination structures of his world. He had nothing (except his life) that his opponents could take from him, threaten him with, or pressure him by. He could not be intimidated, silenced, coopted, or forced to defend the indefensible. The only thing anyone could do to Jesus was kill him. Throughout his public life Jesus was fully in solidarity with the marginalized in explicit and vocal opposition to the domination structures of his world. Jesus opted for the poor.

Religious Life is a prophetic vocation, a particular following of Jesus the prophet, because Religious make the same life choices, and for the same purpose, that enabled Jesus to accept and fulfill his prophetic vocation. Contemplation, which fosters experiential knowledge of God, is at the heart of their life, retaining an absolute priority no matter how pressing ministry becomes. And they choose not to have a family, hold political office, participate in business for profit, possess anything as their own, or seek or hold office in the Church as institution. The conditions of prophecy are intimacy with God, whose word they must "become" so as to be able to speak it in season and out, and social, political, economic, and religious marginality, that is, detachment from those dynamics of the world that are most likely to make the prophet deaf to God's word, blind to the signs of the times, and complicit in the *status quo.* Not all Religious achieve the fullness of their prophetic vocation just as not all married people achieve the fullness of faithful and fruitful love. But the lifeform Religious undertake is prophetic by nature and exists to foster and support its members in that calling.

As we have seen, the community life of Religious is itself prophetic, part of the task of criticizing the domination systems of Church and culture and energizing hope for an alternative future. By the choice of possessionlessness and egalitarian sharing of power, Religious construct and live in the "alternate world" that renounces the oppressive dynamics of the kingdom of Satan that have such pervasive influence on the surrounding culture. Walter Wink describes the Reign of God realized on earth as follows:

> ...we can speak of God's reign as a domination-free order characterized by partnership, interdependence, equality of

opportunity, and mutual respect between men and women that cuts across all distinctions between people. This egalitarian realm repudiates violence, domination hierarchies, patriarchy, racism, and authoritarianism: a total system detrimental to full human life.[24]

This is the life Religious try to create and embrace as their own life context and it is prophetic precisely because it proclaims the Good News of the Reign of God already operative in this time and place. The egalitarian community of interdependence and freedom both realizes and bears witness to the domination-free Reign of God.

It is in ministry, however, that Religious, like Jesus himself and his full-time ministerial band of disciples, live most publicly and even dangerously the critical face of prophecy. This is where they encounter head-on the dynamics of the evil world and are challenged to obey God alone even unto death. Ministry is therefore, for Religious, as it was for Jesus and his original disciples, the sphere in which they experience the greatest tension not only with their own secular culture but also with the institutional Church. And, precisely because Religious live in and from the heart of the Church as Body of Christ, as followers of Jesus who lived in and from the heart of Judaism, ministry is the place where confusion, guilt, doubt, despair, and suffering are most likely to challenge and even overwhelm them.

Prophetic witness, as Old Testament scholar Walter Brueggemann has taught us, involves two interrelated moments. First, by public lament the prophets try *to pierce the numbness*, the "royal consciousness," the sense that things have to be the way they are, which oppressive regimes generate to legitimate the domination system. This sense of inevitability, even of divine approval, of the domination system is rooted in an economics of affluence in which all material resources are in the hands of the elite, a politics of oppression in which the small elite control power, and a religion of immanence in which a domesticated god underwrites the *status quo* so that it cannot be contested. Second, the prophets strive to *energize hope* against the helpless despair of the people who succumb to this "royal consciousness" which makes the oppressive *status quo*, no matter how unjust, appear to be "the only game in town."[23]

The prophet laments by confronting situations of oppression and injustice and energizes hope by recalling for the oppressed the resources from their history, from their experience with a liberating God, that assure them that something different *is* possible. The prophet seeds the imagination of the people with new images, teaches them a new language, and evokes new dreams that generate hope for a different world and energy to pursue it. As we will see, this two-pronged prophetic task was Jesus' primary work during his earthly ministry. It became the shape of ministry among his original band of full-time disciples. And it is the primary model of ministerial Religious Life today.

Both state and Church regimes demand submission to their claims to power disguised as a call to "obedience." Both are purveyors of the "royal consciousness" which strives to create the hopeless conviction that the *status quo* is God's will, or at least inevitable and irresistible. Religious, however, are much better at unmasking the dominative agenda of secular power structures than they are at confronting the abuse of power masquerading as authority in the Church. Perhaps no dimension of ministerial Religious Life today has more need of sound biblical foundation, theological clarity, and moral steadfastness than the issue of obedience in ministry.

In looking to Jesus as model and source for their own practice of prophetic obedience, Religious must resist the temptation of "literary docetism": of thinking that Jesus spoke and acted as he did because, being God, he knew all the answers and was following a preestablished script that he knew would end in Resurrection, vindicating him against all his opponents. Jesus in his public life was speaking not *as* God but *for* God as the prophet always does, not in the sense of relaying a divine message available only to the prophet but in the sense of witnessing to the priority of God and God's will in the conflictual situation in which both people and prophet are involved. Especially when he confronted religious authorities who, like those in our day, held legitimate hierarchical office and exercised legitimate religious authority according to divine Law in Israel, Jesus ran the same risks we do: of being wrong, of possibly giving scandal, of punishment. Jesus was just as much in danger when he called the scribes and Pharisees "hypocrites" or Herod a "fox" (more like "skunk" in our language) as we would be if we leveled such a charge at the local bishop or the governor. Jesus is not a divine puppet for a ventriloquist God but a very real flesh and blood prophet sent by God to a very real people including officeholders and peasants.

B. Jesus: Model of Prophetic Obedience in Ministry

Although Jesus was not, historically, a priest or any other kind of religious official and was most reticent about accepting the attribution of king or messiah, he not only accepted the designation of prophet from others but also presented himself as such. By briefly looking at Jesus' prophetic lineage, call, work, and fate we can discern more clearly the model of prophetic ministry to which Religious are called. In Jesus the prophet we see total obedience to God lived freely in the service of God's people, even unto death at the hands of the Empire and the Temple elites colluding in the support of the Satanic domination systems Jesus had been sent to dismantle.

1. Jesus' prophetic lineage

As Moses was the paradigmatic prophet of the Old Testament, so Jesus is of the New Testament where he is pervasively presented, especially in John's Gospel, as the messianic "prophet like Moses" promised in Deuteronomy 18:15–19. But Jesus is also compared, implicitly and explicitly, to Isaiah, Jeremiah, Hosea, Ezekiel, and Jonah among others.

In John 4:19 the Samaritan Woman recognizes Jesus as "a prophet" and in John 9:17, 33 the Man Born Blind proclaims to the Jewish officials that the one who cured him is "a prophet" who is "come from God." After his Resurrection, when Jesus asks the two disciples on the way to Emmaus what they are discussing, they reply "Jesus of Nazareth, who was a prophet mighty in deed and word before God and all the people" (Luke 24:19). We find in these texts testimony to the faith conviction of Jesus' contemporaries but especially of his post-paschal disciples about his identity. While Jesus was not exclusively a prophet, this was his primary identity and role during his public life, and was embodied in his teaching, healing, and exorcising ministries.

Jesus himself, according to the Gospels, claimed to be a prophet, most notably in Luke 4:16–19 when he read the passage from Isaiah 61:1–2 in the synagogue of Nazareth:

> When he came to Nazareth, where he had been brought up, he went to the synagogue on the sabbath day, as was his custom. He stood up to read, and the scroll of the prophet Isaiah was given to him. He unrolled the scroll and found the place where it was written: "The Spirit of the Lord is upon me, because he has anointed me to bring good news to the poor. He has sent me to proclaim release to the captives and recovery of sight to the blind, to let the oppressed go free, to proclaim the year of the Lord's favor."

Jesus claimed that the Old Testament prophet's description of his mission, to bring good news to the poor by word and deed, was being fulfilled in Jesus himself. He responded to the indignation this claim aroused by quoting the proverb that a prophet is not without honor except in his hometown (v. 24) and then he went on to compare himself to Elijah and Elisha (Luke 4:25–27) whose prophetic ministries overflowed the boundaries of Israel.

This prophetic self-identification so fueled the ire of his already-enraged neighbors that they tried to kill him. We need to note that this first attempt on his life[25] occurred at the very outset of his ministry and precisely because of his claim to be sent by God as prophet. Jesus also predicted that he would suffer the fate of the prophet, namely, execution in the Holy City (see Luke 13:33). In short, Jesus was fully aware of his prophetic lineage and identity, his mission and his fate, and he was recognized as a prophet during his lifetime as well as after his Resurrection.

2. Jesus' prophetic call

The great prophets of the Old Testament are presented as called to their special vocation in a dramatic "inaugural vision" (e.g., Isa 6; Ezek 1–3; Jer 1:1–10; Hos 1; Amos 7:14) or revelatory encounter with God in which they were chosen, strengthened for mission, and sent to the people. Although couched in vivid narratives which give the reader the substance but not necessarily the historical details of their vocational experience, the point of these inaugural events is twofold: that the prophet is *not self-appointed nor the inventor of his own message* and the prophet also is *not simply a puppet*, a divine "mouthpiece" parroting a set message from another realm. The prophet is chosen by God for a particular work in a particular historical time and place to deal with particular crises in the life of God's people. But the prophet must, despite fear or natural inability, freely choose to accept the divine mission.

Jesus' prophetic ministry began with the revelatory experience of his baptism when the Spirit descended upon him, he heard God's voice claiming him as "beloved Son," and he was led/driven immediately into the desert to face Satan in a proleptic struggle that foreshadowed his life work that would end only with his death (Matt 3:13—4:11 and pars.). In the triple temptation, Jesus was enticed to enlist among the oppressor elite, to commit himself to the domination program by which the human race is held captive to the evil world which Satan rules. Three times Jesus chose God's project of liberation and justice in solidarity with the poor.

But, as Luke 4:14 tells us, Satan was not definitively banished from Jesus' life in this programmatic encounter. The prophet does not, by the initial acceptance of vocation, become immune from temptation or defeat. The struggle is joined from the start, but its outcome is not decided. The prophet's whole life will be consumed in the struggle to subvert the demonic dynamics operative in the situation, structured by sin, to which she or he is missioned, and to foster the coming of the Reign of God.

3. Jesus' prophetic work

Between his prophetic calling at the Jordan and his prophetic death in Jerusalem, Jesus carried on a ministry of speaking and acting in the classic prophetic mode. His method of teaching, unlike that of the scribes (see Mark 1:22) with its appeal to and reliance on text and tradition, was typically prophetic, that is, original rather than derivative, and uniquely authoritative, based on the personal integrity of the prophet speaking out of his intense experience of God. He acted out by mighty deeds reminiscent of the Old Testament prophets the meaning of the Reign of God. His speaking and acting included both the negative, critical, lament dimension of prophecy that questioned the domination systems of the kingdom of Satan, and the positive, hopeful, energizing dimension that revealed the alternative Reign of God, assuring his hearers that it was real, possible, and meant for them not in some remote afterlife but in the here and now. We cannot examine the whole of Jesus' public ministry but I want to highlight certain features of it which can illuminate the struggles of Religious today, not only with the injustice and oppression of secular society but especially with the exercise of power in the Church.

Jesus' parables and aphorisms, which we find especially in the Synoptic Gospels, are the classically prophetic forms of teaching. Short, pithy sayings (aphorisms) such as his lament over Jerusalem (see Luke 13:33 and par.) and his Woes against the hypocritical religious officials (see Matt 23:13–29 and par.), as well as the Beatitudes addressed to the victims of the domination systems (see Matt 5:3–11) were elaborated in wonderful symbolic stories (parables) that often asked his hearers to decide what they would do about the conundrums the stories posed. Is it just for the eleventh-hour workers to receive the same pay as those who had worked all day? Was the father of the prodigal a God-image or just a weak-willed enabler? Jesus the prophet was calling his hearers to moral autonomy, challenging them to move beyond the royal consciousness, the authoritative version of reality promoted by those in power, to a revolutionary view of reality seen through the eyes of a liberating God.

These stories and sayings were often not about religious realities but about daily political, economic, and social affairs such
as farming and taxes, childbirth and parenting, baking and
dinner parties, prostitution and money lending. They were
exposures of wicked kings and dishonest landowners and abusive patriarchs. When they did touch explicitly on religion they
were not exhortations to more exact liturgical practice, to
humble submission to the authorities who were God's representatives, or to financial support of the Temple. They were
characteristically directed against the hypocrisy of religious
officials who talked a pious game but did not practice what they
preached (see Matt 23:3), and against the ritualistic practices
used to cover over hard-hearted moralism imposed on people
whose grinding daily reality could not "measure up" to elitist
demands (see Luke 13:9–14).

In one rare "theological" discussion of Jesus with his disciples Jesus simply swept aside the whole legal code of ritual
purity surrounding food (see Mark 7:14–23). He did not claim
divine revelation on this subject. He had, apparently, come to
the conclusion on his own—the Law to the contrary notwithstanding—that nothing we eat nor the way we eat it can corrupt
the human spirit. What we take into ourselves from outside,
with hands washed or unwashed, from clean or unclean vessels
cannot defile us. It is we who defile ourselves and all we touch
by the impurity of our intentions and desires and the violence
of our behavior.

For religious people, who tend to think that the validity of
ecclesiastical regulations, especially if presented as law, is self-
evident since "God's representatives formulate them" this is a
stunning example of Jesus' own moral autonomy. Jesus, a
deeply religious Jew who knew and observed the Law and even
taught it, sometimes made void manmade religious traditions
in order to witness to God's real concerns. It was the counter-
point to his accusation against the authorities that they made
void the law of God for the sake of their traditions (see Mark
7:8–13). Jesus' moral compass was so truly calibrated, so fixed
on God alone, that he apparently felt confident to declare
humanly defined "evil" good and "good" evil when he per-

ceived that truth was being sacrificed to the agenda of power, that divine authority was being invoked to buttress human oppression. He was utterly free of the royal consciousness which succumbs helplessly to the "way things are," the conviction that those in authority must "be right," to the moral weakness in the face of power that masquerades as "obedience."

Jesus' stories offered his hearers alternative visions of hope for the final subversion of the domination systems, whether political or economic, social or religious. He played off the "hard master" who reaped where he did not sow (Matt 25:14–30) with the generous vineyard owner who paid a full day's wage to the eleventh-hour workers (Matt 20:1–16). He subverted the social vengeance and the economic privilege of primogeniture of the elder son with the picture of the father whose womb-like compassion for his once-lost younger son cast patriarchal honor to the winds and poured out his wealth in wanton prodigality at his son's return (Luke 15:11–32). He extolled equally the joy of the shepherd who found the erring sheep and that of the householder who found her lost coin suggesting both that the joy of the finding God is not conditioned by how the found got lost and that the God who seeks is neither male nor female but simply indefatigable divine love (Luke 15:7–10). Jesus offered visions of the fruitfulness of a tiny mustard seed (see Luke 13:19), the secret fertility of a crop growing unaided in the night (Mark 4:26–28), the amazing power of a flicker of faith that moves a mountain (Matt 17:20) or uproots a tree (Luke 17:6), and the silent action of the leaven in a mass of dough (Matt 13:33) to reassure his hearers that what seems little, indeed nothing in the hands of our weakness, is all that is needed in the powerful hands of God. He even challenged the most self-evident assumptions of the social domination system by making Samaritans (see Luke 10:30–37; 17:12–19; John 4:1–42) and Canaanites (see Matt 15:22–28) and Romans (see Matt 8:5–13) heroes in his stories.

In short, Jesus was "parabling" into the imaginations of the oppressed God's future into which they were called. He lamented, critiqued, excoriated, condemned the seemingly all-powerful oppressive political domination by the Roman

Empire, the unjust economic system of crushing debt and poverty that divided Palestinian society into the tiny class of Jewish "haves" and the masses of Jewish "have-nots," the patriarchal social system based on the powerless suffering of women, children, and slaves, the hypocritical religious system that claimed divine sanction for the hierarchy's domination of the "ignorant people of the land" who "do not know the Law" (see John 7:49). But at the same time he was also drawing a glowing imaginative picture of an all-inclusive Reign of God. There the last would be first (Matt 19:30), the hungry filled (Luke 1:53–54), the sorrowing consoled (Matt 5:4), the rejected welcomed to inclusive table fellowship.

But it was not only by his powerful speech but also by his mighty deeds and his daily prophetic practice that Jesus encouraged the oppressed to hope for a liberation in their time like that of the Exodus. Some of his symbolic prophetic actions were one-time master strokes, such as the anti-Temple action which John makes an inaugural act at the very beginning of Jesus' public life (see John 2:13–22) and the Synoptics make the final affront to the Temple authorities that led to his arrest (e.g., Mark 11:15–18). This public anti-temple symbolic action was twinned with a public anti-imperial action. Jesus, on the Sunday before his death, rode meekly on a donkey into the Holy City (see Matt 21:1–11), fulfilling a messianic prophecy that salvation would come through a humble pastoral emissary of God (cf. Zech 9:9), not through the "horses and chariots" of Rome's legate, Pilate, who entered the city at the same time amid royal pomp and splendor.

Others of Jesus' prophetic acts were repeated with variations many times over. He showed his followers what salvation meant as he exorcised the demon-possessed (see Matt 12:25–27), opened the eyes of the blind and the ears of the deaf and loosed mute tongues (see Matt 15:30–31; Luke 7:22), restored cleansed lepers to community life (Mark 1:40–41), fed the hungry (Mark 6:35–44 and pars.), forgave the sins of those who feared they were beyond the pale of God's mercy (Luke 7:36–50), blessed children (Matt 19:13–15), and even raised the dead (Luke 7:11–15). By all these actions and the words that accompanied them, he proclaimed Good News to the poor, that God was with them in Jesus and that the Reign of God was not "pie in the sky bye and bye" but God's *shalom*, the fullness of well-being, emerging in their very midst. They had only to believe that the Kingdom of God was among them and, like children, to accept what was being freely offered.

Perhaps the most striking of Jesus' prophetic signs was the simplest and the most challenging to the religious domination system of his time: his ever-open table fellowship. The quintessential, repeated criticism of Jesus was that he "welcomed sinners and ate with them" (Luke 15:2). To share table fellowship with another was to establish community with that person. The whole religious domination system of second Temple Judaism was based on the purity laws, the structures of inclusion/exclusion that undergirded the socioreligious hierarchies. By subverting the boundaries, indeed permanently abolishing them, Jesus was establishing a single community in which there was to be no up and down, no in and out, no clean and unclean, no center and periphery, no male and female, no free and slave, no rich and poor, no pious and sinner, no Jew and Gentile, no well and sick, even no alive and dead—no divisions of any kind except the self-segregation of those who chose to wall themselves in when they could no longer wall others out. For Jesus all the provisions of the Law and teaching of the prophets were summed up in "Love the Lord your God with your whole being and your neighbor as yourself" (see Matt 22:33–41; Mark 12:28–34). The neighbor was now every human being simply because they were human and therefore children of God (see Luke 10:36–37).

In effect, Jesus was proposing the reordering of society politically, economically, socially, religiously. The Sanhedrin was perfectly correct when it judged that if Jesus were not stopped it would be the end of the nation, or more exactly the end of "world," the social and religious reality construction in which the powerful and the elite, religious and secular, had their secure places (see John 11:48). Jesus the prophet was subverting the domination systems and evoking an alternate world, the Reign of God. He was not promising it for some vague time and place after a lifetime of powerlessness, poverty, suffering, and religious oppression. He was calling it into existence right in the midst of Satan's world.

One narrative in the Gospel tradition epitomizes Jesus' prophetic work of universal inclusiveness based on a new kind of justice rooted not in vengeance but in compassion. Because it is specifically about the confrontation of Jesus with the religious institution of his time, the Judaism to which he belonged, whose tradition he honored and obeyed, whose leaders he respected and instructed others to respect, and which he never attempted to invalidate or overturn, it is especially illuminating for those involved in prophetic ministry in the contemporary Church. This narrative of the "Woman Taken in Adultery" is an "orphan text" that is found now in John's Gospel (John 7:53— 8:11) that has appeared in different places in the New Testament in the course of the transmission of the canonical text.[26] Its checkered textual career may testify to the fact that it was too shocking to early Church officials to be easily admitted as Scripture and too cherished by believers to be successfully suppressed. In it we see perhaps the starkest confrontation of Jesus as prophet with the religious authorities.

The story begins with the religious officials dragging before Jesus a woman taken in the very act of adultery. She is, without doubt, guilty of breaking one of the most serious commandments of the Law. Adultery was a capital offense (see Deut 22:23–24) and the scribes and Pharisees, the religious elite, test Jesus by asking him what he says about the stoning prescribed by the Law of Moses as penalty for this sin. "Are you for it or against it?"

If Jesus agrees to her execution he aligns himself with the elite of the religious establishment; he agrees that God is indeed a just judge who is unrelenting toward sinners, not the "spineless" parent of the prodigal that Jesus, according to Luke, had been preaching! If he opposes her execution, he opposes the Law of Moses, thereby proving that he does not come from God or speak for God, that is, that he is not a true prophet. At the very least, if he agrees that she deserves to be stoned but refuses to participate in it (since Rome apparently denied to the Jews the power of capital punishment), he is showing that his real allegiance is to the Empire rather than to Judaism or God. The three-way trap is well set with the woman as bait.

Jesus, however, does not take the bait. He does not enter into an argument about the nature of God or sexual morality, about the validity of the Law or about the authority of the hierarchy to enforce it, or even about the reach of Roman jurisdiction. He simply turns the focus from the admittedly guilty sinner to the religious officials themselves. Rather than accepting their framing of the case as religious authority righteously executing the Law, he reframes it as abusive hierarchical power hypocritically vindicating itself by scapegoating the helpless. He does not say adultery is all right or that the woman is innocent. He does not even ask if she is repentant. He says in effect, "The facts of the case may be exactly as you say. The problem with your adjudication of it (and implicitly of other cases of the condemnation of sinners by human authority) is, who is qualified to judge and to apply the penalty? Is there one among you (or in the whole human race?) who is sinless and is therefore in a position to judge and punish a sinner?"

They all depart, validating Jesus' stunning prophetic challenge to the religious domination system, and leaving him and the woman face to face. Jesus, however, does not claim for himself the dominative power he has denied to the authorities. The right question is not who can condemn, but who can forgive: namely God, to whose true character Jesus the prophet witnesses and whose forgiveness, therefore, he can mediate. Jesus seems to be saying that in God's dispensation condemnation itself stands condemned. It has no place in the Reign of God because it just shores up the system of violent retaliation, every act of which perpetuates the futile system. God is the one whose justice is manifested in endless compassion that makes what is wrong, the human predicament, right again. God makes the sun shine and the rain fall on the just and the unjust, and welcomes sinners home without conditions. His forgiveness precedes conversion and thereby makes it possible. He asks only that those whose infinite debts are freely forgiven forgive those whose debts against them (see Matt 18:21–35).

Jesus' prophetic act, in short, seems to say something about God that is inconceivable in a framework of law, sin, judgment, retribution, punishment—in the human program of how to run a tight moral ship in a religious institution. He seems to be suggesting in relation to the religious order, as he did with the parable of the Prodigal Son in relation to the patriarchal social order, and that of the servant whose entire debt was forgiven because he could not pay it in relation to the oppressive economic order, that God is operating in a framework that is radically different from ours. In God's justice, which is compassion, there is no place for wrath, coercive power, vindictiveness, or violence. Indeed, he seems to be saying that our image of God acted out in our version of "justice" says much about *us* but virtually nothing true about *God.*

Jesus leaves his interlocutors to decide for themselves which regime they want to live in and promote: the religious, economic, social, political domination systems in which they can rely on the rules to keep those who keep the rules, or the Reign of God in which there seem to be no rules except the Law of Love over which we have no control. Why, we have to wonder, would anyone choose the former? But the catch is that if one opts for compassion, inclusion, and forgiveness for oneself, one cannot deny them to one's fellow human beings, and that demands a conversion so radical that risking condemnation for the security of being empowered to condemn can seem the safer choice.

4. Jesus' prophetic fate and destiny

Books have been written about why Jesus was executed. Until New Testament scholars began to study intensively the social world of Jesus, that is, the political-economic-social-religious context of Palestine in the early first century, it was easy enough to believe that "the evil Jews" were so resistant to Jesus' spiritual message of God's love that they killed him out of jealousy. Anti-Jewish and otherworldly biblical interpretation has long maintained that Jesus was not involved in politics or economics. He was simply trying to bring about a spiritual conversion from sin, especially from the religious hypocrisy practiced by the scribes and Pharisees who preferred their "Law" to God's love.

This, of course, is a very superficial view of Jesus' mission and ministry, a reading of a myopic and ahistorical Christian version of religion, to say nothing of Christian anti-Judaism, back into Jesus' first-century world. Religion in first-century Palestine was not separate from the social, political, and economic dimensions of society. Religion was "embedded" in the culture that included all of these aspects in intimate interaction. The segregation of economics, politics, religion, and more, into distinct and even separate compartments was a much later sociological development.[27]

Furthermore, "the Jews" were not reducible to "the scribes and Pharisees," and the scribes were not all hard-hearted legalists (see, e.g., Mark 12:28–34 on the wise scribe), nor all the Pharisees hypocrites (see, e.g., John 7:50–53 on Nicodemus). The ordinary peasants, the vast majority of the Jews in Palestine in Jesus' time, were the victims of their own rapacious Jewish overlords and self-serving religious leaders who, as puppets of the Roman Empire, were charged with keeping the lower class in political submission to Rome. There was no "middle class" in our sense of the term. The domination system into which Jesus was born included a miniscule group of wealthy, powerful, socially prominent, and religiously influential Jewish males in collusion with the politically supreme Roman Empire reigning over the vast majority of the people who were basically powerless against these oppressors. Jesus quickly emerged as a leader of a short-lived mass movement among the peasants. There were other movements and groups operative in Palestine at the same time; some collaborators, some violent insurrectionists. Jesus was neither. He was what Borg calls a "religious revolutionary."

Jesus was executed because he was "stirring up the people" (see Luke 23:5) as the Jewish leaders claimed when they demanded that Pilate crucify him. This was the same charge, in other terms, that Caiaphas and the Sanhedrin brought against him when they said that unless Jesus was stopped, the people (the "whole world") would follow him *en masse*, which would bring down the ire of the Empire on Jerusalem and the

Romans would take away "our place and our nation," that is, the Temple and Jewish "autonomy" (see John 11:47–50 with 18:14). In other words, Jesus was executed by the collusion of the Roman occupying regime with the Jewish Temple hierarchy, both of which owed their position to the Roman Emperor.

Jesus was carrying out the prophetic task of challenging the domination system—the politics of oppression in liaison with the economics of material exploitation and religious tyranny—rooted in the socially violent ground of pervasive patriarchal inequality. He was leading its victims to claim their true identity as God's People and to throw off the yoke of oppression. He was a new Moses challenging a new Pharaoh and if he were successful the result would surely be the end of the *status quo* within which the ruling elites held their dominant positions.

As Palestine teetered on the brink of social upheaval and chaos, which would surely have been crushed by Pilate's forces and resulted in the destruction of the Temple and the definitive suspension of even minimal Jewish self-rule—exactly what did happen a few decades later in 70 CE when Jerusalem was leveled—Jesus became the designated scapegoat whose murder would bring about a return of order and civic calm.[28]

Jesus was a "religious revolutionary" because the resources for his critique of the society of his day and the content of the alternate world he was proposing was the experience of Israel as the People of God. Jesus believed that God would rescue God's people. He was drawing on the liberating potential of the Hebrew Scriptures and his own profound religious experience of the One he called "Abba," and was obviously convinced that only fidelity to the God of the Exodus and the Covenant could free his people for life in the Reign of God.

In that respect, Jesus is properly distinguished from the violent political movements for liberation seething around him as well as the collusion of the religious authorities with the Empire. He was also in a very different place from the hopeless victims of the *status quo* who had given up any thought of resistance or hope for change. Jesus' resistance was deeply religious, nonviolent, and God-centered in its sources, resources, strategies, and tactics. But it was neither a counsel of submission to the powers of Temple or Empire nor a promise of otherworldly salvation in exchange for patient endurance of unending injustice in this world.[29]

The program of Religious in ministry in contemporary society is very analogous to that of Jesus in his time. So it is sobering to note that Jesus' *fate*, which he also predicted for the disciples who would take up his mission as prophetic ministers (see John 16:2), was execution at the hands of the political empire in complicity with the religious hierarchy working to stabilize and protect the *status quo*. Jesus' true destiny, however, was to take up his risen presence among his disciples in order to continue his struggle for the liberation of humanity; the struggle that Religious down through the centuries have joined.

But the full emergence of ministerial Religious Life in the aftermath of Vatican II casts that participation in Jesus' project in a new light. I am suggesting that the prophetic identity of ministerial Religious today, while not new in an absolute sense, is new in that women Religious are "in and for the world" in a way they have not been able to be before. This has precipitated tensions with the institutional Church, which have rarely been completely lacking but also have rarely been as pronounced or explicit as they are today.

C. The Prophetic Ministry of Religious and the Vow of Obedience

On the eve of his Passion Jesus forewarned his inner circle of disciples, "They [the religious authorities] will put you out of the synagogues. Indeed, an hour is coming when those who kill you will think that by doing so they are offering worship to God" (John 16:2). The "those" in the text are "everyone" or "whoever" but in the context, the reference is to the religious authorities who, that very night, would arrest Jesus whom they would hand over to the political authorities who had the power to execute him. In other words, the enemies of the prophets come from both inside and outside the religious establishment because the domination systems which are the object of prophetic challenge are mutually sustaining.

Very shortly after the Resurrection Jesus' first disciples experienced exactly what he had predicted:

> Now many signs and wonders were done among the people through the apostles.... Then the high priest took action; he and all who were with him [that is, the sect of the Sadducees], being filled with jealousy, arrested the apostles and put them in the public prison. But during the night an angel of the Lord opened the prison doors, brought them out.... [T]hey entered the temple at daybreak and went on with their teaching. Then someone arrived and announced, "Look, the men whom you put in prison are standing in the temple and teaching the people!".... The high priest questioned them, saying, "We gave you strict orders not to teach in this name, yet here you have filled Jerusalem with your teaching and you are determined to bring this man's blood on us." But Peter and the apostles answered, "We must obey God rather than any human authority." (Acts 5:12–29)

This episode gives the pattern of prophetic ministry: proclamation by word and deed of the Good News of liberation; opposition by authorities (religious or secular or both) who sense that this message is subversive of the domination systems of which they are both the protagonists and the beneficiaries; use of force to stop the prophetic work; the choice by the prophets to "obey God rather than [the human authorities]" who often claim to speak for God.

The outcome is swift:

> When they had called in the apostles, they had them flogged. Then they ordered them not to speak in the name of Jesus, and let them go. As they left the council, they rejoiced that they were considered worthy to suffer dishonor for the sake of the name. And every day in the temple and at home they did not cease to teach and proclaim Jesus as the Messiah. (Acts 5:40–42)

The persecution continues. But the disciples are undeterred as they follow in the footsteps of Jesus, the executed prophet. Their definition of obedience is not submission to coercive power presenting itself as divinely sanctioned authority, even when it is exercised by the religious hierarchy, but listening to God, discerning God's will, and doing it courageously regardless of the consequences.

This pattern provides the context for our consideration in the rest of this chapter of what it means for Religious today to live prophetically the politics of the Reign of God in ministry to Church and world. Although there are myriad aspects of this topic that require consideration, I will concentrate on two: discerning ministry in contemporary Religious Life and exercising prophetic ministry in the contemporary ecclesiastical context.

As we have seen, some people fear that obedience has ceased to be a factor in the ministerial life of Religious. Religious today, it is lamented, find their own "job," inform their superiors, and live according to their own choices. This view is seriously erroneous. Because Religious do not practice obedience the way it was practiced in 1950 does not mean that they are simply "doing their own thing" any more than the fact that they are now paid a salary for what they do means that they are financially independent employees or that they are "charging" for ministry.

As we discussed in part 2 regarding its economic aspects, ministry is not "a job." It is not "baptized" gainful employment. By the same token ministry is not an independent career, an exercise in individualism. Rather, ministry is the free proclaiming, by word and work, of the good news of the Reign of God. How and where the individual Religious proclaims that word is a response in obedience to God's will discerned within the Congregation, according to its charism, and validated by the missioning of the Religious by the Congregation's leadership.

1. The change in the understanding of obedience in ministry

The underlying theological assumptions and actual practices of obedience in ministry during the standardization period of modern Religious Life embodied the monarchical and military models of Religious community discussed in chapter 6. Even if the superior's assignment of a Religious was a massive error in judgment or, God forbid, a deliberate exercise of oppression, the Religious "never erred in obeying" because s/he was doing God's will which could only work for her or his ultimate sanctification. In other words, especially in regard to the apostolate, the Religious Congregation was a sacralized domination system.

This system was in the service of the Church Militant, whose mission was to protect in the faith its own members and convert those outside its pale. Hence, the military precision with which Religious were deployed in function of these objectives made sense. Unfortunately, in preconciliar Religious Life, this military organization often enough generated pervasive discouragement and a sense of perpetual failure in those who could never achieve the desired level of discipline and performance.

As we have seen, this system changed radically in the decades following the Council. Whatever negative effects, financial and communitarian, this change of ministerial context caused, the precipitous end of the monarchical-military model of ministry also prompted some major positive developments in theology that have brought about a virtually complete reconceptualization of the ministerial dimension of Religious Life. Intrinsic to this rethinking of ministry has been a new understanding of the role and practice of obedience in relation to ministry. This development, in my opinion, is not a reluctant accommodation to unfortunate negative influences but a quantum leap forward in the theology and living of Religious Life and especially the vow of obedience. In other words, precipitating factors are not necessarily primary causes. Sometimes they are conditions of possibility of a newness that would not occur if the inertia of "what we have always done" were not disturbed by an outside challenge that has to be met.

The most important developments concerning ministry in the 1960s to 1980s were ecclesiological and missiological. As Religious embraced the two-fold understanding of the Church as the pilgrim People of God in history and as the Body of Christ called to transform the world into the Reign of God here and now, they quickly began to reconceptualize their community not as an absolute divine right monarchy fielding an army of conquest against an evil world but as a discipleship of equals called to freely proclaim the Good News to the whole world which God so loved as to give the only Son (see John 3:16–17). This was not only revolutionary and radical for the communities but is also at the root of the tensions and even conflicts between Religious Congregations and the Vatican, which we will discuss in the next section.

In a discipleship of equals modeled on the community Jesus founded no one is ontologically superior to anyone else. Those who hold office are elected by the community, and not appointed from above. Their authority is not the capacity to exercise coercive power over their sisters or brothers. Rather, they are called to serve the community by facilitating its self-government and ongoing discernment of God's will, mediating conflicts, articulating consensus, and coordinating the execution of its Gospel-inspired choices. In other words, authority and obedience, as we discussed above, have become correlative terms describing the mutual relationships of all the members of the community among themselves.

Congregations revised their Constitutions to reflect this renewed theology of authority and obedience in a community of equal disciples. They developed collegial structures of team leadership, ways to facilitate total participation in decision making and governance including representative councils. They initiated processes for nonviolent conflict resolution, for consultation with members on all that affected them, for discernment and consensus building in preference to majority rule. They rejected unilateral command-submit dynamics, the use of secrecy and withholding of information as control mechanisms, coercion, and threat as instruments of domination. Obedience came to be understood as whole-hearted cooperation in the achieving of the common good rather than blind submission of some to the absolute will of others.

Renewing Religious Congregations have moved forward steadily and fairly swiftly to implement theological developments and the actual revision of structures and procedures that flowed from them. This theological reenvisioning of community as a discipleship of equals has led to a completely different understanding of how ministry is discerned in the Religious community. It no longer begins with a set of institutional positions to be filled by a set of available workers but with a prophetic inquiry into the real needs of the Church and world in the here and now. Discernment is not the work of the solitary monarch deploying interchangeable objects to fill the institutional positions but of all those who will be involved in the ministry, both leaders and members. In the dialogical process of discernment all have voice (authority) and all are called to open attentiveness (discernment) to the "signs of the times" and the resources available for response, and to shared active responsibility for the ultimate decisions and their implementation (obedience).

The result of such discernment is often the choice of individualized ministries in which one Religious may be the animator of a project involving lay partners. It can give rise to inter-Congregational ministries, sharing in interdenominational or interreligious projects, or engagements outside official Church boundaries. Thus responsibility and accountability to Congregational leaders might be very different from the "chain of command" processes of earlier times. In other words, many of the "new" features of the way that Religious choose and carry out ministry today are not manifestations of the disappearance of obedience, the rejection of accountability, or individualistic independence in relation to community. They are expressions of the transformation of the dynamics of relationship in communities. Authority and obedience, the dynamics of the vow Religious profess, continue to structure their ministerial involvement as it does their community life. But the theological basis of the understanding and practice of obedience is the ecclesiology of the People of God as a discipleship of equals in mission rather than of the Church as a divine right monarchy. And this has made all the difference.

2. Authority and obedience in ministerial discernment

The contemporary process of ministerial discernment and commitment involves the interaction of three factors: the discernment of the needs of the Church and the world; the resources and needs of the Congregation itself which missions its members; the ministerial potential and spiritual needs of the individual Religious who will minister in the name of the Congregation. This interaction, rather than unilateral assignment by superiors and submission by subjects in function of institutional needs, constitutes the dynamic of authority and obedience in community and ministry today.

The *needs of the Church and world today* may not be what they were in the standardization period. Furthermore, as I argued in part 2, ministry is not simply a "baptized" paying job. Nor is it merely "good work" that keeps the Religious usefully occupied between periods of monastic practice. Proclaiming the Reign of God is a matter of utmost urgency. Both Church and world are in desperate need of prophetic witness that challenges the *status quo* of domination systems and energizes hope for the inbreaking of God's Reign of liberation and *shalom*. The limited personnel as well as material resources available for this crucial work make careful discernment essential so that the very best use can be made of all available resources.

It is no longer self-evident, as it once seemed to be, that this or that institution needs to be staffed virtually exclusively by Religious or that wherever ecclesiastical authorities ask a Congregation to do is "God's will" for it. Discerning the Congregation's priorities in ministry is the work of the whole Congregation gathered in Chapter or operating through other processes. Several features of the present situation, which might not have been taken into account during the standardization period, need to be recognized today.

First, institutional Church ministries, especially ministries to Catholics (who are much better educated today than they were in the nineteenth century and have much wider access to resources for their own ongoing formation in their faith) do not necessarily have the priority for Religious in ministry that they do for the ordained whose pastoral office is primarily directed to the Catholic community itself. Religious minister from the heart of the Church, as Jesus did from the heart of Judaism. But as Israel was called to be a "light to the nations" (Isa 42:5–9) so the Church is sent "into all the world [to] proclaim the good news to the whole creation" (Mark 16:15). Now that many lay Catholics are aware of their baptismal vocation to ministry and are being formed to offer many of the services that Religious once provided, especially in parishes and other Catholic institutions, Religious need to look anew at the visions of their founders in relation to the needs of the world.

Founders of Religious Congregations were moved to respond to the often-inarticulate needs of those overlooked or rejected by society and often by the Church itself. The call today as in the past is to go where others cannot or will not go: to the most abandoned souls, to the unevangelized, the marginalized, the excluded, the poor and oppressed, those who are suffering physically, emotionally, and spiritually. Religious do not begin by asking what religion (if any) people profess but rather what they need. Conversion is not the price of their ministry, which Jesus said, must have no price, financial or otherwise. As Religious have freely received, so must they freely give (see Matt 10:7–8).

Responding to such needs will raise all the economic issues we discussed in the chapters on poverty in part 2. But unless Religious see themselves as **called by preference**, individually and corporately, **to minister to the underserved,** they might not recognize the challenge to do the creative financial planning necessary to make those ministries possible. Especially in first world countries it seems imperative for the Religious to ask, when discerning her ministry, whether she is starting her individual or corporate discernment process with her own needs for the personal support of family or friends, for economic security, for proximity to cultural resources, for racially or ethnically comfortable contexts, which might draw her to environments where there is already a concentration of religious and spiritual resources, or starting with the desperate needs of our time which may take her into unfamiliar or uncongenial situations.

Second, a priority of prophetic ministry, indeed one face of its primary task, is naming, unmasking, and engaging "the principalities and powers," **subverting the domination systems**—political, economic, social, religious—which express and promote the kingdom of Satan. Like Jesus, Religious must

492 • BUYING THE FIELD

pierce the numbness; challenge the "royal consciousness" that breeds resigned despair in the victims of secular and religious oppression. They must energize hope by recalling God's liberating intention and helping people believe that change is possible so that they are willing to work for it.

In the concrete, this prophetic ministry can put Religious in real danger. It may be physical danger as they oppose repressive economic, political, and military regimes in missionary settings, as did Dorothy Stang, SNDdeN, in Brazil, or the Maryknoll women in El Salvador, or the Cistercian monks in Algeria. It could bring ecclesiastical persecution such as that visited on theologians like Roger Haight, SJ, Elizabeth Johnson, CSJ, and Ivone Gebara, OSA, or activists like Roy Bourgeois, MM, or those like Joan Chittister, OSB, or Theresa Kane, RSM, who have spoken out in the Church in defense of gay people, women called to ordained ministry, married priests, the divorced and remarried, or other victims of ecclesiastical repression.

Rather than regarding such disapproval and persecution as something to be ashamed of, something that should not and would not happen if Religious were "being obedient," much less allowing it to deter them from prophetic witness, Religious should be in the forefront of those who speak truth to power in society and Church. With the same courage that strengthened Jesus in his confrontations with the oppressive Temple hierarchy, with Pilate and Herod enforcing Roman domination, with the economic overlords who were exploiting their own people for material gain, Religious must stand in solidarity with the people to whom they are sent regardless of the consequences.

Third, the **individualization of Religious ministries** may be an important positive development in our understanding and embrace of prophetic ministry. This individualization is not simply a response to the fact that Religious are too few in numbers to continue collective ministries in large Catholic institutions. Jesus worked "alone" in the sense of carrying on a ministry outside the collective structures of the Jewish hierarchy or contemporary monastic groups such as that of Qumran. He formed around himself a group of committed followers whom he apprenticed in prayer and virtue, imbued with a vision of the Reign of God, sent out on mission and "debriefed" on their return in order to empower them further. Placing one Religious at the center of a ministerial project involving lay colleagues, paid or volunteer, *ad hoc* or more permanent, might be a better use of personnel today than committing a group of Religious to a single project such as a school or hospital.

In short, discerning ministry, individually or corporately, should start with the question of what is needed, not where we would like to be, whom we would like to be with, or what we have traditionally done. The urgency that drove Jesus from town to town, the burning zeal that moved founders of ministerial Congregations across oceans and continents, must be the "love of Christ [that] urges us" (see 2 Cor 5:14) today.

The second factor that must come into play in ministerial discernment is *the Congregation itself.* Religious may minister individually, but they do so as integral participants in their Congregations, which carry into the world a particular charism. Although defining "charism" is not easy and beyond our purposes here, Religious know by participation that there is a "deep story," a corporate "personality," a "founding vision," a shared "spirit," something that functions as a touchstone of identity and a criterion of fidelity in which all members participate and which links the generations of the Congregation throughout time.

Congregations no longer tend to identify their charism with a particular work such as "educating youth" or "ransoming slaves." Today we realize that these works were expressions of the founder's insight into a particular way the Gospel responds to concrete needs: preaching, teaching, presence, healing, empowerment, liberation, and so on. Contemporary members are carrying into the present ministries of their Congregations that originating graced insight of their founders, which may be embodied in ministries that the founder could not have envisioned.

So, questions that must be raised as an individual member discerns his or her ministry are "How does this ministry embody the charism of the Congregation?" and "How does this ministry relate to other ministries in the Congregation?" A member may not be actually physically or geographically ministering with any other members of the Congregation, but any one member should be able to say of his or her ministry, "Where I am, the Congregation is." The corporate[30] impact of the Congregation's ministry is a function of all the ministries in which its members are engaged. No member should be a "lone ranger" who is simply "doing her or his own thing." It is a major mistake to equate individualized ministries of members who are deeply involved in the Congregation's mission with the estrangement from the community of "fringe" people who have actually "left without dispensation."

This second dimension of discernment also includes **the needs of the Congregation itself**, in terms of both financial resources and personnel. Keeping in mind all that was said in the discussion of the vow of poverty, especially that ministry is not "gainful employment" (whether or not the minister receives remuneration) and that the ability of those to whom we minister to pay for our services must not be a determining criterion of ministry, it remains the case that the economic well-being of the Congregation is the responsibility of every member. How a ministry will be supported financially, and what effect its support will have on other ministries, are necessary and important issues in discernment for which there is no single formula.

Furthermore, every Congregation has intra-Congregational ministries that require personnel. Elected leadership, central financial services, health care of elderly and infirm members, administration of Congregational properties, formation, and vocation work may make a legitimate demand on an individual member who has the gifts necessary for the ministry in question but might be powerfully attracted elsewhere. No member should consider her or himself exempt from considering the request to discern a call to Congregational ministry. It is in the nature of the case that the people required for such ministries are usually precisely the people who are valued and sought for other ministerial endeavors. The chronically "unemployed," the people who are always available for Congregational service because they have made a career of being "in transition," those who are too financially or personally irresponsible to be able to "hold a job" in the real world, are not likely to be elected to Congregational office or invited to serve as novice director. Whoever moves into such positions will do so, in all likelihood, at the personal cost of other positions and interests that might be much more attractive to her or him and for which they are admirably suited.

In short, Congregational belonging is a necessary and critical factor in ministerial discernment. The Congregation is not a loose association of independent agents. It is not a network of professionals, each of whom is pursuing a personal career. It is a ministerial body composed of many members with diverse gifts and limitations united by a shared charism, committed to a single prophetic vocation of proclaiming the Gospel of the Reign of God. Each member's ministry is an integral part of that common mission.

The third factor which needs to play a role in the discernment of ministry is *the Religious her or himself.* In former times, any expression of personal ministerial attraction by a member was regarded as ambition, selfishness, or pride. Sometimes people were diverted from ministries for which they had real aptitude precisely because of that aptitude! Fortunately, those days of gratuitous frustration for the sake of virtue are over in most Congregations. If every member of the Congregation plays an integral part in its common mission it only makes sense to utilize the very best each person has to offer personally and professionally in responding to the needs of the Church, the world, and the Congregation itself.

Furthermore, other things being equal, people grow and develop in holiness and ministerial effectiveness when they are activating their God-given gifts and responding to the passions the Spirit inspires in them. Religious are not cogs in a machine, employees in a workforce, or foot soldiers in an army. They entered Religious Life in a quest for God that must retain its absolute priority throughout their lives. Their own articulation of where they are in that quest, what would foster it and what retard it, where and how they sense God is calling them is of great importance as they discern their ministerial involvements with their leaders and peers.

If the community as a whole has a priority role in discerning the ministerial direction of the Congregation itself and elected leaders have a priority role in regard to the Congregational dimension of personal discernment, the Religious her or himself must be accorded priority in relation to the personal or individual dimension of discernment. The directiveness appropriate in helping a newly professed in ministerial discernment becomes less appropriate as a person grows in holiness, experience, generosity, prayerfulness, zeal, and clarity. Other things being equal, mature Religious should be respected and trusted as the best interpreters of their own ministerial call.

The challenge of integrating these three factors—the needs that become evident in the signs of the times, the Congregation's identity, vocation, and current requirements, and the personal God-quest of the individual Religious—is ongoing. But it is clear that the new understanding of obedience within which ministerial discernment goes on today is better grounded biblically and theologically, more psychologically and sociologically sound, and probably at least as effective for the proclaiming of the Good News as its monarchical-military predecessor.

V. Summary and Conclusion: Prophetic Obedience in Community and Ministry

Although it is not true, as we noted that some people both inside and outside Religious Life and especially in the hierarchy fear, that obedience has "withered away" in Religious Life, it is certainly true that the understanding and practice of authority and obedience have changed radically since the middle of the twentieth century. We are now in a position to see more comprehensively what has changed and how, why it has changed, and especially what prophetic obedience has come to mean today. I will gather this summary together under two headings: Religious Life as a *charismatic lifeform* in relation to the Church as institution; and the *prophetic character of Religious community and ministry* in relation to the institutional Church as patriarchal and hierarchical.

A. Religious Life as Charismatic Lifeform

As Vatican II insisted, Religious Life[31] is not an office in the Church. It does not belong to the hierarchical structure of the Church as a "*tertium quid*" between the ordained and the lay classes in the institution. Rather, it is a charism, given by the Holy Spirit to the Church as a manifestation of and contribution to its holiness.[32] The Church as institution, in other words, did not create Religious Life. Initiative in regard to the life, therefore, rests with the Spirit and the persons freely responding to the vocation, not with the ecclesiastical institution or its officials.

In the exercise of its pastoral ministry, the ecclesiastical institution has some responsibility to help foster and protect Religious Life. This responsibility carries corresponding authority to regulate some aspects of the life insofar as the common good of the Church and the good of Religious Life itself requires. But there is no justification for interpreting this authority as unilateral, totalitarian, universal, or coercive power to control the life itself in every detail and dominate the individuals within it. No one is obliged to enter Religious Life and therefore the freedom that people exercise in responding to a Religious vocation should not be understood as undertaking an obligation of blind subservience to overwhelming institutional power.

The Spirit created Religious Life by inspiring in some individual members of the Church the desire to give themselves totally to God in Christ through lifelong Profession of the vow of consecrated celibacy to which other vows, especially of poverty and obedience, were eventually added. Some Religious chose to live community in a sociologically visible way in groups, while some others chose to live community individually as hermits, anchorites, consecrated virgins, and so on. Some chose to devote themselves exclusively to withdrawal from the world and prayer (in "stabile monastic life") and others to integrate prayer and service in the world (in "mobile ministerial life").[33] Beginning in the first centuries of the Church's life, Spirit-inspired (i.e., charismatic) individuals, like Benedict of Nursia, founded corporate forms of the life, which would eventually be called Orders and Congregations and which embodied a foundational charism to which other individuals were attracted. In short, Religious Life as a theological-spiritual reality was created by the Spirit and invented as a lifeform by charismatic founders. It is not a function or offshoot of the ecclesiastical institution even though it is an ecclesial reality situated within the Church.

At different times throughout history, various kinds of relationships developed between Religious and the office-structure of the Church. However, it is important to realize that, unlike ordained ministry to which one is called by the institutional Church to serve its spiritual and temporal needs in a public and official capacity, Religious Life is a gift offered to a person by God alone. While one needs permission to be ordained, no one needs permission to commit oneself totally to God and the service of God's people. A person might be refused permission to enter a particular (or even any) Religious Institute because of incompatibility between the individual and that group, but one cannot be forbidden to undertake the substance of Religious Life even if one does so privately. And, of course, no one can be coerced to undertake this life publicly or privately.

In the course of history, especially as the Church became a worldwide sociological entity requiring institutional organization, a process of "approbation" or "approval" of Religious Congregations developed. Approval, however, does not equal permission to exist. Canon Law does not constitute or establish the theological reality of Religious Life in the individual or the group and no one can keep a group from coming into existence or its members from making and living a vowed life in community and ministry. The Law codifies the reality of Religious Life as it has developed under the influence of the Spirit and through the long practice of the life by Religious themselves. It also describes and sets conditions for relationships with, including approval as a Religious Institute by, the institutional Church. Refusal or withdrawal of approbation may mean that the group is not canonically recognized as a Religious Institute, but it does not mean that it does not or may not exist, profess and live the vows, and serve its neighbors.

Numerous communities of apostolic life existed, functioned, and were accepted as Religious by the people they
served and even by the ecclesiastical authorities in whose areas
of jurisdiction they lived and ministered, for decades and even
centuries without ecclesiastical recognition, which only
became available for non-cloistered groups in 1900 and was not
sought in some cases until much later.[34] However, no one, least
of all the members themselves, doubted that the hundreds of
apostolic Congregations founded in the 1800s in North America, for example, were truly Religious. In short, there is nothing
that belongs to the theological substance of Religious Life that
the baptized do not have a right to be and do. Ecclesiastical
approbation, approval, or recognition confers a certain public
canonical status on the group, but not permission to live the
life because that requires no permission.

The process of recognizing Religious Orders or Congregations, a legitimate organizational development in the Church's
life, led naturally to the development of relatively standard criteria for approving these groups, that is, for constituting them
public and recognized instances of Religious Life in the canonical sense of the term. But these criteria were essentially articulations of the features that characterized the life as such (such
as, vows, community, prayer, ministry, and so on) as well as certain supports of these features (such as, that people must be
free, be legally of age, and undergo adequate formation in
order to validly make public vows). These provisions of Canon
Law help insure the integrity of the life across diverse Congregations as well as its orderly integration into the life of the
Church as an institution. However, it must be remembered that
these provisions flow from and are theologically dependent on
the life itself. Canon Law codifies a life that springs charismatically from the Holy Spirit. It does not create the life, determine
its constitutive features, nor validate it as such.

It follows, then, that using the approval process as a canonical weapon to coerce Religious into appropriating understandings of their freely chosen life that are contrary to the
intentions of their founders, violate their charismatic identity
and historical self-understanding, conflict with their legitimate

traditions, or have no essential relation to the life itself (e.g., regarding what clothes they will wear, what devotions they will practice, where they will live, what ministries they will exercise, etc.) is simply an abuse of power. On this grounds, I would argue that the requirement, in Canon Law, that all Religious constitutions must interpret their vow of obedience as constituting the pope the highest superior of every Religious *in virtue of her or his vow* (Canon 590), is also an abuse of power.[35]

Religious, like other Catholics, are subject to the immediate jurisdiction of the pope that was definitively established at Vatican I[36] (although this interpretation of papal primacy also has been seriously questioned on theological grounds since its definition) but this has nothing to do with the vow of obedience made by Religious. The vow is not analogous, much less identical to, the promise of obedience that the ordained make to their hierarchical superiors. The Religious vow of obedience is made only to God according to the Constitutions of the Order. The Constitutions derive from the intention and understanding of the founder (charism) and the historical development (legitimate tradition) of the Congregation. The pope has no authority—even if he has the power—to rewrite the Constitutions of every Congregation to endow himself with supreme immediate authority over every member *in virtue of their vow* if this was not the intention of their founders, not part of their tradition, and not their own intention in making the vow. This is an example of "creeping primacy" universalizing personal papal power, analogous to the "creeping infallibility" that attempts to make ordinary Church teaching binding in conscience and irreformable. Both are an abuse of power, not a legitimate exercise of authority.

If the vow of obedience self-evidently or by its very nature made the pope the highest superior of every Religious, the Jesuits could never have chosen to make a special fourth vow of obedience to the pope (one cannot vow to do what one is obliged to do) nor limited the object of that vow to matters of mission (since it is already universal in virtue of the vow of obedience itself). In other words, what ecclesiastical officials, including the pope, have the coercive power to impose and enforce does not necessarily establish what they have the authority or a moral right to do. And when Religious judge, after serious and prayerful communal discernment, that their legitimate autonomy as individuals and/or Congregations is being violated (which many Congregations did when required to include Canon 590.2 or its substance in their revised Constitutions), they are not being disobedient or insubordinate by respectfully protesting and, if necessary, resisting this violation of their rights.

The foregoing observations bear directly on the emotionally charged issue that Religious are reluctant even to acknowledge, much less confront openly: the question of "losing canonical status" as a Religious Institute if they do not submit totally to absolute Vatican control of their life and ministry. The launching of the "Apostolic Visitation" of U.S. women's apostolic Congregations in 2009 makes avoiding this issue virtually impossible. In my opinion, it is better for Religious Congregations to face this traumatic possibility before they are confronted with the necessity to make a decision about it so that they are not "blindsided" by a *fait accompli* in relation to which they have developed no options. A favorite hierarchical tactic which has been used repeatedly in recent times is to present an individual or group with two equally impossible options, insist they are bound in conscience to choose one, and then claim that they "freely chose" something which they unwillingly accepted as less onerous than the other option. The most egregious recent example is the mass dispensation from vows of the Los Angeles IHMs, but the expulsion of individual Religious from their Congregations, interdict and excommunication, and similar penalties are disturbing instances of this tactic. Religious need to know, before this tactic is used, what their real options are and how to exercise them.

If the tension between the Vatican and a particular Congregation reached the point at which the Congregation were required to choose between infidelity to its charism, distortion of its life and mission, or violation of the consciences of its members on the one hand, and the loss of Vatican approbation on the other, the Congregation might be well advised to choose the latter, no matter how painful that choice might be. Jesus supplied the principle for dealing with such life and death choices in Luke 9:25: "What does it profit them [literally: a person] if they gain the whole world, but lose or forfeit themselves?"

The context (vs. 24) of this aphorism is Jesus' challenge to his disciples to take up their cross and follow him. He says, paradoxically, that "saving one's life" can be, in fact, "losing one's life," and vice versa. It depends on what one considers "one's life." The question is, what is the ultimate value you must protect at all costs? If it is your physical life (or any of the goods that sustain that life) and you preserve it at the expense of fidelity in discipleship, the price is too high. If you lose your earthly life to preserve the spiritual integrity of your discipleship you have, in fact, gained your real life. But then, Jesus universalizes the maxim. The "whole world" means anything you value or even everything you value. "Yourself" means your personhood, your identity, your integrity. If the price of canonical approval becomes compromise of the integrity of the Congregation and/or its individual members, the price is simply too high.

Deprivation of canonical status as an ecclesiastically recognized Religious Institute would be a real loss to a Congregation,[37] but not of anything absolutely essential to their life as a community of vowed members in mission and ministry, unlike the ecclesiastical institution that would no longer have canonical access to the community. A Congregation, especially one which is experienced and mature, deeply rooted in its charism and history, which is coerced against its will into such a choice, would continue, one would hope, to live its life as before (though without external interference). Experience, both historical and contemporary, seems to suggest that the laity in general, who tend to relate to Religious in terms of their charism and ministry rather than in terms of juridical legalities, would not have a problem with the "status" of such a community.[38] One would hope that other Congregations would continue to relate to the community as before. If such punitive action were taken against a critical mass of Congregations, Religious Life itself as a charismatic reality in the Church would undoubtedly survive (as it has a succession of secular and ecclesiastical assaults in the past) but the Church as institution would be seriously impoverished by its loss of structured relationship with and influence on a powerfully charismatic element in the Church.

Religious Life is profoundly ecclesial and Religious Congregations clearly are not courting conflict with, much less separation from, the Vatican. They have in the past and undoubtedly will continue to make every effort, even when their efforts are not welcomed or reciprocated, to dialogue openly, responsibly, and respectfully with ecclesiastical authority. However, in the long run, it is not good for Congregations to allow their integrity to be impugned, their identity to be distorted, their vocation to be denatured, or themselves to be intimidated or bullied for the sake of a recognition which, however useful and desirable, is not theologically or spiritually essential to their life.

Perhaps equally important, it is not good for the Church for individuals or groups to be codependent enablers of the abuse of ecclesiastical authority. Religious, called to a prophetic vocation in the Church that specifically entails the effort to dismantle domination systems of all kinds, has to be willing, if integrity demands it, to follow Jesus, who desired ardently to avoid execution by the hierarchical authorities of his own religious tradition, but who desired even more to do the will of the One who called and sent him (see Luke 22:42). His execution was the public statement by the hierarchy of his religious tradition that he was a blasphemer and heretic, cursed by God. That judgment was repudiated by his Jewish followers and eventually by the worldwide movement that we call the Church. The only behavior we can finally control is our own, and trying to "buy time" by surrender of one's integrity rarely converts the oppressor.

B. The Prophetic Character of Religious Community and Ministry

The burden of this chapter has been understanding what Religious obedience means (and does not mean) as a Gospel way of handling one of the major coordinates of human experience, namely, freedom and power. With evangelical poverty, the "economics of the Reign of God," as a Gospel way of handling material goods, and consecrated celibacy as a Gospel way of living relationships, prophetic obedience as the "politics of the Reign of God," helps constitute the alternate world in which Religious live and from which they minister in and to the Church and the world.

The charismatic character of Religious Life, as we have just seen, creates a certain prophetic tension between this life and the Church as institution. In this final section, we will examine this tension in greater detail by looking first at how the fundamentally *egalitarian nature of Religious community* and its resulting collegial functioning contrasts with the fundamentally patriarchal structure of the ecclesiastical institution and its monarchical functioning. Second, we will look at how the *prophetic nature of Religious ministry* contrasts with the hierarchical approach to ministry of the institutional Church. The charismatic and prophetic element in the ecclesial community, especially as it is publicly and corporately embodied in Religious Life, will always present a challenge to the institutional and hierarchical ecclesiastical structure. This challenge is necessary if the Church is to be a living organism and not simply a bureaucracy.

1. Egalitarian community in a patriarchal institution

As I discussed in the preceding chapter, the historical development of Religious Life in a world and Church that were "naturally" patriarchal largely accounts for its appropriation of the patriarchal familial, military, and monarchical models of organization. But, intrinsic to the life of nonclerical Institutes, as we saw in section 3 above, was an egalitarian dynamic that needed only the proper soil and nurture to develop into a definitive rejection of patriarchy and all its hierarchical manifestations. As we have also seen, conditions at the beginning of the twentieth century in both Church and world, and especially Vatican Council II, provided that impetus.

Contemporary Religious Life, especially among women in the first world and increasingly in the developing world, is deeply egalitarian. This is not a political option for a democratic form of government (which is hardly egalitarian!) but a theological and spiritual option for the kind of nonhierarchical community Jesus founded and for its collegial rather than monarchical structure and function.

The New Testament gives striking witness to Jesus' rejection of patriarchal patterns of relationship. It was not only that he reproved his disciples for any attempt on their part to establish hierarchy among themselves, and rejected their assumption of the right to exercise coercive power over others, but he also rebuffed any attempt of others to project dominant power on himself. When the disciples argued among themselves over who was greatest or first among them Jesus gave them the examples of a little child who could claim nothing (see Luke 9:46–48), of the person in the last place at table (see Luke 14:8–11), of the master who is among his subordinates as one who serves (Luke 22:26–27). He insisted that among his disciples there were to be no fathers, teachers, rabbis; that is, no patriarchs (see Matt 23:5–10), because they were all sisters and brothers, children of one Parent in heaven. When they wished to drive little children away from him (see Mark 10:13–14), to get rid of a mere woman crying after them (see Matt 15:23), or one presuming to converse with him (see John 4:27), to forbid someone to minister in his name without their permission (see Mark 9:38–40), or to call down fire on an unreceptive Samaritan town (see Luke 9:52–55), Jesus overrode them every time.

Some passages that get little notice in ordinary preaching are even more thought provoking because they show Jesus himself rejecting efforts to treat him as superior. His refusal to allow the crowds to make him king is well known (e.g., John 6:15). When two brothers ask him to settle an inheritance dispute between them Jesus replies, "Who set me to be a judge or arbitrator over you?" (Luke 12:13–14). In other words, he says he has no natural or conferred authority over other people's lives and does not wish to assume it. When an inquirer greets him with a divine attribute, "Good Teacher," Jesus replies, "Why do you call me good? No one is good but God alone" (Mark 10:17–18). In effect, he says, "Do not project upon me divine attributes that will free you from the responsibility of making your own decision about what it means to keep the

Law. We can both read and we are equally responsible for our interpretation." When his disciples ask him to pronounce on eschatological matters—who will sit where in the kingdom of God (Matt 20:23) or when or how the end will come (Mark 13:32)—he says that he has no knowledge of what belongs in God's disposition alone.

Most strikingly, Jesus refuses to be drawn into participating in the administration of divine justice in the case of the woman taken in adultery. He says that all humans, among whom he obviously includes himself ("then neither do I condemn you"), are finally under the judgment of God but none are under the judgment of each other (see John 7:53—8:12). And in the remarkable scene at the Last Supper, when Jesus washes his disciples' feet and Simon Peter objects that it is outrageous that Jesus assumes such a menial position in relation to his followers, Jesus calmly insists that serving them is not a renunciation of his identity or role. It is Peter who cannot understand that neither serving nor being served has anything to do with superiority or inferiority (see John 13:1–17). Inequality, including his own superiority, does not seem to be part of Jesus' understanding of community.

These and other stories and teachings in the same vein are not examples of Jesus pretending to a false humility in order to give his inferiors a good example. He is simply living fully his humanity, which makes him like his brothers and sisters in all things except sin. Although there are natural or conferred differences (beauty, intelligence, strength, wealth, office, responsibility, etc.) among humans, and even special roles assigned to some by God, there is no real inequality among them. No one is to lord it over others in the Christian community and claim that they are doing the community a favor. That is the attitude and behavior of pagans, Jesus said. Among his disciples it is not to be that way (see Mark 10:43). Thus Jesus who, as Word, is "one with" the Father (see John 10:30) acknowledges that as one who shares our flesh, "the Father is greater than I" (John 14:28).

In Jesus, the legitimacy of patriarchal domination came to an end and with it the claim to legitimacy of all domination systems. No human takes God's place among his or her fellow human beings. Any such claim is blasphemy and to acknowledge it is idolatry. The choice by Religious to live the equality Jesus established by his Incarnation among us, by his example and by his teaching, and by his entrance into our death at the hands of human overlords whose patriarchal domination could not vanquish him, is a rejection of domination not because it is painful to those at the bottom of the structure but because it is incompatible with their identity as Christians and with their mission to be and preach Jesus among their fellow human beings.

In practice, Religious are trying to live an understanding of authority and obedience that poses a challenge to the understanding and practice of this relationship not only in the world with its domination systems but also in the institutional Church. Authority and obedience refer not to domination and submission but to the variety of roles and variations in process, interchanging constantly and reciprocally, that interact in the collaborative effort to discern God's will in community and ministry and to do it faithfully. It is hardly conceivable that living this conviction within the Church as it currently functions will fail to cause tension and even some conflict at times between Religious Congregations and ecclesiastical authority.

The choice by Religious to reject from their life the patriarchalism that continues to function robustly in the institutional Church, to structure their community life in the radical egalitarianism of Jesus, to govern themselves not monarchically but collegially, and to live "without fathers" as brothers and sisters of Jesus and one another, is a prophetic witness to both Church and world. Religious are proclaiming that it is possible to live the "politics of the Reign of God" which rejects all "power over," right in this world of "wheat and weeds" where the domination systems of Satan control virtually every human institution and project—political, social, economic, educational, even at times ecclesiastical.

2. Prophetic ministry in a hierarchical institution
In section 4 we examined in depth the meaning of prophetic obedience in ministry including the meaning of prophecy

itself, Jesus' prophetic identity and ministry, and the prophetic ministry of Religious. Although Religious Life as such is a prophetic lifeform in the Church, the salient feature of *ministerial* Religious Life is the Incarnation of that prophetic charism in full-time ministry which is constitutive of the life itself rather than being a kind of part-time "overflow" of a basically monastic lifeform. This is the innovation that was finally recognized when non-cloistered, nonclerical Institutes received official approbation as canonical. But we are only today facing the real challenge of what it means to live nonclerical ministerial Religious Life in an institution which does not really recognize genuine authority that is not institutionally controlled as part of the hierarchical structure. Religious, who stand outside the hierarchical chain of command of the institution, remain a mystery to some hierarchs in both the higher and lower clergy and a serious threat to some of them.

In the living of their charismatic prophetic identity in ministry, ministerial Religious, like Jesus, remain deeply rooted in their Christian tradition, respond to a personal vocation to proclaim Good News to the poor, and do so by bringing the Word to bear in concrete situations in which God's will must be interpreted in terms of the signs of the times. As we have seen, often the situations which Religious must help people confront are new, perhaps unprecedented, not easily brought into clear relationship with official Church teaching that was formulated in general if not abstract terms and often in long-past circumstances not comparable to those in which current decisions have to be made. Jesus frequently found himself in such situations in which there was a clear law (Sabbath, purity, etc.) and something else was evidently called for.

Religious today do not minister exclusively to Catholics in Catholic institutions. Like Jesus, they find themselves dealing with people outside their tradition or in conflict with the hierarchical Church, and, as was frequently the case for Jesus, do not feel called to make conversion, institutional or moral, the purpose of or a requirement for their ministry. As we have seen, they do not see themselves as "agents of the institution" whose job is to enforce Church discipline. They are called to make the nonjudgmental, unconditional compassion of Jesus present and active in this world in the lives of people who are suffering, whether they are suffering from their own sinfulness or from the inflexibility of ecclesiastical discipline that excludes them from the Eucharistic table, marginalizes them in the Church, or threatens them with punishment even beyond the grave because they cannot in conscience or in their life situations meet the demands of the law.

The prophetic identity and role of Religious, especially women, as they read the signs of the times and respond individually and as Congregations to the social and religious "untouchables" of our time, is increasingly unacceptable to the extreme traditionalists in the Church, both lay and Religious, and especially to some of the hierarchy as many Vatican II bishops who had learned to lead by dialogue have been replaced by dogmatic and moral absolutists. The resulting increasing polarization in the Church is often articulated in terms of authority and obedience understood as absolute and unilateral coercive power of the hierarchy demanding total and unquestioning submission from the laity, including Religious. Efforts at dialogue at both the universal and local levels have frequently foundered on the equation of "Church" with "hierarchy" and the refusal of any real recognition that there could be a prophetic function in the Church that is not identical with or exercised by the hierarchy.

The hierarchy often demands of Religious, as individuals or as Congregations, that they function as agents of the institutional Church, as quasi-clerics in the hierarchical chain of command. But Religious often enough cannot with integrity impose or enforce positions which the official teachers themselves cannot present persuasively enough to evoke reception by even the majority of Catholics, such as on the ordination of women, homosexuality, the salvific power of non-Catholic traditions, contraception, the use of condoms for the prevention of disease transmission, and the like. Many Religious, in their personal ministries (as distinguished from official positions in chancery, parish administration, or the like, where they do have responsibility to represent accurately the official position), are unwilling to present as nonnegotiable truth sanctioned by excommunication or damnation that which is impossible for many reasonable people of good will to believe or do. The tensions in the contemporary Church run very deep as the intellectual and moral divide between the official teachers and the majority of believers widens and the credibility of the teachers is subverted by the moral corruption in the hierarchy and the clergy, especially in regard to sexuality and finances. The solidarity of Religious with the people of God often puts them at variance with institutional power, and the tension can be energy draining, fear inspiring, and dangerous for both the individual Religious and his or her Congregation.

However, it is critical for Religious to recognize that this tension is not a matter of disobedience or rejection of authority any more than were Jesus' acceptance of the ministrations of the "public sinner" who washed his feet with her tears in the presence of the righteous Pharisee who thought Jesus was obliged to rebuff her (Luke 7:36–50), his sharing table fellowship with tax collectors and sinners, his eating with unwashed hands (see Mark 7:1–15) and laying his healing hands on the religious untouchables (Matt 8:2–3), his telling parables about the free salvation of those religious pariahs who need a physician rather than the righteous who do not (see Luke 5:31), his overturning of the legitimate money changers' tables in the temple, or his calm rejection of both the accusations of the religious authorities and the threats of their political ally, Pilate. Jesus the prophet was in fairly constant tension with the domination systems, both political and religious, of his day. Part of the reason that the prophet is so threatening to the denizens of these systems is that the prophet is not only subverting the power systems that oppress the helpless but also exposing the hypocrisy of the oppressors who, in their own eyes, are the sole reliable representatives of God's will. The prophet, like Jesus with the woman taken in adultery, is not only rescuing the victims of the *status quo* but also implicitly calling into question the legitimacy of the program that is victimizing them.

Religious desperately want this tension with ecclesiastical authority to cease. They can sometimes find themselves longing nostalgically for the days when they were the "favorite daughters (or sons)" of the institutional Church. And they can easily be tempted to think that official disapproval must mean they are doing something wrong, even sinful. Learning to live as fallible, and even unwelcome, prophets in a sinful Church is much more difficult than living as the "perfect" in a Church shining with absolute truth enforced with absolute power. Part of the prophetic contribution of contemporary Religious Life to the Church is its living into reality of a redefinition of authority-obedience as the free fidelity in community and mission of those willing to lay down their lives for those to whom they are sent.

Chapter Nine

Making Room in the Church for the Prophetic Vocation

I. Introduction

A. Transition

As I have proposed several times in this work, Religious Life is constituted by the total consecration of the members to God in Jesus Christ through the perpetual Profession of the vows lived in community and mission. Profession is a unitary and unifying act by which a person involves her or himself totally in the project of creating, living in, and ministering from an "alternate world" which is an effective imaginative construction of world as Reign of God realized in history as a particular, concrete sociological reality. But each of the vows makes a distinct and particular contribution to this unitary project.

In volume 2 we looked at consecrated celibacy as the primordial vow which distinguishes Religious Life from other life-forms in the Church by specifying the way Religious live the relational dimension of their lives within the transcendent community of friends, the discipleship of equals that is bound together not by blood, economic gain, or power but by the shared faith, rooted in baptism, that they express by their life-long commitment in their Congregation.

In this volume, starting from a theology of the world which God so loved as to give God's only Son in whose mission Religious share, I have been trying to develop a contemporary spirituality of world involvement in which evangelical poverty and

512

prophetic obedience, as the economic and political dynamics of the Reign of God, shape the relation of Religious to material goods and to freedom and power as these are operative in community life and in ministry.

These three foundational relationships—to persons, to material goods, and to power—are the constitutive coordinates of all human life. All faithful Christians choose how (not whether) they will direct these relationships toward their participation in and fostering of the Reign of God. By the distinctive way Religious choose to handle them they create the "alternate world" in which Religious live and out of which they minister. Regarding the vows of celibacy and poverty, we have attended to their incarnation in community, in ministry, and in the spirituality of the unitive God-quest that is the fundamental dynamism of the life. Our concern in the third part of this volume has been prophetic obedience.

We looked first (in chapter 7) at the contemporary cultural and ecclesiastical context in which we are trying to reflect on and live Religious obedience today. We also reviewed the history of this vow as it has developed through the centuries leaving the residue, both creative and distorting, of various models of obedience (familial, military, monarchical) that have been in the ascendancy at different periods. Then (in chapter 8) we explored the biblical foundations of a theology of prophetic obedience as the politics of the Reign of God lived in community and in ministry. We come finally to the third dimension of the vow, the unitive or mystical. It is here, in the individual's personal practice of obedience as integral to her or his single-hearted quest for God in Christ, that many of the contemporary challenges confronting Religious in the day-to-day living of this vow in the context of Church and Congregation come into view.

B. Subject and Scope of this Chapter

The number and variety of angles from which to approach the spirituality of Religious obedience make any comprehensive treatment, or even a schematic summary, impossible.[1] So, with my focus on the spirituality, that is, on the unitive dimension, of this vow, I am making some strategic choices about what to discuss in these final two chapters, hoping that these choices will touch some of the more challenging aspects of the experience of prophetic obedience in Religious Life today and that they will feed into reflection and discussion about aspects not treated here.

In the following section, the second part of this chapter, I will attempt to "clear a space" theologically and spiritually for the constructive work to follow in chapter 10. Throughout this work, I have taken the approach that Religious Life is one Christian lifeform among others (such as matrimony), neither superior to nor normative of the others, but complementary and necessary for the full ecclesial expression of the universal Christian vocation to holiness of all the baptized. Therefore I will first raise the question of how Religious obedience incarnates the broader reality of *Christian obedience* that is common to all. In the process I will propose *a contemporary understanding of Christian obedience* as an exercise of freedom in discernment rather than as a blind submission to or compliance with heteronomous authority.

Second, I will attend to the *distinctiveness* of the vowed obedience of Religious arising from their ecclesial situation as participants in a *public state of life* in the Church. Understanding what this means, and perhaps even more importantly what it does not mean, is crucial to "clearing a space" for a contemporary approach to the spirituality of prophetic obedience.

In the first part of chapter 10, I will describe what I think is the *major change in the understanding (not in the theological meaning) of obedience* that was initiated by the conciliar reform, discuss the challenge that change has raised and how it might be met, and harvest from this consideration a renewed vision of the meaning of obedience in postconciliar Religious Life. This will entail some consideration of what I will call the "*privileged mediations*" of God's will and their role in the ongoing practice of Religious obedience.

In the second part of chapter 10, I will make some tentative suggestions, intended more to encourage discussion than to lay out any kind of map or plan, about how *obedience actually shapes the experience of Religious in the three main phases of Religious*

Life, namely, initial and ongoing formation, the period of active ministerial life, and the final phase of life when the self-abandonment which comes to its fullest expression in death plays a larger role.

II. Clearing a Space for a Unitive Spirituality of Obedience

A. A Contemporary Theology of Christian Obedience

Just as all Christians are called to chastity and detachment and the consecrated celibacy and evangelical poverty of Religious are a distinctive form of this basic stance toward relationships and material goods, so prophetic obedience is a distinctive form of the obedience all Christians are called to live in imitation of Jesus. All the baptized are called to participate in Jesus' identity and mission as "prophet, priest, and king [or pastor and suffering servant]," that is, to participate as active agents in God's saving work in the world, the coming of the Reign of God. In all aspects and dimensions of his life Jesus, as Son of God incarnate, did always the will of his Father who sent him (see John 8:28–29).

In the last chapter we examined in some detail the role of obedience in the prophetic identity and mission of Jesus, which is the model of the prophetic obedience of Religious in community and ministry. Taking that material for granted, I want in this chapter to look more deeply into the personal spirituality of Jesus, his relation to the one he called "Abba," insofar as the Gospel allows us to glimpse this sacred relationship. What did it mean for Jesus, Son of God by nature and a human being by Incarnation, to be obedient? What does his obedience mean for ours?

From his earliest years Jesus grew in wisdom, age, and grace by his obedience to the human parents God had appointed for him (see Luke 2:51). He learned his own religious tradition as a member of the covenant community of Israel not only from his Law-observing parents (see Luke 2:22–24) but also from the official teachers of his Jewish tradition (see Luke 2:46–47).

Jesus began his public ministry by confronting and banishing Satan, who tried to subvert his obedience to God in favor of his own well-being and profit (see Matt 4:10). He instructed his disciples to respect, as he did, the authority of the religious leaders even when those leaders were unworthy of the office entrusted to them (see Matt 23:2–3). Jesus prayed before making important decisions (see Luke 6:12–13) and in agony in the face of suffering (Luke 22:42). He was finally obedient unto death, even unto death on a cross (see Phil 2:8), and "although he was a Son, he learned obedience through what he suffered" (Heb 5:8).

But Jesus also sometimes found himself, not only in his adult and public life but also in his personal and familial life, in apparent or real conflict with the agents and exercises of authority in his life. Even as a child he chose to stay behind in the Temple despite his parents' anguish over his disappearance and he even called into question any absolute claim of parental authority over him when he felt called to do God's will in another way (see Luke 2:41–52). This same pattern appeared in his adult life when he resisted the natural authority of family, even of his own mother, in favor of God's unique claim on his life (see John 2:1–4; Matt 12:46–49).

In his public life, as we saw in the last chapter, Jesus frequently set aside even the most serious demands of the Law in favor of his own discernment of God's will, for example, the prescriptions of the Law governing contacts with unclean persons such as Samaritans, Gentiles, lepers, the dead, sinners (see John 4:8–10; Mark 7:24–31; Matt 8:2–3; Luke 7:12–16 and 36–50); kosher dietary practices (see Mark 7:1–23); and even the most sacred laws of Sabbath observance (see Matt 12:1–8 and 9–13; John 5:1–19; 9).[2]

Jesus challenged not only the official interpretation of the Law, but also the exercise of official authority by the religious leaders who guarded and enforced it. He refused to explain or defend his exercise of personal authority contrary to the Law when challenged by religious officials intent on trapping him, instead challenging them to account for their own willful ignoring of God's call to conversion through John the Baptist

(Matt 21:23–27). One of his most striking challenges to the authority of the religious leaders, and perhaps even to the Law itself, was his refusal to condone their application of the death penalty prescribed in Mosaic Law to a woman taken in adultery (see John 8:2–11). And Jesus' response to both the High Priest during the religious inquisition after his arrest (John 18:19–23) and to the Roman governor, Pontius Pilate, during his legal trial (see especially John 19:9–11) were clear challenges to both the religious and the political authority structures of his time[3] as well as to the officials exercising that authority.

From this very complex relationship of Jesus to familial, legal, religious, and political authority, we can glean at least two fundamental principles governing Jesus' personal practice of obedience, the model of all Christian obedience. First, Jesus, while respectful of legitimate authority, both of persons and of laws, and generally compliant in his response to its exercise, **did not absolutize any human authority**, no matter what its basis or claims or content. It is a mistake—indeed, it is a type of naïve docetism[4]—to attribute Jesus' freedom in relationship to authority to the fact that he was God's Son and therefore not subject to mere humans, much less to corrupt religious hypocrites and venal political tyrants. On the contrary, Jesus was a real human being who, as a child, needed his parents' guidance and was subject to them as much as any child. As a believing Jew he was subject to the religious authority structures of the community of Israel. And those who sit on the seat of Peter today, or who hold public religious or civil office in our times, are no more or less intelligent, virtuous, or altruistic—nor divinely preserved from error—than were those sitting on the seat of Moses or wielding the scepter of the Roman Empire in Jesus' time. In other words, Jesus was not God playing at being human and his obedience was not a pious charade intended to give his followers a good example. Consequently, we need to recognize that Jesus' practice of obedience involved both complying with the exercise of legitimate authority and refusing to comply with such exercise.

If we take the Incarnation seriously, we have to recognize that Jesus, and later his followers, faced the same personal dilemmas and challenges we do today in the face of legitimate authority, whether well or badly exercised. For us, as for Jesus, legitimate religious and secular authority addresses to conscience a genuine claim for obedience. But whenever such authority claims an absolute right to blind and total submission it has exceeded its mandate. The person today who, in conscience, resists such claims is acting as Jesus did, and as did his first disciples in imitation of Jesus. When the latter were forbidden by the Jewish authorities to preach the Risen Jesus they fearlessly responded, "We must obey God rather than any human authority" (Acts 5:29), just as Jesus had answered the high priest at his inquisition and Pilate during his trial. God alone has absolute authority in relation to human beings. To arrogate such authority to oneself is blasphemous and to acquiesce in such a claim by another is idolatrous.

The second conclusion from an examination of Jesus' relationship to human religious and civil authority is an implication of the first, namely, that if no human authority is absolute then **office does not make the teaching, commands, or actions of the officeholder, *ipso facto*, expressions of the will of God**. Consequently, just as resistance to such commands is not necessarily disobedience, **submission or compliance cannot be simply equated with obedience**. Refusing to form one's own conscience, that is, to come to a personal moral judgment (with all the prudential and theological qualifications involved in such judgment) about the right course to follow in a given situation, because it seems safer to assume that submission equals obedience, is not virtue but irresponsibility or cowardice, and can even be complicity in evil.[5] This teaching, which is both deeply biblical and traditional and was newly articulated by Vatican II,[6] can be highly conflictual for Christians in general, and particularly for vowed Religious.

As the late German Protestant political theologian Dorothee Soëlle pointed out, both Catholics and Protestants in the Western world were, until quite recently, raised in rigidly patriarchal families, societies, and churches in which they were educated to believe that sacralized obedience, due by definition to all persons in authority, trumped even charity as the highest duty in the moral life.[7] Catholics grew up in a Church claiming infallibility for its pope (the very strict limitations of which were poorly if at all understood by many) and by extension nearly absolute authority for its bishops and even lower clergy in their own domains. They were indoctrinated into an all-or-nothing ethos of ecclesiastical as well as familial "blind obedience." And very recent conflicts between bishops on the one hand and theologians, Religious, hospitals and social service agencies, and individual believers on the other, have occasioned assertions of virtually absolute ecclesiastical authority that are shockingly devoid of historical and theological knowledge as well as pastoral nuance or sensitivity. The drastic and even violent penalties for dissent, such as silencing, destruction of careers and reputations, interdict, defrocking of clerics, or even excommunication, reinforce the erroneous idea that all dissent equals seriously sinful disobedience.

The tradition of Religious Life also inculcated a largely unqualified understanding of obedience to superiors, Rule or Constitutions, and even customs, as virtually absolute. In effect, Religious were taught that they must make only one moral decision in their adult lives, namely, the decision to make a vow of obedience. After that, intellectual and moral submission to and behavioral compliance with not only official Church teaching and law but also the "particular law" of their Institute and the will of their superiors assured Religious that they were always fulfilling the will of God. The only exception, namely, if they were commanded to do something sinful, was largely theoretical, since the commands of superiors rarely bore upon anything having to do with sin and subjects were assured that in cases of doubt "it is always better to obey."

As we have already seen, the horrified recognition by many, in the aftermath of World War II, of the complicity of large numbers of Christians in the Nazi Holocaust, under the guidance of their pastors, initiated the subversion of the making absolute of human authority in the secular sphere. The equation of the commands of secular superiors with the will of God was further undermined during the next several decades by the civil rights movement in the United States, the anti-war movements during the Vietnam era, the revolutions of colonized countries and the rebellions against totalitarian regimes worldwide, the final challenge to apartheid in South Africa, and most recently the uprisings of the "Arab Spring." These contestations of authority have taught several generations of Christians the meaning and legitimacy of "civil disobedience," a misnamed but strikingly effective strategy of nonviolent resistance to lawfully constituted authority in which citizens, on the basis of conscience, defied such authority and freely accepted the consequences of noncompliance. Despite its name this resistance, many came to understand, was actually not "disobedience" at all but obedience to God rather than to humans.

Within the Church, Vatican Council II finally, and for the first time in Catholic history, promulgated unambiguously the principle of inviolable freedom of conscience and indeed the duty to follow even an erroneous conscience.[8] By their human nature as well as by divine law people are, the Council taught, required to act according to their conscience and forbidden to act against it.[9] Consequently, not only secular but also religious authority must respect that freedom by abstaining from coercion of conscience even when the authority believes the individual is in error.

While the Council, in *Dignitatis Humanae*, was addressing primarily the question of freedom of conscience in relation to faith commitment, the issue of conscience in relation to morality was raised starkly in the immediate aftermath of the Council when Paul VI, in July 1968, overriding the decisive majority of the papally appointed commission on artificial birth control, published *Humanae Vitae*[10] which declared all forms of "artificial" contraception intrinsically immoral. Immense turmoil of conscience and discipline engulfed the Church in the wake of that encyclical. Not only married couples who found the teaching humanly impossible to implement but also pastors and theologians who found the teaching incoherent and indefensible[11] and its pastoral imposition destructive, finally, and by a very large majority, rejected the teaching in practice (in technical language, did not "receive" it) on the grounds of conscience. This practical rejection, which is still not recognized in official ecclesiastical circles, emerged quickly and clearly despite the pope's explicit appeal to pastors, confessors, and moral theologians to honor their obligation to give an example to the faithful of "sincere obedience, inward and outward…to the Magisterium of the Church" (*Humanae Vitae* 28). In other words, the pope was commanding in virtue of obedience and the Church, the majority of the People of God including large numbers of the clergy, was refusing to submit in virtue of conscience.

Painful as this event has been for all concerned, it has initiated many if not most educated Catholics into a process of moral maturation that had been retarded, if not stymied, for centuries. The decision by the overwhelming majority of Catholics not to receive the solemn teaching of the magisterium on birth control involved the assumption of personal responsibility for forming and following one's conscience even when it opposed Church doctrine and law. While some Catholics who took this position considered themselves to be automatically excluded from Church membership, most did not. And their pastors confirmed them in this decision, while reputable theologians defended their moral reasoning and their right and even obligation to followed their conscience. In other words, many faithful Catholics acted on the realization that no human authority, including that of the pope, is absolute; that what is commanded by those in authority is not necessarily the will of God; that noncompliance or the withholding of submission, even when the command comes from the highest authority in the Church, is not necessarily disobedience.[12] This repudiation in practice of the erroneous understanding of authority and obedience, and of its foundation in the (mis)understanding of the will of God which had held unquestioned sway among Catholics for centuries, may turn out to be more important than the subject matter that occasioned it.

The conclusion of this rapid exploration is that the most fundamental and nonnegotiable moral obligation of every Christian who is called to holiness in imitation of Jesus is to accept the challenge and the responsibility to form her or his conscience through discernment and to act according to that conscience. Personal discernment is necessary precisely because there is no mechanical way, such as appeal to legitimate authority or blind submission to such authority, for a person to establish the will of God (i.e., what is morally good or evil) in any particular situation. The repeated assertion by some ecclesiastical authorities that any judgment of conscience at variance with an official magisterial position is, by definition, malformed and therefore not to be followed, amounts to a denial of the personal moral responsibility of believers and the absolute priority of conscience, and is theologically untenable.[13] If conscience consisted exclusively in compliance with the commands of authority it would be unnecessary. But genuine obedience to God is, by definition, the acting out of the judgment of conscience. Hence, it cannot be equated reductively with compliance. This basic theological position regarding the Christian practice of obedience is not abrogated by the vow of obedience.

Although, as we will see, various exercises of authority do play an important role in discernment, they cannot be simply substituted for it. Consequently, compliance with the commands or demands of officeholders, no matter how highly placed, is no guarantee that one is obeying God. Like Jesus, his followers are predisposed to respect authority, but they do not—because they may not—offer to any human being or human system of law the obedience they can offer morally only to God. So, if "blind obedience" to authority is no guarantee that one has discovered or is doing God's will and if personal discernment remains a moral obligation, where can Christians expect to find resources and guidance for such discernment?

The expression the "will of God" suggests to the imagination of many that God influences human choices and behavior, as well as natural events like disease and earthquakes, by propositional imperatives. Thus, they imagine, God "wills" one to marry this person rather than that one, follow this particular vocation, develop this fatal disease, or be rescued (or not) from this natural disaster. Discernment, in this understanding of God's will, is then a process of figuring out what God "knows" but is not telling or recognizing as divinely intended the (usually negative) occurrences in and around us.

This voluntaristic and positivistic understanding of the will of God is actually a highly distorted literalizing and anthropomorphizing of God as an all-powerful absolute monarch. As Australian theologian Denis Edwards explains well in his recent book,[14] God's initiation of and ongoing engagement with Creation is much better understood as noninterventionist, that is, as God's loving self-bestowal in Creation, not as an imposition from without of absolute explicit divine imperatives on either the macro- or the micro-scale.

What happens in the natural world as well as in our individual lives is the unfolding of natural causality in infinitely complex patterns of interaction bringing about all manner of events and experiences from the cosmic to the intimately personal. God participates in these events not like a supreme master issuing orders, a cosmic engineer manipulating the forces of nature, or a puppeteer pulling the strings on helpless human marionettes, but as the sustaining and enabling power of the unfolding universe and the loving, companioning support of the rational and free creatures who are participants in this process. The challenge of discernment is not to figure out what God wills, commands, or imposes so that we can execute or submit to it, but to work out in our concrete situations, under the ongoing guidance of the Holy Spirit, how best to participate in and promote the flourishing of all Creation including ourselves because this is always what God "wills."

A mature theological understanding of "obedience to the will of God" is, therefore, more complex and demanding than up-or-down submission to persons in authority or compliance with laws or teaching. But for some people, both those in authority and those for whom they feel responsible, who vainly seek a degree of security not available to humans, such an assertion appears to be a dangerous hole in the moral dike that protects civil and ecclesiastical order from the floodwaters of total chaos. For such people who simplistically equate human authority with the divine will, submission to authority is an all-or-nothing proposition. They prefer even suffering, causing suffering to others, or moral incoherence to the insecurity of taking personal responsibility for a conscience decision at variance with the commands of authority.

But the call for discernment is not a repudiation of either obedience or authority. Obedience, as has been said, is the *appropriate response to* (not the rejection of) authority understood not as the power to coerce submission or compliance but as a legitimate *claim or right to be heard and heeded.* When the person addressed has attended carefully, using the necessary means—both personal and communitarian—to form a valid judgment, to the teaching or command of the one holding authority or to the applicable law, and has decided in conscience that the appropriate response is to withhold compliance or even to do something other than or contrary to what is commanded (e.g., Jesus listening to the stoners of the woman taken in adultery and deciding not to cooperate in her execution [see John 8:2–11]), the person is not being disobedient but actively obedient to God, whose will, when that of humans is judged to conflict with it, must be preferred. In such a case, it is better (indeed imperative) to obey God rather than humans.

This does not guarantee that the conscience judgment of the one disagreeing is correct nor even that the behavior that follows from that judgment is objectively morally good. Nor does it guarantee that there will be no consequences for noncompliance. It does mean that in this case the one commanded is freely choosing to follow her or his conscience, that is, to obey God's will as one has discerned it, rather than to submit to human authority.

However, the judgment that the law or the command of a superior is not, in a particular case, a true expression of God's will must derive from competent moral reasoning utilizing some serious indication(s) that another course of belief or action is called for. When we judge that human authority, religious or secular, fails as indication of God's will, where do we look for resources for more valid discernment?

First, on the **natural level**, we need to attend to *Creation* itself (our own as humans and the rest of Creation). God created us in God's own image and likeness, intelligent and free, and it can never be God's will that we abdicate or renounce these gifts. We are not allowed to simply abandon our own responsibility into the hands of someone presumed to "know better" always and in all matters by virtue of office or eminence or divine inspiration. Even a vow of obedience, as we will see, cannot be correctly understood as such an abdication of freedom or responsibility. The resistance, for example, of many members of the Church to some official ecclesiastical positions on homosexuality is based on their convictions that God did not create any human beings as naturally morally deformed by objective disorder.

Second, as Vatican II reminded us, *history* itself is a complex and ambiguous unfolding of the divine will.[15] What Jesus called the "signs of the times" (see Matt 16:1–3) are the signals in the development of human experience and the unfolding of consciousness of the divine vocation to fullness of being and life that God addresses to all humanity. For example, Pope John XXIII, in his encyclical *Pacem in Terris*,[16] called the increasing human insight into the ascendency in human experience of equality and love over domination and fear a global "sign of the times" in the twentieth century to which the Church needed to attend (39–43). He singled out three movements in particular, namely, the claim to their rights of working people, of women, and of nations, as characteristics of our times (126–129) indicating the unfolding of God's design in history. The struggle of women for sacramental equality in the Church may not be welcomed by some in the hierarchy but their attempt to subvert or suppress it, by teaching, law, or sanction, is being resisted in good conscience by many women (as well as men) as not only not God's will for the human race or for the Church but as an area of necessary contestation.

Third, conscience is formed immediately in the nuanced interaction of the personal judgment of the individual with the *community* of which one is a part.[17] We must recognize the indications of God's will in the "givens" of our own personal situation but as persons in relationship. Health, family circumstances, personal gifts and limitations, economic conditions, education and professional qualifications, as well as freely assumed or unavoidable major obligations of all kinds influence our choices because they are part of our unique situation before

God. Among these "givens" is the influence of what I have called "privileged mediations" of God's will arising from one's particular vocation. For example, the needs of one's children and the particular circumstances of one's own marriage might not be compatible with some general ecclesiastical law or directive concerning reproduction. The dissenting response of many married couples to the Church's official position on contraception articulated in *Humanae Vitae* was, in many cases, not a theoretical judgment about contraception in the abstract or about the legitimacy of the ecclesiastical magisterium or its authority, but a discerning response to the privileged mediation of God's will in their lives constituted by their concrete marriage and family.

Beyond the natural level, divine revelation, especially as we internalize Scripture in personal prayer, participate in liturgy, strive to live habitually in moral integrity, and share faith with others in the Christian community and beyond, is a place where we listen for the voice of God sounding within us as conscience.[18] For hundreds of years prior to Vatican II, Catholics were taught to distrust their personal experience of God, to be wary of "private interpretation" of Scripture because they were ill-equipped to understand it. Although this misguided alienation of believers from Scripture, which Vatican II called the "the pure and perennial fount of spiritual life,"[19] was officially reversed at the Council, many leaders of the institutional Church still have hesitations about the personal appropriation of revelation, biblical or otherwise, by the nonordained. Nevertheless, many believers, profiting over the past half century from the work of biblical scholars and pastoral theologians, as well as other sources of Christian formation, have internalized through their own reflection and prayer new and deeper understandings of God, Christ, Church, morality, sacraments, and ministry that do not always reflect exactly the official positions and practices of their local parishes or even the wider official Church.

In short, in seeking to know and do God's will, that is, to obey God in ordinary life and extraordinary situations, the individual believer cannot simply "look up the answers" in the catechism or meekly "ask Father." The unnuanced equation of

Christian obedience with submission to Church authorities is childish at best and irresponsible or even sinful at worst. To be sure, the "default" position of the conscientious believer is respect for Church leadership, openness to and acceptance of official teaching, compliance with ecclesiastical discipline, and submission to promulgated law. In times past many if not most Catholics thought they needed to look no further. Increasingly, believers know that official positions, even when they are the starting point of conscience formation, are not the end.

Some people, those in office as well as some "magisterial fundamentalists" among the faithful, regard such an appeal to conscience as a manifestation of "cafeteria Catholicism" precisely because it does not take a uniformly compliant stance with regard to all official teaching and legislation. But as Catholic sociologist Jerome Baggett has shown through his qualitative analysis of objective data about American Catholics in various situations and social classes,[20] this variety in belief and practice is actually a manifestation of the increasing human and moral maturity of Catholics who now form their consciences in relation to a variety of indications of God's will in their lives. This position, which is the analog in the moral sphere of the recognition of a "hierarchy of truths" in the theological sphere, is becoming more the norm than the exception.

Religious, whatever we must soon say about their particular and distinctive place in the Church and the distinctive features of their practice of obedience, are first of all baptized Christians who must, like all believers, discern God's will and form their consciences accordingly by attending to the natural indications of God's will (Creation, history and the signs of the times, the communities to which they belong, and the givens of their experience including the privileged mediations of God's will in their own vocational situation as Religious) in the light of the indications of divine revelation (mediated by Scripture, prayer, available theological knowledge, and shared Christian experience). For Religious, learning to affirm this conviction peacefully and courageously and to act responsibly in accord with this conviction is essential to clearing a space for a re-imagining of Religious obedience today.

B. The Specification of Religious Obedience by State of Life

Although the prophetic obedience that Religious vow is grounded in the Christian obedience to which all the baptized are called in imitation of Jesus, by Profession Religious also enter a distinct state of life in the Church which has implications for their relationship with ecclesiastical authority as well as in relationship to the specific community they enter. In the course of history, these implications often have been more implicit than explicit, and often understood to entail virtual total control by the hierarchy of Religious, individually and as Institutes, in regard to their personal, spiritual, material, financial, and ministerial lives. One of the most expansive and repressive of such exercises of ecclesiastical control was the imposition of perpetual papal cloister on all women Religious by Boniface VIII in the thirteenth century.[21] This papal edict retarded the full development of ministerial Religious Life for women by several centuries. Indeed, only because some highly creative founders—having discerned that they and their companions were called by God both to Religious Life and to active ministry incompatible with cloister—found ways to circumvent Boniface's edict did this form of Religious Life flourish in our time.

Today Religious, especially women, are much more aware of their right to legitimate autonomy, especially in regard to the internal affairs of their Congregations and the personal and spiritual lives of their members, and are more inclined to question assumptions of arbitrary power over their personal and corporate lives in relation to affairs that have no implications for the Church as institution. The revision of Canon Law in 1983, following the Council, allowed much of the unnecessary and intrusive minute regulation of Religious to disappear, equalized (at least in principle) the treatment of women and men Religious as Religious, abolished mandatory status distinctions between choir and lay Religious, and placed most of the decision making and regulation of the internal affairs of Congregations in the competence of the Congregations themselves through their "proper law" expressed in their documents and governmental structures, and applied by their leaders.

Much of the assumption of hierarchical control of women Religious throughout history was simply the application in regard to unmarried women in the Church of the cultural norms for all adult women prior to the beginning of women's liberation in the 1800s. Based on the commonly accepted natural inferiority and incompetence of women in relation to men and affairs, the husband virtually owned his wife, controlling her associations, living situation, movements within and outside the home, dress, finances, and all the details of her personal life. He assumed control of her productive and reproductive capacities for his ends and benefit, and had the right to discipline her as he saw fit and punish any infractions on her part. Unmarried women remained under the control of adult male relatives. Those women who renounced marriage and left the paternal home to give themselves to God in Religious Life were presumed to be under the same patriarchal arrangements in relation to the institutional Church which "owned" these women, exercising through an all-male clergy and hierarchy virtually total control of their persons and lives.

Patriarchal absolutism, whether paternal, marital, or ecclesiastical, was of course never totally accepted by all women (nor even by all enlightened men). And women Religious, because of their freedom from the responsibilities of child-raising, their solidarity in community life, and often their superior educations, were in a better position to resist such total control than most individual married women.[22] Nevertheless, the assumption that the institutional Church, through the agency of its hierarchy, had a divinely established right to virtually total and unilateral control of women Religious in their personal and corporate lives and that the women had no rights except those bestowed upon them by ecclesiastical legislation was basically unquestioned in theory until very recently.

In the last two centuries, as women in society (especially Western society) have emerged from patriarchal domination or at least from universal acceptance of such domination, women in the Church have begun to resist the patriarchal structure and function of the ecclesiastical institution in relation to their lives. Women Religious, although perhaps a little slower to realize that they were persons and women as well as Religious, have definitely made up for lost time in the past half century. They are well aware today of their dignity and fundamental rights as human beings, their giftedness as women, their competence as educated professionals and ministers, and their equality as Christians not only among themselves and in relation to the laity but also in relation to the clergy and the hierarchy.

Restrictions and intrusions, coercion that sometimes reached the level of bullying, financial manipulation, use and abuse in ministerial situations, unilateral demands for submission without dialogue, and outright psychological and spiritual violence (and in some countries egregious physical and sexual abuse to which Church officials turned, and continue to turn, a blind eye) began to appear clearly for what they were: totally unacceptable domination of women by men in the name of God and sacred power.

Although there are some women Religious who accept the patriarchal ecclesiology that undergirds their own subordination, the vast majority of women Religious, especially in the first world but increasingly elsewhere, have definitively repudiated their second-class status in the Church and its behavioral implications (while attempting to maintain respect for their brothers in the clergy and hierarchy who have not yet grasped the qualitatively different level of human development represented by the emergence of women from subservience to men). This has led to rising levels of tension between the hierarchy and Religious and these tensions have become increasingly public. The Apostolic Visitation of United States women Religious launched by the Vatican in 2009 without any consultation or dialogue with the leadership of the Congregations was perceived as an unjustified assault on Religious and was resisted to a degree that would have been unthinkable even a few years ago. The official effort to present this unilateral invasion as an "ecclesial dialogue" expressed clearly[23] the failure of those who initiated it to understand the qualitative changes that are taking place among women Religious.[24]

This situation makes it imperative to raise the question of whether there is any theological basis for the assumption of special hierarchical authority (i.e., beyond that over the non-ordained in general) over Religious because they are Religious. In other words, does their identity and role as professed Religious influence or modify the meaning of Christian obedience in their lives as Catholics? Are Religious, because they are Religious, bound to a different kind or degree of obedience than other Catholics in relation to Church authorities and law?

Many traumatic experiences in the sphere of "obedience" in the postconciliar history of Religious, particularly women, have originated in the conflictual understanding of the "place" of Religious in the Church. A classic example was that of the "twenty-four signers." For decades, precisely because of the moral pluralism that was deeply dividing American Catholics, many lay Catholics in the United States had publicly raised questions about the absolutism of the Vatican's position on abortion, and over a hundred Catholics signed a 1984 *New York Times* public advertisement calling for open dialogue in the Church on the subject (note: not for a change of teaching or law but merely for honest dialogue). Yet only the Religious signers were ordered to publicly recant their participation in the call for dialogue or be expelled from their Congregations.[25] They were being singled out for coercion and discipline not as Catholics but as Religious. Significantly, two major papers delivered at the 1985 National Assembly of the Leadership Conference of Women Religious by the two best-known women Religious moral theologians in the American Church at that time located this struggle squarely in the realm of moral decision making by Religious as such: Anne E. Patrick, SNJM, "The Moral Decision-Maker: From Good Sisters to Prophetic Women"[26] and Margaret Farley, RSM, "From Moral Insight to Moral Choice: Discernment and Decision-making in the Christian Community."[27]

Again, there have been repeated altercations between Church officials and Catholic politicians on various issues in recent times but only a few extremist bishops have attempted (usually without success) to discipline lay Catholics for what those bishops see as "disobedience" to Church law or teaching. But the Leadership

Conference of Women Religious has been subjected to a "doctrinal evaluation" by the Congregation for the Doctrine of the Faith for even listening to informational presentations at their annual assemblies on such "forbidden" topics as homosexuality, the ordination of women, or interreligious dialogue.

This double standard obviously expresses a conviction by at least some Church officials that Religious are obliged to submit to Church authority, whether of persons, legislation, or teaching, in a way that non-Religious are not. I would suggest that the basis of this double standard is an erroneous understanding of Religious as "public persons" in the Church arising from a lack of clarity about how people function as representatives of the Church, which persons are official agents of the Church as institution, and what "public" means when applied to people in different states of life in the Church.

The confusion is understandable because the distinctions are probably, in a certain sense, new, and also because there are unavoidable areas of overlap. We are, as a Church, slowly emerging from a time when all authority in the Church was seen as vested exclusively in the hierarchy and their subalterns and anyone in any role in the Church was seen as totally subservient to whatever exercises of authority the officeholders chose to use. Since the Council this absolute distinction between the ordained as active and all the nonordained as passive has been somewhat altered as the laity, including women, have assumed some functions previously reserved to the ordained and women Religious have come into considerable prominence in the Church's ministries. Much more nuance, differentiation, and clarity is needed in the Church as a whole. However, it is particularly imperative for Religious if they are to be able to justify their prophetic ministry in the Church against frequent and arbitrary charges of "disobedience" accompanied by threats or actual imposition of sanctions.

1. Who represents the Church and how?

The term "represent" has several quite different meanings. For example, all Americans represent the country when they travel abroad. If they act like "ugly Americans" they damage the image of the country and make things difficult for other Americans who travel. An extremist pastor in the United States burning a Koran in 2011 has incited large-scale violence against Americans in Muslim countries. However, such "ugly Americans" or bigots, people justly despised by non-Americans as representatives of the United States and repudiated by most Americans as a disgrace to their country and fellow citizens, cannot be arrested by the United States government simply for being a counter-witness to the values of the United States.

However, the ambassador of the United States to the Court of St. James represents the country in an altogether different way. The ambassador as ambassador is not a private citizen. She or he is deputed by the highest authority in the United States and officially received by the highest authority in Great Britain. The ambassador represents, in international law, the "person" of the head of state and thus the country itself, and is empowered to negotiate in the name of the United States and take actions that affect the country as a whole. Assassinating an ambassador can be an act of war.

In between these two ends of the spectrum, that is, the private citizen and the official ambassador, are people like heads of large companies or educational institutions, carrying various kinds of credentials from the government or American accrediting agencies, whose actions can have repercussions, financial, economic, and even political and social, for both countries well beyond the influence of a private citizen.

By analogy, every baptized Catholic as a member of the Body of Christ represents the Church as the People of God. Others encounter and judge the Church by the words, actions, and omissions of its members. Ordinary lay Catholics can "preach the Gospel without words" in their daily activities or alienate people from the Church by myriad forms of hurtful behavior like religious bigotry, dishonesty, or viciousness.

There are also official representatives of the institutional Church such as members of the hierarchy and clergy who have been established in office by ordination and who make binding decisions about the institutional Church's position on matters of doctrine and morality, receive people into the Church and excommunicate them, officiate at its celebrations, judge its cases, and so on. Obviously, there is a vast difference between the official representation of officeholders in the institutional Church and the informal representation by the laity of the Church as the People of God.

In between these two poles there are people and institutions, like Catholic schools or social justice agencies and their officers who represent the Church more formally than the individual Catholic but not in virtue of ecclesiastical office, who may have some form of recognition from the institutional Church that makes their Catholic identity more public in some ways than that of the individual lay Catholic, but which is less explicit and formal than that of the ordained.

If all members of the Church represent the Church in some way, either individually as members of the Church as People of God or formally as officers of the institutional Church, some in both categories do so more privately and others more publicly. Those who, like members of the clergy, represent the institutional Church in virtue of office are agents of the institution. They are appointed to formally teach the Church's approved doctrine and administer its laws within their sphere of authority, and they are responsible to represent the official positions of the institution and empowered, when necessary, to enforce its teaching and laws. They are admitted to and established by ordination in office according to criteria of Church law; they make a promise of obedience to their ecclesiastical superiors; they draw their livelihood from the institutional Church. In secular parlance they "work for the Church" exclusively and full time.

Some nonordained persons may be called to participate in some of the official functions of the institution such as serving as chancellor of a diocese, as lay administrator of a parish, as Canon Lawyer, or as director of a sacramental preparation program. They become quasi-public representatives of the institution, sharing the obligations of agents of the institutional Church in respect to the fulfillment of their duties. It is often unclear to what extent their private lives must conform to Church teaching to the same extent that a cleric's must. For example, can an openly gay person living with his or her partner be a catechist? Can a divorced and remarried person serve as a pastoral associate? Can an unmarried pregnant woman be fired from her position as a teacher in a Catholic school? When they are removed from such positions is it because their personal lives are considered "scandalous" or because they are, in virtue of their private lives, unfit for the office? Or are they simply being punished for disobedience as vengeance against them or as a warning to others?

Most of the laity, in any case, are not public representatives of and agents of the institution as official personnel (though more and more are), but are private or personal representatives of the Church as the People of God. Often they bond together in virtue of shared interests and may act or speak collectively. Their large numbers of members might make a group "public" in the ordinary and informal sense of visible and influential, but it does not make them public in the formal sense of official representatives of the institution with an obligation to support its positions and act as its agent. Voice of the Faithful, Call to Action, FutureChurch, Dignity, Catholics for Choice, the Association for the Rights of Catholics in the Church, or a meta-group such as Catholics Speak Out are such unofficial but quite public (in the nonofficial sense) groups. Their influence derives not from office, and not from any approval by the institutional Church (which has sometimes officially condemned them), but from the actual credibility of their faith and commitment, their concern for the Church, their competence, and their willingness to suffer for the good of the Church; that is, from their membership in the Body of Christ and their baptismal share in the identity and mission of Jesus.

Because such groups and their members are not official representatives of the institution they cannot be suppressed or disciplined as a member of the clergy can be silenced or removed from office, nor can they exercise any coercive power over others in the name of the Church. Such groups are often ignored or even harassed by Church officials but they have considerable influence among the laity and in relation to other Christians who often see them as better representatives of the truth of Catholicism than the officials who are attempting to discredit them.

As anyone active in the Church knows, seemingly neat distinctions such as I have been describing, are hardly clear, clean, and airtight categories. In general, we can say that all the baptized represent the Church in some way, either informally (privately or in associations) or formally (publicly either in virtue of Orders or by incorporation into some of the official functions of the Church as institution). Where are we to locate Religious who are not a third category between the ordained and the lay in the hierarchical ordering of the Church and who are not simply secular laity in terms of state in life? We are again in a "gray area," and one which has become much more controversial since Vatican II, when the "total institution" and semi-cloistered model of Religious Life which kept Religious out of the public sphere gave way to the fully ministerial identity and functioning of non-enclosed Religious in the Church and society.

2. Are Religious public persons in the Church?

Just as the notion of "representation" is complex rather than univocal, so is the notion of "public." The question of whether Religious are public persons in the Church is important because if they are assimilated to the clergy as public representatives of the institutional Church then they are agents of the institution with an obligation to formally teach the Church's approved doctrine and enforce its laws. They would be quasi-"clerics" in regard to obligations although remaining "lay" with regard to rights. In fact, Religious, as Religious, do not belong to the hierarchical structure of the Church but to its life and holiness. I would suggest, then, that the "private or public" distinction is both inadequate to describe the situation of Religious in the Church and dysfunctional when attempts are made to apply one or the other, especially in rigid or exclusive ways.

First, Religious have a certain "public" status in the Church, in the ordinary sense of that word, which is not that of the ordained even though it has tended, historically, to be assimilated to the clerical status in some respects. At the same time, Religious are not, in the secular lay sense, simply "private citizens" in the Church because they are members of Religious Institutes which are canonically "juridical (therefore public) persons." The Religious Institute has rights and responsibilities in the Church, specified in Canon Law, different from those of individual lay persons, and those who enter a Religious Institute have some rights and responsibilities different from those characteristic of all the baptized. In other words, by making public Profession Religious enter a distinct and recognized state of life in the Church which is neither that of clerics nor that of the secular laity, but which is in some sense more "public" than the latter in terms of recognizability and influence.

Second, Religious are not members of Secular Institutes whose special characteristic is to remain "anonymously" among the lay faithful in regard to their occupations, their way of supporting themselves, their lifestyles, and so on. Religious (especially those in apostolic or ministerial Congregations) are committed to publicly exercised and often explicitly Christian corporate ministry in a publicly recognized community whose members are economically interdependent. So, Religious, by their membership in a juridically recognized Religious Institute, are persons who are "public" in the Church in a way that neither the secular laity nor members of Secular Institutes are. In short, while the Religious state is a public state of life in the Church, and the Religious Congregation is a juridical public person, the individual Religious is not a public person in the sense of being an official representative or agent of the hierarchical Church but an ecclesial person who is public in the common sense meaning of that term.

Although the mixing of the clerical state with Religious Life in many men's Orders creates all kinds of complexities that have tended to flow into discussions about men's and women's (i.e., Brothers' and Sisters') Religious Life, it is critical to recognize that Religious *as* Religious are not ordained. Religious as such do not hold office in the Church and are not its official representatives or agents (although a certain Religious, like a particular secular lay person, might be appointed to an office in the Church, which carries other implications).

Religious Life does not belong to the hierarchical structure of the Church and Religious are not part of the "chain of command" that structures the Church as institution. Religious Life was not created by the hierarchy but given to the Church by the Holy Spirit, nor are Institutes, even if founded by someone who is a cleric, given their charismatic identity by the hierarchy. The hierarchy does not control the entrance of members into the Religious Institute. There are some general requirements for entrance such as adequate age, freedom, membership in the Catholic Church, and the like, but the Congregation that admits or declines to admit the candidate determines suitability for Religious Life and the particular Congregation. The official Church recognizes Profession but one is admitted to Profession by the Congregation, not by hierarchical authority; Profession is made to God, not to the hierarchy; it is made through the Congregation's leaders, not through the bishop or his representative; and it is made according to the particular Constitutions which are approved but not formulated by Church authority. The institutional Church, unlike in the case of the ordained, does not support Religious financially, either individually or as a Congregation; does not control the formation or education of the members; and does not decide the Congregation's mission (which derives from its charism),[28] nor assign its members within that mission.[29]

In other words, unlike the ordained, Religious do not "work for the Church." Religious represent the Church in which they participate, as do all members of the Church: the People of God, the Body of Christ acting in this world to bring about the Reign of God. They do not, as Religious, represent the Church as institution, that is, as official instrument of teaching, ruling, and sanctifying. They are, at least in some cases, "public" in terms of visibility and influence, as are many other non-ordained people who are involved, especially in leadership roles, in Church-related activities, but that does not make them official representatives of the institutional Church.

Perhaps the best analogy, at the individual level, would be to Catholics who are "married in the Church," that is, those who have undertaken the public state of sacramental marriage called matrimony. This has some juridical consequences (e.g., in regard to divorce) but it gives the hierarchy no blanket or minute control over the ordinary functioning, the internal choices, or the participation in public life of the spouses. This has become much clearer in recent years as the majority of married Catholics have repudiated the claim to control by the ordained of their reproductive choices. The non-reception of *Humanae Vitae* was a rejection of the official Church's attempted self-insertion into the interiority of matrimony.

All this being said, however, Religious have a visibility or publicity in the Church, as members of their Congregations, that lay people as individuals usually do not have, although certain prominent lay people, for example the United States ambassador to the Holy See, probably have more visibility than does a Religious simply as a member of her Congregation. And because the Institute itself is a "canonical person," it has a more explicitly ecclesial identity than lay groups such as Voice of the Faithful do. Thus there is a certain formal (though not official) "public" quality to Religious Life and its members, corporate and individual, that it would be naïve to deny.

Some members of the hierarchy, even some in the Vatican, collapse the distinction between Religious and the ordained and between the presbyterate and the Congregation in relation to the issue of public ecclesial identity, and confuse the representative character of individual Religious with that of official agents of the Church. Such officials think that all Religious and their Congregations are official agents of the institutional Church when it comes to representing exactly, only, and explicitly the official positions, theologically and legally, of the Vatican or the diocese and enforcing those positions to the extent they are able. Thus, for example, a bishop might attempt to forbid a Religious Congregation to invite to its college a speaker who has contested the official Church position on contraception or who favors the ordination of women, or that it fire a teacher who has made his or her gay identity public.

Resistance to such demands is increasingly frequent and forceful, not because Religious Congregations have no respect for episcopal authority or are indifferent to the moral obligations of Catholics but because they are convinced that the bishop is exceeding his authority in attempting to make the Religious Congregation a coercive arm of the institutional

Church. (And usually those in the hierarchy most insistent on the "official" responsibilities of the Congregation are least ready to accord these same entities any "official" rights in the determination of policy, positions, or practice.) Receiving and listening to someone representing, in word or lifestyle, a contested position in the Church does not constitute ecclesiastical endorsement of that position because Religious as individuals and as Congregations are not agents of the Church. In their capacity as adult believers they are exercising their right to hear and think about alternate positions and they are rejecting a kind of blanket mind control that would forbid such engagement with controversial topics.

Religious Congregations are not instruments of the ecclesiastical institution even though there is a sometimes very complex overlap, in virtue of ministry, between diocesan authority and Congregational autonomy. Serious conflict in this sphere might require the Religious Congregation to withdraw from diocesan ministry or even public ministry in a diocese but it does not give the bishop the right to force the Congregation out of the diocese, to minister according to his directives, or to cease to carry on its internal activities. The bishop might dismiss an individual Religious from a diocesan position because of her expressed beliefs that are contrary to his understanding of Church teaching, but he cannot dismiss her from her Congregation nor, except in rare cases, expel her from the diocese[30] (any more than he can expel a divorced and remarried Catholic from the diocese or legally dissolve the second marriage even though he may dismiss the person from his or her position as a catechist). Though delicate negotiations are sometimes necessary, and some tensions irresolvable, my point here is that it is not a foregone conclusion that hierarchical authority extends always and absolutely to the life and ministry of Religious Congregations and their members.

I would suggest that the proper analogy for the "public" character of Religious, as members of Congregations which are "public persons" in the Church according to Canon Law, is neither the individual private lay person on the one hand nor the individual public ordained minister on the other but derives from the prophetic nature of Religious Life in the Church. Religious are, in fact, in an analogous relationship to the contemporary ecclesial reality as the prophets, including Jesus, were to Judaism. Jesus was not a priest, a Levite, a judge, a Pharisee, a scribe, or a lawyer. That is, he held no official hierarchical position in Judaism. Like the prophets before him, Jesus was not an official representative or agent of the Temple or of its personnel. However, he was certainly a high-profile, very "public" (in the sense of visible and influential) charismatic figure, and his expressed Jewish identity and explicitly religious ministry were never in doubt. He was accorded the honorific "rabbi" or teacher in Israel even though that was a recognition of his religious influence (like that of many Religious today such as Joan Chittister or Theresa Kane) rather than an "office" in Judaism.[31] There was nothing "private" or anonymous (in the sense of secret or unrecognized) about his participation in the religious life and affairs of the Judaism of his time, so much so that his religious activities, especially his teaching, led finally to his arrest and execution at the hands of the political and religious authorities.

Often disapproved of and castigated by the religious authorities, Jesus was both a faithful member of the Jewish religious community and frequently a challenge to its leadership. He was an original interpreter of the Law in favor of those whom the Law had officially interpreted as oppressed. He stood in creative tension with the official Temple worship. He taught on his own authority, in accord with the truth, not by quoting precedent or engaging in the legal polemics of the schools (cf. Matt 7:29; Mark 1:22). He engaged his official challengers in critical and dissenting argument and invited his disciples and the crowds not to stricter observance of the Law as the way of salvation but to participation in the new world, the Reign of God that he parabled into their imaginations in stories and similitudes and symbols which disturbed and sometimes outraged the officials.

In short, Religious both are and are not "public" persons in the Church. As Religious they are publicly recognized as belonging, through their Congregations, to a distinct state of life in the Church and their ministries are normally situated not in the secular but in the ecclesial, if often not in the ecclesiastical, sphere. Public ministries in the Church, those belonging to the official teaching, ruling, and sanctifying offices, and which are sometimes exercised by Religious, are under the authority of the bishop of the diocese who is responsible for their proper function and coordination; but bishops are urged by Canon Law to respect the rightful autonomy of Religious Congregations concerning the apostolates entrusted to them, and the proper authority of the Religious superior in relation to the members of the Institute serving in the diocese.[32]

On the other hand, Religious are not ordained and their vocation is not to exercise authority or office in the Church. This is not a clear-cut and absolute distinction because, as has been said, a Religious (like other nonordained) may exercise an official ministry in a diocese and the highest officer in a Religious Congregation exercises an ecclesiastical (though not hierarchical) office. But, all the overlapping and interlacing notwithstanding, the Religious vocation is charismatic, not institutional, and prophetic, not official or hierarchical. Women Religious particularly need to consistently resist the tendency of the hierarchy to treat them, in regard to obligations though not in regard to power or privilege, as they do ordained male Religious who, *as* ordained (not as Religious) fall under hierarchical authority beyond the boundaries of their Congregations.

All this being said, things are rarely perfectly neat and unambiguous when it comes to human beings in human institutions. Because of the way the Church is currently organized, the history of Religious Congregations in certain dioceses, the way Religious have been formed, the way religion functions in first world societies, and the economic challenges facing Congregations today, it is often the case that Religious will be involved, at least to some extent, in ministries that are functions of the Church as institution. A Religious might be a Canon Lawyer in the diocesan tribunal, a diocesan vicar, a superintendent of Catholic schools, a parish administrator or associate, an RCIA director, or a principal of a parish school. Insofar as she or he is functioning as part of the diocesan ministerial structure her ministry will be to a greater or lesser degree governed by the provisions that organize the ministries in the diocese. A non-ordained Religious may actually have a certain amount of juridical authority over some clerics but will probably have less real leverage in a case of conflict than her subordinate, which can lead to irresolvable bureaucratic tangles.

Nevertheless, as a Religious she or he is subject to her or his own superiors, not to ecclesiastical authority beyond what is owed by other non-clerics in virtue of some ministerial position held in the diocese. In other words, she may be subject to the diocesan hierarchy because and insofar as she is a chancery official, but not as a Religious. And she is no more subject because she is a Religious than she would be as a lay chancery official. In case of irresolvable conflict the leaders of the Religious Congregation cannot force the diocese to treat the Religious justly, but they can remove the Religious from the diocesan position and thus from the ministerial jurisdiction of the bishop.

Ministerial participation in the ecclesiastical structure, especially if there is a reasonable bishop, does not necessarily stifle or compromise the prophetic dimension of the ministry of a Religious, but it is more likely to lead to tensions of various sorts when the individual Religious is ministering in a diocesan institution such as a parish. The postconciliar experience of Congregations has involved egregious and repeated violations of the persons and rights of their members, especially women, as they have been used and abused for ecclesiastical purposes before being summarily dismissed without severance or recommendations, usually in favor of threatened clerics. Other things being equal, Religious running their own Congregational non-diocesan educational institutions, spirituality centers, health care facilities, inner-city poverty, art, and social justice ministries, and so on are much more likely to be able to minister according to their own charisms and with the autonomy and mobility that fosters truly prophetic engagement with the issues of the day in both society and Church. They might, however, have to avoid establishing such works as "ministries" in the name of the Institute to circumvent canonical restrictions.[33]

On the other hand, Religious can often exercise a critical prophetic role in diocesan affairs that their ordained colleagues cannot. Thus, it is a prudential decision on the part of Religious in discernment with their own leadership whether, when, how, and under what circumstances they will undertake ministries that integrate them to some degree into official ecclesiastical structures. But it seems to me that maintaining their essentially prophetic role in the Church requires that they not get themselves into situations in which they must surrender to a unilateral, extra-Congregational control of their prophetic witness by a hierarchical claim that they are official public representatives of the institutional Church and therefore subject to absolute control by the ordained.

It is not likely that the tensions I have been describing between Religious who are a public prophetic presence in, but not owned by, the local Church, and some bishops and clergy who believe that their jurisdiction in the local Church or parish is universal, that their authority absolute, and that Religious are, or should be, simply an "obedient" work force available for ecclesiastical projects will be resolved any time soon. Nor, probably, will the struggles cease between Religious and some Vatican officials who still do not take women Religious seriously as adult subjects of their own lives but continue to see them as troublesome minors who must be controlled by a unilateral exercise of patriarchal authority demanding unquestioning "obedience."

This situation is discouraging at best and there have been increasing discussions of late among Religious about whether the struggle of remaining canonically Religious, remaining "public" figures, even in a nonofficial sense of that term, in an institutional Church that is often so abusive and obstructive, is worth the suffering. Although there are many angles from which this question can be, and has to be, approached, the one I am concerned with in this chapter is spirituality.

If Religious Life is simply a humanitarian project bringing together talented people committed to contributing to a sustainable future for the universe and a better world for its denizens then the answer is probably no. Involvement with the institutional Church is too often an unnecessary and unproductive obstacle to effective pursuit of this objective. If, however, Religious are people personally called by Jesus Christ both to a single-hearted communitarian quest for God and to participating through the creation, by public Profession, of an alternate world within the Church for the sake of the world, then the answer is probably yes. The question facing Religious, in my view, is not primarily a political one: can we survive in a dysfunctional and often corrupt institution? Rather, it is deeply spiritual: does God's mission in the world need the prophetic witness that is Religious Life in the Church as the People of God and, if so, are we willing to pay the price Jesus did to embody that witness in our own time and within our own religious tradition? If we choose to follow in the footsteps of Jesus the prophet, we need a spiritual maturity and commitment well beyond that of embattled subjects in a sometimes totalitarian institution.

III. Conclusion

In this chapter I have tried to shed some light on two very thorny issues which have bedeviled the spirituality of Religious obedience for most of its two-thousand-year history: first, the absolutist understanding of Christian obedience itself; and second, the blanket implications of their "public" status in the Church for the obedience of Religious. The lack of nuance in regard to both issues still has a powerful grip on the Catholic imagination.

The first simplistic assumption is that all legitimate authority is absolute and obedience must respond in kind. The "because I said so" of parent to child is carried forward into adult life, at least in respect to figures (and their laws) who claim participation in the sacral authority of the "parent God," namely, those holding office in the Church. One is either "obedient," that is, does as one is commanded, thereby obeying God, or one is "disobedient." Disobedience is always wrong, even when there are extenuating circumstances. The response of married Catholics to *Humanae Vitae*, to such absolute obligations as weekly Mass attendance, annual confession, and attempts to control their voting or other exercises of civic responsibility is serving notice with increasing emphasis that this "all or nothing" theology of obedience is no longer accepted by the majority of believers. In a voluntary society, even the Church, the authority of the leaders is undermined by the general disregard of their teaching and commands by the members of the society,[34] and the leaders are ill advised to promote such disregard by unreasonable or abusive uses of authority.

The second simplistic assumption is that Religious, because they belong to a Religious Institute which is juridically a "legal person" in the Church, are completely subject in all respects to ecclesiastical authority extending downward from the pope to the bishop to the parish pastor. Religious, in this understanding, are simply an extension, a basically mindless mouthpiece of the hierarchy's position on all matters. As long as Religious accept this understanding of authority and obedience they will, quite simply, be ecclesiastical slaves.

Religious freely vow obedience to God, in the hands of the elected leaders of their Congregation, and according to the Constitutions of their Institute. Religious Congregations have a right to claim legitimate autonomy and the right to internal self-determination and self-governance that cannot be simply usurped by ecclesiastical authorities by virtue of their claiming it. Requesting approval of the Congregation's Constitutions does not cede total control of the members and their life, individually or corporately, to the hierarchy any more than getting married in the Church places the couple under the absolute control of those officials in regard to their married life.

Just as married people have had to resist unwarranted intrusions by Church authority into the exercise of their marital rights and obligations, so Religious have to resist unilateral definitions of their life and its obligations by those outside the Congregation, including ecclesiastical officials. If Religious are living their Constitutions, are not giving public scandal (which is not the same thing as calling a Church official's position into question), and are exercising their ministries according to the intention of their Religious superiors and in appropriate cooperation with the ordinary of the diocese, they are free to determine for themselves, within their Congregation, how they will pursue the holiness proper to their state in life. Repeated examples in recent years of Religious superiors refusing to expel members who have displeased priests or bishops, even though the Religious have not violated the obligations of their Religious state, and of Religious as individuals and groups refusing to submit their conscience decisions to ecclesiastical officials are making the point that simply being a Religious does not suspend one's freedom of conscience or the right and obligation to act according to it.

No doubt this struggle will not end soon. Many in the hierarchy are still operating within a premodern model of society, that of the Church as a divine right monarchy in which authority flows in one direction only, namely, downward, and can be exercised absolutely on the assumption that the subordinates have no rights except those bestowed upon them by the superiors. Religious in general are operating within a different model, one that has developed over the past two centuries in nontotalitarian societies and that was, in principle, enshrined in the documents of Vatican II in its recognition of the equality of all the baptized in the Church and the inviolable freedom of conscience. This equality and freedom are the basis for a theology of obedience as an exercise of asymmetrical mutuality rather than abject subordination.

I would suggest that part of the prophetic witness of Religious Life in the Church today is the calm but unyielding insistence that its integrity and that of its members be respected. That insistence grounds the implication, and supports the assumption, that the same theology of mutuality, equality, and freedom is the only acceptable theology of obedience in the Church of Jesus Christ. Jesus came not as a legitimator of human domination, much less of domination in the name of God, but as the Truth who sets us free.

Chapter Ten
Unitive Discernment in the Quest for God

I. Re-imagining Religious Obedience in the Quest for God

The purpose of the previous chapter was to "clear a space" for meditating on the contemporary spirituality of Religious obedience by proposing that Religious obedience is not primarily or essentially about the relationship of Religious to the official authority structures or personnel of the institutional Church. It is essentially participation in the obedience of Jesus who did always the will of the one sending Him. Jesus was not a slave or subordinate of an all-powerful God but the loving coequal Son of God who fully embodied God's saving design for humanity. Christian obedience, then, which Religious share with all the baptized, is not constituted by blind submission to officials or compliance with laws but by a discerning self-gift to God in all the circumstances of one's life, including one's response to legitimate authority.

The purpose of this chapter is to analyze the changed understanding of obedience that emerged among Religious in the wake of the Council in order to see how the contemporary approach to obedience has changed significantly and yet has remained substantially continuous with the meaning of this vow in the history of the life. Once again, both the continuity, which relates contemporary Religious Life to its own history,

548

and the discontinuity, which validates the real developments the life has undergone and is undergoing, are important.

A. Preconciliar Religious Life as "Enchanted Universe"

1. The role of cloister

Religious, by their vow of obedience, specify their Christian obedience in ways other Christians do not. As we have just seen, that specification is not, as some Church officials continue to claim, an essentially different relationship to official Church authority,[1] but rather a particular relationship to the authority structures and personnel *within their Congregations*— they make Profession according to the Constitutions—leading them deeper and deeper into the unitive quest for God that Religious Life is all about. In other words, our concern here is with the particular "privileged mediations" of God's will which become operative in the life of a Religious because of the vow she makes, analogously to the way certain specific mediations of God's will, in relation to one's family, become operative when one marries. How do these specific mediations, by the response they evoke in the Religious, foster and nurture the deepening union with God in Christ which is the ultimate purpose of Religious Life?

The pre-renewal understanding and practice of Religious obedience contrasts so starkly with our experience today that some people, in and outside of Religious Life, wonder if, in fact, this vow has become *de facto* inoperative. When most Religious alive today entered the convent every detail of life from the rising bell in the morning until the signal for the "great silence" at night was governed by obedience to Constitutions, custom book, horarium, bell, or the explicit or implicit commands of superiors, all seen as the characteristic special mediations of God's will for Religious. They not only got up and went to bed according to schedule but also wore always and only the habit of their order down to the regulation number of pins and pleats; ate when, where, and only what they were served; fulfilled exactly the tasks assigned in the convent and in their apostolates; recreated always and only with the assigned persons in the assigned place and in the approved way; lived where they were sent with those sent to the same house, and left the house only with permission, with a companion, and with a specific destination and purpose. Their prayer was determined as to hour, place, length, and to a large extent form and content as they moved in time with the bell from meditation to liturgy to examen to adoration to spiritual reading to office or common vocal prayers. They studied what and when they were assigned to study and ministered where they were missioned, usually without any consultation or consideration of their preferences. Virtually any activity not specified by Rule, superior, horarium, or custom required explicit permission. The ideal of obedience was that it be unquestioning, prompt, and exact, interior and wholehearted as well as external and effective. In practice, little distinction concerning seriousness of obligation was made among the various mediations through which the Religious knew clearly what God desired of her at any given moment.

Today, astounding as it may seem when we consider how recently this model of obedience was in full force, virtually none of this practice of obedience any longer characterizes Religious Life. Clothing, daily schedule, prayer, recreation, relationships, and most activities are largely decided by the individual, and she participates extensively and substantively in the determination of her living situation as well as her choice of, preparation for, and exercise of ministry. Small wonder, then, that some people feel that Religious obedience has virtually "withered away" in the process of renewal. I think it is precisely in evaluating this judgment that we may come to a renewed understanding of the vow of obedience, which is both in radical substantial continuity and significant discontinuity with what most Religious today lived until the mid-seventies or even later.

First, we need to realize that the uniformity and regularity just described was not—at least among mature Religious— slavishness, scrupulosity, or rigidity, much less a witness to an impoverished imagination or childish dependence. Furthermore, despite some lamentable abuses, it was not the expression of a control agenda on the part of power-hungry superiors.

People entered Religious Life freely, knew before they made Profession what it involved, and, if they stayed, found human and spiritual happiness and fulfillment in this highly regulated and ordered life. Rather than being a masochistically ascetical structure the life was, in fact, especially in regard to the obedience that governed its every detail, the expression of a particular worldview that had largely disappeared outside the convent.

This convent worldview was inherited from earliest monasticism and passed through the Middle Ages[2] into preconciliar Religious Life without substantial modification while, outside of Religious Life, culture had undergone a profound process of modernization in the post-medieval period. This transition has been called, picturesquely but accurately, the transition from a premodern "enchanted worldview" to a modern and now postmodern "secular worldview."

The premodern worldview was "enchanted," not because it was magical or superstitious, but because its denizens interpreted all reality, no matter how mundane, as full of, saturated by, the spiritual or the transcendent. In some way, everything was permeated by that which transcended the total grasp or full control of humans.[3] Nothing was purely secular, that is exclusively immanent, in our contemporary sense of that term. Thus, because all reality was an expression of God in the world, all life should be a response of praise to God. The "veil" of appearances between what we today would call the mundane and the more-than-mundane was diaphanous. God, whether experienced as beneficent or threatening, was palpably present and active in all of life. The medieval mystery plays in which the three-tiered stage revealed simultaneously to the viewer heaven, earth, and the underworld was a faithful image of real life for the person of faith, and in some sense that meant virtually everyone.

Preconciliar Religious Life was distinct from surrounding Catholic life as well as from secular society because, by virtue of cloister, it had been able to retain much of the medieval "enchanted" worldview that had been passing away since the Renaissance in the fifteenth century and was virtually nonexistent, even for religious people, by modern times. But because the culture of Religious Life during this emergence of modernity evolved much more slowly (or even not at all) in relation to the surrounding culture, it acquired a certain, increasingly exotic character (that it did not have in the Middle Ages, when its worldview coincided more fully with that of its cultural environment). In other words, Religious, largely because of the physical, psychological, and social separation effected by cloister, could and did maintain not only a somewhat medieval lifestyle in the concrete details of convent living, but also a medieval religious worldview, even as they participated selectively in their actual modern cultural setting (such as using modern educational methods in their schools).

I have described preconciliar Religious Life sociologically as a "total institution" which disintegrated in the wake of the renewal as Religious turned toward the "world" which God so loved and from which they had previously seen themselves as totally separated. This sociological isolation from the world and secular culture made possible and fostered the religious and spiritual climate of the "enchanted universe." No matter how deeply secularization was permeating culture outside the convent, inside the cloister the sacralization of every aspect of life continued.

By means of the habit which she donned each morning—each piece of which, especially the veil and scapular, Religious had worn for centuries—the Religious *person* "put on Christ" from head to foot. The horarium, regulated minutely by the bell heard as the "voice of God," related every moment of *time* to eternity. Real time in the Religious house was not measured, as it was for the participants in industrial modernity, by weekend respite from the drudgery of daily work, but by Sunday, when the implicit worship of the ordinary apostolate was taken up in the explicit worship of the Lord's Day. The year was not punctuated by secular holidays as times of festival but unfolded joyfully and solemnly in the liturgical year with its major Christmas and Easter seasons, and Ordinary Time marked by the sanctoral cycle celebrating persons and events, many of which were special to the Congregation. The *space* of the cloistered dwelling was free of all secular activity and closed to all secular people. *Manual work* was care of God's property, which, no matter how poor or lowly in function, was to be handled, as St. Benedict had exhorted, with the reverence due to the vessels of divine worship. And the *apostolate* was not a job or profession but a sacred task entrusted to the Religious. The superior was not just the administrator of a community, much less the boss of a work force, but God's *representative* expressing the divine will in solicitude, instruction, direction, or even correction. The Rule was God's special and specific *covenant law* for this community and the community itself was a *chosen people* among whom the individual Religious was privileged to be numbered.

In short, cloister was critical to the creation, maintenance, and life-giving power of this sacralized world, whether absolute in the enclosed monastery or somewhat mitigated in "apostolic Orders." Cloister, which kept the Religious inside and everything that was not Religious Life outside, protected the sacralized world from the questions and challenges which might relativize the self-evident validity of the life. Cloister was the sacred safeguard of the sociological reality of the "the total institution," and the total institution protected the enchanted universe.

Such measures as keeping family names and other details of pre-convent life of the members as well as the contents of the Rule, customs, and practices from secular scrutiny, protected the individual members as well as the group from any challenge to their way of life. What went on in the convent, however intriguing to outsiders, remained a mystery to them. The serenity, in-group loyalty, ministerial generosity and effectiveness, and public piety of the Religious had to suffice as justification of the life to the external world. Whatever Religious were living, seculars were to conclude, it must be good because it produced, generally speaking, good, generous, and happy people.

2. The role of obedience

The second feature of pre-renewal Religious Life that played a constitutive role in maintaining the "enchanted world" was the understanding of obedience described above. The all-embracing obedience which governed every moment of the life integrated the members into the structure and function of this sacralized environment, which could only continue to exist if everyone believed in and lived it fully and there was no serious challenge to it from the outside. In other words, obedience was both an expression and a sustainer of the total institution which cloister protected. The resulting "world" was the enchanted universe, the sacred environment in which faith illuminated every aspect of life whose details, in turn, mediated the will of God to the obedient Religious on a moment-to-moment basis.

Before discussing how the premodern understanding and practice of obedience helped create and maintain the enchanted or sacralized world, and why the postconciliar changed understanding of obedience definitively subverted that world, it is important to recall that the basically cloistered form of apostolic Religious Life came to a fairly abrupt end with the "turn to the world" initiated by Vatican II. We have discussed at length in previous chapters why and how the Church, at the Council, reversed its centuries long rejection of and estrangement from "the world," the expression of this reversal, particularly in *Gaudium et Spes*, and the challenge this reversal raised for Religious who were urged by the Church not only to update certain outmoded practices in their lives but to reconceptualize their life and mission as participation in the Church's own newly espoused mission in, to, and for the world.

The "return to the sources" of apostolic Religious, which revealed the non-cloistered and ministerial intentions of the founders of many of their Congregations, required the practical reenvisioning of the life. This reenvisioning began with the postconciliar Chapters and the resulting renewal effectively ended cloister for ministerial Religious. Without cloister the sociological model of Religious Life as total institution could not be maintained and the "enchanted universe" that it protected quickly dissipated. More and more Religious, for a variety of reasons, undertook individualized or inter-Congregational ministries outside hierarchically controlled institutions, and this often entailed non-collective living situations with the necessity for Religious to assume more personal responsibility for their lifestyle. Congregations undertook to rewrite their premodern, highly detailed, behavior-focused Constitutions in terms of their deepened understanding of the Gospel, renewed vision of the ministerial motivation of their founders, and increased appreciation of the vocation to human maturity and personal spirituality of their members.

Experientially, for the Religious themselves, "convent (i.e., semi-enclosed monastic) life" disappeared. The sacred dress (habit), sacred time and space (horarium and cloister), exclusive company of other Sisters in their own Congregation, daily collective prayer, meals, work, and recreation within the house (common life), as well as ministries in Congregationally owned and operated institutions (apostolates) were no longer possible. The minute-by-minute external mediation of the divine will—in other words, an entire conception or imagination of Religious Life itself as enchanted universe—had disappeared.

3. Expressions of a crisis in the understanding of obedience

As Religious began to assume personal responsibility for the details of their own lives, both mundane and spiritual, and to participate in major ways in their choice of ministry and living situation—all of which had once been minutely regulated by obedience to external authority—many began to doubt that obedience any longer had a significant role in their lives.

This sensed disorientation has led to at least three disturbing reactions with which we are still dealing. Some few Congregations chose a *rigidly traditionalist* path. After making a few evidently necessary minor modifications, especially in the externals of their lives, they called a halt to renewal and reaffirmed what they regarded as the essential elements of Religious Life such as Congregational group living for all members, traditional common life in regard to prayer, work, horarium, and especially habit, and institutional Church ministries preferably operated by their own Congregations in dependence on the hierarchy. Their theology of obedience called for a reaffirmation of the preconciliar understanding and practice. Theologically they lined up with the emerging restorationism of the John Paul II papacy, reaffirmed their commitment to a certain type of preconciliar theology of Religious Life, and became very vocal in their opposition to the renewal in other Congregations.

The divergence of their choices from what was happening in the vast majority of renewing Congregations, and their sense of being a final, and perhaps threatened, bulwark against the disintegration of the life under the influence of the renewal, led, in the United States, to the formation of a separate organization of major superiors of these traditionalist groups, the Council of Major Superiors of Women Religious. CMSWR unfortunately took an increasingly antagonistic stance toward the mainstream Leadership Conference of Major Superiors (LCWR) in which most Congregations participated. This self-separation and antagonism, warmly encouraged by restorationist elements in the Vatican as well as the most conservative elements in the Church in the United States, has tended to produce a regrettable and unnecessary rift within women's Religious Life in the United States,[4] which many regard as totally unnecessary and hope will be short-lived.

A second development was a *romanticist* movement among both women and men that led to the foundation of a few new and highly traditionalist communities, some by clerics or bishops eager to organize young recruits for John Paul II's "new evangelization" agenda and "theology of the body" moral theology, and some by Religious themselves as separatist movements within, or break-offs from, established Congregations. With an emphasis on conspicuous attire, uniform group prayer, group living, common apostolates, traditional forms of penance, unquestioning loyalty to superiors, blind obedience, and magisterial fundamentalism, these groups appealed directly to the most enthusiastic type of young people whom John Allen of the *National Catholic Reporter* has called the "new Catholic evangelicals." These idealistic youth (they are overwhelmingly in the "adolescent/emerging adulthood" stage, which differentiates them from the traditionalists described above who have been in Religious Life since before the Council), like many of their contemporaries in various religiously tinged (or deeply dyed) youth movements, are in search of clear, unproblematic, publicly recognized social identity and emotionally expressive peer-group belonging. They are drawn to authority figures they can trust for unquestioned truth on important issues and who can assure them of meaning in this life and eternal salvation in the next if they are totally obedient to their superiors, ecclesiastical and Religious. They often identify themselves as "the pope's youth," "brides of Christ," or religious "soldiers" in a holy war. They seem to enjoy the media's attention to their unusual choices and behaviors and evince a sense of joyful solidarity with one another in a great counter-cultural adventure open only to the elite. They are often deeply attracted to mysterious ritual, repetitive vocal prayer in foreign languages, and public forms of piety including corporal penitential practices from earlier times.

A third troubling development has taken place within mainstream Religious Congregations that have pursued in depth the conciliar agenda of renewal. These individuals are not organized groups but "lone rangers" who have become pervasively *secularized and marginalized* without juridically separating from their Congregations. Probably every Congregation has a few such members who, concluding that obedience has no real meaning in Religious Life today and therefore that there is no central organizing dynamic at work in the Congregation, have drifted to the fringe (or beyond the fringe) of Congregational life.

These isolated members ignore directives about financial or ministerial accountability, seldom if ever participate in Congregational meetings or respond to corporate consultations, take no role in local, intermediate, or general structures or processes of governance. Because general ordinances or directives with attached sanctions are not emanating from superiors they consider as optional any consultation about, much less compliance with, Congregational policies about travel, study, transportation or dwellings, health care, vacations, recreation or anything else that would formerly have come under the heading of obedience. Many of these "members," who in effect have left the Congregation without formally seeking dispensation, have relocated their personal commitments outside the Catholic Christian faith in various kinds of nondenominationalism or eclectic spiritualities, ecological commitments, politically motivated social justice or feminist projects, or simply taken up professional careers that are unrelated to religion, Church, or the Congregation.

The fact that such a situation, even if it involves only two or three members of a Congregation, can continue for relatively long periods unless Congregational leaders act decisively is a worrisome testimony to the real possibility of individual Religious totally (mis)understanding the renewed theology of obedience as the abrogation of the vow. It underscores the importance at this historical juncture of clearly articulating a life-giving theology and spirituality of the vow of obedience both for newer members who never lived in the preconciliar sacralized environment and for those who have experienced, but perhaps not reflected on, the meaning of obedience in contemporary Religious Life.

B. The Transition in the Understanding of the Vow of Prophetic Obedience

1. The privileged mediations of God's will in preconciliar Religious Life

Christian obedience, as we have said, is the disciple's quest for ever-deepening union of will with God. By discerning attention to the natural and supernatural mediations through which God's will is made known and responding to that will in freedom, the disciple grows in the holiness to which all the baptized are called. But differing life situations, such as the vocations of marriage or Religious Life, diverse existential factors such as age, education, and capabilities, diverse historical contexts such as developed or developing world situations, and so on, introduce what I have called "privileged mediations" of the will of God which are particular to the vocation and circumstances of the individual or group in question.

Until recently the particular privileged mediations that characterized Religious Life included all the indications of God's will that together constructed the "enchanted universe" we have just described. Superior, Constitutions, customs, bell, horarium, cloister, daily common life in regard to meals, prayer, apostolic assignment, recreation, and so on—all particular to Religious Life as such—wove every moment of every day into a seamless robe clothing the life of the Religious in holy obedience the way the holy habit clothed her body from head to toe.

What all these mediations of God's will, diverse as they were in objective importance, subject matter, and medium, had in common was their *heteronomous character, including sanctions* (positive and negative) that they entailed. They were all extrinsic to the Religious, addressed to her as exercises of external authority, and had to be internalized by her as obedience defined virtually always as submission and compliance. Such obedience was rewarded in many ways while disobedience was punished. Coercion, possible or actual, was intrinsic to the relation of obedience to authority. Thus, obedience in the enchanted universe of preconciliar convent life, no matter how free and willing, was not a relationship between equal adults seeking God's will together but an intrinsically hierarchical relation of domination (ideally benevolent) and subordination (ideally willing) between "superior" and "subject."[5] The superior commanded in God's name; the subject responded to God by submission to the superior.

The very heteronomy of the exercise of authority was often invoked as an indication, if not proof, that submission itself actually *constituted* obedience. As long as one was *not* "doing one's own will" one could be sure that one *was* "doing God's will." Even in situations in which compliance might be wrong, "in doubt, it was always better to obey." From the novitiate on Religious, were taught, "Even if the superior errs in commanding, the subject never errs in obeying unless the action commanded is certainly sinful." The Religious who "keeps the Rule" could be sure that the "Rule will keep her." Even the bell was referred to as "the voice of God." In other words, a rejection or surrender of one's own "will"—whether spontaneity, freedom of choice, or even deep spiritual desire—that was rooted in a profound mistrust of one's own intelligence and motivations was inculcated from formation onward. Thus, obedience consisted in the suspension or even renunciation of one of the fundamental resources for moral development through genuine obedience to God, namely, one's own created nature as an intelligent and free subject.

The primary casualty of this understanding of obedience was maturity of conscience. Conscience, understood as the ongoing exercise in community of personal prudential judgment regarding the moral character and value of proposed choices and actions, was, in effect, "sacrificed" on the altar of obedience. The deleterious effect of this paralysis of conscience was, in many cases, a moral immaturity that manifested itself embarrassingly (if not worse) in the lack of prudence and good judgment that characterized the behavior and relationships of some Religious in their first renewal-inspired ventures into the "outside world." Without the regimentation of convent life and the continual surveillance of a superior, some Religious who had not had to govern their own personal lives (in contrast, often, to their demanding apostolic/professional lives) since they were teenagers were simply unable at first to make the mature personal decisions demanded by life outside the total institution.

Another unfortunate result of this understanding of obedience as intrinsically heteronomous and coercive was that some Religious were unable to make the transition to more consensual and collegial discernment of God's will in their lives, from sanctioned submission to external commands to voluntary and responsible cooperation as the expression of adult obedience to God's will. For them, what was not explicitly mandatory was, by definition, optional.

2. Renewal of the theology of mediation and discernment

We have already seen, in various contexts, that it was not the case that obedience disappeared from Religious Life in the course of the conciliar renewal. Rather, the *understanding and therefore the practice of obedience changed* in light of new theology, the changed social situation of Religious which occurred with the dissolution of the total institution, and the socioreligious context of feminist consciousness. Religious are still called to holiness through union of will with God, but the mediations through which God's will expresses itself have *expanded in range and changed in mode.* And, correspondingly, the *process of discernment* is significantly modified.

a. THE EXPANDING RANGE AND CHANGED MODE OF MEDIATION OF GOD'S WILL

Without repeating descriptions of these developments already discussed, let us simply recall that the theology of the Council initiated an extraordinary openness of the Church to the "other": to people of different denominations and religions,[6] to the whole spectrum of human cultures in which the Church lives, to the world itself as the place of God's salvific self-revelation, and to new developments in science, media, and communications. No longer were the spiritual antennae of believers to be attuned only to Church teaching or their duty to God to be satisfied by religious observances. Rather, they were to be alert to what God is revealing in the events of their time; to the struggles, joys, and hopes of the whole human race; to the traces of God's finger in the unfolding of the universe itself.

Religious who had been sheltered from the news media, cultural expression in films and the other arts, and from politics, economic developments, and social movements now realized that these were not "distractions" or "secular temptations" but genuine "places" of God's involvement with humanity, loci of ongoing revelation. And the complexity, moral ambiguity, and sheer volume of this information called for ongoing discernment that vastly exceeded accepting blindly the rather black-or-white simplicity of earlier official Church pronouncements about what was or was not God's will for Catholics in general and Religious in particular.

Besides this vastly expanded range of challenges to discernment common to all in the Church, Religious Life also faced the particular challenges to renewal addressed to it by the Council. Among the realities that emerged in the life of Religious in the wake of the Council was the awareness of the urgency of ministerial commitment beyond the borders of the Church and its in-house concerns. Social justice issues, approached systemically, rose to the top of the ministerial agenda. Sisters marching with Martin Luther King, Jr., going to prison for civil "disobedience," protesting war, opening their suburban schools to the children of undocumented immigrants, speaking out for gay rights, and so on were in stark contrast to their immediate elders (or even their former selves) who would not have known the details of the Civil Rights struggle or been able to apply just war criteria to the Vietnam conflict, much less justify opposing the opinions and even orders of clergy and hierarchy on numerous issues.

In short, the range of mediations of God's will, both those common to all Christians and the privileged mediations particular to Religious Life, was vastly expanded by the openness to the world in all its complexity called for by the theology of Vatican II, and the dissolution of the total institution in which Religious had been enclosed. Furthermore, the mode of this mediation was no longer limited to authoritative, externally delivered, explicit expressions of God's will by superiors, texts, structures, and convent routines. Those expressions of God's work in the world no longer came with a clear *imprimatur* or *nihil obstat* that would obviate the need for personal evaluation of the phenomena which appeared on one's moral horizon. The whole of reality was now seen as God's address to the minds and hearts, that is, to the consciences, of Jesus' disciples, and was required to be heard and heeded. The nightly news was now as much a call to obedience as was the horarium of the house or the order of a superior in former times.

b. THE CHANGING UNDERSTANDING OF THE PROCESS OF DISCERNMENT

The sheer scope, complexity, and ambiguity of the historical and ecclesial reality, which Religious now understand as mediating into their lives in ever new ways the challenge of fostering the Reign of God in the field of this world, brought into renewed focus a process which has always been, at least theoretically, important in the practice of Christian obedience; namely, discernment. However, in the preconciliar Church, self-enclosed against the modern world and providing for its members a full "menu" of obligations, devotions, and teachings transmitted and enforced by clerical officials whose authority was largely unquestioned, most believers considered "what the Church says" about any topic as all they really needed to know on the subject. In other words, personal or corporate discernment was largely superfluous. Authority discerned and decided and the rest obeyed. And in the convent every detail of daily life was explicitly regulated by privileged mediations such as Rule, superior, and horarium. Even without the stimulus of the firestorm of controversy stirred up by *Humanae Vitae,* the expanded engagement of Catholics with the modern world would probably sooner rather than later have precipitated a felt need for individuals to take much greater personal responsibility for moral decision making.[7] For Religious, the transition from the "enchanted world" of semi-monastic life into the larger Church and world made this need imperative.

Discernment is an exercise of the virtue of prudence. It is neither mechanical (a process of totting up the positive and negative dimensions of a situation and going with the former) nor esoteric (an arcane process reserved for specialists). It is a difficult process required in any situation in which we must make a judgment or decision about *what is the right thing to do in the present situation.* Notice, the question is not about what is, in principle, right for a theoretical subject in some generic situation (e.g., a person must not kill) but rather what *I* am called to do, *here and now,* in response to the *concrete situation* in which I find myself (e.g., whether to enlist to fight in a war of choice, procure an abortion, vote for capital punishment).[8]

Discernment is never an isolated process. Even when the decision being made primarily affects the individual rather than the community, it is *always communal* in the sense that a valid conscience decision must take into account the persons and groups to whom one is related in ways relevant to the situation (e.g., for Religious, their own community and its particular law), the influence of one's decisions on others, and so on.[9] Furthermore, discernment is not a matter of simply "making up one's own mind." A prudent person recognizes the need to *"form one's conscience,"* that is to consult, to familiarize oneself with the biblical, moral, historical, and theological data relevant to the issue to the extent that this is realistically possible, to attend to good example, to examine circumstances carefully, and to do whatever else it is possible to do to bring to bear in the decision-making process all the data relevant to the situation within the limits of time and warrants of importance of the question.

As moral theologians unanimously teach, a well formed, even if erroneous, conscience not only *can* but *must* be followed. Experienced people know that any conscience judgment, no matter how carefully achieved, can be erroneous. No one, from pope to peasant, has absolute knowledge of absolute truth, although Church teaching is sometimes erroneously presented as if there were a strict equation between official teaching and the mind of God and thus that no dissent can ever be a good moral choice. No matter how frequently this position is reiterated, explicitly or implicitly, this is simply not the case. If it were, conscience would not be necessary. So, acting morally— that is, trying to discern God's will and act accordingly—is never risk-free. We are always doing the best we can in full knowledge of both our finitude and our sinfulness, in the confidence that God never asks of us what is impossible.

Finally, and directly relevant to the issue of obedience in the context of Religious Life, women Religious in general have assimilated the analysis of patriarchy that feminism was developing during the period just before and after the Council. To the distress of some of the hierarchy these women have applied this analysis in and to their own lives. This has meant not only realizing that as women in the most relentlessly patriarchal institution in the Western world they have been and continue to be systemically oppressed in their own Church, but also that the structures and functioning of their own Congregations were, until very recently, deeply impregnated with the principles and practices of patriarchy. The issue of obedience to hierarchical authority in the Church, both local and universal, has indeed been increasingly conflictual as women have assumed rightful autonomy as adult believers and Religious. But perhaps more important and urgent in the long run has been the radical reenvisioning of the understanding of obedience in their own communities, most of which were mini- "divine right" monarchies modeled on that of the institutional Church.[10]

C. Prophetic Obedience in Contemporary Religious Life

Almost fifty years after the Council the renewal of Religious Life in the vast majority of first world Congregations (and increasing numbers in developing areas) has resulted in an understanding of obedience that may constitute the most profound difference between pre- and postconciliar living of this vocation. It is certainly the flashpoint of the accusations and laments by champions of the restorationist agenda—hierarchical, Religious, and lay—that contemporary Religious Life has disintegrated. Although space prevents a thorough description and analysis of this new understanding, virtually all of its features have been discussed at various points in this volume and its predecessors. Here I want to pull together the salient features in their interrelationship as a background for the final, and most important, section of this chapter, namely, the evolution of obedience in the personal spirituality of Religious.

Obedience, as it has been discussed in this work, is the appropriate response to authority. Religious authority and obedience are correlative rather than separate and juxtaposed. They are free and active exercises of attention, initiative, and cooperation. The dynamic of obedience is an ongoing dialogue by means of which a person attempts to follow Jesus in doing always the will of God. The will of God, however, is not some heteronomous imposition of divine commands. It is God's loving self-gift to humanity, for our good. Obedience is the loving response by which the person, in self-giving response, becomes increasingly one with the self-giving God. "The will of God," says Paul, "is your sanctification" (see 1 Thes 4:3). It is the fullness of divine life, which God offers us in Christ and enables us in the Spirit to accept and live. The will of God is a lure, a lodestar, drawing us forward through the challenges and opportunities, the sufferings and joys of earthly life toward the Resurrection life to which we are called.

The will of God, because it is not a list of imperatives but a

comprehensive reality that envelops and saturates our experience, must be continuously discerned in our ongoing life.
Authority is the characteristic of anyone or anything that mediates the divine will. In other words, authority is the quality we
recognize in the appeal to our freedom of some aspect of experience. Authority is the claim of a person, a law, an experience,
an opportunity, a gift, or some other reality to be heard and
heeded, to be attentively considered as an indication of God's
creative work in our life with which we are called to cooperate.
As we have seen, Religious share with all believers the global
and ongoing indications of God's will that address us in our historical circumstances and the ongoing life of the Church in
which we participate.

But Religious Life itself, the alternate world that Religious
enter and within and through which they engage the world
from their distinctive place within the Church, presents the
Religious with those privileged mediations that are characteristic of and particular to the life itself. Some of these privileged
mediations are unique and singular, such as the foundational
vocation to Religious Life. Others are habitual, such as the
responsibilities undertaken in virtue of the Constitutions of the
Congregation. Some are constitutive of the life, shaping it from
within on a daily basis, such as the vows, community life, and
ministry. Others are time-limited and circumstantial, such as the
requirements of a particular ministry, or a call to leadership, or
the obligation to participate in a Congregational process.

The vow of obedience is, then, a commitment to be continuously attentive to the claims of reality, general and personal,
that must be heard and heeded as expressive of God's will in
one's life. Discernment is necessary not only to recognize *that*
our experience is the locus and manifestation of God's appeal
to our freedom, but also to figure out *what* is being revealed,
offered to us, or asked of us in that ongoing experience.

It is not a foregone conclusion, for example, that the request
of a community leader, a particular stipulation of Constitutions
or custom, an invitation to consider Congregational leadership, or a specific ministry is purely and simply God's will at this
moment. The presumption is in favor of those indications that

are integral to one's vocation. Listening attentively to what is asked in such circumstances is the first act of obedience. Heeding this indication will normally mean acceding to the request or invitation. But heeding responsibly might sometimes entail bringing up other or counter considerations. It could even mean, on rare occasions, respectfully declining to comply or meeting the request differently than was originally proposed.

There are some significant differences, however, between the preconciliar understanding of how we attend to the manifestation of God's will and the contemporary understanding. One is a certain necessary *individualization* in the way common obligations are discerned and fulfilled. For example, all members are obliged to participate according to the Constitutions in the governance structures and procedures of the Congregation such as the general Chapter, which is a primary way Congregational authority is collegially exercised today. The obligation to participate, even if it cannot be fulfilled at a given time, does not obviate the obligation or make participation optional. It simply makes it, in this particular instance, impossible even though it remains obligatory.

A second difference is that many Religious Congregations, recognizing the fundamental equality and mutuality of all members, whether they are in office or not, have transformed monarchical structures of domination and submission into genuinely *communitarian and collegial* ones, and authority is no longer normally exercised by sanctioned commands. Again, this does not mean that the provisions arrived at by consensus, adopted collegially, and articulated as shared vision and projects are not binding on all the members. It simply means that all are equally responsible for the life and mission of the Congregation even though some individuals are asked by the community to exercise particular responsibilities of leadership at particular times or in relation to particular aspects of their shared life. When these leaders address individual members in relation to these corporate responsibilities they are exercising a legitimately authoritative function to which Religious owe professed obedience.

A third difference is the contemporary realization that different privileged mediations of God's will in the community have *differing weight and importance*. For example, the basic openness of one's relationship with leadership, including responsibility and accountability, is more important than absolute exactitude in filling out a particular form or hanging the car keys on the appointed hook. Members are expected to make appropriate decisions about matters that were once the subject of specific and sanctioned rules and regulations among which distinctions regarding the seriousness of obligations were seldom made. But again, that does not mean that someone can decide whether or not she is obliged by community decisions but only how she fulfills her obligations when conflicts of value arise.

There are certainly other differences, but the point is that obedience is just as pervasive and probably more demanding in the life of a contemporary Religious—especially in terms of personal and communal discernment, renunciation of personal preferences in favor of the common good, responsibility, accountability, and cooperation—than it was in the context of the total institution with its emphasis on uniformity, heteronomy, coercion, and dominative power. Precisely because there is much personal choice involved in being obedient it can be more demanding than conformity that permitted no choice. When authority is exercised in mutuality and equality as a service among equals rather than as domination of inferiors by superiors, and it addresses itself to the freedom rather than the fear of the members, those practices do not eviscerate, much less obliterate, obedience. Rather, they encourage the genuine and free obedience of adult sons and daughters of God whose model is Jesus who was obedient unto death.

Something that has not changed is that the most personally challenging aspect of obedience today is still the interpersonal experience of mutual cooperation in relation to other members of the Congregation and to Congregational leaders. It is much easier to make a thoughtful determination in regard to conflicting behavioral obligations than to negotiate with a person with whom we disagree. As we saw in chapters 7 and 8, the free integration of the individual into a community of equal adults who commit themselves to one another for life and in which leadership is a necessary and important ministry to the whole will require, at times and perhaps often, active listening, the disposition to cooperate at the cost of one's own plans and even convictions, and effective commitment to participating in the Congregation's life and mission as it is discerned and articulated by the community and implemented by the leaders.

As we will see in a moment, the role of obedience will vary as a person progresses not only in integration into the community but in the spiritual life. But at every stage obedience is just as all pervasive in the life of the Religious as are the singlehearted love expressed in consecrated celibacy and the total nonpossession of evangelical poverty. Together the vows create and structure the alternate world, the concrete realization in history of the Reign of God, in which Religious live the reality of community and from which they minister to the world.

II. Growing in Obedience: A Spirituality of Unitive Freedom

Throughout this work I have tried to promote a basic understanding of Religious Profession in which the vows are not understood as punctual acts by which the Religious assumes certain specific supererogatory obligations but as the total and integrated self-gift to God. The vows are understood as symbolically inclusive expressions of total commitment to the God-quest. Each of the vows, as we have seen, situates the Religious in relation to one of the fundamental coordinates of human existence: relationships (consecrated celibacy shaping the dynamic of love), material goods (evangelical poverty shaping the dynamic of desire), and power (prophetic obedience shaping the dynamic of freedom). And the living of each of the vows has at least three dimensions or three contexts in which it functions: the communitarian, the ministerial, and the unitive. In this chapter we are examining the unitive dimension of prophetic obedience, the understanding of which has undergone major transformation in theory and practice during the past fifty years. The task of this section is to look at the lived experience of obedience in the spirituality of Religious concentrating especially on the *developmental* characteristic of this experience.

For reasons already discussed, the theory that the relationships in the Religious Congregation are intrinsically and necessarily hierarchical—understood until fairly recent times as the only possible way to organize any stable social entity and as God's sole model for human societies—in which some people hold virtually absolute power over others in the name of God, and subordinates therefore owe unquestioning interior and exterior submission to superiors, is theologically faulty, psychologically retarding, socially dysfunctional, and spiritually stunting. The Religious community, I have argued, is a voluntary society of equal adults, not a primary family of parents and children, a feudal fiefdom of masters and serfs, an army under military discipline, or a divine right monarchy. We need not revisit here the arguments against these secular hierarchical/patriarchal models of obedience. In what follows I am talking about Religious obedience in an egalitarian community that has communally chosen leadership structures and in which all members are co-responsible for the life and mission of the Congregation even though their roles in that shared enterprise are diverse and changing.

In this section I want to concentrate on the actual experience of the positive role of obedience in the spirituality of Religious throughout their lifetime from initial formation to death. Important to these considerations are some recent major developments in social anthropology and developmental psychology. Today, we have a more nuanced approach to developmental diversity in relation to obedience generally; and in addition the model of human development with which we are working is significantly different from that which was operative when most of today's Religious entered. Erik Erikson's division of the lifecycle into eight stages, although more finely tuned than the earlier division into childhood, adolescence, and adulthood, was already under revision before his death and scholars continue to refine our picture of adult development. This suggests that we can no longer, as in the recent past, assume that the practice of obedience appropriate to a person in her twenties in the novitiate remains the same into her sixties or eighties.

Developmental psychologists have helped us realize that childhood embraces infancy, early childhood, and latency (with a need for different types of schools for children in these different stages because their capabilities and needs are quite different) and that adolescence is not simply early or preparatory adulthood but a distinct stage (including a not yet fully developed brain that makes risky behavior "normal") with its own developmental tasks and challenges. Likewise, today geriatricians, life cycle psychologists, cultural anthropologists, and sociologists are dividing adulthood into emerging adulthood (twenties to early thirties),[11] adulthood I (thirties to sixties), adulthood II (sixties to eighties),[12] followed by old age.

This new staging is at least partly the result of the increased life expectancy in first world countries as well as the widespread improvements in health care that make millions of people today able to function at eighty the way people did at sixty only a few decades ago. Many people in their eighties and nineties are still living independently and productively, well able to care for themselves, sustain their personal relationships at a high level, and contribute to their communities. But especially significant for our purposes is the fact that this expansion of life is not in the period of youth but in maturity. It is adulthood prior to old age that has been greatly expanded by the recognition that there is a decade between the end of adolescence and the beginning of full adulthood (emerging adulthood) and one to three decades between the end of what used to be considered adulthood and the beginning of genuine old age.

The expectation of living two, three, or more decades longer, and more vigorously, than one's grandparents did allows young people to take more time in assuming adult responsibilities such as work, financial independence, marriage and parenthood, and to spend years in education, travel, and experimentation in the realistic expectation that they will still have more than one "life" as an adult ahead of them. Not only is one expected (barring catastrophic illness or accident) to be fully employed, self-sufficient, socially involved, and vigorously healthy until at least seventy or even seventy-five, but most fifty-year-olds also consider themselves, and are considered by others, as quite young. In a youth-worshipping, age-denying culture such as that of the United States this quantitative life extension has major qualitative implications for families, educational patterns, the economy, the structure of the work force, and individual persons.

It also has important implications for Religious Life. We are well aware that, in most cases, people in the first world are entering Religious Life much later than they did in the 1950s and 1960s. Furthermore, those who enter in their late twenties or early thirties are in some ways developmentally more like the late teenager of preconciliar novitiates than the thirty-year-old of that same era who had made final Profession in her late twenties. People entering today in their mid-forties or fifties are very different from the silver jubilarians who were that same age in the 1960s. Likewise, Religious today who are in their late seventies, eighties, and even occasionally in their nineties often are not retirees psychologically, socially, or ministerially, even if they might be such in terms of society's employment structure.

Several questions are raised for Religious Congregations by this still quiet revolution in age-related life development. The most evident cluster of questions concerns the age for entrance.[13] Do we really want "twenty-somethings" in formation if they will very likely be psychologically incapable of perpetual commitment even in their early thirties after a decade of formation? (There are, of course, exceptions but, probably, they will be even fewer in the future.) But, if the early or even mid-twenties is too young, how old is too old for formation? What does "formation" mean when the new arrival is in her thirties and just beginning to accept that she cannot "experiment" for the rest of her life; in her forties but not at all sure she will want to continue for more than a few years in the ministry for which her current graduate school program is preparing her; in her fifties, successfully retired from her first major lifework as a psychologist, divorced with an annulment, three grown children and several grandchildren? And beyond the question of formation, can such rich and varied concrete life experiences, including necessarily lifelong personal commitments to children and grandchildren, be integrated into a perpetual commitment in a celibate lifeform?[14]

A second set of questions that has received much play in the press in the last few years is how we are to understand an "aging community." Is a Congregation composed primarily of adults in their sixties to nineties a dying enterprise? Should its members be withdrawing from active ministry, abstaining from taking new members, planning for the phaseout of its institutions or at least of the presence or involvement of its members within them, and accepting that its role in Church and society is over? Are Religious a "dying breed" and Religious Life a "vanishing lifeform?" Or is such a Congregation actually composed of the real adults in our society, those whom anthropologist Mary Catherine Bateson says are in the "age of active wisdom?" Is Religious Life with its current age configuration the ministerial lifeform required for and suitable to the faith community today when four times as many Americans are over eighteen as under?[15]

These important questions are not unrelated to the question I want to raise here: what does the spirituality of obedience mean in the developmental course of a Religious Life which runs not from eighteen to sixty but from thirty to ninety? Specifically, what does obedience mean in the process of formation, both initial and ongoing? What does it mean for the person in the flood tide of ministerial life, that is, in adulthood I and adulthood II? What does it mean for the Religious in old age? How does the lived experience of prophetic obedience begin, change, develop, mature, and flower over a Religious lifetime that may not begin before the age of thirty and may well extend over a period of fifty years or more?

A. The Spirituality of Pedagogical Obedience: Formation

Regardless of the age or stage in the life cycle of the person entering Religious Life, she or he will spend the first five to ten years in "initial formation." This process is no longer seen as a kind of "boot camp" at the end of which the person is basically equipped for "convent life" which is not expected to change much, if at all, during her lifetime. A lifelong process of "ongoing formation" is now an integral part of Religious Life at every stage. But, contrary to the monolithic definition of obedience as "doing what one is told" by heteronomous "authorities" that was thought valid for all situations and life stages, obedience functions differently not only in different stages of the spiritual life but also in relation to different kinds of authority.

1. Initial formation

From entrance until final Profession the new member is "in initial formation," a process whose necessity or even appropriateness has been challenged in recent years, at least as applied to candidates who enter not as emerging adults but in adulthood I or even in adulthood II. It is certainly true that the formation process has to be individualized in terms not only of the chronological age of the entrant but especially in terms of the person's stage in the life cycle. However, no matter how old or experienced people are at entrance, they are new to Religious Life and, like an adult entering a new profession, the neophyte has to learn how to live the new life she or he is undertaking. I would suggest that there are three overlapping facets of the life, or tasks integral to, this learning project, and because they are about *learning* what one does not yet know, about being a *disciple*, I am calling it a process of "pedagogical obedience."

The first task of initial formation is "*leaving the world.*" Today this term does not refer, as it once did, to definitively leaving the parental home, donning a new outfit, bidding farewell to relatives, and plunging into the total institution of "convent life." As we have discussed, "world" is not so much a place or even a set of relationships but an imaginative reality construction. The world of Satan and the world that we call the Reign of God are diametrically opposed but intimately interwoven constructions of reality, like the wheat and the weeds in Matthew's parable of the field. All Christians at baptism are called to renounce the Satanic version of reality with "all its works and pomps" and to align themselves with Christ's project of promoting the Reign of God.

But the "world" which the aspiring Religious leaves to enter the "world" of Religious Life is not merely Satan's evil world (which, presumably, she has long since renounced) but the secular world as a whole, a good and legitimate reality construction, but one distinguished from the reality construction constituted by the vows. The candidate is setting out on the journey that will become definitive when, by Profession, she embraces the coordinates of the "alternate world" of Religious Life.

She will definitively choose, by vowing consecrated celibacy, to shape her personal God-quest by a self-gift to Christ to the exclusion of any other primary life commitment, including marriage and family, even if she had founded a secondary family before entrance and is still deeply related to her children and their spouses and children.

By the vow of evangelical poverty she will embrace a life of total nonpossession, dispossessing herself of all material goods, both those already possessed or that will be acquired in the future, thereby making the community the sole economic context of her life. Again, this will be a different experience for one who is not financially independent when she enters, one burdened by debt, or one who must divest herself of a home, savings, investments, or a professional practice.

And by vowing prophetic obedience she will shape her freedom in prophetic service of the Reign of God in the context of a community of equal disciples discerning and fulfilling only the will of God in this world. Once again this will present different challenges to younger people who have barely left the parental home and people who themselves have been the authority figures in the workplace or a family.

The task of "leaving the world" is not accomplished on the day of entrance. Some Religious, in fact, have never really left the world and some returned to it long after Profession, with or without formal dispensation from their vows. Learning what it means to leave the secular order and to undertake Religious Life is learning what Profession means, what the individual vows entail and how they relate to one another in the construction of life in the alternate world, and discerning carefully whether one is called to shape one's life in this deeply and radically alternate way.

Although candidates in different stages of the life cycle will have different learning curves as they investigate what becoming a Religious means, all candidates will need to put themselves willingly in the school of Christ mediated by those assigned to teach them what this life means. The teaching is not exclusively intellectual, although candidates need to learn the content, shape, and obligations of the life they will undertake. But the deeper learning is the apprenticeship in the life by which they learn how to relate as celibates to people of both sexes and all ages and orientations, how to responsibly handle money and goods that are not one's own and what it means to hold all things in common, and how to participate as a responsible and accountable equal in all the affairs of community life.

This learning, this growth in discipleship, is necessarily a prolonged process because it is not a matter of mastering facts or getting the rules down but of being transformed from one kind of Christian into another. The formation program is a school that is in session twenty-four hours a day, seven days a week, because being a Religious is not a skill set but a way of being, of living in the alternate world. A novice in any field does have to "learn the scales," but virtuoso performance is not mechanical expertise and no one can teach oneself the complex of skills and art that constitutes "being an artist." Learning Religious obedience is a much more transformative and dynamic process than learning to submit or conform.

A second, and simultaneous, task of initial formation is *socialization into the community*. Every community has an indefinable, intangible, but very real ethos, spirit, way of being and operating that is an expression of its deep narrative, that is, the historical living of its distinctive charism. New members need to imbibe, to "catch," that spirit by being immersed in community life. This aspect has less to do with becoming a Religious as such than with becoming a Sister of St. Joseph or a Dominican of San Rafael. Someone genuinely called to Religious Life might not be called to this community, and part of the pedagogical task of initial formation is to facilitate the discernment of not only the genuineness of the call to Religious Life but the "fit" between the candidate and the particular community. Age, life experience, or psychological maturity cannot render this part of formation unnecessary. In fact, the more advanced in the life cycle the candidate is the more challenging the task of socialization may be precisely because she is more "set in her ways." This has always been part of the hesitation about admitting older candidates and it remains a serious consideration even today.

The third task of initial formation is that of *formal learning,* which is both intellectual and experiential. Initial formation always involves a fairly intensive study of the history of the Congregation complemented by exposure to a diversity of members and ministries, especially the older members who carry the spirit as well as the lore of the group.

Another important area of formal learning is theology. By the end of initial formation the contemporary Religious needs at least the equivalent of a masters in this rapidly developing discipline, not only for competence in ministry (whether or not her ministries will be specifically "religious" in content) but especially as a resource for her own prayer life and tools for dealing with personal struggles with faith, Church, and morality as she develops humanly and ministerially. If there was a time in the past when Religious could depend on superiors to deal with theological or religious questions and could assume that the prayer life one developed in common was adequate, that time is long past. Religious need to develop an intense personal spiritual life which is theologically equipped to grow and develop throughout a lifetime of constantly changing conditions in Church and society, and to acquire the habit and skills of ongoing theological inquiry.

Finally, during initial formation, if it is deep and thorough, most people who have grown up in the complexities of the first world will come face to face with some serious psychological issues such as narcissism, habitual electronic distraction, substance and behavioral addictions, problems with self-discipline and emotional control, sexual compulsiveness or obsessions, relationship issues, social inauthenticity and the need to manipulate and dominate, as well as anger, fear, guilt, anxiety and other problems stemming from unresolved experiences in their pasts. No matter how well adjusted the candidate, or how experienced, the very openness and introspection that formation involves will probably bring areas that require attention into consciousness of both the candidate and the formation personnel. Spiritual direction may need to be complemented by counseling or therapy of one kind or another as the person struggles for the psychological and spiritual maturity that will enable her to discern the call to Religious Life and make a genuinely free choice before God about how to respond.

2. Ongoing formation

Important as are the first years in Religious Life and the intensive period of formation that prepares the person for definitive commitment by Profession, all Religious will spend the rest of their lives growing in union with God through discernment and fulfillment of God's will in their personal and communal life. Consequently, formation is a lifelong process. Only at death do we "graduate" from the school of Christ.

Ongoing formation is not only necessary if the life is to be lived intensely and fruitfully; it is the right of Religious, with a corresponding duty of support on the part of the Congregation, to pursue increasing depth and breadth in their spiritual life, not only their interior life of prayer but also their community and ministerial life. In general, ongoing formation occurs in two ways: **actively**, through initiative on the part of Religious themselves, and **passively**, through their willing engagement of challenging life experience.

As Religious progress beyond initial formation—in which their growth and development was the primary concern of their formators and they received fairly continuous and intensive feedback, as well as input in the form of curriculum, practice, experience, personal and group guidance—they must take greater responsibility in discerning their own growth needs and figuring out how to meet them. The Religious needs to complement a disciplined daily program of personal prayer, nourished by spiritual reading and study and by periodic participation in lectures, workshops, days of reflection, or cultural events which expand her horizons and deepen her engagement, with the theological, ecclesial, social, developmental, cultural, and ministerial dimensions of life. Successful initial formation should disincline the mature Religious to spend her non-"work" time reading pulp literature, parked for hours in front of the television, prowling the mall, surfing the web, or playing computer games. She should, by the end of initial formation, know the difference between healthy relaxation and dissipation or habitual distraction and be able to recognize the warning signs of the latter and do something about it.

The sabbatical, once seen as either a guilty luxury ("taking" something unearned for oneself) or a "reward for a life well spent" (one's right after "all these years" to whatever one has not had a chance to do), is now seen, at least in healthy communities, as a reasonable, indeed necessary, time of refreshment and growth that people involved in intensive ministry should request and be granted at critical points in their lives if they are to stay focused, interiorly alive, energetic, and creative.

Sabbatical or renewal needs are highly individual and community resources are not infinite. But a generous and responsible Religious should not feel that requesting some time for personal renewal of her spiritual life or enrichment of her ministerial competence is selfish or a sign of personal weakness. The same must be said for an occasional prolonged retreat, regular spiritual direction, or some personal growth counseling or therapy in challenging times or circumstances. One should not have to be in crisis, burnout, or on the brink of nervous collapse to recognize the need for some support or assistance, and seeking it is part of the person's responsibility for her or his ongoing formation.

But besides these actively sought growth experiences, simply living a serious spiritual life as a responsible community member and committed minister will inevitably bring the maturing Religious into periods of intensive conversion that she has not foreseen or planned and for which she could not have been prepared. These are experiences of passive formation that are often critical. Taken-for-granted convictions about faith might be seriously challenged by one's reading or by interreligious involvements, resulting in excruciating experiences of religious doubt and uncertainty. Overwhelming professional challenges can sap one's healthy sense of confidence and the bright hope of early ministerial success can become monotonously gray until putting one foot in front of another day after day seems impossible. Misunderstandings or conflict in community can create prolonged tensions, and generate angers that simmer into explosions not easily healed. A long-ignored or rationalized "minor" addiction can suddenly plunge the Religious to "the bottom" in public shame and personal self-loathing that blots out any sense of worth or remembrance of all the generosity of years of ministry, and face her or him with ultimate and impossibly difficult choices. A nourishing friendship can dry up, leaving a trough of loneliness in its wake. Darkness in prayer can be so profound and prolonged that the person wonders how the spiritual life ever could have seemed real or possible. Nonrecognition of one's accomplishments or destructive machinations of jealous colleagues can leave a person's self-confidence in shreds. The dysfunction of the institutional Church and the corruption of its leaders can be profoundly scandalizing and utterly discouraging especially when they touch one's own ministry directly. Sheer rage at injustice can become a habit of exhausting anger as cynicism replaces hope for reconciliation. Some people, perhaps in a period of retreat or through the self-examination encouraged by spiritual direction, or just through sudden or gradual insight into their own experience, may confront unsuspected and deep-seated spiritual evil so entangled in their spirit that they are plunged into a full-blown experience of passive purification which cannot be understood from within the experience itself and from which they can see no exit. Catastrophic illness or the death of a dear friend can precipitate an existential loneliness that time seems powerless to assuage.

This list does not exhaust the possibilities of real passive suffering, some of which will surely enter the life of any serious Religious. Borrowing trouble by trying to anticipate which, or when, or if such things will happen or imagining how one will handle them when they do is foolish and futile. Nor does it usually help in such times to be reminded of Jesus' agony in the garden or Mary's experience at the foot of the cross, to be pointed to the classical texts on interior purification, or to be reassured that "time heals all things" and "everyone goes through things like this." These experiences, whether short or prolonged, whether once in a lifetime or repeated, whether dramatic or almost hidden from the one enduring it, are part of the growth process through which the will, the capacity for self-gift, is slowly pried loose from the iron grip of the sinful ego, progressively purified of the impediments to love that no amount of active asceticism can reach, and finally freed for full union with God. This is the part of ongoing formation over which the person has little or no control, which no prudent person would precipitate, but without which spiritual maturity is unlikely to be achieved. And that is precisely the point of such experience.

In short, formation is a lifelong process that takes place primarily by docile and courageous engagement with influences that enter one's life, invited or uninvited, as "part of the program" or "out of the blue," as painful or exhilarating. In that sense, there is something "external" about that to which one is challenged to respond. And that is why it is "pedagogical" or "formative." Life is teaching the Religious what it means to give oneself to Christ as he gave himself to the one he called Abba, as Mary gave herself to her Son in joy and at the cross. Responding to these influences that enter one's life, invited or uninvited, calls one beyond the personal and spiritual integration so far attained, invites and challenges one to grow, to become more and other than what one has been. Properly engaged, these influences are developmental.

Pedagogical obedience, that is, the willingness and capacity to engage these potentially growth-fostering experiences fruitfully throughout one's lifetime, requires a mature theology of the "will of God." Because we tend to joyfully recognize good influences in our life as "God's grace" there is a tendency to see suffering as God's "doing things to us" to punish us, to test us, or to build our character. But a "theology" of direct, divine primary causality is dangerous in the spiritual life. Sooner or later it will make God the "enemy" who persecutes us or allows us to be persecuted "for our own good," the betrayer who abandons us when we are at the end of our rope, or an indifferent power to which it is useless to pray, and we will find ourselves having to choose between rebellion at this arbitrary treatment or powerless submission to a overpowering force. It is not "God's will" that one is misjudged, blindsided by anger or addiction, unjustly condemned, or that one forms a life-giving friendship or finds a good spiritual director or is successful in ministry. Concatenations of secondary causes of all kinds lead to such finite effects in our experience. God is present, not externally causing or orchestrating events from some celestial computer, but interiorly in our consciousness, in our choices about how to respond to what we experience.

When Paul prayed, "three times" (i.e., insistently) that God remove some impediment in his life, some "thorn in the flesh" that was torturing him, God turned Paul's attention away from the affliction (which God did not cause and would not miraculously cure) and to Paul's response which God was indeed enabling by "my grace [which] is sufficient" for you (see 2 Cor 12:7–10). God is always on our side, whether what is happening in our lives is good or bad, and often we do not know which is which until we have somehow emerged from the struggle. Even when the "bad" is due to our own sinfulness or the "good" is perverted by our pride, God is supporting in us the movement toward discipleship, the obedience to God's invitation to grow, God's teaching us in and through everything that enters our life. God's will is not that it rain on our parade or that we win the lottery. God's will is our sanctification and God is never far from our hearts as we struggle toward holiness.

B. The Spirituality of Dialogical Obedience: Ministry

There is another range of experience that becomes primary in the life of the Religious as she or he leaves initial formation and undertakes the lifelong service of others that is intrinsic to the prophetic dimension of ministerial Religious Life. This type of experience is different, though not always easily distinguished from the pedagogical, in that it is not the individual who is solely the object or the source of the challenge to discern and fulfill the will of God.

In ministry one confronts, on a daily basis, choices and challenges that are essentially relational. Discerning whether or not to take on a particular ministry, or decline it, or withdraw from it involves not only oneself, what is good or growthful for me, but the community, the other people involved in the ministry, the people to be served, institutional requirements and personnel. Deciding how to handle a problem, how to mediate a conflict, when to insist on or refrain from implementing a policy and when to look the other way for a time, how to raise funds, when something is a matter of principle or is something on which one can compromise, and so on are rarely or ever exclusively one's own private affair. They are matters that must be communally discerned taking account of the concerns of all the stakeholders. Even the decision about whether a decision should be made by consensus or by the one finally responsible is not a solitary decision.

Such decision making and implementing, such interaction with and influence upon the lives of other people both colleagues and those whom one serves, is the very stuff of ministry. It is intrinsically dialogical because all who are involved in or impacted by the decisions made must have some place in the process of discernment. When those in leadership do not recognize this dialogical character of ministry, genuine authority is subsumed into authoritarianism at the least and dictatorship at worst. The autocrat who thinks that he or she is invested with divine authority and thus speaks for God, whether that person is a Religious superior, a member of the hierarchy, a pastor, a teacher, or a counselor, is simply deluded. As I tried to show in the last chapter, God does not confer absolute divine authority or power, purely and simply, on any finite being, and all offices, even the highest, have limits.[16]

Dialogical obedience, the disposition to and practice of honoring the claim to be heard and heeded of all those who have a legitimate role in the decisions that weave the fabric of ministry, is the kind of obedience that shapes the life of the minister on a daily and even hourly basis over the whole of her or his ministerial life, just as the incessant give-and-take of spouses gradually shapes their relationship in their marriage. For one who is spiritually mature enough to live fairly habitually in the presence of God, dialogical obedience is as continuous and all-pervasive as was the minute-by-minute obedience of "convent life" in preconciliar days. It is a continuous experience of being "not one's own" which can be a source of alienation, of feeling overrun by the needs and demands of others, or can become a continuous and peaceful sense of "availability " for God's work calling us forth through the needs of others. Like Jesus who turned himself over to the people even when he had not even time to eat (see Mark 3:20) because he had compassion on them for they were like sheep without a shepherd (see Matt 9:36–38), the obedient minister grows daily in the ability to participate in the dialogue between people's needs and his or her ability to meet them.

This dialogue, however, is truly dialogue, not a monologue in which one person (the minister) decides what others need and how to meet those needs. It is sometimes a shock for people who are closet docetists to realize how often Jesus, in his exercise of ministry, was called beyond his first reactions by the address of his interlocutors. He was genuinely surprised at the faith he encountered in people his Jewish training prepared him to find hard of heart or unbelieving, for example, the pagan Royal Official (see Mark 4:45–54) and the Canaanite woman (see Matt 15:27–28). Challenges to his orthodoxy helped him claim the real God of his own faith-experience over the letter of the Law, for example, in the case of the woman taken in adultery (Mark 8:2–11), the Samaritan woman at the well (Mark 4:1–42), or the sinful woman in Simon's house (Mark 7:36–50), the people he cured on the Sabbath (e.g., Mark 3:1–6), or the good thief on Calvary (Mark 23:41–43). On the other hand, the religious officials he had come to see as hypocrites were not all such as he discovered when he talked seriously with the scribe whom he discovered was "not far from the kingdom of God" (Mark 12:28–34).

Dialogical obedience is formative, but not so much because it comes into our experience, as do pedagogical factors requiring us to re-constellate our earlier synthesis to make room for something new. There is less sense that we have, somehow, become a new person. Dialogical or ministerial obedience is formative because of the interaction between who we are, what we think or think we think, our spontaneous attractions and repulsions, our experience and conclusions and what enters into our minds and hearts on the words and concerns of others who, themselves, are being transformed by our contributions. This is an obedience that is both more continuous and less clear cut. We do not always know when it begins and when it ends. There is often not a clear before and after, a defined moment when A becomes B. Rather, the attentive minister is always changing through interaction, through the process of hearing and heeding the claims upon her or his understanding, compassion, authenticity, and fidelity. And, sadly, it is precisely those ministers whose vision expands, whose compassion deepens, who come to realize through their experience that God, not they, are "in charge," who are most likely to run into trouble with the legalism of the system when someone in the secular or ecclesiastical hierarchy insists on the "absoluteness" of positions which, experience teaches, are serious but not absolute.

A mature minister's theology of the will of God is likely to become more subtle and more adequate in this sphere of dialogical obedience precisely because neither party to a genuine ministerial dialogue starts with the presupposition that his or her position is "God's will." One might come into the discussion convinced of one's position, but the very fact of listening authentically to the others presupposes that one has not preemptively equated one's position with God's. It is easy to spot ministers who think they are the "final authority," that they speak for God. They appear to listen but everyone knows that however patiently they wait out the expression of other opinions they are neither hearing nor heeding. The decision was made before the discussion began.

When the dialogue is genuine, when the discernment is careful and the decision is consensual, there is a justified sense that

"God's will" has been discerned. This does not mean that the decision reflects objectively and substantially "what God wants done." This would involve investing our discernment processes with a kind of magical efficacy. The decision itself could be mistaken and later have to be revised. But the people involved are doing what God asks of them in the sincere effort to make the best decision of which they are capable here and now. Once again, God accompanies and supports faithful obedience without our having to believe that mistakes are "God's will" or that God's infallible approval stamps our decisions as irrefutable and absolute.

C. The Spirituality of Relinquishment: Suffering and Loss

A final dimension of the spirituality of obedience, like the two discussed in sections A and B, also is part of the experience of seeking union with the will of God in all stages of development and in all spheres of life. But, like the spirituality of pedagogical obedience which is especially operative in formation and the spirituality of dialogical obedience that is especially significant in ministerial situations, the obedience of relinquishment is particularly salient as the Religious moves closer to the end of life, whether that occurs early due to catastrophic illness or accident or in the later phases of old age.

Many people have come to refer to the experience of old age as a time of "diminishment." I find this rhetoric, which might have originated with Teilhard de Chardin who used it in relation to passivity as contrasted with activity in the spiritual life,[17] as highly problematic. Diminishment, which means literally "getting smaller" or "becoming less" in worth or dignity, or "losing significance," suggests decline, disempowerment, impoverishment, loss of vitality, the fading of life which ends by being finally snuffed out altogether. To regard the final stages and end of a life totally given to God over decades of fidelity and service as "diminishment" is certainly, as Jesus said to Peter who protested Jesus' journey to the cross, "to judge according to human standards rather than God's" (cf. Matt 16:23; Mark 8:33). If our definition of life, like Peter's, is physical power and beauty, influence, wealth, pleasure, and so on, then old age is certainly diminishment. But if life means primarily and essentially that "life in abundance" which Jesus came to share with those who believe, then those who are walking toward the fullness of divine light, life, and love, toward and into the Resurrection we enter through the portal of physical death, are not diminishing but increasing, growing, becoming finally what they were called to become in baptism, which was shaped by Profession, and has been realized by a lifelong quest for the living God in community, ministry, and contemplation.

Nevertheless, the final stages of our human journey are marked by loss and often by suffering, as was Jesus' end. But Jesus' death-Resurrection was not his final defeat, his extinction by darkness; it was the salvation of the world, the ultimate triumph of divine love over human evil, both physical and moral. What is significant about the suffering and loss of human dying is not its painfulness, which is unavoidable, but what the *person is doing* in and through that final encounter with the powers of evil when one must drink to the dregs the finitude of creatureliness. Jesus' prayer in the garden, as he realized that he had come to the end humanly speaking, that there was no way out of death except through it, was "Not my will but yours be done" (Mark 22.42). This prayer is often interpreted as the acknowledgement of a clash between the will of God who decreed Jesus' death and the will of Jesus who wanted to live. Theologically, this makes no sense. God did not will the death of Jesus (which would have been evil) and Jesus, who had done God's will with his whole life, was certainly not at this moment opposing it.

Jesus prays that in everything he will suffer in the next two days—inescapable suffering not willed, much less caused, by God but by the Roman authorities in conjunction with the Jewish hierarchy—he will be faithful, as he has been throughout his life, to God's will which is Jesus' own participation in God's salvific love for all humanity. In the depths of suffering, when physical pain, loneliness, abandonment, betrayal drench every fiber of one's being, the final temptation, as it was for Job and Jeremiah, is to reject God, to curse God whom one wrongly thinks could save one from death but chooses not to. It is to despair of God who has abandoned us and fall back finally on ourselves, choosing to escape what cannot be escaped without rejecting God.

So Jesus prays to be kept faithful to God's will, come what may. He prays that his human will not be the ultimate measure of his fidelity, but that God's will be done in him, no matter what. The Epistle to the Hebrews captures this intimate transaction between Jesus in the deepest experience of his humanity and the infinite supportive love of the One he calls his Abba: "In the days of his flesh, Jesus offered up prayers and supplications, with loud cries and tears, to the one who was able to save him from death, and he was heard because of his reverent submission. Although he was a Son, he learned obedience through what he suffered…." (Heb 5:7–8).

Jesus, like each of us at the moment of death, is heard by God precisely as he hands himself over to God. In death we finally know what obedience, which we have interiorized throughout life in the choices we have made, really means. That is the moment *par excellence* when we must be "saved from death"; not from mortality, from which there is no escape, but from the death Jesus taught his disciples was the only real death, the eternal death to which no human can sentence us as long as we are in the hand of God (see Matt 10:28–29). Jesus learned obedience as a human being through what he suffered as a human being. He had to learn as all humans do how to hand himself over completely, to abandon himself in total faith and trust without reserve or remainder, to the only One who can save us from the final death. And he was indeed heard, and saved from death; both the death of despair on the cross, and physical death itself through Resurrection.

I would suggest that the final phase of life, at whatever age or in whatever circumstances it begins and however it ends, is the time in which we are called to "be made perfect" (see Heb 5:9) as Jesus was by "reverent submission" in a process which might be called "self-abandonment" or "relinquishment." For most first world people, especially Religious who generally live a healthy lifestyle, the stage of elderhood or extreme old age can be quite prolonged. They often live into their eighties, nineties, or beyond a hundred.

Little by little they lose their independence, both because of increasing physical limitations and by being no longer able to safely drive or travel alone. The former Congregational president who must be bathed or dressed by a novice or the college president who cannot answer her own phone or feed herself is, humanly, humiliated by the loss of her professional dignity and reserve. A formerly vigorous, even athletic, Religious now experiences increasing pain and debility while trying to do even simple movements. Someone whose judgment was respected, whose opinion was influential, who was regularly consulted on important Congregational affairs is, for the first time, not a Chapter participant and perhaps no one even remembers to inform him or her of important decisions. Failing senses can rob the elder of the joys of reading and art, films or television, music or conversation with friends. For some people their mind or memory will fail before their body does and such losses are not determined by one's level of education or publication history.

Religious who have watched friends go into this final passage know that the most deeply challenging aspect of it, for those going and those watching, is knowing that it is a one-way journey. Unlike illnesses or injuries in one's youth or adulthood, old age cannot be arrested or reversed. It can only be engaged. And this is what makes it a matter of obedience in a different way than formation or ministry. One does not have the array of options one has in most situations. One cannot choose not to be old, not to suffer, not to lose one's privacy, independence, memory, or senses, not to die. One can only choose whether to accept such suffering or to reject it, to go gently into the deepening night, making it easier for one's friends and caregivers and witnessing to God's steadfast and trustworthy love, or to rage against it.

Once again, it is important to cultivate a sound theology of God's will. God does not will the suffering of illness, the agonies of loneliness and fear and pain. It is never "God's will" that we suffer. "This is the will of God, your sanctification" (1 Thes 4:3). Jesus came only that we might have life, and have it in all its fullness (see Mark 10:10). Union with God is the purpose, from God's point of view, of all the joy and all the suffering we experience.

Old age and death are part of what it means to be finite, a creature, and suffering and loss are part of this process. As we approach death we are called, not to seek suffering or believe that God is punishing or testing us, or is indifferent to or angry with us, but to relinquish literally all in our life that is not God, to abandon ourselves to God's love, trusting that indeed "nothing can separate us from the love of God in Christ Jesus" (see Rom 8:39). In the end, as the saints have said, we go to God with empty hands. We do not present our credentials, our achievements, our strength or beauty, our connections, our awards, or our superior virtues. We offer ourselves, finally disentangled from all the subterfuges and dodges and excuses. This is all God has ever wanted. And the amazing proof of God's respect for our freedom is that we must offer ourselves. God will not take what we do not give. No matter what we do, death will finally take us as it will take all creatures; but God will only *accept* us if we surrender all other things and pray with Jesus, "Into your hands I commend my whole self." That is the meaning of the last stages of obedience.

III. Summary and Conclusion

The purpose of these last two chapters has been to introduce some clarity and nuance into the thinking about Religious obedience which, as has been said a number of times in this volume, is the vow that has been most distorted by historical factors, by the confusion of Religious obedience with sociological and psychological phenomena called by the same name but that have nothing to do with the theological reality, by the power and control agendas of ecclesiastical officials, and by the misinterpretation of Scripture which flows from the inveterate tendency of humans to create God in their own dominative image. So the first task was to clear a space for reflection by disentangling the understanding of Christian obedience in general and Religious obedience in particular from unnuanced assumptions about the univocal and absolutist character of obedience.

I have consistently defined *obedience*, whether human, Christian, or Religious, as the appropriate response to genuine authority (that of God or of human beings, laws, and institutions) and *authority* as a legitimate claim to be heard and heeded. To listen (hear) and engage seriously (heed) the authoritative address demands an appropriate response. The presumption favors compliance or cooperation precisely because the one commanding has some kind of authority, either in general (e.g., the law of the land or of the Church) or as a privileged mediator in a person's life (e.g., a parent in relation to a child or spouses in relation to each other or the Congregational leader in relation to a Religious). This presumption, however, is not total abandonment of responsibility. The one called upon to obey must always make a *discerning conscience decision* about what constitutes the appropriate response in this case. Usually the appropriate response is cooperation and compliance. But sometimes the appropriate response is to decline to comply. The "theology" that claims that no dissent from the teaching, no noncompliance with the command, of authority is ever legitimate is fallacious and must be rejected by mature Religious, in theory and in practice.

The foregoing means that authority is not the right of the powerful to dominate the weak. Among adults, authority-obedience is a mutual relationship between equals in which the two parties have different and correlated rights and responsibilities but in which both remain free subjects responsible before God and others to make good decisions and to act accordingly. This basic understanding of obedience is not suppressed or abrogated because Religious are participants in a public state of life in the Church. Relationships within a Religious community and between the Congregation and ecclesiastical authority can be complex and complicated but that does not justify simplistic "solutions" that deny responsibility or violate consciences, subvert the legitimate autonomy of Congregations or entail complicity with abuses of power masquerading as authority.

Within the space cleared by claiming a theology of obedience as participation in a relationship of equals seeking God's will together we examined the functioning theology of obedience as it had developed in preconciliar Religious Life. The combination of cloister, which facilitated the sociological total institution, and an understanding of every detail of daily life as a privileged mediation of God's will, created the "enchanted universe" of "convent life." The ideal of obedience as minute-to-minute accomplishment of God's will by total submission to heteronomous expressions of that will which were, in principle, virtually all of equal importance generated a conception (and theology) of obedience which could not be maintained outside the total institution.

The dissolution of "convent life" during the renewal, which entailed the end of this conception of obedience, necessitated a renewal of the theology of obedience which involved recognizing a much-expanded range and mode of mediators of God's will and a much-deepened process of discernment. This understanding of obedience is just as all-embracing and demanding as the more simplistic one, but it is more interior, more personally responsible, and above all more complex.

By recognizing the internal diversity and richness of Religious obedience as the lifelong project of seeking union of will with God and the fact that different ways of practicing obedience are more important in different phases and stages of the life of a Religious we were able to distinguish at least three dimensions, or three experiences of the spirituality of prophetic obedience.

Pedagogical obedience, which has a particularly important role in formation, both initial and ongoing, leads the Religious to deeper discipleship through his or her ongoing response to factors, explicit and implicit, which enter the person's life and expand or modify his or her spirituality. Docility, or the willingness to learn God's ways, is the salient mark of pedagogical obedience.

Dialogical obedience is the "normal" mode of obedience among mature Religious. In community life and ministry the person interacts with others as a responsible equal in discerning what to do and carrying out the decisions, which will normally involve compromise, will often be tentative or provisional, and can always be mistaken. There is no mechanical equation possible between what is decided and the will of God. Flexibility in cooperation might be said to be the salient feature of this kind of obedience.

Finally, although the experience of loss or suffering is part of all phases of the life of the Religious, it becomes central for most as old age leads to the end of earthly life. Increasingly the person "has no choice." Or rather, the choice is not whether or not one will lose the relative goods of the active life and finally life itself, but whether one will willingly relinquish these gifts that the life process is now withdrawing in favor of the final gift of eternal life. At the end of life the *obedience of self-surrender* is the final fruit of a life of union with the will of God. Trusting abandonment into the hands of God as one passes through the portals of death into Resurrection life is the salient feature of this ultimate experience of obedience.

To live fruitfully the diversity, the richness, the challenges of prophetic obedience over a lifetime requires that the Religious develop a mature theology of "the will of God" which is not an imposition of irresistible divine power on a passive and helpless subject who must submit or pay the penalty. Nor is the will of God an inscrutable divine program for "educating" hapless victims by testing them with suffering and punishing them into submission. The will of God is always our sanctification, which consists in loving union with the One who loves us infinitely.

Conclusion

Transforming Renewal

Conclusion
Transforming Renewal

I. Introduction

The end of this volume is also the end of a project which has taken almost twelve years to complete, namely, an examination, interdisciplinary analysis, and spirituality oriented theological interpretation of Catholic Religious Life as it has emerged and is continuing to develop from the renewal of Vatican II, and is now manifesting itself with ever-increasing confidence as a renewed and transformed reality in the Church. This renewing lifeform is both deeply continuous with its two-thoursand-year history and startlingly different from anything anyone alive today knew as Religious Life until close to the last quarter of the twentieth century. The conciliar renewal has transformed Religious Life which is, in turn, transforming the conciliar renewal from a dream of the heart to an incarnation of hope, not only in Religious Life itself but in the Church as a whole.

When I entitled the work *Religious Life in a New Millennium* I had no idea it would be more than one volume in length and never suspected it would take more than the first decade of the new millennium to complete. But as this final volume goes to press I discern the breath of the Spirit of God in what has often seemed merely interminable human impediments to finishing the project. If the work had not been able (indeed forced) to take account of the developments of the last decade it would be far less adequate as a treatment of contemporary Religious Life and probably much less usable for the immediate future. The last few years in particular have seen a weaving together, partly under adverse ecclesiastical pressure on American women Religious,[1] but mainly through the increasingly confident appropriation by Religious of what they have been living and becoming since the Council, of many experimental strands into a strong fabric whose pattern is increasingly clear and hopeful. There is today a new sense among many Religious of identity, solidarity, and enthusiasm for the future that feels like the "end of the beginning" of renewal and the beginning of a transformed maturity in the history of this life. This writing project began at the turn of the millennium with the publication of the first volume in 2000 and it will be completed, fittingly enough, with the publication of this third volume in 2013, during the golden jubilee of the Second Vatican Council.

Within the overarching title of the trilogy, *Religious Life in a New Millennium*, each volume has borne a title accommodated from the little parable in Matthew 13:44: "The Reign of God[2] [here applied to Religious Life] is like a TREASURE hidden in a field which a person found and out of joy SOLD ALL s/he had to BUY THAT FIELD." The accommodation of the biblical text, however, is not fanciful or far-fetched. Applying the parable about the Reign of God to Religious Life is recognition that this lifeform is not something other than or separate from the Church (as might have been the image projected by the "otherworldly" preconciliar form of Religious Life), but one way of being Church that is herald, sacrament, and servant of the Reign of God. This distinctive way of being Church is complementary to, but not superior to nor normative of, other ways.

Just prior to this parable (in Matt 13:36–42), Jesus had explained to his disciples the allegory of the weeds and the wheat by saying explicitly that the field in his parables is the world; the Sower is the Son of Man; the wheat are the children of the kingdom; and the weeds the children of the Evil One. So the overall theological interpretation of Religious Life that this work is propounding is that Religious Life is, for those called to it, the treasure of a vocation to a way of life in the Church that demands and consists in the total self-gift to God in Christ for the sake of the world that God so loved.

II. *The Project of Renewal:* Ressourcement, *Development,* Aggiornamento

It has often been remarked that *Perfectae Caritatis*, the conciliar "Decree on the Up-to-Date Renewal of Religious Life," published just before the end of the Council in October 1965, and
a mere twenty-five articles in length, contained very little that
was new or particularly enlightening, galvanizing, or creative.
(This perhaps explains why this rather bland product of a truly
revolutionary Council is a favorite text of those, in and outside
of Religious Life, who found the Council's call to profound
renewal deeply distressing.) But, as John O'Malley pointed out
in his remarkable analysis of the Council, *What Happened at Vatican II*,[3] the decree on Religious Life is the only conciliar document which explicitly mentions all three categories with which
the Council wrestled throughout its history and which continue to fuel the struggles between those in the Church who
embrace the Council and those who have been trying for fifty
years to neutralize or even reverse it.

These three categories, whether functioning individually, in
tension with each other, or in mutual interaction, were invoked
repeatedly in the herculean effort that the Church-in-Council
was making, after centuries of increasingly sterile immobility,
to come to grips with the fact of the Church's historicity. The
transcendent mystery embodied in the Church can only be
preserved, rejuvenated, and effectively communicated in the
changing conditions of temporality. This transcendent mystery,
God's salvific interaction with humanity, is incarnate, historical, and therefore not only immersed in time but also conditioned by change. The three categories, unevenly grasped and
appropriated by the Council Fathers, and embodied in the
documents with uneven success, were first, *ressourcement*
(return to the sources); second, development (real change in
substantial continuity); and third, *aggiornamento* (adaptation to
the changed conditions of the contemporary world).

I would suggest, for reasons I will explore in the next section,
that Religious Life, especially that of women, has embraced

more integrally and creatively this three-pronged agenda than any other group or institution in the Church. This may help explain why women Religious have been, in the past half century, not only a primary source of support and courage for the renewal-minded in the Church but a lightning rod for those in the hierarchy and the laity who are committed to the restoration of the preconciliar version of Catholicism.

Attending briefly to the way in which Religious embraced these three coordinates of conciliar renewal can help us understand both the depth of the transformation of the life that has resulted and the tensions with the institutional Church that the transformation has generated. However difficult the tensions continue to be, for Religious it is the transformation that needs to be claimed, celebrated, and focused if ongoing renewal is to draw Religious Life into the future.

The return to the sources (*ressourcement*) to which the Council urged Religious was twofold. First, they were to return to Scripture, especially the New Testament, which *Dei Verbum*, the dogmatic constitution "On Divine Revelation," called "the pure and perennial source of the spiritual life" (*DV* VI, 21), as the "supreme rule" of their life. Second, they were to return to the charism and vision of their founders, which Religious interpreted expansively as embracing not only the life and writings of the founders themselves but the "deep narrative" in which that heritage has been lived out since the foundation.

Religious enthusiastically plunged into the study of Scripture discovering there a fountain of spirituality that irrigated the often-dry lands of a way of life that had become overly rule-bound and tradition-encrusted. In their encounter with the Word they found life and freedom, creativity and courage, a call to Christian maturity and responsibility for the world that God so loved as to give the only Son (see John 3:16). In the stories—often long obscured, deformed, or even deliberately suppressed—of their foundations they discovered the motivating visions, the imagination and daring, the remarkable courage and creativity of women and men who were years or even centuries ahead of their time. Far too often they (especially women) discovered as well the long process of ecclesiastical domestication that had absorbed those exciting foundational dreams into institutional uniformity and subordination to external authorities.

Updating (*aggiornamento*) both preceded and followed development. What began gingerly as small "experiments" with dress, horarium, titles, or customs, experiments that the authorities assumed could be reverted to preexperiment status if they caused any upset, rapidly became major ventures in personal, community, Congregational, and societal development. Religious Congregations accelerated, expanded, and deepened the education of their members and the members broadened their interaction with the world around them including engagement in political and social concerns once completely excluded from convent life. Religious soon realized what ecclesiastical officials found hard to grasp: that human "experiments" were not controlled laboratory tests that could be reversed or abandoned if they did not "work out" as planned. Action and interaction among humans changes the people and the institutions involved and, while adjustments can be made, reversal is not possible. In many ways, what happened rapidly in the postconciliar period was a "growing up" of Religious, personally, communally, professionally, and societally. One cannot reverse the process of maturation.

Development (which interestingly never had a culturally determined synonym, like *ressourcement* from the French or *aggiornamento* from the Italian, but had to be translated anew into each language) was actually a way of talking about a global approach to human experience based on a historical rather than a classical understanding of the Church and the people who compose it. It is development, finally, whether in an individual person or an institution, which makes that reality actually different from what it had been in its own past. The mature person is still who she or he was in childhood or adolescence but is remarkably, irreversibly, and even substantially different, for example, now capable of producing and raising a family. If such change does not take place, for example, when a thirty-five-year-old still feels, behaves, and relates as a five-year-old, the situation is recognized as abnormal or even pathological.

The return to their roots of Religious and the resulting adjustment of their life to their contemporary situation changed Religious and their Congregations in all the ways we have discussed in these three volumes. Reversing this development is inconceivable, even if individuals or groups desired to do so. Attempting to resurrect the lifestyle, relational patterns, ministerial self-understanding and engagement, spirituality, or even something as external as the archaic dress of earlier times would result not in a restoration of a previous form of the life but in an artificial mimicry like that of the characters in a historical pageant. When Religious say about the renewal of their life that "there is no turning back" they mean simply that life, which is historical and therefore developmental, does not run backward but forward, whether or not one finds the later stage preferable to the former. Even when Congregations have judged that a particular adaptation or new way of being or acting is less productive than they thought or hoped it might be they realize that correcting course cannot be done by reverting to attitudes or behaviors previously abandoned but only by finding better ways to pursue the original goal.

Besides entering with total seriousness into the dynamics of the conciliar renewal Religious also entered deeply into the content of the Council's teaching. Renewing Congregations did not restrict themselves to meditating on the rather thin theological offerings of *Perfectae Caritatis.* Instead, they drew more deeply on chapter VI of *Lumen Gentium,* "The Dogmatic Constitution on the Church," which, though not especially forward-looking from our present standpoint, more adequately situated Religious Life in the context of conciliar ecclesiology. *Lumen Gentium,* which was hotly contested behind the scenes and on the Council floor, reflected the irresolvable tension between the biblical ecclesiology of the Church as Body of Christ and People of God (in chapter II) on the one hand and the preconciliar ecclesiology of the Church as transcendent hierarchical institution, indeed as an absolute divine right monarchy (in chapter III) on the other. Religious resonated much more with the ecclesiology of chapter II as the context for reading chapter VI devoted to Religious Life. However, this major document, and "The Pastoral Constitution on the Church in the Modern World," *Gaudium et Spes*, faced Religious with some of the most important and challenging issues of renewal within Religious Life itself and between this vocation and that of others in and outside the Catholic Church.

In particular, Religious had to come to grips with two features of the Council's teaching that deeply challenged their traditional self-understanding, both within the Church and in relation to the world. First, the Council reaffirmed a long-obscured teaching that all the baptized are equally called to one and the same holiness (*LG* V), which implied that Religious Life could no longer be understood as an elite vocation to a "life of perfection" that made its members superior to other Christians. Second, *Lumen Gentium* (see chapter IV) declared that all believers, in virtue of their baptism and confirmation, are equally called to participation in the prophetic, priestly, and royal mission of Jesus. Religious could no long claim unique access to quasi-official ministries from which the rest of the laity were excluded.

Closely related to these intra-ecclesial challenges to the long-held self-understanding of Religious were those implied in the radical reorientation of the Church as a whole to the world and its history that the Church had for centuries rejected. The "Pastoral Constitution on the Church in the Modern World," *Gaudium et Spes*, renounced the virulent antimodernism that had sealed the Church off from its historical context and alienated it from the great achievements and projects of the post-medieval world for almost four hundred years. For Religious, who had defined themselves in terms of rejection of and separation from the world, this turn of the Church toward the world created an enormous challenge of conversion in self-understanding. The resultant attitudes and behaviors would integrate their life into the conciliar Church's professed project of solidarity with all humanity in its pilgrimage through history. Indeed, in some respects Religious have been more consistent and coherent in their turn to the world than has the institutional Church itself.

The Council's resituation of the Latin Church in relation to its sister churches of the East and of the Reformation as well as to non-Christian religions has led Religious Life not only out of the cloister but also into challenging ecumenical and inter-religious relationships that would have been unthinkable in preconciliar days. This has posed a steep learning curve that Religious have undertaken seriously, unlike some, even among the hierarchy and the clergy, who have sidestepped it. The process of integrating this much wider angle of vision into their understanding of their faith has been profoundly disorientating at times and it has positioned Religious in relation to "the others" in ways that are often not understood nor accepted by ecclesiastical officials.

Finally, and closely related to the preceding, perhaps the most revolutionary teaching of the Council, "The Declaration on Religious Liberty," *Dignitatis Humanae,* opened up social and political questions that had been simply foreclosed in the preconciliar Church. The implications of this new position on freedom of conscience touched not only the personal lives of Religious, demanding a new level of moral maturity and responsibility in relation to the official Church, but also their social and political commitments and their ministries in ecclesiastical institutions.

Religious, in short, did not read their call to renewal narrowly or superficially, attending only to the rather conventional exhortations of *Perfectae Caritatis* explicitly addressed to Religious Life itself. They read that call integrally, mining the implications for their life of the full depth and breadth of the conciliar vision expressed in all the major documents of the Council. They committed themselves, individually and corporately, not just to cosmetic revisions, but also to profound and holistic conversion. One does not emerge from such a process the way one entered it. Indeed, the subject of real conversion does not emerge at all because ongoing conversion becomes a way of life. Furthermore, conversion is not a solitary process. As the person or the group changes, their conversion affects all those with whom they relate. So we should not be surprised that, in a way, the whole Church has been affected by the renewal, the conversion, in Religious Life. For some people the renewal of Religious Life has been a source of scandal and a cause of opposition and even of persecution. For many more people it has been a source of challenge, encouragement, hope, and energy.

III. The Process of Renewal: Turning Toward the World

It would be naïve to think that Religious sat down in 1965, read the Council documents, and set out to systematically reform their life accordingly. Vatican II did not elaborate a new theology from scratch. The theological renewal, especially in the areas of Church history, patristics, liturgy, and Scripture (the "sources" to which the Council appealed), had been underway since the late 1930s and 1940s and was gathering momentum right up to the time of the Council, especially among French and German-speaking scholars in Europe.[4] The most prominent theologians, who were censured and even condemned right through the 1950s for their dangerous "originality" in relation to the Tridentine synthesis, were virtually all present as *periti* or scholarly advisors at the Council. And these *nouvelles théologiens* of primarily historical and pastoral bent were now accompanied by systematic theologians, particularly ecclesiologists, anthropologists, and missiologists. The Council articulated, not always completely coherently but sufficiently so to make its originality excitingly clear, a new theological understanding of the Church in relation to history, the world, and "the others" that had been developing for half a century even while antimodernism and world-rejection continued to exercise its dominance.

Different analysts have proposed different "central insights" as key to the meaning of the Council. The Church historian John O'Malley, for example, identified the issue of coming to grips with historicity as the major challenge faced by the Council. How could "development"—so key to the understanding of the modern world—be integrated into the life and teaching of the Church without invalidating its claim to divine foundation, protection from error, and possession of the fullness of unchanging truth which it alone had been commissioned by God to teach and all people were bound to accept? How could an institution that had understood itself as immutable, atemporal, and transcendent in relation to history situate itself in relation to a world that had changed profoundly over the four hundred years of the Church's antimodern self-isolation and was changing even more rapidly in the twentieth century?

I have suggested that the most significant insight and choice of the Council, at least from the standpoint of Religious Life, was turning the Church toward the world it had rejected, to a large extent, since the end of the Middle Ages. Actually, coming to grips with historicity and turning toward the world are very closely related. For the Church to affirm its temporality, its involvement in change, its historicity, the actual and necessary development in its doctrine and practice, was to immerse itself in the world, to espouse a valid and salvific "secularity" as God in Jesus did by Incarnation. At the Council, the Church as Body of Christ began to renounce a kind of ecclesial docetism and face the difficult consequences of the fact that Christ's mystical body, like his humanity, is not a dispensable material shell housing a timeless spiritual reality, but a time-immersed, historical, developing reality that must grow in wisdom and grace as it ages through the centuries.

Religious were affected by this radical conversion of the Church to the world in a way most other elements in the Church were not, or at least not to the same degree. Religious Life was an extreme embodiment of the Church's antimodern world-rejection. The life was virtually defined by separation from, indeed death to, the world. Consequently, the Council's turn toward the world challenged Religious to a radical redefinition of themselves as well as their life. Religious felt the impact of the conciliar changes in every aspect and detail of their lives.

The business of Religious is precisely religion, which was not, for them, a Sunday interlude in an otherwise largely secular existence. Preconciliar Religious Life was pervasively sacralized, not only interiorly by intention but in all aspects: time, space, dwelling place, work, community life, material goods, even clothing. Religious, as seen by others, did not dress, eat, recreate, converse, get tired, or emote like other earthlings, but lived a mysterious, quasi-angelic life immune to change, unaffected by personal or institutional development, in serene and unquestioning possession of untroubled truth, without the doubts or temptations of ordinary mortals. Indeed, even the sight of a nun sitting cross-legged, playing cards, or eating a hot dog fascinated onlookers as if they were seeing a cocker spaniel typing. A burst of anger from a nun was not just surprising; it was scandalous.

Consequently, and paradoxically, precisely because of its enclosed and hidden preconciliar character, Religious Life became a kind of fishbowl where the effects of the Council's immersion of the Church in the historical reality of the world were more visible—even shocking—than anywhere else. For example, probably the most *conspicuous* change most Catholics observed in the immediate aftermath of the Council, apart from the liturgy, was Religious becoming *inconspicuous* by replacing their strange anachronistic habits with ordinary contemporary clothes. In the demystification of Religious Life, in the reinsertion of those who had "left the world" into the world God so loved, people could see the Church itself in a process of desacralization, of descent from its transcendent heights by engagement with the world of time and change and by increasing solidarity with the people and projects of the modern world. The timeless was becoming temporal, the anachronistic was becoming contemporary, the enclosed and exclusive was becoming open and welcoming, the exalted and unavailable was becoming ordinary and companionable. Like God becoming human in Jesus, the Church was becoming part of the world to which, as the Body of Christ, it was sent. This drawing near of the Church to the world undoubtedly helps explain why the "changes" in Religious Life met with such vehement rejection, even anger, by those elements in the Church, both lay and hierarchical, which resisted or even repudiated the spirit of the Council.

While some Religious thought the opening of their lives toward the surrounding context in the wake of the Council proceeded with glacial slowness, others thought the renewal was occurring with reckless speed. In fact, Religious Life moved out of the total institution and into the full floodtide of renewal in less than two decades, between the end of the Council and the beginning of the 1980s. This was probably one of the most cataclysmic periods in Western history. Feminism, the Civil Rights Movement, the antiwar protests, the Cold War, the student revolts against all forms of authority, and the end of the post–World War II suburban tranquilization of American society were all under way. The space age was dawning, the antennas of the communications revolution were sprouting up like mushrooms after a storm, the younger generation was "going East" in search of enlightenment, psychology was challenging religion as the path to salvation, and the sexual revolution was placing on the silver screen and the front pages of the newspaper language (and the behavior and concepts to go with it) that had rarely if ever been heard in polite society. All of these phenomena were part of the social, economic, and political globalization that was birthing the postmodern world. This postmodern world—not the modern world that the Council thought it was engaging—was where Religious, most of whom had entered the convent in the tame and respectable first half of the twentieth century, found themselves in the aftermath of the Council.

In the wake of the Council those Religious who persevered through the great "exodus" from the convent between 1965 and 1975 were coming to realize in a profoundly new way that their life was meant to be one of free, personal, intense union with God and total self-gift in ministry to the world that God so loved. The uniformity, rigidity, routinization, and control that had marked preconciliar Religious spirituality was giving way to an emphasis on personal prayer, directed retreats, individualized spiritual direction, wide and deep spiritual reading especially of Scripture and the mystics, theological development, psychological exploration arising from personal need and interest, creative forms of community prayer and faith sharing, liturgical experimentation—in short, to a deep personalization and interiorization of the spiritual life. Contemplative prayer was no longer seen as a dangerous domain that the "ordinary" Sister should avoid lest she be drawn into something "singular" but as the cultivation of the relationship with God on which her life was centered. Silence and solitude were not narcissism or flight from community but the necessary context of that relationship.

At the same time, Religious were claiming the intrinsically ministerial dimension of their lives that they had discovered in the "return to the sources" of their Congregations. Many no longer saw themselves as extensions of or adjuncts to the clergy, or as an obedient work force staffing ecclesiastical projects. They were beginning to realize that they were not "founded for" particular tasks such as staffing Catholic institutions but that they were founded to preach the Gospel to every creature, and that the "how" and "where" of that ministry was not necessarily predetermined even by what the Congregation had traditionally done. As individuals and as Congregations, they were assessing the needs of the People of God in a new, postmodern world and trying to find ways to meet those needs. Increasingly they were finding themselves in relationship, even colleagueship, with laity, with non-Catholics, and even with people and in projects that were not explicitly Christian or Church related.

The intensification of the interior life and the diversification and individualization of ministry, which was increasingly recognized as intrinsic to the life rather than an "overflow" or secondary end in relation to a primary end of personal sanctification, was taking place in the context of a reinvention of community life. Religious explicitly espoused the principles the Council had recognized as characteristic of the Church as the People of God; namely, equality, collegiality, and subsidiary, with their consequences of mutuality and co-responsibility. Only in hindsight can we grasp how remarkable was the incorporation of these principles, in the space of a couple of decades, into a life that had been modeled, to a large extent, on the patriarchal family, the military, and divine right monarchy.

The first thirty-five years of the renewal were a profoundly turbulent time in Religious Life. Virtually every aspect of the life changed dramatically if not radically. By the turn of the century the pace and dramatic character of change was decreasing. The ecclesiastical and secular spotlight on Religious Life was less glaring. Those who had stayed through the great exodus were committed for the long haul. It was beginning to seem possible to get enough perspective to reflect, not simply on what Religious Life had once been but no longer was, but on what it was becoming. That was the context for the beginning of this project. I must confess that I had no idea, as I started, how complex that task would be.

IV. Reflecting on the Process: Discernment, Interpretation, and Articulation

A. The Project in Retrospect

Let me briefly recall the stages in the reflection that comes to a close with this volume. In volume one of the trilogy, *Religious Life in a New Millennium*, entitled *Finding the Treasure: Locating Catholic Religious Life in a New Ecclesial and Cultural Context*, I engaged in a "search" within our modern/postmodern context for the *treasure* of Religious Life. This lifeform, once so unmistakably distinctive in the Church and even in the surrounding secular context, seemed to have been "lost" to view or obscured to some extent in the conciliar reconceptualization of the Church, both internally and in its relationship to the modern world. How was this life to be recognized, identified, situated in this new context?

In volume 2, *Selling All: Commitment, Consecrated Celibacy, and Community in Catholic Religious Life*, I dealt with the inner constitution of this treasure for which some people throughout Christian history have been willing to *sell all they possessed*, that is, to give themselves totally. This treasure of Religious Life is, in fact, constituted by the single-hearted quest for God through self-gift to Christ, to the exclusion of all other primary life commitments, which is symbolized (i.e., expressed and effected) by the lifelong commitment in *consecrated celibacy lived in community*.

In this third volume, *Buying the Field: Evangelical Poverty, Prophetic Obedience, and Mission to the World in Catholic Religious Life*, I invite readers to return to the starting point, the postconciliar Church within and missioned to the world. The world is now recognized not simply as modern but postmodern, no longer seen as a foreign context from which we must extract the treasure of Religious Life and then abandon in contempt or fear of contamination. The world is not simply an extrinsic context, positive or negative, of the Church or Religious Life. Rather, the world is that which God so loved as to give the only Son that those who believe in him might not perish but might have eternal life (see John 3:16). The Church's mission is to proclaim, symbolize, and promote the Reign of God in the world and this, *à fortiori*, is the mission of Religious Life. Therefore, the non-enclosed and non-monastic form of Religious Life that is the subject of this trilogy is intrinsically ministerial in nature. Ministry is not an appendage to ministerial Religious Life. It is integral to its *raison d'être*.

The first task of this final volume, then, is to inquire into the meaning of "world." Religious Life had been understood, for much of its history, as antithetical to the world. This negative stance toward the world reflected in a particularly intense way the extreme negativity toward everything outside the Church, which had been so characteristic of the preconciliar ecclesiastical institution. The negativity was especially virulent during the Church's long struggle against "modernity," which escalated from the end of the Middle Ages to its apotheosis in the ultramontane antimodernism of the nineteenth and early twentieth centuries. This volume, then, had to deal with what I have suggested may turn out to be the most profoundly transformative development of the Council, the Church's "turn toward the world." The three chapters of part 1 are devoted to a biblical, historical, theological, sociological, and psychological exploration of the meaning of "world," the identity of Religious in relationship to the world, and the nature and inner dynamics of the mission of Religious to the world.

Part 2 of this volume is devoted to evangelical poverty. Of the three vows, poverty is certainly the most ambiguous because poverty is both an ideal proposed by Jesus to his followers and an evil that Christians are committed to eradicating from human experience. The primary resource for understanding this ambiguous reality is Scripture. Whatever Religious mean by this aspect of their lives must be *evangelical,* that is, Gospel poverty, not human destitution on the one hand or some kind of economic strategy on the other. Against the background of this biblical material, I explore poverty as the economics of the Reign of God and try to put this theological reality into realistic relationship with the concrete facts of the present economic and financial situation in which Religious Life must function, both in terms of community and of ministry. Finally, I turn to the unitive or mystical dimension of evangelical poverty, its role in the spirituality of Religious.

Part 3 of the volume is devoted to prophetic obedience. The daunting challenge of this section was to rethink obedience against the background of the horrors committed in the name of obedience in recent history, the deep ambiguities surrounding obedience in contemporary, especially first world, culture, the highly problematic theology of obedience operative in the Church today, and the long history of inadequate modeling of obedience in Religious Life itself. Philosophy, history, sociology, psychology, and political theory were mined in search of resources for re-imagining the nature of obedience as a human phenomenon. Theology and especially Scripture, particularly the teaching and practice of Jesus against the background of Old Testament prophecy, were used to develop a new prophetic model of obedience and its practice in community and in ministry. The final two chapters are devoted to the unitive or mystical dimension of this vow, its role in the spirituality of the Religious.

Through more than a decade of research, reflection, listening to and consulting with Religious and other interested parties in both the United States and other parts of the world, lecturing and teaching and writing on the subject of Religious Life, I have been struggling to discern and articulate a coherent interpretation of this life in and for a new millennium. In the process, I have come to some convictions about its nature, meaning, purpose, and direction which seem to me to be deeply consonant with its long history but which are also very different from the understandings that had petrified into a kind of Procrustean bed in the two centuries prior to Vatican II.

This preconciliar hardening into a uniformity that was

increasingly airless and narrow was the reflection in Religious Life of the sclerosis in the Church as a whole that the anti-modernist period, especially between Vatican I and Vatican II, had generated. It was this great Roman-centered institutional monolith that had in some ways virtually entombed the People of God that John XXIII wanted to open up to the rushing wind of the Spirit. Through the Council, this Spirit of newness released into the postmodern world the energy of a renewed Church. This conciliar Church no longer understood itself primarily as an essentially hierarchical institution, perfect, finished, and unchanging, but as People of God on its pilgrim way to the fullness of life that Jesus came to bring. Religious, especially women, were eagerly poised to respond.

But no one could have predicted how the Council's call to renewal—not just to a superficial "updating" of externals but to profound interior conversion—would challenge Religious Life itself and its members. Huge numbers of Sisters, for various reasons related partly to what was happening in the Church but also to what was happening in the world, left Religious Life in the decade immediately following the close of the Council. Those who stayed struggled with the wrenching emotional losses of cherished companions and institutions, drastically reduced personnel and financial resources, confidence-destroying ecclesiastical persecution by an increasingly right-wing hierarchy, deep spiritual darkness precipitated by theological upheavals that undermined the massive unquestioned synthesis upon which their life had been built, while the long-overdue shift of ecclesiastical attention to the laity and their parochial context left Religious increasingly invisible and often "placeless" in the Church. The necessarily piecemeal and unevenly paced experimentation with renewal subverted the reassuring sense of total coherence that had characterized preconciliar Religious Life itself creating a pervasive sense of continual disorientation and even, at times, a seeming loss of meaning.

It is now fifty years since the Council opened. At least two generations of younger people were born after the greatest event in modern Church history closed and cannot really grasp what "all the fuss was/is about." A vigorous and disheartening restorationist program, promoted by John Paul II (and now kept in motion by his successor) and bolstered by a well-financed and ideologically unified contingent of Tridentine laity, was underway within two decades of the end of the Council and its energy is far from spent. In this half-century Religious Life, especially that of women, has undergone a sea change unparalleled by anything in its history. And most of the people in Religious Life today have lived through this entire development, well able to remember the preconciliar life that has changed so radically.

Now what, if anything, can we say with clarity and confidence about ministerial (i.e., non-monastic) Religious Life? Attempting to answer that question has been the burden of this three-volume work, which obviously cannot be summarized in a few pages. However, I want to articulate, as succinctly and clearly as I can, what seems to me to be a valid, and I hope life-giving, interpretation of Religious Life at this point in what, surely, will be an ongoing process of renewal. I want to examine not only clear gains but also ongoing problems, not only answers but also unanswered questions. I will speak at times in the first person by way of taking responsibility for my own articulation even though nothing I am suggesting is "mine" in any exclusive sense. But I want to recognize that there is wide pluralism among Religious in regard at least to emphases and often enough with regard to substance, and my interpretation has no claim to exclusivity or superiority. In the midst of a lively and ongoing conversation about this life, a conversation that must and will continue probably long after this work is out of print, I offer these conclusions, confidently but also tentatively, as one way of understanding what Religious Life has become.

I am confident, even though these conclusions constitute a "still take" on a moving reality, because virtually everything that has finally come to expression in this work has been tested against the experience of the people who are currently living this life. In many ways I feel more like a "scribe" of our collective experience than an individual theorist working in the abstract. As long as readers realize that what is here proposed is an existential picture of an evolving lifeform and not an essentialist definition or prescriptive formulation meant to arrest further development, this relatively coherent picture based on theological reflection on shared experience can perhaps provide a standpoint for ongoing progress. But I offer these conclusions tentatively precisely because they are necessarily provisional conclusions about a living reality whose continuing development no one can predict. In other words, I hope that articulating what seems relatively clear, at least to me, at this point can be a basis for continuing the process of interpretation that must go on as long as the life is a life and not just a fossil in a museum.

B. Articulating a Synthesis

The conviction underlying this entire trilogy is that, in its deepest reality, **ministerial Religious Life is a Christian mystical-prophetic lifeform, given to the Church by the Holy Spirit for the sake of the world, and constituted by perpetual Profession of consecrated celibacy, evangelical poverty, and prophetic obedience lived in transcendent community and ministry**. Without trying to summarize or even recall the salient points of three volumes of reflection I will try to indicate the crucial issues to which each element of this global description points. In some cases, for example, the vows, very little remains to be said since whole chapters have been devoted to the topic. But in other cases, such as the Christian and ecclesial character of the life, I have taken this feature for granted but not engaged the contemporary problems and controversies surrounding it. In regard to the first category, I invite the reader to return as desired to the much lengthier developments that have led to this point and pursue the discussion, perhaps with the aid of the Study Guide, with others involved with the topic. In regard to the second category I will give the topics careful attention here in order to complete and conclude the global presentation of a theology of Religious Life which is the purpose of this trilogy. My objective in this concluding chapter is to articulate positively what is distinctive about ministerial Religious Life in order to affirm the life and to support the hope of those who live it and those who look to Religious for companionship on the journey. At the same time, and actually for the same purpose, I will also acknowledge honestly the painful, at times agonizing, tension between Religious Life as a charismatic lifeform in the Church and the Church as ecclesiastical institution, with confidence that there is power in truth for progress toward reconciliation and resolution.

1. *Religious Life is a* lifeform

In earlier times Religious Life was called a "state of life." This term, which is still useful in some contexts, can risk suggesting that the life is static and its constituent features fixed and unchanging. In choosing "lifeform" I have tried to suggest that the life is organic; not an extrinsic combination of essential elements but a living entity whose unity is achieved and maintained by the complex, ever-changing interaction of related and ordered features, coordinates, dynamics, experiences, processes, and so on. My imaginative model has been a living being, whose identity is internally structured and dynamic, that is in creative interchange with its ever-changing environment, rather than an immutable and lifeless construction fixed in a setting to whose vicissitudes it is basically immune.

Religious Life as a lifeform is not, in the first place, an organization. It is not a club, a business, a political party or civic project, an institution or benevolent association, a task force, a committee, a tribe or an army. It is not a family, either primary or secondary. Nor is it simply a loose network whose members interact for mutual benefit or in common projects on an "as needed" basis. Perhaps the closest analog is marriage; a shared life in which the partners, through their loving, egalitarian, faithful, and permanent union gradually become who they are together and out of that identity-in-union give life in unique ways. But while this analogy captures many features of Religious Life there are obvious important differences, so it cannot be used as an adequate, much less an exclusive, model. The important point, however, is that Religious Life is a life, not a thing. And it is a particular kind of life. Its identity is not artificial; its unity is not external or mechanical; its motivation is not instrumental. "A Religious" is something one is, not something one does. And "Religious Life" is the organic shared lifeform of such persons.

Among the **important implications** of the fact that Religious Life is a lifeform in the Church is that it is recognizable and therefore *public*. However, its public character does not arise from any ecclesiastical office, assigned role, or official function in the Church. Religious as public persons in the Church are not clerics, quasi-clerics, or substitute clerics, much less part of the hierarchy. They are not agents of the Church as institution.

Furthermore, within their freely chosen lifeform, which no one in the Church is obliged to undertake, and which has no official role or function in the hierarchical structure of the Church, they have *the right to self-definition in regard to their life* (within the framework of the Gospel and Church law) and to *legitimate autonomy* in the internal life and governance of their communities.

The *lifelong commitment* they make by Religious Profession is not a regulation or requirement set up by law. It is intrinsic to the character of Religious Life as a lifeform rather than some kind of organization or association which one joins and leaves at will. This dimension of Religious Profession was treated in detail in volume 2, part 1.

2. Religious Life is a Christian *lifeform*

Describing Religious Life as Christian is not a mere formality. Its Christian and Catholic character has been assumed throughout this work. However, it may be the most problematic term in this description and this is the place to acknowledge the problems, describe and analyze them, and attempt to justify "Christian" and "Catholic" as defining characteristics of the life. Describing the lifeform as Christian grounds several important distinctions as well as establishing certain connections. It implies specific features and commitments and qualifies certain assumptions that have been taken for granted by Religious and Church authorities for centuries. It also raises some extremely important theological issues that are problematic for communities as well as for individual Religious today in a way that would have been unimaginable even fifty years ago.

As has been said before, most literate religions throughout history have given rise to some form of contemplative or ascetic virtuosity lived in eremitical or cenobitical monastic life. Ministerial Religious Life, however, is a Christian *novum* precisely because of its intrinsically ministerial character, which implies that it is non-monastic.

It is also important to realize that Christian Religious Life is not unique to Catholicism. The life arose in Eastern Christianity where it exists to this day both in rites united with Rome (Eastern Catholics) and others not in union with Rome. Religious Life, in various forms, is also important in the Orthodox tradition, which definitively distinguished itself from the Latin or Roman Church in the eleventh century. It has been reborn in a number of churches of the Reformation despite Luther's strong polemic against it and it was never fully extinguished in Anglicanism where it remains important today. So the ministerial Religious Life treated in this trilogy is neither synonymous with "monasticism" nor strictly identical with Christian Religious Life. Calling it a Christian lifeform recognizes its connection with all other forms of Christian Religious Life while distinguishing it from non-Christian monasticism.

More important, perhaps, "Christian" correctly puts the emphasis on what is most foundational to the faith commitment of the lifeform we are discussing. Its Catholic character is, of course, important, but Catholicism is a particular way of being Christian, not vice versa. When the Council declared that "the final norm of the religious life is the following of Christ as it is put before us in the Gospel" and therefore that the Gospel (not the pope, the hierarchy, Canon Law, the Constitutions or traditions, or the opinion or regulations of the clergy or local bishop) "must be taken by all institutes as the supreme rule" (*P.C.* 2) of their life, it was making precisely this point. Religious are not super-Catholics, nor a special kind of Catholic, nor bound to be Catholic in a way different from that of other members of the People of God. They share with other Catholics their Christian identity that Catholics in general share with other Christians.

In preconciliar times Religious Life had become so idiosyncratic and even esoteric in its lifestyle that it sometimes seemed more like a "sect" (or even a cult) than a form of Christian life. Religious practiced a spirituality beyond and often different from that of the ordinary baptized. They even celebrated the sacraments in the privacy of their cloistered dwellings rather than with communities of "secular" Catholics, and their attitudes toward "seculars," even members of their own families, suggested that their non-Religious fellow believers were a danger to their vocation if not to their faith. Such practices as daily Mass, weekly confession, and a vast array of devotional observances were regarded as just as obligatory (and sometimes in practice more obligatory) than fundamental Christian virtues. Perhaps most serious was the virtual suspension of personal conscience in deference to ecclesiastical authority, to which Religious considered themselves bound in a special, even absolute, way. This expanded authority was often inserted into the internal life of communities in highly questionable ways.

Postconciliar Religious, like other well-educated Catholics, have learned to make appropriate distinctions between faith and human traditions, divine and ecclesiastical authority, God's law and ecclesiastical law or regulations, Church office itself and fallible officeholders, genuine teaching of faith and morals and arrogant or ignorant abuse of power, and so on. Religious have also learned that there is a hierarchy of religious truths, some of which belong to the very core of Christian faith expressed in the Creed while others range from solidly probable theological and moral positions to the idiosyncratic interpretations of ecclesiastical extremists, some of whom, unfortunately, are highly placed in the Church's official structure. In other words, not everything associated with Catholicism, even when propounded by Church officials, is necessarily Christian or obligatory, and Religious, like other Catholics, have a right to make such distinctions and act accordingly.

However, the other side of this coin is that explicit Christian faith is the nonnegotiable foundation of Catholic Religious Life. The Gospel of Jesus Christ is its supreme rule. A Catholic Religious cannot be, authentically, "spiritual but not religious" and the religious commitment in question is Christianity, not a vague personal religiosity or a self-constructed synthesis of beliefs, practices, texts, and teachings from a variety of traditions. In terms of the faith which grounds their life-commitment, Catholic Religious cannot be simply feminists, ecologists, undeclared spiritual "seekers," peace and justice activists, poets, artists, nature mystics, or agnostics. This is not because there is some law against these options but because a non-Christian Catholic Religious is as much an existential contradiction as a sacramentally married polygamist or a monotheistic atheist. And Christian faith is not a vague, general, or nondescript commitment to positive values that is basically interchangeable with any and all constructive life stances. Christianity is a specific and particular religious commitment. It is a scriptural, sacramental, doctrinal, communitarian, morally committed faith that one either freely accepts and practices or does not.

If this work had been written fifty years ago the Catholic Christian character of the life would have been so self-evident to its members as well as its observers that talking about it at all would have been equivalent to discussing the wetness of water. The basically cloistered and ghettoized preconciliar form of Religious Life and its sociological character as a total institution kept the Life and its members sufficiently out of contact with the surrounding culture, either religious or secular, so that no real challenge to the monolithically Catholic character of the life could have been imagined. In the theologically anti-modernist, ecclesiologically ultramontane, and socioculturally self-enclosed context of nineteenth- and early twentieth-century Catholicism, Religious were virtually hermetically sealed off from anything that would or could have challenged the doctrinal and practical uniformity of their life and faith.

This situation changed radically as the modern age began to give way to the postmodern sometime in the mid-twentieth century. Theologically, the lead-up to Vatican II, and scientifically, the opening of the "Space Age" and the explosion of the natural sciences that began symbolically with the launching of the Russian spacecraft *Sputnik* in 1957, marked the beginning of the end of the Church's four centuries of isolation from "the world" which we discussed at length in chapter 1 of this volume.

Two major pressures—no doubt not the only ones—resulting from the conciliar reengagement of the Church, and therefore Religious Life, with the world have created significant challenges for many contemporary Religious concerning their Catholic identity. The first was the emergence of a new cosmic context for human existence, sometimes called "the universe story," with its scientific, ecological, theological, and spiritual implications. The second was the originally ecumenical but increasingly interreligious contacts between Catholics and the people and beliefs of other religious traditions.

Although these issues have not surfaced on the formal agendas of most Congregations, these two radical expansions of the traditional Catholic Christian theological framework of Religious Life are having major and often highly disruptive influence in communities. My purpose here is to raise this issue to the surface in hopes of stimulating open discussion. Religious Life cannot survive a basic subversion of common faith, whether it is subverted by silence or by open disagreement. Discussion of these issues and the development of a way of dealing with them is crucial.

All religion—whether the nature religions of primal peoples, the mystical religions of the East, or the historical religions of the West—is cosmically situated. Underlying and structuring belief in transcendence or the Transcendent, whether personal or otherwise, is a fundamental understanding of the world in which the believer or practitioner lives. Whether this world is believed to be pervasively inhabited and controlled by spirits or powers that transcend the human, to be an illusory and opaque veil between the individual human and true reality, or to be the creature of a benevolent creator who is manifested historically, symbolically, or otherwise in and through the world itself, the imaginative world-construction underlies and structures the human relation to ultimate reality. Consequently, when the operative world-construction is seriously impacted, for example, by natural catastrophe, encounter with ideas or practices which call the validity of the tradition into question, or scientific or philosophical discoveries that seem incompatible with what has heretofore been "known," religious belief is affected. Sometimes the effect is such that it destroys the religious tradition, as seems to have been the case of the major pagan religions in the Greco-Roman world under the impact of Christianity and rational philosophy. But this is not the only possible result.

Christianity, even in its modern period, has undergone, and so far survived, several major changes in "worldview" that the Church strenuously resisted at the time precisely because of the massive implications for faith of the new understanding of reality. The Galileo saga is one of the most illustrative because Galileo's theories were suspect precisely because of what they implied regarding the "world." Following Copernicus (1473–1543), Galileo (1564–1642) defended the thesis that planet Earth was not the stable center of the universe but that the sun was the center and Earth (as well as other planets) moved in orbit around it. Significantly, the written formulation of this theory for which Galileo was brought before the Inquisition in 1632 was *Dialogs on the Two Chief **World Systems*** (emphasis added). In other words, Galileo realized that he was challenging the reigning worldview. Although Galileo was forced to recant his theory it has, of course, proven true and Galileo is recognized as a, if not the, central figure of the Scientific Revolution. Whatever was involved scientifically in Galileo's theory, the Church's objection to it was not fundamentally a concern about its science but about the implications of the theory for the truth of the Bible and what was believed to be biblical revelation about the world. In other words, Galileo's theory seemed to undermine the world-construction in which the Christian religion operated and on which, according to its leaders, that religion therefore depended.

The struggle of the Christian churches with the naturalist Charles Darwin (1809–1882), who formulated, published, and defended the theory of the origin of species by natural selection (evolution), is structurally similar. Darwin's thesis appeared to imply that human beings were perhaps not specially created by God as Genesis seems to say they were, and that humans may not all be descended from one original pair, Adam and Eve. The struggle over Darwin's theory continues to play itself out in contemporary classrooms, churches, and courtrooms. Even though the *Index of Forbidden Books* (to which Darwin's writings were consigned by the Catholic Church) no longer exists, the battle between "evolutionists" and "creationists" and between the hypotheses of "evolution" and "intelligent design" continues to pit believers against each other, depending on whether they think the implications of this scientific theory are compatible or not with the world-construction within which their faith can make sense.

Pierre Teilhard de Chardin (1881–1955), a Jesuit scientist whose major life work as a paleontologist consisted in his effort to integrate natural science, specifically evolutionary biology, with Christian theology, launched a movement that has been swelling ever since and is perhaps cresting in our time. Chardin, who finally had a significant influence on the thinking of the Fathers of Vatican II, proposed a cosmic theory according to which evolution, including that of humans, was directed toward the earth's culmination as the fullness of Creation achieved in love, which is ultimately the love of Christ. Somewhat younger than Chardin, Thomas Berry (1914–2009), a Catholic priest who called himself a "geologian" (rather than theologian), developed his theory of the "Universe Story" which, with the help of Brian Swimme, a mathematical cosmologist, has achieved a powerful grip on the religious imagination of our time. They have persuasively presented the challenge of contemporary humanity, "the Great Work" as they call it, as the human service of the earth in the context of the expanding universe. In the same line James Lovelock (1919–), a renowned life sciences and geophysiologist, elaborated his "Gaia hypothesis" which proposes that the earth is a living system made up of smaller systems which "she" integrates into herself for her own well-being. Humanity is one of these systems, an extremely powerful one, with the capacity to foster or undermine, perhaps even destroy, Gaia's ultimate project.

These theologians and scientists are at the theoretical cutting edge of a developing worldwide revolution of consciousness. The reality-threatening anthropocentrism that has run amok in the aftermath of the Scientific Revolution and the Enlightenment must be reversed before the destructive trajectory humans have launched destroys the earth or makes it uninhabitable for future human beings and other creatures. These scientists are in league with public intellectuals, ecologists, writers and artists, theologians and philosophers, scientists, politicians and activists—some of whom are Christian but many of whom are not and many of whom lay primary blame for the fragile state of the cosmos on biblical religion—who are urgently pressuring humanity to see the earth (the cosmos) in the context of the story of the universe within which humanity is a fleeting moment in a history that is billions of years old. This "new science" is a quantum leap beyond the incremental progress of one scientific theory building on another that characterized the so-called Scientific Revolution. The new science is challenging the entire human race to reverse our perspective, to see ourselves as dependent upon and responsible for our world rather than as god-like masters enthroned at the pinnacle of reality, for whom nonhuman creation exists, and which we have the right to subordinate, use, abuse, and dispose of solely in terms of its utility for us.

People who recognize the truth in this new perspective on reality, and among whom women Religious are prominent, often have a difficult time integrating this new universe consciousness with Christian faith and theology which centers God's creative plan for the world (if not the whole universe) on the salvation of humanity through the Incarnation of God in a first-century Jewish human being, Jesus of Nazareth. Some are convinced that just as humanity must cede its place at the center of reality, so must Christianity, including Jesus, Scripture, Church, sacraments and even God be "retired" in favor of a new cosmic commitment to Gaia as the ultimate principle of being and understanding. The whole Christian "thing" can suddenly seem too small, too provincial, too historically young and institutionally old, too self-centered and self-serving to be worth bothering about as they turn their attention to the preservation of the natural universe and the fostering of right relationships among all species, among which there is nothing special about humans except that we are more destructive than any other species. For some people there is no choice but to replace *"Gloria in excelsis Deo"* with the song of the universe, "Everything is connected."

In short, we are in the midst of a major change in worldview as reality construction. Just as the contemporaries of Galileo and Darwin were being challenged to integrate into their Christian worldview new theories which relativized the notion of planet Earth as the center of the universe and humanity as the unique species qualitatively separate in origin and nature from all the rest of the biological world, so we are being challenged to reconceive our place in Creation and cosmos.

Some people now, like the guardians of the faith in the sixteenth and seventeenth centuries, are digging in against the new science, denying its truth and its consequences, convinced that if they refuse to believe in something it will disappear. They refuse to accept that they are responsible for the earth rather than nature existing to fulfill their every desire; that they are actually involved in deciding what will be available, if anything, for future generations; that the cosmos itself depends on their restraint and active care. They simply deny the fact of global warming, its already deleterious effects and its disastrous potential; they consider reducing waste and recycling as optional "fads" for which they have no time and certainly no obligations. Urban farmers are, in their opinion, romantics with too much time on their hands. And it is certainly counterproductive in their minds to regulate production or consumption today in view of some mythological future threat.

Other people, however, have been so fascinated with what seems like a "fresh start" in relation to a Church grown old in corruption, grizzled with patriarchy, and paralyzed by lack of imagination, that they are more than willing to turn in their baptismal certificates as children of God in exchange for citizenship papers in the earth community. There is among these enthusiasts much back-to-nature romanticism, irresponsible and even disrespectful religious eclecticism, and glib theory-spinning that is scientifically and theologically fuzzy at best and incoherent at worst. Ecstatic primitivism often stands in for liturgy while the martial arts become sacraments. Any elevating text can function as Scripture and deities of nature religions or heroes of political movements can stand in for the living God, Jesus, and the saints of Christian tradition. The Holy Spirit is simply the life force of plants and animals. Any invocation of the Trinity as divine or Jesus as God made human is embarrassingly old-fashioned, exclusivist, or provincial and easily replaced by worship of the four directions and invocation of the spirits of animals and ancestors.

Although I know of no surveys or studies of Religious on this subject, my fairly wide contacts suggest to me that there are relatively few Religious at the far end of the resistance scale. In fact, some publications have opined, on the basis of considerable evidence, that Religious, especially women, are in the vanguard of propagation of the universe story, serious study of the new cosmology, ecological and environmental activism, and the attempt to promote a sense of interconnectedness and responsibility for the earth and all creatures among those to whom they minister.

I also strongly suspect that the number of those at the other extreme—those who have rejected revealed religion in general and Catholic Christianity in particular in favor of some form of nature worship, agnosticism, or unbelief—is quite small. However, these enthusiasts have influence out of proportion to their numbers, at least in the public forum, because they present themselves as the visionaries of the future, the champions of change, development, and new thinking. Few of their fellow Religious, no matter how deeply Christian, want to even appear to contest such "progressive thinking" lest they be assimilated to the restorationist guardians of orthodoxy whose fossilized version of "Catholic truth" is so problematic, especially for women Religious.

Attention to earlier crises in Christianity, like those associated with Galileo, Darwin, and de Chardin when a shift in imaginative world-constructions has seemed to subvert the very foundations of faith can perhaps be instructive for our present situation. Let me suggest a few points for reflection and discussion.

First, any attempt to forbid the study of new ideas, to simply deny what the physical or human sciences are discovering, or to establish human knowledge by *fiat* is worse than pointless. Silencing Galileo did not make the earth stand still and condemning Darwin did not establish that a single couple was the ultimate parent of all humans. The only way to deal with new theories is to engage them, which begins by trying to understand them. And if the matter is really important and transformative it will not be able to be understood by the reading of a couple popular articles or watching an uplifting video. Study, discussion, and time will be required before one is in a position to make serious decisions about the implications of new knowledge for major intellectual and religious convictions. Herd-mentality enthusiasm is hardly a valid or rational position. And while one studies and explores, one can accept many implications of a new scientific position such as the importance of ecological responsibility, even before being in a position to make decisions about its implications for the nature of God, the divinity of Christ, or the reality of salvation.

Second, there seems to be a direct relation between intellectual rigidity and literalism (even fundamentalism) on the one hand and the tendency to "replace" traditions as a whole, especially ancient religious ones, with "new" orthodoxies, simplistically swallowed whole. More subtle minds whose Christian theology is deep, nuanced, and complex will approach new knowledge, whether scientific or religious, with the same subtlety and nuance. The fact that the compatibility of a new idea or theory with what is already known is not immediately obvious does not require a black or white decision that for the new to be true the known must be false. Unlike paradigm shifts in the physical sciences in which a new theory, if true, simply replaces its predecessor, developments in the humanities are more dialectical. New knowledge modifies previous knowledge which in turn has implications for the new knowledge until a synthesis emerges which seems to take better account of experience and data. And no theory is final in the sense that further new data cannot modify it.

Careful reflection should make it clear that what we know by revelation cannot, in the nature of the case, be proved or falsified by what can be known scientifically. Science modifies our limited frames of reference, our categories for understanding revelation, not the revelation itself or that which is revealed, such as the nature of God, the inspiration of Scripture, or the efficacy of the sacraments. It is not always immediately clear how to integrate new data into a previous synthesis, and it certainly does not take place by hearing a lecture or seeing a film. People who are, whether they know it or not, literalists (or fundamentalists) about their Christian faith can only replace it with something new which seems incompatible or reject the new in stubborn protection of frameworks they need to feel safe. Theologically sophisticated believers can see other ways to deal with new data, well aware that such engagement will not be swift or total or self-evidently and unarguably "true."

Third, Christian faith, while it always operates within some worldview and is therefore affected by changes in worldviews, is not a *theory* about God, the world, or humanity. It is a *relational universe* in which the believer actually experiences God, Jesus, community, revelation, personal spiritual development through prayer, sacramental participation, aesthetic-spiritual engagement with Christian Scripture as a revelatory text, and ongoing conversion. An experienced Christian believer already lives in a sacramental universe and even if that universe expands dramatically it does not necessarily cease to exist or cease to mediate the One it has made present in previous experience. Such a person may not see immediately how certain new data about the evolving universe can be integrated with the relationships that constitute her Christian faith universe but she or he has at least as much reason to maintain those relationships as to openly engage new data that requires integration.

The second pressure on the Christian faith of Religious (as well as other Catholics) arises from the openness to "the other" that the Council legitimated and encouraged. Part of the turn toward the previously rejected world outside the institutional Church was a tentative but sincere outreach not only to Protestant "sister churches" from whom the Catholic Church had become alienated in the aftermath of the Reformation, but also to Orthodox, to Jews and Muslims, to religions outside the monotheistic "family," and even to "nonbelievers." In other words, the embrace of the other was not simply ecumenical (already a huge step beyond the absolute rejection of preconciliar times) but interreligious and even extra-religious.

Catholics had very little preparation for relating to people they had grown up regarding as heretics, schismatics, and even reprobates whose salvation depended on conversion to or reunion with Catholicism, to say nothing of "perfidious" Jews, Muslim "barbarians," Hindu and Buddhist "pagans," agnostics and atheists. Once they began to mingle with these previously "off-limits" people, especially since many Catholics already had considerable experience of such non-Catholics through mixed marriages in their families, their children's friends in public schools, and so on, Catholics came to respect and even admire the human and religious quality of these new conversation partners. Some people who had been regarded as reprobate and even virtually demonized were clearly people of sterling integrity, sometimes-heroic goodness, fidelity, generosity, and kindness. How was it possible to continue to hold that Christianity was the only true religion and Catholicism the only true Church when whatever religion was supposed to profess clearly existed in those who were neither Christian nor Catholic?

As Religious interacted in greater depth with these "outsiders" they could not avoid the conclusion that these people were not good in spite of their "false religions" but precisely because of what they believed and practiced. The incompatibility of this obvious truth with what Catholics had been taught and what, in occasional postconciliar documents like "*Dominus Jesus*"[5] was—with some softening but not real change—reiterated, led to a sense among some Catholics that "all religions are essentially the same" and none, including one's own, is necessarily superior. For those (among whom most Religious would probably be numbered) sufficiently sophisticated to realize that there is more to religion than personal morality, that all religions are certainly not the same or interchangeable, and that the category of "superiority" is more problematic than illuminating, it nevertheless could seem to be the case that any religion (or even no religion) could be salvific for a sincere believer or practitioner.

Once again, Religious who had spent decades in the hermetically sealed total institution of preconciliar convent life were ill prepared to handle the suddenly expanded pluralistic religious world in which they found themselves. Again, the dualism characteristic of Western rationality has not served them well. If what Buddhists, Unitarians, Muslims, Quakers, or Jews believed was true (and it must be if it made people in those faiths good), then what Catholics believed that was different must be false. Or perhaps none of these faiths, including Christianity, were actually true but simply a variety of ways of thinking about ultimate reality and there was no reason except tradition or habit to prefer one's own. A richer experience could be had by experiencing a variety of practices and entertaining a variety of faith positions, or none. How could one continue to believe that one's faith had real content, was true in some ultimate sense, when obviously a huge proportion of the human race was getting along quite well without it?

Let me, once again, make some suggestions that might stimulate fruitful discussion. First, faith is not like political party allegiance, something one holds as long as it works but can abandon if something more cogent or effective comes along. Faith is more like friendship, or love. One does not trade one's friends in for "better" options. Furthermore, comparing relationships makes little sense. They are not based on a comparative evaluation of pluses and minuses. Love is a response of the whole self to the whole of the other. No comparisons among relationships are really possible or desirable.

Second, religious faiths are "wholes," experiential universes, not collections of separable elements. Only someone who believes in the triune God, for example, can make believing sense of the Incarnation of the Word of God in Jesus, and only on the basis of a christologically based faith does the Church as Body of Christ make sense. The sacraments are not "rituals" which can be interchanged with rituals of other religions but encounters with Christ in his paschal mystery, which itself is meaningless unless Jesus is who Christians believe him to be.

What is true for Christianity is true for other religions. The fact that there are analogous contacts between religions (e.g., that most religions revere certain texts as sacred) does not make those aspects of each religion "detachable" from their faith matrix and interchangeable. The Christian Bible and the Muslim Koran are analogous in that both are sacred texts, but in fact the Koran is for Islam what Jesus (not the Bible) is for Christians.

In short, there are profound questions raised by the pluralism of religions. The theology of religions is a specialization that is immensely complex and subtle. The preconciliar approach that simply declared the Catholic faith true and all others false is simplistic in the extreme, and in any case, not even possible for people who have actually experienced the beauty and truth in traditions other than their own. Once the child ventures beyond his or her own backyard, there is no way to pretend that all people are the same color, speak the same language, accept the same customs and so on. Catholics, including Religious, left the ghetto half a century ago and religious pluralism is irrevocably part of their consciousness.

Both the encounter with the "universe story" and the encounter with other religions are part of a process that cannot be reversed; namely, a widening and diversification of the frame of reference within which we know and deal with ultimate reality. When the frame of reference within which we deal with any reality changes we are challenged to re-see, to see differently, to reevaluate and appropriate anew, everything within that frame of reference. When a family that was previously only the couple has a child everything changes; it is not just a matter of adding furniture or rearranging the schedule. Values, preferences, behaviors, ways of handling money or time or energy, social life, priorities, especially relationships, including that of the parents to each other, change and all the changes are themselves interrelated.

Catholics, including Religious, live in a different faith world than they did in the 1950s, and it is not at all clear exactly how everything that is part of that new world is related to everything else. It is not even clear what some things, new and old, mean.

Simply jettisoning the faith synthesis that has shaped and resourced one's relationship with God, with self, with fellow-Christians, with the world over a lifetime because new thinking, resynthesizing, reexamination of even fundamental concepts and constructs, reevaluations of commitments and relationships and much more have become necessary in light of the changed frame of reference, makes as much sense as getting a divorce and putting the new baby up for adoption when one realizes things are not and can never be the same as they were before the child was born. This realization does not invalidate the experience of the relationship before the new arrival. But it might well change one's evaluation or understanding of some of that previous experience.

Somehow, it seems to me, Religious need to find a way to discuss, at deep levels of trust and sharing, how their faith life has changed over the past several decades. Who is God for each of us? Who is Jesus? What is Church? What type of prayer is most meaningful? Where, when, and how do we experience the Spirit in ourselves, our Church, our world? What is most distressing for us? What kind of liturgy is meaningful? What is the relationship between personal faith and ministry? What spiritual disciplines help us stay on course? Conversation at such depth can only happen if there is a serious mutual commitment to listen to each other, to genuinely entertain the possibility of what the other is saying without attempting to "correct" or "convert" and without feeling oneself judged by what the other is saying. If we need to defend our own current position or prove the position of the other deficient, even if we do not express this, the conversations will become stalemates. People develop at different rates. Different aspects of faith are centrally important to different people. We did not have to contend with this kind of diversity in the past; it may well have existed but it was submerged in a uniform practice and language so we did not know and did not need to know what others thought. Now we do.

At risk of serious objection, I would suggest that there is a real need at this stage in the development of ministerial Religious Life to fearlessly and confidently affirm our Christian, even Catholic, faith in language, ritual, iconography, and practice. Unless we start from who we are and where we have been together it is hard to see how we can move to new places we can really share. Even when we pray together "through Christ our Lord" there will be diversity in what that means to different people. But there will also be something in common on the basis of which we can talk about the differences.

Within this shared context of genuinely Christian faith many commitments that are not specifically Christian or religious, such as that to feminism, ecological sustainability, peace and justice, and human development, are not only compatible with Christian faith and practice but can be powerfully motivated and sustained by it. And reciprocally, Christian faith can be enriched and deepened by such commitments and by dialogical engagement with and even influence by other faith traditions. Contemporary science and philosophy raise challenging questions for traditional Christian images of God and can nuance, expand, and deepen understandings of various aspects of Christian faith. There are many inspiring sacred texts deriving from non-Christian traditions that can offer spiritual nourishment also to Christians, including Religious. But Catholic Religious Life is not a benevolent association of people practicing a variety of private religions (or none) who simply agree not to tread on each other's beliefs while working together for a better world.

On the contrary, Christian Religious Life is a vibrant, integrated, coherent religious and spiritual lifeform in which the members draw personal sustenance and strength for ministry from shared faith in the triune creator God revealed in Jesus Christ and poured forth in their hearts by the Holy Spirit. They celebrate and nourish this common life in the Spirit in many ways, but most importantly through Eucharistic celebration illuminated by the only text Christians hold as canonical, that is, not only as true (which many other texts are) but also as ultimately normative of their faith: the Christian Scriptures. The morality to which they hold themselves and one another accountable is not a vague inoffensiveness, a private code of conduct, or even a robust commitment to virtue, but the imitation and following of Jesus Christ. Christians believe that when Jesus told his followers to "do this [i.e., Eucharist] in memory of me" and to "love another as I have loved you" (i.e., unto the laying down of one's life), he was not exhorting them to generic virtue in the religion of their choice but to a specific commitment centered on his Person and participating in his salvific work through sharing in his paschal mystery.

Finally, we have to recognize the serious problem raised for Religious by the contemporary ecclesiastical situation that makes sacramental practice for women in general and women Religious in particular often unavailable, and when available, alienating and oppressive. The Eucharist, sacrament of unity, is often for women much more a participation in the suffering and death than in the Resurrection of Jesus. It is naïve to pretend that this experience is not frustrating, contradictory, and even infuriating, especially when Religious try to celebrate together in ways that all can appreciate. Acknowledging this reality among ourselves is not a solution to the problems but can perhaps help us to share our suffering rather than increase each other's by blaming ourselves or one another for problems we did not create. And, slowly, we are finding creative ways to deal with these problems, which, though not ideal, at least are less compromising than blind submission to abusive power operating under the label of "ministry." No matter how difficult participation in the public worship life of the Church is at the present time, however, I am suggesting that definitive alienation from the believing community and abandonment of sacramental life is not a viable option for a Catholic Religious.

An **important implication** of the fundamentally Christian character of Religious Life is that while it is specifically and integrally *Catholic*, it is so in an *inclusive Christian* rather than exclusively denominational way. The Catholicism of Religious does not turn them inward in an ecclesiastical exclusivism that precludes engagement with anything that is not explicitly and officially Catholic. Religious are not "official" representatives of the institution who must avoid anything not publicly and officially "on the books."

Religious have been leaders in the raising of feminist consciousness, in ecumenical sharing, in engagement in interreligious dialogue and even well-considered interreligious practice, in ecology and environmentalism, in engagement with the new science and its cosmological expansion of consciousness, in the use in their ministries of healing of techniques and the integration of forms of spiritual practice that do not derive from explicitly Catholic sources. One of the great gifts of Religious Life to the Church is its combination of intensive faith and practice of Catholic spirituality with openness to spiritual resources and non-Christian dialogue partners that the official Church often hesitates to engage. Their Profession does not commit Religious to proselytize. They are committed to offer, as attractively as possible, the Gospel to any and all whom they encounter. "Attractively" will sometimes mean explicitly, and even in Catholic formulation. At other times it will mean indirectly, at least until their interlocutors indicate a desire to go further.

3. *Religious Life is a* mystical-prophetic *lifeform*

The description of Religious Life as a mystical-prophetic lifeform points to several important features of the life, particularly those which have been appropriated most deeply in the process of conciliar renewal. Religious Life, as has been said in various contexts throughout this work, is modeled on the life of Jesus. All Christian spirituality consists in the imitation and following of Christ, as we discussed in some detail in chapter 4, sections 6 and 7 of this volume. But different states of life raise to visibility in a particular way different aspects of the life of Jesus.

I have suggested, and want to reemphasize here, that it is the prophetic character of Jesus' life rooted in his mystical union with God, the life into which he initiated a small band of itinerant disciples who left all to follow him during his earthly ministry, that provides the particular and distinguishing model for Religious Life. This mystical-prophetic character of the life was muted, perhaps even obscured, during the period of virtually total ecclesiastical institutionalization of apostolic Religious Life in the nineteenth and early twentieth centuries. Only since the beginning of the renewal, especially in the American

Church, has there been a major reassertion of the prophetic character of the life that was much clearer at the origins of this form of the life in Europe in the seventeenth and eighteenth centuries and then in North America.

At the heart of Jesus' prophetic life is the mystical reality of deeply experienced personal union with God. Especially in the Gospel of John Jesus speaks of being so completely united with the One who sent him that those who see him truly see God (see John 14:9). The term "mystical" in this formulation has nothing to do with esotericism or paranormal phenomena. Rather, it points to the experiential character of the deeply contemplative and unitive core of Jesus' life, which is also central to the life of Religious. Jesus cultivated this mystical dimension of his life through participation in the prayer life of his Jewish tradition, in frequent and prolonged solitary prayer, and in constant discerning and courageous obedience to the will of God in his life and death. It is this same spirituality, nourished by the liturgical life of the Christian tradition, by a life of personal contemplative prayer, and by discerning and faithful obedience that grounds and finds expression in the life and ministry of Religious.

Emphasizing the mystical character of the life calls attention to the fact that the spirituality at the heart of this life is experiential rather than purely theoretical, moral, or even primarily ascetical. Again, during the long century when apostolic Religious Life was highly institutionalized, contemplative prayer was seldom emphasized and often even discouraged as "singular," incompatible with the heavy monastic schedule of common vocal prayers and spiritual exercises, and a distraction from the time-consuming demands of maintaining institutional ministries.

Jesus' mystical life consisted in his intense unitive experience of God, but it came to expression in his prophetic mission in which he was engaged from the moment of his public emergence as an adult until his last breath on the cross. He carried out that mission in a multiform ministry of proclamation, teaching, healing, consoling, challenging, and confronting evil wherever it manifested itself, in or outside Judaism, in high places as well as among the ordinary people. This is precisely the ministerial ideal Jesus proposed to the itinerant band of disciples whom he apprenticed to himself during his public life and commissioned to carry on his own ministry after his departure (see Matt 10:8).

Personal mysticism and prophetic public ministry are two "faces" of a single lifeform. Mysticism has never been easy for institutional religion to handle precisely because it is the foundation of prophecy. This was true of Jesus and it has been true of the Church throughout the ages. The Church may canonize mystics after their deaths but it is far more likely to persecute and even execute them during their lives. One of the first things his contemporaries said of Jesus was that he taught and acted from a source of authority that the institution, its tradition and its laws and its officials, did not control (see Matt 7:29; 9:6, 8; 21:23–24, 27; and par. in Mark and Luke). In this he was following in the footsteps of the Old Testament prophets who were equally unsettling to kings and priests and for the same reason. The source of prophetic speaking and acting is the direct relation of the prophet to God, that is, the mystical or contemplative union that is not mediated by institutional personnel or processes and, finally, cannot be controlled by them. Joan of Arc is a singularly clear example of this tension between God's "voice" (in her case claimed literally) and the "voice" of ecclesiastical authority claiming to speak "for God."

This is the essence of the tension between the charismatic and the institutional. Both are necessary dimensions of religion as it functions in history. But they will never be comfortable companions. The prophet will always find the institutional constraining if not oppressive, overly self-seeking and too little concerned with the People of God, and the officials in charge will always find the charismatic uncontrollable and dangerous, "stirring up the people" who should be obeying official authority. In one sense, the Old Testament makes it clear that Jesus could hardly have ended up any differently than he did. And Religious Life, imitating and following Jesus precisely in his mystical-prophetic vocation within an institutional Church, can expect to share his fate in one way or another.

In the Old Testament, the opposite of the true prophet was the band or school of court prophets. These were groups of religious figures who, from the relative anonymity of the collective, were willing to tell the king what he wanted to hear and thus lend religious legitimacy to his projects, even when they were contrary to God's will, in exchange for their own safety and status in the religio-political system. They were religious functionaries who knew who was paying their salaries and convinced themselves that God's will must be reflected in the will of God's anointed representative, the king or priest. True prophets like Jeremiah and Amos would not play institutional ball and suffered the fate that Jesus would suffer.

The two features of the true prophets of Israel, reflected in Jesus, and which distinguished them from the bands of court prophets, were that they were individuals who had to stand up to power unbuffered by anonymity and unprotected by "group think," and when they challenged institutional authority they refused to succumb to official power. The measuring rod of their message was not what would keep them safe or in the good graces of those in power but what "God said." The prophets never claimed to speak in their own name. Their oracles began, literally or by implication, with "Thus says the Lord."

One of the most salient features of the renewal of Religious Life has been the reemergence, after a very long period of hyper-institutionalization and over-identification with the hierarchical-clerical element in the Church, of the charismatic, prophetic dimension of their vocation. To some extent this correlates with the individualization of ministries that has characterized the renewal and that has emphasized the corporate rather than collective nature of the mystical-prophetic lifeform, and it certainly owes much to the deepening of the contemplative spirituality of Religious and their much sounder theological formation. Conflicts between individual Religious and Church officials, often embroiling their Congregations in the struggle, have multiplied and intensified in recent years. This experience has been profoundly troubling, even traumatic, for Religious and the tragedies, personal and corporate, have been agonizing. But, in my opinion, the courage and perseverance of Religious in the face of ecclesiastical persecution and even violence is bearing fruit in a deepened sense of corporate solidarity, peace, steadfastness, willingness to lay down their lives in many ways for those to whom they are sent, and even to pay the price that Jesus paid for speaking truth to power.

Two other **important implications**, besides those implicit in what has been said above, can be mentioned. They have been discussed at some length in various places in this trilogy so I merely recall them here for the sake of completeness. The essentially charismatic rather than institutional source of Religious Life makes it fundamentally *egalitarian rather than hierarchical*. Religious are not part of the chain of command of the institution. They are neither superior to others in the Church nor subject, in their life and vocation, to Church officials. They are neither agents of the official Church nor a work force for ecclesiastical projects.

Furthermore, within their own Congregations there is a fundamental equality among the members in a completely voluntary community. All leadership, although important and respected, is provisional and exists for the sake of service. No one holds ontologically based power over the others and the only real "superiority" and "power" is service (see Matt 23:11). Religious have an important role in witnessing in the Church to the possibility of a truly egalitarian Church like that of Jesus' first disciples in which even Jesus, "teacher and lord" that he was (see John 13:13), washed his disciples' feet, not in a pantomime of ecclesiastical pomp but as a servant giving them an example of how friendship strips away even a "legitimate" claim to dominance.

One other implication that has emerged with clarity from the renewal and reappropriation of their mystical-prophetic vocation is that ministerial Religious are committed to a ministry that is *itinerant* and *free*. Distinguishing ministerial Religious Life from monastic life has allowed the former to replace the "total institution" model of community with the freedom to be among those they serve, as Jesus was. Without a "home of their own," special clothes or honorific titles, a uniform prayer life, institutional apostolates requiring all to do the same work in collective settings, or controllable forms of income, ministerial Religious can follow more closely the One who had nowhere to lay his head. They follow the One who allowed himself to be pursued even into his brief respites for rest and prayer; who sometimes had not even time to eat but went wherever God led him, even if that meant to the outlaws and the sinners and the foreigners and the reprobates whose uncleanness prohibited their presence in sacred space or participation in sacred ritual; who shared table fellowship with the poor and the outcasts and the rich and the powerful, and charged no one for the Word of God.

4. Religious Life is a gift of the Spirit to the Church for the sake of the world

This brings us to the other central affirmation in the description of Religious Life that I have proposed. We have had occasion to say a good deal throughout this work about the pneumatological origin of Religious life which was reemphasized by Vatican II. Religious Life is neither a human invention nor an office in the Church's structure but a charism given to the Church as the Body of Christ for the sake of the world.

As we saw at length in volume 1, chapters 9 and 10, charism characterizes Religious Life on various levels: in the individual, in the foundation and deep narrative of the particular Congregation, in various types of Religious Life that have arisen throughout history, and in the lifeform itself. At all levels the charisms pertaining to Religious Life are gifts of the Spirit to the Church, enriching its life and ministry, but the Council was referring particularly to the last when it spoke of Religious Life itself as a gift of the Holy Spirit to the Church.[6]

Individual Religious in a community will die. Congregations, for various reasons, can and do go out of existence. Even forms of the life diminish almost to the vanishing point. But Religious Life itself, which arose in the first decades of the Church's history, has never been totally absent from the Church's life.

This persistence of Religious Life in the Church, which I suggest is not simply an interesting historical phenomenon but an aspect of the Spirit's care for the People of God as the Body of

Transforming Renewal • 641

Christ, should be a source of strength and clarity of purpose for Religious and their communities in times of trial, persecution, scarcity of material resources, dearth of personnel, or decline of apostolic influence. The Church needs Religious Life, but not necessarily any particular Congregation. Therefore, the efforts of Religious to ensure the future of their Congregations should be vigorous and creative because we do not know what is or will be needed in the Church, but not frenzied or desperate. The first order of business for any Congregation is not self-perpetuation but fidelity of the Congregation to its charismatic vocation.

A charism is a grace that is bestowed by the Spirit not primarily for the sake of the individual or group receiving it but precisely for the building up of the Church in itself and in mission. Therefore, the charism of Religious Life does not exist primarily for its own sake nor is the life that embodies it an independent enterprise that can be situated anywhere. Religious Life exists for the sake of the Church in mission to the world.

Religious Life and its public witness may be more necessary in the Church today than it was in the new world in the 1800s when the Church's need to protect the faith of waves of immigrants occasioned the enormous increase in numbers of Congregations and candidates. Religious today are carrying a particular (though certainly not exclusive) responsibility for the preservation of the conciliar renewal that is being threatened by a backlash of restorationism, the lack of an adequately catechized and ecclesially inculturated younger generation of Catholics, massive moral scandal and loss of credibility of Church leadership from top to bottom, and a riptide of attrition in membership, all exacerbated by increasing financial strain and decrease in numbers of clergy relative to numbers of members.

The prophetic vocation, whether that of Moses in relation to Israel, Jesus in relation to Judaism, or Religious in relation to the Church, is a vocation within and in service to the community so that the community can fulfill its vocation to be "a light to the nations." This means that Religious Life is intrinsically an ecclesial vocation. I have insisted that it is not a particularly ecclesiastical, that is, hierarchical and institutional, vocation. It is not concerned especially with Church order, providing ecclesiastical services, running the institutions and operations of the corporation. But ecclesiality—to borrow an evocative term and concept from Orthodoxy—is not merely an accident of history (that Religious Life happened to arise in the Christian Church) nor is its ecclesial identity purely sociological or cultural (that it was "born Catholic" but has outgrown, or could depart from, its family of origin without substantial loss). Ecclesiality is a constitutive feature of Catholic Religious Life. This is a very challenging statement in the current historical context.

The paradigmatic temptation of the prophet is to abandon the chosen community that refuses to listen. As the story of the desert journey in Exodus makes abundantly clear, Moses was often driven to the point of wanting to give the "stiff-necked" Hebrew people back to the God who had brought them out of Egypt. Jeremiah wanted to flee into the desert and build himself a hermitage where he could weep for the people of Judah whom he could not convert (see Jer 9:1–2). Jesus wondered "why should I even speak to this adulterous generation" (see John 8:25) and wept over the city of Jerusalem that, even as Jesus' ministry moved to its close, still "did not know the time of its visitation" (see Luke 19:41–44 and elsewhere).

Anyone living Religious Life in the Church today has heard from companions or herself voiced this characteristic temptation of the prophet: "Why should we continue to relate to an institution which neither appreciates nor supports Religious Life? Why not sever the canonical bond—some have suggested, the way an abused spouse severs the marriage bond—which gives the hierarchy power to undermine our life and mission, and get on with the work of preaching the Gospel within and beyond the Church?"

This question expresses the agonizing paradox of the deeply ecclesial identity of Religious Life within the Church as People of God and the dilemma of its prophetic vocation to speak truth to power and minister to the victims of the abuse of that power within the often self-serving Church as institution. Dealing honestly with this conundrum is a real and urgent challenge for many Religious as well as for anyone thinking of entering Religious Life today. I would suggest that the answer to the "why" Religious should stay is clear enough: "for the sake of the world that God so loves." The answer to the question of "how" to stay without being personally crushed, spiritually compromised, or so ministerially undermined as to be useless is not at all clear and has to be rearticulated in every situation of tension, conflict, or abuse as it arises.

I want to offer several considerations which, while they neither prove the validity of the claim that Religious Life can only be authentic, faithful to its prophetic vocation and identity, as an ecclesial reality (which is a matter of faith, not logic), nor solve or resolve the ongoing tensions between Religious Life and ecclesiastical power structures, might supply some motivation for continuing in the struggle.

First, only in the Church can Religious Life witness to and participate in the paschal character of salvation, which cannot be reduced to any human enterprise no matter how highly motivated. Religious commit themselves, to the exclusion of any other primary life commitment, and for the whole of their one and only life, to the project Jesus committed to his Church, the transformation of this world into the Reign of God. In the nature of the case, this project is infinitely larger than any political, sociological, or humanitarian endeavor and exceeds the lifetime of any individual or any human efforts no matter how strenuous. The structure of this mission is "paschal," including suffering and death, which is the only path to the Resurrection life Jesus offers. By committing their whole lives to this humanly unachievable project, whose final success they will never see, Religious witness to the real nature and meaning of Jesus' saving work and the validity of complete and selfless faith commitment to it. This witness of Religious Life, in and through its members' personal perseverance, by its totality, its renunciation of personal success, its active faith in a victory unseen, helps sustain the efforts of others and of the Church as a whole. This witness can only be given in and as an ecclesial reality.

Second, because Religious Life is a visible and public lifeform within the Church, which is not, however, an office in the hierarchical Church, it can operate more easily at, and even across, ecclesiastical boundaries. Religious involved in ecumenical and especially in interreligious dialogue are not private, anonymous, or purely personal agents promoting tolerance, mutual understanding, and even a sharing of spiritual gifts. Religious operate specifically and publicly as the Body of Christ reaching out to the "others" whom God loves just as God loves us.

Once again, the example of Jesus—who was profoundly Jewish but not a member of the Jewish hierarchy and who held no office among his people—is instructive. Jesus originally so strongly appropriated his Jewish religious particularity that he understood himself as sent "only to the lost sheep of the house of Israel" (Matt 15:24) and he remained clear, even in dialogue with those estranged from Judaism, that "salvation is from the Jews" (John 4:22). But in his ministry he discovered that, while the prophet arises from the Chosen People, ministers to and among them, and witnesses to the Word of God entrusted to that community, his mission is not necessarily limited to that community. Jesus encountered faith outside the community of Israel that exceeded any he had encountered within it and he responded to that faith with the same offer of eternal life he had extended to his fellow Jews (see Matt 8:10; 15:28; Luke 7:9; John 4:53). The Gospel does not tell us how Jesus resolved this paradox theologically. Perhaps he never did. Each time it happened, he was "amazed." But he went where God led him, recognizing the truth even when and where it was not supposed to exist.

Religious, though called primarily in and for the Church, have increasingly discovered, as Jesus did, that they are often called to move beyond the ecclesiastical frontiers into dialogue with and service to people outside the official Church, even outside Christianity. Sometimes their welcome by and among "outsiders" is more sincere than their reception among their own. And ecclesiastical authority is not always approving of the extra-institutional and interreligious activities of Religious whom they often tend to regard as an in-house work force. This, also, was Jesus' experience: that the prophet is not without honor except among his own people (see John 4:44; Mark 6:4; Matt 13:57).

A third and extremely important reason why Religious Life, in my judgment, needs to remain an ecclesial reality, not only despite but especially because of the tension between Religious and the ecclesiastical institution, has become much clearer to me in the course of working on this study. Religious Life as a lifeform, especially as it is lived by nonclerical Religious, is a concrete, visible realization in the contemporary Church of a communitarian ecclesiology that is older and more biblically substantiated than the monarchical ecclesiology that has been characteristic of the Church since the Middle Ages and remains dominant in the Church as institution today. Unless this communitarian ecclesiology survives as a minority position and becomes the normative self-understanding of the Church, there may be no Church worth struggling over in the not too distant future. It may have become a ghetto of ideologues rather than an inclusive community of equal disciples, the people of God on its pilgrim way through time to which belong the Catholic faithful, "others who believe in Christ, and finally all mankind, called by God's grace to salvation" (*LG* II:13).

Vatican II, in chapter II of *Lumen Gentium*, the dogmatic constitution on the Church, entitled "The People of God," attempted to reemphasize this communitarian ecclesiology to which the New Testament clearly attests and which continued to function vigorously through the first millennium and right up until the medieval period in the West and to this day in the Eastern Church. In the struggle of the Great Schism (1378–1415), with its factions and anti-popes that raised sharply the question of the collegial and mutually authoritative relationship between Council and pope, this communitarian ecclesiology, later pejoratively labeled "conciliarism," was condemned and rejected in favor of a rigidly and exclusively monarchical ecclesiology. The pope claimed absolute and unilateral power in the hierarchy and direct personal jurisdiction over every individual member of the Church and rejected accountability to anyone on earth.

The epitome of this almost exclusively hierarchical understanding of the Church as institution, begun in the confusion of the fifteenth century and furthered at the Council of Trent in the sixteenth, was the crowning of absolute papal primacy by the definition of papal infallibility at Vatican I in the nineteenth century. Unfortunately, this ultramontane, exclusively hierarchical understanding of the Church was reaffirmed in chapter III of *Lumen Gentium* even though in its extreme form it is, at least in the mind of many well-balanced ecclesiologists, in serious tension with the collegial ecclesiology expressed in chapter II of the same document.[7] Although the official position of the Vatican and the last two popes has been that there is really no tension, much less contradiction, between the two ecclesiologies in *Lumen Gentium,* the experience "on the ground" is that, in fact, it is difficult to reconcile the two even rhetorically much less practically, and compromise is clumsy and inadequate at best and nonexistent at worst.

A striking postconciliar development, especially in the renewal of women's Religious Life, has been a reappropriation in their own Congregations of the communitarian ecclesiology that was characteristic of Religious Life from its earliest cenobitic realizations in the sixth century, which was muted but never fully suppressed among Religious.[8] The foundation of this essentially nonhierarchical ecclesiology is an understanding (discussed above in relation to the mystical character of the life) of the community as a voluntary society of intrinsically equal members. I explored this unique constitution of the nonclerical Religious community in chapter 7 where I argued that the monarchical model of authority and obedience was never really verified in principle in such Religious Congregations[9] despite the continuous efforts of ecclesiastical authority, down to our own day, to "monarchize" these communities in practice.

Intrinsic to this communitarian ecclesiology are the principles of collegiality, subsidiarity, and co-responsibility that Religious Congregations have written into their renewed Constitutions. Despite dire warnings from the Vatican that only chaos could result from such developments, most renewed Religious Congregations have successfully stabilized their community lives based on these principles. This development has been strengthened, as the renewal has progressed in nonclerical Congregations, by the realization that many founders, especially those who predated the total triumph of papal absolutism in the nineteenth century and were not members of clerical male Orders who stamped a hierarchical pattern on the women's communities they influenced, actually originally understood their communities in much more communitarian than monarchical terms.

In other words, deepened exposure of Religious to the vision of Church and community in Scripture and the documents of Vatican II supported the wide and deep experimentation with new forms of relationship and government within communities. This experimentation, never without its challenges from within and without, affirmed the intuitions of Religious that the model of Religious community life they were developing (or recovering) was faithful to the founding insights of their Congregations, more authentically rooted in the conciliar renewal, more faithful to the New Testament, more psychologically healthy, and more ministerially effective.

As I mentioned above and have developed at some length elsewhere,[10] the postconciliar virulence of hierarchical persecution of women's Congregations derives, at least in part, from the fact that women Religious have been the primary "carriers" of the vision and spirit of Vatican II, particularly its ecclesiology. Nonclerical Religious Congregations are an organized and thus visible embodiment in the very heart of the contemporary Church of the understanding of the Church as the People of God, a voluntary community of fundamentally equal disciples who are called to be the Body of Christ in this world and thus to announce the Good News of Jesus Christ to all nations. Religious Life is no longer, in its own self-understanding, a "state of perfection" deriving a claim to elite status in the Church from its mirror reflection of and unquestioning submission to the hierarchy. Rather, it is part of the Church as Pilgrim People making its way faithfully but fallibly toward the eschatological New Jerusalem which it neither claims to be, nor recognizes the Vatican to be.

In my view, this intra-ecclesial vocation of witness to an "alternate ecclesial world" is as important today as the extra-ecclesiastical witness of Religious Life as "alternate reality construction" of the Reign of God in the "field" of this world. For Religious to abandon their ecclesial location, identity, and vocation in the face of ecclesiastical misunderstanding and even persecution would be not only infidelity to a corporate mission but also a tragic loss for the Church. This realization and, I hope, the courage to face the opposition that fidelity to the Council's much expanded vision of Church requires do not obviate the suffering this entails for Religious. Publicly acknowledging that suffering can be a healthy refusal to be complicit in their own oppression or to see themselves as helpless victims. Actual participation in the suffering of Christ the prophet is at least as important to the life of the Church as ritual enactment of Christ's role as priest.

Practically speaking, it seems to me that Religious, for at least two reasons, are in a better position today to handle this suffering resolutely and creatively than they were in the first decades of the renewal, when some of the most egregious violations of Congregations and individual Religious occurred.[11] Religious no longer need to see themselves caught in no-win dilemmas between integrity and abusive power. New insights can give them a "place to stand" when submission to the demands of authority unjustly or dysfunctionally exercised as coercive power is presented as the only option.

The first insight is the increasing realization, just discussed, that the communitarian ecclesiology that is predominant in Religious Congregations today is biblically based and theologically legitimate. Even when power is invoked and exercised in unjust and violent ways by ecclesiastical officials, Religious know that they have a right, based in Scripture and the teaching of the Council, to live out of that communitarian ecclesiology within their own Congregations and in relation to other elements in the Church. That conviction can ground a confident adherence to principle and even appropriate resistance in the face of abuse when that is necessary. Like Jesus before the Sanhedrin and before Pilate, being unjustly treated need not lead to the acceptance of guilt or internal submission.

The second insight is that this communitarian ecclesiology is the theoretical and practical framework for an alternate understanding of obedience, discussed at considerable length in chapters 8 to 10 of this volume. The fundamental principles of this theology of obedience are the basic equality of all the baptized and the absolute primacy of conscience. These principles ground a much wider and more nuanced range of options than the "*either* (do/believe as you are commanded) *or* (leave or be dismissed)" theology of obedience that is still functional in the monarchical system. Religious, both individually and as Congregations, have gradually built up a reservoir of options in the face of illegitimate, coercive, or abusive exercises of ecclesiastical power whether based on ignorance or on more morally suspect motives.

Important implications flow from this reflection on Religious Life as charismatic gift of the Spirit to the Church for the sake of the world. First, its *ecclesial identity* and location flow from its prophetic character, which Religious live in imitation of Jesus, prophet among his own people, who paid the ultimate price for calling Israel to its vocation as "light to the nations." The ministry of Religious through the Church to the world God so loved is grounded in their identity as *members of his Body* and it is this identity which gives meaning and efficacy to all they do to mediate eternal life in all its fullness to those to whom they are sent.

Second, the institutional Church itself needs—even when its officials reject it—the prophetic presence and witness of Religious to the *nature of the Church's divine mission and to an alternate communitarian ecclesiology*. It also needs the *ministry on the margins* that Religious as public persons who are not institutional agents can exercise.

Third, the most glorious periods in the history of Religious Life have not been those in which Religious have been the darlings of the hierarchy. Unqualified approval by those who wield power too often comes at the price of a conspiracy of silence or cowardly complicity in institutional corruption. Such complicity leads to domestication and cooptation, to the transformation of God's messengers into "court prophets." One of the things that may have changed permanently, and for the better, among Religious in the past fifty years is that, as a lifeform, they *no longer suffer from a paralyzing need for ecclesiastical approval.*

Fourth, the same conviction that enabled Jesus to remain faithful to his prophetic vocation unto death is basic to the *ecclesial fidelity* of Religious who have chosen to stay. They believe that the Church, like themselves imperfect in so many ways, is called to be a "light to the nations." Living that conviction will lead to their participation, in large ways or small, in Jesus' destiny, which included not only his execution but also his ultimate vindication by the God to whom he was faithful.

Fifth, in situations of conflict and struggle, it is well to remember that Religious do not believe in the *Church*; they believe *in* the Church. The Church as People of God and Body of Christ is the context of their faith and their fidelity in ministry, but Jesus, not the Church as institution, is the object of their faith.

5. *Religious Life is* constituted by perpetual Profession of the vows

The Catholic Christian, ecclesial, mystical and prophetic properties of Religious Life as a lifeform are global characteristics that have been discussed from numerous points of view and in relation to various topics throughout these three volumes. They therefore needed to be identified for themselves and discussed at some length in this conclusion. The following features—perpetuity, Profession, the vows, community, and ministry—have been considered separately and at some length in different parts of the work. Consequently, the conclusions already articulated on these subjects need only to be referred to or presumed here rather than repeated or discussed in detail. I am picking up these features here for the sake of completeness and to keep them in the forefront as readers bring their reflections to a close.

Perpetual Profession was discussed in detail in volume 2, part 1, especially chapter 3. Perpetuity is characteristic of the two forms of consecrated life in the Church, matrimony and Religious Life, precisely because these life choices are the undertaking of a lifeform, not the entrance into an organization or the taking on of a project. The "project" undertaken by matrimonial or Religious vows is one's whole life, which now will be lived entirely in function of the great love at its center. The Religious, by perpetual Profession, is declaring that the whole of her or his life will be devoted to the quest for God to the exclusion of all other primary life commitments, including marriage and family, career or profession, or projects of any kind.

This commitment is neither a function of some kind of fore-knowledge of the challenges one could or will face nor a hubristic conviction that one will be able, by dint of determina-tion and personal courage, to meet all challenges, come what may. It is really not about the content of the future at all. What will eventuate in one's Religious life is unknowable when one makes Profession, as is the content of the life initiated by mar-riage vows. Profession is about the present. Perpetual commit-ment is a total self-gift in love, here and now. The totality of the gift, whether life lasts an hour or a century beyond the cere-mony, is expressed in terms of all the dimensions of one's life: time, gifts and talents, possessions, self-determination, health and longevity or lack thereof, success and failure, and whatever else will characterize that life.

Two things should be recalled about the three vows that make perpetual Profession concrete even as they embrace the vast "unsaid" of the life. These three vows—consecrated celibacy, which was treated in detail in volume 2, part 2; and evangelical poverty and prophetic obedience, which were dis-cussed in this volume, parts 2 and 3 respectively—are not a list of particular, limited and specified "supererogatory obliga-tions" which the Religious assumes. They are, as has been said, global metaphors referring to the three major dimensions of human life: relationships, possessions, and freedom and power. By one's self-disposition concerning these basic coordi-nates of life one enters into the "alternate world" that realizes the Reign of God in the midst of historical reality. By Profes-sion, Religious determine how they intend to live in commu-nity, in society, in the Church, in the world for the rest of their lives.

The way these basic dimensions of human life are understood differs from culture to culture. How institutionalized Religious Life handles them changes as a function of changes in society and Church. But humans will always construct their lives in terms of persons, possessions, and power. And I have suggested in my treatment of the three vows that there is a characteristic way that Religious relate to these fundamental spheres of human experience which may call for very different concrete behaviors in different places and at different times. I have tried to capture, by use of the traditional names for the vows combined with a descriptive adjective for each, both the characteristic way the vows have been understood over time and the flexibility of the modes and behaviors in which that characteristic approach is embodied.

The specification of the traditional vows by descriptive adjectives was also necessary because of the intrinsic ambiguity of each of the vows if its name was left unspecified. Celibacy, the condition of being unmarried, says nothing by itself about motive, perpetuity, or the sexual behavior of the celibate. Poverty, the lack of possessions, can be voluntary or imposed against one's will, range from simplicity to destitution, be the result of one's own or someone else's sinfulness, have good or bad consequences for oneself and others. Obedience, the taking into account of the will of another in one's own life, choices, and behavior, can be free or imposed, collaborative cooperation or cowardly alienation of responsibility, a help in discernment or violent coercion, growth-producing or infantilizing, a help to development in attentiveness to the will of God or depersonalizing oppression.

By referring to celibacy as "consecrated" I tried to emphasize freedom of choice, motivation by the love of God, totality and exclusivity of the self-donation and therefore its intrinsic perpetuity as constituting a state of life, the relationship of that state of life to the quest for God, and the global moral obligations of chastity that express the commitment. I also looked at the ramifications of this free commitment in the relationships of the celibate within and outside the community. In effect, consecrated celibacy is not simply a choice regarding sexuality. It is the total self-donation in love, to the exclusion of any other primary life commitment, to the quest for God. This is why I present it, as some others discussing Religious Life do not, as not only intrinsically perpetual but as the defining feature of Religious Life.

By referring to poverty as "evangelical," that is, Gospel poverty, I intended to emphasize that the poverty undertaken by Religious and which consists in a choice of complete self-dispossession of material goods, is not primarily a socioeconomic condition, whether simplicity or communal sharing or deprivation or destitution or anything else on the scale of material well-being. It is an imitation and following of Jesus as he appears in the Gospel and according to his own teaching on this subject. This teaching, which is a major theme of the Gospel, is concerned not with how much money or other goods one has but with the complete detachment of the heart from material goods and their possession. Such Gospel poverty is manifested in the absence of anxiety that is rooted in total trust in God. Nothing, large or small, present or absent, can be allowed to become "Mammon" in one's life, an idol that takes God's place in the heart, because what one's heart seeks betrays the true "treasure" of one's life. The state of total nonpossession is a condition of freedom that allows the person to live, act, go, be, according to God's desires. Thus, the ongoing education of desire is central to the spirituality of the Religious and involves a lifelong engagement with the dynamics of creaturehood in its gradual acceptance of divinizing dependence on a loving Creator.

"Prophetic" obedience, perhaps the most misunderstood of the vows and a source, for centuries, of serious deformation of consciences and infantilization in ministry and community, required major rethinking to remove it from the framework of blind submission to human power claiming to hold God's place in the life of Religious and place it in the framework of enlightened discernment.

A renewed theology and spirituality of obedience requires Religious to return to Jesus the prophet, in his obedience to God, as their authentic model. Obedience, then, has to be re-imagined as the commitment to hear and heed all indications and intimations of the will of God, both within and outside the community, as Jesus attended to the One who sent him. This careful listening and commitment to heeding what one hears calls for discernment which, while inclined preferentially toward legitimate authority and other privileged mediations of God's will, never becomes mindless surrender, through laziness or cowardice or ulterior motives, to anything masquerading as God's will. We thus come to understand that authority is not a sacralization of oppressive power, and obedience is not perpetual irresponsible immaturity and subjection. Rather, discernment takes place in the dialogue of authority and obedience as a shared search for the will of God. Furthermore, the will of God ceases to mean the imposition of irresistible divine power on powerless pawns, being rather God's ongoing involvement, through cooperating human subjects, in the unfolding of God's plan of salvation.

We also took time to examine the formative process by which obedience, in practice, changes and develops as the Religious progresses from initial formation through active ministerial involvement into the gradual self-abandonment to God in sickness, old age, and death. The spirituality of the Religious is thus shaped, over a lifetime, by the single-minded self-gift to God in consecrated celibacy, the education of desire for the one thing necessary by evangelical poverty, and the gradual attunement of the will to God's loving guidance in prophetic obedience.

6. Religious Life is lived in transcendent community and ministry

It may be that nothing in Religious Life has changed as noticeably and as profoundly in the process of renewal as the understanding of community and ministry. The changes in these two dimensions were intimately interrelated and, in hindsight, the reasons for this are not hard to discern. Both community understood as traditional common life, and ministry understood as highly institutionalized common and even identical apostolates, were monastic in origin and form and collectivist in realization. They required and worked well in the "total institution" but could not continue as that sociological model of the life came to an end.

The deconstruction of Religious Life as a total institution in the wake of the increasingly clear distinction of the ministerial form of Religious Life from the enclosed monastic form brought an end, in the former, to cloister and its requirements and practices, and it integrated ministerial involvement in the world into the fundamental self-understanding of Religious Congregations and their members. Postconciliar ministerial Religious Life was individualized, both in terms of community and of ministry.

For a few decades this transformation was extremely destabilizing, because Religious had no experience of anything other than common life and institutionalized apostolates and there was no articulated theological frame of reference within which to understand the new developments. It looked to many, including those involved, like the dissolution of the life itself into a terminal individualism when, in fact, it was the deconstruction of a sociological and theological frame of reference that was *de facto*, but not *de jure*, coterminous with the life prior to the renewal. So entrenched was that model that most people took the model for the substance and could not, for some time, imagine a new way of conceptualizing the situation.

Volume 2, part 3, was a detailed examination of the meaning of community in ministerial Religious Life. We began by affirming essential continuity with the traditional understanding of Christian and, therefore, Religious community as based in the theology of the Trinity. But, by calling it "transcendent" community I also intended to distinguish it from other realizations of Christian community. While this term can present problems if it implies or connotes otherworldliness, dualism, or superiority, I have not been able to find another single term better able to capture the distinctiveness of Religious community.

Unlike other types of Christian community which are rooted not only in the sharing in divine life initiated in baptism but also in natural conditions, Religious community has no "natural" or "necessary" basis. It is neither rooted in nor productive of blood relationships and it is not required either for survival in this world or for salvation. Nor is it "intentional" community in the sense of being a mutual selection of members by one another. The fact that Religious communities are, by and large, monosexual, celibate, affectively inclusive, permanently intergenerational, totally economically interdependent on the basis of shared total dispossession of the members, and that the deepest bond that unites the members is not natural affinity but solely the love of Christ to the exclusion of any other primary life commitment, makes the Religious community unique. I have suggested that the unique bond is a particular kind of Gospel friendship that transcends any of the natural foundations for human community.

Once the basic coordinates of Religious community are established, both in terms of what it has in common with other forms of Christian community and what is distinctive about it, the question that arises immediately concerns how that unique or transcendent community is, can, or must be sociologically embodied. Prior to the renewal it seemed self-evident that Religious community was synonymous with "common life," that is, group/collective living under the same roof and to the exclusion of nonmembers. The diversification and individualization of ministries in the years immediately following the Council led to a parallel change in living situations. But even those involved in such new living situations, to say nothing of those who objected to them, considered anything other than traditional collective common life as, at best, an "exception" which might be necessary for particular reasons but should be rectified as soon as possible.

No such "rectification" has occurred and it is probably accurate to say that most ministerial Religious no longer think that such is necessary or desirable. While terminology is slow to change, the emotional freight of the language might change before it is linguistically modified. The term "living alone," once loaded with negative connotations, and which I tried to rename as "living singly" or "living individually," has not disappeared, but it no longer automatically carries the implication of isolation, alienation from the community, self-marginalization, resistance to Congregational responsibility and accountability, and so on. It has become, for most people, simply a description of a *de facto* living situation, which can be as life giving or problematic as any other type, including group living. Many Religious live individually because it is most conducive to handling their ministerial or educational responsibilities. They do not feel obliged to pretend that this is a temporary or abnormal arrangement that they long to "correct"; nor do they feel that they need to defend it against implied accusations. It is one lifestyle among others for ministerial Religious. And those living this lifestyle are just as likely (or unlikely) as those living in Congregational groups to be fully participative members of the community, economically responsible and accountable, celibate in practice, and prayerful.

One linguistic modification that has been slowly creeping into the usage of Religious, and that I consider quite significant, is the tendency to speak not so much of living "*in* community" as of "*living* community." It reflects, I would suggest, that we are becoming less inclined to define community by *where* a Religious lives (under the same roof with other members of the Congregation) and more by *attitudes and behaviors* in relation to the community. One can live community intensely and faithfully no matter where one dwells. And one can dwell in the same house with five or fifty other members of the Congregation and be isolated, marginal, negative, or subversive.

The same thing seems to be happening in regard to mission and its embodiment in ministry. The term "mission" seems less and less to mean where one is "stationed" or the fact of being "assigned" to that location, and more the corporate calling, identity, and commitment of the Congregation as a whole. As Anthony Gittins has expressed it in numerous places, "Mission is not something we have, but something that has us."

"Ministry" has largely replaced "apostolate" as a designation of one's personal involvement in that corporate mission. It matters much less today whether one's ministry is within an institution of one's own Congregation, or shared with other Religious across Congregational lines, whether it is an individual or group ministry, in an officially Catholic or even religious setting or not. It matters much more whether one's ministry is integral to the mission of the Congregation, which is defined in terms of its charism, traditions, and current priorities. It seems to me that these changes in language reflect some deep changes in theological understanding of what it means to live Religious Life in community and ministry.

The current volume has been concerned especially with this final aspect of the description of Religious Life: that it is a life "lived in community and ministry." We began this volume by reexamining the meaning of "world" and the conciliar re-orientation of the Church and therefore of Religious from a stance of world-rejection to one of world-involvement. In light of that renewed, and in some ways genuinely new, understanding of what the mission of Religious means today I have tried to reconceptualize and rearticulate the meaning of what I have called the "vows of community life and mission," that is, evangelical poverty and prophetic obedience.

If consecrated celibacy is the mystical heart of Religious Life as total self-gift to God to the exclusion of any other primary life commitment, then evangelical poverty and prophetic obedience are the community-structuring dynamics that equip Religious Life for the prophetic ministry that carries Jesus' mission into the world that God so loved as to give the only Son that all who believe in him may not perish but may have eternal life.

Notes

Preface

1. Sandra M. Schneiders, *New Wineskins: Re-Imagining Religious Life Today* (New York/Mahwah, NJ: Paulist, 1986).

2. Throughout the work, unless the context clearly stipulates otherwise, I will use "lay" to refer to baptized Catholics who are not ordained or vowed members of Religious Institutes. This is not a pejorative designation, as I explained at length in volume 1, chapter 7, but recognition of the fact that Religious have rights and obligations under Canon Law that other members of the laity (in the sense of "nonordained") do not. That means that Religious constitute a canonical category distinct in some ways from other nonclerics. Laity is, at least potentially, a positive term whereas non-Religious is a privative term and open to more negative connotations than laity.

Introduction

1. When I speak of world-engagement in what follows, I am assuming that the engagement of Religious with the world is always from within the Church. At times Religious engage the Church directly and often prophetically, but even when their primary concern is engagement with the world itself, they do so as Christians and specifically as Catholic Religious.

2. To distinguish the Resurrection of Jesus from that of his followers, that is, the originating event from subsequent participation in that event, I will uppercase the term for the former.

Chapter 1

1. There is increasing debate among New Testament scholars over when the break between Christians and Jews became definitive and whether it was a "one way" excommunication on the part of the Jews or a reciprocal process of mutual alienation and estrangement,

or even a self-marginalization by Christians. In particular, the theory of J. Louis Martyn, in *History and Theology in the Fourth Gospel*, 2nd ed. (Nashville: Abingdon, 1979) and Raymond E. Brown in *The Community of the Beloved Disciple* (New York: Paulist, 1979) that there is evidence in the Gospel of John of a definitive rejection of Christians by Jews is being contested. See a brief, cogent presentation of the theory and arguments for and against it in Adele Reinhartz, *Befriending the Beloved Disciple: A Jewish Reading of the Gospel of John* (New York/ London: Continuum, 2001), 37–53.

2. The exact reason for the definitive break between first-century Judaism and fledgling Christianity (if indeed there was such a break) has never been determined to the satisfaction of Jews or Christians. Increasingly, scholars doubt that the Christian identification of Jesus as Messiah, even in a post–Second Temple Judaism that was less tolerant of diversity than it had been in Jesus' day, is at most part of the explanation. I find very convincing the argument of Carey C. Newman, "Resurrection and Glory: Divine Presence and Christian Origins," in *The Resurrection: An Interdisciplinary Symposium on the Resurrection of Jesus*, ed. Stephen T. Davis, Daniel Kendall, and Gerald O'Collins (Oxford: Oxford University Press, 1997), 59–89, that it was the Christian attribution to the Risen Jesus of the glory which was a unique divine attribute, in other words, the attribution of divinity to Jesus, that established a nonnegotiable threshold between the two religious groups. However, in a brilliant article on Jewish "binitarianism" Daniel Boyarin, "The Gospel of the Memra: Jewish Binitarianism and the Prologue to John," *Harvard Theological Review* 94/3 (July 2001): 2243–84, demonstrates that belief in a Word of God who was divine is not as much of a Christian *novum* as has been suggested. The problem is less trinitarian than incarnational.

It should be mentioned that there are some students of this period who question whether there actually was a "break" between the two communities. See Adam H. Becker and Annette Yoshiko Reed, eds., *The Ways That Never Parted: Jews and Christians in Late Antiquity and the Early Middle Ages* (Tübingen: Mohr Siebeck, 2003), 1–24.

3. Acts 6–7 recounts the eloquent defense of Christian faith and resultant violent death of Stephen, the proto-martyr, who died for the faith within a decade of the Resurrection. His martyrdom was followed shortly by that of James (see Acts 12:2), and somewhat later that of Paul and Peter.

4. Paul's exhortation to submission to civil authority in Romans

13:1–7 functioned as a primary biblical justification for racial apartheid in South Africa in the twentieth century.

5. See Elisabeth Schüssler Fiorenza, *In Memory of Her: A Feminist Theological Reconstruction of Christian Origins* (New York: Crossroad, 1983), especially chapters 7 and 8 on the household codes and the effects on the Church of early Christian acceptance of the codes.

6. See the discussion of this point in chapter 1 of Sandra M. Schneiders, *Finding the Treasure: Locating Catholic Religious Life in a New Ecclesial and Cultural Context*, vol. 1 of Religious Life in a New Millennium (Mahwah, NJ: Paulist, 2000), 19 including n. 27.

7. In February 380 they jointly published the edict that all their subjects should profess the faith of the bishops of Rome and Alexandria (*Codex Theodosius* XVI, I, 2).

8. For a loyal and compassionate but very incisive analysis of the inherent weaknesses of the imperial ecclesiastical system, see Donald Cozzens, *Sacred Silence: Denial and the Crisis in the Church* (Collegeville, MN: Liturgical Press, 2002, esp. chs 3, 7, 9.

9. A fine study of the spirituality of the early desert monastics, including its asceticism, can be found in Douglas Burton-Christie, *The Word in the Desert: Scripture and the Quest for Holiness in Early Christian Monasticism* (New York: Oxford, 1993).

10. See the new study by Fergus Millar, *A Greek Roman Empire: Power and Belief under Theodosius II, 408–450*, Sather Classical Lectures 64 (Berkeley and Los Angeles: University of California, 2006).

11. Although there are still desert hermits, mostly Orthodox and living in Egypt, today this form of Religious life is relatively rare. Vatican II restored the hermit life (see Canon 603 of the 1983 *CCL*) but contemporary Catholics espousing this ideal tend to live in cities, not deserts, and to live lives only remotely reflective of that of the early desert dwellers. The eremitical ideal of solitude, prayer, and penance was carried forward in cenobitic Orders such as the Carmelites, Carthusians, and Camaldolese, but none of these actually espouses the kind of lifestyle developed in the desert.

12. In 1870 when the Papal States were taken over by Italy and the pope, just declared infallible, lost the geographical basis of his political power in Italy and therefore in the world at large, Pope Pius IX declared himself "the prisoner of the Vatican" and, until Pope John Paul II began the worldwide travels of his lengthy pontificate the popes exercised their personal influence only by the written and spoken word, never venturing out of the tiny Vatican city-state.

13. Boniface VIII in 1298 issued the papal bull *Periculoso*, which

imposed papal enclosure in perpetuity on all women Religious. However, the struggle of women to develop a noncloistered form of apostolic Religious Life began shortly after this time. *See Finding the Treasure*, 290–97, for a brief sketch of the emergence of this form of life.

14. For a fuller treatment of the complex history of the development of apostolic Religious Life for women, see *Finding the Treasure*, chapter 9.

15. Leo Cardinal Suenens (1904–96) was, at his death, the retired Cardinal Archbishop of Mechelen-Brussels and former primate of Belgium. He was the major influence in changing the direction and the agenda of Vatican II from the narrow-mindedness of the original working documents to the open-mindedness of the agenda that replaced them in the first session of the Council. He served as one of the four moderators who presided over the Council. Among the causes he supported were the renovation of women's Religious Life, the expanded role of the laity in the Church, open discussion of married priests and contraception, the reform and decentralization of the Curia.

16. Joseph Cardijn (1882–1967) was a Belgian priest who, from his youth, was deeply concerned about the de-christianization of young workers. He founded the Jeunesse Ouvrière Chrétienne (Jocists), which eventually enlisted over a million Young Christian Workers all over the world. The strategy he developed of organizing youth in "cells" which worked through his "see, judge, act" model for social change was one of the most powerful developments among lay Catholics in the period leading up to Vatican II.

17. Yves Congar, OP (1904–95), was one of the most important of the European theologians who, for thirty years or more, prepared the Church for Vatican II. His avant-garde theological writings cost him years under suspicion before he emerged as a major architect of a number of the Council's documents. His *Divided Christendom: A Catholic Study of the Problem of Reunion*, trans. M. A. Bousfield (London: G. Bles, 1939) on ecumenism; *True and False Reform in the Church*, rev. ed., trans. Paul Philibert (Collegeville, MN: Liturgical, 2011), on Church reform; and *Lay People in the Church: A Study for a Theology of the Laity*, 2nd ed., trans. Donald Atwater (Westminster, MD: Newman, 1965), were groundbreaking contributions.

18. For a detailed discussion of the meaning of the terms *lay* and *secular* and how they are related to each other and to *clerical* and *Religious*, see *Finding the Treasure*, chapter 7.

19. Pope Pius XI gave Catholic Action its classic definition in his

"Discourse to Italian Catholic Young Women," *L'Osservatore Romano*, March 21–22, 1927. For a concise summary of how he developed and used the term throughout his pontificate, see the article on "Catholic Action" by D. J. Geaney in *New Catholic Encyclopedia*, 2nd ed., vol. 3 (Detroit: Gale, 2002), 275–78.

20. The development of understanding of the lay apostolate from its narrowly "Catholic Action" incarnation to the theology of Vatican II's "Decree on the Apostolate of Lay People" was facilitated by the important address of Pope Pius XII to the Second World Congress of the Lay Apostolate, "Guiding Principles of the Lay Apostolate," Oct. 5, 1957, in which he clearly stated that Catholic Action was a subset of the lay apostolate that belonged to all the baptized in virtue of their baptism and confirmation. Lay persons could appropriately take initiative in the apostolate as partners with the ordained and they were urged to do so especially in the secular sphere. He thus sanctioned the type of theology of the laity that developed in the decades prior to the Council and came to strong expression in *Apostolicam Actuositatem (A.A.)*, "Decree on the Apostolate of Lay People" (Flannery, vol. 1). Henceforth, all conciliar documents will be cited from Austin P. Flannery, editor, *Vatican Council II: The Conciliar and Postconciliar Documents*, 2 vols. (Grand Rapids: Eerdmans, 1975/1984) by the initials of the Latin title followed, where appropriate, by chapter and paragraph numbers and the indication of the Flannery volume in parentheses.

21. The Bill of Rights was ratified on Dec. 15, 1791.

22. A sobering exhibit on Ellis Island documents, through placards, handbills, newspaper articles, and other materials from the period, the virulent anti-Catholicism of the nineteenth century as Catholics from Ireland, Italy, and Poland came into the country. For many Americans, from the foundation of the country until the mid-twentieth century, "American" meant "Christian" and "Christian" meant Protestant, white, and Anglo-Saxon or at least northern European in background. It was not until the election to the presidency of John F. Kennedy in 1960 that Catholics achieved, symbolically, full recognition as Americans. See Mark Massa, "Anti-Catholicism: The Last Acceptable Prejudice?" in *American Catholics, American Culture*, ed. Margaret O'Brien Steinfels, 149–54 (Lanham, MD: Rowman & Littlefield, 2004).

23. See *Dignitatis Humanae (D.H.)*, the conciliar "Declaration on Religious Liberty" (Flannery, vol. 1). An excellent analysis of the conciliar process leading to *D.H.* and the fallout from the declaration in the developing "culture wars" in the Church of the late sixties and beyond was presented by American Church historian Joseph Chinnici,

OFM, as part of the celebration of the hundredth anniversary of the births of Karl Rahner, SJ, Bernard Lonergan, SJ, and John Courtney Murray, SJ, the latter a major contributor to the conception and production of *D.H.* The paper, "The Problem of John Courtney Murray," received by me from author, has not been published.

24. The classic New Testament text on this subject is Romans 2:15–16.

25. Since the Council, with the increasing militancy of Islam in some places, the appeal of the Church to "freedom of religion" and therefore, effectively, to separation of Church and State, has become more and more frequent.

26. Both documents are available in Flannery, vol. 1.

27. See *Nostra Aetate* (*N.A.*), Vatican II's "Declaration on the Relation of the Church to Non-Christian Religions" (Flannery, vol. 1).

28. The negativity of the Church toward the modern world which had been building since the Protestant Reformation in the early sixteenth century achieved explicit formulation in the "Syllabus of Errors" of Pius IX issued on Dec. 8, 1864, which was followed by the syllabus of errors of Pius X, *Lamentabili Sane*, of July 3, 1907, and supplemented by the encyclical *Pascendi Dominici Gregis* against Modernism of Sept. 8, 1907, and the "Oath Against Modernism" of Sept. 1, 1910.

29. See *D.V.* 6:24 (Flannery, vol. 1).

30. The exact figures are as follows: Fourth Gospel = 78; Johannine Epistles = 24; Revelation = 3; Synoptic Gospels = 14; Pauline Epistles = 48; Catholic Epistles = 13. In Paul the term is concentrated in 1 Corinthians (21 times) and Romans (9 times) and appears seldom elsewhere, whereas in John the usage is pervasive.

31. Two recent studies of the term κόσμος in John make distinctions that are slightly different in nuance from mine because they are concerned with other contexts (translation and theology) in which the word is used. However, they are complementary rather than contradictory to my distinctions. See D. J. Clark, "The Word *Kosmos* 'World' in John 17," *Practical Papers for the Bible Translator* 50 (October 1999): 401–6, and Stanley B. Marrow, "Κόσμος in John," *CBQ* 64 (2002): 90–102. See also the study by John Painter, "Earth Made Whole: John's Rereading of Genesis," *Word, Theology, and Community in John*, ed. John Painter, R. Alan Culpepper, and Fernando F. Segovia (St. Louis: Chalice, 2002), 65–84, in which the primary focus is contemporary ecological concern.

32. The genitive of the masculine and neuter third person pronoun are the same (αὐτοῦ) and the antecedent "light" (φῶς) is

neuter. However, the use of the masculine accusative (αὐτοῦ) in verse
10 makes it clear that although "the true light" is grammatically
neuter in verse 9 the intended referent is either the word (λόγος
which is grammatically masculine) or the Word Incarnate, Jesus (who
is biologically masculine).

33. Because "incarnate" and "incarnation" have numerous meanings in contemporary English I will uppercase the word when it refers
to the mystery of God becoming human in Jesus.

34. Although first-century Christians did not have our twenty-first-
century sense of the universe they did think of the world as one
"story" of a three-story creation that included "heaven" or the realm
of the divine and "Hades" as the realm of the dead or even the
demonic. Consequently, "world" is a metonym for the whole of Creation and not a designation of planet Earth in isolation.

35. For a fuller exploration of how the "doctrine of Creation" as
such is an expression of the conviction that the universe is a form of
divine revelation see Sandra M. Schneiders, *The Revelatory Text: Interpreting the New Testament as Sacred Scripture*, 2nd ed. (Collegeville, MN:
Liturgical Press, 1999), 36–40.

36. For a fuller treatment of the Nicodemus story see Sandra M.
Schneiders, *Written That You May Believe: Encountering Jesus in the
Fourth Gospel*, 2nd rev. ed. (New York: Crossroad, 2003), 117–25.

37. This is the only passage in which the expression "Reign of
God" (βασιλεία τοῦ Θεοῦ) is used in John. It is used as the object of
"see" (3:3) and "enter (3:5) and both times it is qualified by the stipulation "unless one is born anew" and "unless one is born of water and
the Spirit."

38. It is also important to note that John's Gospel is talking about
Jews (and a Samaritan and a Gentile in chapter 4) who are in interaction with the pre-Easter Jesus. The evangelist is probably ignorant of
the existence of people outside the Mediterranean world and is not
concerned with people who have never met nor heard of Jesus. God
doubtless has ways of leading to salvation people of other traditions.
To address to the gospel questions about which it could not possibly
have been aware raises issues that the text, by definition, cannot solve.

39. For a fuller treatment of this pericope, see Schneiders, *Written
That You May Believe*, 149–70.

40. The theology of "original sin" as the explanation for the human
tendency to actual sin is rooted in the Pauline teaching that the universal need of salvation is due to the universal inclusion in the sin of our
first parents. As in other areas such as Christology and ecclesiology, the

early Church and the New Testament, which arose from the experience of the earliest communities, developed a variety of soteriologies, or theologies of salvation. The notion of original sin, which, especially under the influence of Augustine's theology, eventually prevailed as the primary understanding of the human proclivity to evil and need for salvation, is not the only theological position in the New Testament. John's theology is an important complement to the Pauline theology because it focuses attention on other aspects of theological anthropology and soteriology. For an excellent contemporary study of the history and theology of original sin, see Tatha Wiley, *Original Sin: Origins, Developments, Contemporary Meanings* (New York/Mahwah, NJ: Paulist, 2002).

41. Obviously, this clarity about the meaning of the world is important for all Christians called by the Gospel and by the Council to affirm and promote the world, but our concern in this volume is with the particular problems the notion of "world" has raised for Religious.

42. See 12:31; 14:30; 16:11.

43. Cf. 8:44.

44. Cf. 13:27.

45. This principle of evil is presented in John as masculine (cf. texts cited in previous note), thus emphasizing the personal character of Jesus' opponent. But this agent is not biologically gendered any more than the Word or the Spirit or God is. The use of gendered pronouns in English is virtually necessary to underscore a personal rather than purely material character or impersonal cosmic agency.

46. The effect of the Prince of this World is not personal sin but "darkness," which is a condition in which people can choose to dwell. Thus, Satan's control is not a given. It is something one submits to, chooses. It is obviously closer to humans' connatural situation than the more strenuous choice of doing the truth and coming to the light. However, it does not seem to be a condition into which one is simply born.

47. See e.g., Ray L. Hart, *Unfinished Man and the Imagination: Toward an Ontology and a Rhetoric of Revelation* (New York: Seabury, 1979); Gordon Kaufman, *An Essay in Theological Method* (Missoula, MT: Scholars, 1975) and *The Theological Imagination: Constructing the Concept of God* (Philadelphia: Westminster, 1981); David Tracy, *The Analogical Imagination: Christian Theology and the Culture of Pluralism* (New York: Crossroad, 1981); Walter Brueggemann, *The Prophetic Imagination* (Philadelphia: Fortress, 1978).

48. In the Gospel, of course, the "truth" is the Truth, Jesus. People who had no experience of Jesus or of the Covenant of Israel were not within the purview of the evangelist. The Gospel should not be read

as a narrow exclusion from salvation of contemporary people who have never heard of Jesus or who are members of other religious traditions. John's theology of salvation by coming to the truth through the doing of the truth (see John 3:20–21) offers valuable resources for imagining the path to salvation of those outside Christianity.

49. The most comprehensive treatment of this world of evil in the New Testament is Walter Wink's three-volume work, *The Powers* (Philadelphia: Fortress, 1984–92). It includes *Naming the Powers* (1984); *Unmasking the Powers* (1986); and *Engaging the Powers* (1992).

50. A powerful and illuminating description of the "world" as it operates in the globalized economy in contrast to the Reign of God is Aloysius Pieris, "Ecumenism in the Churches and Unfinished Agenda of the Holy Spirit," *Spiritus* 3 (Spring 2003): 53–67.

51. Although some contemporary Christians tend to think of Creation primarily as the universe within which planet Earth, the human race, and human affairs are a late and relatively minor development, the people of Jesus' time thought of the Earth and humans as the center of non-divine reality, with the sun, moon, stars and the rest of the universe as our "context." Hence, although it is possible to point to texts that use "world" to denote the vast universe itself, regardless of human existence and action, for our purposes the world with which the Gospel is concerned is the human world. It is humans who must broaden our vision to include much beyond ourselves but it is still we who must do this.

52. I am using "natural world" as a shorthand way to designate the universe other than human beings. Of course, humans are also "natural" and the universe denotes more than the "world." But our concern here is not with how to shape an appropriate discourse on reality as a whole but how to think and act in relation to reality as given and as constructed. When I speak of "material creation" in contrast to humanity I am distinguishing between that part of reality, namely humans, whose rational activity affects nonrational creation and that which is affected by such activity, even though, of course, human are also material. Our very difficulty in making appropriate linguistic distinctions is a sign of our increasing awareness that we, as human beings, are not totally *sui generis* in creation but participants in a reality which is far more differentiated and interrelated than the classical "chain of being" suggests.

53. Thomas of Celano, *The Remembrance of the Desire of a Soul*, ch. CLX, in *Francis of Assisi: Early Documents*, vol. 2: *The Founder*, ed. Regis

J. Armstrong, J. A. Wayne Hellmann, William J. Short (New York/ London/Manila: New City Press, 2000), 382–83.

54. An excellent treatment of nonreligious spirituality can be found in the introduction by Peter H. Van Ness, ed., in *Spirituality and the Secular Quest,* World Spirituality, vol. 22 (New York: Crossroad, 1996).

55. Sandra M. Schneiders, "Religion vs. Spirituality: A Contemporary Conundrum," *Spiritus* 3, no. 2 (Fall 2003): 163–85.

56. See, e.g., Ronald Rolheiser, *The Holy Longing: The Search for a Christian Spirituality* (New York: Doubleday, 1999).

57. Christian theologians have, in the past decade, devoted serious attention to the plight of the earth, and to the role of religion in general and Christianity in particular in both the precipitation of the ecological crisis and the effort to address it constructively. An excellent resource for appreciating the breadth and depth of this work is available in *Christianity and Ecology: Seeking the Well-Being of Earth and Humans,* ed. Dieter T. Hessel and Rosemary Radford Ruether, Religions of the World and Ecology Series, ed. Mary Evelyn Tucker and John Grim (Cambridge, MA: Harvard University Press, 2000).

A particularly important contribution is Elizabeth A. Johnson's Presidential Address to the Catholic Theological Society of America, "Turn to the Heavens and the Earth: Retrieval of the Cosmos in Theology," Proceedings of the Catholic Theological Society of America 51 (1996): 1–14. The paper was reprinted as "The Cosmos: An Astonishing Image of God," *Origins* 26, no. 13 (Sept. 12, 1996): 206–12.

58. The best-known exponent of Creation spirituality as an alternative to a redemption spirituality is Matthew Fox, whose numerous publications since the late 1970s have largely defined the field. See his *On Becoming a Musical Mystical Bear: Spirituality American Style* (New York: Paulist, 1976); *Whee! We, Wee All the Way Home: A Guide to a Sensual, Prophetic Spirituality* (Santa Fe: Bear & Co., 1981); *Creation Spirituality: Liberating Gifts for Peoples of the Earth* (San Francisco: HarperSanFrancisco, 1991) as examples of his approach. Fox has also attempted to show that Creation spirituality as he understands it is rooted in the Christian mystical tradition through studies on medieval mystics such as Thomas Aquinas, Meister Eckhart, Julian of Norwich, and Hildegard of Bingen. See *Western Spirituality: Historical Roots, Ecumenical Routes,* ed. Matthew Fox (Notre Dame, IN: Fides/Claretian, 1979).

Another proponent of this position who has attempted to enlist new cosmological theory and Creation spirituality in his reflection on

Religious Life is Diarmuid O'Murchu. See, e.g., his *Poverty, Celibacy, and Obedience: A Radical Option for Life* (New York: Crossroad, 1999); *Consecrated Religious Life: The Changing Paradigms* (Maryknoll, NY: Orbis, 2005).

59. See, e.g., Michael Guinan, *To Be Human before God: Insights from Biblical Spirituality* (Collegeville, MN: Liturgical Press, 1994).

60. Elizabeth Johnson offers an analysis of the present crisis and a feminist, Catholic approach to it in her 1993 Madeleva Lecture on ecospirituality, *Women, Earth, and Creator Spirit* (New York/Mahwah, NJ: Paulist, 1993).

61. We will consider the Resurrection and its implications for Religious Life in detail in chapter 2. Here our concern is with the grounding of faith in the Incarnation in the Resurrection.

62. This conviction among the early Christians of the divinity of Jesus comes to expression in a number of New Testament texts (e.g., John 1:14–18; Col 2:9; Phil 2:5–11; Heb 1:1–3).

63. James D. G. Dunn masterfully traces the development of a fully incarnational faith in the early Church in his classic work, *Christology in the Making: A New Testament Inquiry into the Origins of the Doctrine of the Incarnation* (Philadelphia: Westminster, 1980). It actually took the Church nearly five centuries, through the first ecumenical councils, to bring its faith in the Incarnation to explicit articulation, and the task of unfolding that articulation for subsequent generations is a task for the Church in every age. A recent important contribution to this task is Roger Haight, *Jesus, the Symbol of God* (Maryknoll, NY: Orbis, 1999).

64. For a fuller treatment of the Christian specificity of Catholic Religious Life in contrast to the monasticism of other traditions, see *Finding the Treasure*, 5–18.

65. One of the best known of Teilhard de Chardin's expressions of this is his "The Mass on the World," which is available in its entirety and final form in Pierre Teilhard de Chardin, *The Heart of the Matter*, translated by René Hague (New York/London: Harcourt Brace Jovanovich, 1978), 119–34.

66. For references to places in his writings where de Chardin's theory that "union differentiates" or that "true union does not fuse: it differentiates and personalizes" is explained, see, Siôn Cowell, *The Teilhard Lexicon: Understanding the Language, Terminology and Vision of the Writings of Pierre Teilhard do Chardin—The First English-Language Dictionary of His Writings* (Brighton, UK/Portland, OR: Sussex Academic Press, 2001), 57, 201.

67. The mystery of the mutual indwelling of Jesus and his disciples, modeled on that of Jesus and his Father, is presented throughout the last discourses (John 14–17). This mystery of indwelling, Jesus says, is the model for the relationship among the disciples themselves.

Joseph Bracken has used process theology to explore the implications of trinitarian theology for cosmology. See *The One in the Many: A Contemporary Reconstruction of the God-World Relationship* (Grand Rapids, MI: William B. Eerdmans, 2001) and *Society and Spirit: A Trinitarian Cosmology* (Selinsgrove, PA: Susquehana University Press, 1991).

68. A beautifully illustrated and accessible introduction to this story is Sidney Liebes, Elisabet Sahtouris, and Brian Swimme, *A Walk Through Time From Stardust to Us: The Evolution of Life on Earth* (New York: John Wiley & Sons, Inc., 1998). See also Owen Gingerich, *God's Universe* (Cambridge, MA: Harvard University Press, 2006) for a brief introduction to cosmology from the standpoint of science in dialogue with religious faith.

69. The geologian Thomas Berry, who has made extremely valuable contributions to our religious understanding of the universe, has also suggested (erroneously in my view) that Christians need to suspend their involvement with the Bible and the Jesus story until they have sufficiently immersed themselves in the universe story. For example, in a lecture entitled "Creating a Culture of Meaning," given to the Foundation for a Global Community, Palo Alto, CA, on Feb. 10, 1997, Berry said, "My suggestion is to put the Bible on the shelf for at least twenty years and get on with reading the primary scripture, the world around us" (from a tape of the lecture). Berry was calling attention to the fact that starting with the Bible, especially understood propositionally as verbal revelation, can blind people (as it did the first European settlers in North America) to what is already there, namely, the natural context which is indeed revelatory. This can (in this case, did) lead to insensitivity and violent disregard for nature. However, in my opinion, Berry is overstating the case in a way that can be very misleading. The misunderstanding of Scripture should not be pitted against a proper understanding of the natural world. Revelation is of a piece. Creation is indeed revelatory as is scripture. Both are needed. A Christian would say that the hermeneutical key to both is Jesus Christ, the Word (revelation) of God incarnate.

70. The strongest contemporary statement of this position is probably Richard Dawkins, *The God Hypothesis* (London: Bantam, 2006).

71. An excellent path into the theological and religious questions arising from post-Darwinian biological studies is provided by John F.

Haught, *God after Darwin: A Theology of Evolution* (Boulder, CO: Westview Press, 2000). One of the most prominent thinkers on the interface between post-Newtonian physics and religion is Ian Barbour. His 1989–1991 Gifford Lectures on the subject are available in a revised and expanded form as *Religion and Science: Historical and Contemporary Issues* (San Francisco: HarperSanFrancisco, 1997). The physicist who became an Anglican priest, John C. Polkinghorne, has written a number of very accessible books on the possibility of rethinking Christian faith in light of "big bang" theory. Notable is his *Belief in God in an Age of Science* (New Haven, CT: Yale University, 1998). See also Owen Gingerich, *God's Universe* (Cambridge, MA: Harvard University Press, 2006).

72. Paul Knitter provides a very good basic introduction to the work of these scholars in *Introducing Theologies of Religions* (Maryknoll, NY: Orbis, 2002). For a very thorough, balanced, and exhaustively documented treatment of the subject see Jacques Dupuis, *Christianity and the Religions: From Confrontation to Dialogue*, translated by Phillip Berryman (Maryknoll, NY/London: Orbis/Darton, Longman and Todd, 2000).

73. The issue of revelation will be taken up in the next chapter.

74. The Wisdom literature's presentation of personified Wisdom is rich and complex. Not all the material is completely consistent within itself or with other reflection on wisdom in the Old Testament. For an excellent introduction to the subject and analysis of the data as well as some indication of how personified divine Wisdom as Word and Spirit functions in the incarnational theology of the Gospel of John, see Nozomi Miura, "A Typology of Personified Wisdom Hymns," *BTB* 34/4 (Winter 2004): 138–49.

A fascinating article suggesting that there may have been reciprocal influence between John and the Wisdom tradition in Alexandria is Barbara Green, "The Wisdom of Solomon and the Solomon of Wisdom: Tradition's Transpositions and Human Transformation," *Horizons* 30/1 (2003): 41–66.

75. For a profound and beautiful theological treatment of Jesus as the incarnation of Sophia, divine Wisdom, see Elizabeth A. Johnson, *She Who Is: The Mystery of God in Feminist Theological Discourse* (New York: Crossroad, 1992), 150–69.

For an approach to science through the lens of divine Wisdom, see Dennis Edwards, *Jesus the Wisdom of God: An Ecological Theology* (Maryknoll, NY: Orbis, 1995).

76. The pivotal Old Testament texts on personified Wisdom are Job 28, Proverbs 8, Sirach 24, Wisdom 7–9.

77. The primary and explicit text on this subject is the Prologue (1:1–18) of the Gospel of John where Wisdom, as Logos or Word, is said to "become flesh," that is, human, and to dwell among humans.

78. J. A. T. Robinson, *The Body: A Study in Pauline Theology* (Chicago: H. Regnery, 1963), 51. Robinson prefers "analogy" to "metaphor" which he obviously regards as a literary device. Contemporary reflection on the role of metaphor as a heuristic device, a semantic expansion, would not hesitate to recognize "Body of Christ" as metaphor in the strong sense of that word.

79. One of the best treatments of this theme I have found is Mary Coloe, *God Dwells With Us: Temple Symbolism in the Fourth Gospel* (Collegeville, MN: Liturgical Press, 2001).

80. This is essentially the same message carried by Matthew 25:40: "whatever you did to the least of my brothers and sisters, you did to me" or Paul's conversion vision in which Jesus identifies himself as "Jesus, whom you are persecuting" in the Christians Saul was apprehending (Acts 9:5).

81. Thomas à Kempis, *The Imitation of Christ: A New Reading of the 1441 Latin Autograph Manuscript* by William C. Creasy (Macon, GA: Mercer University Press, 1989), 21. The actual context of this quotation (which was not original with à Kempis but cited by him) is the chapter "Of the Love of Solitude and Silence" and is not about the dangers posed by the other but the dissipation of the Religious who spends "a long time in idle chatter." However, the unnuanced interpretation, which was common in preconciliar Religious Life, was that relationships with other people were usually a threat to intimacy with God.

82. A very interesting social-scientific interpretation of the "family rejection" texts in the New Testament is Carlos J. Gil Arbiol, "Overvaluing the Stigma: An Example of Self-Stigmatization in the Jesus Movement (Q 14:26–27; 17:33)," *BTB* 34 (Winter 2004): 161–66. The author uses the category of self-stigmatization to show how a charismatic leader, like Jesus, could undermine the control mechanisms of society by over-identifying with characteristics that the society regarded as negative, thereby making them values. Hence, Jesus and his followers took on, as a badge of identity, alienation from family, which was one of the primary means of social control. In any case, these texts have to be handled very carefully so that, on the one hand, they are not voided of their radical challenge and, on the other hand, do not promote animosity toward those to whom special love and care are due.

83. This position was actually defined as dogma by the Council of Trent but the teaching of Vatican II on the universal call to holiness as well as its failure to cite the Tridentine position suggests an abandonment of the position in fact. For details of this historical development and references, see *Finding the Treasure*, 375, n. 2.

Chapter 2

1. I remind the reader that, as in the first two volumes, I write Religious with a capital letter when I am referring to the specific life-form of vowed members of canonical Congregations, and with a lowercase letter when I am using the term globally. Hence, this title, if it were part of a sentence, would be written: "Religious Life as a religious reality."

2. From now on, and differently from the usage in chapter 1, I will write "world" or "the world" within quotation marks when I am speaking of the negative or evil reality construction of Satan. I borrow this usage from the practice of many New Testament scholars who write "the Jews" this way when they are referencing the negative epithet in the Fourth Gospel in order to distinguish this epithet and its referent from the more general use of the term Jews to refer to people who are ethnically and/or religiously Jewish but are not those who have "refused the light" of revelation. I will use the term *world* without quotation marks to refer to the world as Creation and/or humanity (in other words in any neutral or good sense) and to the world as the Reign of God or eternal life or some equivalent to refer to the reality construction which is opposed to "the world" in its negative sense. I hope this will eliminate the need for constant paraphrase or explanatory clauses.

3. The facts of this episode are detailed in William H. Shannon, *Silent Lamp: The Thomas Merton Story* (New York: Crossroad, 1992), 199. Merton's struggle around this event is recounted in his own words in letters he wrote to Dorothy Day, James Forest, and James Douglass which can be found in *The Hidden Ground of Love: The Letters of Thomas Merton on Religious Experience and Social Concerns*, ed. William H. Shannon (New York: Farrar, Straus, Giroux, 1985). On pages 148–50, he writes to Dorothy Day about his attempt to withdraw his name from the list of sponsors of the Catholic Peace Fellowship because of the "suicide," and that his friends "Jim Forest and above all John Heidbrink interpreted this as a knife in the back..."; on

pages 285–94, where he discusses the situation with Jim Forest and also rescinds his decision to cut his ties with the CPF but not his objection to the means chosen by LaPorte; and on pages 162 to 63, he discusses his resignation with Jim Douglass and recounts that "Heidbrink told me I had no business trying to say anything about the peace movement."

4. A very informative testimony to this struggle in which Merton engaged over much of his Religious life is the correspondence from August 1966 to December 1967 (thus at the very end of Merton's life) between the monk and the young theology professor Rosemary Radford Ruether, who seriously challenged Merton about the validity of being safely in his monastery when some of the most important struggles for justice and peace of the twentieth century were unfolding in the United States. The correspondence in its entirety as well as helpful opening and closing essays are available in *At Home in the World: The Letters of Thomas Merton & Rosemary Radford Ruether*, ed. Mary Tardiff (Maryknoll, NY: Orbis, 1995).

5. Postmodernism was dealt with at some length in Sandra M. Schneiders, *Finding the Treasure* (New York/Mahwah, NJ: Paulist, 2000), chapter 3. See also the very accessible treatment of the subject in Paul Lakeland, *Postmodernity: Christian Identity in a Fragmented Age* (Minneapolis: Fortress, 1997).

6. This resistance to coherence is not a perverse penchant for irrationality but arises from the recognition that coherence and unity are products of human construction and that power agendas are seldom absent from such constructions. Because such constructions are ways of defining reality they often function as control mechanisms by which those who have developed them oppress those defined as inferior. Deconstruction is the attempt to expose the constructed character of such syntheses and the hegemonic agenda and tactics they create, sanction, and disguise from view. Once recognized as constructed such systems lose their "sacred" character and become susceptible to criticism and revision.

7. For a very insightful and appreciative explanation of contemporary nonreligious spirituality, see Peter H. Van Ness, "Introduction: Spirituality and the Secular Quest," in *Spirituality and the Secular Quest*, ed. Peter H. Van Ness, vol. 22 of World Spirituality: An Encyclopedic History of the Religious Quest (New York: Crossroad, 1996), 1–17. This volume has articles on such nonreligious spiritualities as the following: New Age spirituality, holistic health, psychotherapies, Twelve

Step spirituality, feminist spirituality, gay spirituality, ecological spirituality.

8. The "universe story," as noted in chapter 1, is shorthand for the account of reality offered by the new cosmology with its particular attention to the place of humans within rather than above the rest of Creation. It has been made widely available to non-scientists through the writing and lecturing of Thomas Berry, a Passionist priest who refers to himself as a "geologian," and his disciples such as Brian Swimme, Matthew Fox, and Miriam Therese MacGillis. Creation spirituality, sustainability, deep ecology, ecofeminism, and other movements are concrete offshoots of this new realization that as humans we are part of Creation rather than its lords and that the earth is our bountiful but fragile home rather than an inert source of disposable wealth or a dump for the byproducts of our greed.

9. The most comprehensive and balanced resource I am aware of on this subject, written from a Catholic theological perspective, is Jacques Dupuis, *Toward a Christian Theology of Religious Pluralism* (Maryknoll, NY: Orbis, 1997). Other important Catholic contributors to this conversation are Paul Knitter and James Fredericks.

10. For a presentation of Griffiths' tentative efforts in this direction, see Bruno Barnhart, editor and commentator, *The One Light: Bede Griffiths' Principal Writings* (Springfield, IL: Templegate, 2001). Shirley DuBoulay, *Beyond the Darkness: A Biography of Bede Griffiths* (New York: Doubleday, 1998) gives a good sense of the profundity of Griffiths' struggle for a unity that did not deny his Christian faith commitment but embraced the Hindu vision he found so compelling.

Thomas Merton, as is well known, died while attending an interreligious monastic conference. His *Asian Journal*, edited from his original notebooks by Naomi Burton, Patrick Hart, James Laughlin, and consulting editor Amiya Chakravarty (New York: New Directions, 1973) is his final testament to his long journey into interreligious dialogue and his deep experience of Zen Buddhism.

Raimon Panikkar is a Catholic priest who, as the child of a bi-religious family, has long considered himself both Hindu and Christian and has proposed a distinctive way of understanding the relationship between Christianity, Hinduism, and Buddhism. A number of well-known theologians discuss his christotheandric theory in *The Intercultural Challenge of Raimon Panikkar*, ed. Joseph Prabhu (Maryknoll, NY: Orbis, 1996).

11. The challenge of religious pluralism is qualitatively different

from the traditional question of how non-Christians can be saved. The question now is how non-Christian religions are salvific. No one claims to have solved this problem but the contributions to the discussion are enlightening. See the recent essay by Claude Geffré, "The Christological Paradox as a Hermeneutic Key to Interreligious Dialogue," *Who Do You Say That I Am? Confessing the Mystery of Christ,* ed. John C. Cavadini and Laura Holt (Notre Dame, IN: University of Notre Dame Press, 2004), 155–72.

12. A fine introduction to interreligious praxis is Judith Berling, *Understanding Other Religious Worlds: A Guide for Interreligious Education* (Maryknoll, NY: Orbis, 2004). Berling discusses different approaches to other religions appropriate for students or inquirers with different agendas and different levels or kinds of preparation.

13. Richard Woods, in "What Is New Age Spirituality?" *Way* 33 (July 1993): 176–88, pointed out that "new age spiritualities" which are the current embodiment of this approach to "private religions" are actually predominantly composed of elements borrowed from Christianity but combined in idiosyncratic and often inconsistent if not incoherent ways.

Two very influential writers in contemporary spirituality, Joan Chittister, OSB, and Ronald Rohlheiser, OMI, have been recognized as deriving much of their power as spiritual leaders from the fact that they are critical but faithful committed Catholics who offer the riches of the tradition without dilution or apology even as they recognize and prophetically challenge the faults and foibles of the institutional Church and the sinfulness of its leaders and members, themselves included. Martin Marty, a Protestant, in his "Forward" to Joan Chittister's *In the Heart of the Temple: My Spiritual Vision for Today's World* (Erie, PA: Benetvision, 2004), x–xi, says, "What stands out in this book? First, Joan Chittister is Catholic [which he distinguishes from catholic]….Second, she is religious [which he differentiates from "pick-and-choose" religiosity]….Third, to the core, she is Benedictine…."

Ronald Rolheiser in *The Holy Longing: The Search for a Christian Spirituality* (New York: Doubleday, 1999), after listing the four non-negotiables of a genuinely Christian spirituality (private prayer, social justice, mellowness of heart and spirit, and community) [53], devotes two foundational chapters to Christ and the Incarnation.

14. For a lengthier treatment of the contemporary discussion of this issue, see Sandra M. Schneiders, "Religion vs. Spirituality: A Contemporary Conundrum," *Spiritus* 3, no. 2 (Fall 2003): 163–85.

15. Rudolf Otto, *The Idea of the Holy: An Inquiry into the Non-Rational*

Factor in the Idea of the Divine and Its Relation to the Rational, 2nd ed., trans. John W. Harvey (London/New York: Oxford University Press, 1958. This classic, although it has been contested and refined in many ways since the death of its author in 1937, continues to call attention to what Otto called the *a priori* character of genuine religious experience.

16. Although I am speaking about it in the singular for the sake of simplicity and clarity, religious experience is often not singular and punctual. It can unfold gradually or be mediated through a variety of types of experience. Our point here is not the phenomenology of religious experience but the fact of the inbreaking of the wholly other.

17. This inbreaking need not be in the form of paranormal experience. God has been experienced in the beauty of nature, the intensity of human relationship, the depths of personal prayer, imageless meditation, and so on. But revelation has the character of "otherness," of coming not from oneself or through one's own power but as a gift.

18. One need not take the narrative of the burning bush literally in order to take it seriously as a way of recounting Moses' revelatory encounter with the God to whom the Israelites attributed their liberation, exodus, and covenant.

19. It would be too cumbersome to keep making the necessary distinctions between "religion" in the etymological theistic sense and traditions such as Buddhism or Confucianism that function for their adherents as religions do for theistic communities but which, in fact, do not posit a personal deity; between "faith" in the sense of self-donation to God and the vision of reality which calls for self-commitment but not necessarily to a personal Other, and so on. My interest here is Christianity so I will presume the reader is aware that speaking universally of the world's great religions is not possible and will know where major qualifications are required.

20. I am basing this approach to religion on the definition developed by cultural anthropologist Clifford Geertz in his very influential essay, "Religion as a Cultural System," available in *The Interpretation of Cultures: Selected Essays by Clifford Geertz* (New York: Basic Books, 1973), 87–125. The definition appears on p. 90. The essay was originally published in *Anthropological Approaches to the Study of Religion,* ed. M. Banton (London: Tavistock Publications Ltd., 1966), 1–46.

21. Clifford Geertz uses as an epigraph for his article "Religion As a Cultural System" (see n. 20 above) a quotation which perfectly cap-

678 • BUYING THE FIELD

tures the point I am making here about Christianity as a unitary worldview: "Any attempt to speak without speaking any particular language is not more hopeless than the attempt to have a religion that shall be no religion in particular....Thus every living and healthy religion has a marked idiosyncrasy. Its power consists in its special and surprising message and in the bias which that revelation gives to life. The vistas it opens and the mysteries it propounds are another world to live in: and another world to live in—whether we expect ever to pass wholly over into it or no—is what we mean by having a religion": quotation is by George Santayana, *Reason in Religion* (New York: Dover, 1982), 5, 6. As we will see, I am proposing in this volume that Religious Life is an attempt to "pass wholly into" that "other world" of Christianity, the Reign of God, even in this historical context.

22. The recent literature on the Resurrection of Jesus is voluminous. A major Catholic contributor to the discussion is Gerald G. O'Collins, whose *The Resurrection of Jesus Christ* (Milwaukee: Marquette University Press, 1993) is an excellent, biblically sophisticated theological treatment that takes into account the contemporary discussion.

The proceedings of the ecumenical symposium, the Resurrection Summit, held at Dunwoodie, NY, April 7–10, 1996, are published as *The Resurrection: An Interdisciplinary Symposium on the Resurrection of Jesus*, ed. Stephen T. Davis, Daniel Kendall, and Gerald O'Collins (Oxford: Oxford University Press, 1997).

Discussion of resurrection, that of Jesus and of his followers, is also lively in the scientific community. See the volume of studies by theologians and scientists, *Resurrection: Theological and Scientific Assessments*, ed. Ted Peters, Robert John Russell, Michael Welker (Grand Rapids, MI: W. B. Eerdmans, 2002).

23. In the Old Testament (1 Kgs 17:17–24) there is the story of the raising of the dead son of a widow by Elijah and in the New Testament we read that Jesus raised the son of the widow of Naim (Luke 7:11–17) and the daughter of Jairus (Mark 5:21–43 and Luke 8:49–56). The most striking account is the raising of Lazarus in John 11, because, unlike the other two whom Jesus raised prior to their burial (in a time and place where embalming was not practiced and burial took place almost immediately after apparent death) and who might, therefore, have been actually still alive, Lazarus is "certified" by Jesus himself (11:11–4) and by the evangelist through Martha (11:39) as really dead since he has been in the tomb for more than three days.

24. For a fuller development of the meaning of the Resurrection of Jesus for the spirituality of the Christian, see Sandra M. Schneiders, "The Resurrection (of the Body) in the Fourth Gospel," *Life in Abundance: Studies in John's Gospel in Tribute to Raymond E. Brown, S.S.*, ed. John R. Donahue, SJ (Collegeville, MN: Liturgical Press, 2005), 168–98.

25. See 1 Corinthians 15:35–57 and Luke 24:13–35 (the Emmaus story); John 20:11–18 (the appearance of the risen Jesus to Mary Magdalene); John 20:24–29 (the appearance to Thomas).

26. See Sandra M. Schneiders, "The Resurrection of Jesus and Christian Spirituality," in *Christian Resources of Hope*, ed. Maureen Junker-Kenny (Dublin: Columba, 1995), 81–114, for a more extensive discussion of the imaginative challenge to resurrection faith and its implications for Christian spirituality.

27. See, e.g., the remarkable account in *Teresa of Avila: The Book of Her Life*, trans. and ed. Kieran Kavanaugh and Otilio Rodriguez, intro. Jodi Bilinkoff (Indianapolis/Cambridge: Hackett, 2008), ch. 27, pp. 175ff.: "...the following happened to me....I saw, or, to put it better, I felt Christ beside me...it seemed to me that Christ was at my side—I saw that it was he....It seemed to me that Jesus Christ was always present at my side....I felt very clearly that He was always present at my right side, etc." She continues to explain this intellectual vision of the living Christ who is, in his own person, present to her.

One of Bernard of Clairvaux's most lyrical expressions of Jesus mysticism is his famous hymn, "Jesu Dulcis Memoria" which begins, "Jesus, the very thought of thee / With sweetness fills my breast; But sweeter far Thy face to see, /And in Thy presence rest" and concludes, "Jesu, our only joy be Thou / As Thou our prize wilt be; Jesus, be Thou our Glory now / And thru eternity." This is not a hymn to a memory but to a person experienced as present.

28. The texts of the early Church Fathers are accessible on the Internet. Search by the name of the author, e.g., Ignatius of Antioch.

29. An important witness is Justin Martyr, *First Apology*, ch. 15, where he speaks of Christians, both men and women, who have remained chaste (i.e., unmarried for the sake of Christ) from childhood and are now sixty or seventy years old. Justin (100–165) was writing in or before 150 and thus the virgins he describes must be dated back to the last decades of the first century.

30. It might be the case that the essentially ascetical form of Religious Life developed by the monastics who fled to the desert in the aftermath of the Constantinian legalization of Christianity and the

subsequent assimilation of the Church to secular culture was, in fact, a kind of self-chosen martyrdom. But this was not the original motivation for consecrated virginity, which was seen primarily as "marriage to Christ," not as martyrdom.

31. The context of this quotation should make it clear that this logion is not a prediction that the relationship of spouses is terminated in the afterlife. The context was a test question to Jesus about the application of the levirate law, which was not about the relationship between spouses but specifically about reproduction to continue the family. The brother of a deceased husband was to raise up descendants to his dead brother through his brother's widow. When his opponents ask Jesus which of seven brothers who successively married their one deceased brother's widow would have her in eternity, Jesus declares the whole issue of reproduction in the afterlife to be as irrelevant in the dispensation of the Resurrection as reproduction among angels.

32. At a recent international symposium on Jesus in the life of Christians, Elizabeth A. Dreyer, a spirituality scholar at Fairfield University, contributed a paper entitled "Jesus as Bridegroom and Lover: Critical Retrieval of a Medieval Metaphor," *Who Do You Say That I Am?: Confessing the Mystery of Christ*, ed. John C. Cavadini and Laura Holt (Notre Dame, IN: University of Notre Dame Press, 2004), 207–35. Besides stressing the fundamental importance of this metaphor as mediation of the central datum about Christ, that he is the expression of God who is love, she shows how, far from being a "God and me" privatized spirituality, in the medieval mystics Jesus-mysticism was both deeply trinitarian, outwardly oriented toward community and ministry, and "Creation centered." Hildegard of Bingen is a classic exemplar of all of these features of spousal mysticism.

33. See Colin Thompson, *St. John of the Cross: Songs in the Night* (Washington, DC: Catholic University of America Press, 2003), 57.

34. See Sandra M. Schneiders, *Selling All: Commitment, Consecrated Celibacy, and Community in Catholic Religious Life*, vol. 2 of Religious Life in a New Millennium (New York/Mahwah, NJ: Paulist, 2001), ch. 8.

35. Some very important research is being done by New Testament scholars taking a social science approach to the Jesus Movement and its successor, the Church. Particularly valuable are the studies of Jesus' "anti-family" attitudes and teaching as integral to his proposal of a new model of community, a "family without fathers," a faith-based kinship of equals. See, e.g., Carlos J. Gil Arbiol, "Overvaluing the Stigma: An Example of Self-Stigmatization in the Jesus Movement

(Q 14:26–27; 17:33)," *BTB* 34/4 (Winter 2004): 161–66; Santiago Guijarro, "The Family in the Jesus Movement," *BTB* 34/3 (Fall 2004): 114–21.

36. See *S.A.*, ch. 3, 100–113.

Chapter 3

1. *L.G.* IV, 31 (Flannery, vol. 1).

2. See *FTT*, chs. 9 and 10; *SA*, passim.

3. This line, often quoted against the romanticizing of nature, is from Alfred, Lord Tennyson's 1849 poem "In Memoriam A. H. H.," Canto 56.

4. See *G.S.*, esp. 1–11 (Flannery, vol. 1).

5. For example, some separatist conventicles like the Essenes separated from mainstream Judaism to form eschatologically oriented communities. It has been hypothesized that both John the Baptist and Jesus might have spent some time, prior to their own public ministries, at Qumran in such an Essene community.

6. For a very striking exposition of this Christian *novum*, that death was nonexistent in Jesus' imagination because the God he called "Abba" simply "is entirely without any relation to death: that death is for God something that is not," see James Alison, *Raising Abel: The Recovery of the Eschatological Imagination* (New York: Crossroad, 1996), esp. ch. 2, "The Living God."

7. By the time of Jesus (going back at least as far as the book of Daniel, second century BCE) many Jews, notably the Pharisees and those who shared their interpretation of Scripture, had come to believe in some kind of resurrection of the dead at the end of time. However, prior to that event both good and evil were consigned to Sheol, a kind of non-life that was not-quite-total extinction. Furthermore, the nature of the hoped-for resurrection was ambiguous. (For a good explanation of the Pharisaic position in contrast to that of the Sadducees who rejected the notion of resurrection, see Alison, *Raising Abel*, 35–41.) The resurrection that Jesus announced and which was revealed in him was altogether different. It began in this life as "eternal life" already possessed and was not abrogated at death.

8. For a brief but very insightful introduction to the Wisdom of Solomon, see Diane Bergant, "Wisdom Reading Guide," *The Catholic Study Bible* (New York/Oxford: Oxford University Press, 1990), RG 276–82.

For a deeper treatment of the theology of Wisdom of Solomon in re: the issue of life and death, see Barbara Green, "The Wisdom of Solomon and the Solomon of Wisdom: Tradition's Transpositions and Human Transformation," *Horizons* 30/1 (Spring 2003): 41–66.

9. There are two myths of Creation in Genesis (1:1—2:4a and 2:4b—3:24) but we are interested in the second one which includes the story of the fall, the expulsion of Adam and Eve from the Garden of Paradise, and is followed by the story of the murder of Abel by Cain in chapter 4.

10. Unfortunately, Drewermann's voluminous work has not been translated into English. However, an excellent synthesis of his work, especially as it bears on our topic here, is available in Matthias Beier, *A Violent God-Image: An Introduction to the Work of Eugen Drewermann* (New York: Continuum, 2004). See esp. ch. 1, "Fear, Evil, and the Origins of a Violent God-Image," 23–130.

11. In the 200 or so years prior to the coming of Jesus Judaism developed some ideas of life after death including the picture of Sheol, the possible bodily reconstitution of the martyred at least long enough for justice to be done to persecutors and the persecuted to be vindicated, and a more mystical union of the deceased with God that is reflected in the psalms which declare that, however it might be accomplished, the hope of the pious for life with God could not be finally frustrated. These theories are certainly part of the theological background of Jesus and his contemporaries but none of them can be considered a real precursor of the belief in the Resurrection based on the appearances of the Risen Jesus to his disciples after his death.

12. A very readable and clear survey of the various soteriologies in the New Testament is provided by Marcus J. Borg, *The Heart of Christianity: Rediscovering a Life of Faith* (San Francisco: HarperSanFrancisco, 2003), 91–96.

13. This is not an original theory on my part but a synthesis of the soteriologies of an increasing number of theologians and biblical scholars struggling with the evident problems of a theory of atonement as divine retribution.

14. See *FTT*, ch. 10. I developed this argument at greater length in Sandra M. Schneiders, *Prophets in Their Own Country: Women Religious Bearing Witness to the Gospel in a Troubled Church* (Maryknoll, NY: Orbis, 2011), henceforth, *Prophets in Their Own Country*.

15. I discussed, at greater length, this issue of the shape of renewed ministerial Religious Life in connection with the opening of the exhibit "Women & Spirit" in South Bend, IN in 2011. See *That*

Was Then…This Is Now: The Past, Present and Future of Women Religious in the United States (Saint Mary's College, Notre Dame, IN: Center for Spirituality, 2011).

Chapter 4

1. Marie Augusta Neal, SNDdeN, a sociologist who conducted very inclusive surveys of United States women Religious, especially those in ministerial Congregations, in 1966 and 1982, found that despite congregational statements and commitments to work with the materially disadvantaged and for social justice most Religious did not feel called to personally minister to the economically marginal or socially oppressed. See Marie Augusta Neal, *Catholic Sisters in Transition: From the 1960s to the 1980s* (Wilmington, DE: Michael Glazier, Inc., 1984), 24–28.

2. Scholars and spiritual writers continue to debate whether the choice by the young French mystic, Simone Weil, to practice such literal solidarity with the poor that she precipitated her death through starvation was an act of heroism or misguided extremism. See Jillian Becker, "Simone Weil: A Saint for Our Time?" *The New Criterion* 20/7 (March 2002): 15–23, who raises serious doubts, compared to Eric O. Springsted, *Simone Weil and the Suffering of Love* with preface by Robert Coles (Cambridge, MA: Cowley, 1986), who delves deeply and appreciatively into the spirituality of Weil, who lived as an ethnic Jew and unbaptized Catholic in the climate of the Holocaust.

3. *Federal Register* 76/13 (January 20, 2011): 3637–38.

4. *At Home in the World: The Letters of Thomas Merton and Rosemary Radford Ruether*, ed. Mary Tardiff (Maryknoll, NY: Orbis, 1995), 80–81.

5. *At Home in the World*, 83–84.

6. In our time one of the most powerful reflections on what the combination of material destitution with meaningless labor does to the human being is Simone Weil's writing on "affliction." See Springsted, *Simone Weil and the Suffering of Love*, for an attempt to explicate this aspect of Weil's thought.

7. The vocabulary of poverty in the Old Testament is extensive and variegated. A valuable vocabulary study can be found in Augustine George, "Poverty in the Old Testament," *Gospel Poverty: Essays in Biblical Theology*, translated and prefaced by Michael D. Guinan (Franciscan Herald Press, 1977), 4–6. See also Michael Guinan, *Gospel Poverty:*

Witness to the Risen Christ, A Study in Biblical Spirituality (New York/Ramsey, NJ: Paulist, 1981).

For a more detailed discussion of these terms, an excellent overview of biblical material on poverty, and a carefully selected and annotated bibliography, see John R. Donahue, SJ, *What Does the Lord Require? A Bibliographical Essay on the Bible and Social Justice,* rev. ed. (St. Louis: Institute of Jesuit Sources, 2000). I am heavily indebted to this work in what follows.

8. For a fascinating presentation by a well-known Old Testament scholar of how the "remembering" process which underlies the casting of traditional material in scriptural form might have taken place, see the novel by Barbara Green, *Mindful* (order from www.booksurge.com), 2008.

9. The term *Anawim* is Hebrew for "poor ones" in general but became a quasi-technical term for a particular type of person and a particular spirituality that developed among postexilic returnees from the Babylonian captivity to Jerusalem in the sixth century BCE, their co-religionists among those who were not deported to Babylon, and their spiritual successors down to the time of Jesus. We will examine this phenomenon in section B, 2 following. Henceforth, unless specified otherwise, I will use the term capitalized and without italics or quotation marks to denote this particular type of person or spirituality.

10. Cf. Alice L. Laffey, "The Priestly Creation Narrative: Goodness and Interdependence," *Earth, Wind, and Fire: Biblical and Theological Perspectives on Creation,* ed. Carol J. Dempsey and Mary Margaret Pazdan (Collegeville, MN: Liturgical Press, 2004), 24–34. This volume contains a number of essays pertinent to our theme.

11. Theologians have traditionally distinguished natural from moral evil. The first is due to the limitations inherent in created reality. It is not totally preventable and not ultimately disastrous whereas the second is due to human free will and is, at least in theory, both preventable and able to undermine God's creative intention. Teilhard de Chardin was faulted by his critics for being too sanguine about the reality of natural evil that wreaks such havoc upon humans and not sufficiently concerned about moral evil that he tended to present as a by-product of the evolutionary process of struggle between unity and multiplicity. Teilhard de Chardin's positive appreciation of evolving reality which took passivity and diminution very seriously was a healthy antidote to the Jansenistically tinged preconciliar theology of the human relation to matter but an underestimation of the reality, power, and human responsibility for evil can lead to a naïve optimism

that can replace responsible commitment in the face of human evil with romantic rhapsodizing about the beauties of nature.

12. See Guinan, *Gospel Poverty*, 19–20.

13. Some contemporary writers in the field of spirituality would like to ignore this strand and concentrate exclusively on a "Creation-centered spirituality." But this is faithful neither to scripture nor to human experience.

14. When an epic past is constructed to give meaning to the present and hope for the future it usually is presented as an ideal time peopled with heroes and heroines who are larger than life, events that are soul-size, and deeds of evil and good that are scarcely imaginable in ordinary times. Although the account of the Exodus includes much sin, alienation, rebellion, and suffering it is also presented in the Old Testament as the time of Israel's espousal to Yahweh. Later Israelites looked back to the desert as a time when they were educated by Yahweh as a young bride is initiated into her new role. We do not need to demythologize this account because what it affirms is precisely what we are seeking in this examination of Old Testament material, namely, Israel's theological reflection on the human relation to material goods and the role of that relationship in spiritual experience.

15. Some contemporary Old Testament scholars have serious doubts about the historical facticity of the "conquest," but the presentation of the crossing of the Jordan and taking possession of the land is a way of signaling that something new was beginning. Subsequently, possession or loss of the land in the Old Testament is a narrative device that carries the spiritual theme of fidelity-infidelity. When Israel is faithful to the covenant, she dwells securely with Yahweh in the land that is a garden of prosperity and peace; when she is unfaithful she is banished from the garden with its fertility and abundance and goes into exile in various wildernesses.

16. The quintessential expression of Torah was the book of Deuteronomy; hence the story of Israel's infidelity to the Covenant is called the "Deuteronomistic History" although it is not really a history but a paraenetic interpretation of Israel's experience from the entrance into the Promised Land through the establishment of the monarchy and into the Exile.

17. For a good brief introduction to the Wisdom literature, see Roland E. Murphy, "Introduction to Wisdom Literature," *NJBC* 27: 447–52. The reference above is from page 447, paragraph 5.

18. The confines of this brief overview do not allow for a study of

the Psalms that include the quintessential prayers of the Anawim. For a very fine introduction to the spirituality of the Psalms, including those which scholars identify with the Anawim, see John C. Endres and Elizabeth Liebert, *A Retreat with the Psalms: Resources for Personal and Communal Prayer* (New York/Mahwah, NJ: Paulist, 2001).

19. For the development of the notion of the pious/poor (the growing synonymity of the two terms) see Walter E. Pilgrim, *Good News to the Poor: Wealth and Poverty in Luke-Acts* (Minneapolis: Augsburg, 1981), 30–31, 35–36.

20. The "classic" on Anawim spirituality, Albert Gelin's *The Poor of Yahweh* (Collegeville, MN: Liturgical Press, 1964), is an inspiring and scholarly treatment of all the major texts relevant to the subject. However, contemporary Old Testament scholarship raises serious doubts about the sociological construction of the Anawim as a distinct community(ies) as well as introducing caveats about the tendency to "spiritualize" or "idealize" poverty that is inherent in the construction. Gelin himself is alert to this danger but those who have found rich spiritual nourishment in his work have not always been as careful.

21. See Gelin, *The Poor of Yahweh*, chs. 2–3, 27–61, for a succinct history of the development of the religious category of the Anawim and the spirituality of this group. Later scholars have been hesitant to follow Gelin completely because of the lack of the kind of historical certitude about postexilic Israel that would allow for the kind of confident historical development Gelin proposes and also, as pointed out in the previous note, because of the danger of romanticizing poverty or idealizing the poor. (On this point, see Pilgrim, *Good News to the Poor*, 30–31.) It is, in my opinion, possible to avoid this latter danger without ignoring the immense spiritual wealth Gelin and others have uncovered in this Old Testament tradition.

22. Guinan, *Gospel Poverty*, 53. For references to the material in the Psalms and the Wisdom literature stemming from the postexilic period see the excellent annotated bibliography of John Donahue, *What Does the Lord Require?* 38–41.

23. George, "Poverty in the Old Testament," 19.

24. I find it useful to appropriate from Marcus Borg, *Meeting Jesus Again for the First Time: The Historical Jesus and the Heart of Contemporary Faith* (San Francisco: HarperSanFrancisco, 1994), 15–17, the terms "pre-paschal" and "post-paschal" (equivalently, pre- and post-Easter) to designate Jesus' life before the Resurrection and his life after the Resurrection respectively. The traditional term "earthly Jesus" can set up a theologically dubious dichotomy between the "Jesus of history"

and the "Christ of faith" and implicitly deny the ongoing presence of the Risen Jesus among his contemporary earthly disciples.

25. On this subject see Raymond E. Brown, *The Birth of the Messiah: A Commentary on the Infancy Narratives in the Gospels of Matthew and Luke*, rev. ed., The Anchor Bible Reference Library (New York: Doubleday, 1993), esp. 346–66.

26. This is not in any sense to deny the extreme suffering and lack of all material and even spiritual resources that Jesus experienced in the Passion. Rather, it is to recognize that the material deprivation at the culminating moment of his life was the real symbol of the *kenosis* of the Incarnation and not a model for an actual lifestyle among his followers.

27. As D. Fiensy, "Leaders of Mass Movements and the Leader of the Jesus Movement," *JSNT* 74 (1999): 3–27, has well documented, leaders of mass movements of peasants around the time of Jesus were virtually never, themselves, peasants. They were usually "outsiders" in the sense of having resources and influence that the poor did not. It has been noted that, in our own time, this pattern also obtains. Liberation theologians who have articulated the theoretical basis of the option for the poor are well-educated professionals. The actual leaders (e.g., Martin Luther King, Jr., Dorothy Day, Cesar Chavez, the Salvadoran Jesuits, the four martyred Church women of El Salvador, Oscar Romero, etc.), although in solidarity with the poor and often enough martyred for that solidarity, bring to their work with the poor and marginalized precisely the resources to which the poor do not have access.

28. Mark does tell us that Jesus and his disciples sometimes were so overwhelmed by ministerial demands that "they could not even eat" (Mark 3:20) but this implies that they were in the habit of eating regularly, a routine interrupted by the crowds.

29. See the concise summary on Jesus' personal attitude toward material goods in Walter E. Pilgrim, *Good News to the Poor: Wealth and Poverty in Luke-Acts* (Minneapolis, MN: Augsburg, 1981).

30. For a good description of the social and economic situation of Palestine in the time of Jesus, see Pilgrim, *Good News to the Poor*, 39–63.

On Jesus as leader of a peasant mass movement, see Fiensy, "Leaders of Mass Movements and the Leader of the Jesus Movement," which includes further bibliography.

31. Santiago Guijarro, "The Family in the Jesus Movement," *BTB* 34/3 (Fall 2004): 114–21.

32. Carlos J. Gil Arbiol, "Overvaluing the Stigma: An Example of

Self-Stigmatization in the Jesus Movement (Q 14:26–27; 17:33)," *BTS* 34/4 (Winter 2004): 161.

33. I developed this theory at some length in *Written That You May Believe: Encountering Jesus in the Fourth Gospel*, rev. ed. (New York: Crossroad, 2003), 184–201.

34. Guijarro, in "The Family in the Jesus Movement," argues that the partnership between the itinerant missionaries of the Jesus Movement and the households to whom they first announced the Gospel is precisely what assured the continuity of the Movement after the dispersal of the crowds by the crucifixion. In other words, the role of families increased dramatically in the second stage of the Movement and has remained crucial ever since.

35. It is important to remember that Acts is not a literary "videotape" of the first days of the Church. It is part of the diptych Luke-Acts that was composed late in the first century and it reflects the theology of the Gospel of Luke that we will examine shortly. However, Luke presents the material as the story of the immediate post-Resurrection community and it is the only such narrative we have.

36. For a good, relatively brief, accessible synthesis of Pauline theology, see Joseph A. Fitzmyer, "Pauline Theology," *NJBC* 82:1382–1416.

37. The passage in 1 Corinthians 7:1–16 in which Paul wishes that "all were as I myself am" (v. 7), i.e., presumably unmarried, is in the context of a strong affirmation of not only the right of all to marry but also of the duty of the married to remain with their spouses and to practice the sexual morality appropriate to the married.

38. See Philip Seidensticker, "St. Paul and Poverty," *Gospel Poverty: Essays in Biblical Theology*, trans. Michael D. Guinan (Chicago: Franciscan Herald Press, 1977), 92–95, on the Pauline collection. This article is a very good, brief summary of the Pauline literature in relation to poverty.

39. Seidensticker, "St. Paul and Poverty," 99.

40. This is noticeable not only concerning class issues but also in regard to slavery and the equality of women. Paul seems to have been able to affirm the equality in the Christian community of all the baptized without drawing the sociopolitical consequences concerning changed social structures and practices. No one, even Paul, can do everything! Today's Christians need to continue into concrete social reality the trajectories Paul initiated spiritually. If in Christ there is no "slave or free, male and female" then these hierarchies need to be abolished in historical fact as well as in spiritual principle.

41. See Seidensticker, "St. Paul and Poverty," 112–14 for a summary of Paul's teaching and practice in regard to material goods.

42. See Pilgrim, *Good News to the Poor*, 110–11. Throughout this section I am indebted to Pilgrim's book.

43. The interpretation of this parable is considerably enriched by placing it in the context of Greek moral philosophy (particularly Cynicism with its evaluation of virtue above wealth and hedonism) and the Greek novel, as has been done by Ronald F. Hock, "The Parable of the Foolish Rich Man (Luke 12:16–20) and the Graeco-Roman Conventions of Thought and Behavior," *Early Christianity and Classical Culture: Comparative Studies in Honor of Abraham J. Malherbe*, ed. John T. Fitzgerald, Thomas H. Olbricht, L. Michael White [Supplements to *Novum Testamentum*, 110] (Leiden/Boston: Brill, 2003), 181–96. However, for our purposes its biblical context is primary.

44. Pilgrim, *Good News to the Poor*, 121.

45. Ibid., 125–29.

46. See Robert J. Karris, "The Gospel According to Luke," *NJBC* 43:148, 707–8.

47. Douglas E. Oakman, "The Radical Jesus: You Cannot Serve God and Mammon," *BTB* 34/3 (Fall 2004): 122–29. Citation is from p. 124. This excellent article with helpful bibliography makes the connection between the Jesus of Luke and the contemporary situation in first world capitalist societies.

48. See *L.G.* V (Flannery, vol. 1) on the universal call to holiness.

49. Cf. Matt 27:52; Acts 9:13, 32, and elsewhere; Rom 1:7; 1 Cor 1:2; 2 Cor 1:1; Eph 1:18; Phil 4:22; Col 1:12; and many other places in the Pauline corpus.

50. Elisabeth Schüssler Fiorenza, *In Memory of Her: A Feminist Theological Reconstruction of Christian Origins* (New York: Crossroad, 1983).

51. Simon Légasse, *L'appel du riche (Marc 10, 17–31 et parallèles): Contribution à l'étude des fondements scripturaires de l'état religieux* (Paris: Beauchesne, 1966). Légasse gives a brief synopsis of the argument, available in English, in "The Call of the Rich Man," *Gospel Poverty: Essays in Biblical Theology*, 53–80.

52. As Légasse points out, this is a clearly redactional addition by Matthew since the second great commandment is not an "eleventh" following the ten but the complement of the first great commandment. Its addition at this point serves to emphasize the orientation to the neighbor of the Christian pursuit of "the good."

53. Paul refers in Romans 12:2 to Christian behavior in contrast to the way of the world as doing "what is God's will, what is good, pleas-

ing and perfect." God's will, good, perfection are strictly equivalent terms.

54. Légasse, "The Call of the Rich Man," 74.

55. I am using the NIV translation of this text.

56. Douglas E. Oakman, "The Radical Jesus: You Cannot Serve God and Mammon," *BTB* 34/3 (Fall 2004); 123, says that the Aramaic behind the Greek of this text suggests "*the* Mammon." "Mammon is set in stark contrast to 'God,' without the suggestion at all that there could be a 'Mammon of Justice,' an acceptable and legitimate Mammon...." In parallel with my usage regarding *Anawim*, I will use the term *Mammon* henceforth capitalized but without italics or quotation marks.

57. John of the Cross, *The Ascent of Mount Carmel*, I, 11, in *The Collected Works of Saint John of the Cross*, rev. ed., trans. Kieran Kavanaugh and Otilio Rodriguez (Washington, DC: Institute of Carmelite Studies, 1991), citation on 143. John says: "This [being unable to "fly" to God] is the lot of those who are attached to something; no matter how much virtue they have they will not reach the freedom of the divine union." This is verified in the story of the Rich Young Man who had kept all the commandments but remained attached to his "many possessions."

Chapter 5

1. The question of the nature of the "Devil" or "Satan" or the "Evil One" is beyond the scope of this study. The Fourth Gospel, from which this terminology is derived (see ch. 1) explicitly affirms the existence of this evil power and clearly regards "him" as a personal agent. This captures the important point that moral evil is not simply "what happens" as nature and history take their course but that personal volition in opposition to God's salvific will is at work in the world. Jesus is said to overcome both the "Prince of this World" and "the world." Thus, there is a meaning of "world" which is synonymous with the embodiment or symbolic expression of the principle of evil at work in human history. By referring to this principle by name or title, the evangelist both simplifies the way of talking about evil and affirms the personal moral agency involved in it. My intention, when I speak of Satan or the Evil One is the same. I am not entering into the question of how to describe this agent phenomenologically or ontologically. The point is the *fact* rather than its description or explanation.

2. From now on, to avoid repetition, I will use the term *poverty* to mean evangelical poverty unless otherwise specified. Evangelical poverty is the object of the vow Religious make, which is the subject matter of this chapter.

3. For a full treatment of Religious Profession, see Sandra M. Schneiders, *Selling All: Commitment, Consecrated Celibacy, and Community in Catholic Religious Life*, vol. 2 of Religious Life in a New Millennium (New York/Mahwah, NJ: Paulist, 2001), 78–114.

4. The juridical, indeed legalistic, understanding of the vows that was adumbrated in the *Catechism of the Vows* (for example, Pierre Cotel, *A Catechism of the Vows for the Use of Religious* [Westminster, MD: Newman Press, 1962, c. 1926]) was somewhat offset by the treatment of the "virtue of the vows," which tried to express the ideal embraced by the one making Profession but, in fact, most Religious who went through formation prior to the Council equated the vows with the assumption of carefully specified legal obligations that exceeded those of other Christians (i.e., were supererogatory).

5. Although the documents of Vatican II frequently specify Christian commitment as arising from baptism and confirmation, I have chosen, for reasons of conciseness, to use "baptism" ordinarily to refer to Christian initiation. Baptism, confirmation, and Eucharist—the Easter sacraments—were originally considered three dimensions of the same mystery.

6. The distinction between Profession as a global life-orientation and the vows as specific expressions of this orientation is clear from the fact that one can undertake Religious Life in different Congregations and Orders by Profession of a variety of different vows. Some groups, such as male Dominicans, make one vow. Others, such as Jesuits, make several vows. In most Congregations, the members make three vows and sometimes a fourth pertaining to a specific ministry. Profession, in other words, is the act by which one becomes a Religious. The vows are ways of unfolding the potentialities of the act.

7. The vast amount of work on the parables in recent biblical scholarship was launched by the pioneering work of scholars like Amos N. Wilder, *Early Christian Rhetoric: The Language of the Gospel* (Peabody, MA: Hendrickson, 1999). A particularly enlightening treatment is that of Sallie McFague, *Metaphorical Theology: Models of God in Religious Language* (Philadelphia: Fortress, 1982), especially chapter 1 on metaphorical language and chapter 2 on parables. See also John R. Donahue, *The Gospel in Parable: Metaphor, Narrative, and Theology in the Synoptic Gospels* (Philadelphia: Fortress, 1988).

692 • BUYING THE FIELD

8. We cannot here go into a discussion of postmodernism, which is increasingly the context of first world Religious Life and is making inroads, through globalization, into other cultural situations, but the fragmentation which is characteristic of this worldview poses special problems for any theory of Religious Life as a unitary project. See Schneiders, *Finding the Treasure*, 110–19 for a fuller discussion of the characteristics of postmodernity and some of its implications for Religious Life. A good introduction to the characteristics of postmodernity as it impacts faith is Paul Lakeland, *Postmodernity: Christian Identity in a Fragmented Age* (Minneapolis: Fortress, 1997).

9. The sociological category of "total institution" was proposed by Erving Goffman, "The Characteristics of Total Institutions," *A Sociological Reader on Complex Organizations*, ed. Amitai Etzioni and Edward Lehman (New York: Holt, Rinehart and Winston, 1980), 319–39. See the discussion of Religious Life as a total institution in Schneiders, *Selling All*, 357–59.

10. See *G.S.* 1 and 3 (Flannery, vol. 1).

11. Dorothee Soëlle, *The Silent Cry: Mysticism and Resistance* (Minneapolis, MN: Fortress, 2001). [Originally published in German as *Mystik und Widerstand: "Du stilles Geschrei"* (Hamburg, Germany: Hoffmann und Campe Verlag, 1997)], trans. Barbara and Martin Rumscheidt. See esp. ch. 13, "Possession and Possessionlessness."

12. See chapter 4 above on the pericope of the rich man.

13. It is difficult to find appropriate terminology to distinguish countries that are income wealthy from those which are income poor even though the latter may be much richer in other respects. Terms such as *first* world and *third* world are hangovers from the Cold War era that no longer fit well. *Developed* vs. *developing* is loaded with value judgments about the nature of development. *Northern* or *western* contrasted with *southern* or *eastern* is fraught with exceptions since countries like Australia and Japan (and others) that are income-rich defy the locational identification of "northern" or "western." The fact remains that there is a huge disparity between economically wealthy and economically poor or even destitute regions of the world and there is a sizable proportion of the world's peoples who are not clearly in either of those two categories. So, in order to stay focused on my "target audience" of women Religious in ministerial Congregations based in "first world" contexts, I have to rely on the reader to remember that, by that term, I mean North America north of the Rio Grande and south of the Arctic Circle, western Europe including the United Kingdom and Ireland, and Australia and New Zealand as well

as some regions in otherwise "third world" countries influenced by Congregations from these areas. By "third world" I usually mean Latin America (though not all countries in Latin America would be in this category), Africa, and much (but not all) of Asia. Regarding Religious Life the category of "second world" remains significant because of the role of Pope John Paul II and Cardinal Franc Rodé, both from former Soviet Bloc countries, who have had so much (largely negative) effect on first world Religious precisely because of their "second world" understanding of the life.

14. Lewis Hyde, *The Gift: Imagination and the Erotic Life of Property* (New York: Random House, 1983).

15. My concern here is with the stark contrast between the type of economy in which Religious in the rich nations live and that which they undertake by Profession. Consequently, I cannot make the finer distinctions that would be necessary if this were an in-depth analysis rather than a broad-stroke description of the commodity economy. I recommend the now classic text of John F. Kavanaugh, *Following Christ in a Consumer Society: The Spirituality of Cultural Resistance*, 25th anniversary edition (Maryknoll, NY: Orbis 2006), for a much more adequate, and sobering, treatment.

16. This is especially true of *laissez-faire* capitalism. In democratic capitalist societies there has often been a political balance to the market economy responding to a recognition that an unhampered market does not attend to many of the needs of a society, for example, for education, health care, and so on. In such societies a concern for the public welfare leads, in many cases (unfortunately, less in the United States than in many other societies), to a redistribution of resources through taxation and the provision of public services.

17. Catholic social teaching, as many other traditions, has recognized that material goods are often better cared-for when they are privately owned and therefore there is a right to private property. This right, however, is not absolute (as is maintained by some extreme *laissez-faire* capitalists) but is relative to the needs of others. One of the remarkable insights of early Benedictine monasticism is that a better motivation for the care of material goods than private ownership is a disposition to treat all the goods of the monastery as one treats the vessels of the altar. In other words, if goods belong to God or exist for God's service reverence is the proper attitude toward them and care flows from reverence.

18. See Kavanaugh, *Following Christ*, chapter 1, for some chilling

statements of just how totally defined by one's possessions the denizens of a commodity economy can be and actually are.

19. The implosion of the economy in 2008–2009 was a stunning verification of the interconnectedness of the entire globalized economic system, not just in one country but throughout the world.

20. For a fascinating description and analysis of the economic interdependence in an Amish community and its integral relationship to the community's spirituality, see D. B. Kraybill, S. M. Nolt, D. L. Weaver-Zercher, *Amish Grace: How Forgiveness Transcended Tragedy* (San Francisco: John Wiley, 2007).

21. Although in theory, and sometimes in practice, the rising tide of increasing economic resources lifts all boats, the failure of the "trickle-down" economics of the Reagan era (the 1980s) in the United States as well as the statistics showing how the wealthiest one percent of Americans have progressively monopolized an ever-increasing proportion of national wealth, far outstripping the bottom 40 percent of the population and increasingly impoverishing even those who once composed the "middle class," makes it clear that what is theoretically possible is not happening in the richest nation on earth. For statistics, see Kavanaugh, *Following Christ*, 14. Although it is well known that the resources and methods exist to end poverty worldwide, there is, as yet, not a political will to do this.

22. This is, incidentally, one of the distinctions between Religious and secular Institutes. While the latter participate in the commodity economy as individuals, like other secular Christians, Religious do not, as we will see.

23. Catholic social teaching recognizes three dimensions of justice, commutative (which governs such issues as just pay which is the concern of the early hour workers), distributive (which the vineyard owner is exercising in providing adequately for all workers), and social justice. For a clear description of these dimensions of justice see the Pastoral Letter of the U.S. Bishops, *Economic Justice for All: Catholic Social Teaching and the U.S. Economy* (issued November 18, 1986), chapter 2, numbers 68–75. A tenth anniversary edition was published by the National Conference of Catholic Bishops in 1997 and is available from the USCCB office in Washington, D.C. It is also available in David J. O'Brien and Thomas A. Shannon, *Catholic Social Teaching: The Documentary Heritage* (Maryknoll, NY: Orbis, 1992).

24. Personal property, traditionally called *patrimony*, refers to monetary, real, and other goods that a prospective Religious owns prior to entrance, the administration, use, and revenue of which she must

cede before first Profession. Before perpetual Profession she makes a will. The effect of these acts, which are usually binding in both Canon Law and civil, is to terminate any involvement of the Religious in acts of ownership in relation to this property that, legally, she continues to own. See Canon 668 and the commentary on it in *NCCCL* (2000), 834–37.

25. As the commentary on Canon 600, "Regulation of Personal Property" states: "Once these instruments [ceding of administration and revenue and the making of a will] are in place, the religious should have no further involvement with the property or its revenue," *NCCCL* (2000), 835.

26. Although the Religious still legally owns her patrimony or personal property, and this arrangement can be very important if she leaves the Congregation, the actual effect is that she has no property of which she can make use or from which she can receive revenue.

27. Although a member can appoint someone outside the Congregation as the administrator of her patrimony she cannot deal with that agent without the knowledge and permission of her lawful superiors.

28. Patrimony, of course, is still legally owned but the Religious has no access to or use of it or its revenue. See notes 13–15 above.

29. The term "apostolic Congregations" is the designation of Congregations, which, without cloister, were approved canonically as Religious in 1900. They were distinguished from their monastic predecessors by their undertaking of active ministry outside their convents. I have preferred to call those apostolic Congregations that have undergone major, even substantive, renewal (rather than simply updating or modernization) "ministerial Congregations" in order to emphasize that active service of the neighbor is intrinsic to their identity while avoiding the connotation that they were "founded to do a particular work" or "apostolate." However, I will occasionally use the traditional term in what follows for reasons of clarity or convenience.

30. The Matthean logion is addressed by Jesus to the twelve; the Lukan one to the seventy. This is important because it marks Jesus' instructions as addressed to all ecclesial ministers whether or not they are ecclesiastical officers (i.e., clerics or hierarchy).

31. This fund, generated by a nationwide annual Sunday collection, was initiated in 1988 (and has been extended to 2017) by the U.S. Bishops Conference to help Religious Congregations that are not fully funded for retirement of their members (which is most Congregations) to plan for the future well-being of their members. To

date it has generated more than $500,000,000. It was preceded by the establishment of a lay-initiated collection called Support Our Aged Religious (SOAR), which was founded in 1986 and which annually collects several hundred thousand dollars. The reason for the inability of Religious to provide for their retired members is now acknowledged by both ecclesiastical leaders who used the services of Religious to carry out the Church's ministries without adequately compensating their Congregations, and by many lay people, now successful in their various lines of work, who profited from the services, freely or at minimal cost rendered by Religious. The fact that the bishops' collection is the most "popular" collection taken up by the United States Church is a warm testimony to the character of the service Religious have offered as ministry in the name of Christ rather than as paid service.

32. Most commentators believe that this description of ecclesial communism was either an idealistic presentation of the economic implications of the Gospel that might have been lived by a small group, or a very short-lived experiment. Religious, however, have actually formed communities in which none own and all are supported.

33. The fact that there are two references to this economic common life in Acts, 2:44–45 and 4:32–37, suggests that there was at least some experiment with this type of life at least among the first Christians in Jerusalem. However, it was not obligatory (cf. Acts 5:4) and as we saw in chapter 4 was not taken up in the communities outside Jerusalem. This may suggest that the kind of economy which Religious embrace is, as I have proposed, a singular way of embodying the Gospel call to detachment. As with consecrated celibacy, the Gospel value is proposed to all but the particular way of living that value in Religious Life is distinctive.

34. Hannah Arendt, *The Human Condition* (Chicago/London: University of Chicago Press, 1958).

35. The reception, both enthusiastic and critical, given Cardinal Léon Joseph Suenens' book, *The Nun in the World* (Westminster, MD: Newman Press, 1963) and the founding of the Sister Formation Movement, and other developments in the 1950s and 1960s, testified to this intensifying self-identification of women Religious as ministers. For a well-informed and insightful telling of this chapter of the history of apostolic Congregations in the United States, see Kenneth A. Briggs, *Double Crossed: Uncovering the Catholic Church's Betrayal of American Nuns* (New York: Doubleday, 2006), 41–66. See also the sociological analyses

of the increasingly apostolic orientation of Religious during this period by Marie Augusta Neal, SNDdeN, *Catholic Sisters in Transition From the 1960s to the 1980s,* Consecrated Life Studies, vol. 2 (Wilmington, DE: Michael Glazier, 1984) and *From Nuns to Sisters: An Expanding Vocation* (Mystic, CT: Twenty-Third Publications, 1990). The development of the Conference of Major Superiors of Women into the Leadership Conference of Women Religious is described and analyzed by Lora Ann Quiñonez, CDP, and Mary Daniel Turner, SNDdeN, in *The Transformation of American Catholic Sisters,* Women in the Political Economy, ed. Ronnie J. Steinberg (Philadelphia: Temple University Press, 1992). This increasingly ministry-oriented transformation of women Religious was strenuously resisted by some of the hierarchy, the most notable case being that of the struggle between the Los Angeles IHM Sisters and Cardinal James F. McIntyre who attempted to force the Religious who were implementing the renewal directives of Vatican II back into preconciliar, more cloistered Religious Life. This story is now available in Anita M. Caspary, IHM, *Witness to Integrity: The Crisis of the Immaculate Heart Community of California* (Collegeville, MN: Liturgical Press, 2003).

36. It should be noted that there were Orders of teaching and nursing Brothers in existence. Although usually highly monastic in lifestyle at the time of their founding these groups, like the Christian Brothers or the Xaverian Brothers, are more like women's ministerial Congregations today than they are like clerical Orders of men. It is interesting that women's apostolic Congregations, if founded by men, were founded by clerics (Religious or not) rather than by Brothers. Consequently, Congregations of Brothers never seemed to have been seen as models for women's apostolic Congregations. Brothers and Sisters have discovered their commonality in the last few decades.

37. The financial situation was different in hospitals and social service agencies but essentially the same pressures led to the need for these institutions also to resituate themselves in relation to secular peer institutions or be simply taken over.

38. See the extended description and analysis of this phenomenon in Schneiders, *Finding the Treasure,* chapter 8.

39. Patricia Wittberg has provided a remarkable resource for studying the institutionalization and de-institutionalization of faith-inspired ministries in her *From Piety to Professionalism—And Back? Transformations of Organized Religious Virtuosity* (Lanham, MD/Boulder/ New York, et al.: Rowman and Littlefield, 2006). Her sociologi-

cal analysis of the paradoxical and reciprocal effect of institutions on the Congregations and their members is especially interesting because she studies the phenomenon among Protestant as well as Catholic "virtuosi."

40. The prayer and suffering of the aged and infirm is certainly a continuation of their active ministries. And although "work" does not seem to be the appropriate category for this involvement in the mission and ministry of the Congregation it is no less strenuous than active ministries.

Chapter 6

1. In a wonderful essay, "Word and Spirit," in *On Christian Theology* (Oxford: Blackwell, 2000), 121, Rowan Williams writes, "To be 'Son of God' in the world of violence *is* to be the crucified victim: the sonship of Jesus is in no sense a 'cushion' between him and the felt absence of God in the world. To do the Father's will in the world is to refuse the authority of the 'the kings of the Gentiles', and this leads inexorably to the importance of suffering; and the Father cannot 'rescue' Jesus from outside because that would be the victory of coercion."

2. For a good overview of how the approach of New Testament scholars to the issue of poverty in Luke has developed in the 20th century, see John R. Donahue, "Two Decades of Research on the Rich and the Poor in Luke-Acts," *Justice and the Holy: Essays in Honor of Walter Harrelson*, ed. Douglas A. Knight and Peter J. Paris (Atlanta, GA: Scholars Press, 1989), 129–44. The article also offers an excellent bibliography on the topic.

3. An inspiring treatment of the real meaning of Jesus' relation to God as "Abba" and specifically in terms of his total trust in and confident dependence on God is Albert Nolan's *Jesus Today: A Spirituality of Radical Freedom* (Maryknoll, NY: Orbis, 2007), esp. ch. 13.

4. Robert J. Karris, "The Gospel According to Luke," *NJBC* 43:676.

5. For background on Matthew's community, see Benedict T. Viviano, "The Gospel According to Matthew," *NJBC* 42:630–74, esp. paragraph 24 on the Beatitudes. See also Daniel Patte, *The Challenge of Discipleship: A Critical Study of the Sermon on the Mount as Scripture* (Harrisburg, PA: Trinity Press International, 1999), which is particularly concerned with how critically responsible exegesis can lead to committed Christian response.

6. New Testament scholars refer to a hypothetical pre-Gospels

document containing sayings of Jesus as "the sayings source." "Source" in German is *Quelle* so this "document" is usually referred to as "Q." When material is identical or very similar in Matthew and Luke but not found in Mark (which is thought to have been a source for both Matthew and Luke) the hypothesis is that Matthew and Luke had another common source, the hypothetical "Q." Although the existence of "Q" cannot be proved, the hypothesis remains useful because it allows scholars to raise the question of how and why each evangelist used the same material in diverse ways. This process of "redaction criticism" helps reveal the particular theological and spiritual concerns of the different Gospels.

7. See Acts 6:8—7:60. The martyrdom of Stephen is presented in Acts as the beginning of the persecution of the early Church. He is the "beginning" both paradigmatically in that his death mirrors that of Jesus which is how the early Church understood martyrdom and chronologically because "That day [Stephen's death] a severe persecution began against the church in Jerusalem...."

8. See Walter Brueggemann, *The Prophetic Imagination* (Philadelphia: Fortress, 1978).

9. As should be clear from my use of *corporate* throughout this work, I am using the term in the Pauline sense deriving from "corpus" or "body." My use has no reference to the way the term is used in the business world to talk of "corporations" as legal persons. The emphasis is on the organic integration of the members of the Religious Congregation into a community of diverse but equal members who make various contributions to the well-being of the whole and who share a life, a mission, an identity, an agency that is unified by their charism rather than by any external features such as uniform clothing or shared dwelling.

10. As we discussed in chapter 3, the notion of "mimetic desire," that is, the rivalry set in motion by the desire of one person to possess what another has simply because the other values it, has been proposed by René Girard, the French literary scholar, as the root cause of human violence. Girard says, "Acquisitive desire divides by leading two or more individuals to converge on one and the same object, with a view to appropriating it" (*Things Hidden from the Foundation of the World* [London: Athlone, 1987], 26). Numerous thinkers in the fields of anthropology, sociology, literary studies, and especially theology and spirituality have found Girard's theory of desire convincing as a foundational explanation of the character and dynamics of the human predicament. See Gil Bailie, *Violence Unveiled: Humanity at the*

Crossroads (New York: Crossroad, 1995) and especially James Alison, *The Joy of Being Wrong: Original Sin through Easter Eyes* (New York: Crossroad, 1998). For an introduction to Girard's theory in relation to biblical studies see Robert Hammerton-Kelly, *Sacred Violence: Paul's Hermeneutic of the Cross* (Minneapolis: Fortress, 1992), 19–39.

11. I borrow the use of the term *virtuoso* for Religious from Patricia Wittberg who uses it as a sociological term in her writings on Religious Life. I explained my own use of it, and how I think it illuminates certain features of Religious Life, in *Finding the Treasure: Locating Catholic Religious Life in a New Ecclesial and Cultural Context*, vol. 1 of Religious Life in a New Millennium (New York/Mahwah, NJ: Paulist, 2000), 32–38. In that section I also attempted to purify the term of hierarchical and elitist overtones while stressing its usefulness in pointing to the "specialization" that helps make Religious Life a distinct lifeform in the Church.

See also the work of Ilana Friedrich Silver, *Virtuosity, Charisma, and Social Order: A Comparative Sociological Study of Monasticism in Theravada Buddhism and Medieval Catholicism* (Cambridge: Cambridge University Press, 1995) and the application of the category to the community that produced the Gospel of John by Timothy J. M. Ling, *The Judaean Poor and the Fourth Gospel* (New York: Cambridge University Press, 2006), esp. ch. 3, "Judaea and 'virtuoso religion,'" and 165–216 on Johannine virtuosity.

12. John of the Cross is the classical exponent of the role of desire in the spiritual life as well as the need for its radical reordering if one is to make progress in union with God. John of the Cross' treatise on the subject, *Ascent of Mount Carmel*, discusses active asceticism while his *Dark Night* discusses the passive purification which "follows." For an accessible but very lucid exposition of John of the Cross' difficult text on active asceticism, see Iain Matthew, *The Impact of God: Soundings from St. John of the Cross* (London/Sydney/Auckland: Hodder & Stoughton, 1995).

13. See Matthias Beier, *A Violent God-Image: An Introduction to the Work of Eugen Drewermann* (New York: Continuum, 2004), 23–130.

14. A strikingly original exploration of the human dilemma and the solution God offers in Jesus is Alison, *The Joy of Being Wrong*. Alison is indebted to René Girard and his theory of desire for the theoretical framework of this biblical/theological exploration of original sin as the condition we only recognize as we are being extricated from it by grace.

15. It is not amiss to note that this position has implications for the

ancient question of whether the Incarnation was part of God's plan from the beginning or is a kind of "Plan B" that God devised after humans, by Original Sin, wrecked "Plan A." I am clearly opting for the first position, that God "knew" from the beginning that it would not be enough to gift humans with divine life but that God would have to reveal the all-sufficiency of divine love in a way the human creature could understand; that is, in human terms. Jesus is God's human discourse on the subject of how creatures are related to the Creator: not as slaves to a master but as children to a parent.

16. As pointed out in chapter 4, the infancy narratives are not historical accounts of Jesus' birth, but midrashic constructions designed to reveal the theological significance of Jesus' birth.

17. For a wonderfully thought-provoking poetic meditation on this parable, see "The Father Empties His Coffers" in *Yahweh's Other Shoe* by Kilian McDonnell (Collegeville, MN: Saint John's University Press, 2006), 35–45.

18. See note 10 above for a brief description of Girard's thesis.

19. R. G. Hamerton-Kelly, *Sacred Violence: Paul's Hermeneutic of the Cross* (Minneapolis: Fortress, 1992), 19–24.

20. See Martin Laird, "The Fountain of His Lips: Desire and Divine Union in Gregory of Nyssa's *Homilies on the Song of Songs*," *Spiritus* 7:1 (Spring 2007), 40–57, for a brief but clear exposition of this theme in Gregory of Nyssa. Although each of the mystics has her or his own take on this dynamic of desire, its perversion and its healing, and its redirection to its true end, God, we find the same teaching in Origen, Augustine, Teresa of Avila, John of the Cross, Mechtilde of Magdeburg, Francis of Asissi, Clare, Francis de Sales, and many others. A contemporary writer on this subject of the healing of desire is Constance FitzGerald. See her "The Desire for God and the Transformative Power of Contemplation," *Light Burdens, Heavy Blessings: Challenges of Church and Culture in the Post Vatican II Era. Essays in Honor of Margaret R. Brennan, IHM*, ed. Mary Heather MacKinnon, Moni McIntyre, and Mary Ellen Sheehan (Quincy, IL: Franciscan, 2000), 201–22.

21. This famous line from the *Confessions* of St. Augustine appears on the first page of Book One and is the leitmotif of the whole work.

22. A particularly good treatment of this dynamic of perverted desire based on the teaching of John of the Cross in *The Ascent of Mount Carmel* is Part III of Iain Matthew, *The Impact of God: Soundings from St. John of the Cross* (London/Sydney/Auckland: Hodder & Stoughton, 1995), 35–50.

23. For references to Eckhart's treatment and commentary on it, see Bernard McGinn, "Theological Summary," *Meister Eckhart: The Essential Sermons, Commentaries, Treatises, and Defense*, translation and introduction by Edmund Colledge and Bernard McGinn, preface by Huston Smith [The Classics of Western Spirituality] (New York/Ramsey, NJ/Toronto: Paulist, 1981), 60–61.

24. This episode is recounted in Raymond of Capua, *The Life of Catherine of Siena*, trans. Conleth Kearns (Wilmington, DE: Michael Glazier, Inc., 1980), 121–22, pp. 115–18.

25. See Bernard McGinn, *The Mystical Thought of Meister Eckhart: The Man from Whom God Hid Nothing* [The Edward Cadbury Lectures, 2000–2001] (New York: Crossroad, 2001), 157–61, for an extended commentary on Eckhart's teaching on the indissoluble unity of activity and emptiness which is characteristic of perfection.

26. See McGinn, *The Mystical Thought of Meister Eckhart*, 160.

27. The interesting project begun by Nancy Sylvester, IHM, called "Engaging Impasse: Circles of Contemplation and Dialogue," arose from the sense of impasse in social justice ministry experienced by her and many women Religious in the 1990s. See the remarkable testimonies to the fruits of the first year of this ongoing process, *Crucible for Change: Engaging Impasse through Communal Contemplation and Dialogue*, ed. Nancy Sylvester, IHM, and Mary Jo Klick (San Antonio, TX: Sor Juana Press, 2004).

28. A remarkable prayer, attributed to Oscar Romero, acknowledges that we can never accomplish what we set out to do in ministry, but that we are finally called just to begin.

29. See Raymond of Capua's *Life*, 92, p. 85, and also Suzanne Noffke's translation of *The Prayers of Catherine of Siena* (New York: Paulist Press, 1983), 11, p. 95.

30. See the description, in John of the Cross, *Dark Night* II, 9, 4, of how the person being prepared for union with God must pass through the experience of "emptiness and poverty of spirit" due to the loss of "every natural support, consolation, and apprehension, earthly and heavenly."

31. Although somewhat marked by its origin in the mid-1960s, Dominic M. Hoffman's *The Life Within: The Prayer of Union* (New York: Sheed and Ward, 1966) is a valuable treatise on this experience because, rather than proposing John of the Cross' spiritual theology as an enclosed system, it presents a well thought out synthesis of Thomistic philosophical psychology, John's spirituality, and Freudian

psychological thought through the lens of what is obviously an extensive experience in spiritual guidance.

Also useful for understanding this experience, and probably more accessible to Religious familiar with post-Freudian and specifically Jungian and transpersonal psychology is Edward F. Edinger, *Ego and Archetype: Individuation and the Religious Function of the Psyche* (Boston/London: Shambala, 1992).

32. Karen Horney's classic on psychological growth, *Neurosis and Human Growth: The Struggle toward Self-Realization* (New York: W. W. Norton, 1950), as well as others of her treatises are still worth more than cursory study.

Chapter 7

1. The term *first world* is increasingly problematic, but it is difficult to find a workable substitute. Not only was there serious tension between Religious in countries like the United States, Canada, Australia, New Zealand, the United Kingdom, Ireland, and many European countries (erstwhile "first world" countries) and their missions and provinces in other parts of the world on the one hand and the "second world" mentality of the Vatican under John Paul II and the office for Religious under Cardinal Franc Rodé on the other hand, but there is considerable difference between Religious in first, second, and third world countries because of economic, cultural, social, and spiritual experiences and sensibilities. For the moment, the terms, despite their outmoded evocation of "cold war" politics and their insensitivity to the realities of globalization, seems the best shorthand for the discussion in certain contexts.

2. The development and promulgation (April 23, 1978) of the Vatican document *Mutuae Relationes* (Directives for the Mutual Relations Between Bishops and Religious in the Church) by SCRSI (now CICLSAL) begins by noting that "totally new problems have arisen" in the wake of the Council, one of which is that of the "mutual relations between Bishops and Religious" (*M.R.* 1, Flannery, vol. 2).

3. For a much fuller discussion of the biblical meaning of prophecy and the prophetic vocation, see Sandra M. Schneiders, *Finding the Treasure: Locating Catholic Religious Life in a New Ecclesial and Cultural Context*, vol. 1 of Religious Life in a New Millennium (New York/Mahwah, NJ: Paulist, 2000), ch. 10.

4. "Individuation" is the Jungian term for maturity, as process

and product. Other schools of psychology use different terms but all propose the movement toward autonomy (or interdependence) in some form as "growth" and continued dependency or hetero-determination as stagnation or regression. For further study of this concept as well as references in the rest of this chapter to post-Freudian, especially Jungian, psychology I would suggest the good overview provided by Murray Stein, *Jung's Map of the Soul: An Introduction* (Chicago and La Salle, IL: Open Court, 1998) in conjunction with Edward F. Edinger, *Ego and Archetype: Individuation and the Religious Function of the Psyche* (Boston/London: Shambhala, 1992).

5. See the article by Dennis Rupert at http://www.new-life.net/milgram.htm entitled "The Milgram Experiment: A lesson in depravity, the power of authority, and peer pressure" (7/09/08) for a description of the experiment and further experiments which attained results virtually identical to the original.

6. For the experimenter's own report on his research, see Stanley Milgram, *Obedience to Authority: An Experimental View* (London: Travistock, 1974). Seventeen editions of the book have been published.

7. See *A Catechism of the Vows for the Use of Religious* by Peter Cotel, revised by Bernard Fennelly (Westminster, MD: Newman, 1962 [orig. 1926]), 47, which was a formation manual for preconciliar novices: "...Superiors cannot command that which would be a sin, even venial....However, in doubt, the inferior is obliged to obey until a superior authority decides." Notice, that even when the subject suspects the command is sinful he or she alienates responsibility "upward" in the chain of command and, in the meantime, continues to obey.

8. Dorothee Soëlle, in *Beyond Mere Obedience*, trans. Lawrence W. Denef (New York: The Pilgrim Press, 1982 [orig. 1968]), provides a profound meditation on the deformation of the Christian conscience by the exaltation of obedience to pride of place in the Christian hierarchy of moral virtues.

9. For a chilling description and illuminating examination of the connection between mass violence and sacralized obedience, see Gil Bailie, *Violence Unveiled: Humanity at the Crossroads* (New York: Crossroad, 1995), 260–72.

10. It is important not to confuse or conflate "new forms of Religious Life" with the canonical language introduced into the 1983 revised Code of Canon Law of "new forms of consecrated life." The latter refers not to canonical Religious Life but is, rather, a "catch-all"

category for experimental communities that have not received canonical approbation as either Religious or Secular Institutes.

11. The publication on Aug. 15, 1969, by SCRSI of *Venite Seorsum* ("Instruction on the Contemplative Life and on the Enclosure of Nuns," in Flannery, vol. 1), was as upsetting to many communities of contemplative nuns who were in a process of conciliar-mandated renewal as *Essential Elements* published in 1983 (see n. 20) was to apostolic Congregations and for the same reasons. Both documents were experienced by many Religious as repressive attempts to regulate minute details of the internal life of communities in an effort to prevent any change or development in the direction of renewal or modernization.

In February 2009, CICLSAL announced an "Apostolic Visitation" of all Congregations of apostolic women Religious in the United States. Although the Vatican's rhetoric was "pastoral" very few Religious, members or leaders, in ministerial Congregations were reassured. The select object of the visitation suggested an investigative motive, especially since there were no "charges" being leveled at these Congregations other than a decline in numbers that was paralleled in other forms of Religious Life, the clergy, and among men as well as women. For a more extensive treatment of the visitation itself, its initiation, the response of women Religious and others, and reflection on motivation, and so on, see Sandra M. Schneiders, *Prophets in Their Own Country: Women Religious Bearing Witness to the Gospel in a Troubled Church* (Maryknoll, NY: Orbis, 2011).

The suspicion that the Vatican's intentions were not entirely benign was confirmed when, in April of the same year, it launched a "doctrinal evaluation" of the LCWR stating its fear that the leaders of women's Congregations were not as zealous as the Vatican would like in promoting non-infallible Vatican positions which were widely non-received among ordinary Catholics.

12. The primary and eloquent initiator of this move was not a woman Religious but Brussels Cardinal Leo Suenens whose book *The Nun in the World: New Dimensions in the Modern Apostolate* (London: Burns & Oates, 1962) called for the integration of women Religious into the "new dimensions of the modern apostolate" where they would influence those who "run the world, create the climate of opinion and the atmosphere we all breathe...The adults who in their turn will form, or deform, the coming generation" rather than spending all their time with small children or the sick and dying. He was a voice crying in the wilderness at the time but his vision is precisely that

which motivates ministerial Religious today. For discussion of the voices raising the issue of a deeper renewal of Religious Life, especially of women, than the Council eventually mandated, see Maryanne Confoy, *Religious Life and Priesthood: Perfectae Caritatis, Optatam Totius, Presyterorum Ordinis,* Rediscovering Vatican II, ed. Christopher Bellito (New York/Mahwah, NJ: Paulist, 2008), 177–84.

13. See the discussion in Schneiders, *Finding the Treasure,* chapter 7, on the two different uses of "lay" in relation to Religious Life. If "laity" denotes the nonordained, the term includes nonordained Religious. If the term is used for the secular baptized, that is, for those who do not make public Profession of the evangelical counsels, it does not include Religious who are in a different state of life.

14. This is explicitly stated in *L.G.* 33 and incorporated in the Code of Canon Law (1983) in Canon 225.

15. The Sister Formation Conference was founded in 1954. It was a response to concerns about the inadequate formation of women Religious for the apostolates, such as teaching and nursing, which they exercised. Over the next decade this "grassroots" organization helped bring about a dramatic change in the status of these women within the Catholic Church and within American society as a whole, by such means as the *Sister Formation Bulletin* (the first publication "by sisters, for sisters," in the words of its editor, Sister Ritamary Bradley) and workshops on spiritual and professional development. Sisters were well prepared to receive the Second Vatican Council because they already had been engaged for a decade in the *aggiornamento* it mandated. Its name was changed in 1976 to Religious Formation Conference to reflect the addition of men formation personnel to its membership.

16. See Anita M. Caspary, *Witness to Integrity: The Crisis of the Immaculate Heart Community of California* (Collegeville, MN: Liturgical Press, 2003), xiv, for a clear statement of the relation of ministry to the issue of self-determination. Had this courageous and visionary initiative not been driven from canonical recognition as a Religious Institute by hierarchical shortsightedness armed with violent power the movement toward a new form of women's Religious Life (which Sister Anita quite clearly identified as such) would undoubtedly have been faster and suffered far fewer setbacks. All Religious owe this community, which continues to thrive as a dedicated lay community, a deep debt of gratitude.

17. The brutal process by which the Cardinal forced the separation of most of the Sisters, including their general superior, from

canonical Religious Life makes shocking reading even today. It is fully documented in Caspary, *Witness to Integrity*.

18. SCRSI, which was the predecessor of CICLSAL, published *Essential Elements in the Church's Teaching on Religious Life as Applied to Institutes Dedicated to Works of the Apostolate* on May 31, 1983 (*Origins* 13:8, 133–42). This document was never officially promulgated because it could not obtain the requisite number of signatories, a clear demonstration of how out of touch it was with the development of Religious Life at that point in history.

19. It should be noted that the small minority of traditionalist Congregations that are united in the Conference of Major Superiors of Women Religious (CMSWR) regard this document as foundational for their understanding of Religious Life. The document plays no role in the self-understanding of the approximately 80 percent of Congregations affiliated through the Leadership Conference of Women Religious (LCWR).

20. Archbishop John Quinn headed the Vatican commission that was deputed in 1984 to examine the condition of women's Religious Life in the United States. He succeeded in bringing that investigation to a close without disciplinary action against Congregations and the ensuing peace allowed the renewal to continue.

21. See, e.g., Phyllis M. Kittel's insightful narrative of the transformation of the Sisters of the Precious Blood in *Staying in the Fire: A Sisterhood Responds to Vatican II* (Boulder, CO: Woven Word Press, 2009).

22. These Congregations separated from the LCWR in 1970–1971 to form the Consortium Perfectae Caritatis, which became the Conference of Major Superiors of Women Religious in 1992. In 1995, CMSWR was recognized by the Vatican as an official organization parallel to LCWR creating an unprecedented situation of double representation of women Religious of a single country in relation to the Vatican and, in effect, formalizing the tension between the two conferences.

23. These restorationist groups have to be distinguished from groups like the Society of Pius X (Lefebrites) who are formally in schism.

24. Interestingly, this "new monasticism" movement seems strong, and growing, among non-Catholic Christians as well as among Catholics.

25. Canon 605 provides for the discernment and eventual canonical recognition of "new forms of Consecrated Life" which would be, probably, neither Religious nor Secular Institutes but which, if canon-

ically recognized, would be classed under "Institutes of Consecrated Life."

26. Both the English translation of the Decree (*P.C.*) and its implementing documents are available in Flannery, vol. 1.

27. *G.S.* and *L.G.* are available in English translation in Flannery, vol. 1.

28. An excellent brief summary of the types of ministerial involvement characteristic of ministerial Religious is the article by Joan Chittister, "If They Really Mean It, It's About Time," published online in the *National Catholic Reporter*. She wrote this in response to the announcement in mid-February 2009 that the Vatican was undertaking an "apostolic visitation" of U.S. women's Religious Congregations. Her article constitutes a fairly clear illustration of the distinction I have been trying to describe between the "apostolates" of preconciliar Religious and the "ministries" of ministerial Religious.

I have addressed the same issue, at somewhat greater length, in a published address. See Sandra M. Schneiders, "That Was Then...This Is Now; The Past, Present, and Future of Women Religious in the United States" (Saint Mary's College, IN: Center for Spirituality, 2011.)

29. The principles underlying these requirements are generally outlined in the first four articles of *P.C.* and more practical aspects of renewal appeared in the implementing documents that followed between 1969 and 1971. All of the documents are available in Flannery, vol. 1.

30. *L.G.* 6, 44: "The state of life, then, which is constituted by the profession of the evangelical counsels, while not entering into the hierarchical structure of the Church, belongs undeniably to her life and holiness." See Rose M. McDermott, introductory commentary to Part III: Institutes of Consecrated Life and Societies of Apostolic Life, of Book II of *NCCCL*, 741: "While they are gifts of the Spirit and an integral part of the life and holiness of the Church, these institutes and societies do not belong to its hierarchical structure...."

31. This universal call of the baptized to participate in the mission of the Church is reiterated in a number of places in the conciliar documents, but one clear statement is in *Apostolicam Actuositatem* (Decree on the Apostolate of Lay People) available in Flannery, vol. 1. "Inserted as they are in the Mystical Body of Christ by baptism and strengthened by the power of the Holy Spirit in confirmation, it is by the Lord himself that they are assigned to the apostolate" (*A.A.* 3).

32. This document was prepared by SCRSI and SCB (Flannery, vol. 2).

33. A particularly neuralgic case was the conflict many Congregations, in the process of revising their Constitutions, experienced over
the interpretation of their vow of obedience in Canon 590 as obliging
them to obedience to the pope in virtue of their vow. Although
forced to incorporate this Canon into their Constitutions under
penalty of non-approval, many Congregations continue to have serious reservations about this interpretation of their vow that is historically and theologically highly questionable.

34. This was certainly not always the case. The *Catechism of the Vows*
originally published in 1926 (see n. 9 above for complete reference to
1962 edition) was a major educational instrument in the formation of
preconciliar Religious. It was largely a compendium and expansion
through explanation of the 1917 Code of Canon Law for Religious
and most Novices learned the meaning of their life, its obligations,
and to some extent its ideals from this basically juridical document.
This created the unfortunate perception that law proposes the ideal
when it fact it prescribes the minimum.

35. I discussed the issue of the canonical status of Religious Institutes at some length in *Finding the Treasure*, 257–64.

36. Avery Dulles, *Models of the Church* (New York: Doubleday,
1974). Dulles expanded the book in 1987, adding to the original five
models a sixth, the "church as community of disciples."

37. A still useful study of the succession of forms of Religious Life
from the period of desert eremitism to the emergence of apostolic
Congregations is Lawrence Cada, Raymond Fitz, Gertrude Foley,
Thomas Giardino, and Carol Lichtenberg, *Shaping the Coming Age of
Religious Life* (New York: Seabury, 1979). A limitation of the treatment
is its failure to recognize that consecrated virginity was a form of Religious Life that predated the desert form.

38. Theologically, the Church's government is collegial (see *L.G.*
3), governed by the "apostolic college" of bishops with the pope at
their head. But see note 42 below on the actually monarchical understanding and functioning of the institutional Church.

39. For a discussion of the distinctions between Religious Life as
such, and its various dimensions as community, Congregation, and
Institute, see Sandra M. Schneiders, *Selling All: Commitment, Consecrated Celibacy, and Community in Catholic Religious Life,* vol. 2 of Religious Life in a New Millennium (New York/Mahwah, NJ: Paulist,
2001), 17–33.

40. As Richard McBrien says in *The Church: The Evolution of Catholicism* (New York: HarperCollins, 2008), 41, the Church as it is pre-

sented in the New Testament was never a monarchy theologically nor was Peter's authority absolute. However, as the Church developed from the New Testament era through Vatican I the institution became ever more pyramidally hierarchical. The claim for papal primacy as an absolute and unaccountable universal power over the whole Church and every individual in it, combined with the doctrine of papal infallibility, made the Church, functionally, a divine right absolute monarchy.

41. I am using the masculine form as normative here because Benedict legislated for monks. Benedict's twin sister, St. Scholastica, headed a monastery for women about five miles from Benedict's monastery at Monte Cassino. Probably the women monastics followed the Benedictine Rule but this is not documented. In the later medieval and early modern period women monastics adopted and adapted the Rule to themselves. However, the Rule as it was formulated for men remains the norm.

42. See the major work of New Testament scholar Mary Coloe, *Dwelling in the Household of God: Johannine Ecclesiology and Spirituality* (Collegeville, MN: Liturgical Press, 2007), for the New Testament development of the Old Testament theme of the temple into a familial ecclesiology.

Still the best book-by-book exegetical study of this theme in the New Testament is Elisabeth Schüssler Fiorenza's classic, *In Memory of Her: A Feminist Theological Reconstruction of Christian Origins* (New York: Crosssroad, 1983).

43. The Greek is ἀδελφοί, which is masculine in form when it applies to male siblings (there is a feminine noun ἀδελφή for a sister), but when the noun in the plural refers to a group comprised of siblings of both genders the noun becomes collective, like the archaic *brethren* in English. The proper English translation of the collective word, therefore, is "siblings" or better "brothers and sisters" when it is important to emphasize that the group includes both.

44. The Greek is καθηγητής, which means one who leads. Since διδάσκαλος, which is "teacher" in the strict sense, is used in apposition to "Rabbi" in verse 23:8 it is redundant to use "master" in the sense of "teacher" in 23:10. The point of the text is that among themselves Christians are not to assign titles of hegemony: teacher, father, leader to members of the community.

45. Timothy Fry, ed., *The Rule of St. Benedict in Latin and English with Notes, RB 1980* (Collegeville, MN.: Liturgical Press, 1981), ch. 2.

46. For a moving explanation of the familial character of Benedic-

tine life that clarifies its formative affective influence on those who live it, see Rembert G. Weakland, OSB, *A Pilgrim in a Pilgrim Church: Memoirs of a Catholic Archbishop* (Grand Rapids, MI: Eerdmans, 2009), ch. 2.

47. The work of feminist New Testament scholars has been critical in establishing that Jesus, by his use of *abba* for God, did not sacralize patriarchy or the patriarchal family but definitively subverted it. For a brief and concise treatment of this topic see Sandra M. Schneiders, *Women and the Word: The Gender of God in the New Testament and the Spirituality of Women* [1986 Madeleva Lecture in Spirituality] (New York/Mahwah, NJ: Paulist, 1986).

48. This is particularly clear in the relationship between Jesus and his Mother in all four Gospels. His relationship to her, from the time of the boyhood appearance in the Temple in Luke 2: 46–49 through the various "disassociations" of Jesus from his mother during his public life (see, e.g., Matt 12:48–50; Mark 3:33–35; Luke 11:27–28; John 2:1–11) to the final transformation of their relationship at the foot of the cross (John 19:25–27), is clearly presented as primarily a faith rather than a blood relationship. For a complete treatment of this subject, see *Mary in the New Testament: A Collaborative Assessment by Protestant and Roman Catholic Scholars*, ed. Raymond E. Brown et al. (Philadelphia: Fortress, 1978).

49. This is expressed quite poignantly and powerfully in the funeral liturgy in which the prayers for the deceased, including a child or parent, are for "our brother" or "our sister" with the baptismal name rather than for "our mother" or "our son/daughter." The role in the community of the deceased bishop is recognized not by praying for him as our "father" but as "servant," the only other designation that is properly applied to all who are called by baptism to wash one another's feet, and *à fortiori* to those in positions of spiritual authority.

50. For a more extended treatment of metaphor in the context of religious discourse, and for bibliography on the subject, see Sandra M. Schneiders, *The Revelatory Text: Interpreting the New Testament as Sacred Scripture*, 2nd ed. (Collegeville, MN: Liturgical Press, 1999), 27–33.

51. For an extended treatment of the biblical and theological character of Religious community as transcendent, see Schneiders, *Selling All*, ch. 8.

52. For a more complete treatment of evangelical friendship as

the bond of Religious community Life, see Schneiders, *Selling All*, 288–305.

53. "Just War" theory was reiterated as acceptable in the United States Bishops 1983 Peace Pastoral, *The Challenge of Peace: God's Promise and Our Response* and more recently was treated at length in the *Catechism of the Catholic Church* (1993, 1997). Paragraph 2309 gives the criteria for just war.

54. The vexing problem of violence in Christian history and Scripture is far from solved, but a remarkably illuminating treatment of the subject can be found in S. Mark Heim, *Saved From Sacrifice: A Theology of the Cross* (Grand Rapids, MI: William B. Eerdmans, 2006), ch. 9, "The Bad News about Revelation: Two Kinds of Apocalypse."

55. The NRSV has "until an opportune time." In any case, the defeat of the devil in the desert was not definitive.

56. Gil Bailie's *Violence Unveiled: Humanity at the Crossroads* is a remarkable analysis of this cycle of violence. His thesis is precisely that this cycle, unless its dynamics are unveiled and arrested, will destroy humanity. For a direct application of this theory to soteriology, see Heim, *Saved from Sacrifice*, 297–302. For a cogent discussion of the God-image problem, see Matthias Beier, *A Violent God-Image: An Introduction to the Work of Eugen Drewermann* (New York: Continuum, 2004).

57. For an illuminating presentation of this salvific strategy, see James Alison, *Knowing Jesus,* rev. ed. (London: SPCK, 1998).

58. See Erving Goffman, "The Characteristics of Total Institutions" in *A Socoiological Reader on Complex Organizations*, edited by Amitai Etzioni and Edward Lehman (New York: Holt, Rinehart and Winston, 1980), 319–39.

59. It is interesting that St. Ignatius originally called his followers "The Company of Jesus" to evoke the image of the military unit sharing a common mission.

60. An interesting testimony to how pervasive the military model was in the preconciliar Church is the incidental, descriptive remark in *L.G.* 43 that Religious "are bound together in [brotherly] communion in the army of Christ" (in Flannery, vol. 1).

61. Frederick Buechner, *Wishful Thinking: A Theological ABC* (New York: Harper and Row, 1973), 95.

62. One of the most enlightening explanations that I have read of the mind-set that had to be overcome by the Council in order to enter into the relationship with the modern world expressed in *G.S.* is chapter 2, "The Long Nineteenth Century," in John W. O'Malley,

What Happened at Vatican II (Cambridge, MA: Harvard University Press, 2008), 53–92.

63. See the now famous opening paragraph of *G.S.* The next paragraph explicitly links this new attitude toward the world to the Council's rearticulation of the nature and mission of the Church expressed in *L.G.*

64. The critical source for conciliar teaching on the hierarchical structure of the Church is *L.G.* 3 (Flannery, vol. 1). For a brief commentary on this *Dogmatic Constitution on the Church,* and an account of the divergence of the final document from the original draft on the issue of the collegial rather than monarchical structure of the Church, see Richard P. McBrien, *Catholicism,* rev. ed. (San Francisco: HarperSanFrancisco, 1994), 669–71.

65. For a brief treatment of this evolution see McBrien, *The Church.* This is perhaps the best nontechnical one-volume work on the subject in English.

66. Two important works on the subject of the Curia as problem and challenge are John R. Quinn, *The Reform of the Papacy: Costly Call to Christian Unity* (New York: Crossroad, 1999), and Michael J. Buckley, *Papal Primacy and the Episcopate: Towards a Relational Understanding* (New York: Crossroad, 1998). Both were responses to the admission of John Paul II in the encyclical *Ut Unum Sint* (*Origins* 25:4, 49–72) that the exercise of the papacy was a major impediment to Christian unity. He asked for help in the process of trying to find a way to exercise the primacy that would be more conducive to the unity for which Jesus prayed. In this John Paul II was following Paul VI who, in an allocution to the Secretariat for Promoting Christian Unity, April 28, 1967, said, "The pope, as we well know, is undoubtedly the gravest obstacle in the path of ecumenism."

67. John Quinn, retired Archbishop of San Francisco, in the conclusion of his important book, *The Reform of the Papacy,* says that decentralization of Church government is the only road toward the reform in the exercise of the papacy that is necessary for reunification of the Church and that "Once the decision is made to move toward decentralization, the substantial reform of the Roman Curia will be inevitable," (180). The question is, as Quinn implies, will this decentralization and reform occur before the papacy simply loses control of the Church because of the inability of any such centralized government to respond to changing circumstances on a worldwide scale with the requisite speed and flexibility.

68. See *L.G.* 27 (Flannery, vol. 1), which affirms the "proper, ordi-

nary and immediate" power of bishops and denies that they are to be regarded "as vicars of the Roman Pontiff." The railroading of the English-speaking bishops of the world into a pastorally and theologically incompetent "reform" of the liturgy, effected in 2011, is a very clear example of the reduction of the bishops, not only individually but as conferences, to valet status in relation not only to the pope but to the Curia.

69. Recent scholarship has made us aware that there probably was no clear, simple, recognizable "break" between early Christianity and Judaism. There were certainly tensions, and the believers in Jesus came to be called "Christians" even during the New Testament period. This distinctiveness is important for our purposes but should not be understood simplistically. See Adam H. Becker and Annette Yoshiko Reed, eds., *The Ways That Never Parted: Jews and Christians in Late Antiquity and the Early Middle Ages* (Minneapolis: Fortress Press, 2007).

70. Benedict XVI dropped the title "patriarch" in 2006.

71. See Richard P. McBrien, *Catholicism*, 755–56, on the escalation of the papacy in the Middle Ages.

72. For an excellent treatment of the history of this strong collegial current in the Church see Francis Oakley, "History and the Return of the Repressed in Catholic Modernity: The Dilemma Posed by Constance," *The Crisis of Authority in Catholic Modernity*, ed. Michael J. Lacey and Francis Oakley (Oxford/New York: Oxford University Press, 2011), 29–56.

73. This complicated history and its attendant theology, which I have adumbrated very concisely here, can be studied in greater detail in Patrick Granfield, "Pope," *The New Dictionary of Theology*, edited by Joseph A. Komonchak, Mary Collins, Dermot A. Lane (Wilmington, DE: Michael Glazier, 1987), 779–84, and McBrien, *Catholicism*, section XX, "Special Questions in Ecclesiology," 739–82. See also the much more detailed theological and historical presentation of the papacy in McBrien's *The Church*, Part IV: Ecclesiology from Vatican I to the Threshold of Vatican II.

74. This conviction, and the extraordinarily dysfunctional results of its implementation, have been on lurid display in the clergy sexual abuse scandal for the past decade. Bishops can exercise no real control or influence on fellow bishops, no matter how egregious the crimes of the latter are. And the refusal of the bishops to accept that they are in any way accountable to the people who have been hurt by the malfeasance of clergy has been lamented and excoriated across the world. But, in fact, there are no mechanisms in the monarchical

system to redress these grievances. Only the pope can do anything to rein in rogue bishops and he shows very little inclination to do so.

75. See note 73 for resources.

76. This famous quotation is from Lord Acton writing to Bishop Mandell Creighton in 1887 about Pope Pius IX.

77. This remarkable departure from the eighteen previous centuries of Church belief and teaching that "error had no rights" with the extension that the person in error had no rights in regard to the "error" was enshrined in *Dignitatis Humanae* (Declaration on Religious Liberty) of Vatican II (*D.H.* available in Flannery, vol. 1). It is widely acknowledged that it was the American experience and the ability of American theologians such as John Courtney Murray to articulate that experience which led to this recognition by the Church of the right of every person to follow her or his own conscience in relation to religion.

78. The abortion debate in the U.S. Church, in which some laity and bishops believe that voters and lawmakers can and should be spiritually punished (e.g., by excommunication or refusal of sacraments) for their political behavior, contrasts with the settled acceptance of abortion rights in some traditionally Catholic countries in Europe, demonstrating that the issue of whether the Church can claim political control of its members is definitely not settled.

79. See *L.G.* 2, 10 (Flannery, vol. 1).

80. *L.G.,* chapter 3, is notable for this juxtaposition of collegial and primatial theology that are hard to harmonize.

81. Dylan Thomas, "Do Not Go Gentle into That Good Night," in *The Collected Poems of Dylan Thomas* (New York: New Directions, 1957 [17th printing]), 128.

82. See Elisabeth Schüssler Fiorenza, *In Memory of Her: A Feminist Theological Reconstruction of Christian Origins* (New York: Crossroad, 1983), who traces through the New Testament the development (or regression) in the first two centuries of the Christian era from the Church as a discipleship of equals into a patriarchal ecclesiastical institution. See especially Part III: Tracing the Struggles: Patriarchy and Ministry.

83. *L.G.* 10 (Flannery, vol. 1).

84. Although this arrangement was often-enough circumvented by power groups in Congregations who managed to control elections and keep a cabal in power over long periods, this was neither legitimate nor intrinsic to the governmental structure.

85. This power was often used illegitimately and even violently, but it was not contested as invalid.

86. The distinction which was enshrined in some Orders in the distinction between solemn and simple vows often had to do with intellectual ability and/or formation which determined the kind of work members were able to do.

87. Canon 622 designates them "supreme moderators" but this generic term, probably intended to avoid "canonizing" the particular terminology of any Institute or Order, is rarely used by women Religious who tend to find the coupling of "supreme" and "moderator" amusingly ironic.

88. This preference for consensus is not without problems since it can be used to manipulate dissenters or make dissent invisible. Many Congregations recognize a balance between consensus and secret balloting as a better option. But the point is that the hallmark of modern democracy, "one person one vote," is not the governmental ideal in Religious Congregations.

Chapter 8

1. Dorothee Soëlle's, *Beyond Mere Obedience*, trans. Lawrence W. Denef (New York: Pilgrim, 1982) examines the role of Christian theology in the exaltation of obedience to a place in Christian teaching and practice that made the behavior of the Nazis appear virtuous.

2. See Hannah Arendt, *Eichmann in Jerusalem: A Report on the Banality of Evil* (New York: Penguin Books, 1964; rev. 1976).

3. For a brief introduction to feminism and its embrace by Christian/Catholic women (and men) see Sandra M. Schneiders, *Beyond Patching: Faith and Feminism in the Catholic Church,*. 2nd ed. (New York/Mahwah, NJ: Paulist Press, 2004).

For an excellent analysis of the notion of "domination systems," see Walter Wink, *Engaging the Powers: Discernment and Resistance in a World of Domination* (Minneapolis: Fortress, 1992). This is volume 3 of his trilogy on The Powers.

4. There is more than one way to understand "hierarchy." But the way most people, including many within the ecclesiastical governance structure, tend to understand it is as a sacralized domination system. Understood this way it is contrary to the Gospel and the object of Jesus' challenge and opposition; it is opposed to the discipleship of equals that Jesus inaugurated.

5. The attempt to supply a biblical basis for the exclusion of women from ordination foundered when the Pontifical Biblical Commission, after extensive investigation of the question, declared that Scripture does not preclude the ordination of women. See "Biblical Commission Report *Can Women Be Priests?*" in *Women Priests*, ed. Leonard Swidler and Arlene Swidler (New York/Mahwah, NJ: Paulist, 1977), 338–46.

6. See *D.H.* 1, n. 2 (Flannery, vol. 1).

7. Margaret A. Farley, *Commitments: Beginning, Keeping, Changing* (San Francisco: Harper and Row, 1990), esp. 14–19 on commitment. See also Schneiders, *Selling All*, ch. 3, "Commitment and Profession," esp. 82–96.

8. See Elisabeth Schüssler Fiorenza's classic, *In Memory of Her: A Feminist Theological Reconstruction of Christian Origins* (New York: Crossroad, 1983), on this development within the New Testament times. In Richard P. McBrien, *The Church: The Evolution of Catholicism* (New York: HarperCollins, 2008), Parts II and III describe the post-biblical development up to the mid-nineteenth century. By Vatican I, the Church had become a full-fledged monarchy. McBrien insists that the "The Catholic Church is not an absolute monarchy. Its governmental structure is communal and collegial...." (101). However, in my opinion, this is more a theological than a historical statement. When papal primacy, which should be a "primacy of service" among a communion of churches governed collegially, is combined with papal infallibility, especially as it has been exercised since Vatican I, it functions as divine right monarchy and is viewed that way not only by secular political scientists but also by other Christian communions. Absolute (as opposed to constitutional) monarchy as a government is essentially characterized by the concentration of the executive, legislative, and judicial branches in a single office exercised by a single ruler. Vatican II attempted to reinstate the collegial and communal character of the Church but virtually all provisions for the exercise of episcopal collegiality (synods, episcopal conferences, etc.) within episcopates, or of the episcopate with the papacy, have been rescinded or neutralized in the postconciliar period.

9. The incompatible ecclesial models in chapters 2 (on the people of God) and 3 (on the hierarchy) of *Lumen Gentium* are the clearest locus of this contradictory development in ecclesiology. Efforts to present the two models, one monarchical and the other collegial, as complementary are laudatory, but not very successful. Hierarchy that is based in ontological dualism between the superiority of

the ordained and the powerlessness of the laity makes even collegiality among the hierarchs extremely difficult to imagine or achieve and genuinely egalitarian community between leaders and members almost a contradiction in terms.

10. The Apostolic Visitation of U.S. apostolic Congregations of women Religious and the "doctrinal assessment" of the Leadership Conference of Women Religious, both launched in 2009, were, respectively, a judicial proceeding against the Congregations and a virtual heresy trial of the LCWR. Attempts to present the former as a "pastoral" initiative in fostering Religious Life have been fruitless since the very nature of an Apostolic Visitation is disciplinary and implies guilt or well-founded suspicion of guilt (see Sandra M. Schneiders, *Prophets in Their Own Country: Women Religious Bearing Witness to the Gospel in a Troubled Church* [Maryknoll, NY: Orbis, 2011] for a fuller discussion of this event). And the "doctrinal evaluation" is seen by many as part of a long effort of the Vatican to supplant the renewal-minded LCWR which represents some 80 percent of U.S. women Religious with the more compliant and traditionalist Conference of Major Superiors of Women Religious (CMSWR) which represents about 15 to 20 percent. The agenda of the investigations is widely perceived among Religious and laity as an attempt to neutralize the force for renewal that women Religious in the U.S. represent.

For more detailed discussion of the Vatican investigations see the links under http://ncronline.org/apostolic visitation. The heading "Stories about the apostolic visitation" contains an archive of virtually all the stories on the investigation published by *NCR* with internal links to other resources.

11. For an exposition of Catholic Gospel-based feminism, see Schneiders, *Beyond Patching: Faith and Feminism in the Catholic Church.* Unfortunately, most Vatican officials and many in the hierarchy have not been able to grasp the real distinction between secular and Christian feminism and have sustained a consistent animosity toward feminism as a threat to the Church rather than capitalizing on it for renewal in the Church. One of the major reasons for the tension between the Vatican and LCWR has been the suspicion of the former that women Religious in general and their leaders in particular were in the grip of a dangerously anti-Catholic feminism.

12. Léon Joseph Suenens, *The Nun in the Modern World: New Dimensions in the Modern Apostolate* (London: Burns & Oates, 1962). For a good explanation of the effect of Suenens' thinking on the Council but especially on Sisters themselves, see Maryanne Confoy, *Religious*

Life and Priesthood: Perfectae Caritatis, Optatam Totius, Presbyterorum Ordinis [Recovering Vatican II] (New York/Mahwah, NJ: Paulist, 2008), especially Section III on "Perfectae Caritatis."

13. Important contributions include the groundbreaking work of Schüssler Fiorenza (see n. 8 of this chapter). Subsequent compilations which provide insight into the work of the immediate postconciliar decades include *The Bible and Feminist Hermeneutics*, edited by Mary Ann Tolbert, *Semeia* 28 (Chico, CA: Scholars, 1983); *Feminist Interpretation of the Bible*, edited by Letty M. Russell (Philadelphia: Westminster, 1985); *Feminist Perspectives on Biblical Scholarship*, edited by Adela Yarbro Collins, Society of Biblical Literature Centennial Publications (Chico, CA: Scholars, 1985). For further references, see Mary Paula Walsh, *Feminism and Christian Tradition: An Annotated Bibliography and Critical Introduction to the Literature* (Santa Barbara, CA: Greenwood, 1991).

14. Particularly noteworthy are the contributions of Elizabeth A. Johnson, *She Who Is: The Mystery of God in Feminist Theological Discourse* (New York: Crossroad, 2002 [orig. 1992]) and Catherine M. LaCugna, *God for Us: The Trinity and Christian Life* (San Francisco: HarperSanFrancisco, 1991).

15. See, e.g., *A Just and True Love: Feminism at the Frontiers of Theological Ethics: Essays in Honor of Margaret Farley*, ed. Maura A. Ryan and Brian F. Linnane (Notre Dame, IN: University of Notre Dame, 2007).

16. See, e.g., *Religion and Sexism: Images of Woman in the Jewish and Christian Traditions*, ed. Rosemary Radford Ruether (New York: Simon and Schuster, 1974) and Ruether's own *Women and Redemption: A Theological History* (Minneapolis, MN: Fortress Press, 1998).

17. Important in this field is Rosemary Radford Ruether. See especially her *Sexism and God-Talk: Toward a Feminist Theology* (Boston: Beacon, 1993) [orig. 1983], which was one of the first attempts to see all of Christian systematic theology through a feminist lens. Likewise, *Freeing Theology: The Essentials of Theology in Feminist Perspective*, ed. Catherine Mowry LaCugna (San Francisco: HarperSanFrancisco, 1993), brings together biblical, systematic, historical, moral, liturgical, and spirituality contributions to feminist theology. See also the overview *Feminist Theologies: Legacy and Prospect*, ed. R. R. Ruether (Minneapolis: Fortress, 2007). On liturgy and preaching, see Mary Catherine Hilkert, *Naming Grace: Preaching and the Sacramental Imagination* (New York: Continuum, 1997).

18. Since I devoted all of chapter 10 to Religious Life as prophetic in *Finding the Treasure: Locating Catholic Religious Life in a New Ecclesial and Cultural Context*, vol. 1 of Religious Life in a New Millennium

(New York/Mahwah, NJ: Paulist, 2000), I am only recalling here the general lines of this subject.

19. See Albert Nolan, "Structures of Sin," in *Hope in an Age of Despair: And Other Talks and Writings*, edited and introduced by Stan Muyebe (Maryknoll, NY: Orbis, 2009), 150–67.

20. See Marcus Borg's remarkable book, *Jesus: Uncovering the Life, Teachings, and Relevance of a Religious Revolutionary* (San Francisco: HarperSanFrancisco, 2006), esp. ch. 5, "The Shaping of Jesus: His Experience of God."

21. For an in-depth treatment of this subject, see Walter Wink, *Engaging the Powers: Discernment and Resistance in a World of Domination*, Part 1, 3–104. For a briefer treatment, see Marcus Borg, *Jesus*, chapter 9.

22. Albert Nolan has written very insightfully on the meaning of the "option for the poor" as "taking the side" of the oppressed in imitation of Jesus who was not romanticizing poverty or canonizing the poor but recognizing that their cause, no matter their morality or attractiveness, demands solidarity. See *Hope in an Age of Despair*, chapters 5 and 6.

23. See Walter Brueggemann, *The Prophetic Imagination*, 2nd ed. (Philadelphia: Fortress, 2001) [orig. 1978].

24. Walter Wink, *Engaging the Powers*, 107.

25. Actually, according to Matthew, Herod had attempted to kill Jesus immediately after his birth but the midrashic literary genre of the infancy narrative makes the historical facticity of this episode unlikely. Nevertheless, Luke does portray Herod as an opponent of John the Baptist whom he has killed and later of Jesus. Therefore, Matthew's midrashic account probably captures an historical opposition between Herod and Jesus.

26. See Pheme Perkins, "The Gospel According to John" in *NJBC* 6:115.

27. For a good, succinct description of the social world of Jesus, see Borg, *Jesus*, ch. 4, "The Shaping of Jesus: Jewish Tradition in an Imperial World."

28. This analysis relies on the theory of mimetic violence of René Girard which authors like Walter Wink have used extensively to explain the dynamics of the Passion. I subscribe to it and it forms the background and substrate of this section on Jesus as prophet, but it would take us too far afield to explore it in this volume. However, I have written at some length about it in "Whose Sins You Shall Forgive....The Holy Spirit and the Forgiveness of Sin(s) in the Fourth Gospel," *The Spirit in the New Millennium: The Duquesne University*

Annual Holy Spirit Lecture (Pittsburgh, PA: Duquesne University, 2009), 14–21, and in "The Lamb of God and the Forgiveness of Sin(s) in the Fourth Gospel," *CBQ* 73/1 (January 2011): 1–29.

For an excellent in-depth treatment of the meaning of the death of Jesus analyzed in terms of Girardian theory, see S. Mark Heim, *Saved from Sacrifice: A Theology of the Cross* (Grand Rapids, MI: Eerdmans, 2006).

29. See Borg, *Jesus*, chapter 4, for a more detailed discussion of Jesus' social world, his religious context, and his prophetic self-understanding within it.

30. It is important to remember that, as I explained at greater length in *Selling All*, especially chapters 9 and 10, "corporate" in this sense does not refer to a business model but is used in the Pauline sense of all believers being "one body" (*corpus*). The Congregation is a corporate, or organic, rather than mechanical or purely organizational reality and its mission is corporate rather than collective. All the ministries of its members are expressions of that corporate identity.

31. When I speak of Religious Life (upper case) I am speaking of the theological-spiritual reality of the vast movement throughout Christian history constituted by the total dedication of free individuals by perpetual Profession of consecrated celibacy (and eventually other vows) to God in Christ. This movement has been concretized in all kinds of individual and group developments, in Orders and Congregations, and other communities, some of which have never sought ecclesiastical approval and many of which have received such approval. When I want to talk specifically and exclusively of a particular canonically approved group insofar as it is juridically recognized I use the canonical term, "Religious Institute."

32. See *L.G.* 6, 43, 44 (Flannery, vol. 1).

33. I dealt at some length with these two forms of the life, traditionally called "contemplative" and "active," and why these descriptive terms are both inadequate to the reality and misleading today, in *Finding the Treasure*, 301–11.

34. For a brief history of the development of apostolic Religious Life of women up through the 1600s including a discussion of their history of relationship with the institutional Church, see Patricia Ranft, *Women and the Religious Life in Premodern Europe* (New York: St. Martin's, 1996), esp. 95–131.

35. Canon 590 in the revised Code was actually a quasi-repetition of the substance of Canon 499 in the 1917 Code. Interestingly

enough, there is no "track" of references in the 1917 Code that would indicate that this understanding of Religious obedience has any history in the tradition of the Fathers, older commentaries, previous law, and so on. (My thanks to Canon Lawyer Francis Morrisey, OMI, for pointing this out to me.) It needs to be remembered that the 1917 Code was an attempt (quite remarkably, but not wholly, successful) to put some order into the vast body of diverse laws known as the *Corpus Iuris Canonici*. It followed by only a few decades Vatican Council I, which reaffirmed papal primacy and defined papal infallibility, the most wide-ranging extensions of absolutist understandings of papal power in the history of the Church, and perhaps the least widely accepted conciliar provisions in modern history. This history suggests that Canon 590, especially since John Paul II whose autocratic interpretation of papal power was well-established by this time apparently exercised some personal influence to have it retained and personally assured that it would be a criterion for approval of Constitutions, should be regarded with some skepticism if not suspicion. It is certainly out of "sync" with the spirit of collegiality and the principle of subsidiarity promoted by Vatican II. The widespread resistance to it by Religious Congregations, many of whom accepted it only under threat of denial of approbation of their renewed Constitutions, i.e., under severe coercion, is a good indication that Religious in general did not and do not understand their vow this way. As John Beal says in the conclusion of his illuminating article, "Something There Is That Doesn't Love a Law: Canon Law and Its Discontents," *The Crisis of Authority in Catholic Modernity*, edited by Micahel J. Lacey and Francis Oakley (New York: Oxford University Press, 2011): "Not all of canon law's discontents can be blamed on dark outside forces or disobedient members of the church. There are internal tensions and contradictions within the law itself that the promulgation of a new code not only cannot paper over but also has inevitably exacerbated" (p. 154).

36. For a brief history of the development of papal primacy in the Western Church and what it has come to mean, see Richard P. McBrien, *The Church: The Evolution of Catholicism* (New York: HarperCollins, 2008), 98–101. To understand the extremity of the development of papal monarchy and absolutism by the eve of the Council see Michael J. Lacey, "Leo's Church and Our Own," *The Crisis of Authority in Catholic Modernity*, 57–92.

37. I discussed at some length, in *Finding the Treasure*, 257–64, the advantages to a Congregation that canonical status as a Religious

Institute offers and the disadvantages of being deprived of such status so I will not repeat that material here.

38. Laity and even bishops recognized communities as Religious before apostolic Congregations were officially accorded such canonical status in 1900. Communities such as Sisters for Christian Community (founded in 1970 and made up predominantly of former members of canonical Congregations who decided that the control exercised over Religious by the Vatican was too serious an impediment to ministerial Religious Life) today have little trouble living and ministering as Religious even though they are not officially a Religious Institute in the canonical sense of the term.

Chapter 9

1. For a good overview of the development of the vow of obedience and especially of the immediate preconciliar and postconciliar developments leading into a contemporary approach to the vow drawing on Scripture, theology, a healthy form of communion ecclesiology, and contemporary psychological theories of human development, see Judith K. Schaefer, *The Evolution of a Vow: Obedience as Decision Making in Communion*, Communicative Theology, vol. 2, ed. Bernd J. Hiberath, Bradford E. Hinze, Matthias Scharer (Berlin: LI [North American distributor: New Brunswick, NJ: Transaction Publishers], 2008), 203.

2. On Jesus' relation to the Jewish Law see John P. Meier, *A Marginal Jew: Rethinking the Historical Jesus: Law and Love* (New Haven, CT: Yale University Press, 2009).

I have dealt in some detail with this subject of Jesus' relationship to authority in *Prophets in Their Own Country: Women Religious Bearing Witness to the Gospel in a Troubled Church* (Maryknoll, NY: Orbis, 2011), ch. 4, esp. 80–97.

3. It is somewhat anachronistic to talk of "religious" and "political" spheres of authority in first century Palestine as such powers were not freestanding "institutions" but embedded functions of a theocratic society under foreign domination. But speaking of them this way simply points out that the Jewish authorities made their claims (however politically interested they might have been) in the name of religion and Pilate made his (however religiously oppressive they were) in the name of the Roman Empire.

4. Docetism is "[t]he view of some early Christians that Christ's

human nature, life, and suffering were only apparent." See *The New Dictionary of Theology*, edited by Joseph A. Komonchak, Mary Collins, Dermot A. Lane (Wilmington, DE: Michael Glazier, 1987), 291.

5. For an up-to-date, non-polemical, pastorally sensitive, and theologically sophisticated treatment of conscience, see Linda Hogan, *Confronting the Truth: Conscience in the Catholic Tradition* (New York/Mahwah, NJ: Paulist, 2001), especially, for our purposes, chapter 6, "Living with Contradictions: Disagreement and Dialogue in the Church."

An excellent treatment of conscience, its nature as process, its exercise in community, and its relationship to authority is Anne E. Patrick, *Liberating Conscience: Feminist Explorations in Catholic Moral Theology* (New York: Continuum, 1996). This is a particularly good resource for Religious because of its balanced appropriation of the contributions of feminist and liberationist learnings and because it pays particular attention to the struggles of women Religious with the Vatican since the Council.

6. On this subject of conscience Richard McBrien offers a short but clear summary of Church teaching in relation to theology against a brief background treatment of the relevant biblical material in *Catholicism*, rev. ed. (New York: HarperCollins, 1994), 968–80.

For a good historical treatment of the development of the theology of conscience, from the patristic through the medieval and modern periods and Vatican II, see Hogan, *Confronting the Truth*, chs. 2–4.

The most important postconciliar Church document treating conscience is the 1993 encyclical by John Paul II, *Veritatis Splendor*. See the excellent treatment of this document, both its strengths and its very significant weaknesses, by A. E. Patrick, *Liberating Conscience*, 145–69.

7. See Dorothee Soëlle, *Beyond Mere Obedience*, trans. by Lawrence W. Denef (New York: Pilgrim, 1982 [German orig. 1968]), esp. ch. 2, 7–10. Soëlle points out that this formation in blind obedience was a direct and powerful contributor to the disastrous triumph of Nazi fascism in Germany.

8. *Dignitatis Humanae* 2–8 (Flannery, vol. 1). The primary object of the affirmation of freedom of conscience by the Council was, in fact, the freedom to follow one's conscience in regard to religious affiliation that, for centuries, had been denied by the Church on the grounds that choice of any religion other than Catholic Christianity was the exercise of an erroneous conscience and "error had no

rights." But the principle of freedom of conscience, once affirmed, clearly applies also to other exercises of this freedom.

9. See *G.S.* 16 citing Rom 2:15–16 (Flannery, vol. 1).

10. Paul VI, *H.V.*, July 25, 1968 (Flannery, vol. 2).

11. Michael Dummett recently published an article in *Commonweal* 138/3 (February 11, 2011) entitled "Indefensible: Moral Teaching After 'Humanae Vitae'" in which he argues that the prohibition of use of "the pill" has created an anomaly in Catholic moral teaching that resists resolution.

12. Interestingly, Joseph Ratzinger (later Pope Benedict XVI) wrote in the *Commentary on the Documents of Vatican II*, ed. H. Vorgrimler, vol. 5 (New York: Herder and Herder, 1967), 134: "Over the pope as expression of the binding claim of ecclesiastical authority, there stands one's own conscience which must be obeyed before all else, even if necessary against the requirement of ecclesiastical authority. This emphasis on the individual, whose conscience confronts him with a supreme and ultimate tribunal, and one which in the last resort is beyond the claim of external social groups, even the official church, also establishes a principle in opposition to increasing totalitarianism."

13. By way of example, as Anne Patrick, in *Liberating Conscience*, p. 161, says, "The most serious limitation of this encyclical [*Veritatis Splendor*] that would celebrate 'The Splendor of Truth' is a theological one. Repeatedly the document conflates the transcendent Truth associated with the Deity with the pronouncements of the hierarchical magisterium."

14. Denis Edwards, *How God Acts: Creation, Redemption, and Special Divine Action* (Minneapolis, MN: Fortress, 2010).

15. See *G.S.* 4–10 (Flannery, vol. 1).

16. Pope John XXIII's, encyclical *Pacem in Terris* (Peace on Earth) was published on April 11, 1963. It is available in English as *Pacem in terris. Peace on Earth; Encyclical Letter of His Holiness Pope John XXIII*, ed. William J. Gibbons (New York: Paulist Press, 1963).

17. In A. E. Patrick's, *Liberating Conscience*, chapter 1 is an excellent treatment of the community as necessary context and interlocutor in valid discernment.

18. *G.S.* 16 (Flannery, vol. 1).

19. *D.V.* 21 (Flannery, vol. 1).

20. Jerome Baggett, *Sense of the Faithful: How Americans Live Their Faith* (New York: Oxford University Press, 2008).

21. The papal bull *Periculoso* was published by Boniface VIII in 1298 imposing papal enclosure on all women Religious in perpetuity.

22. For a fascinating history of women in monastic life in the Middle Ages, in which their self-determination despite ecclesiastical domination is well highlighted, see *Crown and Veil: Female Monasticism from the Fifth to the Fifteenth Centuries*, ed. Jeffrey F. Hamburger and Susan Marti (New York: Columbia University Press, 2008 [orig. German 2005]).

23. The replacement of Cardinal Rodé who initiated the investigation with Archbishop João Bráz de Aviz as Prefect of CICLSAL and Archbishop Joseph Tobin, CSsR, as Secretary changed this situation qualitatively. Neither of these men pretended that the Apostolic Visitation was justified in the first place and both have recognized publicly the harm to relationships between the Vatican and women Religious that resulted from both the fact and the mode of the Visitation.

24. I have described and analyzed this unfortunate episode in recent Church history in *Prophets in Their Own Country*, especially in the "Introduction," 1–27.

25. For a fuller treatment of this case, specifically concerning the maturation of women Religious in regard to moral decision making, see Lora Ann Quiñonez, CDP, and Mary Daniel Turner, SNDdeN, *The Transformation of American Catholic Sisters* (Philadelphia, PA: Temple University Press, 1992), 133–40.

A. E. Patrick in *Liberating Conscience*, 118ff., explores this incident specifically from the standpoint of conscience and of the differential treatment of lay and Religious in this case.

26. This paper is available as "Anne E. Patrick, SNJM, 'The Moral Decision-Maker: From Good Sisters to Prophetic Women,'" *Records of the Leadership Conference of Women Religious*, 1985, CLCW 79/20, Archives of the University of Notre Dame.

27. This paper is available as "Margeret Farley, RSM, 'From Moral Insight to Moral Choice: Discernment and Decision-making in the Christian Community,'" *Records of the Leadership Conference of Women Religious*, 1985, CLCW 79/20, Archives of the University of Notre Dame.

28. Church authority, in giving approval to the foundation of a Religious Institute and its Constitutions, recognizes the mission it has received through its founder(s) and the Institute is responsible to preserve and persevere in this mission (see Canons 578 and 587.1). However, as is abundantly clear from the developments in the mis-

sion and ministry of Religious Institutes in the wake of Vatican II, how such mission and ministry are understood and lived in various times and places has varied widely.

29. Historically, there have been all kinds of over-stepping of appropriate boundaries of Religious Congregations by the hierarchy and lower clergy. But this has been due to the assumption of unbounded authority of the ordained over everyone in the Church and the fact that Religious often had no idea that they had rights in relation to Church authorities. So abusive practice in the past is no argument for its continuation.

30. See Canon 679, in which the stringently restrictive conditions for such expulsion are specified.

31. As John Meier says in *NJBC* 78:14: "Jesus was addressed honorifically as 'Rabbi' but the title in pre–AD 70 Judaism was more loosely used than later on." It was an honorific used for charismatic leaders, e.g., for John the Baptist in John 3:26.

32. See *CCL* (1983), 678.

33. Religious Congregations cannot operate institutional ministries (e.g., Catholic schools, etc.) in a diocese in the name of the Institute without the authorization of the diocesan bishop. However, once established, such ministries are much easier to keep under the control of the Religious Congregation than is the ministry of an individual Religious working in a diocesan ministry such as a parish or the chancery office.

34. I highly recommend the volume edited by Michael J. Lacey and Francis Oakley, *The Crisis of Authority in Catholic Modernity* (New York: Oxford University Press, 2011), especially "Prologue: The Problem of Authority and Its Limits" by Francis Oakley; "Something There Is That Doesn't Love a Law: Canon Law and Its Discontents," by John Beal; "Magisterial Authority," by Charles Taylor; "American Catholics and Church Authority," by William V. D'Antonio, James D. Davidson, Dean R. Hoge, and Mary L. Gautier. The essay by Leslie Woodcock Tentler, "Souls and Bodies: The Birth Control Controversy and the Collapse of Confession" deals specifically with this issue. These articles and others in the volume deal with the impasse between a premodern conception of authority and the nonacceptance of that conception by modern Catholics.

Chapter 10

1. Although Canon 590, 2, claims that Religious, by virtue of the vow of obedience, are subject to the pope as their highest superior, there are very good reasons, which I have discussed several times in preceding chapters and will not repeat here, to question the theological coherence, if not the validity, of this claim. The massive coercion applied to force the inclusion of this Canon's content in revised Constitutions, by itself, raises moral as well as theological questions. But in any case, this imposition of a meaning not intended by the founders nor by generations of Religious making vows to God according to the Constitutions of their Institutes would seem to be a *de facto* violation of the appropriate self-determination of the Congregation and deforms the understanding of the vow and the intention in making it of generations of Religious. In my opinion, no matter what legal weight it may have, it cannot be used as any kind of basis for theological reasoning about the meaning of the vow of obedience or the spirituality of obedience in the life of Religious. Slavery was perfectly legal, and even declared moral by the Church, for centuries. And the Church, in the name of God, helped enforce it. But that did not make it theologically or morally valid. Bad laws do not become good because they are "on the books" or because there exists a power capable of enforcing them.

2. For a fascinating, scholarly treatment of medieval female Religious Life and the effects, both fruitful and restrictive, of the fact that all female Religious were cloistered (which I will be suggesting was a major factor in the development of the theology of obedience), see *Crown and Veil: Female Monasticism from the Fifth to the Fifteenth Centuries*, ed. Jeffrey F. Hamburger and Susan Marti, trans. Dietlinde Hamburger (New York: Columbia University Press, 2008 [orig. in German 2005]).

3. Charles Taylor in his Templeton Prize—winning study, *A Secular Age* (Cambridge, MA: Harvard University Press, 2007), traces and analyzes, in extraordinary breadth and depth, the passage of western humanity from the "enchanted universe" of premodernity into the secularized universe of the modern world giving way to the postmodern. I cannot adumbrate in a few pages this 900-page exploration, but the mere scope of his work suggests how profound the shift from the medieval to the modern worldview has been. I am suggesting here that this shift is precisely what underlies the evolution (or revolution)

in the understanding of Religious obedience through which contemporary Religious are living.

4. For a good sense of the ethos, style, major concerns, and theological-spiritual perspectives on Religious Life of these types of Congregations, see *The Foundations of Religious Life: Revisiting the Vision* by members of the Council of Major Superiors of Women Religious (Notre Dame, IN: Ave Maria Press, 2009). Authors of the individual essays are leaders of this group. Justin Rigali, former cardinal archbishop of Philadelphia, provides the forward, and George Weigel, Charles Chaput, and Alice Von Hildebrand provide endorsements.

5. See the substantive and nuanced discussion of the difference between a patriarchal model of obedience and an egalitarian model in Anne E. Patrick, *Liberating Conscience: Feminist Explorations in Catholic Moral Theology* (New York: Continuum, 1996), especially chapter 3, which contrasts the two models, and chapter 4, where she applies the contrast to the analysis of recent episodes of conflict between Catholics and the magisterium.

For an excellent explanation of the fundamentally hierarchical understanding of the Church, which was basic to the understanding of the Religious Congregation, in which an ontological difference between ordained and lay is believed to ground an unalterable inequality and necessary control and command structure, and which underlies the revised (1983) *Code of Canon Law* as it did the earlier Code, see John P. Beal, "Something There Is That Doesn't Love a Law: Canon Law and Its Discontents," *The Crisis of Authority in Catholic Modernity*, ed. Michael J. Lacey and Francis Oakley (New York: Oxford University Press, 2011), 135–61.

6. See John W. O'Malley, *What Happened at Vatican II* (Cambridge, MA/London: Harvard University Press, 2008) for an excellent analysis of the effect of Vatican II on the Church. The "Introduction" is particularly succinct and clear in describing the major currents that run through all of the Council's work.

7. See A. E. Patrick, *Liberating Conscience*, for an account of the rapid development of the Catholic conscience in the wake of the Council.

8. For a succinct summary of what is meant theologically by discernment as part of the virtue of prudence, see Richard P. McBrien, *Catholicism*, rev. ed. (New York: HarperCollins, 1994), 975–77, including the bibliographic references.

9. A. E. Patrick in *Liberating Conscience* devotes her first chapter to "Conscience and Community."

10. For an illuminating documentation and analysis of some of the more dramatic confrontations between the United States hierarchy/the Vatican on the one hand and theologians and women Religious on the other hand, see A. E. Patrick, *Liberating Conscience*, esp. ch. 4, "Contested Authority: The Cases of Charles Curran and the Vatican 24," 102–33. This entire book is a much more detailed treatment than I can give here of the issues of conscience, discernment, and obedience and could profitably be studied by all Religious in relation to the vow of obedience.

11. A major study of this recently recognized stage of the life cycle is *On the Frontier of Adulthood: Theory, Research, and Public Policy* [John D. and Catherine T. MacArthur Foundation Series on Mental Health and Development], edited by Richard A. Settersten (Chicago: University of Chicago Press, 2008).

12. See Mary Catherine Bateson, *Composing a Further Life: The Age of Active Wisdom* (New York: Random House, 2010); Sara Lawrence-Lightfoot, *The Third Chapter: Passion, Risk, and Adventure in the 25 Years After 50* (New York: Farrar, Straus and Giroux, 2009); Betty Friedan, *The Fountain of Age* (New York: Simon & Schuster, 1993) for a variety of approaches to what is being called a new stage of the life cycle.

13. In this section I am discussing first world experience. Maturation patterns as well as life cycle experience is quite different in some other cultures.

14. It is helpful to remember, however, that many founders of Religious Orders, male and female, took up Religious Life after having raised a family, been widowed or abandoned, or exercised a public career. The pattern of eighteen-year-olds entering right from the primary family context is not normative even though it has been the most common pattern in the first world for several decades.

15. The census statistics are extremely interesting. American women who were fifty-five years of age in 2007 had a typical life expectancy of eighty-three; those seventy-five could expect to live to eighty-seven; those eighty were expected to live to eighty-nine.

In 2010, 76,504,000 Americans were fifty-five years old or older (24.7 percent of the total population) and by 2020 that number is projected to be 97,807,000 (28.6 percent).

The median age of Americans in 2010 was 36.9 and by 2020 is predicted to be 37.7. In other words, about half the population is under and half over forty.

But the percentage of Americans between eighteen and twenty-four, which is the "traditional" age of entrance into Religious Life, is about 9 percent, whereas the percentage of the population over fifty-five years of age is roughly 25 percent.

These statistics suggest that the vast majority of Religious today are in roughly the same age bracket as the majority of Americans. This raises questions not only about desirable age of entrance, but also about the age of people to whom ministry needs to be directed, the kinds of ministry needed, etc. A twenty-three-year-old teaching seventy third-graders with fifty more on the waiting list might have made the recruitment of large groups of people in their twenties eminently reasonable and the teacher well-qualified for her ministry. It might not make much sense today when three-fourths of the population is out of high school and people in their twenties are not generally professionally or psychologically likely to be capable of ministering to their elders.

16. Charles Taylor, in a short but profound essay, "Magisterial Authority," in *The Crisis of Authority in Catholic Modernity*, 259–69, suggests that this is as true of the pope as of others in the Church and that when hierarchs fail to recognize and observe their limits they do not increase their power or authority but undermine it.

17. Pierre Teilhard de Chardin, *The Divine Milieu*, Perennial Classics Edition (New York: HarperCollins, 2001). See especially "The Passivities of Diminishment," 46–62.

Conclusion

1. See my treatment of one extreme example of this pressure, the 2009 Apostolic Visitation of U.S. Women Religious, in *Prophets in Their Own Country: Women Religious Bearing Witness to the Gospel in a Troubled Church* (Maryknoll, NY: Orbis, 2011) for a fuller treatment.

2. Actually, the text says "Kingdom (or "reign": βασιλεία) of the heavens." "Heaven" is a Matthean euphemism to avoid use of the divine name. But since I avoid, when possible, patriarchal language, and the meaning is the same, I prefer to use "Reign of God."

3. See John W. O'Malley, "Conclusion," in *What Happened at Vatican II* (Cambridge, MA: Harvard University Press, 2008), esp. 298–313.

4. For a good overview of the persons, writings, and concerns of this period during which the conciliar reform was germinating, see Jürgen Mettepenningen, "Yves Congar and the 'Monster' of Nouvelle Théologie," *Horizons* 37 (Spring 2010): 52–71.

5. "Dominus Jesus," the Declaration of the Congregation for the Doctrine of the Faith "On the Unicity and Salvific Universality of Jesus Christ and the Church," undoubtedly authored by its then-prefect, Cardinal Joseph Ratzinger (later Pope Benedict XVI), was promulgated on August 6, 2000. Within the context of recognition that the Council had modified somewhat the kind of "outside the Church no salvation" ecclesiology and soteriology of preconciliar times, it reiterates the substance of the previous rejection of any kind of religious pluralism that would assign real salvific significance to non-Christian religions. The document was, and remains, a locus of contention for theologians of religions.

6. The treatment of Religious Life in *Lumen Gentium* VI is more adequate than that in *Perfectae Caritatis* in trying to articulate how Religious Life and its members are integrated into the Church. It tried to both elevate Religious Life as "special" in the Church without contradicting what it had already said about the role and dignity of the laity; to deny hierarchical status to Religious and assert the hierarchy's rights in regulating the life without denying that the life enjoys a genuine autonomy, and so on. In places it seems to grasp what the life should mean to and for the Church at large, but the framers of the document were divided about whether there should be a separate chapter on Religious when there were already chapters on laity and hierarchy. (In other words, was there anything distinctive to say about Religious Life?) The conservative minority at the Council probably had a disproportionate role in the synthesis. In general, the treatment of Religious Life by the Council was deficient at best and, in my judgment, more theoretical mileage and practical wisdom concerning Religious Life is gained by working with the context provided by the Council in its treatment of the Church, the relation of the Church to the World, freedom of conscience, and relations with "the others" (Christian sister-Churches and non-Christians) than by attempting to derive a coherent theology of Religious Life from *LG* VI and/or *PC*. A very good contextual presentation of the Council's treatment of Religious Life is Maryanne Confoy, *Religious Life and Priesthood: Perfectae Caritatis, Optatam Totius, Presbyterorum Ordinis,* Rediscovering Vatican II, ed. Christopher M. Bellitto (New York/Mahwah, NJ: Paulist, 2008), Section III on Religious Life.

7. An excellent historical study of how the basically communitarian ecclesiology which characterized the first millennium of Church history was gradually repressed in the Church in favor of an increasingly absolutist monarchical ecclesiology until the former was almost

obliterated in the Conciliarist controversy that followed the Great Schism is provided by Francis Oakley, "History of the Return of the Repressed in Catholic Modernity: The Dilemma Posed by Constance," *The Crisis of Authority in Catholic Modernity*, ed. Michael J. Lacey and Francis Oakley (New York: Oxford University Press, 2011), 29–56. The four centuries that followed the Protestant Reformation, from Trent to Vatican I, saw a constant effort to canonize the theory of an absolute divine right monarchy as the sole legitimate form of ecclesiastical government. The effort seemed to have been successful in the definitions of papal primacy and infallibility, but the historical and theological effort revived at Vatican II has again called for a reevaluation of the question. The tension between chapters 2 and 3 of *Lumen Gentium* show that the issue is still very much alive.

8. See Oakley, "History and the Return of the Repressed," 42–43.

9. This is a major reason that many, if not most, Religious Congregations strongly resisted the move by John Paul II through the reinsertion in the revised Code of Canon Law (1983) [Canon 590, 2] to "monarchize" their vow of obedience by unilaterally redefining the nature of their vow as including in its object obedience to the pope as their highest superior thus making the pope, by *fiat*, the highest superior of every Religious Congregation. There is no historical or theological basis for this understanding of Religious obedience as such and it is certainly not what founders intended or Religious have understood by the their vow, even back as far as the Rule of St. Benedict in the sixth century. If the vow, by its nature, included the acceptance of the pope as the highest superior in the Congregation and of every individual Religious the Jesuits would not, indeed could not, have created a fourth vow of obedience to the pope, nor could they have limited that vow to matters of mission. The question this anomaly raises is, "What options does a person or group have, when it is forced by the threat of "ecclesiastical capital punishment" (in this case, non-approval of their Constitutions) to act contrary to what they know to be the truth?" This parallel in ecclesiology to Galileo's dilemma in astronomy is striking, and illuminating.

10. See *Prophets in Their Own Country: Women Religious Bearing Witness to the Gospel in Troubled Church* (Maryknoll, NY: Orbis, 2011), esp. ch. 4.

11. We need only remember the suppression of the IHM Congregation of Los Angeles, the protracted struggle over the signing of the *New York Times* advertisement on abortion by "the twenty-four," the Agnes Mary Mansour conflict, and so on.

Works Cited

Abbo, John A., and Jerome D. Hannon. *The Sacred Canons: A Concise Presentation of the Current Disciplinary Norms of the Catholic Church (In Paraphrase)*. St. Louis: Herder, 1951.

Alison, James. *The Joy of Being Wrong: Original Sin Through Easter Eyes*. New York: Crossroad, 1998.

——. *Knowing Jesus*. London: SPCK, 1998.

——. *Raising Abel: The Recovery of the Eschatological Imagination*. New York: Crossroad, 1996.

Arendt, Hannah. *Eichmann in Jerusalem: A Report on the Banality of Evil*. New York: Penguin Books, 1964.

——. *The Human Condition*. Chicago/London: University of Chicago Press, 1958.

Augustine of Hippo. *Confessions: Books I–XIII*. Rev. ed. Translated by F. J. Sheed. With an Introduction by Peter Brown. Indianapolis: Hackett, 1993.

Baggett, Jerome. *Sense of the Faithful: How Americans Live Their Faith*. New York: Oxford University Press, 2008.

Bailie, Gil. *Violence Unveiled: Humanity at the Crossroads*. New York: Crossroad, 1995.

Barbour, Ian. *Religion and Science: Historical and Contemporary Issues*. San Francisco: HarperSanFrancisco, 1997.

Barnhart, Bruno. *The One Light: Bede Griffiths' Principal Writings*. Springfield, IL: Templegate, 2001.

Bateson, Mary Catherine. *Composing a Further Life: The Age of Active Wisdom*. New York: Random House, 2010.

Beal, John P., James A. Coriden, and Thomas J. Green, eds. *New Commentary on the Code of Canon Law*. New York/Mahwah, NJ: Paulist Press, 2000.

Becker, Jillian. "Simone Weil: A Saint for Our Time." *The New Criterion* 20, no. 7 (March 2002), 15–23.

Beier, Matthias. *A Violent God-Image: An Introduction to the Work of Eugen Drewermann*. New York: Continuum, 2004.

Bergant, Diane. "Wisdom Reading Guide." In *The Catholic Study Bible*, 276–82. New York/Oxford: Oxford University Press, 1990.

Berling, Judith. *Understanding Other Religious Worlds: A Guide for Interreligious Education.* Maryknoll, NY: Orbis, 2004.

Borg, Marcus. *Uncovering the Life, Teachings, and Relevance of a Religious Revolutionary.* San Francisco: HarperSanFrancisco, 2006.

———. *The Heart of Christianity: Rediscovering a Life of Faith.* San Francisco: HarperSanFrancisco, 2003.

———. *Meeting Jesus Again for the First Time: The Historical Jesus and the Heart of Contemporary Faith.* San Francisco: HarperSanFrancisco, 1994.

Boyarin, Daniel. "The Gospel of the Memra: Jewish Binitarianism and the Prologue to John." *Harvard Theological Review* 94, no. 3 (July 2001): 243–84.

Bracken, Joseph. *The One in the Many: A Contemporary Reconstruction of the God-World Relationship.* Grand Rapids, MI: William B. Eerdmans, 2001.

———. *Society and Spirit: A Trinitarian Cosmology.* Selinsgrove, PA: Susquehanna University Press, 1991.

Briggs, Kenneth. *Double Crossed: Uncovering the Catholic Church's Betrayal of American Nuns.* New York: Doubleday, 2006.

Brown, Raymond E. *The Birth of the Messiah: A Commentary on the Infancy Narratives in the Gospels of Matthew and Luke.* New York: Doubleday, 1979.

———. *The Community of the Beloved Disciple.* New York: Paulist Press, 1979.

Brown, Raymond E., Karl P. Donfried, Joseph A. Fitzmyer, and John Reumann, eds. *Mary in the New Testament: A Collaborative Assessment by Protestant and Roman Catholic Scholars.* Philadelphia: Fortress, 1978.

Brueggemann, Walter. *The Prophetic Imagination.* Philadelphia: Fortress, 1978.

Buckley, Michael J. *Papal Primacy and the Episcopate: Towards a Relational Understanding.* New York: Crossroad, 1998.

Buechner, Frederick. *Wishful Thinking: A Theological ABC.* New York: Harper and Row, 1973.

Burton-Christie, Douglas. *The Word in the Desert: Scripture and the Quest for Holiness in Early Christian Monasticism.* New York: Oxford University Press, 1993.

Cada, Lawrence, et al. *Shaping the Coming Age of Religious Life.* New York: Seabury, 1979.

Caspary, Anita M. *Witness to Integrity: The Crisis of the Immaculate Heart Community of California.* Collegeville, MN: Liturgical Press, 2003.

Catechism of the Catholic Church. Collegeville, MN: Liturgical Press, 1994.

Catholic Church. *Code of Canon Law, Latin-English Edition: Translation.* Washington, DC: Canon Law Society of America, 1983.

Cavadini, John C., and Laura Holt, eds. *Who Do You Say That I Am? Confessing the Mystery of Christ.* Notre Dame, IN: University of Notre Dame Press, 2004.

Chittister, Joan. "If They Really Mean It, It's About Time." *National Catholic Reporter* 45, no. 10 (March 2009): 15–20.

———. *In the Heart of the Temple: My Spiritual Vision for Today's World.* Erie, PA: Benetvision, 2004.

Clark, D. J. "The Word *Kosmos* 'World' in John 17." *Practical Papers for the Bible Translator* 50 (1999): 401–6.

Collins, Adela Yarbro, ed. *Feminist Perspectives on Biblical Scholarship.* Chico, CA: Scholars, 1985.

Coloe, Mary. *Dwelling in the Household of God: Johannine Ecclesiology and Spirituality.* Collegeville, MN: Liturgical Press, 2007.

———. *God Dwells With Us: Temple Symbolism in the Fourth Gospel.* Collegeville, MN: Liturgical Press, 2001.

Confoy, Maryanne. *Religious Life and Priesthood: Perfectae Caritatis, Optatam Totius, Presbyterorum Ordinis.* Rediscovering Vatican II. New York/Mahwah, NJ: Paulist Press, 2008.

Congar, Yves. *Vraie et fausse réforme dans l'église.* Paris: Du Cerf, 1968. Translated with Introduction by Paul Philibert under the title *True and False Reform in the Church* (Collegeville, MN: Liturgical Press, 2011).

———. *Jalons pour une théologie du laïcat.* Paris: Éditions du Cerf, 1953. Translated by Donald Attwater under the title *Lay People in the Church: A Study for a Theology of the Laity* (Westminster: Newman, 1965).

Cotel, Peter. *A Catechism of the Vows for the Use of Religious.* Westminster, MD: Newman, 1962.

Council of Major Superiors of Women Religious. *The Foundations of Religious Life: Revisiting the Vision.* Notre Dame, IN: Ave Maria Press, 2009.

Cowell, Siôn. *The Teilhard Lexicon: Understanding the Language, Terminology and Vision of the Writings of Pierre Teilhard de Chardin—The First English-Language Dictionary of His Writings.* Brighton, UK/Portland, OR: Sussex Academic Press, 2001.

Cozzens, Donald. *Sacred Silence: Denial and the Crisis in the Church.* Collegeville, MN: Liturgical Press, 2002.

Creasy, William C. *The Imitation of Christ: A New Reading of the 1441 Latin Autograph Manuscript.* Macon, GA: Mercer University Press, 1989.

Davis, Stephen T., Daniel Kendall, and Gerald O'Collins. *The Resurrection: An Interdisciplinary Symposium on the Resurrection of Jesus.* New York: Oxford University Press, 1997.

Dawkins, Richard. *The God Hypothesis.* London: Bantam, 2006.

Donahue, John R. *What Does the Lord Require? A Bibliographical Essay on the Bible and Social Justice.* St. Louis: Institute of Jesuit Sources, 2000.

———. "Two Decades of Research on the Rich and the Poor in Luke-Acts." In *Justice and the Holy: Essays in Honor of Walter Harrelson,* edited by Douglas A. Knight and Peter J. Paris, 129–44. Atlanta, GA: Scholars Press, 1989.

———. *The Gospel in Parable: Metaphor, Narrative, and Theology in the Synoptic Gospels.* Philadelphia: Fortress, 1988.

Dreyer, Elizabeth A. "Jesus as Bridegroom and Lover: A Critical Retrieval of a Medieval Metaphor." In *Who Do You Say That I Am?: Confessing the Mystery of Christ,* edited by John C. Cavadini and Laura Holt, 207–35. Notre Dame, IN: University of Notre Dame Press, 2004.

DuBoulay, Shirley. *Beyond the Darkness: A Biography of Bede Griffiths.* New York: Doubleday, 1998.

Dulles, Avery. *Models of the Church.* New York: Doubleday, 1974.

Dummett, Michael. "Indefensible: Moral Teaching After 'Humanae Vitae.'" *Commonweal* 138, no. 3 (February 11, 2011): 15–17.

Dunn, James D. G. *Christology in the Making: A New Testament Inquiry into the Origins of the Doctrine of the Incarnation.* Philadelphia: Westminster, 1980.

Dupuis, Jacques. *Toward a Christian Theology of Religious Pluralism.* Maryknoll, NY: Orbis, 1997.

Eckhart, Meister. *Meister Eckhart: The Essential Sermons, Commentaries, Treatises, and Defense.* Edited by Edmund Colledge and Bernard McGinn. New York/Ramsey, NJ/Toronto: Paulist Press, 1981.

Edinger, Edward F. *Ego and Archetype: Individuation and the Religious Function of the Psyche.* Boston/London: Shambala, 1992.

Edwards, Denis. *How God Acts: Creation, Redemption, and Special Divine Action.* Minneapolis: Fortress, 2010.

———. *Jesus the Wisdom of God: An Ecological Theology.* Maryknoll, NY: Orbis, 1995.

Endres, John C., and Elizabeth Liebert. *A Retreat with the Psalms: Resources for Personal and Communal Prayer.* New York/Mahwah, NJ: Paulist Press, 2001.

Farley, Margaret A. *Commitments: Beginning, Keeping, Changing.* San Francisco: Harper and Row, 1990.

———. "From Moral Insight to Moral Choice: Discernment and Decision-Making in the Christian Community." *CLCW* 79, no. 20. *Records of the Leadership Conference of Women Religious,* 1985. University of Notre Dame Archives.

Fiensy, D. "Leaders of Mass Movements and the Leader of the Jesus Movement." *Journal for the Study of the New Testament* 74 (1999): 3–27.

FitzGerald, Constance. "The Desire for God and the Transformative Power of Contemplation." In *Light Burdens, Heavy Blessings: Challenges of Church and Culture in the Post Vatican II Era: Essays in Honor of Margaret R Brennan, IHM,* edited by Margaret R. Brennan, Mary Heather MacKinnon, Moni McIntyre, and Mary Ellen Sheehan, 201–22. Quincy, IL: Franciscan, 2000.

Fitzmyer, Joseph A. "Pauline Theology." In *The New Jerome Biblical Commentary,* edited by R. E. Brown, J. A. Fitzmyer, R. E. Murphy, 1382–1416. Englewood Cliffs, NJ: Prentice Hall, 1990.

Flannery, Austin, ed. *Vatican Council II: The Conciliar and Post Conciliar Documents.* Vol. 1 of Vatican Collection. Rev. ed. Grand Rapids, MI: Eerdmans, 1988.

———. *More Post Conciliar Documents.* Vol. 2 of Vatican Collection. Northport, NY: Costello, 1982.

Fox, Matthew. *Creation Spirituality: Liberating Gifts for the Peoples of the Earth.* San Francisco: Harper San Francisco, 1991.

———. *Whee! We, Wee All the Way Home: A Guide to Sensual, Prophetic Spirituality.* Santa Fe, NM: Bear, 1981.

———. *Western Spirituality: Historical Roots, Ecumenical Routes.* Notre Dame, IN: Fides/Claretian, 1979.

———. *On Becoming a Musical Mystical Bear: Spirituality American Style.* New York: Paulist Press, 1976.

Friedan, Betty. *The Fountain of Age.* New York: Simon & Schuster, 1993.

Friedrich-Silver, Ilana. *Virtuosity, Charisma, and Social Order: A Comparative Sociological Study of Monasticism in Theravada Buddhism and Medieval Catholicism.* Cambridge: Cambridge University Press, 1995.

Fry, Timothy. *The Rule of Saint Benedict in Latin and English with Notes: RB 1980.* Collegeville, MN: Liturgical Press, 1981.

Geertz, Clifford. "Religion as a Cultural System." In *The Interpretation of Cultures: Selected Essays by Clifford Geertz*, 87–125. New York: Basic Books, 1973.

Gelin, Albert. *The Poor of Yahweh*. Collegeville, MN: Liturgical Press, 1964.

George, Augustine. "Poverty in the Old Testament." In *Gospel Poverty: Essays in Biblical Theology*, translated by Michael Guinan, 3–24. Chicago: Franciscan Herald Press, 1977.

Gil Arbiol, Carlos J. "Overvaluing the Stigma: An Example of Self-Stigmatization in the Jesus Movement." *Biblical Theology Bulletin* 34, no. 4 (2004): 161–66.

Gingerich, Owen. *God's Universe*. Cambridge, MA: Harvard University Press, 2006.

Girard, René. *Things Hidden from the Foundation of the World*. Translated by Stephen Bann and Michael Meteer. Stanford, CA: Stanford University Press, 1987.

Goffman, Erving. "The Characteristics of Total Institutions." In *A Sociological Reader on Complex Organizations*, edited by Amitai Etzioni and Edward Lehman, 312–40. New York: Holt, Rinehart and Winston, 1980.

Green, Barbara. *Mindful*. Charleston, SC: Booksurge, 2008.

———. "The Wisdom of Solomon and the Solomon of Wisdom: Tradition's Transpositions and Human Transformation." *Horizons* 30, no. 1 (2003): 41–66.

Guijarro, Santiago. "The Family in the Jesus Movement." *Biblical Theology Bulletin* 34, no.3 (2004): 114–21.

Guinan, Michael. *To Be Human Before God: Insights from Biblical Spirituality*. Collegeville, MN: Liturgical Press, 1994.

———. *Gospel Poverty: Witness to the Risen Christ: A Study in Biblical Spirituality*. New York: Paulist Press, 1981.

Haight, Roger. *Jesus, Symbol of God*. Maryknoll, NY: Orbis, 1999.

Hamburger, Jeffrey F., and Susan Marti. *Crown and Veil: Female Monasticism from the Fifth to the Fifteenth Centuries*. New York: Columbia University Press, 2008.

Hammerton-Kelly, Robert. *Sacred Violence: Paul's Hermeneutic of the Cross*. Minneapolis: Fortress, 1992.

Hart, Ray L. *Unfinished Man and the Imagination: Toward an Ontology and a Rhetoric of Revelation*. New York: Seabury, 1979.

Heim, S. Mark. *Saved from Sacrifice: A Theology of the Cross*. Grand Rapids, MI: Eerdmans, 2006.

Hessel, Dieter T., and Rosemary Radford Ruether. *Christianity and Ecology: Seeking the Well-Being of Earth and Humans.* Cambridge, MA: Harvard University Press, 2000.

Hilkert, Mary Catherine. *Naming Grace: Preaching and the Sacramental Imagination.* New York: Continuum, 1997.

Hock, Ronald F. "The Parable of the Foolish Rich Man (Luke 12:16–20) and Graeco-Roman Conventions of Thought and Behaviour." In *Early Christianity and Classical Culture: Comparative Studies in Honor of Abraham J. Malherbe,* edited by John T. Fitzgerald, Thomas H. Olbricht, and L. Michael White, 181–96. Leiden/Boston: Brill, 2003.

Hoffman, Dominic M. *The Life Within: The Prayer of Union.* New York: Sheed and Ward, 1966.

Hogan, Linda. *Confronting the Truth: Conscience in the Catholic Tradition.* New York/Mahwah, NJ: Paulist Press, 2001.

Hyde, Lewis. *The Gift: Imagination and the Erotic Life of Property.* New York: Random House, 1983.

John of the Cross. *The Ascent of Mount Carmel.* In *The Collected Works of Saint John of the Cross.* Rev. ed. Translated by Kieran Kavanaugh and Otilio Rodriguez. Introductions by Kieran Kavanaugh. Washington, DC: Institute of Carmelite Studies, 1991.

John Paul II, Pope. "*Ut Unum Sint.*" *Origins* 25, no. 4 (June 8, 1995): 49–72.

Johnson, Elizabeth A. "The Cosmos: An Astonishing Image of God." *Origins* 26 (September 13, 1996): 206–12. Also published as "Turn to the Heavens and the Earth: Retrieval of the Cosmos in Theology," *Proceedings of the Catholic Theological Society of America* 51 (1996): 1–14.

———. *Women, Earth, and Creator Spirit.* Madeleva Lecture in Spirituality, 1993. New York/ Mahwah, NJ: Paulist Press, 1993.

———. *She Who Is: The Mystery of God in Feminist Theological Discourse.* New York: Crossroad, 1992.

Karris, Robert J. "The Gospel According to Luke." In *The New Jerome Biblical Commentary,* edited by R. E. Brown, J. A. Fitzmyer, and R. E. Murphy, 675–721. Englewood Cliffs, NJ: Prentice Hall, 1990.

Kaufman, Gordon. *The Theological Imagination: Constructing the Concept of God.* Philadelphia: Westminster, 1981.

———. *An Essay in Theological Method.* Missoula, MT: Scholars, 1975.

Kavanaugh, John F. *Following Christ in a Consumer Society: The Spirituality of Cultural Resistance.* Maryknoll, NY: Orbis, 2006.

Kittel, Phyllis M. *Staying in the Fire: A Sisterhood Responds to Vatican II.* Boulder, CO: Woven Word Press, 2009.

Knitter, Paul. *Introducing Theologies of Religions.* Maryknoll, NY: Orbis, 2002.

Komonchak, Joseph A., Mary Collins, and Dermot A. Lane, eds. *The New Dictionary of Theology.* Wilmington, DE: Michael Glazier, 1987.

Kraybill, Donald B., Steven M. Nolt, and David Weaver-Zercher. *Amish Grace: How Forgiveness Transcended Tragedy.* San Francisco: John Wiley, 2007.

Lacey, Michael J., and Francis Oakley, eds. *The Crisis of Authority in Catholic Modernity.* New York: Oxford University Press, 2011.

LaCugna, Catherine Mowry, ed. *Freeing Theology: The Essentials of Theology in Feminist Perspective.* San Francisco: HarperSanFrancisco, 1993.

————. *God For Us: The Trinity and Christian Life.* San Francisco: HarperSanFrancisco, 1991.

Laffey, Alice L. "The Priestly Creation Narrative: Goodness and Interdependence." In *Earth, Wind, and Fire: Biblical and Theological Perspectives on Creation*, edited by Carol Dempsey and Mary Margaret Pazden, 24–34. Collegeville, MN: Liturgical Press, 2004.

Laird, Martin. "The Fountain of His Lips: Desire and Divine Union in Gregory of Nyssa's Homilies on the Song of Songs." *Spiritus* 7, no. 1 (Spring 2007): 40–57.

Lakeland, Paul. *Postmodernity: Christian Identity in a Fragmented Age.* Minneapolis: Fortress, 1997.

Lawrence-Lightfoot, Sara. *The Third Chapter: Passion, Risk, and Adventure in the 25 Years After 50.* New York: Farrar, Straus and Giroux, 2009.

Légasse, Simon. "The Call of the Rich Man." In *Gospel Poverty: Essays in Biblical Theology*, translated by Michael Guinan, 53–80. Chicago: Franciscan Herald Press, 1977.

————. *L'Appel du riche. (Marc 10, 17–31 et parallèles): contribution à l'étude des fondements scriptuaires de l'état religieux.* Paris: Beauchesne, 1966.

Liebes, Sidney, Elisabet Sahtouris, and Brian Swimme. *A Walk Through Time: From Stardust to Us: The Evolution of Life on Earth.* New York: John Wiley & Sons, 1998.

Ling, Timothy J. M. *The Judean Poor and the Fourth Gospel.* New York: Cambridge University Press, 2006.

Marrow, Stanley B. "Κόσμο in John." *Catholic Biblical Quarterly* 64, no. 1 (2002): 90–102.

Martyn, Louis. *History and Theology in the Fourth Gospel.* Nashville: Abingdon, 1979.

Massa, Mark. "Anti-Catholicism: The Last Acceptable Prejudice?" In *American Catholics, American Culture: Tradition and Resistance.* Vol. 2 of American Catholics in the Public Sphere, edited by Margaret O'Brien Steinfels, 149–54. Lanham, MD: Rowman & Littlefield, 2004.

Matthew, Iain. *The Impact of God: Soundings from St. John of the Cross.* London/Sydney/Auckland: Hodder & Stoughton, 1995.

McBrien, Richard. *The Church: The Evolution of Catholicism.* New York: HarperCollins, 2008.

———. *Catholicism.* Rev. and updated ed. San Francisco: HarperSanFrancisco, 1994.

McDonnell, Kilian. "The Father Empties His Coffers." In *Yahweh's Other Shoe,* 36–48. Collegeville, MN: Saint John's University Press, 2006.

McFague, Sallie. *Metaphorical Theology: Models of God in Religious Language.* Philadelphia: Fortress, 1982.

McGinn, Bernard. *The Mystical Thought of Meister Eckhart: The Man from Whom God Hid Nothing.* New York: Crossroad, 2001.

Meier, John P. *A Marginal Jew: Rethinking the Historical Jesus.* 4 vols. Anchor Bible Reference Library. New York: Doubleday, 1991–2009.

Merton, Thomas. *The Hidden Ground of Love: The Letters of Thomas Merton on Religious Experience and Social Concerns.* Edited by William H. Shannon. New York: Farrar, Straus, Giroux, 1985.

———. *Asian Journal.* New York: New Directions, 1973.

Merton, Thomas, Rosemary Radford Ruether, and Mary Tardiff. *At Home in the World: The Letters of Thomas Merton and Rosemary Radford Ruether.* Maryknoll, NY: Orbis, 1995.

Mettepenningen, Jürgen. "Yves Congar and the 'Monster' of Nouvelle Théologie." *Horizons* 37, no. 1 (2010): 52–71.

Milgram, Stanley. *Obedience to Authority: An Experimental View.* London: Travistock, 1974.

Millar, Fergus. *A Greek Roman Empire: Power and Belief Under Theodosius II (408–450).* Berkeley/Los Angeles: University of California Press, 2006.

Miura, Nozomi. "A Typology of Personified Wisdom Hymns." *Biblical Theology Bulletin* 4, no. 4 (2004): 138–49.

Murphy, Roland E. "Introduction to Wisdom Literature." In *The New Jerome Biblical Commentary*, edited by R. E. Brown, J. A. Fitzmyer, and R. E. Murphy, 447–52. Englewood Cliffs, NJ: Prentice Hall, 1990.

National Conference of Catholic Bishops. *Economic Justice for All: Pastoral Letter on Catholic Social Teaching and the U.S. Economy* (1986). In *Catholic Social Teaching: The Documentary Heritage*. Rev. and exp. ed. Edited by David J. O'Brien and Thomas A. Shannon. Maryknoll, NY: Orbis, 2010.

Neal, Marie Augusta. *Catholic Sisters in Transition: From the 1960's to the 1980's*. Wilmington, DE: Michael Glazier, 1984.

Newman, Carey C. "Resurrection and Glory: Divine Presence and Christian Origins." In *The Resurrection: An Interdisciplinary Symposium on the Resurrection of Jesus*, edited by Stephen T. Davis, Daniel Kendall, and Gerald O'Collins, 59–89. Oxford: Oxford University Press, 1997.

Nolan, Albert. "Structures of Sin." In *Hope in an Age of Despair: And Other Talks and Writings*, 152–67. Maryknoll, NY: Orbis, 2009.

———. *Jesus Today: A Spirituality of Radical Freedom*. Maryknoll, NY: Orbis, 2007.

Oakman, Douglas E. "The Radical Jesus: You Cannot Serve God and Mammon." *Biblical Theology Bulletin* 34, no. 3 (2004): 122–29.

O'Collins, Gerald G. *The Resurrection of Jesus Christ*. Milwaukee: Marquette University Press, 1993.

O'Malley, John W. *What Happened at Vatican II*. Cambridge, MA/London: Harvard University Press, 2008.

O'Murchu, Diarmuid. *Consecrated Religious Life: The Changing Paradigms*. Maryknoll, NY: Orbis, 2005.

———. *Poverty, Celibacy, and Obedience: A Radical Option for Life*. New York: Crossroad, 1999.

Otto, Rudolph. *The Idea of the Holy: An Inquiry into the Non-rational Factor in the Idea of the Divine and Its Relation to the Rational*. 2nd ed. New York: Oxford University Press, 1958.

Painter, John. "Earth Made Whole: John's Rereading of Genesis." In *Word, Theology and Community in John*, edited by J. Painter, R. A. Culpepper, and F. F. Segovia, 65–84. St. Louis: Chalice, 2002.

Patrick, Anne E. *Liberating Conscience: Feminist Explorations in Catholic Moral Theology*. New York: Continuum, 1996.

———. "The Moral Decision Maker: From Good Sisters to Prophetic Women." *CLCW* 79, no. 20. *Records of the Leadership Conference of Women Religious*, 1985. University of Notre Dame Archives.

Patte, Daniel. *The Challenge of Discipleship: A Critical Study of the Sermon on the Mount as Scripture.* Harrisburg, PA: Trinity Press International, 1999.

Perkins, Pheme. "The Gospel According to John." In *The New Jerome Biblical Commentary*, edited by R. E. Brown, J. A. Fitzmyer, and R. E. Murphy, 942–85. Englewood Cliffs, NJ: Prentice Hall, 1990.

Peters, Edward N. *The 1917 Pio-Benedictine Code of Canon Law.* San Francisco: Ignatius Press, 2001.

Peters, Ted, Robert John Russell, and Michael Welker, eds. *Resurrection: Theological and Scientific Assessments.* Grand Rapids, MI: Eerdmans, 2002.

Pieris, Aloysius. "Ecumenism in the Churches and the Unfinished Agenda of the Holy Spirit." *Spiritus* 3, no. 1 (2003): 53–67.

Pilgrim, Walter E. *Good News to the Poor: Wealth and Poverty in Luke-Acts.* Minneapolis: Augsburg, 1981.

Pius XII, Pope. *Guiding Principles of the Lay Apostolate: Address of Pope Pius XII to the Second World Congress of the Lay Apostolate, October 5, 1957.* Washington, DC: National Catholic Welfare Conference, 1957.

Polkinghorne, John C. *Belief in God in an Age of Science.* New Haven, CT: Yale University, 2006.

Prabhu, Joseph. *The Intercultural Challenge of Raimon Panikkar.* Maryknoll, NY: Orbis, 1996.

Quinn, John R. *The Reform of the Papacy: Costly Call to Christian Unity.* New York: Crossroad, 1999.

Quiñonez, Lora Ann, and Mary Daniel Turner. *The Transformation of American Catholic Sisters.* Philadelphia: Temple University Press, 1992.

Ranft, Patricia. *Women and the Religious Life in Premodern Europe.* New York: St. Martin's, 1996.

Reinhartz, Adele. *Befriending the Beloved Disciple: A Jewish Reading of the Gospel of John.* New York/London: Continuum, 2001.

Robinson, John A. T. *The Body: A Study in Pauline Theology.* Chicago: H. Regnery, 1963.

Rolheiser, Ronald. *The Holy Longing: The Search for a Christian Spirituality.* New York: Doubleday, 1999.

Ruether, Rosemary Radford. *Feminist Theologies: Legacy and Prospect.* Minneapolis: Fortress, 2007.

———. *Women and Redemption: A Theological History.* Minneapolis: Fortress Press, 1998.

————. *Sexism and God-Talk: Toward a Feminist Theology.* Boston: Beacon, 1993.

————. *Religion and Sexism: Images of Woman in the Jewish and Christian Traditions.* New York: Simon and Schuster, 1974.

Russell, Letty M., ed. *Feminist Interpretation of the Bible.* Philadelphia: Westminster, 1985.

Ryan, Maura A., and Brian F. Linnane, eds. *A Just and True Love: Feminism at the Frontiers of Theological Ethics: Essays in Honor of Margaret Farley.* Notre Dame, IN: University of Notre Dame, 2007.

Santayana, George. *Reason in Religion.* New York: Dover, 1982.

Schaefer, Judith K. *The Evolution of a Vow: Obedience as Decision Making in Communion.* New Brunswick, NJ: Transaction Publishers, 2008.

Schneiders, Sandra M. *Prophets in Their Own Country: Women Religious Bearing Witness to the Gospel in a Troubled Church.* Maryknoll, NY: Orbis, 2011.

————. "Whose Sins You Shall Forgive…The Holy Spirit and the Forgiveness of Sin(s) in the Fourth Gospel." *The Spirit in the New Millennium: The Duquesne University Annual Holy Spirit Lecture.* Pittsburgh, PA: Duquesne University, 2009.

————. "The Resurrection (of the Body) in the Fourth Gospel." In *Life in Abundance: Studies in John's Gospel in Tribute to Raymond E. Brown, S.S.*, edited by John R. Donahue, 168–98. Collegeville, MN: Liturgical Press, 2005.

————. "Religion vs. Spirituality: A Contemporary Conundrum." *Spiritus* 3, no. 2 (2003): 163–85.

————. *Written That You May Believe: Encountering Jesus in the Fourth Gospel.* 2nd ed. New York: Crossroad, 2003.

————. *Selling All: Commitment, Consecrated Celibacy, and Community in Catholic Religious Life.* Vol. 2 of Religious Life in a New Millennium. New York/Mahwah, NJ: Paulist Press, 2001.

————. *Finding the Treasure: Locating Catholic Religious Life in a New Ecclesial and Cultural Context.* Vol. 1 of Religious Life in a New Millennium. New York/ Mahwah, NJ: Paulist Press, 2000.

————. *The Revelatory Text: Interpreting the New Testament as Sacred Scripture.* 2nd ed. Collegeville, MN: Liturgical Press, 1999.

————. "The Resurrection of Jesus and Christian Spirituality." In *Christian Resources of Hope*, edited by Maureen Junker-Kenny, 81–114. Dublin: Columba, 1995.

————. *Women and the Word: The Gender of God in the New Testament and the Spirituality of Women*. Madeleva Lecture in Spirituality, 1986. New York/Mahwah, NJ: Paulist Press, 1986.

Schüssler Fiorenza, Elisabeth. *In Memory of Her: A Feminist Theological Reconstruction of Christian Origins*. New York: Crossroad, 1983.

Seidensticker, Philip. "St. Paul and Poverty." In *Gospel Poverty: Essays in Biblical Theology*, translated by Michael Guinan, 81–120. Chicago: Franciscan Herald Press, 1977.

Settersen, Richard A. *On the Frontier of Adulthood: Theory, Research, and Public Policy*. Chicago: University of Chicago Press, 2008.

Shannon, William H. *Silent Lamp: The Thomas Merton Story*. New York: Crossroad, 1992.

Soëlle, Dorothee. *The Silent Cry: Mysticism and Resistance*. Minneapolis: Fortress, 2001.

————. *Beyond Mere Obedience*. New York: The Pilgrim Press, 1982.

Springsted, Eric O. *Simone Weil and the Suffering of Love*. Cambridge, MA: Cowley, 1986.

Stein, Murray. *Jung's Map of the Soul: An Introduction*. Chicago and La Salle, IL: Open Court, 1998.

Suenens, Cardinal Léon Joseph. *The Nun in the World*. Westminster, MD: Newman Press, 1963.

Swidler, Leonard, and Arlen Swidler. "Biblical Commission Report: Can Women Be Priests?" In *Women Priests*, edited by Leonard Swidler and Arlene Swidler, 338–46. New York/Mahwah, NJ: Paulist Press, 1977. Also published in *Origins* VI, no. 6 (July 1, 1976): 92–96.

Sylvester, Nancy. *Crucible for Change: Engaging Impasse through Communal Contemplation and Dialogue*. San Antonio, TX: Sor Juana Press, 2004.

Taylor, Charles. *A Secular Age*. Cambridge, MA: Harvard University Press, 2007.

Teilhard de Chardin, Pierre. *The Divine Milieu*. New York: Harper-Collins, 2001.

————. "The Mass on the World." In *The Heart of the Matter*, translated by René Hague, 119–34. New York: Harcourt Brace Jovanovich, 1978.

Teresa of Avila: The Book of Her Life. In *The Collected Works of St. Teresa of Avila, Vol. 1: The Book of Her Life, Spiritual Testimonies, and Soliloquies*. 2nd ed. Translated with notes by Kieran Kavanaugh and Otilio Rodriguez. Washington, DC: Institute of Carmelite Studies, 1987.

Thomas of Celano. "The Remembrance of the Desire of a Soul." In *Francis of Assisi: Early Documents, Vol. 2, The Founder*, edited by Regis J. Armstrong, J. Wayne Hellmann, and William J. Short, 231–393. Hyde Park, NY: New City Press, 2000.

Thompson, Colin. *St. John of the Cross: Songs in the Night.* Washington, DC: Catholic University of America Press, 2003.

Tolbert, Mary Ann. *The Bible and Feminist Hermeneutics.* Chico, CA: Scholars, 1983.

Tracy, David. *The Analogical Imagination: Christian Theology and the Culture of Pluralism.* New York: Crossroad, 1981.

Van Ness, Peter H. *Spirituality and the Secular Quest.* New York: Crossroad, 1996.

Viviano, Benedict T. "The Gospel According to Matthew." In *The New Jerome Biblical Commentary*, edited by R. E. Brown, J. A. Fitzmyer, and R. E. Murphy, 630–74. Englewood Cliffs, NJ: Prentice Hall, 1990.

Vorgrimler, H., ed. *Commentary on the Documents of Vatican II.* Translated by Lalit Adolphus, Kevin Smyth, and Richard Strachan. New York: Herder and Herder, 1967–1969.

Walsh, Mary Paula. *Feminism and Christian Tradition: An Annotated Bibliography and Critical Introduction to the Literature.* Santa Barbara, CA: Greenwood, 1991.

Weakland, Rembert G. *A Pilgrim in a Pilgrim Church: Memoirs of a Catholic Archbishop.* Grand Rapids, MI: Eerdmans, 2009.

Wilder, Amos N. *Early Christian Rhetoric: The Language of the Gospel.* Peabody, MA: Hendrickson, 1999.

Wiley, Tatha. *Original Sin: Origins, Developments, Contemporary Meanings.* New York/Mahwah, NJ: Paulist Press, 2002.

Williams, Rowan. "Word and Spirit." In *On Christian Theology*, 107–27. Oxford: Blackwell, 2000.

Wink, Walter. *Engaging the Powers: Discernment and Resistance in a World of Domination.* Philadelphia: Fortress, 1992.

———. *Unmasking the Powers.* Philadelphia: Fortress, 1986.

———. *Naming the Powers.* Philadelphia: Fortress, 1984.

Wittberg, Patricia. *From Piety to Professionalism—And Back?: Transformations of Organized Religious Virtuosity.* Lanham, MD: Lexington Books, 2006.

Woods, Richard. "What Is New Age Spirituality?" *Way* 33 (July 1993): 176–88.

Index